BEAUTIFUL ANGIOLA

BEAUTIFUL ANGIOLA

The Lost Sicilian Folk and Fairy Tales of Laura Gonzenbach

Translated and with an
introduction by

Jack Zipes

Routledge
Taylor & Francis Group
New York   London

Published in 2006 by
Routledge
Taylor & Francis Group
270 Madison Avenue
New York, NY 10016

Published in Great Britain by
Routledge
Taylor & Francis Group
2 Park Square
Milton Park, Abingdon
Oxon OX14 4RN

© 2006 by Jack Zipes
Routledge is an imprint of Taylor & Francis Group

Printed in the United States of America on acid-free paper
10 9 8 7 6 5 4 3 2 1

International Standard Book Number-10: 0-415-97722-3 (Softcover)
International Standard Book Number-13: 978-0-415-97722-7 (Softcover)
Library of Congress Card Number 2005016194

Library of Congress Cataloging-in-Publication Data

Sicilianische märchen. English 2005
    Beautiful Angiola : the lost Sicilian folk and fairy tales of Laura Gonzenbach / translated and edited by Jack Zipes ; illustrations by Joellyn Rock.
        p. cm.
        "Chapters 1 to 50 originally appeared in Beautiful Angiola: The Great Treasury of Sicilian Folk and Fairy Tales Collected by Laura Gonzenbach, translated with an introduction by Jack Zipes. Published in 2003 by Routledge. Chapters 51-90 first appeared in The Robber with a Witch's Head, translated and with an introduction by Jack Zipes. Published in 2004 by Routledge."
    Includes bibliographical references.
    ISBN 0-415-97722-3 (pbk. : alk. paper)
    1. Folklore--Italy--Sicily. 2. Folklore--Italy--Sicily--Classification. 3. Tales--Italy--Sicily. I. Gonzenbach, Laura, 1842-1878. II. Zipes, Jack David. III. Title.

GR177.S5S53 2005
398.2'09458--dc22   2005016194

Taylor & Francis Group
is the Academic Division of Informa plc.

Visit the Taylor & Francis Web site at
http://www.taylorandfrancis.com

and the Routledge Web site at
http://www.routledge-ny.com

To Luisa Rubini
With Gratitude and Admiration

CONTENTS

Contents

Contents

Contents

Laura Gonzenbach's
Buried Treasure

Jack Zipes

It may be misleading to call Laura Gonzenbach's collection of Sicilian fairy tales a buried treasure. After all, her book, *Sicilianische Märchen* (1870), received favorable reviews from Italian and German scholars when it appeared in Germany. In addition, her stories played a prominent role in the American folklorist Thomas F. Crane's book *Italian Popular Tales* (1885). However, ever since then her work has been more or less forgotten if not indeed buried. Indeed, why pay attention to a book of Sicilian fairy tales published not in Sicilian or Italian, but in German by a Swiss woman born in Messina with no academic or literary standing? In the twentieth century, Gonzenbach was dismissed by most of the leading Sicilian and Italian folklorists, partly because she had stolen their fire and published "their" precious native tales in a foreign language before they did in their own. Only in 1964 did her granddaughter, Renata La Racine, try to recall the significance of her grandmother's undertaking by publishing the first Italian translation of a selection of the Sicilian tales with her publication of *Tradizione popolare nelle fiabe siciliane di Laura von Gonzenbach*, but to no avail. Not long after, in 1979, the German folklorist Rudolf Schenda endeavored repeatedly to point out the great value of her collection in two important essays.* Some ten years later, in 1989, a truncated version of *Sicilianische Märchen* without introduction or notes was published by Greno in Nördlingen. Though it, too, sought to restore the fame of the collection, it was largely ignored. Finally, in 1999, the gifted Italian folklorist Luisa Rubini published the first complete Italian translation, *Fiabe siciliane*, with an insightful introduction and comprehensive notes. Yet even this superb book has drawn little notice by the general public in Europe. What will it take, I have asked myself, to honor the Gonzenbach collection of tales as perhaps the most important collection of fairy tales, legends, and anecdotes in the nineteenth century, more important perhaps than the Brothers Grimm? Why is it really so pertinent today for understanding folklore and popular culture?

It may seem an exaggeration to assert that Gonzenbach's book is much more interesting and important than the *Children's and Household Tales* (1812–1815) of the Brothers Grimm or to privilege the Gonzenbach work over other fine and useful nineteenth-century European collections, but I am not exaggerating. Gonzenbach's collection is uniquely authentic and fascinating: though published in high German, the tales were literally written down from the mouths of Sicilian peasant and lower-middle class women. They represent more genuinely and more candidly the female if not feminist perspective on life, reveal social conditions from the point of view of an oppressed lower class, and do so with gusto, bitterness, and even hope. Such a partisan viewpoint is not evident in most collections of the nineteenth century with the exception of the dialect tales collected by the great Sicilian folklorist, Giuseppe Pitrè. In this regard, Gonzenbach's narratives are in stark contrast to the highly stylized and censored tales of the Brothers Grimm that were constantly changed and edited by Wilhelm. Unlike him, Laura Gonzenbach did not mediate as censor, philologist, and German nationalist. She may have edited the tales somewhat to bring out her own progressive views about women. We do not know this for sure. Certainly she did *not* purge the tales of their sexual inferences, brutality, violence, and frankness the way other Sicilian and mainstream European collectors did. She was not as prudish as many of the male folklorists in the nineteenth century. Unfortunately, we know

---

*See Rudolf Schenda, "Laura Gonzenbach und die Sicilianischen Märchen: Bemerkungen zu den deutsch italienischen Volksliteratur-Beziehungen im Risorgimento," *Fabula* 20 (1979): 205–216, and Rudolf and Susanna Schenda, "La donna e il lavoro nelle fiabe siciliane raccolte da Laura Gonzenbach e Giuseppe Pitrè," in Rudolf Schenda, *Folklore e letteratura popolare: Italia—Germania—Francia*, trans. Maria Chiara Figliozzi e Ingeborg Walter (Rome: Istituto della Enciclopedia Italiana, 1986), pp. 279–287.

little about Laura Gonzenbach's editorial work and personal life because most of the family papers were destroyed in the Messina earthquake of 1908. Yet, what we do know is definitely worth recalling before I deal in greater detail with the significance of her collection.

Laura Gonzenbach was born in Messina, a city of approximately 90,000 inhabitants, on the island of Sicily on December 26, 1842,[*] the day after Christmas. Her father, Peter Viktor Gonzenbach (1808–1885), was a commercial agent from St. Gallen, Switzerland, and her mother, Julie Aders (1806–1847), was originally from a respectable middle-class family in Elberfeld, Germany. Gonzenbach moved to Messina in his adolescence about 1823 and quickly made a successful career for himself working for Swiss and German textile firms. After he met his wife in the late 1820s, they married on June 24, 1830, in Malta and had seven daughters and one son: Magdalena (1831), Ludwig David (1833), Emilie (1834), Anna (1836), Gertha Elisabeth (1839), Clara Victoria (1840), Laura (1842), and Elisa (1846). Three of the girls died at a very young age, and the son passed away at twenty-one.

An ambitious and gifted individual, Peter Viktor Gonzenbach, known as Don Vittorio, began developing his own mercantile business during the 1830s and also served as the Swiss consul in Messina, which was a thriving port city with a small elite class of German, Swiss, and French merchants. Laura profited, as did her sisters, from the family's privileged position in this society and received an excellent education at home and in a small private school attached to the German-Swiss community in Messina. The person most responsible for Laura's education was her sister Magdalena because their mother had died in 1847, when Laura was only five. Magdalena was an extraordinary young woman. Cosmopolitan, trained in all the arts, classical literature, and the sciences, she took charge of the household and the family salon after her mother's death, and her father, a liberal democrat, gave her free rein. A woman ahead of her times, she supported suffragette causes and later had close connections to women's journals in Italy. In 1870 she translated into German the important feminist Fanny Lewald's book, *Für und Wider die Frauen* (*For and Against Women*) and later founded a school for girls in Messina, the first of its kind.

---

[*] For the most comprehensive study of Laura Gonzenbach and her work, see the excellent book by Luisa Rubini, *Fiabe e mercanti in Sicilia: La raccolta di Laura Gonzenbach. La comunità tedesca a Messina nell'Ottocento* (Florence: Leo S. Olschki, 1998). See also Rudolf Schenda, "Laura Gonzenbach e la sua raccolta di fiabe siciliane. Considerazioni sugli scambi italo-tedeschi in tema di letteratura popolare all'epoca del Risorgimento," in *Folklore e letteratura popolare: Italia—Germania—Francia* (Rome: Istituto della Enciclopedia Italiana, 1986), 265–278.

Her influence on her younger sister Laura, with whom she was very close, cannot be underestimated. By the time she was a teenager, Laura could speak four languages (German, French, Italian, and Sicilian) fluently, play musical instruments, and was well versed in literature and the arts. Because she could not attend a university (it was not customary to provide a higher education for young women at that time) she participated in the cultural activities at her father's house and in other salons in Messina and was esteemed as an exceptional storyteller. At the age of twenty-seven, she married the Italian colonel François Laurent La Racine (1818–1906), originally from Savoy, and had five children with him. Soon after her marriage she moved with her husband to Naples. Nothing is known about her life with La Racine or the conditions under which she died on July 16, 1878, in Messina. There is, however, a tombstone in Messina marking her young death at age thirty-six.

The Gonzenbachs were Protestants, and there were two small German Protestant communities in Messina and Palermo. When the position of minister became vacant in Messina in 1860, Peter Viktor Gonzenbach, head of the community, recruited Dr. Otto Hartwig (1830–1903), a theologian and historian, who had recently completed his studies in Marburg, to fill the position. Hartwig was obligated to hold services on Sundays for the German and Swiss community and to attend to their religious needs for a period of five years. His duties also included participating in soirées at different homes, joining a bowling club, attending concerts, and, in general, taking part in the cultural life of the community. His primary contacts were with the European merchants, doctors, and teachers, very little with the Sicilians, but he did undertake research for a book about Sicilian history and took various trips on the island. Among his acquaintances was Laura Gonzenbach, whom he regarded as a formidable teller of fairy tales. After he fulfilled his contract and left Sicily, he called upon her to help him collect tales for one of his books, for he had decided to include some in an appendix to demonstrate the special character of Sicilian culture. As he explained to Laura in a letter, he wanted just a few tales for the second volume of his history of Sicily, *Aus Sizilien: Kultur- und Geschichtsbilder* (1867–1869).

Unlike Hartwig, who never mastered the Sicilian dialect, Gonzenbach had grown up on the island with a thorough knowledge of Sicilian, and she had met numerous Sicilian peasant women in Messina and Catania and in the small villages near Mt. Etna, where she spent summer vacations. Because these women were generally reticent about talking to outsiders, especially men, Gonzenbach had a unique opportunity to form acquaintances with them and win their trust. Most of the tales she collected for Hartwig were told to her by peasant women with the names of Lucia, Cicca Crialesi, Nunzia Giuffridi, and Bastiana, but she also wrote down stories told to her by lower middle-class informants such as Antonia Centorrino and probably young single women such as Elisabetta and Concetta Martinotti, Francesca Rusullo, Peppina Guglielmo, and Caterina Certo. In addition there was at least one male storyteller, a peasant named Alessandro Grasso, who shared tales he had learned from his mother. Assisted by her older sister, Magdalena, Gonzenbach endeavored to write the tales down just as she had heard them. In a letter to Hartwig, she stated:

> Now I'd like to tell you that I've done my best to write down the tales exactly as they were told to me. However, I've not been able to recapture the genuine charm of these tales that lies in the manner and way the tales are told by these Sicilian women. Most of them tell the tales in a lively fashion by acting out the entire plot with their hands making very expressive gestures. While talking, they even stand up and walk around the room when it's appropriate. They never use "he says" because they change the people's voices always through intonation.[*]

Familiar with the folk tradition of storytelling, Gonzenbach also knew German literary tales, probably the tales of the Brothers Grimm, perhaps even French tales. This background enabled her—even though she never lived in Germany or Switzerland for any length of time—to find a suitable literary voice for her translation of the dialect tales. In practice, Gonzenbach translated these tales immediately into German and had to find an adequate style of narration. One cannot say that her tales are "authentic" folk tales, especially because she made some stylistic changes as did Hartwig and Reinhold Köhler (1830–1892), who eventually provided the notes to her edition.[1] Nevertheless, they are probably as close as one can come to the Sicilian oral tradition, with the exception of the dialect collections of Sicilian tales and legends published by Giuseppe Pitrè.[2] Their "naiveté," their use of direct expressions, proverbs, quick transitions, sudden breaks, and lack of

---

[*] Laura Gonzenbach, *Sicilianische Märchen*, ed. Otto Hartwig. Notes by Reinhold Köhler, 2 vols. (Leipzig: W. Engelmann, 1870), p. ix.

[1] See Köhler's notes in the original edition, Laura Gonzenbach, *Sicilianische Märchen. Aus dem Volksmund gesammelt* (1870).

[2] See Giuseppe Pitrè, *Otto Fiabe e Novelle populari siciliane* (Bologna: Tipografia Fava e Garagnani, 1873); *Fiabe, novelle e racconti popolari siciliani*, 4 vols. (Palermo: Pedone Lauriel, 1875), Vols. 4–7 of *Biblioteca delle tradizioni popolari siciliane*; *Fiabe e Leggende popolari siciliane* (Palermo: Pedone Lauriel, 1888).

long explications indicate clearly that the tales are more stamped by oral modes of narration than literary. Moreover, Gonzenbach remained faithful to the ideological perspective of women from the lower class whose struggle against oppression is a major theme in the tales.

Through Hartwig, Gonzenbach was well aware, even though she was twenty-eight with no formal academic training, that there was a strong scholarly interest in collections of Italian folk tales, songs, and stories in Germany. Therefore, after he wrote her in 1868 and she agreed to help him show German readers how fascinating Sicilian folk-lore was, she eagerly sought to provide him with as many tales as she could. At first she sent him about ten, and then, to his surprise, another eighty-two tales in 1868. To his credit, Hartwig realized how extraordinary they were and decided to publish them separately as a book, not as an appendix, but the collaboration on this project could not be completed in 1868. Although a brilliant scholar, Hartwig was primarily a historian, and, indeed, wrote an important essay on the history of the Sicilian language and its relationship to the growth of nationalism to introduce Gonzenbach's collection. Yet he knew little about folklore and therefore recruited Reinhold Köhler, at the time Germany's foremost scholar on international folklore, to write the significant notes for each one of the tales. This was a great boon for the edition, which was finally published by Wilhelm Engelmann in Leipzig at Christmas in 1869, but with the publication date of 1870.

What distinguishes Gonzenbach's collection from most others of the nineteenth century is the variety of the tales, their proximity to the oriental and occidental storytelling traditions, the dominance of female informants, and the abundant references to Sicilian peasant customs and beliefs. There are explicit details of ferocious familial conflicts, arbitrary violence, sadistic punishment, and immoral love—in short, an acknowledgment of aspects of life generally censored in most nineteenth-century collections. Moreover, as I have emphasized, the tales have a distinct feminine if not "feminist" lower-class perspective. All the more reason they are so significant: they explicitly and implicitly reveal the desires and complaints of women whose voices are difficult to hear in the nineteenth-century collections assembled by male scholars. But it is not only this female perspective that makes them so interesting—and I shall address this aspect shortly—it is the manner in which the tales are framed without happy endings, for the Sicilian tales make a clear distinction about who can be happy and who will not be happy until social conditions are changed. It is the candor of these tales that is so striking, and I want to say a few words about this social candor before turning to a discussion of the unusual representation of women and lower-class figures in Gonzenbach's collection. It is truly astonishing that Laura Gonzenbach could accomplish what she did in her twenties, that is, to capture the tone and atmosphere of Sicilian oral tales in a foreign "high" language, namely *Hochdeutsch*, with a literary bent that retains a fresh if not sassy outlook on life.

In his book, *Customs and Habits of the Sicilian Peasants*, Salvatore Salomone-Marino, a contemporary of Laura Gonzenbach who collaborated with Giuseppe Pitrè to preserve the folklore of Sicily at the end of the nineteenth century, depicts many instances in the daily lives of the peasants when they entertained themselves with songs, poems, and all sorts of stories. At one point he remarks:

> On winter evenings the streets are dark, cold, silent: the whole life of the rustic family is concentrated around the hearth, where great firebrands burst out. These are not the meetings in the company of the neighborhood; now every family stays by itself. The womenfolk spin or reel; grandma or the mother keeps the children's mouths hanging open with her skill, mimicry, and incredible emotion: "'. . . they relate of ancient times Tales of sorcerers and Queens.' The boys who request these stories and want to learn are the pretext; the narrator is quite willing and addresses her words even to the adults, who are known always to be pleased to listen at length for the thousandth time as she tells of the fantastic and strange supernatural beings, those men of valor and peerless bravery—to ineffable delight and the fantasies they excite."[*]

Although Salomone-Marino at times romanticizes the life of the peasants, he is for the most part an accurate observer of their customs and traditions. He reports that there were specific occasions like sowing and harvesting when men would also tell the stories. Within the family, however, the prominent storytellers were women, which is why women also figure predominantly as the narrators in the dialect collections of Pitrè and Salomone-Marino and in Gonzenbach's book. Most importantly, the tales preserved by these women reveal a great deal about the central historical role played by storytelling in Sicily to maintain customs and belief systems; they demonstrate fascinating interconnections with tales from other cultures; and they provide a candid perspective on the hard lives led by the Sicilian peasants.

---

[*] Salvatore Salomone-Marino, *Customs and Habits of the Sicilian Peasants*, ed. and trans. Rosalie N. Norris (Rutherford, N.J.: Fairleigh Dickinson Press, 1981): 6–7.

Given the long history of various conquests of the island and colonization by the Greeks, Italians, Arabs, Normans, Spaniards, French, Austrians, and English throughout the past twenty centuries or more, the stories that entered the oral tradition of storytelling in Sicily evince an astonishing cross-fertilization and are clearly international in nature. At the same time, the tales were constantly altered to reflect the changing conditions on the island so that they became closely tied to Sicilian customs and practices. Tales told in Sicilian evolved during the late Middle Ages. A Sicilian dialect did not really begin to flourish until the time of the Norman invasions of the eleventh and twelfth centuries when numerous Italians also emigrated to Sicily, and gradually different forms of a Sicilian dialect became the lingua franca of the country. There was never one standard form of dialect, just as customs varied from region to region on the island. The Sicilian peasants did, however, share other things in their daily lives up through the twentieth century— exploitation, deprivation, and suffering. The invasions and wars fought on Sicilian soil were constant, and often entire cities and villages were wiped out and destroyed, not just by foreign soldiers but by rival communities. There were famines and plagues that almost every generation of Sicilians experienced from the Middle Ages to the twentieth century. The forests and fertile land were gradually devastated and exploited by the nineteenth century; roads were not built; irrigation was limited; and the peasants were always obliged to work for landlords who took most of their produce. The homes of the peasants consisted generally of a large room with partitions, and some of the animals, vital for their survival, slept in this room as well. The peasants ate very little meat, and they generally divided the labor, with the men working cooperatively in the fields or woods, and the women weaving, spinning, taking care of the children, and performing most of the domestic chores.

Although we cannot claim to know fully what the tales they told meant to the Sicilian peasants, they clearly used them to comment on their lives and on how they wished to change them. What is striking is the stark realistic perspective of the storytellers in the Gonzenbach collection. Almost all the tales begin with a lack or grave catastrophe: a king and queen cannot have children, and when they do, they give birth to a snake, beast, or a child who is cursed; children are abandoned or kidnapped by clouds, ogres, and sorcerers who abuse them; young girls and boys are beaten or threatened by a teacher or another authority figure; a family is so poor that the children decide to leave home or are sent away to find their fortune; women encounter men who often prey on them or want to humiliate them; jealous sisters and brothers plot to bring about the downfall of their more fortunate sibling; daughters or stepdaughters face mothers and stepmothers who want to kill them; young men and women must fulfill impossible tasks, otherwise they will be eaten.

Almost all the tales end with similar formulaic refrains such as:

- And then they all lived happily and content, but we were left without a cent.
- She remained happy and content, but we still can't pay the rent.
- And they remained rich and consoled, and we just sit here and are getting old.
- They continued to live happy and content, but we were left empty-handed.
- The king and Maruzza lived for a long time still, rich and consoled, and we have nothing as we get old.
- Indeed, they all celebrated a splendid wedding and remained happy and content, but we just sit here and gaze at each other, and our day is spent.

Perhaps the latent reality of the peasants' oppression and their hatred for their situation explain the often brutal punishment of the evildoers at the end of the tales: a nasty and ugly daughter has her head chopped off and pieces of her body are served as salted tuna fish to her wicked mother; another sinister mother is boiled in oil; a traitor has his head chopped off; a stupid king burns himself to death; an evil queen is cooked in oil and thrown to the dogs to be devoured; a lascivious priest is burned at the stake and has his ashes strewn to the wind.

Yet such fantasies of violent retribution that might usher in a more just world never quite make it to the surface of the tales. The tellers remain dispassionate and choose a style that emphasizes distance: whatever has happened—good or bad—did not happen to them. At most they were witnesses. More often than not their stories belong to another time. As storytellers their main task is to make the extraordinary seem ordinary, to integrate the miraculous into their listeners' lives and so to insist on the possibility of sudden radical change in spite of seemingly insuperable odds. They make clear, however, that if someone happened to become rich or fortunate, the storyteller and her family did not share in the good fortune. They are always left behind, poor, without a cent, getting older.

Are these what we call fairy tales?

Well, not all the stories in the Gonzenbach collection are fairy tales. There are legends, fables, and folk anecdotes. The majority are indeed fairy tales, and despite the realistic concise telling of tales that are often lurid and terrifying, they are also filled with hope and intended to make listeners yearn for better days. There are also lessons to be learned, and many are wish-fulfillments that exhibit a profound belief in magic and the miraculous. Most of the Sicilian peasants had to live by their wits and do severe manual labor, and if they fell upon hard times, they called upon miraculous intervention. It is therefore interesting to see how the narrators did not disguise the injustices they suffered and the viciousness of class conflict in their tales because miracles rarely did occur. The peasants had to take fate into their own hands.

Peasants are indeed the protagonists in tales such as "Ferrazzanu," "Sciauranciovi," "The Shepherd Who Made the Princess Laugh," to name but a few. The lower-class figures are clearly smarter than their lords and masters, and they inevitably find ways to embarrass them, avoid punishment, and even kill them. For instance, Sciauranciovi has no qualms about deceiving a nobleman three different times and finally leading him to his death. He deals with the upper class just as the aristocrats dealt with him and his friends. For instance, the intriguing queen in "Prince Scursini" has no scruples in lying to the parents of artisans and feeding their daughters to their ruthless bestial sons, who murder them. No wonder the peasants respond in kind and perhaps with more justification by taking brutal revenge.

Lies and deceit abound in all the tales, and if there is one major theme that unites them, it concerns the *Word*—giving one's word, not a written word. One's word is one's life. Words can literally determine one's fortune and fate. For instance, there are several tales in which a prince leaves a woman, his true bride, after she has liberated him, to go to his parents' castle and to fetch garments for her that will make her look more respectable and beautiful for the people at the court. She warns him that if he is kissed by his mother or anyone at the castle, he will forget about her. The prince gives her his word that he will remain true to her and tells her not to worry. However, he is always unavoidably kissed and always forgets his true bride until she finds a way to break the spell cast on him through her own words, which recall his pledge. Curses can only be broken by words that count in one's life.

Certainly, this is one of the reasons why the narrators kept these tales alive, for the words have a relevance not only within the plot and narrative strategy of the tale, but they bring out the pertinence of the stories in such a way that the hearers will remember to tell what has a meaning for their lives. The words of the tale touch them emotionally and are absorbed by them, for they are weapons of the weak. They bear messages for survival. They bare some naked truths and demand that we pay attention to why we use words the way we do, and how we can use words to resolve discomforting social conditions. Words are given in trust. Words form the curses, spells, and vows that determine the action of all the protagonists.

One prime example is the legendary scoundrel, Giufà, a folk figure, whose antics were first recorded in Arabic tales during the late Middle Ages but were readily adapted and spread in Sicily and southern Italy. Indeed, Giufà is related to many other bumpkins and rascals in the European tradition in tales about Hans (German), Pietro (Italian), Pierre (French), and Jack (British and American). Giufà takes words literally, and consequently he has a limited sense of the world, for he cannot grasp how words are used metaphorically and idiomatically to articulate commands, wishes, instructions, and so forth, which don't mean what they bespeak or express. He rarely catches the inferences and implications of words; he is apt to make foolish mistakes and kill people or animals without thinking that he has committed a mistake. He even kills his baby sister and a shepherd without much remorse. Some of his own words are fortunate because he coincidentally discovers things with malapropisms that most people do not notice. His mother, a wise peasant woman, is the only one who can more or less control and save him because she understands the duplicity and ambiguity of words, and that her son lives by the literal word. Giufà is really not a dunce. He is someone who believes in the literal meaning of words and does not know how to communicate with a world that uses words and clothes to veil the meanings of its actions. This is why he ridicules his relatives when they are not hospitable because he does not wear the proper garments. This is why he exposes a greedy bishop and tricks some robbers.

The fairy tales in the Gonzenbach collection—and not only in her collection—keep words alive in narrative form that otherwise might have disappeared. The narrators want us to recall events and situations that should never be forgotten, for they mark what is still lacking in our lives—trust in words, social justice, and human compassion. Many of the tales have a religious aspect due to the influence of the Catholic religion in Sicily. However, the use of such figures as Saint Joseph, Jesus, and Mary has very little to do with religious orthodoxy. For instance, Saint Joseph is more like a wizard or sorcerer than a pious man, and he is consequently more fascinating because he is also more human. He is a favorite in many of the tales because he brings work and food to the poor and helps offset injustices. The faith that the characters demonstrate in God is always repaid because the Lord does not break his word. Miracles occur if one keeps the faith, and one's goose will be cooked if one presumes too much or questions the order of the world. Humility is necessary for salvation, but not always. It is generally the theme of the legends and religious fairy tales. It is also generally reserved for women as in "The Humiliated Princess," but it is a contested topic, and throughout Gonzenbach's collection there are a number of stories that inform us about an insurrection in the making, a longed-for change in the relations between men and women, or about the need to discard humility and to defend oneself against abuse.

In fact, the metaphorical struggles in the tales do not only pit peasants against their aristocratic masters and so project class conflict, they also speak to gender conflicts and expose men as oppressive masters. Here again it is worth quoting some passages from Salomone-Marino's *Customs and Habits of the Sicilian Peasants*:

> Husband and wife do not caress openly; they outwardly treat each other with a certain gravity, the more pronounced in him, but not because their feelings are less strong. She keeps the best for him, the most useful, the finest things. But things do not always go so smoothly and sweetly. On some days the husband is in a bad humor, whether because household matters go badly, or various other reasons supercharge him with electricity, awaiting only a light for him to go off violently. Woe to the wife who, in such moments, does not do her work well, breaks a household utensil, dares to make a remark to her man, or is lacking in the least regard and obedience due him as a master! He suddenly loses the light of reason and his traditional calm, and the wife must submit in holy peace, often undeservedly, to the nastiest insults, bestial punches, kicks, beatings, or blows given with the first object the furious man grabs hold of. She bears bruises, swellings, sometimes wounds and fractures, but still she does not let out a cry; she puts up no resistance, doesn't weep at all for fear of worse, nor does she spread in public the woes and hell she endures in her family. And the husband is truly an absolute master. After such mistreatment and blows, he claims that the woman is humbled (which she is willingly) to accord her peace; and he jeers at her into the bargain, trying to justify his bestial behavior; a dozen sound beatings (he always says) are as necessary as bread; if nothing else, it is handy way to stretch your skin, so you will eat more and get fat! *

If the situation of Sicilian peasant women was more or less the way Salomone-Marino describes it—and we have no reason to doubt him—it becomes more clear why the female narrators depict many young women in their tales who seek to break away from home and

---

*Salvatore Salomone-Marino, *Customs and Habits of the Sicilian Peasants*, ed. & trans. Rosalie N. Norris (Rutherford, N.J.: Fairleigh Dickinson University Press, 1981), pp. 42-43

determine their own fates. This is not to say that the storytellers intentionally changed tales to project the possibility of liberation for women. However, when compared to many of the tales in the Grimms' collection and other nineteenth-century books of folk tales, there is clearly a preponderance of audacious, smart, independent, and resourceful female protagonists in the Gonzenbach collection.

Sorfarina serves as the model of the "emancipated woman" among the tales recorded by Laura Gonzenbach, one of the reasons that I placed her story first in the collection. She is an unusual figure in the European folk-tale tradition. An educated woman, beautiful and smart, she marries a belligerent and revengeful prince, who behaves like a stubborn brute. Why Sorfarina loves him and does not abandon him is an open question. Perhaps it is because she never finished educating him while they were in school together. Perhaps she sees something in him that others cannot see. She tolerates him while sitting in a well and seduces him as a prostitute in different cities. Then she uses her magic powers, her art, to form the type of life she desires. However, toward the end of the tale, she cannot trust the prince who tries to kill her, and when he thinks he has done the foul deed, he tries to commit suicide. Their reconciliation at the very end is bittersweet. Sorfarina is in control of the situation, but she must forever be on her guard, for here is a man who relentlessly wants to prove he is the absolute master of his household and will stop at nothing—even though his wife has borne him three children—to establish his manhood.

Sorfarina refuses to be humiliated, and there are numerous tales such as "The Green Bird," "The Snake Who Bore Witness for a Maiden," "Betta Pilusa," "Beautiful Cardia," "The Daughter of the Sun," and others in which the female protagonist is audacious and uses her wits to gain what she wants. The threat of violation and exploitation remains constant, but the experience gained by the young woman in fending for herself is a kind of guarantee that she will not tolerate abuse in the future.

In contrast to what was allowed in Sicilian society, whether a woman came from the lower or upper class, many of the heroines in these tales travel or wander by themselves. As a rule, Sicilian women were actually prevented from leaving their homes unless they married. In the tales, however, many leave their homes for different reasons and are often glad to do so: some run away from jealous sisters or mothers and find work in a castle; some are orphans and must seek work as a secretary or maid; some are forced to work as nurses in dangerous situations. They all seek their own fortune that will generally be of their own making. Yet they are invariably threatened by predators who try to violate them. In tales such as "The Story of Oh My" and "The Robber with a Witch's Head," we have different versions of young women who leave home only to be confronted by sadistic killers who murder females because they do not act like slaves. Such brutality may very well be a representation of how badly women were treated during this period in Sicily. Whatever the case may be, the tales are liberating alternatives to the actual conditions suffered by the women, perhaps even by the storytellers themselves.

Just how unique and different, that is, emancipatory the Gonzenbach tales are in contrast to the classical Grimm tales can be demonstrated easily by comparing some of the same tale types such as "Beautiful Angiola" with "Rapunzel," "Lignu di Scupa" with "Rumpelstiltskin," "Betta Pilusa" with "All Fur," or others. In the Grimms' final version of 1857, Rapunzel is essentially a passive victim, unable to break away from the witch, and, consequently, she is severely punished for wanting to escape her prison. In Gonzenbach's tale, Angiola defies the witch and escapes with the prince. She continually outwits her mother/witch, and though she is cursed, she uses an intermediary, the dog, to gain the happiness that she desires. The ending is particularly interesting because the witch shows her defiant daughter compassion. This ending may have something to do with a woman's more considerate perspective on a tale that traditionally makes women appear hapless and hopeless.

Of course, it would be a grave mistake to characterize the Gonzenbach collection as feminist or politically subversive. Like the best of the dialect collections, although they were not recorded in dialect, the tales do not mince words, and because they were not heavily edited or adapted to make them appropriate reading for children and bourgeois families, they are startling in the frank and brusque manner in which they portray internecine strife and class struggles. They may be startling for us, but they were accepted and appreciated by the listeners to the tales, which included children of all ages. Then, as now, children are exposed to all kinds of stories, whether we approve of the narratives or not; and then, more than now, these stories along with songs, dance, and music were their major form of entertainment and means of learning about their lives and ways to change them.

Because Laura Gonzenbach and the two men who assisted her, Hartwig and Köhler, did not alter the tales very much, that is, they did not sweeten them or tone down the violent conflicts and the depiction of feisty women, her collection never became the proper bedtime reading or school reading for German children who were weaned on tales by the Grimms, Ludwig Bechstein, and Hans Christian Andersen. Luisa Rubini refers to Gonzenbach's narratives as "Buchmärchen" or book fairy tales, similar to the designation that some scholars have applied to the Grimms' texts. This is generally a term that tries to define the difference between "authentic" oral tales (*Volksmärchen*) and literary fairy tales (*Kunstmärchen*), to distinguish the peculiarity of tales that stem from the oral tradition but are recorded in high German and stylized according to the artistic gifts of the collector. Certainly this is the correct term for the Grimms' tales, for the brothers made vast changes in tales they wrote down from their informants, combined different versions, censored them, and took many of their texts from literature. This is not exactly how Rubini uses this term when discussing the tales of Laura Gonzenbach. She is more concerned with distinguishing them from modern methods of collecting through the use of tape recorders and cameras that do not pay attention to general rules of punctuation and grammar. The modern recordings on paper have different marks to indicate changes, movements, and breaks, and all the pauses, mistakes, and repetitions of the storyteller are noted. In contrast, Gonzenbach's book tales were intended to make the reading flow more smoothly for the reader without adding other versions and constantly rewriting the original texts. At the same time, she did her best, as she frankly wrote, to recapture the authenticity of the tales as she heard them.

This is impossible, and she even admits it. And because we do not know exactly how she went about her collecting, we are left with many intriguing questions that can never be answered but are worthwhile posing. Did Gonzenbach sit there with pen in hand and immediately translate the dialect tales she heard into high German? Did she just listen and then return home and write them down from memory? How much did Magdalena help her, for we know that she spent the summer vacation with Gonzenbach while she was collecting the tales? How intimate was her relationship to the peasant women? To the slightly more affluent storytellers? Who told her which tale, for she did not write down the name of the informant for each tale? What went on in her mind as she heard these tales? Did she discuss them with her sister Magdalena? Which were her favorites? Did she make some slight changes to make the tales more emancipatory, or were most of the tales truly recorded as they were told? Did she delete details of a scatological or erotic nature? To what extent did Hartwig and Köhler edit the tales? Hartwig insists that he made very few changes. Is there really a great difference between the manner and content of tales told by women and those by men?

We can make some important comparisons with the dialect tales in the resplendent collections of Giuseppe Pitrè. In Gonzenbach's own collection there are two dialect tales at the very end that were not sent by Gonzenbach and are similar to two of her texts.

The dialect text of one story called "The Story of the Three Sisters," recorded by Salvatore Morganti, ends this way:

> "I remember everything," he responded, "and I fall to your feet and ask you to pardon me for all the suffering that I've caused you. I have changed, and I shall be your loyal and tender lover until death. Pardon me, my love."
>
> They made peace and went to sit down at the table to eat, but as he approached her to throw himself into the arms of his lover, the maiden quickly took out a dagger and stabbed him in his heart.
>
> "I'm dying," he said as he fell, "by the hands of a traitor."
>
> The maiden grabbed him by his hair and dragged him down to the foot of the stairs where she buried this lover. The three sisters became owners of this rich palace, but they were not happy because the price of blood is always bitter.

The Gonzenbach tale with the title "The Courageous Maiden" ends somewhat differently:

> So the nobleman went upstairs. When he saw her two sisters, he asked who they were.
>
> "My chambermaids," she answered, and she kept the nobleman there through her polite conversation until it became evening.
>
> "Can I also have the honor of dining with you tonight?" she said, and the nobleman stayed. During the meal, however, she handed him the bottle with the sleeping potion. As soon as he drank a little of it, he sank into a deep sleep. Then she took a little knife and slit his throat so that he died for his sins without confession or absolution. Afterward the maiden called her sisters, and all three dragged him to a deep well and threw him into it. At midnight the door opened once again, and the dark figure entered and said to the youngest sister, "You have saved me through your courage, and now all these treasures belong to you. Live well. Tonight I have come for the last time because now I have found peace."
>
> Upon saying this, she disappeared and never returned. Meanwhile, the three sisters remained in the magnificent castle, and each one of them married a fine gentleman. Indeed, they remained happy and content, and we were left without a cent.

What are we to conclude when we compare the different styles and endings? The version by Morganti is more succinct in its style and appears to capture the vindictiveness of the dead woman, whose murder is avenged by a maiden who shows no mercy to the repentant murderer. The story by Gonzenbach is more elaborate and explanatory. There is a sense that the young women, who were very poor, will be happy. Morganti's text cannot envision happiness smeared by blood. His text presents the woman as first subjecting herself completely. She apparently embraced her subservient position to her lover. Gonzenbach's tale does without such a scene of abject submission. Moreover, she shows a kind of sisterhood with the ghostly woman, and her protagonist seems to emphasize the need and reward for women's communal action against oppressive masters. Instead her ending suggests peace and contentment—at least for the tale's protagonist and her sisters as immediate beneficiaries.

But both tales are bloody, and both are more similar in tone and style than different. Gonzenbach does not minimize the brutal crime suffered by the dead lady; she does not really soften the way the youngest sister kills the nobleman and has his body discarded. Both tales are about ruthless revenge and the reward reaped by three hard-working sisters. The versions by male and female storytellers do not contradict each other. In fact, it may be that the Gonzenbach tale was also told by a male. We cannot be sure, but we can say that while the tales are not exactly feminist, they are not book tales, and they are candid about the humiliation and oppression that women did not want to suffer. Morganti's tale resembles a great deal of the popular broadsides and colportage of the time and has a strong moral conclusion, as if to protect the reputation of Sicilian folklore. The Gonzenbach version envisions a happier end brought about by women who have solidarity with one another. This is, indeed, quite a difference.

As Laura Gonzenbach herself stated, it is difficult on the printed page to capture the flavor and the gesticulations that a storyteller imparts when she tells a tale. We cannot imagine the emphases, shifts of voice, movements of the body, the eye contact, articulated meanings, or the interruptions by the listeners. Nor can we envision the context. Was it the hearth or dinner table? Whose home? Who was there? Nevertheless, the tales that she collected are riveting because she gave them a voice that will continue to resonate today. Her tales, recorded on a tiny island that was the crossroad between oriental and occidental worlds for hundreds of years, recall how cruelty and viciousness have always marred our daily lives, and how words can hold us spellbound for magical moments and alleviate our suffering if we take them seriously and search for the fortunate alternatives they propose.

A Note on the Translation and Acknowledgments

We do not know how Laura Gonzenbach would have ordered the tales when she sent them to Otto Hartwig, but we do know that Reinhold Köhler determined the organization and the placement of the narratives according to tale types. Such categorization is certainly helpful to the scholar, but most other readers will probably find the artificial repetition of plots and motifs in the two-volume German publication of *Sicilianische Märchen* boring. The tales were not told to Laura Gonzenbach to bore her or other listeners. Therefore, I have taken the liberty of mixing the tales according to my taste. I chose the first three tales because I believe that they emphasize the central role women play in many of the narratives and enable readers to grasp how strongly the female narrators were invested in their tales. I have also brought to the front, so to speak, many of the tales that one finds in the classical collections of Charles Perrault, Mme d'Aulnoy, the Brothers Grimm, and Ludwig Bechstein, so that readers familiar with the literary fairy-tale tradition, may readily compare the so-called classics with the "deviant," if not devious, Sicilian analogues. Otherwise, my ordering is arbitrary. That is, I mixed most of the tales without a conceptual purpose except to present more of a kaleidoscope of stories than an orderly progression.

The translation itself did not present major problems because Gonzenbach's style is not complicated, and her command of German was excellent as well as her knowledge of standard phrases, motifs, and topoi. Nevertheless, her translation of Sicilian dialect tales into high German raises some issues, which is why Sicilian folklorists like Giuseppe Pitrè, Salvatore Salmone-Marino, and Giuseppe Cocchiara, to name but a few, were reluctant to acknowledge Gonzenbach's achievement. Certainly, in their eyes, her translation was a kind of betrayal if not an illegitimate expropriation of what belonged to the Sicilian people.

But there is always a struggle for appropriation, adaptation, and authenticity whenever tales are translated and printed. This is what makes them so interesting, especially if we admit to their conflicting nature.

In his brilliant forward to Zora Neale Hurston's *Every Tongue Got to Confess: Negro Folk-tales from the Gulf States*, John Edgar Wideman remarked: "How speech is represented in writing raises more than questions of aesthetics. An ongoing struggle for authority and domination is present in any speech situation interfacing former slaves with former masters, minority with major culture, spoken with written. Such interfaces bristle with extralinguistic tensions that condition and usually diminish mutual intelligibility" (p. xv). As much as a translation may seek to recuperate words, language, customs, and proverbs of a particular dialect used by an oppressed people to form bonds and understanding, it also destroys, omits, and obfuscates the historical conditions and context in which the oral tales were told and appreciated. Authentic or definitive renderings of oral folk tales in written languages are virtually impossible, even if the collector takes down the story in the vernacular with signs denoting tone and gesticulation. The contextual moment cannot be recaptured. The relevance cannot be completely discerned. Sometimes, one must ask oneself, why collect? Why translate and transliterate? Why trespass?

Dialects and so-called minor languages are dying, and they are doing so rapidly. The early folklorists—many of them amateurs or philologists—began recognizing this during the latter part of the nineteenth century and so helped bring into being folklore as a profession. As much as they could, they wanted to preserve languages, customs, belief systems, and artifacts in the original to document the everyday life of communities. The people or common folk could speak for themselves, but they had not been educated to write and organize things for themselves. Therefore, educated scholars, no matter how colonialist or condescending their attitude toward the common folk, committed themselves to inscribing into history those narratives that might have otherwise died or undergone such momentous changes that they would be rendered unrecognizable.

To collect, transcribe, and translate folklore is to recognize the values of common people and to esteem their position in the world even if one does not comprehend fully what the words of these people represent in the web of relations of power and authority. When Laura Gonzenbach went to the peasant women in the region of Catania and Messina, she did so as an authority figure of the upper class who had, at best, a dim understanding of what it meant to lead the life of a peasant or common laborer. Nevertheless, she inspired trust among her informants, who provided her with more tales than she had ever imagined she would receive, and they would have told her even more if she had so desired. Perhaps they trusted her because she showed them respect, gave them money, and demonstrated that she cared for them despite all differences of rank and experience. We don't know. Perhaps she even shared some of their attitudes and beliefs and felt a bond with them as women. Perhaps she had a deep affection for sounds of the first tongue she encountered and used before she learned German, for most of the European children in privileged homes learned Sicilian first from nurses, nannies, and servants before they were introduced to the "cultivated" language of their parents. We have no concrete information on any of that, but we may wonder what Laura Gonzenbach felt and thought as she heard these marvelous tales—tales she may have even heard when she was very young—and then wrote them down in German.

There is not one trace of dialect in Gonzenbach's German translation. The language she uses is literary German. As she recorded the tales on paper and sought the appropriate German words and expressions, she more than likely thought about what an educated German might expect as he or she read folk tales. Her primary and intended reader was such a man, Otto Hartwig, the German theologian turned historian. She had to find the forms and words that he would approve, and she probably also censored herself, unless the peasant women already censored themselves by omitting curse words, sexual inferences, and other speech that had no place in the literature of this era's polite classes. Traces of Gonzenbach's desire to capture the language of her informants, however, survive in her many footnotes and explanations of Sicilian terms.

Because I am familiar with many of the extant Sicilian dialect versions of the tales Gonzenbach collected, I know how different they are from her high German renderings. At the same time, I have been surprised at how closely Gonzenbach held to the plots and the terse and abrupt manner in which the tales were obviously told. The dialect tales give a good indication of the tone and color of the tales, and, fortunately, her German equivalents do not embellish or improve the tales with smooth transitions and clearer motivation. Gonzenbach respected the "authorial" and ideological perspective of the narrators, and I have tried to follow her example, for the value of the translated narratives lies in the manner in which they retain the viewpoint of the lower-class perspective and style. There is no clear uniform ideology in the tales, but Gonzenbach's translation keeps alive the anger, disappointment, hope, and hardiness of the storytellers, who view life from the bottom and do not mask their sentiments.

It is foolish to generalize about translation, for each text brings its own demands and difficulties. For an educated woman such as Gonzenbach, translating tales told by lower-class informants, mainly women, into an upper-class language was not only a very particular process of retention, but it also meant to confront how discontented people thought and spoke and contended, or wished to contend, with oppression. Despite the different languages, Sicilian and high German, Gonzenbach managed to convey the spirit of insurrection and provocation with which the tellers imbued their tales. I sincerely hope I have managed to retain this spirit from Gonzenbach's words in this English translation.

My work on this project would not have been possible if I had not been guided and assisted by the very gracious Luisa Rubini, who has paved the way for scholars seriously interested in Gonzenbach and Sicilian folklore. As usual, Bill Germano, a superb editor and friend, has been closely involved in this project. I have also benefitted from the advice and suggestions of Nancy Canepa, Carol Dines, Carmelo Lettere, and Patrizia McBride. Last but not least I want to thank Alan Kaplan for overseeing the production of this book and Rebecca Condit for the careful and meticulous editorial work.

Jack Zipes
Rome, June 7, 2003

1

SORFARINA

Once upon a time there was a king and queen who had only one
son. Because they wanted him to learn everything that a son
should know for someone of his social class, they sent him to a
teacher in a school. Many other children also attended this school, and
among them a merchant's daughter more beautiful than the sun, and
she was called Sorfarina. Not only was she beautiful, but she learned her
lessons better than any of the other children, including the prince, and
the teacher was very proud and fond of her.

Now, one day, the teacher had to take a trip and did not know who
to place in charge of the school during his absence. While he was con-
templating this matter, Sorfarina asked, "Teacher, what's the matter?"

"Oh, Sorfarina, I have a great dilemma. I have to take a trip, and I
don't know who to place in charge of the school."

"Place me in charge," Sorfarina said. "I'll teach the students while
you're gone."

The teacher thought this was a good solution, and he departed,
while Sorfarina kept the school going. However, one day as she was
teaching the prince, he refused to pay attention. She became impatient
and gave him a slap in the face. The prince did not react at all, but he
remembered the insult in his heart.

Many years passed. The prince no longer attended the school, and
Sorfarina had become a marvelously beautiful maiden, so beautiful that
he fell passionately in love with her. One day he went to his father and

said, "Dear Father, I've found a bride whom I like very much. I want Sorfarina to become my wife."

His father would have preferred to see him marry a princess, but because he could never deny him anything, he said, "All right, my son, if you want her, take her."

So a splendid wedding was celebrated with many festivities, and the prince married the beautiful Sorfarina. However, when they went into their bedroom to sleep, he said, "Sorfarina, do you remember the slap in the face you gave me when we were younger? Tell me, do you regret it?"

"No," she answered.

"I didn't regret it, and I don't regret it now.

"And if you want another slap, you'll get one and how!"*

"What?" the prince cried out, extremely angry. "You dare say something like that to me! Well, then I don't want you in my bed!"

Upon saying this, he kicked her out of the bed, and Sorfarina had to sleep on the ground. However, because he loved her so much, his heart troubled him when he saw her lying on the cold stones, and he said to her, "Dear Sorfarina, tell me, don't you really regret it?"

"No," she answered.

"I didn't regret it, and I don't regret it now.

"And if you want another slap, you'll get one and how!"

No matter how many times he asked and no matter how tenderly he spoke to her, she always gave him the same answer so that he finally became furious and cried out, "All right, then stay where you are!"

The next morning he ran to his mother and told her everything.

"Just think," he said, "after Sorfarina slept the entire night on the cold floor, she still won't say that she regrets the slap in the face that she gave me!"

"My son," she responded, "let it go! That's something which has long since passed."

"No, Mother," he declared. "I want her to say it to me once and for all."

Then he ran back to Sorfarina and said, "Sorfarina, tell me, don't you regret it?"

"No," she answered.

"I didn't regret it, and I don't regret it now.

"And if you want another slap, you'll get one and how!"

---

*Nun m'aju pintuto, e nun mi pintirò,
　　Se n'autra ci ni voli, ti la darò.

"Oh, Sorfarina," he complained, "how stubborn you are! Do you know that I'm going to have you thrown into the well if you don't say it?"

"Well, have me thrown into the well!"

In short, even though he ran back and forth to her many times during the day and tried this way and that, he wasn't successful in getting another answer from her. Finally, he became so angry that he had her thrown into the empty well, which was in the courtyard. Yet, he kept running back to her every second to say: "Sorfarina, I beg you. Tell me that you regret it."

"No," she answered.

"I didn't regret it, and I don't regret it now.

"And if you want another slap, you'll get one and how!"

"Do you know that I'm going to take a long trip far away, and I'm going to leave you here in the well?"

"Go as far as you want," she replied. "Just do me a favor before you leave and tell me whether you're going to travel by land or by sea."

Many days passed this way, and Sorfarina could not be moved either through pleas or threats to say she regretted what she had done. When the prince realized how stubborn she was, he reached the end of his patience and cried out to her, "Farewell! I'm going to Rome."

"Have a nice trip! Are you going by land or by sea?"

"By sea."

"Good," Sorfarina thought to herself, "I'll go by land."

The prince departed, and as soon he left, she climbed out of the well and traveled by land to Rome. Once there she rented a pretty house across from the inn in which the prince was staying. When he looked out his window in the morning, he saw her standing on the balcony across from him. Indeed, he stared at her in astonishment and thought, "Oh, what a beautiful lady! If I hadn't left my wife Sorfarina in the well, I'd say that it was she."

Then he greeted her, and she responded to him in a friendly way. After a few days he went over to her house, and in a short time they formed such an intense friendship that, within a year, a handsome baby boy was born. They called him Romano. Meanwhile, the prince had told her that he had a beautiful but stubborn wife at home who would not bring herself to say to him she regretted giving him a slap in his face.

"Oh," Sorfarina said, "why don't you forgive the poor woman and take her out of the well?"

"No, I want her to do what I demand, just once."

One day, when the little boy was a few months old, Sorfarina said to the prince, "Why don't you go home and see if your poor wife is still sitting in the well? Perhaps she has now reconsidered things for the better."

So the prince departed for home by sea, while Sorfarina left her child with the fairies, who served her because she could do magic, and traveled home by land. When the prince arrived, she was already sitting in the well.

"Now, Sorfarina," he said, "do you still want to be stubborn? I beg you. Tell me that you regret it."

"No," she answered.

"I didn't regret it, and I don't regret it now.

"And if you want another slap, you'll get one and how!"

The prince was completely despondent, for he loved Sorfarina very much, and yet she refused to do his will. One day he said to her, "Sorfarina, if you won't regret it, then I'm going to travel to Naples today."

"Have a nice trip! Are you going by land or by sea?"

"By sea."

"Then I'll go by land," she thought, and no sooner did the prince depart than she climbed out of the well and also traveled to Naples. Once she was there, she rented a house across from the inn in which the prince was staying. When he went to the window, she was standing on the balcony across from him, and he stared at her in amazement.

"What's this now? If I hadn't left my wife in the well, and my lady friend in Rome, I would have to say that this beautiful woman is one of them."

He greeted her, and she responded in a friendly way. In short, after a year, the prince had another baby boy named Napolitano. When the child was a few months old, Sorfarina said to him, "Why don't you go home and see if your wife has reconsidered everything?"

So the prince traveled home, but Sorfarina was faster than he was, and when he came to the well, his wife was already standing there and asked him, "Well, have you had a delightful time in Naples?"

"Oh, Sorfarina, if you would only do what I say, you can't imagine how much I'd love to stay with you. Please, dear Sorfarina, tell me that you regret it!"

However, Sorfarina gave him the same answer, no matter how much he pleaded with her or threatened her. One day he became so furious that he went to her and said, "Sorfarina, either say it or I'm going to travel to Genoa today!"

"Have a nice trip!" she cried in a mocking tone, and as soon as he had departed, she climbed out of the well and arrived in Genoa at the same time he did. Once again she rented a house across from the inn in which her husband was staying, and the first thing he saw when he looked out his window was the beautiful lady standing across from him on her balcony.

"Something's not right here!" he cried. "Here's another woman who looks just like my Sorfarina. If I hadn't left my wife in the well, and my lady friend in Rome, and my other one in Naples, I'd have to think that she was one of them."

Now he greeted her. She thanked him. Soon they formed a friendship, and before a year had passed, a little daughter saw the light of day, and they called her Genova. One day, when the girl was a few months old, Sorfarina said, "Why don't you go back home and see what has happened to your poor wife? Who knows, perhaps she has reconsidered everything!"

So, the prince traveled home, but Sorfarina was not lazy, and when he came to the well, she was already standing in it.

"Dear Sorfarina," he begged, "you're certainly not stubborn anymore. I beg you, tell me that you regret it."

"No," she answered.

"I didn't regret it, and I don't regret it now.

"And if you want another slap, you'll get one and how!"

No matter how often the prince went to the well, Sorfarina always gave him the same answer.

"Sorfarina!" he finally said, "if you don't do what I want, I'm going to take another woman for my wife!"

"Take her!" she answered.

So, he sent for a beautiful princess, and plans were made for a splendid wedding celebration. But the prince could not forget his beloved Sorfarina, and he ran back to her and begged, "Sorfarina, out of love for me, do it. I'm serious about taking another woman for my wife, and tonight there will be a great ball the royal castle."

"Have a wonderful time," she answered. "Do what you want."

That evening, however, she wished for her three children, and all at once they stood before her. They were the finest looking and most handsome children imaginable, and they were wearing magnificent royal garments. She also wished the most glorious gown for herself and the richest jewelry, and many servants, who washed her with water that had a pleasant aroma, and who dressed her with great care. Finally she wished for a golden carriage with four horses and everything else that went along with it. Then she climbed into the carriage with her three children and drove to the castle.

When she arrived and entered the grand ballroom with her three children, everybody looked at her in amazement, for she was the most beautiful of all the women, and her gown was magnificent. The prince rushed to her and wanted to dance with her. Then she called out in a high voice: "Romano and Napolitano, take your sister Genova by the hand and dance with her."

When the prince heard these names, he stood there as if he were struck by thunder, and when he looked at Sorfarina more closely, he recognized her all at once and cried out, "Oh, Sorfarina! Is it you? Were you also the lady in Rome, Naples, and Genoa?"

"Yes," she answered. "It was me. So this was the way you spent your time while you left your wife sitting in the well?"

And she gave him a slap in the face in front of all the people at the ball.

Now you can imagine how disturbed the prince was when he was treated this way in front of all these people. However, he could not do anything but ask for forgiveness, and when he saw his children there, he embraced them full of joy and said to Sorfarina, "Well, now you are to remain my dear wife."

So he had to send the princess from the foreign country back to her home, and the prince took Sorfarina as his wife once again to honor her. But she was smart and kept thinking, "Who knows whether he really has forgiven me?"

Later she went into their bedroom before him and made a large doll out of sugar and honey about her size. The doll had a string around its neck, and when she pulled on it, the doll nodded with its head. Sorfarina placed the doll into their bed and then hid beneath it with the string in her hand. Shortly thereafter, the prince came into the room and went over to the bed and asked her, "Well, Sorfarina, are you finally going to say that you regret it?"

Sorfarina pulled the string so that the doll shook its head as if to say "no."

"What?" he yelled. "Even now you're still stubborn?"

He became so furious that he pulled out his sword and cut off the doll's head. When he ran the blade through his mouth to wipe off the blood, it tasted so sweet that he became sad and cried, "Oh, your blood was so sweet, my dearest Sorfarina, and I've killed you! Well, I don't want to live any longer!"

Just as the prince was about to stab himself with the sword, Sorfarina jumped out from beneath the bed, embraced him, and cried, "Stop! I'm still alive. Let's eat this dove of honey and sugar as husband and wife."*

The prince hugged his wife full of joy and said, "Well, you've led me on quite a trip up to this point, and I forgive you everything."

"And I want to say to you that I regret having given you the slap in the face," she cried.

Now the joy was really great, and they remained happy and content with their children, but we're still sitting here without a cent.

---

* E la palumna di zuccaru e meli, ni la manciamu maritu e mugghièri.

2

THE GREEN BIRD

O nce upon a time there was a king who had just one daughter named Maruzza, and he loved her more than anything in the world. One day, when he was playing with little Maruzza on the terrace, an astrologer walked by, and when this man caught sight of the little princess, he shook his head. The king became furious and ordered the astrologer to be seized and brought to him.

"Why did you shake your head when you looked at my daughter?" the king asked him.

"Oh, your majesty," he responded. "I was only lost in my thoughts."

"If you don't tell me the truth right away," the king said. "I'll have you thrown into the dungeon."·

So the poor astrologer had to obey and said, "When the princess turns eleven, her destiny will take a terrible turn."

Now the king became very despondent and had a tower built without windows in a desolate region, and he had his daughter locked inside with her nurse. He came and visited her often. In the meantime, Maruzza grew and became more beautiful with each passing day. At mealtimes, however, they gave her meat without bones so that she

---

*In German, Burgverließ; in Italian, trabano; in French, fr. oubliette

wouldn't harm herself. They also took everything away from her that might cause her harm.

When she was almost eleven years old, her nurse came to her one day and brought her a piece of roast goat in which a sharp bone was still lodged. Maruzza found the bone and wanted very much to play with it, and because she knew that her nurse would take it away from her, she hid it behind a box. Later, when she was left alone, she took the bone out and began to scratch the wall with it. There was a hollow place in the wall exactly where she had begun scratching so that she had soon made a little hole. She continued to dig with the bone so that the hole became so large she could stick her head outside. All at once she saw the beautiful flowers, the blue sky, and the sun, and she was so happy about all of this that she spent the entire day just looking through the hole. However, when the nurse came into the room, she hung a little curtain over the hole. From then on, whenever the nurse was absent, Maruzza kept looking through the hole for days on end. On the very day of her eleventh birthday there was a rustling in the air, and a beautiful, glistening green bird flew through the hole and said, "I'm a bird and want to be a man," and all at once the bird was transformed into a handsome young man. When Maruzza saw him, she was terribly frightened and wanted to scream, but he soothed her with friendly words, "Noble maiden, don't be afraid of me, I'll do you no harm. I'm an enchanted prince and must stay under a magic spell for many more years. If you'll wait for me, I'll make you my wife one day."

Gradually, the prince managed to calm Maruzza, and after an hour had passed, he became a bird again and left her with the promise to return the next day. From then on he came to her each day at noon, and when the clock struck one, he left her again.

After one year had passed, the king thought, "Now the danger for my Maruzza must be over," and he went to the tower in a beautiful coach and brought her back to the castle. Even though Maruzza was now living in her father's splendid castle, she became very sad, for the beautiful, green bird did not come to her any more, and she became so melancholy that she could no longer laugh and continually stayed in her room. So the king issued a proclamation that was sent throughout his entire realm: "Whoever can get the princess to laugh will be richly rewarded."

Well, an old woman who lived on top of a mountain heard about this and set out for the king's castle. Along the way she met a man driving his mule loaded with sacks filled with money.

"Give me a handful of your money," she requested.

The mule driver replied, "I can't give you anything here. If you come with me to the castle where I have to deliver the sacks, then I'll give you some."

So the old woman went with him, and he led her to a marvelous castle inhabited by twelve fairies. When the mule driver and the old woman climbed the steps of the castle, the man opened the sacks and let a few coins fall to the ground. There were so many, however, that the old woman was satisfied by the mere sight of the money and she did not demand any coins. She went through the rooms and saw the valuable treasures that were gathered there. All the chairs, tables, and beds were made of pure gold. Finally, she entered a room that had a table covered with twelve gold plates and twelve gold cups. Then she went farther and came to the kitchen where there were twelve fairies standing in a row, and each one was in front of a hearth with a gold kettle of soup being heated by a fire. When the soup was done, they took their kettles off the fire and placed them on to the table. Because they ignored the presence of the old woman, she became bold and said, "My noble ladies, you haven't said anything, so don't be insulted if I help myself to the soup."

So the old woman took a gold spoon and helped herself to some of the soup. But when she lifted the spoon to her mouth, the soup splashed into her face and she burned herself very badly. At the very same moment there was a rustling in the air, and the green bird flew into the room.

"I'm a bird and want to be a man!" said the bird, and he was transformed immediately into the handsome prince. He began groaning right away and cried out, "Oh, Maruzza, my Maruzza, have I completely lost you? Why can't I find you anywhere?"

The fairies gathered around him to console him, but the old woman left the castle unnoticed and thought, "I've got to tell the young princess this story. If this does not cause her to laugh, then nothing ever will."

When the old woman arrived at the royal castle, she had herself announced to the king and said she had come make his daughter laugh. The king led her to his daughter's room and left them alone. Now the old woman began to tell how she had been taken to the beautiful castle by the mule driver, and how she had burned her mouth as she had tried to taste the soup. Upon hearing all this, Maruzza broke into laughter, and the king, who was listening outside, was very happy that someone

---

*In Sicily it is considered a terrible violation of hospitality if a stranger is not invited to eat when one sits down at the table.

had finally succeeded in making his dear child laugh. However, the old woman said, "Listen to the end of my story, my little lady!" And she told her about the green bird that changed itself into a handsome prince and continually asked about the whereabouts of his dear Maruzza.

Then Maruzza became even more cheerful and said, "My father will give you a beautiful gift, and you will receive just as much from me if you come here tomorrow at the same hour and secretly lead me to the castle of the twelve fairies."

The old woman promised to do this, and on the next day she came and led the princess a long way over a mountain and through a valley until they came to the castle of the twelve fairies. Once again the fairies were sitting in front of their gold hearths, and the soup had just been finished and taken from the fire in gold kettles.

"Just look, my girl," the old woman said, "this was the way I tried to eat the soup," and she took some of the soup with a gold spoon. But when she wanted to put the spoon into her mouth, the soup splashed into her face.

"Let me try," Maruzza said, and she took the gold spoon, dipped it into the soup, and guess what happened! She could easily put the spoon of soup into her mouth.

All of a sudden there was a rustling in the air, and the green bird flew into the room and changed itself into the handsome prince. When he began to groan, "Oh, Maruzza, my Maruzza!" the princess rushed into his arms and cried out, "Here I am!"

But the prince became very sad and said, "Oh, Maruzza, what have you done? Why have you come here? Now I must depart and must fly around seven years, seven days, seven hours, and seven minutes without any peace or rest."

"What?" the poor Maruzza cried. "Do you want to leave me now after I've been so sad because of you and have traveled so far just to see you?"

"I can't help you," the prince answered. "But if you want to release me from the spell, I'll tell you what you must do."

Then he led her onto a terrace and said, "If you wait for me here seven years, seven days, seven hours, and seven minutes, and if you can withstand storms and sunshine and don't eat, drink, and speak, then I can be released from the magic spell, and you'll become my wife."

Upon saying this he became a bird once more and flew away. Now, poor Maruzza sat on the terrace, and when the fairies came and asked her to come back into the castle, she shook her head and remained seated in a corner. She did not eat or drink, and she did not utter a word. This was the way she remained for seven years, seven days, seven hours, and seven minutes in rain and storm and in the glowing heat of the sun, and her fine white skin became black, and her face became ugly and distorted, and her tender arms and legs became stiff.

When the long time of the enchantment was over, there was a rustling in the air, and the green bird came flying down to the terrace and became a handsome prince. Then she rushed into his arms, wept, and cried out, "Now, you're free, and now all our sufferings have come to an end!"

However, when he saw how ugly she had become and how black, he did not love her any more, for all men are like this. So he shoved her brusquely away and said, "What do you want from me? I don't know you."

"You don't know me?" Maruzza wept and said. "I left my old father because of you! And yes, because of you, I sat here for seven years, seven days, seven hours, and seven minutes and withstood rain and sunshine. I didn't eat or drink. I did not even utter one word!"

"And you did this all for a mere mortal? You lay here on this terrace like a dog?" he said. "You let all of this happen to you?" He spit two times into her face, turned away, and left her.

Poor Maruzza fell to the ground and wept bitter tears. Then the fairies came, consoled her, and said, "Keep up your courage, Maruzza. You'll become even more beautiful than you were and get revenge on this wicked man."

They brought her back into the castle and washed her with rose water for many days until she became completely white and so beautiful once more that no one could recognize her as she had been before. Then Maruzza traveled to the country where the prince lived with his mother, the old queen, and the fairies accompanied her with all their precious things. Once there, the fairies built a marvelous palace for Maruzza overnight, which faced the royal palace.

When the prince looked out of his window the next morning, he was astonished to see the beautiful castle that was much more beautiful than his own. While he was wondering how the castle had been created, Maruzza appeared in the window across from him. She was wearing splendid clothes and was so beautiful that the prince could not take his eyes off her. Because he did not recognize her, he bowed to her and wanted to address her. However, Maruzza slammed her window and shut it right before his nose.

"Oh," the prince thought, "who is this lady who thinks she is better than I am?" He called his mother and asked her whether she knew the woman, but she did not know anything about her, and no matter who and where he asked, he could not gather any information about her.

Every morning, when he caught sight of her by her window, he moved to his balcony, but when he tried to greet her and speak to her, she proudly turned her back on him and slammed her window shut. The prince became sad because he would have liked to have made the beautiful woman his wife.

"Mother," he said to the old queen one day, "do me a favor and go over to the beautiful lady who lives across from us, and take her your most beautiful headband in my name and ask her if she would like to become my wife."

The old queen set out and went to the beautiful Maruzza's castle, and a servant carried the golden headband, which glistened with pearls and precious stones, on a silver plate. When Maruzza heard that the queen was there and wanted to speak with her, she rushed toward her and said, "Oh, your majesty, why didn't you ask me to come to your castle? Why have you made such a fuss on my behalf? It was I who should have asked permission to see you." Then she led the queen with many flattering words into her best room, which radiated with gold and precious stones.

"How may I serve you, noble queen?" Maruzza asked.

"My son has sent me to you," the queen responded. "He has fallen passionately in love with you and asks for your hand in marriage. He has also sent you this valuable headband."

"What an honor!" Maruzza replied. "But your son deserves the richest and most distinguished queen, not a poor maiden like me. I'm not worthy of this honor."

While she was speaking, she took the valuable headband, plucked it apart into into small pieces, and called out "Kur, kur, kur," and the twelve fairies entered the room. They had transformed themselves into twelve little geese and swallowed the gold kernels greedily as well as the precious stones. When the old queen saw this spectacle, she was so outraged and astounded that she could not utter a word.

"Your majesty," Maruzza said, "why do you look so furious? I usually feed my geese with pure gold."

While she said this, she signaled a servant who brought her costly jewelry, headbands, and armbands on a platter, and she plucked them apart into a thousand little pieces and spread them on the ground for the geese.

In the end, the queen returned to her home fully irritated and feeling that she had been put to shame. Meanwhile, the prince was already standing on his balcony again and looking for the beautiful maiden. After Maruzza had accompanied his mother to the door, she rushed back to her room and stepped out on her balcony. When the prince sought to greet her, she turned her back on him and slammed the window shut. Right away the prince realized that she had rejected him before his mother could even bring him her answer, and he was deeply dejected. However, he could not keep himself from going on to his balcony every day and looking for the beautiful Maruzza, even though she continued to turn away from him and slam her window shut.

After some time had passed, the prince spoke to the old queen once again, "Mother, do me a favor and go one more time to the beautiful lady and ask her if she will be my wife."

"Oh, my son," his mother answered, "think of how cruelly she insulted me last time. I can't go back to her."

But the prince said, "Mother, if you really love me, you'll do as I request and bring her my crown in my name."

Then he took the crown off his head and gave it to his mother, and the old queen let herself be persuaded to visit the beautiful Maruzza one more time.

When Maruzza saw the queen coming, she rushed toward her and received her with great hospitality, and when they were alone with one another, Maruzza asked again, "How may I serve you, noble queen?"

"My son is passionately in love with you," she responded, "and he's sent me here to ask you whether he may have the honor of becoming your husband. As a sign of his love, he's sent you his gold crown, which he took off his head."

"Oh, noble queen," Maruzza said, "how could I accept this honor? A poor maiden like me is not fit to become the wife of your son."

As she said this, Maruzza called her cook and said, "Come over here and take this gold crown. I think it will be the perfect cover for my kettle." When she saw that the queen was once more disturbed and filled with anger, she continued. "Noble queen, why are you so disturbed? I'm accustomed to having gold crowns for my kettles." Then she signaled to the cook, who brought several kettles with gold crowns.

So the queen returned to her home thoroughly upset once more and feeling that she had been put to shame, while Maruzza rushed to the window to give the prince his usual insult.

Eventually the prince became sick from anger and sorrow, and he stayed in bed for an entire month. No sooner did he get better than he crept straight to his balcony, and when he saw Maruzza standing across from him, he tried to greet her again. She again turned her back on him and slammed her window shut right before his nose. Then the prince said to his mother, "If you really love me, go to the beautiful lady and ask her if she will be my wife."

The queen did not want to go, but he continued to beg her so much that she finally said "yes." So he took his heavy gold chain from his neck and gave it to his mother to take to the beautiful lady. The queen was greeted by Maruzza once again with great hospitality, and Maruzza asked, "How may I serve you, noble queen?"

The queen told her once more that the prince wanted to make her his wife and had sent his gold chain, but Maruzza explained once again that she was too poor and too low for the prince. Then she signaled to one of her servants, gave him the chain, and said, "Put it around the dog's neck."

When the queen stood there speechless because of the new insult, Maruzza said, "Your majesty, why are you so furious? All my dogs have collars made of pure gold." Then she signaled to her servant who brought a platter with many dog collars made of gold. They were all thick and large.

The queen had to return home once again without having accomplished a thing while Maruzza rushed to the balcony. When she saw the prince, who looked at her with a sad face, she turned her back on him and closed the window.

Now the prince became so sick that everyone believed he would die. After a long time, however, he became better and said right away to his mother, "Mother, I beg you to go to the beautiful lady just one more time and plead with her to be my wife. Tell her that if she rejects me and closes the window with so much disdain, I shall fall down dead before her very eyes."

The queen did not want to go at all, but because she saw how weak and sick her son was, she decided to see the beautiful Maruzza despite it all. Once again she was received in a friendly way and said to Maruzza, "Noble lady, I've come with a request that you must not refuse. My son is more than ever passionately in love with you and wants you to be his wife. If you, however, reject him and slam the window shut before his nose, he will fall down dead before your very eyes. Without you he cannot live."

Then Maruzza answered, "Tell your son that, if out of love for me, he decides to let himself be carried in a coffin from his house to mine and has the death bells ring in the entire city and is accompanied by priests who sing funeral songs, I shall have a priest waiting here, and he will perform the marriage ceremony."

The queen returned to her son with this answer, and he immediately had a beautiful coffin built and lay down inside. Death bells were rung in the entire city, and the prince was carried in the coffin accompanied by priests with burning candles who also sang funeral songs. Maruzza

16

stood there in regal adornment on her balcony and watched the funeral march with pride.

When the coffin was beneath her window, she leaned down and yelled with a loud voice, "How could you lower yourself out of love for a mere mortal? Even though you're alive, you're now good as dead in a coffin," and she spit twice into his face.

It was then that the prince finally recognized her and cried out, "Maruzza, my Maruzza!"

As he continued to shout her name, she rushed down from the balcony and said to him, "Yes, I'm your Maruzza, and I wanted you to feel all the sorrow and grief that you caused me. Now we're even, and the priest is waiting to marry us."

Indeed, a splendid wedding was celebrated, and the prince became king, and Maruzza became queen.

3

THE SNAKE WHO BORE
WITNESS FOR A MAIDEN

Once upon a time there was a poor woman, so poor that she had to live in a very wild and desolate region. She had just one daughter, who was more beautiful than the sun. The mother gathered herbs and took them into the city where she sold them, while her daughter generally remained at home and cooked and washed.

One day, when the mother had gone into the city again with her herbs, the daughter remained all alone at home, and the king's son happened into this wilderness. He had been hunting and had become separated from his entourage. When he caught sight of the little cottage, he got off his horse, knocked on the door, and asked for a glass of water because he was so thirsty. The maiden did not open the door, but instead opened the window and handed him the glass of water through the window. As soon as he saw how strikingly beautiful she was, he was overcome by a dark desire and impetuously demanded that she open the door for him. She refused, but he was driven by his wild desires and broke down the door. He forced his way into the house and overpowered the maiden. She yelled and cried, but no one heard her. As she was looking around for some help, she noticed a snake crawling by. "Since nobody hears me in my need," she said, "I'm calling upon you, oh snake, to bear witness for me: prince, may you never marry anyone but me!" After she said this she yielded to the prince's will. He then left the cottage, and she never told her mother anything about this.

Not long after this event a rumor spread that the prince was soon to marry a beautiful princess. One day, after the mother had gone to the city again to sell herbs and returned in the evening, the maiden asked, "Tell me, dear Mother, what's new in the city?"

"Oh, my child," her mother said, "I've heard such an unusual story, nobody believes it. Just think, the prince has a snake wrapped around his neck, and nobody can chase it away, and when anyone tries to pry it loose, the snake only tightens itself around the prince's neck so that he has almost been strangled to death."

When the daughter heard this, she knew quite well what snake it was and set out early the next morning for the city without saying anything to her mother, and went straight to the castle.

When the guards saw her and asked her what she wanted, she said, "Announce me to the king. I have a way to free the prince from the snake that's wrapped itself around his neck."

The guards began to laugh and said, "Many doctors and wise folk have already tried this, and nobody has succeeded. Now you want to try!"

But she responded, "Just announce me to the king."

When the king heard the noise, he asked what was happening.

"There's a maiden down below," his servants told him. "She boasts that she has a way to free the prince from the snake."

"Well, let her come up," the king said. "Even if she doesn't have a way, it won't harm to let her try."

So the beautiful maiden was led to the king, and the king conducted her into his son's room and left her there alone with his son. She stepped up to him and said, "Look at me. Do you recognize me?"

"No," the prince replied, but as he said this, the snake tightened itself around his neck.

"What?" she continued. "Have you forgotten how you charged into my house and forced me to do your will? Don't you recall how I called on the snake to bear witness so that you would not be able to marry anyone else but me?"

He would liked to have responded "no" again, but the snake tightened itself even more, so that he finally said "yes." Then the snake released its grip a little.

"And now you want to marry a princess and abandon me?" the maiden asked.

"Yes," he answered. As soon as he said those words the snake wrapped itself more tightly around his neck until he finally promised that he would not marry the princess.

"Now swear to me that you'll marry me," the maiden said.

The prince swore, and just as he did the snake released itself from his neck and disappeared. The prince rushed to the king and said, "Dear Father, send my fiancée back to her father. This maiden has freed me from the evil snake, and she is the one who will be my bride."

The prince married the beautiful maiden, and she had her mother come to the castle. They lived happy and content, but we have nothing to pay the rent.

4

The Sister of Muntifiuri

Once upon a time there was a brother and a sister who had neither mother nor father, and they lived alone with one another and cared for each other with great love. The brother was a handsome young man and was called Muntifiuri. His sister was more beautiful than the sun.

Now, one day the king happened to be looking for a new valet, and he was told that Muntifiuri was a handsome young man. So, the king sent him a message ordering him to come to the court because he wanted him to become his valet. Before Muntifiuri departed he had a portrait of his sister made and took it with him. The king quickly took a great liking to his servant, kept him in the best of circumstances, and always wanted to have Muntifiuri at his side. When the young man had nothing to do he often went to his room, looked at the picture of his sister, and wept. The other servants were jealous of the favor the king showed to Muntifiuri, and thought of ways to bring about his downfall. Therefore, they went to the king and said, "Muntifiuri is always sitting in his room, and nobody knows what he's doing there because he won't let anyone enter."

The king became curious and went to his servant's room and secretly looked through the keyhole. There he saw Muntifiuri looking at a portrait and weeping. Later, when Muntifiuri left his room, the king asked him, "Whose portrait are you always looking at? I want you to show it to me at once."

Muntifiuri did not want to show the picture because his sister was very beautiful. The king threatened him, "If you don't show me the portrait right away, I'll have your head cut off."

So Muntifiuri had to fetch the portrait, and when the king saw it, he asked, "Who is that?"

"Your majesty, that's my sister," Muntifiuri answered.

"Is she really so beautiful?" the king asked.

"Even a thousand times more beautiful," said Muntifiuri.

"If she's really a thousand times more beautiful," the king cried, "have her come here. I want to make her my wife."

So Muntifiuri went to his sister and said, "Just think, dear sister, the king wants to elevate you and make you his wife. Now your fortune is made."

"Oh," she answered, "how can I go to the king? I can't travel by sea. You know that when I was a little child, an evil sorceress cast a spell on me and said, 'May the siren of the sea* fetch you!'"

So, her brother had a large ship built that was boarded up on all sides, and told her, "See, dear sister, you can travel safely in this ship because there are no windows or openings, and the siren cannot come in and fetch you."

Now, there was a wicked woman who happened to live next to the brother and sister, and she saw the good fortune that had befallen Muntifiuri's sister with jealous eyes. She also had a daughter who was uglier than sin, and she went to Muntifiuri and said, "We've always been good friends, Muntifiuri, so do me a favor and let my daughter accompany your sister. She can stay with her as a servant."

Muntifiuri agreed with this proposal. He sent his sister and the ugly companion off in the ship enclosed by walls from top to bottom so that his sister would arrive safely at the king's court. However, the evil neighbor had given her daughter a drill and told her, "When you're at sea, I want you to drill a hole in the wall of the ship so that the siren of the sea can enter and fetch the future queen. Then you'll become the queen."

This is exactly what the ugly daughter did. She drilled a hole in the wall of the ship, and all at once the siren came and took Muntifiuri's beautiful sister. Then the neighbor's daughter put on the beautiful maiden's clothes. When the ship sailed into the harbor, Muntifiuri ran onto the deck and had the cabin opened so he could fetch his sister.

---

*Sirena du mari.

However, he only found the neighbor's ugly daughter who looked even uglier in the magnificent clothes of his sister.

So Muntifiuri went to the king, fell at his feet, and said, "Your majesty, my sister slipped into the water along the way and died, and I have only brought my neighbor's daughter."

The king was very depressed when he heard this and said, "If your sister has died, then I shall marry your neighbor's daughter."

The neighbor's daughter was led before the king, but when the king saw her, he was horrified by her ugly face. However, because he had promised to marry her, he did not want to break his royal word. Indeed, he wed the ugly maiden and celebrated with a splendid party.

Now the young queen began thinking of a way to murder Muntifiuri because of the king's fondness for him. She went to her husband and said, "Muntifiuri boasts that he can do great things. He's even begun to build a marvelous fountain on the large square in front of the castle. It will have running water and will be beautifully decorated, and he says he can finish it overnight."

So the king had his faithful servant summoned and said to him, "Muntifiuri, you've boasted that you're going to build a fountain overnight on the square, and it's going to have running water and be beautifully decorated. Either you do as you said you'll do, or I'll banish you from my service."

Muntifiuri became very distressed and went to the seashore where he began to weep bitter tears, "Oh, sister, my sister, things are going very badly for me!"

All of a sudden a beautiful figure emerged from the waves. It was his sister, who was more beautiful than ever before. She had three beautiful maidens on her right side and three on her left, but she was the most beautiful of them all. Unfortunately, she was wearing a golden chain on her foot, which the siren held tightly so that she could not escape.

"Why are you weeping so bitterly, my brother?" she asked.

He poured out all his troubles, but she said, "Put your mind at rest and go home and sleep. Tomorrow morning the fountain will be finished with running water, and it will be beautifully decorated."

Muntifiuri was relieved and went home. During the night his sister came with her six maidens, and it took only a moment for them to erect a marvelous fountain with running water and beautiful decorations. However, she was still wearing the golden chain on her leg, and the siren continued to pull her down into the sea.

When the king awoke the next morning and caught sight of the beautiful fountain, he was extremely pleased and praised his faithful servant. The young queen, however, continued to think of a way she could harm Muntifiuri, and she said to the king, "Muntifiuri is boasting about his talents again. He's already begun planting a marvelous garden all around the fountain and claims there will be trees and flowers from the entire world in this garden."

The king summoned his faithful servant again and ordered him to build a garden around the fountain overnight, and it was to contain all the trees and flowers of the world. If he did not do as the king said, he would be thrown into prison.

Once again, Muntifiuri went to the seashore, wept, and called his sister. She appeared above the water and asked what he wanted. When he told her about his troubles, she answered, "Put your mind at rest, go home, and sleep. Tomorrow morning the garden will be finished."

During the night she came with her six maidens and built a garden that was more beautiful than any other garden in the world, and in it were trees and flowers from all parts of the earth. When the king awoke the next morning, he was astonished by the beautiful garden and was very happy about it. The young queen said to him, "Muntifiuri persists in boasting about his talents. He's been so presumptuous as to declare that he can collect all the different kinds of birds that exist on earth and bring them to the garden overnight."

The king ordered poor Muntifiuri to collect all the birds of the earth in his garden by the next morning, or he would have his head cut off. Muntifiuri went to the seashore again, called his sister, and told her his troubles.

"Just go home and sleep," she said. "Tomorrow the king will be satisfied."

During the night his sister came with her six maidens, and all at once the trees were covered with birds of all kinds from all over the earth. Their songs were the loveliest that had ever been heard.

The young queen then became angry that Muntifiuri had accomplished everything, and that she could do nothing against him. So she took twelve ducks, called Muntifiuri to her, and said, "Every morning you must lead these ducks into the field, and if one is missing in the evening, it will cost you your head."

Muntifiuri took the twelve ducks, drove them to the seashore, and called his sister again. She raised herself from the waves and asked what he wanted.

"I'm supposed to lead these twelve ducks out to pasture," he said. "But if you would give them something to eat, I wouldn't have to go so far."

Then she shook her beautiful braids so that pearls and gold kernels fell out, and the ducks began to peck them with great hunger.

When it became evening and Muntifiuri drove the ducks home, they began to sing:

> Quack, quack, quack, we're coming from the sea.
> We're full of pearls as you can see.
> The sun is beautiful, very bright,
> But Muntifiuri's sister shines brighter
> Than its golden light.˙

When the queen heard this, she was horrified and quickly locked up the ducks so that no one could hear their song. The next morning she took a duck, killed it, and gave Muntifiuri only eleven ducks to take with him. Because he was so immersed in sad thoughts, he forgot to count the ducks and went straight to the seashore where he called his sister. She shook her braids again so that pearls and gold kernels fell out, and the ducks ate them until they were full. When Muntifiuri drove them home, they began to sing once more.

> Quack, quack, quack, we're coming from the sea.
> We're full of pearls as you can see.
> The sun is beautiful, very bright,
> But Muntifiuri's sister shines brighter
> Than its golden light.

The queen rushed down the stairs and locked up the ducks, and when she counted them there were only eleven. So she went to the king and said, "Muntifiuri has lost one of my ducks, and therefore his head must be cut off."

The king had to yield to the queen's will, and so he summoned his faithful servant and said, "Muntifiuri, you've lost one of the queen's ducks. Therefore, you must die."

"Very well," answered Muntifiuri, "but grant me one request and let me go one more time to the seashore."

The king granted this request, and Muntifiuri went to the seashore, called his sister, and told her his troubles.

---

*Qua, qua, qua du mari vinemu,
  Chini di perli nui semu,
  E la soru di Muntifiuri
  E cchiù bedda di lu suli.

"My poor brother," she answered. "Now I can't help you anymore. However, have yourself buried in the garden next to the beautiful fountain. Then I shall come three nights in a row and sing the funeral songs for you. That's the only thing I can do for you."

So Muntifiuri went to the king and said, "After my head is cut off, please let me be buried in three coffins, a lead one, a silver one, and a gold one, and let me be buried in the garden next to the beautiful fountain that I had built for you."

The king promised to do this. After the executioner had cut off his head, he had his body divided into three parts for the three coffins as Muntifiuri had wished, and then had him buried in the garden next to the fountain.

During the night his sister came with her six maidens and sat down on the grave. She sang the funeral songs, and they sounded so lovely that the king's gardeners could not get enough of her songs. But when the siren pulled on the gold chain, the beautiful maiden had to return to the sea.

The next night, things went the same way, and the gardeners went to the king and said, "Your majesty, during the last two nights, seven maidens have appeared in the garden. They are all beautiful. The one in the middle, however, is more beautiful than the sun. She wears a gold chain on her foot, sits down on the grave of your servant Muntifiuri, and sings. Truthfully, we have never heard anything more beautiful in our lives. After a while, however, someone pulls on the chain—we don't know who—and the marvelous figure disappears."

The king became curious and said, "I'm going to watch with you tonight."

When it became evening, the king hid himself in the garden. Soon Muntifiuri's sister appeared for the last time and sat down on the grave and sang more beautifully than she had done during the first two nights. All at once the king jumped up and smashed the gold chain in two with his sword.

"Who are you, beautiful maiden?" he asked.

"I'm poor Muntifiuri's sister," she answered. "I didn't drown in the sea. The wicked neighbor's daughter, who is your wife, drilled a hole in the wall of the ship, and the siren of the sea came and dragged me down to the bottom of the sea and has kept me prisoner there with this chain. Now you've released me from her spell by breaking the chain."

"If this is the case, you shall become my wife," the king cried.

So he had the false queen's head chopped off, cut into many little pieces, and salted in a barrel. At the very bottom he placed her hand, which had a ring on it that she had received from her mother. He sent the barrel to the wicked neighbor and had the messenger say to her, "Your daughter, the queen, has sent you this beautiful tuna fish and would like you to eat it out of love for her."

The mother was very happy about this. She opened the barrel right away and began to eat some of the pieces. After she had begun eating, she felt the urge to continue until she began approaching the bottom of the barrel. Now she had a cat and a dog who were continually jumping around her and asking, "Give us a piece, and then we'll help you later when you weep." But she chased them away and refused to give them anything. When she finally came to the bottom of the barrel and found the hand with the ring, she realized that she had eaten her own daughter, and in her sorrow she rammed her head so hard against the wall that she died. The dog and the cat danced in joy around the house and sang, "You didn't give us anything to eat. So we won't help you when you weep."

The king celebrated a splendid wedding and married Muntifiuri's beautiful sister, and they lived happy and content, but we can't even pay the rent.

5

The Story About Ciccu

Once upon a time there was an old man who had three sons. The oldest was called Peppe,[*] the second Alfinu, and the youngest, Ciccu.[†] The man was very poor, and one day he and his sons had nothing more to eat. So he called his three sons and said to them, "My dear children, you know how poor we are. I see no way out other than begging, for I'm old and I can't take on a proper job."

"No, dear Father," the sons answered. "We won't let you go begging. We're the ones who should go begging to support you, but if you permit us, we want to make you a proposal."

"Speak," the father said.

"We want to take you into the forest where you can work with us to cut wood. Then we'll tie it in bundles and carry the wood to sell in the city."

The father agreed, and they made their way into the forest. Because the father was very old and weak, the sons took turns carrying him on their shoulders into the forest. Once they found the right spot, they built a small straw hut[‡] where they could spend the night. From then on the father went every morning to cut firewood, and the sons tied the wood in bundles, carried the wood into the city, and sold it. They used the money to buy their father bread, wine, and other food. While they

---

[*]Giuseppe, Joseph.
[†] Francesco, Frances.
[‡] Pagliaro.

were gone, the father continued to chop wood, and the brothers could therefore travel into the city every morning.

After they had done this for some days they asked their father, "How do you feel, dear Father?"

"Very good," he replied. "We can lead a great life like this."

Several months passed this way, but the father finally became very sick and felt that he was about to die. So he said to his sons, "Fetch a lawyer, my dear children, so that I can make my last will and testament."

When the lawyer arrived the old man said, "I own a little cottage in the village as well as the date tree that stands next to it. I want to leave my house to all three of my sons so that they can live in it. I want to divide the date tree as follows: my son Peppe is to have the branches; my son Alfinu is to have the trunk; my son Ciccu is to have the fruit. I also own an old cover, which I want to leave to my oldest son; my second son is to have an old purse; and my youngest is to be given a horn."

After the father had spoken, he died. Then the brothers talked with one another.

"What should we do now? Should we stay in the forest as we've been doing or should we return to the village? Perhaps it's best to stay here. We've found a good way to earn our living."

So the brothers stayed in the forest, chopped wood, and sold it in the city as they had done before. One evening it turned very hot, and they lay down to sleep in front of the straw hut. Three fairies came by and saw them lying there.

"Just look, dear sisters," one of the fairies said. "Such handsome boys! Why don't we give each one of them a gift?"

"Let's do it," the sisters said.

So the first fairy said, "The oldest has a cover. My gift to him is that when he hangs it around himself and wishes to be any place he wants, he'll be there in a second."

Then the second fairy said, "The second son has a purse. My gift to him is that whenever he speaks to the purse and says, 'dear purse, give me this amount of money or that amount of money,' he'll find it in the purse."

Then the third fairy said, "The youngest has a horn. Whenever he blows on the small end, the sea will swarm with ships. If he blows on the larger end, all the ships will disappear."

Upon saying this the fairies vanished. Ciccu had not slept. Indeed, he had heard everything the fairies had said, and he thought, "Oh, I'd never need anything anymore if I had all these things!"

The next day, when they were working together, Ciccu said to his brothers, "The old cover and the purse are really worthless. Why don't you give them to me?"

The brothers loved Ciccu very much, and because he asked them in such a friendly way, they gave him the cover and the purse. Then Ciccu said, "Listen to me, dear brothers, I've had enough of this life in the forest. Let's move to the city and try to start something there."

"Oh, no, Ciccu, we'd prefer to stay here," the brothers said. "We have it good here. Who knows what would happen to us in the world?"

"We could try it one time," Ciccu insisted. "If things don't go well for us, we'll return to the forest."

So they took the bundles of wood they had just finished tying together and carried them to the city. Ciccu took the cover, the purse, and the horn with him. When they arrived in the city, they discovered that there was a surplus of firewood in the marketplace so that they did not receive much money for their wood, and when they counted everything, there was not enough money even for a midday meal. But Ciccu said, "Come with me to the inn. I'll find a way to pay for our meal."

So they went into the inn, and Ciccu said to the innkeeper, "Bring us a meal with three courses, the best that you have, and some bottles of wine as well."

The brothers became frightened and whispered to him, "Ciccu, what are you doing? How are we going to pay for all this?"

"Let me take care of this," Ciccu answered.

After they had eaten and drunk to their hearts' content, Ciccu said to his brothers, "Why don't you get up and leave? I'll take care of the bill."

The brothers were happy to get away because they thought, "He's certainly going to get a good beating."

But Ciccu simply asked the innkeeper to tell him how much the bill was and then said to his purse, "Dear purse, give me six gulden." No sooner did he say this than he found six gulden in his purse. Then he paid the innkeeper and returned to his brothers in a good mood.

"How did you manage to pay the innkeeper?" they asked.

"What does it matter to you? I managed to get away."

The brothers became anxious and did not want to stay with Ciccu any longer. Then Ciccu said, "I'm going to give you each twenty pounds. Use this money well because I am going to set out alone and want to seek my fortune."

Upon saying this he embraced them and departed. He traveled until he finally came to a city where the king was living. Soon after his arrival he bought beautiful clothes and a wonderful house that faced the royal palace. He closed the gate and had gold from his purse pour all over the stairs until they were fully covered by gold. The rooms were also decorated in a splendid fashion. Soon after he opened the gate once more and began leading a lavish life. The people were astounded by the gold stairs, and everyone in the city could speak about nothing else. The king heard about it and went over to see the beautiful stairs, and Ciccu received him with great honor and showed him around the entire house.

Now the king had a wife and a marvelously beautiful daughter, and they, too, wanted to see the beautiful house with the gold stairs. So, the king sent a messenger to ask whether he could bring his wife to his house, and Ciccu answered that it would be a great honor for him if the queen and her daughter would visit him. When Ciccu saw the beautiful princess, he fell in love with her all at once and wanted to make her his wife, but the princess wanted to know how he had managed to make the stairs into gold. She pretended to like him and flattered him with friendly words until he no longer knew what he was doing. Consequently, he told her about the three fairies in the forest who had cast a magic spell over the cover, the purse, and the horn. Then she asked him to loan her the purse for a few days so that she could learn to make such a purse. Because he loved her so much, he forgot everything and gave her the purse.

The princess took it home and did not think in the least about returning it to him. Meanwhile, Ciccu had used up all the money that he was carrying with him. So he went to the princess and asked her to return the purse. She knew how to put him off until he discovered one day that he did not have a cent to his name. He went to her and said, "Today you definitely must return my purse to me. I need it desperately."

"Oh, leave it with me until early tomorrow morning," she answered. "Then I'll give it back to you for sure."

Ciccu let himself be persuaded once again, but the next morning he did not receive the purse and exploded in anger and swore to revenge himself on the maiden. Since it had become pitch dark, he took a stick in his hand, hung the cover around him, and wished himself to appear in the bedroom of the princess. No sooner did he utter the wish than he was there. The princess was lying in a beautiful bed. Ciccu dragged her roughly from the bed and beat her until she gave him back the purse. Then he wished to be carried back to his house.

Now the princess was furious. She rushed to her father and told him how she had been insulted and how badly she had been treated. The king became enraged and sent his guards to Ciccu's house, where they found him and brought him back to the king.

"You deserve to die," the king said to Ciccu. "But I'll grant you your life if you give me the cover, the purse, and the horn right away."

What could Ciccu do? His life was precious to him. So he delivered the three objects to the king and was once again as poor as he had been before.

Now it was just about this time that the dates were to ripen on the tree, and he thought to himself, "I'll go and see whether the date tree has begun to bear fruit."

When he returned to the little house, his brothers were standing there. They had spent all their money and were living a wretched existence. Ciccu took a basket and wanted to pick some dates, but his brother Peppe said: "Stop! The dates belong to you, of course. However, the branches belong to me, and when you pick your dates, you're not allowed to touch the branches."

Then Ciccu leaned a ladder against the tree in order to reach the dates more easily, but his brother Alfinu called to him. "Stop! The trunk of the tree belongs to me, and you're not allowed to touch it."

When they began to argue about all this and could not come to an agreement, one of them said, "Let's go to the judge and have him decide."

They went to the judge and told him all that had happened, and the judge said to Ciccu, "Since you can't pick the dates without touching the trunk and the branches, I advise you to give the first basket to your brother Peppe, the second to your brother Alfinu, and the rest you can keep for yourself."

The brothers were satisfied, and after they went home, they said to one another, "Let's each bring the king a basket of dates. Perhaps he'll reward us with a gift, and if he does give us something, let's divide it equally among ourselves."

Ciccu picked a basket of the most beautiful dates and gave them to Peppe who set out for the royal castle. Along the way he met an old man who asked him, "What are you carrying in that basket, young man?"

"What's it to you?" Peppe responded. "Mind your own business."

The old man kept asking him, and finally Peppe was so irritated that he yelled, "Dirt!"

"Good," said the little man. "Dirt you've said, and dirt it will be!"

When Peppe arrived at the castle, he knocked on the door, and a servant asked him what he wanted.

"I have a basket of beautiful dates," Peppe said. "Certainly they're not so worthy for a king's table, but I'd like him to accept them to give to all his servants."

The king granted Peppe permission to enter and ordered a servant to bring a special silver platter so that the dates could be placed on it. But when Peppe took the cover off the basket, there were only a few dates on top, and the rest of the basket was filled with dirt. The king exploded in anger and ordered the unfortunate Peppe to be given fifty blows with a cane. When it was over, Peppe was distressed and crept home. However, he did not tell his brothers what had happened to him. Instead, when they asked him what the king had given him, he answered, "After we've all been there, I'll tell you what I got."

A few days passed, and Ciccu picked another basketful of dates and gave them to Alfinu, who set out on his way to the king. Along the way he met a little old man who asked him, "What are you carrying in that basket, young man?"

"Horns!" Alfinu answered.

"Good," the old man said. "Horns you said, horns it will be."

When Alfinu got to the castle he knocked on the door and said to the servant, "I've got a basketful of beautiful dates. Of course, they're not worthy for a king's table, but I'd like his majesty to accept them and give them to the servants."

The king granted him permission to enter and ordered his servant to bring out the special silver platter so the dates could be placed on it. When Alfinu took the cover off the basket, however, there were only a few dates on top, and all the rest had been turned into horns. The king was infuriated by this insult and cried, "Did you think you could trick me? Give him 150 blows with the cane right now!"

When it was all over, Alfinu was distressed and crept home. He did not want to tell what had happened to him and thought, "Let Ciccu try it one time."

After a few days had passed, Ciccu picked the last dates, which were not at all as beautiful as the first ones. Nevertheless, he set out on his way to the king. Along the way he met the little old man, who asked, "What are you carrying in the basket, young man?"

"I have some dates and want to bring them to the king," Ciccu answered.

"Let me see them," the old man said.

Ciccu took the basket off his shoulders and showed the little man the dates.

"I'd like to have one of the small dates," the old man said. "I really have a desire to eat one."

"If I take out one date," Ciccu replied, "they'll notice the missing space."

But because he had a good heart, and the old man kept asking, he could not refuse him and gave him a date. The old man ate it and kept the pit in his hand. Then he asked for another date, then another and another until he had eaten a good portion of the basket.

"How can I take this basket to the king now?" Ciccu asked. "There are so many dates missing."

"Take it easy," said the old man, who threw all the pits into the basket. "Go to the castle and take the basket to the king. Good fortune will shine on you, but don't take off the lid along the way."

So Ciccu took the basket to the king, even though he was anxious and trembling.

"Here are some dates," he said to the servant. "Of course, they are not worthy enough for a king's table, but I would like his majesty to accept them and give them to his servants."

When the king heard there was someone again with dates, he said, "Does he want to trick me too? Well, let him come in here."

When Ciccu took off the cover, the basket was filled with splendid dates. The king was very happy about this and gave him five thalers and a large platter of sweets. Because the king took a liking to the smart lad, he asked him his name and whether he wanted to enter his service, for the king did not recognize him. Ciccu said yes, but first he wanted to take the five thalers to his brothers.

When the brothers were together again, Peppe said, "Now let's see what each of us received from the king. I got fifty blows with a cane."

"I got 150 blows with a cane," Alfinu stated.

"I received five thalers and these sweets," said Ciccu. "You can divide it all among yourselves because the king has given me a position at the court."

Ciccu returned to the castle and served the king, and the king grew more and more fond of him. However, his brothers were jealous of his good fortune and sought to find a way to harm him, so they went to the king and said, "Your majesty, your castle is indeed very beautiful. However, people will only be able to call it regal when you have the saber that belongs to the ogre."*

---

*Dravu or Menschenfresser.

"How can I get it?" the king asked.

"Oh, you just have to tell Ciccu about it," they responded. "He can get the saber for you."

So the king summoned his faithful Ciccu and said, "Ciccu, I don't care how you do it, but you must bring me the ogre's sword no matter what price you may have to pay."

Now, it so happened that there was an enchanted talking horse in the king's stable that was small and gentle. Ciccu loved this little horse very much, and he went into the stable to pet it.

"Oh little horse, little horse," he said, "we're not going to see each other ever again. I've got to go and fetch the ogre's sword for the king no matter what price it may cost."

"Take it easy," the little horse said, "and do what I tell you to do. Ask the king to give you fifty pounds and permission to ride me. Then we'll set out on our way."

Ciccu went to the king, asked him for fifty pounds and the little horse, and rode off that same day. The little horse showed him the way and told him continually what to do. When Ciccu came to the country of the ogre, he called five or six old women and said, "I'll give each one of you a thaler if you fill an entire sack with lice."

After they did this for him, Ciccu went into the ogre's house when the ogre was not there, and he stuck all the lice in his bed and hid himself beneath it. When the ogre came home and wanted to go to bed, he took off his glistening sword. No sooner was he in bed than the lice began to torture him so that he could not stand it anymore. He stood up, and as he roared and raged, he began to look for the lice. This was the moment Ciccu was waiting for, and he grabbed the sword, ran down the stairs, swung himself on top of the little horse, and rode away as fast as the wind. After Ciccu delivered the sword to the king, the monarch was extremely happy, and his fondness for the loyal Ciccu grew even stronger.

However, his brothers went to the king again and said, "Ciccu managed to bring you the sword, but if he could bring you the ogre himself, then this castle would by all rights be able to be called regal."

So the king called his servant again and said, "Ciccu, you must bring the ogre here alive, no matter what it costs you. I don't care how you catch him, but you've got to bring me the ogre."

Distressed, Ciccu went to the little horse in the stable and poured out his sorrows, but the little horse said, "Take it easy and tell the king you need fifty pounds and want to take me with you."

Ciccu did that and set out with the money and the little horse. When they came to the country of the ogre, Ciccu had all the churches ring the death bells and announce everywhere: "Ciccu, the king's servant, has died."

When the ogre heard this he became very happy and called out, "It's good that this villain has died, this thief who stole my sword!"

Meanwhile, Ciccu took an ax and a saw and went into the ogre's forest and began to chop down some pine trees. In response the ogre called out, "Who dares to chop down pine trees in my forest?"

"Oh, noble sir," Ciccu replied, "I've been ordered to build a coffin for Ciccu, the king's servant, and I wanted to use pine wood for this purpose."

The ogre did not recognize him, and because he was so happy about Ciccu's death, he cried out, "Wait a moment. I'll help you."

He ran into the forest, and they both began chopping down pine trees. Then they sawed the trunks, joined the boards together, and soon the coffin was finished. Now Ciccu scratched his head and said to the ogre, "Oh no, how dumb I am! I never measured his size. How can I know whether the coffin is the right size? Wait a second — it just occurred to me that Ciccu was just about as big as you are. Do me a favor and lie down in the coffin so that I can see whether it is large enough."

The ogre fell right into the trap and lay down inside the coffin. Immediately, Ciccu slammed the cover shut, tied a strong rope around it, and loaded it with some effort onto the little horse, which ran like the wind back to the castle, where the king had a large iron cage built for the ogre.

Now it so happened that at the same time the king's wife died, and the king was to marry again, however, he could not find a princess to his liking. Then the jealous brothers came to him again and said, "There is only one lady worthy to become your wife, your majesty. She is the most beautiful woman in the entire world."*

"Where can she be found?" the king asked.

"Oh, tell Ciccu about her. He'll know where to find her."

The king summoned his faithful Ciccu and said, "Ciccu, if you don't bring me the most beautiful woman in the entire world within eight days, I'll have your head cut off."

When he went to the stable to see the little horse, Ciccu was weeping.

---

*A bedda di tuttu lu munnu.

"Oh, dear little horse," he said, "now we shall never see each other again. I must die in eight days if I don't bring the king the most beautiful woman in the entire world."

"Take it easy," the little horse said. "Have the king give you some honey and bread and some money, and take me with you."

Ciccu did exactly that and then set out with the horse. After he had ridden a while, he saw an exhausted bee lying on the ground. It could not fly anymore because it was starving.

"Get off me," the horse said, "and give the little insect your honey."

Ciccu did this and then continued riding. After a little while they came to a stream, and on the bank of the stream there was a fish flapping about on the dry ground.

"Get off, and throw the fish into the water," the little horse said. "It will be of use to you later."

So Ciccu dismounted, threw the fish into the water, and continued riding. A little while later he saw an eagle whose leg was caught in a trap.

"Get off, and free the poor eagle from the trap," the little horse said. "It will be of use to you later."

So Ciccu dismounted and helped the eagle. Finally, they approached a castle inhabited by the most beautiful woman in the world.

"Get off," the little horse said, "and stand on this rock. I must go into the castle alone. When you see me coming out of the castle with the princess on my back, jump on me right behind her, and hold onto her tightly so that she doesn't fall off. If you're not careful and don't do this at the right time, we shall both be lost."

Ciccu dismounted and stood on the rock. The little horse ran into the courtyard and began to dance about in such a dainty way that soon all the people in the castle gathered around to watch the cute animal, which let itself be petted by everyone and was so tame that the king and queen came into the courtyard with their daughter.

"Oh, Father, I'd love to ride this little horse," the princess said, and she was lifted onto the horse that appeared so tame. However, no sooner did she sit on the back of the horse than it sped off, and to keep from falling and hurting herself, she had to grab hold of the horse's mane. When the little horse approached the rock where Ciccu was standing, Ciccu swung himself with one spring onto the horse behind the princess and held her tightly. Then the most beautiful woman in the world took off her veil and threw it onto the ground, and when they came to the stream she took a ring from her finger and threw it into the deep water.

When they returned to the castle, the king was extremely pleased, rushed toward them, and said to the most beautiful woman in the entire world, "Noble lady, now you must become my wife."

"We'll become man and wife when Ciccu brings back the veil that fell off me along the way."

The king summoned his servant and said, "Ciccu, if you don't bring me the veil of the most beautiful woman in the entire world right away, I'll have your head cut off."

Ciccu went back to the little horse in the stall, where he wept and poured out all his troubles.

"Take it easy," the little horse said. "Have the king give you enough food for one day and get on my back."

When they came to the place where Ciccu had freed the eagle from the trap, the little horse said, "Call three times for the king of the birds, and when he answers you, tell him that you want him to bring back the veil of the most beautiful woman in the entire world."

Ciccu called the king of the birds, and after the third time he heard a voice that asked, "What is your desire?"

"Bring me the veil of the most beautiful woman in the entire world," Ciccu cried.

"Wait a moment," the voice responded. "An eagle has been enjoying it and will bring it to you right away."

All of a sudden there was a rustling in the air, and an eagle flew down to Ciccu with the veil in its beak. When Ciccu looked closely at the bird, he realized it was the same eagle that he had rescued. Ciccu took the veil and rushed back to the king, and the king brought it to the most beautiful woman in the entire world and said, "Here is the veil, and now you must become my wife."

"Not so fast," said the princess. "We cannot become man and wife until Ciccu brings me the ring that fell into the stream."

The king summoned Ciccu again and said, "I want you to bring me the ring that the most beautiful woman in the entire world dropped into the stream right away, otherwise I'll have your head cut off."

Ciccu went to the stable once more and poured out his heart to the little horse, and the little horse responded, "Take enough food for one day and get on my back."

The little horse carried him to the stream and said, "Call the king of the fish three times and tell him to fetch you the ring."

Ciccu called the king of the fish three times, and a voice said, "What is your desire?"

"Bring me the ring that the most beautiful woman in the entire world lost here."

"Wait a moment," the voice said. "A fish is enjoying it and will bring it up to you right away."

It did not take long for the water to whirl, and a fish stuck its head out of the water with the lost ring in its mouth. When Ciccu looked closely at the fish, he saw it was the fish that he had rescued from death. So he took the ring and brought it to the king, who gave it to the most beautiful woman in the entire world.

"Here's the ring," he said, "and now you must become my wife."

"We still have time for that," she answered. "Before I marry you, the tile oven has to be heated for three days and three nights, and then Ciccu must jump into it. After he does this, we can become man and wife."

The king called his faithful Ciccu and ordered him to have the tile oven heated three days and three nights, after which he was to throw himself inside.

"If you don't do this," the king said, "I'll have your head cut off."

Ciccu went to the little horse and said, "Farewell, my dear little horse. Now I'm as good as dead. Nothing can save me," and he told the horse about the king's command.

"Don't lose your courage," the little horse consoled him. "When the tile oven is completely heated, get on my back and ride me around long and hard until I begin to drip with sweat. Then jump down, throw off your clothes, and rub the sweat off me with a knife. After you do this, you must cover yourself with the sweat and jump into the oven."

Ciccu did exactly what the little horse said. He rode the little horse around and around until the horse was dripping with sweat. Then he rubbed the sweat off with a knife, covered himself with it, and jumped into the oven before the eyes of the king and the most beautiful woman in the entire world. However, the fire could not harm him, and he came out of the oven more handsome than he had ever been.

When the most beautiful woman in the entire world saw this feat her heart was filled with love for him, and she said to the king, "I still can't become your wife until you do just as Ciccu has done."

"Yes," the king said. "I'll do it."

When the woman was not looking, the king secretly called his faithful Ciccu and asked him, "Ciccu, what did you do so that the fire did not burn you?"

However, Ciccu was mad at the king for sending him on so many dangerous missions, and answered. "I covered myself with a lot of old grease so the fire couldn't do anything to me."

The king believed him and rubbed old grease all over his body and then jumped into the oven, but the grease only made the flames stronger, and the king burned to death. When this was done, the most beautiful woman in the entire world said to Ciccu, "Now we shall become man and wife, and the king can provide the light for us."*

So Ciccu married the most beautiful woman in the entire world and became king. Yes, they became man and wife, but we're still standing like candles without a life.†

---

*Der da kann uns das Licht halten. Chiddi ni fa di cannileri.

† Iddi ristaru maritu e mugghièri,
 E nui comu tanti cannileri.

6

Count Piro

Once upon a time there was a poor man who had only one son, dumb and ignorant. When the father was about to die, he said to the youth, "My son, I must die and have nothing to leave you except this little house and the pear tree that's standing next to it."

The father died, and his son remained in the cottage. Because he could not earn a living by himself, the dear Lord in his mercy let the pear tree bear fruit throughout the entire year, and this is how the young man nourished himself.

Now one day, as he was sitting in front of the door to the house, a fox came by. To be sure it was in the middle of winter, and yet the pear tree was still covered with the most beautiful and largest fruit.

"Oh!" cried the fox. "Fresh pears in this time of the season! Give me a basket of the pears, and your fortune will be made."

"Oh, little fox, if I give you a basket full of pears, what shall I have to eat?" the young man said.

"Be quiet, and do what I tell you to do," the fox answered. "You'll see, your fortune will be made."

So the young man gave the little fox a basket of beautiful pears, and the fox carried it to the king.

"Your majesty, my master sends you this little basket of pears and asks you to have the good grace to accept this fruit," the fox said to the king.

"Pears! In this time of the season!" cried the king. "I've never seen anything like this before! Who is your master?"

"Count Piro," the fox answered.

"How did he manage to get pears at this time of the year?" the king asked.

"Oh, he always gets what he wants," replied the fox. "He's much richer than you are, your majesty."

"What could I give him as a gift to thank him for his pears?" the king asked.

"Nothing, your royal highness," the sly fox responded. "You should know that he would be insulted if you sent him a gift for his gift."

"Well then, tell your count that I thank him for his gorgeous pears."

When the fox returned to the house the young man cried out, "Oh, little fox, what am I supposed to eat if you carry away my pears?"

"Be quiet and let me take care of everything," said the fox and he took another large basket full of the most beautiful pears to the king and said, "Your majesty, since you accepted the first basket so kindly, my master, Count Piro, has taken the liberty to send you another basket full of pears."

"Oh my, how's that possible?!" the king exclaimed. "Fresh pears at this time of the year!"

"Oh, that's nothing," said the fox. "This is just a drop in the bucket compared to the other treasures he has. However, he would like to ask your permission to make your daughter his wife."

"If the count is so rich," the king replied, "I cannot accept this honor at all because he is much richer than I am."

"Forget that, your royal highness," the fox said. "My lord wishes to have your daughter for his wife, and he doesn't care whether your dowry is more or less because he is so wealthy."

"Is he really so rich?" the king asked.

"Oh, your royal majesty, if only I could tell you! He's much richer than you!"

"Well then, let me invite him to come and dine with me."

So the fox went to the young man and said, "I told the king that you are Count Piro and that you would like to marry his daughter."

"Oh, little fox, what have you done?" screamed the poor boy. "If the king sees me, he'll rip the head off my shoulders!"

---

*In German, Graf Birnbaum; in English, Count Pear.

"Let me take care of things, and be quiet," the fox said, and he went into the city to a tailor and said, "My master, Count Piro, wants to have the most handsome suit that is ready to wear. I'll bring you the money for it another time."

The tailor gave him a splendid suit, and the fox continued on his way to a horse trader and was able to obtain, in the same way as before, the most beautiful horse there was to find. Then the young man put on the fine garments, mounted the horse, and rode to the castle, while the fox ran in front of him.

"Oh, little fox, what should I say to the king?" the young man cried out. "I can't speak the way noble people are supposed to speak."

"Let me speak, and you keep quiet," said the fox. "You just say 'good day' and 'your majesty,' and leave the rest up to me."

When they came to the castle, the king rushed toward Count Piro and greeted him with honor. Then he led him to the dinner table where the beautiful princess was seated. However, he remained silent and did not say a thing.

"Little fox," said the king softly to the fox, "Count Piro doesn't seem to speak."

"Of course not," the fox responded. "He's got too much to think about, especially his treasures and all his wealth."

After they had eaten, Count Piro took his leave and rode back to his house. The next morning the fox said to him, "Give me another basket full of pears that I can take to the king."

"Do what you want, little fox," the young man answered, "but you'll see, it's going to cost me my life."

"Oh, just be quiet," the fox cried. "When I say your fortune will be made, I mean it."

So the young man picked the pears, and the fox took them to the king and said, "My master, Count Piro, has sent you this little basket of pears and would like to have an answer to his marriage proposal."

"Tell the count that the wedding can take place whenever he wants it," the king replied, and the fox was very pleased to bring the news to Count Piro.

"But little fox, where am I supposed to take my bride after the wedding?" the young man asked. "I can't bring her to this poor old house."

"Let me take care of it. What's your concern anyway? Haven't I done very well for you thus far?" the fox said.

So a splendid wedding was celebrated, and Count Piro married the beautiful princess. After a few days passed, the fox said, "My master wants to take his young bride to his castle."

"Good," said the king. "I shall accompany them."

Soon after they all mounted their horses. The king brought a large retinue of his knights with him, and they rode off into the plains. Meanwhile, the sly fox ran way ahead of them. When he came to a large herd with thousands of sheep, he asked the shepherds, "Who owns this herd of sheep?"

"The ogre," they answered.

"Be quiet!" whispered the fox. "Do you see all those knights who are following me? If you say to them that the herd belongs to the ogre, they'll murder you. You'd better say they belong to Count Piro."

Shortly after, when the king came riding up to the shepherds, he asked, "Who owns this wonderful herd of sheep?"

"Count Piro," the shepherds cried out.

"Well, I say, he must be rich!" the king explained and was happy.

A little farther on the fox came across a herd of pigs that was just as large, and he asked the swineherds, "Who owns this herd?"

"The ogre."

"Be quiet! Do you see all those knights who are following me? If you say to them that the herd belongs to the ogre, they'll murder you. You'd better say they belong to Count Piro."

When the king reached the swineherds, he asked who owned the herd, and they answered, "Count Piro," and the king was very happy about his rich son-in-law.

A little farther on the fox came to a large herd of horses and asked the men tending them who owned the herd.

"The ogre."

"Be quiet! Do you see all those knights who are following me? If you say to them that the herd belongs to the ogre, they'll murder you. You'd better say they belong to Count Piro."

When the king arrived and asked who owned the horses, the men responded, "Count Piro," and the king was glad that his daughter had married such a rich man.

Meanwhile, the fox kept running ahead and came to a large herd of cattle.

"Who owns this large herd of cattle?"

"The ogre."

"Be quiet! Do you see all those knights who are following me? If you say to them that the herd belongs to the ogre, they'll murder you. You'd better say they belong to Count Piro."

---

*The plains of Catania

Soon after the king came riding by and asked who owned the herd of cattle.

"Count Piro," they said, and the king was happy about his rich son-in-law.

Finally the fox came to the palace of the ogre, who lived there all alone with his wife. Immediately he rushed in to see them and cried out, "Oh, you poor people! You have a terrible fate!"

"What's happened?" the ogre cried out with fright.

"Do you see all those knights who are following me?" the fox asked. "The king has sent them to murder you."

"Oh, little fox, dear fox, help us," the two ogres began to moan and groan.

"I have an idea!" said the fox. "Crawl into that large baking oven and hide. When they have left, I'll call you."

They agreed and crawled into the oven and asked the fox to stuff the opening of the oven with wood so that they would not be seen. This was exactly what the fox had wanted, and he filled the entire opening with wood. Then he stood in front of the door to the palace. When the king came riding up to the door, the fox said, "Your majesty, please get down and rest here. This is the palace of Count Piro."

So they dismounted and went up the stairs and found such great splendor and wealth that the king was completely astounded and thought, "My own palace cannot compare to the beauty of this one." Then he asked the fox, "How come there are no servants here?"

"My master did not want to set up the household without knowing what the wishes of his beautiful wife were," he answered. "She can now do just as she pleases."

After they had examined everything, the king returned to his castle, and Count Piro remained in the beautiful palace. During the night, however, the fox crept to the oven, lit the wood, and started a large fire so that the ogre and his wife were burned to death. The next morning the fox said to Count Piro and his wife, "You're now happy and rich, but you must now promise me one thing. When I die, you must put me into a beautiful coffin and bury me with all the honor I deserve."

"Oh, little fox, don't talk about dying," the princess said because she had become very fond of the fox.

After some time had passed, the fox wanted to put Count Piro to the test and pretended to be dead. When the princess saw the fox, she cried out, "Oh, the little fox is dead. The poor little thing! Now we must quickly have a beautiful coffin made for him."

"A coffin for that beast?" Count Piro cried out. "Take him by his legs and throw him out the window!"

All at once the fox jumped up and screamed, "Oh, you ungrateful dirty beggar, you miserable starving hound! Have you forgotten that it was me who made your fortune? It was me who helped you get everything that you have? You ungrateful wretch!"

"Oh, little fox, just calm down," Count Piro pleaded. "I didn't mean it that way. I just spoke without thinking about what I was saying."

The fox let himself be calmed and continued to live for a long time in Count Piro's palace, and when he really died, a beautiful coffin was indeed made for him, and he was buried with all the honors he deserved. As for Count Piro, he and his beautiful wife lived happy and content, but we were left without a cent.

7

BEAUTIFUL ANGIOLA

Once upon a time there were three neighbors who all became pregnant at the same time. One day while they were all sitting together with four other women, one of them said, "Oh, cousins, I have such a craving for jujubes,* and there are none to be had."

"I'm also yearning for jujubes," said a second woman.

"Me, too. Me, too," the others cried out.

Then one woman said, "Do you know where some beautiful jujubes are growing? Over there in the garden that belongs to the witch. But we can't take any from there. If she catches us, she'll eat us. Besides she has a donkey who guards the garden and would tell on us right away."

The first woman cried out again, "I don't care. I have such a great craving. Just come with me. The witch isn't at home right now and won't notice if we take just a few jujubes. As for the donkey, we'll throw him such juicy grass that he won't even pay attention to us."

The other women let themselves be persuaded, and all seven of them crawled into the witch's garden, threw some beautiful, juicy grass to the donkey, and filled their aprons with the jujubes. Fortunately they escaped safely before the witch appeared.

The next evening the seven neighbors were sitting together again, and once again they had a great craving for the luscious jujubes, and

---

*In Sicilian, zinzuli; in Italian, giuggiole. An edible fruit.

even though they were scared of the witch, they could not resist their urge and crept into the garden a second time. They threw fresh grass to the donkey, filled their aprons with jujubes, and escaped safely before the witch came back.

However, the witch had already noticed that someone had been in the garden because many jujubes were missing. She asked the donkey, but it had eaten the beautiful, juicy grass and hadn't noticed anything. So she decided to stay in the garden on the third day. In the middle of the garden there was a ditch in which she hid and covered herself with leaves and branches. Only one of her long ears stuck out.

The seven neighbors were sitting with one another again. When they thought about the beautiful jujubes, their craving for them returned, but one of them said, "We had better not go there today. The witch could discover us, and then we'd be in for a terrible time."

The others laughed and said, "We succeeded two times. Why should we have bad luck today? Just come along!"

So, she let herself be persuaded, and all seven of them crawled into the garden. As they were picking the jujubes, one of them noticed the long ear of the witch sticking out of the leaves. She thought it was a mushroom, went over, and wanted to pick it. All at once the witch sprang out of the ditch, and the seven women shrieked and fled from the garden. One of them could not run as fast as the rest, and the witch caught her and wanted to eat her.

"Oh!" she cried. "Don't eat me. I had such a craving for jujubes and couldn't find them anywhere else. I promise never to enter your garden again."

"All right," the witch responded. "I'll forgive you this time but only under the condition that you promise me the baby you're carrying. Whether it's a boy or girl, you must give the child to me when it turns seven."

So the woman promised her out of great fear, and the witch let her go free. At home her six neighbors were waiting for her and asked her what had happened.

"Oh," she answered, "I had to promise to give her the child that I'm carrying. Otherwise, she would have eaten me."

When the time arrived, she gave birth to a lovely girl and named her Angiola. The child grew and flowered, and became more and more beautiful with each passing day. After Angiola turned six years old, her mother sent her to school, and she learned how to sew and knit from a teacher. Whenever she went to school, she had to pass by the witch's garden, and when she was almost seven, the witch stood in front of her garden one day, waved to her to come over, and gave Angiola some fruit.

"Do you know, beautiful Angiola," she said. "I'm your aunt. Tell your mother that you met your aunt, and she should not forget her promise."

Angiola went home and told her mother, who became very frightened and said, "Oh, now the time's come, and I must give up my poor child. You know what, Angiola? When your aunt asks you for the answer tomorrow, tell her that you forgot to deliver the message."

When Angiola went to school the next day, the witch was there again and asked her, "Well, what did your mother say?"

"Oh, dear aunt," the child answered, "I forgot to tell her."

"All right then, tell her today," the witch said, "and don't forget."

Well, things went about the same way for the next few days. The witch waited for beautiful Angiola when she went to school and wanted to know her mother's answer. Angiola kept saying that she had forgotten to deliver the message. Well, one day the witch became angry and said, "If you are so forgetful, I'll have to give you a sign to take with you that will make you remember your chore."

The witch grabbed hold of Angiola's pinky and bit it so hard that she took off a big chunk and said, "Now, go home and don't forget to tell your mother."

Angiola ran home weeping and showed her mother her little finger, which was bleeding.

"Oh," thought her mother, "there's nothing I can do now. I must give my poor child to the witch, otherwise she'll eat her out of anger."

The next morning, as Angiola was about to go to school, her mother said, "Tell your aunt that she should do whatever she feels is good for you."

Angiola did this, and the witch said, "Good. Come with me. From now on you belong to me."

So the witch took beautiful Angiola with her and led her far away to a tower without any doors and with only one window. From then on Angiola lived with the witch and led a good life because the witch loved her as if she were her own child. Whenever the witch came home after her excursions, she stood beneath the window and called out: "Angiola, beautiful Angiola, let down your beautiful braids and pull me up!"*

Angiola had gorgeous long braids, which she let down, and then she pulled the witch up with them. Now, one day, when Angiola had grown

---

*Angiola, bedd' Angiola, cala sti beddi trizzi e pigghia a mia.

into a beautiful maiden, the king's son happened to be hunting in the vicinity where the tower was standing. He was puzzled by a house without doors and asked himself, "How do the people go inside?"

Just then the witch came back from one of her excursions, took her place beneath the window, and cried out: "Angiola, beautiful Angiola, let down your beautiful braids and pull me up!"

Immediately the braids fell down, and the witch climbed up. This pleased the prince a great deal, and he kept himself hidden nearby until the witch went out again. Then he went over beneath the window and called out: "Angiola, beautiful Angiola, let down your beautiful braids and pull me up!"

All at once, Angiola threw her beautiful braids down and pulled the prince up to her, for she believed he was the witch. When she saw the prince, she was frightened at first, but he was friendly and asked her to run off with him and become his wife. She let herself be persuaded, and in order to make sure that the witch would not learn where she had gone, she gave all the chairs, tables, and closets in the house something to eat because they were all living creatures and could betray her. The broom, however, stood behind the door, and Angiola could not see it and did not give it anything to eat. Then she took three magic balls from the witch's room and fled with the prince. The witch had a little dog that loved Angiola, and the dog followed her as well.

After a short time had passed, the witch came home and cried out: "Angiola, beautiful Angiola, let down your beautiful braids and pull me up!" But the beautiful braids did not come down no matter how often the witch called, and finally she had to fetch a tall ladder and climb through the window. When she did not find beautiful Angiola anywhere, she asked the chairs, tables, and closets, "Where did she go?"

"We don't know," they answered.

But the broom called from its corner, "Beautiful Angiola has fled with the prince who wants to elevate her and make her his wife."

The witch set out after them and almost caught up with them when Angiola threw a magic ball behind her. A huge mountain of soap arose, and as the witch tried to climb it, she kept slipping back down. But she worked at it until she managed to climb over the mountain and rushed after Angiola and the prince. Then beautiful Angiola threw a second magic ball behind her, and another mountain made of large and small nails arose. Once again the witch had to work long and hard until she climbed over it. When Angiola saw that the witch had almost caught up with them, she threw the third ball behind her, and a roaring river arose. The witch wanted to swim across, but the river became more and more turbulent, and she finally had to turn back. Furious, she cast a curse on beautiful Angiola: "May your beautiful face be turned into the face of a dog!" she yelled.

Within seconds Angiola's beautiful face was transformed into the face of a dog. The prince became very distressed and said, "How can I present you to my parents now? They'll never allow me to marry a maiden with a dog's face."

He took her to a small cottage in which she was to live until the evil curse could be dispelled, and afterward he returned to his parents and lived with them. However, whenever he went hunting, he visited poor Angiola. She wept bitterly over her misfortune until one day the little dog said to her, "Don't cry, beautiful Angiola. I'll go back to the witch and ask her to lift the magic curse from you."

So the little dog set out and returned to the witch. Once there, the dog jumped onto the witch's lap and flattered her.

"Are you here again, you ungrateful beast?" the witch cried out and shoved the dog away. "You left me to follow the ungrateful Angiola."

But the little dog kept flattering her until the witch became friendly and took it on her lap.

"Mother," the little dog said, "Angiola sends her greetings and kisses your hands. She is sad because she's not allowed to go to the castle with a dog's face and can't marry the prince."

"That serves her right!" the witch declared. "Why did she deceive me? As far as I'm concerned, she can keep the dog's face."

However, the little dog kept asking in such a friendly way and insisted that poor Angiola had been punished enough. Finally, the witch gave the little dog a bottle of water and said, "Take this to her, and she'll become the beautiful Angiola again."

The little dog thanked the witch, jumped down from her lap with the bottle, and took it happily to poor Angiola. When the maiden washed herself with the water, the dog's face disappeared, and she became beautiful again, more beautiful than she had been before. So now the prince took her to his castle full of joy, and the king and queen were so delighted by her beauty that they welcomed her with all their hearts and arranged for a splendid wedding. They remained happy and content, but we still don't even have a cent.

8

BETTA PILUSA

Once upon a time there was a rich man, who had a good and pious wife and an only daughter who was very beautiful. After some time passed, his poor wife happened to become ill and was about to die. So she called her husband and said, "Dear husband, soon I shall die, and I am placing our child in your hands. Promise me that you will not marry again until you can find a woman who can wear this ring."

Upon saying this she showed him a ring that she placed with her other jewels and died. His daughter became more beautiful with each passing day, and at one time it occurred to her to take a look at the jewels that had belonged to her mother. When she opened up the little jewelry box, she saw the ring, which her mother had shown to her father on her deathbed, and tried it on. And imagine this! The ring slid very easily onto her finger, but when she wanted to take it off, she could not manage to do it. Now she became scared and thought, "What will my father say?" To make sure he wouldn't see it, she wrapped a piece of cloth around her finger. When her father saw the cloth, however, he asked why she had wrapped her finger with it, and she answered, "It's nothing, dear Father. I just cut my finger."

"Let me take a look," the father said.

She didn't want to let him, but her father became angry and ripped the cloth off the finger. All at once he saw the ring and cried out, "You're wearing the ring. Now you must become my wife."

The maiden was terrified and said, "Oh, dear Father, how could you possibly propose such a sinful thing?"

He did not listen to her and only kept repeating, "You must become my wife."

"At least allow me first to go to my father confessor," she said.

So she went to the priest and began to weep and tell him about her father's desires. The father confessor was extremely shocked and said, "We've got to put him off until he comes to his senses again. I advise you to demand from him a dress the color of the sky with the sun, moon, and stars on it. If he can provide this, tell him you'll become his wife."

The poor girl went to her father and said, "Father, if you bring me a dress with the color of the sky with the sun, moon, and stars on it, I'll become your wife."

The father went and searched for the dress, but no matter what shop he visited, he could not find this particular dress anywhere. He became very sullen and walked into the fields and kept thinking of some way to obtain the dress. All of a sudden a gentleman joined him and asked him why he was hanging his head so low. So the father told him about his troubles.

"Oh," responded the gentleman, "if that's all there is to it, I can get it for you. Just wait here for me."

The man went away, and after a short while he reappeared with the dress. To be sure, the strange gentleman was the devil, who wanted to lure the father into committing a sin. The father took the dress to his daughter and the girl was horrified, but she only said, "Dear Father, I must go to my father confessor again."

So she went to the priest and said, "What am I to do now? My father brought me the dress and still wants to marry me."

"Demand another dress from him," the priest replied. "This time ask him for one that has the color of the sea and all the fish and plants of the sea on it."

So she went to her father and asked him for this particular dress. The father looked for the dress in all the shops, and since he could not find it, he went to the place where he had met the sinister man. Once again he found him there, and when he told him about his wish, the devil brought him the dress with the color of the sea and all the fish and plants of the sea on it.

When he took the dress to his daughter, she said once more: "Dear Father, let me first go to confession."

When she asked her father confessor for advice, he said she should demand a dress from her father with the color of the earth and with all the animals and flowers of the earth on it. She did this, but her father went straight to the devil and had another dress made for her. Now the poor maiden no longer knew what she should do. Once again she went to her father confessor and revealed to him that everything had been in vain. In response the priest said, "Demand a dress made from the fur of a gray cat."

She did this, and her father went once more to the devil, who also provided him a dress made from the fur of a gray cat. Meanwhile, the daughter went to the father confessor and complained that her father still persisted in wanting to marry her.

"Demand that he bring you two barrels full of pearls and jewels," the father confessor advised her.

When she requested the two barrels full of pearls and jewels from her father, he had the devil provide them for him and brought them to her as well. Now she really did not know how she could help herself, and so she decided to flee. She made a bundle out of the first three dresses and the pearls and jewels and waited until morning arrived. As soon as dawn came, she stood up, filled a bowl with water, and placed two pigeons inside. Suddenly, her father knocked on the door and asked her whether she was ready.

"I'm still washing myself, dear Father," she answered while slipping into the dress made of gray cat fur. Then she took the bundle with her and ran through a back door into the open, and because it was still somewhat dark, nobody saw her. In the meantime her father waited for her in his house. Whenever he came near her door, he heard the pigeons splashing and thought that his daughter was still washing herself. Finally he lost his patience and had the door broken down, but there was nobody inside. Her father exploded with rage, but his rage did not help him.

Well, let's leave the father and see what became of his poor daughter.

With tears in her eyes she made her way until she came to a dense forest. It so happened that on this day the young king was hunting in this forest. When he saw the strange-looking creature in the gray fur coat, he thought it was an animal and wanted to shoot it. All at once, however, the maiden cried out, "Don't shoot!"

Now he was even more astonished by an animal who could speak and called out to her, "I swear in the name of God that you had better tell me who you are."

---

*Mondelli.

"Do not swear to God," she replied, "because I am a baptized soul."

"What's your name?" the king asked.

"My name is Betta Pilusa."*

"Do you want to come with me to my castle?" the king asked.

"Yes," she answered. "You can let me be your maid."

So the king took her to his castle and asked her, "Where do you want to live?"

"In the chicken coop," she answered.

From then on she lived in the chicken coop and looked after the chickens. The king went to her every day, brought her delicious bits of food, and conversed with her. One day he came to her and said, "You know, Betta Pilusa, my wedding will take place soon, and there will be three days of festivities. Today there will be a ball. Do you want to come?"

"How could I possibly appear at your dance?" Betta Pilusa grumbled. "Leave me in peace."

When it became evening, however, she threw off the cat fur and wished for a chambermaid, for whoever possessed the three dresses could wish for whatever she wanted, and the wish would be granted. All at once a chambermaid appeared, and she washed and combed Betta Pilusa. Then she helped Betta Pilusa put on the dress with the sun, moon, and stars and adorned her with her mother's jewels. Now Betta Pilusa wished for a coach and beautiful horses and coachmen in uniforms, and they drove her to the ball. As soon as she appeared in the dance hall, she was so stunningly beautiful that everybody stared at her, and the king left his bride standing and danced the entire evening only with Betta Pilusa and gave her a golden needle as a gift. When the ball was finished, however, she broke away from him and drove off in her coach.

"Follow that lady!" the king cried out to his servants, "and find out where she's going."

But Betta Pilusa threw so many pearls and jewels from her coach that the servants were dazzled and could not see where she went. When they were out of sight, the maiden sprang into the chicken coop and hurriedly put on her gray fur coat. When the ball was over, the king came to her again and said, "Oh, Betta Pilusa, if you could only have seen the beautiful lady who appeared at the ball! And nobody knows where she comes from."

---

*In German, Die haarige Bertha; in English, Hairy Bertha.

"What do I care about your beautiful women," grumbled Betta Pilusa. "You've wakened me from my sleep!"

The next day the king came again and said, "Betta Pilusa, today is the second ball. Do you want to come?"

"Do you want to make a laughingstock out of me?" she said. "Leave me in peace."

However, in the evening she dressed herself up even more gorgeous than she had been the first time and wore the dress with all the animals and plants of the sea on it and beautiful jewelry. When she entered the ballroom, everyone was astounded by her stunning beauty, and the king danced with her and gave her a gold watch as a present. Of course, his bride was filled with envy and rage. The king had told his servants in advance to pay careful attention to where the beautiful lady was heading when she bounded away, but once again she threw precious stones at them and they were dazzled. Although the king became very angry, it didn't help. The maiden made her way back to the chicken coop and dressed herself in the gray fur coat. Now the king went to Betta Pilusa once again to tell her about the beautiful lady. In response she just growled at him.

The next morning he came to her again and said, "Betta Pilusa, today there's another ball, and today I must learn who this unknown lady is."

He called all his servants together and said, "If you don't find out tonight who this lady is, you'll all lose your heads!"

That evening Betta Pilusa put on the dress with all the animals and flowers of the earth on it and adorned herself with her jewelry, and when she appeared at the ball, she was even more beautiful than on the previous evenings. The bride was in complete despair, for the king danced only with the strange woman and gave her a precious ring as a gift. When she broke away from him, his servants could not follow her because she dazzled them just as she had done before and fled to the chicken coop. This time, however, she did not take off the beautiful dress. Instead, she pulled the gray fur coat over it. When the king heard that she had disappeared again without a trace, he was furious. The servants fell to their knees and told him that there had been nothing they could do. The beautiful lady had dazzled and blinded them. So the king went sadly to Betta Pilusa and said, "Oh, Betta Pilusa, I'm very sick. The beautiful lady disappeared again without a trace."

But she just grumbled, "What do I care about your beautiful lady? Leave me in peace!"

The king became very melancholy and could only think about the beautiful maiden. The next morning when the cook was kneading the bread that was to be brought to the king's table, Betta Pilusa came into the kitchen and asked for a little bit of the dough. "I'd like to make a bun for myself," she said.

"Go away," the cook answered. "What do you want to bake with your dirty hands? You'd only make a mess of things!"

However, she persisted and kept asking until he finally gave her a piece of dough just to get rid of her. Then she began kneading the bread with her dirty hands while she hid the gold needle, which the king had given to her at the ball, in the middle of it.

"All right," she said, "now you also have to shove this bread into the oven."

The cook did what she said, and imagine what happened! When the cook returned and opened the oven, all the bread had been burned, but the small dirty little bread that belonged to Betta Pilusa had become a wonderful loaf of white bread. The cook called Betta Pilusa and said, "Oh, Betta Pilusa, give me your bread so that I can take it to the king."

"No, no," she answered. "I want to eat my bread myself. What do I care if all your bread has been burned?"

Then the cook pleaded, "Oh, Betta Pilusa, I'll lose my job if you don't give me your bread. Please give it to me."

So she let herself be persuaded and gave him the bread. The cook sent it right away to the king's table. When the king saw the bread, he said, "Today the bread is really beautiful," and he took a slice of it, and the gold needle fell out. The king recognized it immediately and called for the cook. "Who baked this wonderful bread?" he asked.

The cook did not want to tell the truth and answered, "Your majesty, it was me. I was the one who baked it."

The king thought that this was probably not true, but he kept silent and kept the gold needle. The next morning Betta Pilusa went into the kitchen while the cook was kneading the bread and said, "Yesterday you took away my little bread, so now you have to give me some dough again. But today I'm going to eat my own bread."

The cook gave her a piece of dough, and she made bread out of it and stuck the gold watch in the middle. When the time came to take the bread out of the oven, everything had been burned again, and only the dirty dough that Betta Pilusa had kneaded had become a beautiful loaf of white bread. Once again the cook implored Betta Pilusa to give him the bread. She made him beg for a long time, but finally she gave it to him. When the king found the gold watch in the middle of the bread, he summoned the cook and asked him who had baked the bread. The cook replied that it was he who had done it.

The third day Betta Pilusa baked another bread and stuck the ring inside. Just like the other days, the cook's bread was burned, and only the bread with the ring became white and soft. The cook begged Betta Pilusa for her bread, and she refused for a long time. Finally she grumbled but gave it to him. The king thought, "Today the ring must be in the bread," and he was right. When he cut open the bread, he found the ring and summoned the cook. "If you don't tell me the truth about who baked the bread, I'll dismiss you from your job on the spot," he said.

The cook became frightened and told the king about everything that had happened.

"Send Betta Pilusa up to me right away," the king commanded.

When she appeared before the king, he closed all the doors and said, "For three days I've found the gold needle, the watch, and the ring in the middle of the bread that you baked, and these are all things I gave to the beautiful lady at the ball. You're not the simple maid that you want us to believe you are. So now, tell me who you are."

"I'm just plain Betta Pilusa," she answered, "and I don't know a thing about what you're talking about."

Then the king threatened her, "If you don't tell me right away who you are, I'll have your head cut off!"

All at once she threw off the gray cat's fur* and appeared as she really was, young and beautiful in her glistening dress. When the king saw her, he immediately locked her in his arms and said, "You are to become my bride."

Then he called his mother to him, and she was delighted to see her son healthy and cheerful again. Soon thereafter they celebrated a beautiful wedding. The other bride had to return to her home. The king and the young queen lived happily and content, but we were left without a cent.

---

*In another version Betta Pilusa had a wooden chest made for her with moveable legs instead of a dress or coat made of cat's fur. She would hide herself in the chest whenever she fled. Due to her long stay in the forest, the chest became completely covered with moss. She was regarded as a strange talking wild beast at the king's court.

9

LIGNU DI SCUPA*

Once upon a time a woman had a daughter, who was just as beautiful as the sun and the moon. However, the woman was poor and, therefore, sent her little daughter to her own mother, who kindly took her in and kept her in her home. Now the grandmother had a pan, which she usually lent to her neighbors when they wanted to bake something. In turn, they had to give her part of whatever they baked when they brought back the pan.

Now one day the old woman happened to go out and left her grand-daughter alone at home. A neighbor came and said, "I've just received some fish, and I'd like to bake them. Do me a favor and give me the pan."

The maiden gave her the pan, and the neighbor baked the fish, and when she brought back the pan, she also carried along four baked fish on a plate. When the maiden saw the beautifully baked fish that smelled so good, she could not resist the temptation and ate a small piece. Then, because the fish tasted so good, she gradually ate all four fish. When her grandmother came home, she asked the girl right away, "Did our neighbor bring some fish?"

---

*Lignu di Scupa is a "Broomstick."

"I lent her the pan," the maiden said, "but she didn't bring any fish in return."

The grandmother became angry, went over to the neighbor, and cried out, "What's the meaning of this? You took my pan and didn't give me any of your baked fish in return!"

But the neighbor answered, "What are you saying? I laid aside four fish for you and gave them to your granddaughter!"

The grandmother ran quickly back home and scolded and beat her granddaughter so that the maiden screamed and cried. Just at that moment the prince rode by. He had been out hunting. When he heard the terrible noise, he stopped his horse and asked the old woman why she was beating the maiden. The grandmother was ashamed to tell him that her granddaughter had eaten the fish, and she answered, "Your majesty, my granddaughter does nothing all day but spin, and she spins three rolls of flax each day. It's only for her good that I beat her because I want her to put down the spindle awhile and rest."

When the prince heard that and looked at the beautiful maiden, he said, "If your granddaughter is so diligent, I shall take her to my castle where she will become my wife."

So he took her with him to his father's castle, where he told the old king everything that had happened.

"Good," said the king. "If she can spin three rolls of flax every day, she must be able to spin ninety rolls in one month. If she does that, she will become your wife."

The prince led her to a large room in which there was a mass of straw for her to spin ninety rolls of flax. She was locked in this room, and only in the evening did the king have her fetched so she could participate in the evening conversation.* However, the poor maiden wept day and night because it was impossible for her to spin all the straw.

One day as she sat there and wept, a fine gentleman suddenly stood before her. It was none other than Master Paul.†

"Why are you weeping?" he asked.

She told him everything, and the devil answered, "Good, I'll spin all this straw, and on the last day of the month everything will be finished. But when I bring back the yarn on the last day, if you cannot tell me what my name is, you will belong to me and must follow me."

The maiden gave her promise, and Master Paul took the straw and disappeared. Now the poor maiden thought about the stranger's name

---

*Conversazione.

† Mastru Paulu, the devil.

day and night, and since nothing occurred to her, she kept weeping and became skinnier and sadder with each day that passed. When she was led to the king in the evening, she sat there silently, said nothing, and did not laugh. The king was sorry to see her so sad and issued a proclamation throughout the entire country that whoever could get his son's bride to laugh would receive a royal gift.

People came from all over, rich and poor, and told her funny stories every evening, but she did not laugh. Instead, she became even more silent because there were only three days left before the end of the month.

On the last evening an old peasant came to the castle and wanted to go up the stairs.

"What do you want in the king's palace?" the guards asked him.

"I know a funny story that I want to tell the prince's bride so that I can perhaps get her to laugh."

"Oh, come on, you dumb peasant. It's almost a month that people have been coming here every evening to try to get the young queen to laugh, and nobody has succeeded yet. Do you think your foolish story can work?"

The peasant began to scream loudly, "I want to go up and try. Maybe my story is not so foolish!"

When the king heard all the noise, he asked what was happening. His ministers told him that there was a peasant below who wanted to tell the young queen a story, and the guards did not want to let him pass.

"Why not?" asked the king. "Tell them to let him come up."

The peasant went up the stairs, and when he reached the maiden, he said, "Excellency, let me tell you what happened to me. Today I went into the forest to fetch some wood. All of a sudden I heard a strange song, and this is the way it went:

Spin, spin, let's spin our game,
The lady's expected all the same.
Spin, spin, let's spin our game.
Lignu di Scupa is my name.*

---

*Filati, filati, filamu,
  Sta sira a Signura aspettamu,
  Filati, filati, filamu,
  Lignu di scupa iu mi chiamu.

When the maiden heard this song, she realized immediately who had sung it and began to laugh out of joy. Indeed, all at once she became well and cheerful. So the king gave the peasant a beautiful gift and dismissed him with great pleasure.

When the maiden was led back to her room, the king said to her, "Tomorrow you must have the flax finished, and then we shall celebrate your wedding to my son."

Then she sat down in her room and waited for Master Paul. At midnight he appeared on time and brought the flax that he had marvelously spun into yarn and finished.

"Here is the yarn," Master Paul said. "Now, do you know my name?"

"Your name's Lignu di Scupa!" she merrily exclaimed.

So he no longer had any power over her and left her in great anger. The maiden slept peacefully the rest of the night, and when the king entered her room the next morning and saw all the beautiful yarn spun from the flax, he became very happy and said, "Now you will become my son's wife."

They held three days of festivities, and at the end of this time, the prince married the beautiful maiden. Indeed, they remained happy and content, and we were left without a cent.

10

DON GIOVANNI DI LA FORTUNA

Once upon a time there was a man who was very rich, and he was called Don Giovanni di la Fortuna. However, he was a spendthrift and did not know how to hold on to his money and used it all up. When he no longer had anything, he had to go begging and dressed himself as a poor pilgrim and traveled throughout the entire country. One day he met a refined gentleman, who was the devil, and this man said to him, "Do you want to become rich and lead a luxurious life?"

"Yes, why not?" answered Don Giovanni.

"Here's a purse," the devil continued. "Whenever you say to it, 'dear purse, give me some money,'* it will give you as much money as you want. However, you must not wash yourself, comb yourself, cut your beard, or change your clothes for three years, three months, and three days. If you succeed in doing this, the purse will remain yours, and when the time is up, I'll let you keep your soul and take two others instead."

Don Giovanni agreed, took the purse, and moved on. Whenever he ran out of money, he only had to pull out his purse and say, 'Dear purse, give me some money,' and he would have as much money as he needed. But he was not allowed to wash, and soon he was so dirty that

---

*Virzotti miu, nesci danaru.

nobody could look at him anymore, and his beard and hair became long and tangled. His pilgrim's habit became tattered and was full of vermin and bugs.

One day he came to a city and saw a beautiful house, and because the sun was shining so brightly, he sat down on the stairs of the palace and began to search for the vermin and bugs that were on his body. A maid saw this and reported to her master, "Padrone, there is a man down below, and he's the dirtiest creature I've ever seen in my life. Please chase him away so that he doesn't bring all the vermin into our house."

So the master of the house went downstairs and started yelling at him, "You dirty beggar! Get away from this house right now!"

"Don't be so nasty," Don Giovanni replied. "I'm not a beggar, and if I want to, I can force you and your wife to leave this house hand in hand."

"And just how do you think you can do something like that?" the man laughed.

"Do you want to sell me your house?" Don Giovanni asked. "I'll buy it from you right now."

The other man thought that the dirty beggar was crazy, and just to have a little fun with him, he accepted the offer and cried out, "Good. Come with me. Let's go straight to the lawyer and set up a contract."

So they went to the lawyer, and the man sold Don Giovanni the entire house for a great deal of money, which Don Giovanni was to produce within a week. Meanwhile, Don Giovanni rented a room in an inn, and once he was behind closed doors, he kept on saying, "Dear purse, give me some money," and the purse kept on giving him money until the entire room was full of gold by the week's end.

When the owner of the house came to receive his money, Don Giovanni led him into the room full of gold and said, "Well, now take as much as you want."

The other man looked at the gold with an open mouth, and because he had given his word, he had no choice but to accept the money and to let the dirty beggar take over his house. Indeed, he took his wife's hand and left the house with her, just as Don Giovanni had predicted. Meanwhile, Don Giovanni was delighted to move into the house and did not deny himself anything. However, with each day that passed, he became dirtier and uglier.

Now, one day, it so happened that the king needed money, and because he had heard all about the stinking rich Don Giovanni, he sent a messenger to him and asked him to lend him a large sum of money. Don Giovanni agreed immediately, ordered a large wagon to be loaded

with sacks of money, and sent them to the king. Indeed, the king was very astonished and thought, "Who is this man? Why is he richer than I am?" Later, when he was able to earn money on his own again, he had Don Giovanni's sacks filled with money and returned to him. But Don Giovanni spoke to the king's servants, "Tell the king that he's insulting me by doing this. I certainly don't want him to give me back the little money I lent him. And if he doesn't want it, you should keep it."

The servants returned to the king and told him everything, and the king became even more astounded by this rich man. Then, one day he said to the queen, "My dear wife, this man did me a great favor and wouldn't even take back the money that he lent me. Because he's such a rich man, I want to give him our eldest daughter for his wife."

The queen agreed, and the king sent a messenger to Don Giovanni to ask him whether he would do him the honor and accept his eldest daughter for his wife.

"Well," thought Don Giovanni, "that would be a good thing if I could have the king's daughter for my wife," and he agreed.

Then the king sent another messenger to him and asked him to send a portrait because his eldest daughter wanted to see what he looked like. Indeed, Don Giovanni did this, and when the princess saw the picture of the dirty, slovenly pilgrim, she began to scream very loudly, "You want me to marry this dirty beggar!? No, I won't do it! I won't do it!"

"Oh, my child," the king implored her, "how could I know that this rich Don Giovanni was such an ugly man? But I've given my royal word, and there's nothing else we can do. You must marry him."

"No, Father, I won't do it. You can cut off my head, but I won't marry this dirty, no-good beggar."

The queen, too, spoke like her daughter and reprimanded the king for wanting to give their daughter to such a disgusting man. Just then, however, the youngest daughter said, "Dear Father, don't be so sad. If my sister doesn't want Don Giovanni for her husband, I'll take him. By no means should you break your royal word."

The king was now very happy and embraced his dear child, while the queen and the eldest daughter made fun of her.

Now the king sent a messenger to Don Giovanni again and requested that he set the day of the wedding because the princess was ready to marry him.

"Grant me two more months," Don Giovanni replied.

After one month, the three years, the three months, and the three days of his pact with the devil were finished. So Don Giovanni had his long beard cut and took a bath in sweet-smelling water for an entire month. Then he put on some new clothes and became a remarkably handsome young man. Indeed, nobody had ever seen anyone as handsome as he was. Finally, he boarded a magnificent ship and sailed into the harbor of the city where the king lived. As soon as he was in the harbor, the king and queen came out with their two daughters and went onto the ship to greet him. Meanwhile, the eldest daughter and the queen continued to make fun of the youngest daughter because she was about to marry such a dirty man. When they caught sight of the gorgeous young man, however, they were filled with so much anger and jealousy that they threw themselves into the sea and drowned. The devil was waiting and took both their souls. Of course, the king's youngest daughter was very happy about her handsome bridegroom, and they went on land and celebrated a splendid wedding. Later, when the old king died, Don Giovanni became king, and since he still had the purse, he never ran out of money. They remained happy and content, and we never received one cent.*

---

*We never got anything out of this.

11

FEDERICO AND EPOMATA

Once upon a time there was a king and queen who had no children, and yet they would have liked to have had a son or a daughter. One day when they were standing on a balcony, a fortune-teller happened to be riding by. All at once the king called to him to come up to the castle so he could tell the queen whether their wish would come true. The fortune-teller looked at the queen for a long time, and as he did this, he made such a sad face that the king became frightened and asked, "Well? What do you see?"

"Your majesty," he said, "let me depart. I can't tell you what will happen."

But the king ordered him to speak at once or else he would have his head cut off, and, consequently, the fortune-teller was compelled to answer: "The queen will have a son, but when he is eighteen years old, he will have to die."

When the king and queen heard this, they became very depressed and said, "What use is it to have a son if we have to raise him just to lose him after eighteen years!"

"If you want my advice," the fortune-teller added, "have a sturdy tower built and lock your child inside with a wet nurse until he is eighteen. Once he is eighteen, fate will no longer have any power over him."

After saying these words the fortune-teller left the palace. Nine months later the queen became pregnant, and the king immediately had a solid tower built and ordered a noble lady-in-waiting to serve his son in the tower as a replacement for the boy's mother. When the time came, the queen gave birth to a lovely son whom she named Federico. But the king sent the child with the lady-in-waiting and the wet nurse to the tower and had them locked inside. Every morning the lady had to go to the castle and report on how the child was doing, and every morning when the prince was sleeping, the king and queen came to the tower and visited their dear child.

Many years went by like this, and the boy grew rapidly and became more handsome and stronger with each passing day. He believed, however, that the lady-in-waiting was his mother, and did not know anyone but her and the nurse.

Now one morning it so happened that while he was still fast asleep, the lady went to the queen as she usually did, and a voice suddenly cried out: "Federico! Federico!" When the boy awoke, the voice continued to cry: "Federico! Why do you always stay locked in this tower? The lady you call your mother is not at all your mother. Your real parents are actually a powerful king and a beautiful queen who live in a magnificent castle and enjoy their lives, while you have to stay locked up all alone in this tower."

It was fate speaking to the boy, and when Federico heard these words, he began to weep. The lady, who had just returned, ran to him full of fright and asked, "My son, my dear son, why are you crying? Your mother is by your side again."

"Why are you calling me your son?" Federico answered. "You're not my mother at all. My mother is a beautiful queen, and my father is a powerful king, and they live in a glorious castle."

"Oh no, Federico," the lady cried out, "where did you get these crazy ideas? I'm your mother, and you are my dear son."

The lady managed to calm him down with many loving words, but later on she went to the queen with a great deal of anxiety and told her everything.

"Oh, my poor child," the queen said, "now he will be overcome by his fate despite everything we've done to protect him."

Several days passed, but one morning as Federico was still sleeping, and the lady had gone to the queen, the same voice rang out and called, "Federico! Federico!" The prince awoke, and the voice continued: "Federico, don't you want to believe my words? Just look at how alone you are here, and you could be with your parents and enjoy life. Tell this lady, whom you call your mother, that she should take you to your real mother."

Federico began to weep again, and when the lady ran to him, he cried out: "Why are you calling me your son? You're not my mother, and I want to go to my parents in their castle and enjoy my life with them."

The lady began speaking gentle and kind words to him, and she finally managed to calm him down. But when several days passed once more, the voice of fate rang out and repeated the same message. This time the prince would not let himself be calmed down and answered the lady by insisting, "I won't stay here any longer. I want to go to my real mother."

So the lady went to the queen very sadly and told her everything.

"Fate is persecuting my son," the queen replied. "What's the use when we try to protect him against his fate. You might as well bring him to the castle."

So Federico was taken to the castle, stayed with his parents, and grew more and more handsome with each passing day. In the meantime his parents had him guarded wherever he went and never let him go hunting so that he would not be harmed.

One day, when Federico was already seventeen years old, he said to the king, "Dear Father, please let me go hunting today. I want very much to shoot some birds."

His father sought to talk him out of this, but Federico kept asking, and because he was his only son, the king could not refuse him anything. Therefore, he finally let him go hunting with two of his ministers. Before they departed, however, he called the two ministers and said, "You must promise me that you'll always stay at the prince's side and won't leave him for one second."

They promised and went off hunting with the king's son. When they reached the forest, Federico said, "Why should we stay together like this? Each one of us should go off in a different direction, and later we'll see who's shot the most birds."

"Oh no, your majesty, we can't do that. We promised the king not to let you out of our sight for one second."

"Come on, now. I won't go very far, and if anything happens to me, I'll blow on my hunting horn right away so you can rush to my side."

The ministers agreed and went off in different directions, while Federico took a separate path. After he had gone for some time, he saw a bird sitting on a branch.

"Aha!" he said to himself. "What a pretty bird! I'm going to shoot it."

So he got his rifle ready, took aim, and shot. No sooner did he shoot, however, than he was whisked out of the forest and found himself in a large beautiful castle.

The ministers waited for some time for Federico to reappear. Then they became anxious and began calling and searching for him, but Federico was nowhere to be found. Finally, they returned to the castle, fell down at the king's feet, and told him everything. The king and queen put on mourning garments because their son was lost and said, "His fate has overtaken him despite everything."

But let's leave the king and queen and see what happened to Federico.

The castle in which Federico found himself belonged to a powerful sorceress. Her husband was a king of the heathens* and had been suffering from a terrible leprosy for many years. But there had been a prophesy that he could be cured of all his wounds if they were rubbed with the blood of a prince who had to be executed the very same hour that he turned eighteen years old. This is why the sorceress had used her power to abduct poor Federico and wanted to have him executed on the day that he turned eighteen.

Now the sorceress had a very beautiful daughter whose name was Epomata. When she first caught sight of the unfortunate Federico, she fell passionately in love with him, and she felt sorry that the handsome young man would have to be so miserably executed. Because she was scared of her mother, she did not dare to speak to the prince during the day. Instead, she went quietly to his room during the night and advised him what he should do. Federico remained in the sorceress's castle for almost one year and had everything he wanted, but he was never allowed to leave the castle.

One evening, however, Epomata came to him and said, "In three days you'll turn eighteen. Then my cruel mother will have you executed. But don't be frightened. I shall rescue you if you do exactly what I tell you. Tomorrow morning you are not to get up. When the first minister comes to bring you breakfast, you are to say that you have powerful headaches and want to stay in bed. The day after you are to pretend to be even sicker and remain in bed again. That night I shall come to you, and we shall flee."

Federico did everything Epomata had commanded. When the minister arrived with breakfast the next morning, Federico lay in bed and complained that he was sick and didn't want to get up. So the minister left the room and reported this to the sorceress, and she answered, "Grant him what he wants, just so he lives another two days. Then we can bring him alive to the place of execution."

---

*In Italian, Turchi; In English, Turks.

The next morning when the minister went to Federico again, he asked him, "Well, your majesty, how do you feel today?"

"Terrible," answered Federico, "I want to remain in bed again today."

So they let him stay in bed as he wished and thought that he would still be alive for the execution the next day.

But Epomata called a lady from the court whom she trusted and had her bring her a large basket filled with cake, sweets, and many bottles of fine wine, in which she mixed a strong sleeping potion.

Now, the sorceress had two books about magic, which provided her with her power. One was black, the other white. The white one was more powerful than the black one. She always kept these books hidden beneath her pillow. Epomata knew this, and when it became dark, she crept into her mother's room and took the white magic book. Since everyone was asleep, she crawled into Federico's room and brought him some shabby clothes to put on. Then he had to place the basket with sweets and the bottles of wine mixed with the sleeping potion on his head and follow Epomata. The castle was protected by soldiers at seven sentry posts, and Epomata and Federico had to get past them in order to escape. When they came to the first sentry post, Epomata said, "Tomorrow is a holiday because the prince is to be executed. The king will be cured from his leprosy with the prince's blood. Because of all of this, the queen has sent you some sweet cake and good wine so that you, too, can celebrate."

But when the soldiers drank some of the wine with the sleeping potion, they fell into a deep sleep all at once. Epomata did exactly the same thing at each sentry post, and when all the soldiers had fallen asleep, she went to the stable with Federico, saddled two fast horses, and fled.

Early the next morning the sorceress sent her soldiers to bring poor Federico to the spot where the execution was to take place. When they entered his room, however, he had disappeared. Then they ran and told the queen, who cried out, "If Federico has fled, only my daughter could have helped him!"

So she ran to her daughter's room, but it was empty, and no matter how much they searched for Epomata, they could not find her anywhere. "This no-good daughter of mine!" she yelled in anger. "You wait. I'll get my revenge on her! Even if I have lost my power over the prince, Epomata won't get away from me."

She wanted to take her books of magic with her, but she found only the black one because Epomata had taken the white book with her. Now the sorceress became even more furious. She had the horses saddled at once and rode after her daughter and the prince with her ministers at her side. Meanwhile, Federico and Epomata rode as fast as their horses could go. Epomata said, "Federico, turn around and tell me what you see."

As he turned around, he caught sight of the sorceress, who had almost caught up with them, and called out full of fright, "Epomata! Epomata! Your mother is right on our heels."

Epomata immediately opened the book of magic and said, "I'll become a garden, and you'll be the gardener!"

No sooner did she say these words than she was transformed into a garden and Federico was a gardener. When the sorceress came upon the gardener, she asked, "Tell me, my handsome lad, have you seen a man and a woman ride by here?"

"What do you want? Fennel?" Federico answered. "They're not ripe yet."

"No, you didn't understand! I didn't ask for fennel. I asked you whether you've seen a man and woman come riding by here."

"What's that? What? Asparagus. We'll be tying them in little bundles very soon."

"Look, your majesty," one of the sorceress's ministers said. "This man doesn't understand you, and we can't catch up with your daughter and the prince anymore. They're certainly miles away by now."

So they turned around as Epomata and Federico assumed their human shapes once again and continued to flee. As the sorceress rode back to the castle, she opened her black book of magic, and when she read that the garden and the gardener had been Epomata and Federico, she became enraged and said, "I must get revenge on my no-good daughter. Let's turn around and ride after them."

But Federico still continued to look behind, and when he saw the sorceress in the distance again, he called out, "Epomata! Epomata! Your mother is on our heels."

Then Epomata opened her book and said, "I'll become a church, and you'll be the sacristan!"

All at once they were changed into a church and sacristan. When the sorceress came to the church, she asked, "My good man, have you perhaps seen a man and a woman who came riding by here?"

"The priest hasn't come yet. That's why mass has not begun," answered Federico.

"What are you saying? I said nothing about mass. I asked whether you saw a man and a woman ride by here."

"When the priest comes, you can go to confession," Federico responded.

He kept answering her this way until the sorceress lost her patience and turned back. Meanwhile, Epomata and Federico assumed their human shapes and continued riding. But the sorceress read in her book that the church and the sacristan had actually been her daughter and the prince. She became furious and said, "Let's turn around once more, and this time they won't get away from me."

So they rode after them, and for a while Federico had not looked behind him. Then all at once he glanced behind him and saw that the sorceress was right on their heels. "Epomata! Epomata!" he cried out. "We're lost!"

"You shall turn into a pond, and I shall become an eel!" Epomata said quickly, and suddenly Federico was transformed into a pond, and Epomata became an eel that swam merrily in the water. But the sorceress had noticed what they had done, and she bent over the pond and tried to catch the eel. No matter how much she sought to grab the eel, it slipped out of her hands, but she kept trying in vain. Finally, she lost her patience and called out, "May Federico forget you with the first kiss that he receives in his father's house."

After she uttered this curse, she climbed on her horse and rode back to her castle. Meanwhile, Federico and Epomata assumed their human shapes once more. After they rode for a long time, they reached the prince's kingdom, and Federico said, "I belong to the royal family of this realm, and you are to become my wife. But it's not appropriate for you to appear in these wretched clothes in front of my family. Therefore, I'll take you to an inn where you'll stay while I go to my parents and fetch everything you'll need to make your triumphant entrance at the court."

"Oh, Federico," answered Epomata, "don't you remember the curse my mother uttered against you? I implore you not to let yourself be kissed. Remember that with the first kiss you receive, you'll forget all about me."

"Don't worry," answered Federico. "I'll certainly remember."

So he took her to an inn and placed the innkeeper in charge of her. Then he rushed to his parents in the royal castle. As soon as the king and queen caught sight of him and recognized him as their dear son, whom they had thought was dead, they rushed toward him and wanted to kiss him because they were so full of joy. But he called out, "Dear parents, don't kiss me. Otherwise, I'll forget my bride."

His parents were very distressed by this and said, "We've wept over you for many years and thought you were dead, and now that we have you again, shouldn't we be allowed to kiss you?"

But he resisted them and said, "Prepare a beautiful gold coach drawn by six horses, and get my entire entourage ready so that I can go and fetch my dear bride. In the meantime I want to sleep a bit because I'm tired."

Then he laid down and soon fell asleep. Now the lady-in-waiting who had replaced his mother in the tower was there, and she thought, "What's this? I was regarded as his mother for so many years and carried him in my arms. I was actually the one who raised him, and now I'm not allowed to kiss him at all?"

She could no longer hold out and she crept into his room, bent over him, and kissed him while he was asleep. The very moment she did this, he awoke, but Epomata had vanished from his memory.

"Dear son," the queen said. "The coach is ready. Do you want to go now and fetch your bride?"

"My bride? I don't have a bride," Federico answered and insisted he knew nothing about her.

Meanwhile, poor Epomata waited for him, and since he did not appear, she finally thought, "Oh, he's certainly let himself be kissed and has forgotten me."

She called the innkeeper's wife and said, "I shall now have to spend some more time here. Please find me a neat elderly woman who can serve me and accompany me wherever I go."

"Of course," the innkeeper's wife responded. "I know a woman who has been looking for some work, and she will surely please you."

So the innkeeper's wife brought her an elderly woman called Donna Maria, and she stayed with Epomata and served her. Now, the inn stood across from a coffee house in which many cultivated young people gathered. Among them was a young prince. When this man caught sight of the beautiful Epomata and learned that she was alone, he fell passionately in love with her. One day he said to Donna Maria, "I would appreciate it if you would do me a favor and take a message to your mistress."

"I won't take any messages at all," Donna Maria replied curtly and returned to the inn. Later, Epomata asked her, "Whom were you speaking with, Donna Maria?"

The woman did not want to say, for she thought, "My mistress is beautiful and still very young." At the same time, Epomata persisted until Donna Maria answered, "Noble lady, it was a young prince who wanted me to carry a message to you, but I wouldn't listen to him."

"Oh! Why not?" responded Epomata. "Bring me as many messages as he sends."

When Donna Maria went out again, the young prince was waiting outside the door and addressed her, "Oh, Donna Maria, please be so kind and listen to what I want to say to your mistress."

"All right then, tell me what message you'd like me to take to my mistress."

"Tell your mistress I shall honor her with a hundred ounces of gold and give you twenty if she allows me to dine with her this evening and to spend the night with her."

Donna Maria delivered this message to Epomata, who replied, "Definitely. Tell him that I shall expect him."

When it became evening, the prince came and brought Epomata a purse filled with gold coins and twenty for her maid. Dinner was ready, and after they had something to eat and drink, Epomata said, "I'll go into my room first, and after a little while you can join me."

As soon as she was in her room, however, she placed a basin filled with water in the middle of the room, opened her book of magic, and cast a spell on the basin: "One in, one out!" Then she put a chair next to the basin and cast another spell so that it would keep anyone who sat on it from getting off it. Finally, she lay down in bed, surrounded and guarded by sorceresses with drawn swords.

After a while the young prince entered and Epomata said to him, "Noble prince, it is the custom in my fatherland for people to wash their feet before they go to bed. Therefore, I would appreciate it if you would follow our custom and wash your feet in the basin."

The prince sat down on the chair that Epomata had enchanted, and stuck one foot into the water which was so boiling hot that he quickly pulled his foot out with a soft cry and stuck the other into the basin. But he burned this one as well, and when he wanted to stand up, the chair kept him down. Whether he wanted to or not, he had to spend the entire night sticking one foot into the water and one foot out until they were both swollen. Meanwhile, Epomata slept peacefully throughout the night. The next morning, when she woke up, she said, "What! You're still here? Quick, leave the room so that nobody finds you in this condition, or my honor will be ruined."

Then the prince scolded and cursed her and left the room full of anger. But when he returned to his friends who asked him how things had gone, he said to himself, "If I've suffered, why not let them as well?" And he answered, "Oh, things went very well. She's a glorious woman."

When another young nobleman heard this, he went to Donna Maria and said, "Tell your mistress I'll give her eighty ounces of gold and you twenty if she will allow me to dine and spend the night with her."

When Donna Maria brought this message to the beautiful Epomata, she answered, "Tell him he can come whenever he wants."

In the evening the nobleman arrived and brought the money with him. Then they ate, and Epomata was friendly and polite to him. After dinner she said, "I'll go into my room first, and after a while you can join me."

As soon as she was in her room, she placed two lit candles on the table, opened the book of magic, and cast a spell on the candles: "One out, the other lit." Then she cast a spell on the floor so that the nobleman would not be able to move from that spot. Finally she went to bed, and the sorceresses kept invisible guard over her.

After a while the nobleman came into the room, and Epomata said, "Noble sir, the light is hurting my eyes, please put out the candles before you come to bed."

The nobleman put out one of the candles and then the other. The first candle became lit again, and he had to spend the entire night blowing out the candles as they lit up and were blown out. When he tried to leave in his anger, he could not move from that spot. Instead, he had to keep blowing until his lips became thick and swollen. The next morning Epomata awoke and cried out: "What? You're still standing there! Quick, leave my room. If anyone sees you here, my honor will be ruined."

Then he left the room and heaped abuse on Epomata because she had treated him so badly. However, when he returned to the coffee house and his companions asked him how things had gone, he gave them the same answer that the prince had given them: "Oh, things went very well."

Now there was also a merchant's son who went to Donna Maria and said, "Tell your mistress I'll give her fifty ounces of gold and you ten, if she allows me to dine with her this evening and to spend the night with her."

Donna Maria delivered this message to beautiful Epomata, who answered: "Tell him he can come when he wants."

That evening the merchant's son arrived. Epomata received him in a friendly fashion, and they ate together. After dinner she said, "I'll go into my room first, and you can join me in a little while."

Once in her room, however, she opened her book of magic and cast a spell on the window: "Open one, close the other!" Then she cast another spell on the floor so that the merchant's son would not be able to move from this spot. Finally she lay down in her bed and rested calmly because she knew that the sorceresses would keep watch over her.

After a while the merchant's son entered, and Epomata said to him, "Noble sir, the window is still open. Please close it before you come to bed."

But no matter how often he closed one side of the windows the other would open and hit him hard in the chest. This continued the entire night because he could not move from the spot, and his chest became completely bruised and swollen. The next morning Epomata awoke and cried out, "What? You're still there? Leave my room immediately. If anyone sees you here, my honor will be ruined."

So he left the room, heaping abuse on Epomata. Indeed, he crawled down the stairs with difficulty because he could not stand up straight. When his two friends saw him in this condition, they finally confessed that they had both experienced something similar, and all three cursed Epomata and said nasty things about her.

Now, quite some time had passed since Federico had abandoned poor Epomata, and she heard one day that he was going to marry a rich princess, and the wedding was to take place very soon. So she opened her book of magic and wished for two dolls, one a boy who played the violin, and the other a girl who sang. All at once the dolls stood right before her and looked fine and dainty. Then she called Donna Maria and said to her, "Take these two dolls and carry them in front of the king's castle. When you are there, I want you to cry out: 'Beautiful dolls for sale! What beautiful dolls I have for sale! A boy who plays the violin and a girl who sings!' I want you to continue doing this until either the king or his son calls you. Then you are to sell them both dolls."

Donna Maria did what Epomata had commanded her to do. She carried the dolls in front of the royal castle and cried out with a loud voice: "Oh, what beautiful dolls I have for sale! A boy who plays the violin! A girl who sings!"

Just at this moment the king and his son were standing at the window, and Federico said, "Dear Father, do you see the beautiful dolls that woman is selling? I'd very much like to buy them."

So they called the woman to come up to them, quickly settled on a price, and bought the dolls from her. Later, when they were eating dinner, the king said, "Federico, you bought two beautiful dolls today. Why don't you bring them out and show our company how they perform?"

Federico fetched the dolls and placed them on the table. All at once the boy began to play the violin, and soon the girl began to sing and said, "Remember when you were once locked in a tower and your fate spoke to you during the night and told you that you were the son of a rich king? Remember how this kept happening until your parents had to bring you to them? Do you remember this still?"

"No! the boy answered, and "wham!" the girl gave him a hard slap in the face. Federico must have felt this slap, for he let out a loud cry. The girl continued: "Do you remember how you went hunting one day and wanted to shoot a bird, and suddenly you were whisked from the forest to the sorceress's castle? Do you recall how you saw the beautiful Epomata and how she saved you from death when her mother wanted to execute you and how she managed to escape with you? Do you remember this still?"

"No!" answered the boy, and "wham!" He received another resounding slap in the face. Federico felt it so much that he uttered a loud cry.

"Do you remember how you fled with Epomata, and her mother pursued you, and Epomata was transformed into a garden, and you into a gardener? Do you recall how her mother asked you whether you had seen a man and woman come riding by and you answered by asking whether she wanted fennel and asparagus? Do you remember any of this?"

"No!"

And Federico felt another hard slap in the face and uttered a cry.

"Do you remember how the sorceress continued to pursue us and I was changed into a church and you into a sacristan? Do you recall how she asked after us, and you spoke about the priest and confession?"

"No!"

"Wham!"

Federico felt another sharp slap in the face.

"Do you remember how the sorceress caught up with us again, and you became a pond and I was changed into an eel? Do you recall how my mother tried to catch me, and how I continually managed to slip out of her hands until, in her anger, she cast a magic curse on me? She said: 'May he forget you as soon as he receives his first kiss when he returns home.' Do you remember how you swore you would not let anyone kiss you? Do you remember any of this?"

Now when Federico heard these words, he suddenly remembered poor Epomata, jumped up from his chair, stormed out of the house, and rushed to the inn where Epomata was still waiting for him. As soon as he saw her, he fell to her feet and asked for forgiveness.

"Yes," he said. "You are right to reproach me for all the suffering you've gone through. But now I've come and want to take you to my parents. You alone shall become my wife."

While they were speaking with one another, a beautiful gold coach arrived. It had been sent by the king to fetch his daughter-in-law. Epomata put on royal garments and drove with Federico to the castle. When the king and queen saw her, they were extremely delighted by her beauty and said, "Now all preparations should be made for the wedding."

They told the other bride that Federico could not marry her because he already had a bride. Epomata was still a heathen, however, so she first had to be baptized and receive a Christian name. Right before they were to be married, Epomata sent a message to her mother that said, "Dear Mother, forgive me for the way I have wronged you. I have suffered a great deal because of it. I would like it very much if you would forgive me and come to my wedding."

Because a great deal of time had flown by, the anger of the sorceress had vanished, and she fulfilled her daughter's wish and came to the wedding, which was celebrated in great splendor. After a few days went by, the sorceress said to Federico, "Dear son-in-law, I shall now leave you. Follow my command, and you will benefit from it. This evening, when I take leave from my daughter, I shall come into this room. Then you must cut off my head and hang it up on the ceiling. You must cut off my arms and legs and place them in the four corners of this room. My body must be sliced into tiny pieces and strewn around the room."

After hearing this Federico went to Epomata and said, "Your mother has ordered me to chop up her body this evening, but I won't do it. How could I possibly lay a hand on your mother?"

"Why not?" Epomata replied. "You can easily do this with a clear conscience when my mother has commanded you to do it. She is such a powerful sorceress that nothing can ever harm her."

That evening the sorceress took her leave from her daughter and went into her room. Federico followed her and sliced her to pieces the way she commanded him to do. When he entered the room again the next morning, he saw such splendor that he stood there dazzled by it all. Instead of the head on the ceiling he saw a glorious gold crown. The arms, legs, and body had become a huge pile of gold and precious stones. All of this was the sorceress's wedding present to her daughter.

Federico spent the rest of his life with his wife, happy and content, and we still don't have one single cent.

12

THE FEARLESS YOUNG MAN

Once upon a time there was a woman who had enough to live on. Indeed, she did not lack a thing, but she had a son who was fearless and was continually playing dumb pranks. So she said to herself, "I'll take him to my brother-in-law. He's a priest, and certainly he'll be able to make him afraid of something."

She went to her brother-in-law and asked him to take over her ill-bred son and fill him full of fear. The priest agreed and invited the young man to stay in his house. Soon thereafter the priest decided to call a man to help him make the boy frightened of something.

"I'll give you a nice gift," the priest said, "if you pretend to be dead this evening and let yourself be carried in a coffin into the church. My nephew will keep watch over you, and at midnight you must move about in the coffin as though you were alive."

The man promised to do this, and the priest called his nephew to him and said, "A dead man will soon be brought here, and I'd like you to help me set up the platform for the coffin in the church."

After they had set up the platform, the pallbearers came and carried the man who was pretending to be dead, and put him into the coffin on the platform.

"Listen to me," the priest said to his nephew, "I want you to spend the night in the church and keep watch because we cannot leave the dead alone. Are you afraid to do this?"

"Why should I be afraid?" the fellow said and locked himself with the dead man in the church.

At midnight the supposed dead man suddenly lifted an arm and let it sink quickly with a good deal of noise.

"Hey you! Be quiet!" yelled the young man. "I want to get a little sleep."

After a while the man lifted a leg and slammed it against the coffin.

"I think this dead man is coming alive again," the young man thought, and he stood up on the platform and began beating the man with a large club so that the man jumped up, ran to the door, ripped it open, and fled.

The priest heard this racket and came running full of fear because he thought his nephew might have really killed the man.

"What's all this noise?" he asked.

"Just think, uncle," his nephew cried, "the dead man came back to life. I beat him because he became so restless and wouldn't let me sleep, and then he cleared out of here."

"Oh no," the priest thought to himself. "The boy was not the least afraid! I'll have to give that poor man some money to get over the beating he took."

The next evening the priest thought up something else. He took a bunch of skulls, climbed up to the top of the church tower, and placed them along the walls. In each one of the skulls he lit a small candle so that they all looked gruesome. At the highest point of the tower he set up a skeleton and placed the cord to the bells in the skeleton's hand. Then he went downstairs, quickly called his nephew and said, "Run up fast to the top of the tower and ring the bells!"

The young man obeyed, and when he reached the top of the tower and saw the skulls lit in such an eery way, he thought, "Oh, that's really neat! Now I can find my way more easily."

When he next saw the skeleton, he called over to it, "Hey you, what are you doing up here? If you're the one who's supposed to ring the bells, then you can at least get to work, and then I'll go back down. It's either you or me."

Because the skeleton could not move and did not respond, the nephew lost his patience and said, "If you're not going to listen, you'd better take care of yourself," he threw the skeleton down the stairs. Then he began to ring the bells so that all the people came together on the street below and thought that some accident had happened. The priest calmed them down and said, "Dear people, go back home. It's just my nephew. He plays some dumb pranks from time to time. Come down here, nephew!"

Now the priest did not know any longer what he should do and thought, "I'll try one more time, and if he doesn't become frightened, I'll have to send him away."

So he called for another man and said, "Listen, my good friend, I'll give you a nice present if you do exactly what I tell you to do. Tonight you must hide yourself by that wall over there. Toward midnight I'll send my nephew to the well. When he walks by you, I want you to spring from your hiding place and scream: 'Six!' I think such a fright will scare him more than anything else because it's unexpected."

The man promised to do what the priest told him to do, and toward midnight the uncle said to his nephew, "Please go to the well and fetch me a glass of water. I'm so thirsty."

The young man went through the dark night to the well and held a mug in his hand. As he walked by the wall, a dark shape stood up and screamed, "Six!"

"Seven!" responded the boy completely cold-bloodedly, and he whacked the man in his face with the mug. Immediately the mug broke into a thousand pieces, and the man fell to the ground half dead.

When the priest heard the racket, he came running, and when he saw the wounded man lying on the ground, he said, "I can't stand your living with me anymore. Go forth and seek your fortune out in the wide world."

The nephew did not wait for the priest to repeat himself, and off he went in the darkness of the night. He did not take anything with him except the handle of the mug that he still held in his hand. The next morning he found himself in a desolate and wild region. He was thirsty, saw a well nearby, and went over and filled another mug with water and wandered off. Finally he saw a beautiful house standing in the distance, but robbers were living in it. As he headed toward the house, the mug fell from his hand, and the water ran in many little streams here and there. "Five hundred there, four hundred on the other side, six hundred over there,"* he said with a loud voice, and he meant the drops of water.

The robbers thought it was a great general who had come with his army to catch them, so they jumped up and cleared out of the house through the back door. The young man entered the house and found a beautifully covered table, and he sat down and ate and drank to his heart's content. Because he had been traveling the entire night, he wanted to sleep a bit and went into the next room where he found the

---

*Cincucentu di ccà, quattrucentu dda parte, seicentu dda via.

83

thirteen beds of the robbers. He took the beds apart and mounted them against the door. Then he climbed to the top of the beds and took a sword with him that had belonged to the robbers.

After a while the robbers said to one another, "Let's go back and take a look. Perhaps the soldiers have left the house."

When they arrived at the house, the captain of the robbers sent one of them inside to find out how things looked. The robber slipped quietly inside until he came to the door where the beds had been piled on top of one another. The young man who was lying on top of the beds saw the robber coming, drew his sword from the sheath, and called out with a loud voice: "Get out, get out!" And then he beat the robber until he was dead.

The other robbers thought he was calling all his soldiers and ran away from there even faster than they had done the previous time. Then the young man gathered up all the treasures and valuables that were in the house and took them to his mother, who was very delighted that her son had returned and had become such a rich man. Afterward they lived happy and content, but he never learned to fear.

13

CARUSEDDU*

Once upon a time there was a father who had three sons, and the youngest was called Caruseddu. He was also the smartest and the most handsome and was blessed with many magic gifts. Now it so happened that the father died and left his sons in bitter poverty.

"What are we going to do now?" one of them asked.

"Let's set out and earn our living by working in the gardens of rich people."

So they set out, and wherever they saw a beautiful garden, they asked whether they could work there. They managed to earn a meager living this way.

One day they came to a large garden. The owner was standing at his door and called over to them, "Why don't you come in, my good-looking boys. You can work in my garden."

He was very friendly, but he was really an ogre† and intended to eat them during the night.

After the three brothers had worked the entire day, the ogre said, "Why don't you stay with me tonight? Tomorrow you can continue working in the garden."

---

*Caruseddu is the diminutive of Carusu or "young man," but Caruseddu also means a small thing or trifle. It can also denote a clay savings pot.

† Dragu.

He led them into a room where there was a large bed, where all three were to sleep. Now the ogre had three young daughters who slept in the same room as the three brothers, and Caruseddu thought to himself, "The ogre is a bit too friendly, and I'm sure he's going to trick us!" So, when the three maidens and his brothers were asleep, he took the kerchiefs from the heads of the girls and tied them around his brothers' heads and his own, and he put the woolen caps of his brothers on the heads of the maidens. During the night the ogre crept into the room and felt the heads in the beds. First he felt the three kerchiefs.

"Oh," he said to himself. "These are my daughters. I almost made a tragic mistake."

When he went to the other side and felt the caps, he thought they were the three brothers and swallowed his own daughters. After he crept out of the room, Caruseddu woke his brothers and said, "Quick, we must flee right away! I tricked the ogre into eating his own daughters, and when he realizes how I deceived him, he'll kill us."

All three of them ran as fast as they could and were lucky to get away. When they were outside the house, Caruseddu raised his voice and cried out, "Ogre! Ogre! What have you done? You ate your own daughters, and we've managed to get away!"

When the ogre heard this, he tore out his hair and yelled, "Just you wait, you miserable scoundrel! If I ever get my hands on you, you'll have a terrible time!"

The three brothers continued on their way and worked in gardens. Because they were very skilled gardeners, the king heard about them and had them summoned so that they could work for him. After they entered his employ, the king took a great liking to the handsome Caruseddu and said to him, "I want you always to remain with me and be my faithful servant."

Now Caruseddu became the king's faithful servant, and his brothers continued to work in the garden, but they became filled with envy and spoke to one another, "There's our brother, and even though he's the youngest, he's become much greater than we are. What can we do to get him out of the way?"

So they went to the king and said, "Your majesty, you have everything that your heart desires, but there is one thing that you don't have—the talking horse."

"Who has this talking horse?"

"The ogre has the talking horse, and our brother Caruseddu is certainly capable of getting it."

When the king heard this, he wanted to have the talking horse very much and said to him, "Caruseddu, you must do me a favor and fetch the talking horse from the ogre."

"Oh, your majesty, how can I fetch the talking horse? The ogre will swallow me up."

"No, no," the king replied. "He won't do that. Your brothers have told me that you can do anything. Therefore, you must now go and fetch me the talking horse."

What could Caruseddu do? He had to carry out the king's orders. Therefore, he bought a large bag full of sweets and set out on his way to the ogre's house. When he arrived, the ogre was not at home and had also taken his horse with him, so Caruseddu crept quietly to the table and said, "I'm a good Christian and wish to be tiny as a mouse."*

All at once he became as tiny as a mouse and hid beneath the straw. After a short time passed, the ogre returned home, led the horse into the stable, gave it something to eat, and went back into his house. When it began to get dark, Caruseddu said, "I'm tiny as a mouse and want to be a good Christian." He then became a man, crept to the horse, and said, "Little horse, dear horse, do you want to come with me? Look, I'll give you all this sugar and take you to the king."

The horse neighed very loudly to call the ogre.

"I'm a good Christian and wish to be tiny as a mouse!" Caruseddu cried out and hid himself beneath the straw.

Meanwhile the ogre came running and yelled, "What's happened, my little horse?"

"Caruseddu is here and wants to steal me," answered the horse.

The ogre searched the entire stable, but when he could not find anyone, he said, "What? You want to get the best of me?" He grabbed a stick and gave the horse a good beating.

After he went away, Caruseddu assumed his human shape once more, came out of his hiding place, and said, "Do you see how he beats you, little horse? It would be better if you came with me. You would have a good life at the king's court."

The horse neighed loudly again, and Caruseddu had just about enough time to change himself into a tiny creature and hide before the ogre came running into the stable and cried out, "What's happened?"

"Caruseddu's here and wants to steal me."

The ogre again searched the entire stable. When he didn't find anything, he beat the horse mercilessly and cried out, "I'll teach you to

---

*Cristianu sugnu, caruseddu diventu.

try to get the better of me. The next time you neigh so loudly, I'm not going to come."

After the ogre left again, Caruseddu crawled out and said, "Oh, little horse, don't be so dumb. Don't you see, you'll only get another beating."

Now the horse was fed up with the beatings and stood there patiently as Caruseddu untied it. Then the horse followed the sly Caruseddu out of the stable. Once outside, the horse neighed loudly one more time, and Caruseddu cried out, "Oh, ogre! Ogre! How stupid you are! Caruseddu was there and has stolen the horse from you."

"Oh, Caruseddu, you scoundrel! Are you going to come again?" the ogre shouted.

"Of course," answered Caruseddu, who swung himself on top of the horse and rode off.

When he returned to the king, there was great joy at the court.

"Long live Caruseddu! Long live Caruseddu!" the people cried, and the king gave him rich gifts and was more fond of him than ever.

But his brothers became more and more jealous, and they went to the king and said, "Caruseddu has brought you the talking horse. However, the ogre has something much more beautiful. It's the cover with the little gold bell, and only Caruseddu can fetch it for you."

Since the king also wanted to have the cover with the little gold bell, he had Caruseddu summoned and said, "Caruseddu, you brought me the horse, but now you must also fetch me the cover with the gold bell."

"Oh, your majesty," Caruseddu replied. "I can't possibly fetch this for you. The ogre keeps it on his bed!"

"You've got to see to it yourself! You were able to fetch one thing, so you certainly should be able to carry out this task as well."

Caruseddu went into the stable, mounted his horse, and rode to see the ogre. When he reached the gate, he tied the horse to it and crept into the house. Because the ogre had just left, he said, "I'm a good Christian and want to be as tiny as a mouse." Then he hid himself beneath the bed. In the evening the ogre and his wife returned home and lay down to bed. Caruseddu crawled from his hiding place and began to pull the cover very gently.

"Why are you pulling the cover away from me?" the ogre roared at his wife.

"I'm not pulling anything," she answered. "You're the one."

Caruseddu concealed himself quickly under the bed, and when the two had fallen back to sleep, he crawled out and began pulling on the cover again. In short, he kept on pulling until he had dragged the entire cover away from them. In response, the ogre grabbed his wife and began beating her. Fortunately, Caruseddu managed to escape. Once outside the house, Caruseddu shook the cover so that all the bells began to ring loudly.

"It was that scoundrel, Caruseddu," the ogre shouted in great rage. "Caruseddu, are you going to return?"

"Of course, I will," answered Caruseddu, and he swung himself on his horse and rode home.

When he came before the king and laid the cover with the bells at his feet, the king exclaimed, "Long live Caruseddu! Long live Caruseddu!" He gave him a beautiful gift and was more fond of him than ever before. However, his brothers were so envious that they could barely control themselves. "Something strange is going on here," they thought. "He's gone to the ogre twice, and each time he's returned safely. We've got to think up something else."

So they went to the king and said, "Your majesty, wouldn't it be wonderful if we had the ogre here in a cage?"

"That would certainly be a nice thing to see," the king responded. "But who could capture the ogre?"

"Oh, you would just have to send Caruseddu. He can do anything."

The king called for his servant and said, "Caruseddu, I want you to go and bring back the ogre himself. I want to put him in a cage so everyone can see him."

"But, your majesty, that will be the death of me! How can I bring the ogre here?"

"See to it yourself," responded the king. "I'm going to give you three days. Then the ogre must be here!"

Caruseddu went away and disguised himself as a carpenter. He took some boards and tools with him and began working in front of the ogre's house. While he was banging with his hammer and sawing, the ogre came out and asked him, "What are you doing there?"

"Don't you know that Caruseddu has died? I'm making a coffin for him."

"If only he had died ten years earlier, that scoundrel!" the ogre cried out. "He stole my talking horse and my cover with the gold bells. I also ate my own daughters because of him, and he's also to blame for my wife's death. She grieved so much about the loss of the horse and the cover that she eventually died."

The news of Caruseddu's death made the ogre so happy that he wanted to watch the carpenter build the coffin. When the coffin was finally ready and only the top had to be nailed down, Caruseddu suddenly hit himself on his forehead with his hand and cried out, "Oh, how stupid I am! I've forgotten to bring my yardstick with me. Hmm! Caruseddu was about as large as you are. Perhaps you can do me a favor and lie down inside the coffin for a moment."

The ogre was dumb and lay down inside the coffin. As soon as he did, Caruseddu slammed the top down and nailed it shut. Then he loaded the coffin with the ogre onto his horse and took it to the king.

"Here's the ogre, your majesty! Now you can put him in the cage."

"Long live Caruseddu! Long live Caruseddu!" exclaimed the king. "Nobody is your equal!"

The king had the ogre put into a cage, and Caruseddu received many rich gifts. Meanwhile, his brothers became even more jealous because of this and tried to bring about his ruin. They went to the king and said, "Your majesty, you are still unmarried, and your people want you to find a wife. We are certain that we know which princess would be worthy of you. She is the daughter of the queen with seven veils, who is more beautiful than the sun and the moon."

When the king heard this, he thought about nothing but this beautiful princess. As a result he summoned his servant and said, "Caruseddu, you have already done so much, but now you must fetch the daughter of the queen with seven veils because I want to have her for my wife. If you don't fetch her for me, I'll have your head cut off."

Caruseddu went to the stable to his little horse and began to weep.

"Oh, little horse, dear horse," he said. "What should I do? The king wants me to fetch the daughter of the queen with seven veils, and I don't even know where to look for her."

"Just calm yourself," answered the horse. "Get on my back and take enough supplies for you and me."

Caruseddu did this, and he mounted the horse and rode off. After they had traveled for some time, they came across a large ant hill, and the horse said, "Take a loaf of bread and spread some crumbs on the ground for the ants."

Caruseddu did this and rode on. After a while they came to a river, where there was a fish flopping on the bank that could not make its way back into the water.

"Take the fish and throw it into the water," the horse said, and Caruseddu did this.

After they rode some distance, they saw a little bird along the way that was caught in a trap and could not get out.

"Set the little bird free and let it fly," said the horse, and Caruseddu did this.

Finally they came to the city ruled by the queen with seven veils.

"Look," said the horse. "There's the royal palace. Get off my back and lead me by the reins up and down in front of the palace. The princess will feel a great desire to ride me. As soon as she gets on my back, you're to swing yourself on my back right behind her and carry her off."

Caruseddu rode into the city. When he came to the royal palace, he got off the horse and led him by the reins back and forth in front of the palace. Now the princess was standing at a window, and when she saw the marvelous small horse, she was full of joy and called her father: "Look at that cute little horse, dear Father! I'd like to ride on it for a while."

"Good, my child," the king responded. "Do what you like."

So the princess ran down out of the palace and said to Caruseddu, "I want to ride on your little horse. Bring it to me here."

So Caruseddu brought the horse, and the princess got on. No sooner was she on the horse than Caruseddu swung himself up behind her and held her tightly, while the horse sprang away in a gallop. The princess screamed, but it was no use—the horse did not stop running. At the same time the princess ripped the veil from her head and threw it into the air, and when they came to the river, the princess slipped a ring from her finger and threw it into the water. Finally they returned to the king, and Caruseddu said, "Your majesty, here is the princess. I've carried out your command."

When the king saw the beautiful face of the princess, he was extremely happy, praised his faithful Caruseddu, and was more fond of him than ever. Then he turned to the princess and said, "Beautiful maiden, I would like you to be my bride, and as soon as you like, we shall celebrate the wedding."

"Oh, we have a good deal of time before that," said the princess. "Before I become your wife, you must get me my veil that I lost on my way here."

In response the king summoned Caruseddu and said to him, "Caruseddu, the princess lost her veil along the way. You must find it for me within three days, otherwise I'll have your head cut off."

Caruseddu went sadly to the stable and began stroking his little horse and weeping.

"Oh, little horse, dear horse, you helped me one time. Now you must help me again. The princess lost her veil on her way here, and if I don't bring it back here within three days, the king will have my head cut off."

"Stop grieving so much, you fool," the horse said. "Get on my back, and you'll soon find the veil."

So Caruseddu mounted the horse and rode off. The horse ran until it came to the spot where Caruseddu had helped the little bird out of the trap.

"Climb down and shout three times, 'Oh, king of the birds, come out and help me!'" the horse ordered, and Caruseddu got off the horse and shouted three times: "Oh, king of the birds, come out and help me!"

All at once the little bird appeared and asked, "What do you want?"

"The princess lost her veil here, and I'm supposed to take it back to her."

"Two birds are playing with the veil," responded the little bird. "I'll tear it away from them and bring it to you."

Moments later the bird came with the veil in its beak. Caruseddu thanked the little bird, and took the veil to the king.

"Long live Caruseddu!" the king exclaimed. "Even this deed he performed like a hero!"

The king gave Caruseddu rich gifts, and took the veil to the princess and said, "Beautiful maiden, here's the veil, and now the wedding can take place."

"Oh, we've got some time before," the princess replied. "I won't celebrate a wedding until you retrieve my ring that fell into the river."

The king was very despondent that the princess demanded such difficult things, but because she was so beautiful he could not refuse her, and said to Caruseddu, "Caruseddu, now you have a second task to do for me. The princess let her ring fall into the river along the way. I want you to get me the ring."

"But your majesty, how can I find a ring in such a deep river?"

"That's not my problem, and if the ring is not here within three days, I'll have your head cut off."

So poor Caruseddu went to the little horse in the stable and said, "Oh, dear little horse, you helped two times. Please help me this time. I've got to fetch the princess's ring for the king."

"Don't weep," said the little horse. "Just get on my back and don't worry about anything."

Once again Caruseddu swung himself on the back of the horse, who carried him to the river where he had at one time saved the fish.

"Get down and shout three times with a loud voice: 'Oh, king of the fish come out and help me!'"

Caruseddu climbed off the horse and shouted three times: "Oh, king of the fish, come out and help me!"

All at once the water rustled, and a fish swam to the bank. It was the same fish that Caruseddu had saved from death.

"What do you want?" asked the fish.

"The princess let her ring fall into the water, and I'm supposed to take it back to her."

"Is that all you want?" asked the fish. "Right now two little fish are playing with it, but I'll swim between them and tear it way from them."

The fish swam away, and after a few moments passed, he came back and had the ring in his mouth. Caruseddu took it to the king. Now, just imagine how grateful the king had to be, and how many rich gifts he gave to Caruseddu! However, when the king took the ring to the princess and asked her when the marriage would be celebrated she answered, "Oh, not for some time! If Caruseddu cannot sort out an entire warehouse filled with wheat, barley, and oats in three days so that each kind of kernel lies separately and so that the straw is placed in a special pile, I cannot marry you."

The king almost tore out all his hair. "Where does she get all these whims?" he asked himself and summoned his faithful servant again.

"Caruseddu, if you do not sort out this entire warehouse within three days so that each kind of wheat lies separately and the straw in a special pile, I'll have your head cut off."

So Caruseddu went to the little horse and said, "Oh, little horse, you've helped me so often, please help me this time. Now I must sort out an entire warehouse of wheat."

"Get on my back and don't worry," answered the little horse, who carried him to the spot where he had once spread out bread for the ants. "Get down and shout three times with a loud voice: 'Oh, king of the ants, come out and help me!'"

Caruseddu did this three times, and a large ant came crawling out of the ground and asked, "What do you want?"

"The king has commanded me to sort out a whole warehouse full of wheat so that each kind will lay there separately, and the straw is to be gathered into special piles."

"We'll soon take care of this," the king of the ants said and called his ants together. Soon large groups of ants came out from all sides. They crawled into the warehouse, and within three days the work was finished.

"Your majesty," Caruseddu said. "I've carried out your command."

"Long live Caruseddu!" the king exclaimed. "No one can compete with you!"

The king then went to the princess and said, "Beautiful maiden, I've fulfilled your wish. Now we can celebrate our wedding."

But the princess replied, "Caruseddu stole me from my parents, who are still weeping over me and grieving. Therefore he must die, otherwise I won't marry you. Let a lime kiln be heated for three days and three nights, and then order Caruseddu to throw himself inside."

"What?" the king cried out. "After Caruseddu has served me so faithfully and performed so many heroic deeds for me, you want me to kill him?"

"If you don't do it, I won't marry you, and that's it!" the princess answered. But she knew quite well that Caruseddu would come out of the lime kiln unscathed.

The king had his faithful Caruseddu summoned and said, "Caruseddu, I can't help you. The princess has ordered the lime kiln to be heated for three days and three nights, and then you must throw yourself inside. If you won't do this, I'll have your head cut off."

Caruseddu went into the stable and began weeping and petting the horse.

"Oh, little horse, dear little horse, farewell," he said. "Now it's all over. The king wants me dead. He's ordered the lime kiln to be heated three days and three nights, and then I must throw myself inside."

"Don't lose your courage," the horse answered, "and do exactly what I tell you to do. Take a stick and beat me until foam flows from my mouth."

"Oh, little horse," Caruseddu cried out. "I owe you so much, and you want me to beat you? No, my heart won't let me do something like that."

"But you must," the horse said. "Just keep beating. You won't really harm me. However, you must take the foam that flows from my mouth, gather it together, and put it into a pot. When they call you and order you to jump into the kiln, smear yourself from head to foot with the foam, and you'll see that you'll be protected from the fire."

So Caruseddu took a large stick and began beating the horse, and as he did this, he wept.

"Oh, dear little horse, forgive me if I'm hurting you."

"Keep it up," the horse said and snorted so that great streams of foam flowed from his mouth. Caruseddu gathered the foam together in a pot and kept it in a safe place.

When the lime kiln had been heated for three days and three nights, the king summoned poor Caruseddu and said to him, "Now's the time, Caruseddu. Quick, throw yourself into the kiln."

So Caruseddu took off his clothes, smeared himself from head to foot with the foam, and plunged into the lime kiln. And just imagine, the heat did not hurt him, and he came out unscathed and had become even more handsome than he was before!

When the king and all the people saw this, they applauded with joy and yelled, "Long live Caruseddu!"

Now the princess said to the king, "Caruseddu has come out of the lime kiln unscathed. If you really love me, you must jump into the lime kiln as well. Otherwise, I won't marry you."

The king thought, "Perhaps I'll also become younger like Caruseddu. If I only knew what he used to smear himself with."

So he had Caruseddu summoned to him and asked, "Caruseddu, you must tell me what you used to smear on yourself so that the fire did not hurt you."

But Caruseddu thought, "Just you wait. I performed so many deeds for you, and yet you sent me to my death. Now I'll get my revenge on you."

"Your majesty," he said, "I smeared myself with a pot of fat, which saved my life."

"Quick! Bring me two pots full of fat!" the king cried out and thought that he would increase his chances if he smeared more fat on himself than Caruseddu did. When they brought him the pots, he smeared himself all over and threw himself into the lime kiln. When the fire touched him, there was suddenly a high flame, and the king was burned to ashes.

This is exactly what the princess had wanted because the king was old and ugly, while Caruseddu was young and handsome, and she wanted him for her husband.

"Caruseddu," she said, "now I want to celebrate my wedding, and you will be my husband because you did all that work for me."

In the end a splendid wedding was celebrated, and Caruseddu became king. Indeed they remained together, husband and wife, and we just stand like candles without a life.˙

---

*In Sicilian: iddi ristaru maritu e mugghièri, e nui autri comu tanti cannileri. In German: wir sind wie die Leuchter hier stehen geblieben, or, so blieben sie Mann und Frau, wir aber halten ihnen das Licht.

14

HOW SAINT JOSEPH HELPED A YOUNG MAN WIN THE DAUGHTER OF A KING

Once upon a time there was a man who was very rich and had three sons. When he was about to die, he divided his wealth and property among the three brothers and gave each one an equal share.

Now it so happened that the king issued a proclamation in the entire country that whoever built a ship that could sail on the sea and on land could have his daughter for his wife. When he heard about this, the eldest brother thought, "I have such a large amount of money that I might as well try to build this ship."

So he called together all the master shipbuilders in the entire land and had them begin to construct the ship. Older people also came and asked him, "Your lordship, can we also work on the ship so that we can earn a living?" But he turned them away with hard words and said, "I can't use you because you don't have enough strength."

Very young boys and apprentices also came and asked him for work, but he responded, "I can't use you because you're much too weak."

And when workers came who were not very skillful, he chased them away with hard words. Finally, a very little old man with a white beard arrived and said to him, "Are you also going to turn me away like the others so that I can't earn a living?"

Indeed, the young man turned him away like the others.

When the ship was finally finished and was ready to sail, there was a sudden explosion, and the entire ship collapsed. The young man then had nothing, became poor, and returned to his brothers who gave him a place to live and kept him with them. Meanwhile, the second brother thought, "My brother certainly managed things in a clumsy way, and that's why the ship collapsed. Now I'm going to try my luck, and if I succeed, then the beautiful princess will be mine." Shortly thereafter he called together all the master shipbuilders again and ordered them to build a new ship. However, he was just as cold-blooded as his brother, and when old men, young apprentices, or clumsy workers came, he chased them away with hard words. Even the little old man with the long white beard came and asked for work, but he, too, was turned away.

When the ship was finished, there was another explosion, and the entire ship collapsed. The second brother was now just as poor as the older one, and both had to be supported by the youngest, who began to think about the situation: "How shall I be able to support my brothers alone? I want to try my luck, too. If I succeed in getting the king's beautiful daughter for my bride, I'll have enough money for me and my brothers. If I don't succeed, then we shall at least all three be equally poor."

Soon thereafter he called together all the master shipbuilders to construct a new ship for him. When very old people came and asked for work, he said to them, "Certainly, there's enough work here for everyone." And when young boys came and asked, "Master, let us work to earn our bread," he gave them work as well. He did not even turn back the clumsy workers, and also let them work to earn their bread. Finally the little old man arrived and asked, "Let me work to earn my living."

"No, old father,"* he responded. "You're not to work. I want you to manage all the other workers and to oversee the entire construction."

Now the old man was actually Saint Joseph, who had come to help the young man because he was so kind and pious and devoted to the saint[†] and kept a lamp lit at his bedside day and night to honor him.

When the ship was finished, Saint Joseph said to the young man, "Now you can sail away and fetch the beautiful princess."

"Oh, old father," the young man requested, "don't leave me. I'd prefer it if you would accompany me to the king."

"Good," Saint Joseph said. "I'll do that, but only under the condition that you give me half of what you get, whatever it may be."

---

*Patri granni.

† Era divotu di san Guiseppe.

The young man promised to do this, and shortly thereafter they began their journey. The ship sailed on the sea as well as on land, and the young man continued to keep a lamp burning in front of the image of Saint Joseph day and night.

After they had gone some distance, they saw a man who stood in a thick fog. He had a large sack that he was filling with fog.

"Oh, old father," the young man cried out, "what's he doing there?"

"Ask him," answered Saint Joseph.

"What are you doing there, handsome lad?" the young man called out.

"I'm gathering fog in a sack. That's my talent."

"Ask him if he wants to come along with us," Saint Joseph said.

So the young man asked, and the man answered, "Yes, if you'll give me food and drink, I'll come along."

So they took him on board the ship and the young man said, "Old man, there were two of us, and now we're three."

After a while they saw a man coming toward them. He had ripped out half a forest and was carrying all the tree trunks on his shoulders.

"Old father," cried the young man, "just look at that man who's carrying all those trees!"

"Ask him why he's ripped out all the trees."

So the young man asked the man, who answered, "I just wanted to gather together a small handful of twigs."

"Ask him if he will come along with us," Saint Joseph said.

The young man did this, and the strong man answered, "Yes, if you'll give me food and drink, I'll come along."

So they took him on board the ship, and the young man said, "Old father, there were three of us, and now we're four."

After they had traveled another distance, they saw a man drinking out of a river, and he had drunk almost half the river.

"Old father," the young man exclaimed, "just look at how that man can drink!"

"Ask him what he's doing."

So the young man asked, and the other fellow answered, "I've just had a drop of water to drink."

"Ask him whether he'll come along with us."

The young man did that, and the man answered, "Yes if you'll give me food and drink, I'll come along."

So they took him on board the ship, and the young man said, "Old father, there were four of us, and now we're five."

Once more they traveled for a while until they saw a man who stood on the side of a stream and was aiming his gun into the water.

"Old father," the young man said, "what is the man aiming at?"

"Ask him yourself," Saint Joseph said.

So the young man called out to this fellow, "Handsome lad, what are you aiming at?"

"Shhh! Shhh!" the man said and made a sign for him to keep quiet. However, the young man asked him again, "What are you aiming at?"

"Now you've scared it away!" the man said reluctantly. "There was a quail sitting on a tree in the underworld.* I wanted to shoot it. That's my talent. I can hit anything I aim at."

"Ask him whether he'll come along with us."

The young man did this, and the man said, "Yes, if you'll give me food and drink, I'll come along."

So they took him on board the ship, and the young man said, "Old father, there were five of us, and now we're six."

After they had gone somewhat farther again, they saw a man coming their way who took such long strides that he stood with one foot in Catania and the other near Messina.

"Old father, just look at those long strides that man is taking!"

"Ask him what he's doing."

So the young man asked the fellow who answered, "I'm just taking a little walk."

"Ask him whether he'll come along with us."

The young man did this, and the man said, "If you'll give me food and drink, I'll come along."

So they took him on board, and the young man said, "Old father, there were six of us, and now we're seven."

Saint Joseph knew quite well why he took them along, and the ship continued to sail over land and sea due to his power. Blessed are those it carried!†

Finally they came to the city where the king was living with his beautiful daughter. The young man sailed in front of the palace and went to the king and said, "Your majesty, I've fulfilled your wish and built a ship that can sail on land and on water. Now give me the reward that I deserve, namely, your daughter."

But the king thought, "Should I give my daughter to this stranger? I don't know whether he's rich or poor, whether he's a cavalier or a

---

*A munnu suttanu.

† Biatu chiddu, a cu portava.

beggar." He considered how he could keep his daughter from this young man and said, "It's not enough that you've built this ship. You must fulfill one more condition. You must provide me with a runner who's capable of delivering this letter to the Count of the Underworld, and he must bring back the answer in an hour."

"But this condition was not part of your proclamation," responded the poor young man.

"If you don't want to fulfill this condition," the king declared, "I won't give you my daughter."

So the young man became despondent and went straight to Saint Joseph and said, "Old father, the king won't give me his daughter unless I provide him with a runner who's capable of taking a letter to the Count of the Underworld, and he must bring the answer within an hour."

"You fool," said Saint Joseph. "Accept the condition. You can send the man who stands with one foot near Catania and the other foot near Messina."

All at once the young man was happy. He called the man and took him to the king and said, "I want to fulfill the condition, and here is the runner."

The king gave him a letter for the Count of the Underworld, and the man went off with great strides. When he arrived in the underworld, the count spoke to him, "Wait a while until I've finished writing the answer."

However, the man was so tired from so much fast running that he fell asleep while he was waiting and completely forgot about going back. At the same time the young man waited for the runner full of anxiety and worries. Indeed, the hour was nearly up, and the runner still had not appeared. Then Saint Joseph spoke to the shooter who hit everything he aimed at: "Look and see why the runner is staying away for so long."

The shooter looked and said, "He's still in the underworld, in the count's palace, and he's sleeping. I'll wake him right away."

So he shot and hit the runner with a bullet right in his knee. The runner woke up immediately, and once he realized that the hour was nearly up, he jumped up, asked for the answer, and ran back to the palace so fast that he arrived before the hour was gone.

Now the young man was very happy, but the king was bent on keeping his daughter from him and said, "You have fulfilled this condition, but it is not enough. Now you must provide a man who is capable of drinking up half my cellar."

"This condition was not in your proclamation," the young man complained.

"If you don't want to fulfill this condition," the king replied, "I won't give my daughter to you."

So the young man went sadly to Saint Joseph and told him his dilemma.

"You fool," Saint Joseph said. "You can take the man who drank up half the river."

The young man then called the fellow and said to him, "Do you think you can drink up half the cellar?"

"Certainly," the man answered. "I'm so thirsty I could even drink more if there is any more."

They went to the king, who led them into the cellar, and the man drank up all the barrels until they were empty—wine, vinegar, and oil, everything that could be found in the cellar. The king became frightened and said, "I can no longer refuse to give you my daughter, but you must know that I can only give as much dowry as a man can carry."

"But your royal highness," the young man spoke, "even if a man is very strong, he can't carry much more than a hundred or so pounds. What kind of a king's daughter is she?"

But the king insisted: "I'm only going to give her as much as a man can carry. If you won't agree to this condition, I won't give you my daughter."

Once again the young man was distressed and went back to Saint Joseph. "The king will give his daughter only as much dowry as a man can carry. Now I've spent my entire fortune to build the ship. How can I return to my brothers this way?"

"You fool!" said Saint Joseph. "Call the man who carried half the forest on his shoulders."

The young man became very happy and took the man with him.

"Load as much as you can on your shoulders," he said. "You must clean out the entire palace."

The strong man promised to do this and loaded everything on his shoulders that he could: closets, tables, chairs, gold, and silver, even the king's gold crown. When he had cleaned out the entire palace, he ripped the gate from its hinges and threw it on top. Then he carried everything to the ship, and the young man brought the princess there as well, and they sailed away in good spirits. However, the king became furious when he saw his palace empty, and he summoned all his war ships and ordered his soldiers to pursue the young man and regain all his treasures.

When the war ships had almost overtaken the young man's ship, Saint Joseph said to him, "Turn around, and tell me what you see."

When the young man saw all the ships he became scared and cried out, "Oh, old father, I see a lot of war ships following us, and they've almost caught up with us."

All at once Saint Joseph ordered the man who had gathered together the fog to open his sack. As soon as he had done this, a thick fog rose around the ship so that the soldiers could no longer see it and had to return to the king without accomplishing their mission. Meanwhile, Saint Joseph used his power to enable the ship to sail on until it finally reached home safely.

"So," said Saint Joseph, "now you're home again, and I want you to fulfill your promise and give me half of all your treasures."

"I'm glad to do this, old father," the young man responded and divided all the treasures into two equal parts. The last thing was the gold crown, and the young man took his sword and split the crown in two. He took one half and gave the other to Saint Joseph.

"Old father," he said, "I've now divided everything, and there's nothing left."

"What do you mean there's nothing left?" Saint Joseph asked. "You've forgotten the best!"

"The best!" the young man exclaimed. "Old father, I don't see anything more that we haven't divided."

"What about the king's daughter?" Saint Joseph asked. "Wasn't the condition that you would share everything that you got?"

All at once, the young man became very despondent because he had fallen in love with the princess with all his heart. Nevertheless, he thought, "I made a promise, and I've got to keep it."* So he pulled out his sword to slice the princess in half, but when Saint Joseph saw his pious and simple heart, he cried out: "Stop! The beautiful princess is yours, and all the treasures as well. You see, I'm Saint Joseph, and I don't need any of this. I've helped you because I recognized that you have a kind, humble heart. Whenever you're in trouble, just turn to me, and I'll help you."

Upon saying all this, he blessed the couple and disappeared. The young man married the beautiful princess and took his brothers to his home to care for them. He always remained devoted† to Saint Joseph and honored him by keeping a lamp burning day and night.

---

*Non c'è faccia.

† Divotu.

15

THE COURAGEOUS MAIDEN

Once upon a time there were three sisters, who had neither mother nor father. They made a pitiful living through their spinning. Each day they spun a couple of pounds[*] of flax, which they took to their padrona, who was their benefactor. They received two tari[†] for it and had to live on this money alone.

Now it happened one day that they all had cravings for a piece of liver.

"You know what?" the eldest said to her sisters. "Today it's my turn to take the flax we've spun to our padrona. When she gives me the money, I'll buy some liver, bread, and wine so that we can have a delightful day for once."

"Good," her sisters answered.

That evening the eldest sister took the flax to the city. After the padrona gave her the money, the maiden bought a piece of liver, some bread and wine, and placed everything neatly into her basket and set out on her way home.

As she went through a lonely alley, the little basket slipped out of her hand. Immediately a dog jumped upon it, grabbed the entire basket,

---

[*]Rottolo.

[†] Approximately eight silver coins. In German, acht Silbergroschen.

and ran away with it. She ran after the dog but could not catch it, and finally had to return home without any food or wine.

"Didn't you bring anything with you?" her sisters asked.

"Oh, dear sisters," she answered. "There was nothing I could do. Let me tell you what happened to me." And she told them the entire story.

The next day the middle sister went to the padrona and said, "Today I'll bring back the liver."

After she had received the money, she bought liver, bread, and wine, packed it all into her little basket, and headed home. As she walked through a lonely alley, she also let the basket slip out of her hand, and the dog sprang and ran away with the basket so fast that she could not catch up with it.

When she arrived home and told everything to her sisters, the youngest said, "Tomorrow I shall go, and I won't let the dog get away from me."

The next evening she went with the yarn to the padrona, took the money, and bought liver, bread, and wine. When she entered the alley, the basket slipped from her hand. All at once the dog plunged at the basket, grabbed it, and ran off. However, the maiden was more light-footed than her sisters, and no matter how fast the dog ran, she kept up with it and did not lose sight of it. The dog ran through many streets and finally slipped into a house with the maiden right on its heels. She went up the stairs and called out, but nobody answered. She went through all the rooms and saw splendid things. In one of the halls there was a beautifully covered table; in another there were good beds; in a third, treasures and precious things. However, she did not see a single person. Finally she came to a small room, and the dog was sitting on the ground and had the three baskets in front of him. But she no longer thought about the baskets, when she saw all the precious jewels.

As she went farther, she came to a hall where innumerable treasures were stored, drawers and chests filled with gems, and on the ground there were entire sacks filled with gold coins. She then took a sack of the coins, left the castle, and went home with it.

"Dear sisters," she exclaimed full of joy, "now we shall have plenty of things! Look at what I've brought you!"

When the other sisters saw the sack full of gold coins, they were very happy, but the youngest sister said, "Let's give all our possessions to the poor and let our little house stay empty. We can bury the gold here, and then we can go to the castle together and find out why it's there. If things should go badly for us there, we still have the gold that we're going to leave behind here."

This is what they did. They gave away all their possessions and belongings to the poor, buried the gold in the empty house, and went to the mysterious castle. In the first room the beautifully covered table was still standing, and they sat down and ate and drank to their heart's content. Then they looked at all the treasures and splendid things that were stored in the castle. When it became evening, the youngest maiden said to her elder sister, "We can't all sleep here because something might happen to us. Therefore, it's best if you keep a watch the first night, while we two sleep."

Consequently, the two younger sisters lay down to sleep, while the eldest kept watch. At midnight there was suddenly a loud scream that echoed throughout the entire castle.

"Wait! I'm coming up!" a threatening voice cried out.

The sister became so frightened that she quickly jumped into the bed and pulled the covers over her ears. Right after this everything became quiet. The next morning her two sisters asked, "Did you see or hear anything last night?"

Instead of revealing what had happened, she answered, "Nothing at all. It was quiet all night."

The next evening the middle sister had to keep watch, and the two others went to sleep. At midnight the threatening voice cried out again: "Wait! I'm coming up!"

The maiden became very scared, crawled into the bed, and pulled the covers over her head. Then everything became quiet again. The next morning when her two sisters asked her whether she had heard or seen anything, she answered, "Nothing at all. It was quiet all night."

However, she took her elder sister aside and spoke confidentially to her, "Didn't you also hear that terrible cry?"

"Of course," she replied. "But be quiet. If we were scared out of our wits, why should our youngest sister be an exception?"

That evening the two elder sisters went to sleep, and the youngest kept watch. Suddenly, at midnight, the same terrible scream could be heard: "Wait! I'm coming up!"

"As you wish!" answered the maiden.

Then the door opened, and a large beautiful figure in a long dark robe with a long train entered. It went toward her and said, "I see that you're a courageous maiden. If you continue to show the same courage and do exactly what I tell you to do, this palace and everything that is in it will be yours, and you shall be a duchess just like I was at one time."

"Noble lady," the maiden replied. "Tell me what I must do, and I'll make sure everything is done as you wish."

"Look," said the figure, "I'm a duchess and can't find any peace in my grave because the person who murdered me is walking around unpunished. You are to help me gain my peace. In that closet over there you will find many beautiful dresses. You must wear one of them tomorrow and go out on the balcony dressed in it. Toward noon a nobleman will come riding by and will speak to you. Because you will be wearing my dress, he will think you are me. Answer him in a friendly way and ask him to come up. When he is with you, keep him there with polite conversation until it becomes evening and then invite him to dine with you. Take these two bottles. One is wine and the other a sleeping potion. While he is eating, you must give him some of the sleeping potion. When he has fallen asleep, you are to cut his throat with this knife so that he dies for his sins. Just as I cannot find any peace, he shall not enjoy anything blessed in the other life either."

Upon saying these words, the dark figure disappeared, and the maiden remained alone. The next morning she put on a splendid rich gown and stood on the balcony. Toward noon a gentleman came riding by, and when he saw her on the balcony, he called to her.

"Oh! My noble lady, have you been cured? You were ill for such a long time."

"Yes, my noble lord, I am well again. Won't you do me the honor and come up here?"

So the nobleman went upstairs. When he saw her two sisters, he asked who they were.

"My chambermaids," she answered, and she kept the nobleman there with polite conversation until it became evening.

"Can I also have the honor of dining with you tonight?" she said, and the nobleman stayed. During the meal, however, she handed him the bottle with the sleeping potion. As soon as he drank a little of it, he sank into a deep sleep. Then she took a little knife and slit his throat so that he died for his sins without confession or absolution. Afterward the maiden called her sisters, and all three dragged him to a deep well and threw him into it. At midnight the door opened once again, and the dark figure entered and said to the youngest sister, "You have saved me through your courage, and now all these treasures belong to you. Live well. Tonight I have come for the last time because now I have found peace."

Upon saying this, she disappeared and never returned. As for the three sisters, they remained in the magnificent castle, and each one of them married a fine gentleman. Indeed, they remained happy and content, and we were left without a cent.

16

THE HUMILIATED PRINCESS

Once upon a time there was a king who had a very beautiful daughter, but she was also very moody and proud. Indeed, she was never satisfied with any of her suitors. No matter how many came to the castle, she would laugh at them, and they would depart feeling ashamed and cursed. The king reproached her, but she did not listen to him and continued to play the same game with all the suitors who arrived at the castle. Finally, nobody ventured to the castle to court her.

So, the king decided to send pictures of her to foreign countries, where no one knew anything about her. Pictures of handsome princes were sent back to him, but they did not please his daughter. Finally, because the king reproached her so much, she pointed to the picture of a handsome king and said, "Let him come. I'll take him for my husband."

The old king was highly pleased and had the young king brought to his castle with great fanfare and gave him a splendid reception. There were many festivities in his honor, and everything seemed to go well. But one day, when they were sitting at the table, the princess noticed that the young king had taken a chair on which a little feather was lying, and that a drop of sauce fell on his chest while he was eating.

"Oh," she cried out, "feather on the chair, sauce on the breast!" And she did not want him anymore. As a result the young king became

*Pinna in seggia e sarsa in pettu.

very annoyed and returned to his country in great shame. The old king, however, became so enraged that he banished his daughter from his castle and sent her with a chambermaid out into the wide world.

The princess wandered with the chambermaid until they came to a small city, where she rented a small house. Because they had to earn money to live, the chambermaid went about the city and bought some cloth, which she took to the princess, who began sewing clothes. This is the way they lived for some time.

Meanwhile, the young king had fallen very much in love with the princess and could not find peace or quiet without her. When he heard that she had been banished by her father, he disguised himself as a pedlar and wandered with his boxes throughout the entire kingdom in order to find her. One day he came to the city in which she was living, and cried out that he had various things for sale. It occurred to the princess that she no longer had any needles, and she bought some from him. When he saw her, he was very happy and sold her all kinds of things. While they were doing this, he conversed with her, and when he heard that she sewed clothes, he ordered a dozen shirts from her and often came by to see how far she had gotten with the work. Although he was happy to find her, he wanted to gain revenge on her for causing him to be humiliated, and so he did not reveal himself. Rather, he came by always dressed as a peddler.

After some time had passed, he took the chambermaid aside and said to her, "If it is all right with her, I'd like to marry this young maiden. To be sure, I can't marry her yet, but I'd like to take her back to my country because I can't stay here any longer."

The chambermaid went to her young mistress and persuaded her to marry the pedlar.

"If I should die some day," she said to the princess, "you would be alone in the world."

The princess did not really want to get married, but her pride had been broken, and she said "yes" and went with the pedlar out into the wide world. They wandered many, many days until they came to the realm of the young king. The poor princess was so exhausted that she could barely move. Then her husband led her into a miserable little cottage and said, "Here you have my dwelling. We've got to make the best of it."

Now the delicate princess had to do all the work—cook, wash, and sew. Each morning the pedlar wandered about, and when he returned in the evening, he would bring something small to eat and say, "You see, that's all that I earned today."

During the day, however, he remained in the castle with his mother and revealed to her that he had brought the young princess who had upset him so much.

After some time had passed, he went to the princess one day and said, "We have to leave this place because I can't pay the rent anymore. I'm going to the queen to ask her if we can have permission to live in one of the stalls in her stable. She is my patron and won't refuse me."

When he returned later, he said, "The queen gave her permission, and from now on we'll live in a stall."

So now the tender princess had to live in a stall and sleep on straw, but she bore all this with patience and thought, "I've deserved all of this because of my pride." Meanwhile, her husband went away each day with his boxes to sell things, but really went just a few steps out of her sight and through a side door into the castle. He dressed himself as king and always went by her dwelling, but she did not recognize him as her husband. Instead, she recognized him as one of the suitors she had scorned and felt she might sink into the ground out of shame.

One day he went to his mother and said, "The princess hasn't been punished enough for her pride. Let her come up into the castle and work as a seamstress."

"Oh, my son," his mother said, "leave the poor girl in peace and pardon her."

"No," he answered. "I want her to experience the same humiliation that I experienced at her hand."

He then went to his wife and said, "There are a lot of children's clothes that have to be sewn in the castle because the king has married, and his young queen is expecting a child. The old queen has called for you so that you can help with the work."

"Oh, no," she answered. "Please let me stay here. I'm ashamed to let the young king see me."

"Come now!" he exclaimed. "How are we going to make our living? I want you to go right now. The young king won't care about you in the least. And listen to me, don't be stupid. If you can take a little shirt or a bonnet with you, then do it. You'll be needing it soon."

"Oh no," she said. "How could I do such a thing?"

"Don't make me mad!" the husband yelled. "Do what I say. You can hide it beneath your blouse."

The poor princess went to the castle, and because she was afraid of her husband, she stole a little shirt when no one was looking and hid it beneath her blouse. When she was sitting there and sewing, however, the young king suddenly entered the room and cried, "Who is this sewing here? I recognize her as a thief."

The poor princess blushed right away, then turned pale, and the old queen said, "Leave the seamstress in peace, my son. She is a poor maiden who lives in one of our stalls."

"No," he said. "She is a thief, and I'll prove it."

He then grabbed beneath her blouse and pulled out the little shirt. The poor princess was so terrified that she fainted.

"My son," the queen said. "Don't you see how the poor girl is suffering? Now stop torturing her."

"No," he said. "She hasn't been punished enough." And he had her carried down to the stall.

When it was evening again, she wept and told him about her misfortune. She said she would not return to the castle, but he was very stern with her and ordered her to go back to the castle the next morning to steal something else.

"You can hide it under your apron," he insisted.

She wept bitter tears but had to obey him, and the next morning she went back to the castle. When no one was looking, she took two bonnets and hid them beneath her apron. As she was sewing the king entered the room and cried out, "Why have you let this thief come back here? Now I'll show you that nothing can be kept safe from her."

He reached beneath her apron and pulled out the bonnets. The princess fainted, and in spite of the pleas of the old queen, the king had her taken back to the stall.

During that night her time came, and she gave birth to a marvelous baby boy. Her husband brought her some meat broth and said, "The queen has sent you this broth, and these old diapers for our son."

There was a sleeping potion in the broth, and when the princess drank it, she fell sound asleep. The king had her carried back to the castle where a beautiful bed was standing ready for her. He had her dressed in a garment made of the finest cloth and placed in the bed. Next to the bed stood a precious cradle for the baby prince who was also clad in garments fit for the son of a king. Finally, the young king took off the pedlar's clothes and put on his royal garments. When the princess finally awoke, she looked around in astonishment and thought she was dreaming. The king entered and asked her in a friendly way how she was feeling, but she could not look him in the eyes.

"Don't you recognize me?" the king asked. "I'm your husband, the pedlar. I wanted to punish you for your pride. Now all your sufferings are at an end, and you are my dear wife."

When the young queen regained her health, they celebrated a splendid wedding feast, and the parents of the young queen were invited to come and were very happy to see their daughter once again.

They lived happy and content and we're still worrying about the rent.

17

RAGS AND LEAVES

O nce upon a time there was a king who had three daughters and a son. Now at one time the king became so sick that he was going to die. When he felt that his death was near, he summoned his son to him and said, "My dear son, I must die soon, and you will become king after me, so I am placing you in charge of your three sisters. Take care of them until they marry. However, I don't want them to marry according to what they or you think would be good for them. Instead, when one of them reveals a desire to get married, pluck a rose from the beautiful rosebush on the terrace and throw it onto the street. Whoever picks up the rose is to be her husband."

Upon saying these words the king died, and his son became king. After some time had passed, his eldest sister came to him and said, "Dear brother, I'd like to get married and want to choose a husband for myself."

"Do you know what our father ordered on his deathbed?" the king answered, and he told his sister what their father had said. All at once she became angry and said, "Was our father crazy? What is this? I'm supposed to marry any man who happens to pick up the rose? If that's the case, I'd rather not marry at all."

"Do what you want," he said. "I can't help you. This was our father's last will and testament."

When some months had passed, however, the princess became impatient and went to her brother again.

"If this is the way it must be," she said, "I'll do what our father wanted."

Consequently, the king plucked a rose from the rosebush on the terrace and threw it onto the street. He ordered a soldier to keep guard and to bring the first man who picked up the rose into the palace. When the soldier had stood near the rose for a while, a prince came by, saw the beautiful rose lying on the ground, and picked it up, saying, "Oh, what a beautiful rose!"

"Noble sir," the guard said, "the king wishes to speak to you."

So the prince went before the king, who asked him, "Did you pick up the rose that was lying on the street?"

"Yes, your majesty."

"Then you must marry my eldest sister."

"Your majesty!" said the prince very frightened. "I can't do this! The princess deserves to marry the son of a king, and I am only the son of a duke. How is it possible to bestow such an honor on me?"

"No one is talking about honor here," the king answered. "It is simply necessary that my sister becomes your wife."

So the princess married the prince and thought, "Even if he isn't the son of a king, I'm happy because it could have been worse."

After some time had passed, the second princess went to her brother and said, "Dear brother, I'm now at the age when a young woman marries, and I want to search for a man for myself."

"Do you know what our father said on his deathbed?" the king replied. "If you want to get married, you have to do it under the condition that our father set."

"If that's the way it must be, I shall do what our father wanted," the princess said.

So the king plucked a rose and threw it onto the street, and a soldier stood guard over it. For a while nobody came by. Finally a gentleman came along, and when he saw the beautiful rose lying on the ground, he picked it up and smelled it. The soldier went over to him and said, "The king wishes to speak with you."

"Did you pick up the rose from the street?" the king asked.

"Yes, your majesty!"

"Then you must take my sister for your wife."

"Oh, your majesty!" the gentleman exclaimed. "That cannot be. The princess deserves to have a monarch as husband, and I am just a mere subject."

"There's nothing I can do about it," the king said. "My sister must become your wife."

So the wedding was celebrated, and now only the youngest sister was left, and she said, "My eldest sister got a prince for her husband. My middle sister, only a rich gentleman. Who knows what my fate will be! If that's the case, I'd prefer not to marry at all."

So she remained with her brother.

Now it so happened that the king himself married a young woman, and everyone knows, of course, that once a sister-in-law comes into the house, the sister is no longer mistress of the house and must change her life and submit to the sister-in-law. Therefore, the king's sister eventually went to her brother and said, "Dear brother, I'd like to get married, and if I must carry out our father's will, then so be it."

"Take the rose yourself," the king said, "and throw it onto the street."

So the princess plucked the rose and threw it onto the street. A soldier stood guard over it, but nobody came by the entire day. Finally, when it was almost evening, a water carrier with a cane happened to walk by, carrying a barrel of water. He was dirty and ugly as sin, and his legs had leaves and rags tied around them. When he saw the beautiful rose lying on the ground, he picked it up and smelled it. The soldier was shocked and thought, "How can the princess marry this terrible creature?" However, because the king had given him strict orders, he could not let the water carrier move on and had to bring him before the king.

"Did you pick up the rose?" the king asked him.

"Yes, I did, your majesty!"

"Well, then you must marry my sister."

"Oh, your majesty!" the water carrier exclaimed. "You must be joking with me! Don't you see how dirty I am, and how sick my legs are?"

The king was indeed very sad about this, and the princess wept and lamented her misfortune, but nothing helped. She had to marry the dirty, disgusting water carrier.

"I don't want a dowry," he grumbled. "What would I do with it in the mountains?"

So he took his wife with him and led her to the mountains and into a miserable straw hut, inhabited by an ugly old woman.

"This is our home, and that is my mother," he said to the poor princess. From then on she had to live in the small hut, and the mother took away her beautiful garments and gave her a woolen skirt that she had to wear. Moreover, she had to cook and wash like a lowly maid. In

the evening, when her husband came home, she had to untie the rags
and leaves that were around his feet. His mother called him Rags and
Leaves.*

They lived this way a long time, and the poor princess almost wept
her eyes out. Rags and Leaves loved her as if she were his own eyes, and
when he saw her weep, his heart hurt very much.

One evening he saw the princess weeping bitter tears again, and
that night she dreamed she was in a beautiful castle, and many servants
dressed in magnificent garments were at her side and escorted her in a
gold coach drawn by six glorious horses to see her brother. When she
woke up the next morning, she told her husband about her dream, but
he just laughed about it and said, "That was just a dream. How would
you ever get to a rich castle?"

Then she wept again for the entire day, and in the evening she fell
asleep amidst her tears. When she awoke the next morning, she found
herself in a beautiful castle, just as her dream had pictured it. She lay
in a luxurious bed, and many servants stood around her and helped her
to wash herself with sweet-smelling water and dressed her in royal garments. Then she went into another room, where many servants were
standing. They brought her breakfast and asked, "What does your
majesty command?"

"A coach," she answered. "I want to drive to my brother."

"The coach is ready," the servants said, and when she went down
the stairs, a gold coach drawn by six horses stood there. She got in and
drove to her brother, who was standing at his window when she arrived.
As soon as he saw the beautiful coach, the young king thought, "Who's
coming now in such a grand, gold coach?" When he recognized his
sister, he ran toward her with joy and astonishment and asked, "Dear
sister, is it you? How did you manage to get these splendid things? And
where is your husband?"

"I don't know where my husband is," the princess answered, and she
told him what had happened to her.

"Now I've come to fetch you and my sisters," she continued. "Today
I'd like all of you to have dinner in my castle."

The king got into his coach with his wife, his sisters, and their
husbands, and they all drove together in a great entourage to the castle
of the youngest princess. Once there they found a beautifully covered
table, and they sat down and ate and drank to their heart's content. After
the meal came to an end, one of the guests lifted his eyes and saw that

---

*In Sicilian, Pezze e fogghi; in German, Lumpen und Blätter.

there was a large hole in the roof, and Rags and Leaves was sitting in it. Indeed, he was looking down and smiling at the entire company.

"Oh, there's Rags and Leaves!" he cried out.

"Boom!" the entire castle collapsed and disappeared. The king and his entourage found themselves back home, and the youngest princess was wearing her woolen skirt again and sitting in her straw hut on top of the mountain. When Rags and Leaves came home, she poured out her heart to him, but he just laughed and said, "Oh, now you're dreaming even in broad daylight! That was just a dream from the previous night that stuck vividly in your memory."

Now some days passed again, and the poor princess wept a great deal, and when she fell asleep, she dreamed once more that she was in a beautiful castle. It was the very same dream that she had before. When she told her husband about the dream the next morning, he made fun of her and said, "How come you always have the same dream?"

She wept the entire day and cried herself to sleep. The next morning she awoke again in the beautiful castle, and the chambermaids stood around her, and everything happened just as before. She put on royal clothes, drove to her brother, and invited him with his entourage to her castle to dine with her. Toward the end of the meal, however, someone looked by chance at the ceiling, and there was the water carrier in the hole. The guest cried out, "Oh, look! There's Rags and Leaves!"

"Boom!" went the castle, and it collapsed. The king and his entourage were transferred back to the royal castle. The poor princess sat again in her hut on the mountain and wore her poor woolen skirt. When her husband came home, she lamented her fate and said, "Just look. The same thing happened to me a second time. I'm sure you're to blame!"

He just laughed at her and said, "Oh, come on. You're dreaming now day and night."

A month passed, and one evening the princess wept many bitter tears again, and she fell asleep and dreamed the same dream for a third time. The next morning she told it to her husband, who only laughed about it. As a result she wept the entire day and cried herself to sleep, and, just imagine, the next morning she awoke once more in the beautiful castle!

"Now I know what I'm going to do," she thought. "Before I invite my brother, I shall make it a condition that nobody may pronounce the name of my husband." She drove in her gold coach to her brother and invited him to dine with her. "But there is one condition," she said. "Nobody may pronounce the name of my husband in my castle."

"Good," said her brother, and everyone drove to the castle, where a beautifully covered table was already prepared for them. They sat down and ate, and toward the end of the meal the ceiling opened, and Rags and Leaves sat there and looked down from above, but nobody cried out, "There's Rags and Leaves!" When everyone had finished eating, Rags and Leaves came down and sat in the middle of the hall on a beautiful throne. Indeed, he was no longer a dirty water carrier but a handsome young man in royal garments. Rags and Leaves was actually the son of the king of Spain and had been cursed by a wicked sorcerer, but the beautiful princess had broken the magic spell and saved him. For three days there were festivities, and afterward the prince drove with his beautiful wife to Spain. When they left their castle, it disappeared and could no longer be seen. However, the prince and the princess lived happily in Spain, and we were left behind in vain.

18

THE BRAVE SHOEMAKER

Once upon a time there was a shoemaker who worked the entire day and could not earn enough to live without worries. One day he had earned four grani, and someone came by on the street and cried out, "Beautiful ricotta* for sale! Beautiful ricotta for sale!"

"Oh!" thought Master Giuseppe. "I can afford to buy some ricotta for three grani. If I earn yet another grani, I can buy some bread for two grani, and I'll have a splendid meal at noon."

So he bought the ricotta for three grani and put it on the table while he continued to work. It was very hot, and all at once tons of flies settled on the white ricotta. So Master Giuseppe took a piece of leather, whacked the ricotta with all his might, and killed a bunch of flies.

"Oh ho!" he cried. "I'm truly a brave shoemaker. Now I think I'll set out into the world and seek my fortune."

He took a piece of paper and wrote on it: "Five hundred dead and three hundred wounded." He stuck this paper into his vest, took the ricotta, and wandered off. When he came to a city, he pasted the paper on the corner of a street, and all the people were astounded by the brave shoemaker.

---

*Soft cheese made out of curdled milk.

Now it so happened that news of the shoemaker reached the ears of the king, who thought, "I could certainly use a brave man like this," and he had the shoemaker brought to him.

"Are you the man who killed five hundred and wounded three hundred?" the king asked.

"Yes I am, your majesty," replied the shoemaker.

"Well, if you're so brave, you must do something for me," the king said. "You see, in the forest outside the city there's a terrible wild giant, and each year we must sacrifice a human being that the giant eats. Otherwise, he would come into the city and murder every single one of us. I want you to go into the forest and kill the giant. Otherwise, I'll have you beheaded."

"Oh, what a wretched unlucky man I am!" thought Giuseppe. "Now I'll certainly lose my life. Either the giant will eat me, or the king will have me beheaded."

However, because he was cunning and tricky, he did not lose his courage. Instead, he bought some plaster and set out for the forest. Along the way he kneaded some little balls out of the plaster and ricotta and put the balls into his pocket. After he had gone a fairly long way into the forest, he suddenly heard a great deal of noise as if some one were breaking off large branches.

"Aha," he thought, "that's certainly the giant," and he swiftly climbed a tree. Shortly thereafter the giant came, and he was frightening to see.

"I smell the flesh of a human being!" he roared. "I smell the flesh of a human being!"

When he raised his eyes and saw Master Giuseppe sitting in a tree, he said, "So, you're the one. Come down here. I have something to say to you!"

"Go away," the shoemaker cried out. "If you don't leave me in peace, I'll break your neck."

"You little rascal," the giant yelled and laughed. "You dwarf! How do you think you'll manage that?"

"Oh," Master Giuseppe said, "you don't know how strong I am. You see these marble balls. I'm going to squeeze them and make powder out of them with my fingers."

Upon saying this he took the plaster balls, squeezed them with his fingers, and spread the powder onto the ground. The giant really believed they were marble balls and was horrified by the strength of the small man.

"Come down, my cousin," he said, "and stay with me. When two such strong men as we join forces, there is nothing that can stop us."

When the shoemaker now heard the giant call him cousin,* he climbed down the tree with pleasure and said, "Good, we'll join forces. Take me to your hut."

So the giant led him to his hut and said, "Now let's divide the household chores. Why don't you go to the fountain and fetch the water, while I light the fire. The jug is standing over there."

The giant pointed to a jug that the little master could certainly not lift.

"Forget that," spoke the tricky shoemaker. "I'd prefer it if you'd give me a really strong and long rope. Then I'll bring the entire fountain here right away. Otherwise, I'd have to run to the fountain every day."

When the giant heard this, he became even more frightened and thought, "My, what a strong man he is!" Then he said, "All right, forget it. I'll take the jug myself."

While he took the jug and went to the fountain, Master Giuseppe sat in the hut and enjoyed himself.

When the giant returned with the water, he said, "You could at least look for some wood in the forest. Otherwise, we won't have enough. The ax is over there."

It was, however, such a large and heavy ax that Master Giuseppe could not move it from the spot.

"Forget this," he said. "I'd prefer if you'd give me a strong and long rope. Then I could wrap it around an entire tree and drag it here. Then we'd have plenty of wood for a long time."

"My, this man is really strong!" thought the giant and went himself to look for wood because he was scared of the strong shoemaker. Master Giuseppe remained sitting there, relaxed and delighted. When the giant came back with the wood, he placed a large kettle on top of the fire and cooked supper. After they had eaten, he took out a large, thick iron pole and said, "Let's play a little game. Let's see who can carry this pole around the longest."

---

* The giant guaranteed his life by calling him cousin. Family relations are regarded as blood ties and holy in Sicily. Their special patron saint is Saint Giovanni, and one frequently hears the expression, "siamo compari di Saint Giovanni" (we're cousins of Saint Giovanni). There was an event that occurred not long ago in Messina. Two cutlers (coltellatori) reconciled after being enemies for many years, and as a sign to seal their new friendship one of them offered to call the other "cousin," but the other cutler did not accept the offer. As a result, the first cutler, who had made the offer, was convinced that his former enemy still wanted to bring about his death, and one evening, in order to beat him to the punch, he shot him dead.

"Good," the shoemaker said. "But first you must wrap the thick end of the pole very carefully because when I wheel the pole around, I'll go so fast that I can't see what I'm hitting, and I might even smash your skull."

The giant became so terrified when he heard this that he said, "Well, then perhaps we'd better not play this game. Come, let's go to bed."

"Where should I sleep?" asked the shoemaker.

"Just come," the giant replied. "There's space enough for the both of us in my bed."

The two of them lay down in the giant's bed, and soon the giant was snoring as he usually did. The shoemaker was still afraid of the giant, however, and he crawled quietly out of the bed and placed a large pumpkin in the place of where his head had been. Then, he hid beneath the bed.

Shortly thereafter the giant awoke, and because he was afraid of the strong shoemaker, he thought, "The little man is sleeping. Now is the time to kill him. Who knows, maybe he'll murder me?"

All at once he stood up and took the heavy iron pole. He mistook the pumpkin for the shoemaker's head and whacked it with all his might so that the entire pumpkin was squashed. Right at that very same moment Master Giuseppe sighed loudly beneath the bed.

"What's wrong with you?" the giant asked completely frightened.

"Oh, a flea bit me very hard in my ear," Master Giuseppe answered.

Now the giant was completely petrified and lay back down in bed and remained still. Master Giuseppe crawled out from beneath the bed, threw the squashed pumpkin underneath, and lay down as well. He kept trying to find a way to kill the giant because he thought: "I can't stay here forever, and if I return to the city without doing what the king commanded, he'll have my head cut off."

So, listen to what he did.

The next morning he said to the giant, "Today let's just have a huge macaroni meal. Why don't you cook a large kettle full of it, and when we're done eating, I'll cut open my belly first so that you can see that I can eat the macaroni without chewing it, and afterward you have to slice open your belly so that I can see what your macaroni looks like."

The giant agreed, for he was very dumb. He placed a huge kettle of water on the fire to cook a lot of macaroni. Meanwhile, the shoemaker stepped outside and went into the wood. He tied a large sack beneath his neck that sank down to his stomach. When he returned, the giant said, "The macaroni is done. Now let's see who can eat the most."

"Good, let's go at it," the shoemaker said, and both of them began eating. The giant ate very fast, while Master Giuseppe threw all his macaroni into the sack and kept saying, "Keep going. Don't you see that I'm eating much faster than you?"

Finally all the macaroni was eaten, and Master Giuseppe said, "Now, give me a knife. Let's see what the macaroni looks like. I'll begin."

The giant gave him a large knife, and Master Giuseppe sliced open the sack with one powerful cut so that the macaroni fell to the ground.

"You see, I ate my macaroni without chewing it. Now it's your turn," he said and handed the giant the knife.

In turn, the giant made a huge powerful cut in his belly so that his intestines fell out, and he sank to the ground with a great roar.

"That's the way it should be," the brave shoemaker said. "Now you've saved me the trouble of killing you."

Since the giant was now dead, Master Giuseppe stepped up to him and calmly cut off his head, which he took to the king.

"Your majesty, here is the giant's head. The fight was furious, but I finally succeeded in defeating him."

The king became extremely happy, and because he had a very beautiful daughter, he gave her to Master Giuseppe as his wife. They led a glorious life, and when the king died, Giuseppe became king and lived happy and content, and we still can't pay the rent.

19

PRINCE SCURSUNI[*]

Once upon a time there was a king and a queen, who had everything their hearts desired—food and drink, beautiful clothes and coaches, and parties as often as they wanted them. There was, however, one thing lacking: children. In her heart the queen kept saying: "Oh God, each and every animal has young ones, even the spiders, the lizards, and the beetles. Why haven't you given me a child?"

One day she went for a walk in the garden and saw a grass snake crawling around with its little ones.

"Oh God," she said, "look at how many young ones you've given these poisonous serpents, and yet you haven't even granted me one. Oh, if only I could have a son, even if it were a scursuni."

Not long thereafter the queen became pregnant, and there was great joy in the castle and in the entire land. When nine months had passed, the time arrived for her to give birth, and the king immediately sent for the midwife. However, when this woman entered the room where the queen was lying in bed, she fell dead to the ground.

---

[*]Scursuni in Italian; or Ringelnatter in German; grass snake in English, according to the report of a nature expert, who has examined such snakes. In Sicily these snakes are generally regarded as poisonous in contrast to the nonpoisonous *serpe*. In the Fansani dictionary there is the following entry: *scorzone*—serpe nero velenoissimo (*scorezone*—a black snake extremely poisonous). In the folk imagination this snake is also a very dangerous serpent, and the people have a special fear of it. When they talk about this snake, they often use the derogative expression, *Scursunazzu*.

"What's the matter?" cried the king. "Quick, get another midwife!"

The servants brought another woman, but things did not go any better for her. No matter how many midwives they called, all the women fell dead to the ground as soon as they entered the queen's room.

Now there was a poor shoemaker who lived next to the castle, and he had an only daughter who was very beautiful. But she had a stepmother, who could not stand the maiden and constantly thought of ways to cause her ruin. When the stepmother now heard about the great troubles in the castle, she said to the maiden, "Get dressed and go to the castle. I want you to assist the queen who is having labor pains," for she thought that the maiden would die just like the other women.

"Oh," responded the maiden, "how am I to assist the queen? Nobody can come close to her without dying."

"That's not my concern," said the stepmother, and she drove the girl out of the house with harsh words. So the maiden went into the church nearby where her real mother had been buried and lamented, "Oh, blessed be my mother's soul! Oh, dear Mama! Look at how badly I'm being treated! Please help me!"

"Don't weep!" answered a voice, and it was the soul of her mother. "Go to the castle and summon your courage. When you do what I tell you to do, nothing will harm you. Go to the metal worker and have him make you a pair of iron gloves and put them on. Then prepare a large bucket of milk, and when the queen gives birth to her child, grab it with the iron gloves and throw it into the milk."

The maiden was consoled and left the church. She went to the metal worker and had him make a pair of iron gloves for her. She put them on and went to the castle in order to assist the queen. Before she entered the room she asked for a large bucket of milk, which she took with her and placed next to the bed. The queen was still having labor pains, but when the shoemaker's daughter took her in her arms, she could finally deliver her child, and she gave birth to a son, who looked like a very large scursuni. The maiden grabbed him with her iron gloves and threw him into the milk, and the scursuni drank the milk and bathed in it.

From that time on the queen's son became larger and stronger with each day that passed, but he was and remained a scursuni. Many years passed this way until one day the scursuni said to his mother, "Mother, get me a wife. I want to get married."

"Oh now the beast even wants to get married!" the queen cried. "Who would ever want to take you, you ugly scursuni!"

"Mother! That's no concern of yours. I want a wife."

So the queen went to the king and said, "Just think, our son wants to get married. There's a poor weaver who lives next door to us. He has a pretty daughter. Let's summon her without telling her that she's to marry our son."

The king was satisfied with this proposal, and the queen sent for the weaver and said to him, "Master, you have a pretty daughter. Send her to us so she can serve my son and look after his needs. We'll give you plenty of money."

The father was glad to accept the offer and sent his daughter to the castle, where she was locked in a room with Prince Scursuni. In the evening she laid down in bed. At midnight, Scursuni suddenly stripped off his snake skin and was transformed into a good looking well-built man.

"Whose daughter are you?" he asked the maiden.

"The weaver's daughter," she said.

"What! I am the son of a king, and they've brought me the daughter of a weaver for my wife?"

Upon saying these words, he slipped into his snake skin again and stung her to death.

The next morning the queen came into the room and asked Prince Scursuni, "Well now, my son, did you like your wife?"

"What? Did you think she was good enough to be my wife?" he growled. "I'm the son of a king, and I want to marry the daughter of a prince not the daughter of a miserable weaver. Take a look! She's lying over there."

The queen went over to the bed, found the maiden, and wailed, "You're awful! You've murdered the poor girl!"

But she sent a message to the weaver and just said that his daughter had died.

Shortly thereafter Prince Scursuni began demanding a wife again.

"Mother," he said, "I want to get married. Find me a wife!"

"Stop this, you ugly scursuni! Who would want you for a husband?"

"Mother! I don't care. You must get me a wife."

What could the queen do?

"God has sent me this cross to bear because of all my sins," she thought to herself and summoned a poor locksmith who lived near the castle and had a pretty daughter.

"Master," she said, "you have a pretty daughter. Send her to us so that she can be a servant in the castle, and we'll take good care of her."

The locksmith was satisfied with this proposal and sent his daughter to the castle. The queen was very friendly to her and took her into Scursuni's room. In the evening she laid down in bed, and at midnight,

Scursuni stripped off his snake skin and stood there as a handsome man and asked her, "Whose daughter are you?"

"I'm the daughter of a locksmith."

"What? Am I to marry the daughter of a locksmith? I'm the son of a king!"

Upon saying this, he slipped once again into his snake skin and stung the maiden to death.

The next morning the queen was filled with fear and thought, "I hope that the unfortunate Scursuni has not murdered this poor maiden as well." When she entered the room, she said to her son, "Well, my son, how did you like your wife?"

"What? My wife? I want a princess as wife and not the daughter of a locksmith. She's lying over there."

The queen ran to the bed and saw the poor dead maiden stretched out on it.

"You villain!" she wailed. "You've also murdered this unfortunate maiden!"

But she sent a message to the locksmith and just said that his daughter had died.

Now the poor shoemaker was still living next to the castle with his beautiful daughter. However, her wicked stepmother continued to dislike her even more and kept trying to find a way to bring about her downfall. One day she said to her, "Get dressed. I want you to go to the castle and serve Prince Scursuni."

"Oh," answered the daughter, "two girls have already died in his service. Now you also want to see me dead."

"Don't talk back to me!" the stepmother said. "Just get yourself ready, and if you don't obey, I'll chase you out of the house."

The maiden went to the church where her mother was buried and lamented her fate.

"Oh, blessed be my mother's soul!" she wept. "Oh, my dear Mama! See how awful I'm being treated! Oh, please help me!"

"Don't weep!" answered her mother's soul. "Go calmly to Prince Scursuni in the castle. When he asks you, however, whose daughter you are, you're to say that you're the daughter of a great prince and tell him about your wealth and treasures."

So the maiden went with her stepmother to the castle, and the stepmother said to the queen, "Your majesty, I'm bringing you my stepdaughter who would like to serve Prince Scursuni."

The queen received her in a friendly way and led her into her son's room and locked the door. In the evening the shoemaker's daughter laid down in the bed, and at midnight the prince stripped off his snake skin and turned into a large and handsome man.

"Whose daughter are you?" he asked the maiden.

She began to tell him that she was the daughter of a rich prince and talked about her treasures and wealth. Now the prince was very satisfied and said, "A curse has been placed on me. It was caused by my mother when she wished for a son, even if she were to give birth to a scursuni. If I am ever released from this magic spell, you will become my wife."

Then he also laid down, and they slept peacefully until the morning. When daylight came, he slipped into his snake skin again. The next morning the queen entered her son's room full of fear, but the shoemaker's daughter approached her very cheerful, alive, and well, and Prince Scursuni cried out, "Well, Mother, I've finally found a good wife!"

Many months passed like this. The shoemaker's daughter lived with the prince in his room, and he loved her as if she were his very own eyes. Soon she became pregnant, and when the time came, she gave birth to a handsome son. She kept him hidden so that neither the king nor the queen knew about him, but one time during the night, the baby wept. The prince got up, rocked him in the cradle, and sang:

Sleep, my dear, close your eyes.
When grandma knows she will fly
With golden diapers to your side.[*]

Well, the queen heard the song, and the next morning she called the shoemaker's daughter and asked her, "What kind of a song did I hear in your room last night?"

Then the shoemaker's daughter revealed everything to her and said, "Oh, if you only knew what a handsome man your son is! But an evil spell has been cast on him."

"Ask him how you can break the spell," the queen said.

That evening the maiden asked the prince, "What would one have to do to release you from the magic spell?"

"To save me, one would have to spin, weave, and sew a robe made of fine white cloth in one day. Then a lime kiln would have to be heated

---

[*]Dormi, dormi, e fa la ninna
  Si to nanna lu saprà,
  Fasci d'oru ti farà.
  Ninne nanne—nursery rhyme.

three days and nights, and when I strip off my snake skin, someone must throw the robe over me and throw the snake skin quickly into the lime kiln. I would have to be held tightly, otherwise I would throw myself into the fire."

The next morning the shoemaker's daughter told the queen everything, and the queen immediately called together all the workers of the city. They had to spin and weave all the flax on one day and sew a fine robe out of it. Then she had the lime kiln heated for three days and three nights, and when everything was ready, she gave the shoemaker's daughter the robe. In the evening, when Prince Scursuni had stripped off his snake skin, his wife threw the robe over him. At the same moment the servants sprang into the room. Some of them threw the snake skin into the lime kiln. The others held the prince tightly as he fought with people around him and sought to throw himself into the fire. But when the snake skin was completely burned, the magic spell lifted, and he stood there as a handsome young man.

The king and queen embraced their son, full of joy, as well as their grandson and dear daughter-in-law. However, she said to the prince. "I'm not the daughter of a prince as I told you. My father is only a poor shoemaker."

"You have released me from the magic spell," he answered. "And that's why you shall become my dear wife."

And they celebrated a splendid wedding with great festivities, and so they remained content and happy, but all our roots are rotted and empty.

20

MARIA AND HER BROTHER

Once upon a time there was a man whose wife died and left him with two children, a boy named Peppe* and a girl named Maria. Both children were very beautiful, and their father loved them with all his heart. He was, however, a poor man and could only support them by gathering firewood in the forest and selling the wood in the city. Because he never wanted to leave his children alone, he always took them into the forest with him, and they looked for twigs and carried small bundles to their home.

After some time had passed, the man thought about marrying again.

"Oh, Father, don't do it," Maria implored him. "If you bring a stepmother into our home, she'll certainly treat us badly."

"Don't worry, my child," he answered. "After all I'm here, and I'll always protect you and I'll continue to love you as much as I do now."

So he went and married a neighbor, who was a tavern keeper and had a daughter who was very ugly and had only one eye. For a while everything went well, but soon the stepmother became unfriendly toward Maria and her brother. Because Maria was so beautiful and her daughter so ugly, the stepmother clearly could not stand her and thought of ways to cause her ruin.

---

*Giuseppe or Joseph.

One day she said to her husband, "Times are terrible. The bread has become so expensive, and your children eat so much that we'll soon become beggars. Get rid of your children because I'm not going to give them anything more to eat!"

"But where should I send my children?" the father asked.

"Take them deep into the forest tomorrow, to a place where they won't be able to find their way back," the stepmother answered.

"Oh no," said her husband, "how could I commit such a sin and leave my children in the forest all alone? I love them too much."

Well, just as it is customary that wives always get their way with husbands, this husband, too, let himself be persuaded by his wife. So he woke his two children very early the next morning and said, "Come children, I know a beautiful spot in the forest where we can find a lot of wood today."

They set out and took some bread with them and along the way they met a man who was selling lupins.[*]

"Father," said Maria, "give us a senare[†] so we can buy some lupins."

The father gave them the senare, and the children bought the lupins and ate them along the way. As they walked, they threw the shells on to the ground. Finally they reached a certain spot in the forest, and their father said, "Look, children, over there you'll find a lot of twigs. Go there and make some bundles while I chop down this old tree trunk. While the children were gone, the father took a large pumpkin and tied it to the branch of the tree so that it would swing and hit the trunk. Then he crept away and went home. The children worked the entire day, and when they stopped every now and then, they heard the pumpkin hitting the trunk and thought it was their father's ax and cheerfully continued gathering wood.

When evening arrived, Maria said, "Father is working very long today. Let's go and call him."

So they went back to the spot where they had left their father and could not find him. They began calling him, but he did not answer. When they caught sight of the pumpkin, they realized that he had left them alone in the dark forest and began to weep bitter tears.

"Don't cry, Peppe," Maria said. "Early this morning we ate the lupins, and if we follow the path of the shells that we threw on the

---

*Luppini.

† Two centimes.

ground, we'll come to a spot that we know, and from there we can find our way home."

So they followed the path of the shells and found their way out of the forest and arrived happily at their house. In the meantime, their father had sat down at the dinner table and had no desire to eat. He was weeping and lamenting, "Oh, my poor, dear children, I've abandoned you! Now the wild animals will eat you! Oh, my children!"

All at once the children called to him from outside the door, "Father, here we are! Open up!"

And when the father opened the door, he saw his dear children alive and well standing right before his eyes. He embraced them and told them to sit down at the table and was extremely happy that they were there again.

But the stepmother was bitter and angry that they had returned and told her husband once more that he had to take them even farther into the dense forest. Her husband refused, but she screamed at him and threw a fit until he had to promise her with a heavy heart to do what she demanded.

Early the next morning he woke the children again and took them into the forest. Maria was scared that he would leave them alone again, so she filled her pockets and her brother's pockets with beans, and along the way they ate the beans and spread the shells along the path. Their father led them to a spot in the forest where they had never been before.

"Oh Father, how strange and eery it is here!" the children said.

"That's all the more reason we'll find much more wood here," their father answered. "Go farther in the forest to a spot where there are a lot of twigs, and I'll start chopping this tree trunk."

The children went to the spot that their father indicated, but he tied a pumpkin on a branch again and snuck off toward home. When it became evening, Maria said, "Peppe, I still hear Father chopping down the tree, let's go and find him."

When they reached the tree, where the pumpkin was hanging, they did not see him and realized that he had once again deserted them.

"Don't cry, Peppe," Maria said. "We just need to follow the bean shells, and we'll soon find our way home."

So they followed the shells and reached home when it was pitch black. The father sat at the dinner table and moaned about his poor children.

"Father, here we are! Open up," they called from outside the house, and their father opened the door full of joy and embraced his dear children.

But the wicked stepmother became more and more angry that the children had found their way home again despite everything, and she threatened her husband that if he did not abandon his children alone in the forest again, she would chase them away. So the man woke his children early in the morning and said, "Come. Let's go into the forest and look for food."

Maria wanted to fill her pockets once more with beans, but there were no more to be found. So she took a handful of bran and stuck it into her pocket. While she walked with her father, she spread a little bran on the path. The father took them to a very dense and dark spot in the forest and then sent them somewhat farther into the woods to look for twigs. As soon as they departed, he tied a pumpkin to a branch and went home.

When it began to get dark, the children set out to look for their father, but they did not find him and realized that he had again abandoned them.

"Don't cry, Peppe," Maria said. "I spread bran along the way. We only have to follow the trail of the bran, and we'll certainly find our way back home."

However, no matter how much they looked, they did not find their way because the wind had blown the bran from the path, and the children lost their way and went deeper into the dark forest. They began to shed bitter tears and sat down beneath a tree to wait for sunrise. When dawn came, they wandered farther, but they did not find their way out of the forest.

"Oh, Maria, I'm so thirsty," said Peppe. "When we come to a brook, let's get a drink of water."

Soon thereafter they came to a brook, and Peppe wanted to drink. However, Maria heard the brook murmur: "If you drink from my water, you will become a snake and your brother a little serpent."*

"Oh, Peppe," Maria cried, "Don't drink. Otherwise, you'll become a little serpent. We'd better wait a little while."

Farther on they came to another brook, and Peppe said, "Look, Maria, we can get a drink there."

But the brook murmured: "Whoever drinks from my water will become a rabbit."

"Peppe," Maria said, "don't drink, otherwise you'll become a rabbit. We'd better wait a while."

---

*Serpuni.

After they walked some distance, they came to another brook that murmured to Maria, "If you drink from me, you'll become more beautiful than the sun, and your brother will turn into a sheep with gold horns."

"Oh, Peppe," Maria cried out, "don't drink."

But Peppe had already bent over to drink, and no sooner did he take a few sips than he was transformed into a little sheep with pretty gold horns. Maria began to weep, but Peppe was and remained a sheep.

Maria continued to wander with a heavy heart. But before she departed, she also drank some water and became even more beautiful than she had been, more beautiful than the sun. When they had traveled for some time, they came to a cave and crawled inside, and because there were no wild animals there, Maria said, "Let's live here, and during the day I'll go around and look for herbs, and we can live off them."

So Maria made a bed in the cave out of dry leaves and searched for herbs in the forest to nourish herself and her brother.

Many, many years went by this way, and Maria grew to become a very beautiful maiden. Now, one day, the king happened to go hunting and came in the vicinity of the cave. All of a sudden his dogs began to bark and crawled into the cave. So the king sent one of his hunters to see what they had found. When the hunter crept into the cave and saw the lovely maiden, he went back and reported to the king, who shouted, "Come out whoever you may be! We won't harm you."

Maria came out, and when she stood there, she was more beautiful than the sun and moon and the king fell madly in love with her and said, "Beautiful maiden, do you want to come to my castle and become my wife?"

"Yes," she answered, "but my little sheep must come with me."

So the king took the beautiful Maria on his horse and rode with her to his castle, and one of his hunters led the little sheep. When the old queen saw her son appear with this wondrous creature, she cried out in astonishment, "Who's this girl you're bringing out of the forest?"

"Mother, this maiden is to become my wife," the king responded.

To be sure, the queen was not pleased by this, but because she loved her son so much, she let him have his way, and Maria was so beautiful that she soon won the queen's heart. So a splendid wedding was celebrated, and beautiful Maria became queen. But the little sheep still followed her everywhere she went and also had to sleep in her room.

Now that she lived in such glory and splendor, Maria no longer thought about the bad treatment that she had received from her stepmother. On the contrary—she sent her father and stepmother and her stepmother's daughter beautiful presents and had them informed that she was now a queen. Her stepmother's heart, however, became filled with envy because her own daughter had not been as lucky, and she thought of ways to bring about the ruin of the young queen.

When she later heard that Maria was about to give birth, she set out with her daughter on a day that the king had gone off on a hunt. Maria received them in a friendly way, showed them around the entire castle, and finally took them to her own room. There they saw a locked window, and the tricky stepmother said, "Why is that window closed?"

"It's right above the sea," Maria answered, and the king does not want me to open it in case I might fall out."

"Oh, open it up, Maria," the stepmother requested. "I'd like to see the sea from here, and I'll hold onto you in case you're afraid of falling out."

Maria let herself be persuaded and opened the window, and as she was leaning out, her stepmother gave her a push so that she fell into the sea. Right beneath the window was a shark which held open its jaws, and when Maria fell into the water, the shark swallowed her. Then the false stepmother put the queen's nightgown on her daughter and told her to lie down in bed. She herself left the castle in a hurry.

After the king came home and heard that the young queen was lying in bed, he went up to her. But when he looked at her and saw how ugly she was, he was shocked and said, "What happened that's made you so ugly and one-eyed?"

"I'm sick," she answered. "The wicked little sheep rammed me with his horns and knocked an eye out. That's why it's got to die."

The king became furious and had the sheep locked up in the castle dungeon and ordered the cook to sharpen his knives. The dungeon lay close to the sea. All at once the guard heard how the sheep began to moan and to speak:

> Sister, oh sister, oh curly hair,
> They're sharpening the knives and taking great care
> To prepare the kettles to be nice and bright.
> Then they'll cut my throat and create a great sight.*

---

*Soru, soru, aneddi, aneddi,
  Pri mia mmolanu li cuteddi,
  Pri mia mentinu li quaddari,
  Pirchì a mia hannu ammazzari.

All at once, a voice answered from the water:

> Brother dear, I can't help you, I fear.
> The wicked shark has me in his jaw.
> I can't even give birth anymore.[*]

So the guard went to the king and told him what he had heard. The king was astounded and went to the place where the guard usually stood. All at once he heard the little sheep lament:

> Sister, oh sister, oh curly hair,
> They're sharpening the knives and taking great care
> To prepare the kettles to be nice and bright.
> Then they'll cut my throat and create a great sight.

Immediately there was a response from a voice in the sea:

> Brother dear, I can't help you, I fear.
> The wicked shark has me in his jaw.
> I can't even give birth anymore.

The king recognized his wife's voice and had the sheep fetched from the dungeon and said, "Tell me who you were speaking with?"

"With my sister Maria," the sheep answered. "She is sitting in the jaw of a shark because the false stepmother threw her out of the window. Her ugly daughter is lying upstairs in the bed."

The king became very happy and said, "Little sheep, go to the sea and ask your sister how I can rescue her."

The little sheep went and spoke his verse, and after Maria answered him, he continued, "Tell me, Maria, how can you be rescued?"

"You'll need a strong iron hook with a large piece of bread stuck on it," she answered. "When I answer your verse, it will be a sign that the shark is sleeping on the surface of the water and his jaw is open. Then the king must stick the hook into the jaw of the shark so that I can hold onto it while he pulls me out."

And that's what they did. When Maria answered the sheep, the king stood ready with the large hook. He threw it into the jaw of the shark

---

*E iu, fratuzzu, chi ti pozzu fari?
   In vucca sugnu a lu pisci-cani;
   Gravida sugnu e nun pozzu figghiari!

and pulled it toward him with all his might, while Maria held onto the hook and was pulled out. No sooner was she brought into the castle than her time arrived, and she gave birth to a lovely boy. The king was very happy as was everyone in the castle, but the king had the ugly, one-eyed stepsister's head cut off. Then the head was chopped into little pieces and salted in a barrel, which was sent to her mother. The servant who took it to the woman told her: "Your daughter, the queen, has sent this beautiful tuna fish."

When the wicked woman opened the barrel, she found the blind eye of her daughter on top and recognized it right away. Then she ran to the king and demanded to have her daughter back, but the king said, "Just listen to you!" Then he ordered her to be seized and thrown into a kettle full of boiling water.

When Maria was healthy again, the king held a great party, and they remained happy and content, but we've been left without a cent.

21

AUTUMUNTI AND PACCAREDDA

Once upon a time there was a king and queen who ruled over a large beautiful realm. They did not have any children and would have liked to have had a son to inherit their kingdom, so the queen called upon the Mother of God of Autumunti* and said, "Holy mother, if you grant me a son, I'll call him Autumunti and give you his weight in gold as a present."

After a year passed, the queen gave birth to a handsome boy and named him Autumunti, but she did not send the gold to the Lord's mother. Instead, she said, "There's still plenty of time. I can send it to her another day."

Autumunti began to grow, and with each passing day he became more handsome and stronger. When he turned seven years old, the Mother of God appeared to him one time and said, "Autumunti, tell your mother that she should think about the pledge she made."

The next morning Autumunti told his mother that a beautiful lovely lady appeared to him in a dream and told him about her pledge.

"Oh, my child," the queen said, "that was the Mother of God. She's reminding me that I made an oath to give her your weight in gold once you were born."

---

*Of the high mountain.

So the queen had a large lump of gold brought from the treasury, and it was just as heavy as Autumunti.

"I want you to go yourself, Autumunti, and take this gold to the mother of God of Autumunti."

So the boy set out and took the gold to the Mother of God. However, because he was so small he became lost and could not find his way home. Finally he came to a house, and because he was hungry and needy, he knocked on the door. Unknown to him, an ogre and his wife lived in this house, and just before this time a gorgeous young maiden had recently come to them. Her name was Paccaredda, and she had also been lost. When the ogre had seen little Paccaredda, he had wanted to eat her, but his wife had taken such a liking to the beautiful child that she said, "We're going to keep her as our little maid."

Therefore, Paccaredda remained with the ogre and his wife and served them. The witch was very fond of her and treated her as though she were her own child.

Now, when Autumunti knocked on the door, the witch opened it and thought, "Now what a beautiful child! He'll make for a splendid roast."

However, the ogre took pity on him and said, "When Paccaredda came, you didn't allow me to eat her. Now I don't want you to eat Autumunti. Instead, I want him to stay here and serve us."

Indeed, Autumunti remained with the ogre and his wife and served them, but the old witch could not stand him and always gave him more and more difficult tasks to do. One day she went into the forest, tied a large bundle of wood together, and left it in the forest. When she returned home, she sent poor little Autumunti to the spot to fetch some wood, but Paccaredda said to him, "If the bundle is too heavy for you, just say, 'Wood, make yourself light out of love for my sister Paccaredda.'*

Autumunti went into the forest, and when he saw the huge bundle of wood, he became frightened because he could not lift it, not to mention carry it home. Then he said, "Wood, make yourself light out of love for my sister Paccaredda," and just imagine, the wood became so light that he could carry it home without any effort! Whenever the witch ordered him to carry a heavy load from then on, he said the words Paccaredda gave him, and everything immediately became light. As time went by, Autumunti and Paccaredda grew, and gradually they matured and became intelligent young people.†

---

*Ligna, facitivi leggi, pri l'amuri di me soru Paccaredda.

† A l'eta di ragiuni.

Because they had taken a liking to one another, Autumunti said one day: "Do you know, Paccaredda, I'm the son of a great king? Let's escape and go to my father. Then we can marry."

Paccaredda agreed, and that night, when the ogre and his wife were sound asleep, they fled. When the witch awoke the next morning, she immediately thought of Paccaredda, but no matter how often she called her, Paccaredda did not come. When she became aware that the two of them had fled, she became completely enraged, woke the ogre, and cried out: "Your Autumunti, whom you treated as a son, has fled with poor Paccaredda. Quick! Get ready and run after them!"

So the ogre set out, and because he could run faster than Autumunti and Paccaredda, he soon caught up to them.

"Oh, Paccaredda," cried Autumunti, "the ogre is right on our heels!"

"Just calm down," she answered. "I'm going to change myself into a garden, and you into a gardener."

All of a sudden she was transformed into a garden and Autumunti into a gardener. When the ogre came by, he asked Autumunti. "Tell me, good friend, have you perhaps seen a young man and a young woman who came by here?"

"What do you want? Turnips? They're not ripe yet," the gardener replied.

"No. I'm not talking about turnips," the ogre said. "I asked whether you saw two people who came running by here."

"Oh, you want lettuce. Well, then you'll have to come again in a few weeks."

The ogre lost his patience and yelled with irritation: "Go to blazes!"*

Because he did not know what direction Autumunti and Paccaredda went, he returned home to his wife who asked him, "Well, have you brought them back?"

"It was impossible!" he said. "I met a gardener and asked him whether he had seen the two of them, and he only talked about turnips and lettuce. I left him standing there and came back here."

"What's gotten into your head?" his wife yelled. "Go back and get after them!"

The poor man had to set out again and ran after them a second time. In the meantime, Autumunti and Paccaredda had taken on their

---

*Va, fatti benedire!

natural forms again and gone farther. When they saw the ogre on their heels once more, however, Paccaredda said, "I'm going to become a church, and you the sacristan," and so she was transformed into a church, and he into a sacristan.

"Good friend," the ogre said, "Have you seen a young man and woman pass by here?"

"Yes indeed!" replied the sacristan. "Mass will soon begin."

"Who spoke about mass?" the ogre cried out. "I asked you whether you had seen two people come running by here."

"If you want to confess, you'll have to return tomorrow," Autumunti responded.

The ogre lost his patience and yelled, "Go to blazes!" and he returned home.

When his wife asked him what he had done, he grumbled, "Leave me in peace. I asked a sacristan whether he had seen the two of them come by, and he only talked about mass and confession. So, I just left him standing there and returned home."

"No! How dumb can you be?" his wife cried. "You better go back right away and catch the two of them!"

"No, I've had enough now," her husband declared. "Now you can run after Paccaredda yourself!"

So the witch set out and followed the couple and nearly caught up with them. When Paccaredda saw her coming, she cried out, "You'll become a river, and I'll become a fish swimming in it." So, Autumunti became a river, and Paccaredda was transformed into a sprightly fish swimming merrily in the water. However, the witch knew who the fish really was and tried to catch it. No matter how often she got it in her hands, the little fish managed to jump out, and she finally lost her patience and cried out: "All right, go! But when the time comes for you to give birth to a child, I'll have my revenge on you. You won't be able to deliver the baby until I've taken my hands off my head."

Upon saying this, she folded her hands on top of her head and returned home.

Now Autumunti and Paccaredda continued on their way and came to the city in which the king was living. Autumunti was ashamed, however, to show his beautiful bride to his parents in torn clothes, and he said to her, "You stay here outside the city while I go and fetch beautiful clothes for you."

"Oh, no. Don't do this," she replied. "If you let yourself be kissed by your mother, you'll forget me and never return."

But he promised not to forget her and went alone to the castle. Just imagine what joy the king and queen felt when their dear son returned!

He had been gone for so many years that they had assumed he was dead, and now he stood there, a handsome young man. His mother threw her arms around his shoulders and wanted to kiss him, but he stopped her and said, "No, dear Mother, you may not kiss me. Otherwise, you will make me unhappy."

Hungry and tired, he wanted to sleep before he returned to Paccaredda. When he was asleep, the queen decided to satisfy her urge to embrace him. She crept into his room and kissed him, and at the very same moment he forgot Paccaredda, remained with his parents, and led a merry life.

Poor Paccaredda sat and waited for him, and when he did not return, she finally thought, "I'm certain that he let himself be kissed by his mother and has forgotten all about me."

All at once she broke into bitter tears and was very despondent, but she did not lose her courage. Instead she went to the city, bought two doves, and cast a magic spell upon them. Then she took them to the castle and offered them to the prince for sale, and because they pleased the prince, he bought them. Even though he spoke with Paccaredda, he did not recognize her. When he spread something to eat for the doves, one of them began talking to the other one.

"Should I tell you a beautiful story?"

"Yes, do that," the second dove replied.

The first dove told the entire story of Autumunti's life, and how he had lived together with poor Paccaredda at the ogre's house. When the prince heard the name Paccaredda, he suddenly remembered his beautiful bride and quickly set out to find her in a magnificent coach that had gorgeous clothes for her inside. Indeed, he found Paccaredda outside the city and returned triumphantly with her to the castle. Because she was close to giving birth, the queen cared for her as if she had been her own daughter. When the hour arrived to deliver the baby, she could not give birth because of the curse that the witch had placed on her.

In response, the prince called one of his father's loyal servants and sent him to the region where the witch was living. He told the servant to have all the death bells ring, and when the old woman asked who had died, he was to say, "Your daughter, Paccaredda."

"When she takes her hands from her head," the prince continued, "then have all the bells ring the Gloria, and when she again asks you what happened, you are to answer, 'Your daughter, Paccaredda, has just given birth.'"

The servant did as he was commanded, and went to the region where the old witch was living. Once all the death bells began to ring, he stood beneath her window, and she called to him and said, "Tell me, why are they ringing the death bells?"

"Your daughter, Paccaredda, has died," the servant answered.

"Oh my daughter, my dear Paccaredda," the woman lamented and hit her breast with her hands. At that very same moment Paccaredda gave birth to a lovely baby boy. Then the servant had all the bells ring the Gloria, and the witch listened and wondered what was happening.

"Why is the Gloria ringing?" she asked.

"Your daughter, Paccaredda, has just brought a child into the world," the servant said.

The witch realized that she had been deceived and burst in anger. Meanwhile, Autumunti married the beautiful Paccaredda, and they remained rich and content, while we still don't have a single cent.

22

$$\infty 8\!\!\!\%$$

Giufà

Do you want to hear some stories about Giufà? He played many tricks and often caused his mother great embarrassment. Deep down he was quite smart, but his mother was even smarter.

Giufà and the Cloth

One day she called him and gave him a piece of cloth that she herself had woven.

"Take the cloth to the dyer, Giufà, and tell him to dye it a beautiful green."*

Giufà took the roll of cloth and carried it over the countryside. After a while he became tired and sat down on a pile of rocks to rest. All at once a little lizard came and began playing between the rocks.

"Hey," Giufà thought, "what a pretty little green skirt you have on! You must be the dyer. Now listen to me. My mother wants you to dye this stuff a beautiful green just like your little skirt. I'll come back in a few days to pick it up."

Upon saying this, he threw the cloth on to the pile of rocks and departed. When he returned home, his mother asked him, "Where did you take the cloth?"

---

*The peasant women in the vicinity of Messina wear green and blue skirts made out of coarse cloth that they make themselves.

144

"There was a large pile of rocks in the field. Someone was sitting there and wearing such a beautiful little green skirt, and I thought that must probably be the dyer. So I gave him the cloth."

"No, it's not possible. What a dumb thing to do!" she cried. "Who told you to leave the cloth laying in the field? You go right back, and don't return without the cloth!"

So Giufà went back to the pile of rocks, but the cloth had disappeared.

"Listen to me, dyer!" Giufà yelled. "Give me back my cloth, otherwise I'll destroy your house!"

But the lizard had long since crawled away and did not reappear. Therefore, Giufà began to destroy the pile of rocks and continued to yell, "I trusted you with the cloth, and now you had better give it back to me. Otherwise, I'll destroy your house!"

All of a sudden he saw a large pot full of gold coins that had been buried under the pile of rocks. "Well, you must have sold the cloth. So now I'll take the money away."

Giufà picked up the pot with the money and put it in his backpack. On top of it he put a pile of thorns and wandered back home. Along the way people teased him, "Giufà, what are you carrying?"

"Pain,"* Giufà said.

"What is that, pain?" they asked.

"See for yourself,"† Giufà responded.

The people looked and were stuck by the thorns.

"What a beautiful present you're bringing your mother, Giufà," they cried. "She'll certainly be pleased by the thorns!"

When Giufà arrived home, he called his mother and spoke to her quietly so that nobody could hear.

"Look at what I've brought you, Mother!" and he unpacked everything and showed her the money. But his mother was a very smart woman and thought, "I'm sure Giufà will tell everybody that he brought me this money." Then she said to him, "You've done well, my son. Eat your dinner and then go to sleep."

When Giufà was lying in bed, his mother took the pot and buried it beneath the stairs. Then she filled her apron full of dates and raisins, climbed on to the roof, and threw the dates and raisins down through the chimney into Giufà's mouth. All this was a pleasure for Giufà, who ate all that he could eat. The next morning he told his mother, "Just

---

*Guai, Schmerzen.

† Tona e vidirai.

think, Mother, last night the baby Jesus threw me some dates and raisins from Heaven."

Soon thereafter Giufà began to tell everyone: "I brought my mother a large pot filled with money that I found beneath a pile of rocks."

When the people heard this, they went to the court and filed charges against him before a judge. Then the magistrates went to Giufà's mother and said, "Your son has been telling people everywhere that you've kept a pot of money that he had found. Don't you know that one must give the court any money that's found?"

"Gentlemen, oh my gentlemen," yammered the woman, "do you really want to believe everything that my dumb Giufà says in broad daylight? How much more do I have to suffer as his poor mother? My son will be the end of me. I don't know the first thing about a pot with money."

"But, Mother," Giufà cried, "don't you remember? I brought you the pot during the day, and that very same night the baby Jesus threw me dates and raisins down from Heaven."

"Don't you see how dumb he is? He doesn't know what he's saying," his mother declared.

Indeed, the magistrates agreed and went away thinking, "Giufà is truly much too dumb!"

Giufà and the Door

Another time his mother wanted to go to mass and said to Giufà, "Pull the door behind you when you leave, Giufà."

When his mother was in the church for mass, Giufà lifted the door out of its sockets and pulled it to his mother in the church. "Here's the door, Mother," he said.

Giufà and the Hen

There was another time that his mother wanted to go to mass in the church.

"Giufà," she said, "pay attention to the hen and make sure she doesn't leave her eggs. Also, make sure you give her something to eat."

When his mother was away, Giufà gave the hen some bran and in the process became hungry himself. Because he found nothing to eat in the house, he took the hen, slaughtered it, cooked it, and ate it all up. In order to prevent the eggs from getting cold, he sat on them himself. When his mother returned home, she could not find him anywhere and called out, "Giufà, where are you?"

"Cluck, cluck," Giufà answered.

"Did you give the hen something to eat, Giufà?"

"Cluck, cluck," came the answer.

"Where are you, Giufà?"

"Cluck, cluck."

Finally his mother found him sitting on the nest with the eggs.

"Giufà, what are you doing there?"

"I've eaten the hen, cluck, cluck."

"But the eggs will be ruined, you miserable child!"

"That's why I'm protecting them by sitting here. They'll soon be hatched," he answered.

Giufà and the Shepherd

One evening his mother said to Giufà, "I want you to go out and see whether you can get me the animal that sings during the night." She meant a chicken.

So Giufà set out and met a shepherd, who was singing a merry song during the night.

"Stop," Giufà thought. "My mother wants an animal that sings during the night. This must certainly be the one."

At that very moment he murdered the shepherd, picked him up on his shoulders, and took him to his mother.

"Oh, Giufà, what have you done?" his mother cried. "If the magistrates find him, you'll be hanged. Come quickly! We'll throw him into the water tank."

So they threw the dead shepherd into the tank, but while Giufà was sleeping, his mother hauled the dead man out of the tank and instead threw a dead goat into it. The next morning Giufà met the daughter of the shepherd, who was moaning and groaning.

"Some one murdered my father! Some one murdered my father!"

"Did your father sing in the evening?" Giufà asked.

"Yes, sometimes he did," the maiden answered.

"Well, I was the one who killed him, and my mother and I threw him into the tank."

So the maiden went to the court and accused Giufà of killing her father. The magistrates went to Giufà's mother and said, "Your son murdered the shepherd, and you two threw him into the tank."

"Just what are you saying?" the woman exclaimed. "My son is dumb and doesn't know what he's talking about."

"You're wrong, Mother," Giufà said. "Don't you remember that we threw him into the tank?"

The magistrates had Giufà climb down into the water tank to bring up the dead shepherd. When Giufà saw the dead goat, he called up to the maiden, "Did your father have horns?"

"Not at all," the maiden answered.

"Did he have wool?"

"Not at all. That's certainly not my father."

Then the mother said, "You see, gentlemen, last night my son brought home a dead goat that he had found in the field. I feared, however, that people would believe I had stolen it, and therefore I threw it into the sewer tank."

So the magistrates went home and said, "This Giufà is truly much too dumb."

Giufà and His Sister

Giufà's mother still had a little daughter. When she wanted to go to mass once again, she said to her son, "Take care of your sister, and when she wakes up, give her some porridge.* But don't make it too hot, and when she falls asleep again, put her into the cradle."

When his little sister woke up, Giufà cooked the porridge and fed her. However, the porridge was so hot that the child burned herself and died. Because she was so still, Giufà said, "My little sister is sleeping," and he placed her in the cradle. When his mother returned home, she asked him right away, "What's your little sister doing?"

"She's been sleeping for a long time in the cradle," Giufà responded.

So his mother went over to the cradle and found the dead child.

"Oh, Giufà, what have you done?" his mother moaned. "You wicked person. I no longer want to see you!"

Giufà and the Owl

His mother did not want to keep him in the house anymore and sent him to a priest to be his servant.

"How much do you want for your salary?" the priest asked him.

"I only want an egg every day and as much bread as I can eat with it. But you must promise not to send me away until the little owl screeches in the ivy."

The priest was satisfied and thought, "I'll never find a cheap servant like this again."

On the first morning Giufà got an egg and some bread. He opened the egg and ate it with a needle, and each time he licked the needle, he consumed a large piece of bread with it. "Bring me a bit more bread. I

---

*Pane cotto.

don't have enough," he cried, and the priest brought him a large basket full of bread. This is the way things went each morning.

"What a poor wretch I am!" the priest complained. "This fellow will make a beggar out of me in a few weeks."

It was now winter, and many months had to pass before the owl would screech in the ivy. In desperation the priest went and spoke to his own mother.

"Mother, I need you to hide in the ivy this evening," he said, "and then you must screech like the owl."

So the old woman concealed herself in the ivy that evening and began to scream, "Hoo, hoo!"

"Do you hear, Giufà?" the priest said. "The little owl is screeching in the ivy. Now your time is up, and you must leave."

So Giufà took his bundle of clothes and wanted to return to his mother. As he passed by the ivy where the priest's mother was still crying out "Hoo, hoo," he picked up some large stones and yelled in anger:

"Oh, you no good cursed owl,
I hope you feel some pain and howl!"*

He threw the stones into the bushes and killed the old woman. When he appeared at his mother's house, she cried out, "Giufà, where did you come from? I don't want you here anymore. Tomorrow I'll find a new position for you."

Giufà and the Pigs

The next day she went to a landlord who owned a large estate, and convinced him to hire Giufà as his pig keeper. The landlord sent him into a forest very far away and ordered him to take care of the pigs. When they had become fat, he was to bring them back to the manor. So Giufà lived for many months in the forest until the pigs were completely fat. As he began driving them back home, he met a butcher and said to him, "Would you like to buy these beautiful pigs? I'll give them to you for half the price if you'll let me keep the ears and the tails."

Of course the butcher bought the entire herd, and gave Giufà a great deal of money for the pigs as well as the ears and tails. Right after this Giufà went to a swamp and planted two ears next to another and

---

*Chiuzza di mala stasciuni,
  Soffri pene duluri!

about a foot farther he planted a tail. He did this with all the ears and tails. Then he ran very upset to the landowner and screamed, "Oh my lord, just think what bad luck I've had! I had fattened up the pigs so nicely and began driving them home, but they got stuck in a swamp, and all of them have sunk there. Only their ears and tails can be seen."

The landlord rushed with his servants to the swamp where the ears and tails were still sticking out. They tried to pull the pigs out, but no matter how often they caught hold of an ear or a tail, it came out unattached.

"You see how fat the pigs were," cried Giufà. "They're all dead and have sunk in the swamp because they were so fat."*

Finally, the landlord had to leave the swamp without the pigs. Meanwhile, Giufà took the money to his mother and stayed with her again for some time.

Giufà and the Creditors

One day his mother said to him, "Giufà, we don't have anything to eat today. What should we do?"

"Let me take care of things," he said and went to a butcher.

"Cousin, give me a couple of pounds of meat. I'll pay you tomorrow."

The butcher gave him the meat.

Then he went to the baker and said, "Cousin, give me a couple of pounds of macaroni and some bread. I'll pay you tomorrow."

The baker gave him the macaroni and bread, and Giufà went to the oil merchant.

"Cousin, give me a liter of oil, and I'll bring you the money tomorrow."

The oil merchant gave him the oil, and Giufà went to the wine dealer.

"Cousin, give me a quart of wine. I'll pay you tomorrow."

The wine dealer gave him the wine, and Giufà went to the cheese merchant.

"Cousin, give me four grams of cheese, and I'll bring you the money tomorrow."

The cheese merchant gave him the cheese, and Giufà took his mother the meat, macaroni, bread, oil, wine, and cheese, and they had a delightful meal together.

---

*Si sficiru.

The next day, however, Giufà pretended to be dead, and his mother wept and moaned. "My son has died! My son has died!"

He was placed in an open coffin and taken to the church where the priests sang the death mass. When the entire town heard that Giufà had died, the butcher, baker, oil dealer, and wine dealer said, "What we gave to him yesterday is as good as lost. Who is going to pay us now?"

But the cheese merchant thought, "Giufà owes me money for four grams of cheese, but I didn't give them to him as a gift. I'm going to take his cap away as payment."

So he crept into the church where he saw a priest who was still praying beside Giufà's coffin.

"As long as the priest is still there, it's not right for me to take the cap," the cheese merchant said to himself, and he hid behind the altar. When it turned dark, the last priest departed. The cheese merchant was going to come out of his hiding place just as a bunch of thieves rushed into the church. The thieves had stolen a large sack of gold coins and wanted to divide the money in the darkness of the church. As they did this, they began to argue with one another and began to raise their voices and make noise. All of a sudden Giufà sat up in the coffin and yelled, "Get out of here!"

The thieves were terrified when the dead man sat up, and they thought he was summoning other dead people, so they ran from the church in fright without taking the sack with them. When Giufà went to pick up the sack of money, the cheese merchant jumped out of his hiding place and wanted his share, but Giufà insisted, "Four grams is what you get!"*

Outside, the thieves thought he was dividing the money among the dead people, and they said to each other, "Just think of how many he has summoned from the dead if each one of them is only getting four grams."

And they ran as fast as they could from the town. Meanwhile, after Giufà had given the cheese merchant a little money so that he would not say anything, he took the rest of the gold coins to his mother.

---

*Quàttru grani vi toccano.

Giufà and the Fairies

One time his mother bought a large stock of flax and said to him, "Giufà, you could spin the flax a bit just to do something around here."

From time to time Giufà took a strand of the flax, but instead of spinning it, he stuck it into the fire and burned it. In turn, his mother became angry and beat him. Well, what did Giufà do? He took a bundle of twigs and wrapped it with flax like a skirt.[*] He then used a broom as a spindle, sat down on top of the roof of the house, and began to spin. As he was sitting there, three fairies came by and said, "Just look at how nice Giufà is sitting there and spinning. Why don't we give him a gift?"

The first fairy said, "I'm going to give him the power to spin the flax into yarn in one night."

The second fairy said, "I'm going to give him the power to weave into cloth as much yarn as he has spun in one night."

The third fairy said, "I'm going to give him the power to bleach all the cloth in one night."

Giufà heard all this, and in the evening, when his mother went to bed, he went over to her stock of flax, and imagine what happened! Whenever he touched a strand of the flax, it was immediately spun. When all the flax was gone, he began to weave, and as soon as he touched the weaving stool, the woven cloth rolled forth. Finally, he spread out all the cloth on the ground, and no sooner did he knit the cloth together than it became all white. The next morning he showed his mother the beautiful pieces of cloth, and his mother sold the cloth and earned a good deal of money. Giufà continued to do this for several nights, but finally he became tired and wanted to find some other job.

Well now, he hired himself out to a blacksmith, and he was supposed to step on the bellows and squeeze them. However, he stepped on the bellows so hard that he put out the fire. So the smithy said, "Keep off the bellows and forge the iron on the anvil."

But Giufà hammered the molten iron with such power that the iron split into a thousand pieces. Now the smithy became angry, but he could not fire him because Giufà had made it a condition of their contract that the smithy had to keep him for one year. So the smithy went to a poor man and said to him, "I'll give you a very nice present if you go to Giufà and say that you are old Father Death and you have come to fetch him."

---

[*] Cunocchia.

When the poor man encountered Giufà one day, he told him what the smithy had commanded him to say, but Giufà was not easily fooled.

"So, you're Death?" he cried and grabbed hold of the poor man, stuck him into a sack, and carried him to the smithy's shop. Once there he set him on the anvil and began to hammer him.

"How many more years do I have to live?" he asked.

"Twenty years," screamed the man in the sack.

"That's not long enough."

"Thirty years, forty years, as much as you want!" the man cried.

But Giufà continued to hammer away until the poor man was dead.

Giufà and the Clothes

Now Giufà had enough of the work as a smithy's assistant, and he left his master and wandered off. As he went by a house in which his relatives were living, he saw that they were celebrating a wedding. He went inside, but nobody said, "Good day, Giufà, sit down with us." Nobody greeted him. Nobody paid attention to him. So Giufà left and went to a friend and asked to borrow a splendid gold-stitched suit. After he put it on, he went back to see his relatives. No sooner did they catch sight of him than they all stood up immediately to greet him.

"Oh Giufà, how nice it is that you've come! Sit down next to us and eat."

So Giufà sat down next to them, and they placed a beautiful plate of macaroni before him. To their surprise, he took the entire plate and shook the macaroni all over his clothes. Then they gave him some wine, but he shook the wine all over his clothes, and this is what he did with everything they placed before him.

"Giufà, why don't you eat anything?" his relatives finally asked him.

"I'm giving my clothes everything to eat," Giufà answered. "You invited my clothes to eat with you. When I was here a little while ago, nobody greeted me. Nobody invited me to stay."

Later, after the wedding banquet, Giufà returned the splendid suit to his friend, who cried out in pure horror, "Giufà, what have you done to my clothes?"

"Do you want to hold me responsible for what happened?" Giufà answered. "You'd better turn to my relatives. They're the ones who invited your clothes to attend the wedding celebration."

Giufà and the Bishop

One time the bishop of this region announced that he wanted a goldsmith to make a crucifix for him. He declared that the goldsmith who
made the most beautiful crucifix would receive four hundred ounces of
gold, but whoever brought him a crucifix that did not please him would
be beheaded.

The first goldsmith came and brought the bishop a beautiful crucifix, but the bishop said that he did not like it and ordered the goldsmith
to be beheaded and kept the crucifix. The next day another goldsmith
came and brought a crucifix that was even more beautiful than the first,
but his fate was no better than the other goldsmith's. This is how things
went for some time, and many a poor man lost his head. When Giufà
finally heard about this, he went to a goldsmith and said, "Master, you
must make me a crucifix with a terribly thick belly. Otherwise, it's to be
as beautiful as you can make it."

When the crucifix was finished, Giufà took it in his arms and carried it to the bishop. No sooner did the bishop see it than he screamed,
"How can you possibly think of bringing me such a monstrosity! You
just wait. You're going to pay for this!"

"Oh, my honorable lord," Giufà said. "Please listen to me and
understand what happened to me. This crucifix was a model of beauty
when I set out to bring it here. On the way here, however, the stomach
began to swell* out of anger, and the closer I came to your house, the
more awful it began to swell. The worst was when I climbed your stairs.
You should realize that the Lord is furious with you for spilling so much
innocent blood. If you do not give me four hundred ounces of gold
immediately, and if you don't give a life pension to each and every one
of the widows of the goldsmiths, then *your* belly will swell, and God's
fury will be upon you."

The bishop became so frightened that he gave Giufà the four hundred ounces of gold and asked him to send all the widows to him so
that he could endow them with a yearly pension for life. Giufà took the
money and went to each and every widow and said to each one, "What
will you give me if I manage to get the bishop to give you a life pension?"

Each one of the widows gave him a pretty sum of money, and Giufà
took his mother a large pile of money.

---

* Bunchiava.

Giufà and the Friends

One day Giufà's mother sent him to another village where a fair was being held. Along the way he met some children who asked, "Where are you going, Giufà?"

"To the fair."

"Will you bring me a little pipe?"

"Yes!"

"Me, too?"

"Yes!"

"Me, too?"

"Me, too?" the children asked one after the other.

Each time Giufà said, "Yes!"

Finally, the very last boy said, "Giufà, please bring me a little pipe as well. Here's a coin for your troubles."

When Giufà returned from the fair, he brought only one little pipe with him and gave it to the last boy.

"Giufà, you had promised to bring each and every one of us a pipe," the other children cried out.

"But you didn't give me a coin to buy one," Giufà responded.

Giufà and the Robbers

One day Giufà stood on the street doing nothing. All at once a gentleman came up to him and said, "Giufà, will you take this letter for me to Paterno? I'll give you four tari."

"You want me to run to Paterno for four tari?" Giufà asked. "Such a trip is worth at least ten tari."

So the gentleman gave him ten tari and told him where to take the letter. When Giufà returned from Paterno, he had to go through a forest. It had become quite dark, but there was bright moonlight. When the moon hid behind the trees, Giufà cried out: "All right, all right, hide yourself, you rascal. I've already seen you."

Meanwhile, there were thieves in the forest, and they had stolen a fat calf. When they now heard Giufà shouting like this, they thought he had discovered them.

"What should we do?" one of the thieves asked. "When Giufà returns to the town, he'll report us."

"Perhaps we should give him a piece of the calf so that he keeps quiet," another thief suggested.

So they called Giufà to them and said, "Giufà, see this beautiful fat calf. Which part of it would you like?"

"Give me the stomach," Giufà answered.

"What do you want to do with the stomach, Giufà? Take a better part."

"No, no. I want the stomach."

So they gave him the stomach and let him go. No sooner was he far away and they could no longer see him than he laid the stomach on the ground, took a large stick, and beat the stomach with it. As he did this, he screamed as loud as he could: "Oh, don't beat me! Don't kill me! I'll take you to the spot where you can find the rest."

When the thieves heard this, they cried out, "We're done for! Giufà has certainly met the magistrates, and he's going to bring them here."

They ran off in pure horror and left the calf lying there. So now Giufà crept back, and took the entire fat calf to his mother.

Well, as you can see, Giufà has played many foolish pranks, and whoever knows them all cannot stop telling tales about all his adventures.

23

✦

THE MAGIC CANE, THE GOLD DONKEY, AND THE LITTLE STICK THAT HITS

Once upon a time there was a poor bricklayer who had a wife and a lot of children, and he could not earn enough money to support them. One day, when they were crying out of hunger, and the poor man had no work, he said to his wife, "I'm going to set out across the country. Perhaps I'll find work somewhere else and can bring you all back some money and food."

So he set out on his way and wandered about, and when he had gone a good distance, he came to a mountain. All at once he saw a very beautiful woman who said to him, "You don't have to wander any further because I am your good fortune, and I'm going to help you."

She gave him a magic cane as a gift and said, "When you want to eat, you just have to command this cane, and everything your heart desires will stand before you in seconds."

The bricklayer thanked the unknown beautiful woman and headed home in a cheerful mood. But because it was already dark, he could not make it all the way home and had to spend the night in a tavern. So he ordered a table to be brought before him and hit the table with the cane.

"What's your command?" the cane asked.

"I want a plate of macaroni, roast beef, salad, and a good bottle of wine," he said, and all of a sudden everything was on the table before him, and he ate until he was full. Then he thought, "Now I have everything I need for the rest of my life."

However, the tavern keeper and his wife had seen everything, and when the bricklayer was fast asleep, the tavern keeper crept softly into the room, took the magic cane away, and replaced it with an ordinary one. The next morning the bricklayer set out on his way very early and soon arrived home.

"Haven't you brought us anything at all?" his wife asked.

"I've brought something with me that's better than anything I could buy in the shops," he answered. "Quick, set the table."

When the table was set, he hit it with the cane and cried out: "I want macaroni, roast beef, salad, and wine for myself and my family," but nothing appeared no matter how much he called out and commanded. Then his wife began to weep, for she thought that her husband had become crazy. In turn he said, "Well, let it be. I've got to go into the countryside again."

So he set out and wandered until he came to the same mountain and found the beautiful woman who was still there.

"You've lost the cane," she said. "I know it already, but I'm going to help you again. Take this donkey, and when you place it on a piece of cloth, it will spew forth as much money as you want."

So the bricklayer took the donkey, thanked the woman, and went home. However, it had become dark, and he had to spend the night in the same tavern as he had before. He ordered everything his heart desired, and after he had eaten a full meal with wine, he asked for a sheet, took the donkey into his room, and set it on the sheet. Then the donkey spewed forth money until he stopped it. The tavern keeper's wife observed all this through the keyhole, and when the bricklayer was sleeping, the tavern keeper crept inside, took the gold donkey away, and replaced it with an ordinary one.

Early the next morning the bricklayer was delighted to set out on his way home and began calling to his wife from a distance, "Today I'm bringing you something that is better than all the magic canes. Spread out a bedsheet, and you will see something that you've never seen before in your life."

His wife did just as the bricklayer had commanded her to do, but when the bricklayer placed the donkey on the sheet, it did not spew forth any money, and the bricklayer scratched his head and thought: "What's going on here? I'm certain that the tavern keeper and his wife have played a dirty trick on me!"

His wife began to weep, and he said, "Now just be quiet. I've got to seek my fortune one more time."

So he went away again, and when he came to the mountain, the beautiful woman was still there and said, "You've also lost the gold donkey. I know it. This will now be the last time that I'll help you. Take this little stick, and when you say, 'Little stick, start hitting,'* it will keep hitting until you call, 'Oh little stick, enough's enough.'"

The bricklayer took the stick, thanked the beautiful woman, and thought: "With this I can regain my magic cane and gold donkey. But before I do this, I want to see just how strong its power is. Little stick, start hitting!"

As soon as he said this, the stick began beating his back so that he quickly yelled, "Oh little stick, enough's enough!" And the stick became quiet again.

In the evening the bricklayer came to the tavern once more. The tavern keeper and his wife were speaking with one another: "Here comes the same bricklayer, and he's certainly bringing another magic thing with him."

But the bricklayer called out, "Little stick, start hitting!" The stick started beating the tavern keeper and his wife, and all at once they started screaming, "Get the stick off us!"

But the bricklayer answered, "Not before you give me back the magic cane and my gold donkey."

So they ran and fetched the cane and the donkey, and the bricklayer called out, "Oh little stick, enough's enough." And suddenly the stick stopped beating the tavern keeper and his wife.

Early the next morning the bricklayer set out on his way home once again. When his wife saw him coming, she called to him, "Are you bringing us a dirty donkey again that will make the entire room a mess? I just wish you wouldn't ever come again!"

"Little stick, start hitting, but not too hard," the bricklayer said, and the stick beat his wife until she came to her senses again, and her husband ordered the stick to stop. Then his wife silently set the table just as her husband had ordered, and then he hit the table with the cane,

"What is your command?" asked the cane.

The bricklayer asked for a beautiful lunch for himself and his family. All of a sudden everything was there, and they ate together with delight. After the meal the bricklayer said, "Now spread out a bedsheet, dear wife."

---

*Mazzareddi mei, mazziati.

She did this, and when the donkey stood on it, the animal spewed forth as much money as they wanted. From then on the bricklayer lived with his family in joy and splendor, and they did not lack a thing.

However, when the neighbors heard about the good fortune of the bricklayer, they became jealous and went to the king.

"Your majesty," they said, "there is a bricklayer who was always on the verge of dying, and now he's suddenly become a rich man. Something's wrong here."

The king ordered his servants to bring the bricklayer to him, but the man said, "Little stick, start hitting!" And the stick beat all the servants, who ran back to the king and complained that the bricklayer had them all flogged. The king became furious, gathered together his soldiers, and marched with them to the bricklayer's house.

During this time the bricklayer had gone for a walk and met a man with a three-cornered hat that was very odd to look at. "What a strange hat you have on!" the bricklayer said.

"Yes," the man said, "but the little hat has its own special quality. When I turn it, it shoots from all three corners, and no one can resist it."

"I have a little stick," the bricklayer said. "When I say to it, 'Little stick start hitting,' it beats all the people around me, until I tell it to stop and say, 'Little stick, enough's enough.'"

"You know what? Let's let your stick and my hat fight one another, and whoever wins gets both of them."

So the stick and the hat fought against one another, and the bricklayer won, took the hat, and went home very delighted with himself.

No sooner did he arrive at home than the king appeared with his soldiers. They wanted to take him prisoner, but he turned his hat around so that it shot from all three corners and killed all the soldiers. When the king saw how invincible the bricklayer was, he promised to leave him in peace. The bricklayer put on his hat firmly and said, "If you do not disturb me, I promise you as well that I shall come to assist you with my little hat and my stick whenever you have to go to war."

From then on the bricklayer was not disturbed and lived a glorious life, and whenever war erupted, he went to help the king so that the king was always victorious. In the end they remained rich and consoled, while we just sit here and continue to get old.

24

THE SINGING BAGPIPE

Once upon a time there was a king and a queen who had three handsome sons. One day the king and the queen happened to be struck by a serious eye disease. No doctor could help them, and they could find no means to heal this sickness. When the queen went for a walk one time, she encountered a very old woman, who asked for alms. The queen gave her something, and the old woman said, "Your majesty, you have sick eyes, and no doctor can help you. But I know a means to cure you that cannot fail. If you can obtain three feathers from the peacock and rub your eyes with them, you'll be healed from your sufferings."

"How am I to get these three feathers?" the queen asked.

"You have three strong sons," the old woman answered. "Let them set out and search for the feathers."

So the queen called her three sons and said, "My dear children, an old woman has told me that my eyes and the eyes of your father can be cured if our eyes are stroked by three feathers from the peacock. I'd like you to set out and search for the three feathers so that we can regain our sight."

She blessed her three sons, and they began their journey. When they had traveled for a long time, they met an old woman, who was the same one who had given their mother the advice about the three feathers.

"Where are you going, my handsome young men?" the old woman asked.

"We've set out to search for three feathers from the peacock for our parents so that they can regain their vision," responded the brothers.

"Oh, you poor children," the old woman cried, "you'll have to look for a long time before you find them. Indeed, you'll have to wander one year, one month, and one day until you find them."

"If that's the way it must be, we'll just have to wander until we find the three feathers," the princes answered.

When they had wandered for a long time, they encountered the same old woman again, who asked them, "Where are you going my handsome young men?"

They told her how they had set out to search for the three feathers.

"Very well," she said. "When a year, a month, and a day have passed, you will come to a deep cistern. One of you must be let down into it to spend another year, a month, and a day there. Then he'll be able to rip out the peacock's three feathers."

So the brothers wandered farther, and when a year, a month, and a day had passed, they came to the deep cistern. The eldest brother had a piece of rope tied around him and had himself lowered into the deep cistern. He also took a little bell with him, and as soon as he rang it, his brothers were to pull him up. He did not go down very far, for it was so very dark in the cistern that he soon lost courage and rang the little bell as a signal for his brothers to pull him up.

"You try it," he said to the second brother, but things did not go any better for him. He lost his courage in the dark cistern and rang the bell for his brothers to pull him up. Now the youngest brother had himself tied to the rope and said, "Wait here for me a year, a month, and a day. If I don't give you the signal after that time, I'll probably be dead."

So the youngest had himself lowered into the cistern, and even though it was dark, he did not lose his courage. Instead, he continued bravely until he reached the bottom. When he looked around him, he found himself in a large vault, and on the other side he saw a door. He opened it and came into a bright hall where the peacock was living. He stayed with the bird one year, one month, and one day as its servant, and after this long time he finally succeeded in ripping out three feathers from the peacock. As soon as he had the three feathers, he returned to the cistern and rang the little bell. His brothers were just about to leave because they thought, "The poor boy has surely met with his death," but when they heard the little bell, they were very happy and quickly pulled him out of the cistern. All at once he showed them the three feathers, and they set out for their home.

However, the eldest brother was jealous that the youngest was to become king and said, "All three of us worked for this, and so each one of us should give our parents a feather."

The youngest brother agreed, pulled out the feathers, and gave the eldest brother the worst feather because he had stayed in the cistern the shortest time. The second brother received the second best, and he kept the most beautiful for himself. As a result, the eldest brother's heart burned with envy. He decided to kill the youngest and said to the second, "Why did our youngest brother give me the worst feather? After all, I am the eldest. I'm going to kill him because of this."

"Oh, don't do it," the second brother responded. "He worked the most, and so he also deserves the best feather. Why do you want to murder him?"

"No," the other brother cried out. "He must die, and if you don't swear to me your holy oath not to say anything about this to anyone at home, I'll rip off your head right here and now."

So the second brother swore a holy oath and promised he would not reveal anything, and the oldest slew the youngest brother and buried him in the sand on the banks of the Jordan River.[*] The oldest brother had taken the feathers, and the two brothers continued their journey. The younger one, however, kept on weeping and said, "What are we going to say to our parents? How are we going to explain what happened to our younger brother?"

"We'll tell them that he drowned in the Jordan River," the other brother answered.

Finally they returned home and spoke to the king and queen.

"Dear parents, here are the three feathers from the peacock."

Then they stroked their parents' eyes with the feathers so that they could see again.

"Where is your youngest brother?" their mother asked.

"He drowned in the Jordan River," the eldest answered.

The mother became very despondent and wept for her lost son, but the king said, "My eldest son brought me two feathers and his brother only one. So my eldest son shall be king after me."

Now a shepherd had happened to see that the two brothers had buried their brother in the sand and thought, "I'm going to dig him out of the sand and make a bagpipe out of his skin and bones."

He had a dog with him and showed the dog the fresh pile of sand, and the dog dug until it uncovered the dead body of the young man.

---

[*] Sciume Giordano.

Then the shepherd let it dry in the sun and took the bones and skin and made a bagpipe out of them. However, because the young man had died a violent death before his time had really come, his ghost was still restless and remained in the dead body. So, when the shepherd began to play the bagpipe, it gave forth a beautiful song that sounded like this:

> Play me, play me, oh my shepherd,
> Play me merrily, as long as you like.
> On the banks of the Jordan I was killed with a rock,
> All for three feathers from the gorgeous peacock.
> My eldest brother was the one who betrayed me.
> The other's not guilty, not guilty at all.
> It's only the eldest with blood on his hands.[*]

Whenever the shepherd played the bagpipe, it always resounded with this song, which was so beautiful that everyone who heard it was touched by it. The shepherd traveled throughout the country, and his song was heard everywhere, and people gave him a great deal of money for it. Finally he came to the city ruled by the king, and when the news about the beautiful song of the shepherd reached the castle, the king summoned the shepherd to play it before him, the queen, and his sons. When the shepherd played the song, the queen began to weep bitter tears, and the king said, "Let me play the bagpipe."

When he began to play, the bagpipe sang:

> Play me, play me, oh my father, my king,
> Play me merrily, as long as you like.
> On the banks of the Jordan I was killed with a rock.
> My eldest brother was the one who betrayed me.
> The other's not guilty, not guilty at all.
> It's only the eldest with blood on his hands.

After the king finished playing, he gave the bagpipe to the queen and said, "Now you play it."

---

[*]Sonami, sonami, miu viddanu,
   Chiù mi soni e chiù mi piaci;
   E pri tri pinni d'aceddu paùni
   Fui ammazzatu a lu sciumi Giurdanu,
   Di me frati, lu tradituri.
   Lu menzanu nun ci curpa,
   E lu granni va alla furca.

Play me, play me, oh my mother, my queen,
Play me merrily, as long as you like.
On the banks of the Jordan I was killed with a rock.
My eldest brother was the one who betrayed me.
The other's not guilty, not guilty at all.
It's only the eldest with blood on his hands.

After the mother played, the middle son took the bagpipe, which sang:

Play me, play me, oh my brother,
Play me merrily, as long as you like.
On the banks of the Jordan I was killed with a rock.
My eldest brother was the one who betrayed me.
The other's not guilty, not guilty at all.
It's only the eldest with blood on his hands.

When the king heard this song, he cried, "Now our eldest son is to play the bagpipe." Although he refused, the king forced him to play it, and the bagpipe sang:

Play me, play me, oh you filthy traitor,
Play me merrily, as long as you like.
On the banks of the Jordan I was killed with a rock.
My eldest brother was the one who betrayed me.
The other's not guilty, not guilty at all.
It's only the eldest with blood on his hands.

Now it was clear to everyone that the eldest brother had murdered the youngest brother, so the king had a gallows built and ordered his son be hanged. As for the shepherd, he received generous gifts from the king so that he would leave the bagpipe in the castle.

25

GIOVANNI AND KATERINA

Once upon a time there was a rich farmer who had a wife and two children, a boy named Giovanni and a girl named Katerina. He sent Katerina to a school to be taught by a teacher, who was always friendly to her and often asked, "Wouldn't you like me to be your mother?"

Katerina was little and did not understand things very well, so she answered, "Certainly. You give me a lot of sweets, and my mother gives me none."

One day the teacher said to her, "Katerina, if you'd really like me to be your mother, you must do what I say. When you return home today, ask your mother for a date from the large chest. Meanwhile, you're to hold the heavy lid for her, and when your mother bends over the chest to fetch a date, let the lid fall. Then lift it up again, and put a date in her mouth, and you'll see that I'll soon become your mother."

So Katerina went home and asked her mother for a date from the chest. When the mother bent over the chest, Katerina let the lid fall on the woman's neck and broke it. Then Katerina lifted the lid, stuck a date in her mother's mouth, and closed the chest.

When the father came home and saw his wife stuck in the lid of the chest, he ran over and opened the chest. When he saw her with the date in her mouth, he thought, "Her greedy appetite has caused her death."

And all the neighbors said, "Why didn't she just reach in and take the date with one hand the way everyone does?"

But the woman was dead and was soon buried.

After some time passed, the teacher spoke to Katerina again, "If you would like me to be your mother, then tell your father he should marry me. You and your brother would have it good with me."

Katerina told her father, but he answered, "Oh my child, don't believe what the teacher promises you. She would do what all stepmothers do and torment you."

But Katerina kept asking her father to marry the teacher, so her father hung a pair of iron boots over his bed and said, "Only when these boots become worn out will I marry your teacher."

So Katerina went to the teacher to ask for her advice, and the woman responded by saying, "Each morning when your father is in the fields, you must rub the boots in a puddle. Then the rust and dirt will wear them down."

Katerina did what the teacher told her to do, and after some months had passed, the boots had holes in them. Katerina showed them to her father and said, "Now, dear Father, you must marry my teacher."

"Good," the father answered. "But if she tortures and mistreats you afterward, don't come to me and complain."

So the farmer married the teacher, and things went well for the first month. However, the teacher had a daughter who was so ugly and dark that nobody could stand to look at her. Because Katerina became more beautiful with each passing day, the stepmother could not stand her anymore. At first she became cold and indifferent toward her, but soon she began to mistreat and beat her. She gave her very little to eat, and Katerina had to do all the dirty and heavy work. Poor Katerina wept often, but her father said to her, "Why didn't you want to listen to me? Now you'll just have to suffer."

One day the stepmother said to Katerina, "You lazy girl! You always keep your hands in your lap and do nothing. Here's a basket full of flax. I want you to spin it into yarn by this evening, and if you don't finish the job, you'll get a beating and nothing to eat. You might as well look after the sheep as well. If you just sit and spin the entire day, that's merely child's play."

After saying this, the stepmother gave Katerina a basket full of flax, which she would never have been able to spin into yarn in one day. Katerina took the flax and began to weep as she walked to the field where the sheep were grazing, and she sat down. The lead sheep came over and asked her why she was crying. So she told him about her misfortune and how the wicked stepmother was tormenting her.

"Just lie down and sleep," the sheep said. "I'll spin your flax for you."

Katerina lay down to sleep, and when she woke up, the yarn was there in the basket. Then she waited until evening when she went home and took the yarn to her stepmother, who was astonished. "Well now, you lazy girl," she said, "you see you can work when you want to."

The next morning the stepmother·gave her a larger basket of flax and once again sent her into the field where she wept and told the sheep about her troubles.

"Just lie down to sleep," the sheep said. "I'll spin the flax for you."

So Katerina lay down to sleep, and when she awoke, she saw that the flax had all been spun into yarn. Once again the stepmother was astounded when Katerina gave her the yarn, and she decided to follow her on the third day. She gave Katerina an even larger basket, and when Katerina went to the field again, she crept after her. She saw how Katerina lay down to sleep, and how the sheep, instead of the girl, spun the flax into yarn. As soon as the sheep touched the spinning wheel, the flax was immediately spun and turned into yarn. After watching this, the stepmother crawled back to the house, and later, when Katerina bought her the yarn, she said, "Listen, Katerina, tomorrow morning you must bring the lead sheep home because we want to slaughter it."

Katerina broke into tears, and the next morning she continued to weep as she went into the field.

"Katerina," the sheep asked, "why are you weeping again?"

"Shouldn't I weep?" she answered. "This evening I have to take you home with me to be slaughtered."

"Good," said the sheep. "Don't be so sad. When the butcher slaughters me, make sure that he gives you the intestines. Then you're to look for three little gold balls in them. Keep them in a safe place. They'll be of good use to you. But then you must flee the house with your brother because you can't stay there with your stepmother. Make sure, however, that you stay away from the sea. Otherwise, you'll become a sea serpent."

So Katerina took the sheep to the house where it was slaughtered. Katerina made sure she got the intestines and searched them until she found the three little gold balls. Then she called her brother Giovanni, and both of them left the house as quietly as they could.

After they had wandered for some time, they became so tired that they could hardly go any farther. Katerina took the three little gold balls and wished for a beautiful castle with a garden that surpassed even the castle that belonged to the king. She wished that she could live in the castle with her brother. All at once, she and Giovanni were transported to a marvelous castle where they began leading a glorious life, and next to it was a garden much more beautiful than the king's garden. However, the castle was situated on the seashore, and Katerina could never go out on the road nor into the beautiful garden. In fact, she could not even go near an open window and had to remain shut up in the castle.

Now, one day the king happened to go hunting and came by the castle. When he saw the marvelous garden, he stopped his horse and said, "How beautiful that garden is! It's even more beautiful than mine. I wish I could enter for a while."

Giovanni heard this and came to the gate and asked the king what he desired.

"May I go into your garden for a while?" the king asked.

"The garden doesn't belong to me," Giovanni answered, "but to my mistress. I'll go ask her if she will grant you permission to enter."

Then he rushed up to his sister and said, "Just think, Katerina! The king is here and wants to see our garden. Should I let him in?"

"Certainly," Katerina answered.

Giovanni led the king into the garden and showed him the beautiful flowers. The young man pleased the king so much that he asked him whether he wanted to come with him to his castle.

"First I must ask my mistress," Giovanni answered, and he ran to his sister and said, "Just think, Katerina! The king wants to take me to his castle."

"Go, Giovanni," Katerina responded. "I'm safe here. Who knows whether this might be our luck?"

So Giovanni went with the king and lived with him and became his first valet. The king became so fond of him that he treated him as a friend and often said to him, "Giovanni, I won't ever marry a maiden until you recommend her."

One time Giovanni answered, "Well now, your majesty, I have a sister who is as beautiful as the sun and more virtuous than any maiden in existence. She's the one you should marry."

"Very well," the king said. "Go to your sister and tell her that I'll come to fetch her tomorrow."

Giovanni rushed back to his sister and said to her, "Oh, just think, Katerina! Tomorrow the king wants to come to fetch you so that you will become his wife."

"Very good," said Katerina. "But I can't go out on the road. You must have a covered path made that leads from the window of my bedroom to the window in the royal castle."

Giovanni took a huge number of workers, and they had to work the entire day and night to build this covered path.

The next day, when the path was almost ready, two women suddenly knocked on the door of the castle. They were the stepmother and her daughter, who had heard all about the fame of Katerina's beauty. When they entered, they pretended to be very friendly, and the stepmother said to Katerina, "Oh, my dear Katerina, how long has it been since we last saw you! We heard that you had become a rich beautiful lady, and we've come to visit you."

Katerina received them in a polite way and began talking to them. Then, all at once, Giovanni called to her from the covered path. "Katerina, cover yourself in the royal cloak. We'll soon be finished."

Katerina could not understand him very well because she was not allowed to go to the open window, and she asked her stepmother, "What did my brother say?"

"Your brother said," the deceitful woman replied, "that you should step to the window."

As Katerina moved toward the window, she was suddenly transformed into a sea serpent and disappeared. Then the stepmother quickly put the cloak over her own daughter and ordered her to cover her face with her scarf.

When Giovanni was finished with the path, the false Katerina walked through it quickly so he would not have time to see her. Soon she came before the king and had to reveal her face. The king became very angry because she was so dark and ugly, and sent her and her mother to a solitary house in the forest where they had to remain. As for Giovanni, the king banished him. Of course, he did not know what was happening, but when he returned home and went into his sister's room and caught sight of the open window, everything became clear to him. He went to the king and told him what had happened. Because the king was still fond of him, he took him into his employ again and would often say, "Giovanni, Giovanni, you're so handsome and intelligent, but you did disappoint me one time."

As time went on, Giovanni became distressed by this, but he did not know how to rescue his sister.

Meanwhile, the deceitful stepmother lived with her daughter in the forest and thought about how she might also bring about Giovanni's downfall. One day she went to the king and said, "Just think what Giovanni intends to do. He wants to build three fountains in one night in your castle garden. The first fountain will be gushing with water, the second with oil, and the third with wine."

So the king summoned Giovanni and said to him, "I've heard how presumptuous you are. People tell me that you want to build three fountains with water, oil, and wine in one night in my park. Well, if the three fountains are not done by tomorrow morning, I shall banish you."

Giovanni was very depressed when he heard this and went to the beach near the sea. Once he arrived there he began to weep and call his sister, "Oh, Katerina, dear Katerina, what shall I do about my troubles?"

All at once the water began to rustle, and a sea serpent rose out of the water and said, "Here I am. What do you want?"

He poured out his heart about his troubles, and there was nothing left for him to do but to throw himself into the water. But she said, "Don't lose your courage. Take this magic wand and hit the ground in the castle courtyard with it at three different spots. Then three fountains will arise."

Giovanni took the magic wand, and during the night he went and hit the ground in the courtyard in three different places. As soon as he did this, three splendid fountains emerged, flowing with water, oil, and wine. When the king awoke and looked out his window, he was extremely happy about his servant's accomplishments and gave him some rich gifts.

Soon afterward the wicked stepmother came a second time and said, "Giovanni doesn't stop boasting about his talents and has presumed to build a crystal palace in one night, and it is supposed to have everything imaginable in it."

So the king had the poor Giovanni summoned to him and ordered him to build a crystal castle by the next morning. Nothing was to be missing, otherwise he would be banished. Giovanni went to the seashore once more and began weeping and calling for his sister. The sea serpent rose from the waves, and Giovanni told her about the king's new wishes. She gave him another magic wand and said, "If you hit the ground with this magic wand, an entire palace will appear."

In the evening he did this and just then a crystal palace emerged that was more beautiful than the king's palace. When the king saw Giovanni once more, he gave his faithful servant rich gifts and was more fond of him than ever before.

But the wicked stepmother was not satisfied, and went to the king again and said, "Giovanni has succeeded two times. Now he's boasted that he's going to create a major spectacle which seems to me presumptuous. He's said that he would build a huge oven with an enormous fire in one night, and then on his command, all the fish of the sea would come in single file and throw themselves into the flames."

"I'd like to see that," the king cried. He then summoned Giovanni and ordered him to bring about this extraordinary spectacle.

"How can I order the fish in the sea to do this?" Giovanni asked in a shocked voice.

"You've succeeded twice," the king said. "Now you've got to keep your word this time too, otherwise I'll have your head cut off."

Giovanni returned to the seashore, and while he wept, he called his sister. When she came, he poured out his troubles to her.

"Very well," she said. "Take this magic wand, go to the king, and tell him you will be ready to produce the spectacle tomorrow. He is to have some stands built so that the people will be able to see everything more comfortably. Then hit the ground with the magic wand, and the oven will arise. The fish will come tomorrow morning in single file and throw themselves into the fire. Make sure, however, that you do not catch any one of them, even if the king asks you to. At the very end, I shall come. Lean over the opening of the oven so that I can crawl onto your chest instead of throwing myself into the oven. Afterward you are to rush home, prepare a bathtub full of milk, and throw me into it. This is how I'll regain my human shape. Do everything as I tell you to do, otherwise I cannot be saved from this magic spell."

So Giovanni went to the king and asked him to build some stands at the seashore, and during the night he hit the ground with his magic wand. All at once an enormous oven with a gigantic fire emerged. The next morning the king and his court gathered at the seashore and took their places in the stands. Everyone from the city and surroundings had also come to this spot to see the wonderful spectacle. All of a sudden there were countless fish that emerged from the water in single file, the smallest first and the largest at the end. They threw themselves into the fire and shimmered in glistening colors. The king and all the spectators cried out, "Oh, Giovanni, give me this fish, or that one, or this one!"

But he kept answering, "Your majesty has ordered all the fish in the sea to be burned, and I want to burn *all* of them."

Finally the sea serpent came, and the king asked, "Oh, Giovanni, this is the last one. Give it to me."

"I'm supposed to burn all of them, and I shall burn all of them," Giovanni responded.

Upon saying this, he bent over the opening of the oven and, without being noticed, he slipped the sea serpent beneath his shirt next to his chest. Then he rushed home where the bath of milk was standing ready. He threw the serpent into it, and immediately his beautiful sister appeared again, more beautiful than she had been before. Imagine how brother and sister were overjoyed when the magic spell had been broken!

The next morning Giovanni did not go to see the king at his customary time, and when the king awoke, he was furious not to see his faithful servant. He sent a messenger to the castle to summon him. When the messenger knocked at the door, Katerina said to her brother, "Why don't you just rest quietly where you are? I'll answer the door."

When she went to the window, however, the messenger was so struck by her marvelous beauty that he stared at her with an open mouth and could not utter a word. The king sent all his messengers and noblemen one after the other, but none of them returned, for as soon as they caught sight of the beautiful maiden, they were all transfixed on the spot.

Finally the king became impatient, and he himself went to the castle. Katerina saw him coming, withdrew quickly from the window, and said to her brother, "Go down to the door yourself this time and welcome the king."

The king was astounded and asked his servants why none of them had come back. They told him they had seen a maiden who was so marvelously beautiful that they could not move from the spot. At the same time, Giovanni came out and said, "Your majesty, my sister has returned, and if you still want to follow my advice and choose her for your wife, you may have my sister Katerina."

The king went into the castle, and when he saw Katerina, he was so delighted by her beauty that he immediately cried out: "Yes, you and no other shall be my wife."

Then Katerina was dressed in costly royal clothes, and a splendid wedding was celebrated. Meanwhile, the wicked stepmother and her ugly daughter had to remain in the solitary forest until they died.

26

THE SHEPHERD WHO MADE
THE PRINCESS LAUGH

Once upon a time there was a king and queen. They had just one daughter, whom they loved with all their heart. When the princess turned fifteen, she suddenly became very sad and melancholy and refused to laugh anymore. So the king had it announced throughout his realm that whoever could make his daughter laugh, no matter whether he was a prince, a duke, a peasant, or a beggar, he would be given the princess as his wife. Yet no matter how many men tried, none of them succeeded.

Now there was also a poor woman, who had just one son, and he was lazy and did not want to learn any handicraft. His mother finally decided to send him to a farmer to help him look after the sheep. One day, while the young shepherd was driving the sheep over some fields, he came to a fountain, and because he was thirsty he leaned over to drink. As he did this, he saw a beautiful ring lying on the edge of the fountain, and because he liked it so much, he put it on the ring finger of his right hand. No sooner did he do this than he began to sneeze something terrible and could not stop until he accidentally slipped the ring off his finger, when he immediately stopped sneezing.

"Oh," he thought, "if the ring has this power, I can try my luck with it and see if I can get the princess to laugh."

When he stuck the ring on the left hand, it was different—he did not have to sneeze. Well, he took the sheep back to the farmer, demanded his earnings, and traveled to the city where the king lived.

To get there he had to go through a dark forest that was so large that it became evening before he could find his way out.

"If robbers find me here," he thought, "they'll take the ring away from me, and I'll be a beaten man. I had better climb a tree and spend the night there."

So he climbed a tree, tied himself in the branches with his belt, and soon fell asleep. Shortly thereafter thirteen robbers came and sat down beneath the tree in which the shepherd was sleeping. They spoke so loud that he was wakened by them.

"Tell me what each one of you managed to do today," said the chief of the robbers, and each one of them revealed what he had taken. The thirteenth took out a tablecloth, a purse, and a little flute and said, "Today I got the greatest treasures, which I took from a monk, and each one of them has a special power. If you spread out the tablecloth and say, 'Tablecloth, my tablecloth, give me macaroni, or a roast, or whatever food you want,'* everything will appear before you in one second. If you say to the purse, 'Purse, my purse, give me money,'† it will give you as much money as you want. And if you begin to blow on the flute, anyone who hears the music must dance, whether he likes it or not."

"Yes indeed," the robber chief said, "they're certainly valuable things. Now we'll never have to worry for the rest of our lives."

Then he took the tablecloth and spread it on the ground, "Tablecloth, my tablecloth, give me macaroni, some roast beef, a salad, and good wine," and all of a sudden everything stood there.

After they had eaten and drunk some wine, the robbers laid down to sleep, and the chief put the tablecloth, the purse, and the flute next to him. When they were all snoring loudly, the shepherd climbed down from the tree, took the three objects, and crept away from the spot. He was fortunate to have escaped. Indeed, the robbers had drunk so much of the good wine that they slept soundly and did not hear a thing.

The next day the shepherd came to the city where the king was living and went straight to the castle dressed as he was.

"Announce me to the king," he said to the servants. "I want to try to make the princess laugh."

"Oh, don't even bother," they answered. "Many men have tried, and nobody has succeeded yet, and a dirty shepherd like you doesn't have a chance."

---

*Tuvagghiedda mia, nesci maccarruni, stufatu, o zoccu si voli.

† Virzottu miu, nesci dinari.

"Why not?" he demanded. "The king announced that anyone who wanted could try whether it be a farmer or a beggar. Therefore, you've got to announce me."

So they led him to the king, who said, "All right, follow me to the princess."

He went with the king and entered a large hall in which the princess was sitting on a beautiful throne surrounded by all the people of the court.

"If I'm to get the princess to laugh," the shepherd said to the king, "you must first do me the favor of putting this ring on the ring finger of your right hand."

No sooner had the king done this than he started to sneeze something terrible. He could not stop and ran sneezing up and down the hall. Everyone at the court began to laugh, and even the princess could not keep a serious face and ran laughing from the room. Then the shepherd went up to the king, took the ring off his finger, and said, "Your majesty, I've made the princess laugh, and I deserve the reward."

"What!" the king cried. "You good for nothing shepherd! First you made me the laughingstock of the entire court, and now you demand my daughter as your bride? Quick, take that ring away from him and throw him into prison!"

Immediately the servants seized the poor shepherd and threw him into the jail where many other prisoners were sitting. The prisoners received only bread and water every day, but now the shepherd was delighted to take out his tablecloth to wish himself a good meal and share it with all his companions. When the guards saw this, they went to the king and told him about it. The king ran straight to the prison with his servants and had the tablecloth taken away from the shepherd.

"Well," thought the shepherd, "I still have the purse," and the next morning he took it out and said, "Oh purse, my purse, give me some money." And the purse immediately produced as much money as he wanted. He used the money to bribe one of the prison guards, who brought him and his companions some good food and wine.

This is how things went for several days until the other prison guards discovered what was happening and told the king, who came once again with his servants, and they took the purse away from the shepherd.

"Now," thought the shepherd, "if we can't eat anymore, we can at least dance."

So he took the flute out, and no sooner did he begin to blow than all the prisoners began to dance and the guards with them. Soon there was a lot of noise. When the king heard it, he came running once more

176

with his servants, but the servants began to dance right away and the king as well, whether he wanted to or not.

"Take the flute away from the good-for-nothing shepherd," he yelled while he was dancing, and finally one of the servants succeeded in taking the flute away from the shepherd. Gradually they all calmed down, and the king left with the flute. Now the shepherd had nothing more and stayed in the prison for some time until one day he found an old file in the corner of his cell. So he filed some of the iron bars in the prison window at night until he was fortunate enough to escape.

He traveled day and night and finally came to the same forest in which he had already spent the night. Suddenly he saw a large date tree standing before him, and it was bearing some beautiful dates. On one side there were black dates, and on the other, white.

"I've never seen this before," the shepherd thought. "A date tree with black and white dates at the same time. I've got to try them!"

So he picked some of the black dates and ate them. No sooner did he swallow them than he felt something move on his head, and when he ran his hand through his hair he noticed that two horns had sprouted on his head.

"Oh, poor me!" he cried. "What should I do now?"

Because he was still very hungry, he picked some of the white dates and ate them. And imagine what happened! All of a sudden one of the horns disappeared, and when he ate some more white dates, the other also disappeared.

"Now I'm a made man," he thought, "and the king will have to give me back all my things and his daughter as well!"

He set out for the farmer's place and asked him to lend him some other clothes and two baskets, which he filled with white and black dates. Then he disguised himself as a farmer and went to the city. At the marketplace he met the royal cook, who wanted to buy fruit for the king's table. He showed him the beautiful black dates, and they pleased the cook so much that he immediately bought the entire basket.

Later, when the king sat down to eat, and the servant placed the beautiful dates before him, he was very happy and gave some to his wife and some to his daughter, and he ate the rest himself. No sooner did they swallow the dates than they were horrified to see that large horns had grown on their heads. The queen and princess began to weep while the king became infuriated and summoned the cook and asked him where he had bought the dates.

"I got them from a farmer at the marketplace," the cook replied.

"Well, go there and bring him here right away!"

Meanwhile, the shepherd had remained in the vicinity of the royal castle. When the cook came out, he went straight over to the shepherd, who held the basket with the white dates in his hand.

"What bad dates you sold me this morning!" the cook yelled at him. "As soon as the king, the queen, and the princess ate them, large horns grew on their heads."

"Calm down," the shepherd said. "I have an antidote for all this and can drive the horns away. Just lead me to the king!"

So he was led to the king, who screamed at him and told him that he had sold his cook rotten dates.

"Calm down, your majesty," the shepherd said, "and eat this date."

He handed the king a white date, and when the king ate it, one of his horns vanished.

"You see what I can do," the shepherd said. "But before I give you more of these dates, you must give my flute back to me, otherwise the other horn will remain on your head."

Because the king was scared to death, he gave the shepherd the flute, and then the shepherd gave the queen a date. When the one horn disappeared from her head, he said, "Now give me back my purse, otherwise I'll take my dates with me and leave!"

So the king gave him the purse. Next the shepherd drove away a horn from the princess's head and demanded the tablecloth. After the king had returned it to him, he handed the king another date so that the second horn disappeared from the king's head.

"Now give me my ring," the shepherd said. The king had to give him the ring before the shepherd would drive the second horn from the queen's head. Now, only the princess had a horn on her head, and the shepherd said, "Fulfill your promise, and let me wed the princess. Otherwise, she can keep the horn for the rest of her life."

So the princess was obliged to marry the shepherd, and after the wedding he gave her another date to eat so that the last horn vanished. Then they had a huge celebration, and when the old king died, the shepherd became king. And so they were happy and content, and we've remained without a cent.*

---

*In German: Und so blieben sie zufrieden und glücklich und wir wie ein Bündel Wurzeln. Italian: Iddi restaro contenti e felici e noi restammo come un mazzo di radici.

27

BEAUTIFUL CARDIA

Once upon a time there was a king who had three beautiful daughters and one son. When he felt that he was about to die, he called his son to him and said, "My son, I'm going to die, and you'll become king and must take charge of your three sisters. Take care of them and listen to what I have to say. There is a carnation bush on the terrace that will sprout three buds. Pay attention to when the first bud opens. You are to give your oldest sister to the first man who walks by. You are to do this also with your second and third sisters and marry them off to the first men who come by when the buds open."

Then the father died, and his son became king. Every day he went to the terrace and looked at the carnation bush. It did not take long before the bush sprouted three buds that became larger and larger until one morning the first bud blossomed into a beautiful carnation. The young king picked the carnation and leaned over the terrace. At the very same moment a handsome nobleman came by, and the prince called out to him, "Sir, take this carnation from me and give me the honor of your presence in my castle."

When the young man came into the castle, the prince asked him who he was.

"I'm the king of the ravens," the stranger answered.

Then the young king asked him whether he would take his oldest sister as his wife, and the king of the ravens agreed. Soon a beautiful wedding was celebrated, and the king of the ravens took his young wife with him into the countryside. Her brother never heard from her again.

After a few days passed, the second carnation blossomed, and the king picked it and bent over the terrace. Just then a handsome young man came by, and the king handed him the carnation and invited him into the castle. When he asked him who he was, the young man answered, "I'm the king of the wild animals."

So the young king gave him his second sister as his wife, and after the wedding the king of the wild animals and his wife departed. Now the king was alone with his youngest sister and became very sad whenever he looked at the bud that was soon to blossom. He loved his sister very much and did not want to separate from her, but he could not go against the last will of his father. One morning, when he saw that a beautiful carnation had just blossomed on the bush, he picked it and offered it to a handsome nobleman who had just walked by, and he invited him into the castle. When he asked him who he was, the stranger answered, "I'm the king of the birds." The king gave him his youngest sister as his bride, and after the wedding she had to depart with her husband.

Now that the king was left completely alone, he became very sad and could not stop thinking about his sisters. One day he happened to be wandering in a field and was feeling despondent, when he met an old woman who asked him why he was so melancholy.

"Oh, leave me in peace, old woman," he answered. "Isn't it enough that I'm depressed? Do I have to tell you the reason for it?"

The old woman, however, followed him and kept asking him questions until he finally became so furious that he pushed her rudely away from him, and she fell to the ground. Now the old woman was enraged and cried out, "May you forever wander without peace and rest until you have found Cardia, my soul, help me!"*

Then the king became even sadder than he had been, and he was overcome by a great yearning to find this Cardia. Indeed, the yearning grew until he could not bear it any longer, and he set out to search for her.

The king traveled many, many days, but nobody could tell him where he might find Cardia. Finally he came to a dark forest, and when he wandered about for a while, he saw a pretty cottage in the distance. There was a woman standing at the window, and when he approached her, he saw that it was his oldest sister. She recognized him right away and rushed to him and embraced him full of joy.

---

*Cardia, anima mia, dammi riparu.

"My dear brother," she said, "how did you find your way into this wilderness? Oh, if only I could make sure that my husband doesn't see you!"

"Would your husband actually harm me?" the king asked.

"Oh," she replied, "when he comes home, he wants to tear apart anyone he doesn't know. After he has calmed down, he's good and friendly to everyone."

So the sister hid her brother in the cellar, and when her husband came home, he said, "It's as though your brother were here. Well, if he appears, I'll tear him to pieces."

His wife talked him out of this idea, and when he had calmed down, she said, "Now, what would you do if you saw my brother?"

"I would embrace him and give him a hearty welcome."

Then she happily called her brother out of the cellar, and the king of the ravens embraced him and asked him why he was traveling about so alone. The king told him how and why he had set out to search for Cardia, and the king of the ravens gave him an almond and said, "Keep this in a safe place. It will be of use to you."

The king continued his wandering, and after some days had passed, he came once again to a pretty cottage, which was inhabited by his second sister. She was happy to see him, but she had to hide him.

"If my husband sees you," she said, "he'll rip you apart. After he has calmed down, I'll call you."

So she hid him in the cellar, and when her husband came and asked whether her brother had been there, she talked him out of the idea of ripping him apart. Later, when he was calmer, she called her brother, and the king of the wild animals embraced him and gave him a hearty welcome. After he heard that the young king had set out to find the beautiful Cardia, he gave him a chestnut and said, "Keep this in a safe place. It will be of use to you."

Then the king traveled for many days until he finally came to the house where his youngest sister lived. She embraced him with great joy, but things were just as difficult here as they had been with his other sisters. He had to hide in order not to infuriate the king of the birds. When his sister's husband calmed down, she called her brother, and the king of the birds welcomed him with great joy. After he heard why the king had left his realm, he gave him a nut and said, "Keep this in a safe place. It will be of use to you. You are not far from Cardia. If you go farther into the forest, you'll eventually reach a witch's house, which is where Cardia is living. However, there are many other beautiful maidens living there, and whoever wants the beautiful Cardia must be able to choose her from all of them. They are all veiled, but don't worry. Cardia has seven veils. The others have only two. Because you know this, you can't go wrong."

So the king continued on his travels and went deeper into the forest until he came to the witch's house, where Cardia was living. Then he boldly stepped before the old witch and said, "I've come for the beautiful Cardia and want to take her with me as my wife."

"Wonderful," the old witch said, "but whoever wants the beautiful Cardia has to earn her and complete three tasks."

"Tell me what I have to do," the king answered, "and I'll do it."

In the evening the old witch led him into a large cellar filled with beans from top to bottom.

"These beans must disappear by tomorrow morning," she said. "I don't care whether you eat them or what you do with them, but if I find one single bean I'm going to eat you!"

Upon saying this she locked the young king in the cellar, and he stood there helpless staring at the large supply of beans. As he was standing there, he thought, "There's nothing left for me to do except get ready for my death." But then it occurred to him that he had the almond that the king of the ravens had given to him. So he bit it, and as soon as he did, the king of the ravens appeared before him and asked him what he desired. The young king told him about his desperate situation, and the king of the ravens gave a whistle. All at once a large flock of ravens flew into the cellar and asked, "What does our lord command?"

"Eat all the beans you can find, and don't leave a single one on the ground."

The ravens began pecking the beans, and within minutes the cellar was empty and there was not a single bean to be found. However, the ravens and their king had vanished just as fast as they had appeared.

When the witch opened the door to the cellar the next morning, she was already looking forward to roasting the king. But she found him standing in an empty cellar, for he had fulfilled the first task.

"Who helped you?" the witch asked.

"Who could have helped me?" he answered. "You yourself locked the door. I ate all the beans."

That evening the witch led him into another cellar filled with corpses.

"This is your second task," she said. "Do you see all these corpses? They are the corpses of all the princes and kings who tried to win the beautiful Cardia. You have until tomorrow morning to clean the cellar of all these corpses, and if I find even a little bone or a tiny hair, I'll eat you."

She shut the door, and the young king stood there once again without knowing what to do. Then he bit the chestnut, and all at once the king of the wild animals appeared and asked him what he desired. When he told him about his troubles, the king of the wild animals gave a whistle, and immediately the place was teeming with wild animals of the forest.

"What is your command, oh lord?" they asked.

"Clean away all the corpses from this cellar, and don't leave a single one."

The animals plunged on the corpses and devoured them in an instant. Nothing was left to see. Then the animals and their king disappeared just as fast as they had come.

The next morning the witch opened the door and was astonished to see that the king had completed the second task just as she had ordered.

"Now comes the hardest," she said, "and if you can't do the third task, there will be nothing to help you."

She led him into a large room with a lot of empty mattresses on the floor.

"You have until tomorrow morning to fill all these mattresses with the finest, softest feathers. Otherwise, I shall eat you."

After the door was closed, the king quickly grabbed the nut and cracked it open. All at once the king of the birds appeared. When he heard what his brother-in-law wished, he gave a whistle, and a great flock of birds came flying into the room.

"What does our lord command?" they asked.

"Shake off all your fluff, and let it all fall into the empty mattresses."

The birds shook themselves so that their fluff flew into the mattresses until they were all filled. Afterward they disappeared, and the king went with them.

The next morning the witch opened the door and found every single mattress filled with feathers, so the third task had also been completed.

"Now you must choose the beautiful Cardia from among all her companions. Otherwise, nothing will help you," the witch said, and she led the king into a large hall in which there were many beds, and on each bed was a heavily veiled maiden. So the king touched many of the maidens to count their veils, and each time the witch was delighted because she hoped she would be able to eat him. However, he did not say a word until he finally came to a maiden who was covered with seven veils. Then he ripped off the seven veils and cried, "This is my Cardia, and she is to become my wife."

Although the old witch had no choice but to admit that he had selected the right maiden, she kept thinking of a way that she might be able to cause his ruin and said, "Very well, my children, you will marry today. But if, by tomorrow morning, you don't show me a little grandchild that says 'grandmother' to me, I'm going to eat you both."

So the marriage was celebrated, and the other young girls served the beautiful Cardia as bridal maids. Later, after the witch had sent the young married couple into the bridal suite, the young girls made a small doll that Cardia took with her into the bed.

The next morning the witch came at daybreak* and called out, "Well, is my little grandchild there?"

Cardia answered her by disguising her voice: "Grandma, Grandma," and showed the doll to the witch. However, when the witch bent over the bed to see the child, the king jumped up and cut off her head with his sword. Now their joy was complete. The young girls thanked the king, who had freed them from the wicked witch, and they all returned to their homes. The young king and Cardia set out through the forest to return to their realm, and along the way they found the king of the birds, the king of the wild animals, and the king of the ravens, who thanked the king because he had also released them from a magic spell. Now they no longer had to live in the dark forest. Instead, they took their wives and moved with the king and Cardia to their court, and they all lived happily and content.

---

*Pi faci la bona livata.—On the morning after the wedding the young pair is generally visited very early and must offer chocolate to the guests. This means that one does "la buon levata." This was a custom that was also practiced by the upper classes.

28

QUADDARUNI AND HIS SISTER

Once upon a time there were two sisters. One was rich, the other poor. The rich sister had a daughter who was ugly and unfriendly. The poor sister had two children, a son named Quaddaruni, and a daughter who was more beautiful than the moon and the sun. The poor sister went every morning to her rich sister to help her wash, cook, and sew. For all this work, the rich sister gave her leftovers from the meals that she later took to her children. Such was the miserable way she fed her children.

One day, however, she was not feeling well and could not go to her sister. Instead, the rich lady came to see how she was doing, and on this occasion she also saw her beautiful niece.

"What do you give your daughter to eat?" she asked her sister.

"What do you think I give her? I have nothing but what you give me as leftovers," the poor sister replied.

Now, the rich sister went home, and her heart was full of envy because her niece was so beautiful and her own daughter so ugly. When the poor sister soon returned to serve her, the rich woman stopped giving her the measly leftovers. Instead she gave her some bread that was normally baked for the dogs. Still, in spite of the terrible food, the poor woman's daughter continued to flower and became more beautiful with each passing day.

Now, one day the poor woman did not feel well again and became extremely thirsty. She called her son Quaddaruni and said, "Dear son, go to the well and fetch me a jug of water. I'm very thirsty."

"I can't go right now," he answered.

Then her daughter said, "Oh Mother, I'll go, and I'll bring you the water in a jiffy."

"No, no, my child," the mother spoke. "How could you go to the well all alone?"

"Let me go, dear Mother. Nobody will harm me," the beautiful maiden said, and she took the jug and went to the well. After she had filled the jug and was about to go home, she encountered seven young men, who said, "Beautiful maiden, give us something to drink."

She handed them the jug politely with her eyes lowered, and no matter how much they drank, the jug never became empty, for she had met seven wizards.* After they had quenched their thirst, they thanked her and returned the jug to her. Then she departed, and they were impressed by her fine manners. One of the wizards said to the other, "Shouldn't we give this friendly maiden a gift? I want her to become more beautiful with each passing day."

"And I'm going give her a special gift of speech, the second wizard said. "With each word that she utters, a dozen roses will fall from her mouth."

"When she combs her hair," the third one said, "pearls and precious stones will fall to the ground."

The fourth one declared, "She will marry a great king."

In short, each one gave her a gift.

When she returned home, she said to her mother, "Here, dear Mother, I've brought you some fresh water," and as soon as she said this, some roses fell to the ground, and they smelled so sweet that the entire house was filled with their aroma.

"My child, what's happened to you?" her mother cried out in astonishment.

Then she told her mother how seven young men had asked her for a drink of water and how the jug never became empty. With each word she uttered, a rose fell from her lips. When she later began combing her beautiful braids, pearls and precious stones fell out of her hair so that everything shone radiantly.

"Now we shall never need anything," the mother said, "and I'll never have to go to my rich sister anymore."

---

*Fati masculi.

When the poor sister stopped showing up at her rich sister's house, the rich woman went to her one day and asked her why she was no longer coming to her house.

"I don't need to anymore," the sister said.

Just then the beautiful daughter entered, and with each word she spoke, a dozen roses fell from her lips.

"What's happened to my niece?" the rich sister asked.

Then her sister told her how her daughter had gone to the well, and the seven wizards must have given her these magical gifts.*

"Oh," the rich sister thought, "now I'll also send my daughter to this well."

She ran home and said to her daughter, "Dear child, go to the well and fetch me a jug of water. I'm so thirsty."

"Fetch it yourself," her daughter answered in an unfriendly way. But the mother continued to ask her and flatter her until the maiden finally took the jug, while still complaining, and went to the well.

"If someone asks you for a drink of water, make sure that you're friendly," her mother called after her, but the girl went off without paying attention to her mother's words.

After she had filled the jug at the well and wanted to return to her mother, she met the seven young men. They asked her for a drink of water, but she answered, "There's a whole well full of water over there. Go and fetch it yourself."

The seven wizards looked at her as she arrogantly walked by them, and the first one said, "Well now, let's give her some gifts. I'm going to have her get uglier with each passing day."

"With every word that she speaks, filthy things will fall out," said the second.

"When she combs her hair, scorpions, beetles, and snakes will fall out of her hair," declared the third.

"I shall wish that she will only have one eye," the fourth said.

"As for me, I am going to give her a hunchback," the fifth wizard added.

In short, each one of them wished for something bad.

By the time the girl returned home, she was so ugly, hunchbacked, and one-eyed that her mother was horrified.

"Here's the water," her daughter said, and as she said this, filthy things fell out of her mouth. When she combed her hair, scorpions, beetles, and snakes fell out. Her mother tore her hair out and was

---

*La pòttiru infatare.

completely desperate, but nothing helped, and her daughter became uglier with each passing day. In contrast, her cousin became more beautiful with each day, and because a rose fell from her lips with each word she uttered, all the people called her "beauty with the beautiful flowers."*

The roses were so beautiful and smelled so lovely that they were much better than the king's. Therefore, Quaddaruni gathered the roses, made bouquets out of them, and took them to the city to sell. One day he happened to pass by the royal palace just as the king was standing on his balcony. When he saw the roses, he called to Quaddaruni to come up, and he bought all the flowers from the young man.

"Where did you get these beautiful roses?" he asked him.

"I have a rosebush at home, and they grow there," Quaddaruni answered.

"Bring the rosebush to me tomorrow," the king said, "and I'll give you whatever you want for it."

"Oh, your majesty," Quaddaruni replied very frightened, "I can't bring the rosebush to you. I wouldn't sell it for anything in the world."

"If you don't bring me the rosebush, I'll have your head chopped off," the king declared.

Then Quaddaruni fell to the king's feet and said, "Oh, your majesty, I must confess the truth to you. I don't get these flowers from my rosebush. Rather, I have a sister at home who is more beautiful than the sun. With each word that she speaks, a rose falls from her lips."

When the king heard this, he cried, "Bring your sister to me, and if she is really as beautiful as you say, I swear to you that I shall make her my wife."

So Quaddaruni set out and returned to his mother and sister and cried out, "Just think, dear sister, the king wants to see you and swore to me that he would make you his wife! Get ready because tomorrow you must go to the court with me."

When their mother heard this, she was very happy and said, "Yes, my dear son, but take the small boat tomorrow so that your sister doesn't arrive at the court too exhausted. And if the king really chooses her for his wife, let me know so that I can also come to the city."

She began preparing the pretty dress that her daughter was to wear, and on the next morning the brother and sister were to travel to the city. That evening, however, the rich sister came by for a visit out of nowhere, and when she heard that the two of them were going to the

---

*Abedda ddi beddi sciuri.

court, she said, "Dear niece, do me a favor and take my daughter with you. Perhaps the king will take her in his employ."

"What? Your daughter!" Quaddaruni cried. "We don't want to take her! She's much too ugly!"

"My son," his mother scolded. "Don't speak like that. What can the poor maiden do about it if she's so ugly? Take your poor cousin with you."

"But only two people can fit in the little boat," Quaddaruni said.

"Well, let the two girls ride in it, and you go on foot," his mother answered.

And this is what they did.

The beautiful maiden and her cousin sailed in the boat, and Quaddaruni went along the seashore. When they had gone about a mile, he called to his sister:

"Sister, sister of the beautiful flowers,
Wear this kerchief, do it for me.
Cover yourself, for the sun shines brightly,
Or else you won't make your way on the sea."*

Because they were so far from one another, his sister could not hear him very well and asked her cousin, "What's my brother saying?"

"He said that you should take off your veil and give it to me," the deceitful maiden said.

So the beautiful sister took off the veil and gave it to her cousin. After a while Quaddaruni cried out again:

"Sister, sister of the beautiful flowers,
Wear this kerchief, do it for me.
Cover yourself, for the sun shines brightly,
Or else you won't make your way on the sea."

"What's my brother saying?" the beautiful girl asked.

"He said you should take off your dress and give it to me," the cousin replied.

After some more time passed, Quaddaruni cried out again:

---

* Soru ddi beddi sciuri,
  Mettiti stu jancu muccaturi,
  Cuvertiti chi c'è lu suli
  Si no tu non pòi navigà,

"Sister, sister of the beautiful flowers,
Wear this kerchief, do it for me.
Cover yourself, for the sun shines brightly,
Or else you won't make your way on the sea."

"What did my brother say?" the sister asked.

"He said you should look into the sea."

When the beautiful maiden leaned over the boat, the deceitful cousin pushed her into the sea so that she sank right into the water. Now the ugly maiden put on her cousin's dress and covered her face with the veil. When the boat arrived in the harbor, Quaddaruni rushed to it and thought that he was fetching his sister. At the same time he asked what had happened to their cousin.

"Oh, she fell into the water," the false cousin answered, "and she probably drowned."

Then they went to the king, and Quaddaruni said, "Your majesty, here is my beautiful sister."

But when the king lifted her veil and saw her ugly face, he became infuriated and wanted to have Quaddaruni's head chopped off. The poor young man fell to the king's feet and cried out, "Your majesty, that's really not my sister. That's my ugly cousin, and she undoubtedly has thrown my sister into the sea and tricked me and everyone else."

So the king ordered the ugly maiden to be locked in a room and given only bread and water. As for Quaddaruni, he was to remain at the court and look after the king's ducks and geese.

In his sadness, Quaddaruni drove the ducks and geese to the seashore and began to weep, "Oh, my sister, my dead sister, now you're gone! What am I to tell our poor mother?"

All at once the waves began to rustle, and his sister emerged from the water. She had become even more beautiful than before and said, "Dear brother, don't cry. I didn't die. A siren of the sea captured me and has tied me with a golden chain and is holding me tight. However, she's allowed me to come to you for a little while."

Well, Quaddaruni was very pleased and embraced his sister. Then he said, "Oh, I can't stay here. I've got to drive the ducks and the geese out to pasture."

"Don't worry," she said and shook her braids. All of a sudden seeds and barley fell from her hair, and the ducks and geese ate until they were full. Meanwhile, the brother and sister talked until the siren pulled on the golden chain, and the beautiful maiden with the beautiful flowers was dragged back into the sea. Quaddaruni gathered together the ducks and geese, and when he returned to the castle they began to quack,

"Quack, quack, quack,
We've come from the sea
Where we were fed sweetly
Grain and barley
By the beautiful sister of Quaddaruni."*

The servants heard this and were astounded by it, but they did not say anything. The next morning Quaddaruni drove the birds to the seashore again, and when he called for his sister, she arose right away from the water and shook her braids so that seeds and grain fell out and the ducks and geese could eat until they were full. Then she talked with Quaddaruni until the siren pulled on the golden chain and dragged her into the sea. When the geese and ducks returned to the yard, they began once more to quack,

"Quack, quack, quack,
We've come from the sea
Where we were fed sweetly
Grain and barley
By the beautiful sister of Quaddaruni."

This is the way everything went for several days until the servants finally told the king about it. He summoned Quaddaruni and asked him where he drove the ducks and geese, and Quaddaruni told him everything.

"Now, if this is true," the king cried, "ask your sister how she can be released from the siren's magic power, and we shall help her."

So Quaddaruni went to the seashore and called his sister, and when she came, he asked her how he could rescue her.

"I've got to ask the siren," the beautiful maiden said. "Come here tomorrow, and I'll give you the answer."

So she returned to the bottom of the sea, went to the siren, and spoke to her with flattering words, "Dear Mother, I had an idea today. It's not what I want, but just for conversation's sake, I'd like to ask you a question, and yet I also hesitate to ask it."

"Well, speak. Out with it," the siren said.

---

*Qua, qua, qua,
   Di la marina semu vinuti,
   E la soru di Quaddaruni,
   Chi è cchiù bella di lu suli,
   Granu e oriu n'ha datu a mancià.

"You really have to believe that I don't wish to get away," the beautiful maiden said. "I'm just making conversation, but if someone would want to take me away from you, what would he have to do?"

"All right, my child," the siren said. "If I tell this to you, I know you'll leave me."

"Why should I leave you?" the maiden said. "I have it good here, and you're very fond of me."

"Well then," the siren replied, "whoever would want to free you would have to have three sharp swords, seven fast horses, and an iron club.* Then he must lay the golden chain on the iron club, chop it up with the seven swords, and harness the seven horses to a wagon so that he can flee with you as fast as lightning."

"Oh, let it be, Mother," the cunning maiden said, "I don't want to hear anymore. I don't want to think about leaving you at all."

But the next morning, when she heard her brother's voice, she climbed out of the water onto the seashore and told him everything that the siren had revealed to her. Then Quaddaruni went to the king, who said, "Tomorrow, we shall rescue your sister. I'm going to get everything ready right away."

The next day the king, Quaddaruni, and several servants traveled to the seashore and took seven swords, seven horses, and an iron club with them. Then Quaddaruni called his sister, and when she emerged from the sea, she was so beautiful that the king could not take his eyes off her. Meanwhile, the servants quickly placed the golden chain on the club and began to chop it with a sword. As soon as one of the swords broke, they used another. Finally, they broke the chain in two with the seventh sword, and at that very same moment the siren pulled the chain back to the bottom of the sea. When she saw that her prisoner had been set free, she swiftly emerged from the sea and appeared at the seashore, but the king had already put the beautiful maiden into the wagon, and the seven horses carried them away from there as fast as lightning so that the siren could not catch up with them.

The king held three days of festivities and had the mother of his beautiful bride come to the city. Then they celebrated a splendid wedding. As for the false bride, he had her cut into pieces, salted, and stuck into a barrel. Her head was placed on top. Then he had the barrel sent to her mother, and the messenger was to tell her that it was a barrel full of tuna that her daughter, the young queen, had sent her. When the mother received the barrel, she was very pleased and opened it right

---

*Mazza.

away. But when she saw her daughter's head, she was so horrified that she fell dead to the ground.

The king and the queen lived happy and content, and we can't even pay the rent.

29

THE DAUGHTER OF THE SUN

O nce upon a time there was a king and queen who had no children and would have liked very much to have either a little boy
or little girl. So, the king summoned a fortune-teller who had
to predict whether they would have children.

"The queen will give birth to a daughter," the fortune-teller said,
"and in her fourteenth year she will be made pregnant by the sun."

When the king heard this, he was frightened, and he said to the fortune-teller, "If what you predict is true, you will be richly rewarded."

Not long after this the queen noticed that she was going to have
a child. The king thought, "The fortune-teller was right. If one of
his predictions has come true, the other is bound to follow." So he
rewarded the man with rich gifts as he had promised and had a tower
built without windows in a desolate region, and he made sure that the
rays of the sun would not be able to penetrate it.

When the queen gave birth to a beautiful baby girl, the king had
the child locked in the tower with her nurse. It was there that the child
grew up, flowered, and became more and more beautiful with each passing day. When she was almost fourteen years old, her parents sent her
a roasted goat, and as the princess was eating it, she found a sharp bone
in one of the pieces of the meat. She took it, and, just to pass the time,
she began scratching the wall. Soon a small hole was made, and she dug
deeper. All of a sudden a ray of sun penetrated the room and also penetrated her, and because she had just turned fourteen, the fortune-teller's

prophesy was immediately fulfilled. The nurse could not get over her astonishment, and one day, when the king came for a visit, she began to tremble with fear and told him what had happened to the princess.

"It was her fate," the king said, "and she could not avoid it."

When the time came, the princess gave birth to a little daughter who was the most beautiful girl in the world. How could it be otherwise since she was the daughter of the sun? They wrapped the baby in diapers and put her outside in the garden next to the tower, but the king took his daughter back to his castle.

The poor child lay in the garden and would have certainly died of starvation, but it so happened that the prince from a neighboring country had gone hunting this very same day and somehow made his way to this desolate region. As he rode by the garden, he looked into it and saw beautiful lettuce growing inside and had an urge to eat some. So he went into the garden, but when he approached the lettuce, he saw a beautiful baby lying between him and the lettuce. Feeling sorry for the child, the prince picked her up in his arms, called his servants, and said, "Look at this beautiful child! What kind of a despicable mother could abandon her baby this way!"

He took the child with him to his mother and asked her to raise the child. Because the baby had been lying in the lettuce, he called her Lettucia, who became so beautiful that she always brightened everyone's day. When she became older, however, the prince fell passionately in love with her and wanted to make her his wife, so he asked her, "Lettucia, whose child are you actually?"

Lettucia answered:

"I'm the daughter of a dog and cat,
If you don't want me, die and scat."*

"Do you want to marry me?" he continued to ask.

"No," Lettucia responded.

"But, why not?"

"Because I don't want to."

So the despondent prince went to his mother and complained, "Dear Mother, I asked Lettucia whether she wanted to be my bride, and she said "no" to me. When I asked her whose child she was, she

---

*Sugnu figghia di cani e di jatta,
Si no mi voi, mori e scatta.

answered, 'I'm the daughter of a dog and a cat. If you don't want me, die and scat.'"

"There's nothing I can do to help you, my son," his mother replied. "Why don't you wait a while and ask her a second time."

The prince did as his mother advised, but Lettucia answered him abruptly, "No."

"Well, at least tell me whose child you are," the prince asked.

"I'm the daughter of a dog and cat. If you don't want me, die and scat.'"*

Because the queen saw that her son had become so sick out of love for the beautiful Lettucia, she said, "The girl must leave the house. Otherwise, my son will go out of his mind."

So she had a beautiful house built across from the royal palace, and Lettucia had to live there. However, the prince continued to go over and ask her, "Lettucia, will you be my wife?"

But she always answered "no," and the prince would go sadly to his mother and pour out his sorrow. Finally the queen lost her patience and cried out, "If she doesn't want you, just let her go. There are other pretty girls in the world."

So the queen sent out messengers to all the courts and royal houses and had pictures sent to her of beautiful princesses. No matter how many she showed to her son, he could not find any that pleased him. Finally, because he saw that his mother was very sad, and that Lettucia would never have him for her husband, he chose a beautiful princess and said, "Let her come. I'll marry her."

A splendid marriage ceremony was arranged, and the princess came to the court and was married to the prince. When they came out of the church, however, the young bride saw that the prince was disturbed and did not look happy.

"What's wrong with you?" she asked him.

"Oh, I have a sister," he answered, "and she's more beautiful than the sun. I had a fight with her, and that's why she refused to attend the wedding. That's why I'm depressed."

"Oh, if that's all it is," the bride said, "don't let it bother you. Tomorrow we'll send her a large platter of sweets. I'm sure this nice gesture will bring about a reconciliation."

---

*That is, "As far as I'm concerned, just die. I could care less."

Indeed, this is what they did, and the next morning they sent a servant to the beautiful Lettucia with a large platter of sweets.[*]

"Wait a moment," Lettucia said to the servant, "and come with me into the kitchen."

When they were in the kitchen, Lettucia began calling out, "Fire, ignite yourself," and all of a sudden a bright fire was burning in the hearth.

"Pan, come over here," and a gold pan came and jumped onto the fire by itself.

"Oil, come over here," and the oil came as well and poured itself into the pan. When the oil was boiling, Lettucia held her beautiful white hands in the pan for a while, and when she took them out, there were two beautiful gold fish and her hands were not seared at all. Then she placed the fish on the platter, gave it to the servant, and said, "Take the fish to the prince and tell him that he should accept this gift out of love for his sister Lettucia."

The servant went back to the castle, so astonished that he was speechless and his mouth hung wide open.

"Well, tell me what happened!" the prince said.

"Oh, your majesty, you won't believe what I've seen!" and he revealed how Lettucia had prepared the gold fish.

"Oh, is that all?" the young queen said. "I can do that, too."

"Well, if you can do it, then show us," her husband answered.

So she went into the kitchen and called out, "Fire, ignite yourself!" But, no fire appeared on the hearth.

"The fire isn't obeying me today," she remarked and called the cook. "Start the fire for me."

When the fire was ignited, she called for the pan, but the pan did not appear.

"They're all somewhat stubborn today," she said. "Give me the pan," she said to the cook.

The same thing happened with the oil. It was useless for the princess to call the oil. It did not want to come, and the cook had to pour the oil into the pan. When the oil was boiling, she stuck her hands inside, but she burned herself so miserably that she died. The prince then went to Lettucia and said to her, "Lettucia, why did you murder my wife?"

"What did I do to her?" Lettucia asked.

---

[*]After a wedding in Sicily one sends a special platter filled with sweets to all the relatives. It is considered impolite if one does not do this. Cinnamon sticks or canellini form the major part of the candy.

"She heard how you prepared the beautiful gold fish," the prince replied, "and she wanted to do it in the same exact way, but she burned herself so badly that she died."

"Who told her to try what she can't do?" Lettucia answered. "I didn't tell her anything."

"Oh, Lettucia," the prince asked, "don't you want to have me for your husband?"

"No," she answered.

"Well, at least tell me whose child you are."

"I'm the daughter of a dog and a cat, and if you don't want me, die and scat."

She refused to give him any other answer but this, and he returned to his mother somewhat depressed and poured out his sorrows.

"If she doesn't want you, let her go," the queen said and talked with him until he chose another bride and married her. When they came out of the church, however, the prince was once again so disturbed that his new bride asked him what was wrong.

"I have a sister called Lettucia," he said, "and she is more beautiful than the sun. Recently I had an argument with her. That's why she didn't come to the wedding, and that's why I'm depressed."

"Oh," his bride answered, "tomorrow we'll send her a platter full of sweets and canellini. That should pacify her."

The next morning they sent a servant to Lettucia once again, and he carried a platter filled with sweets. Lettucia ordered the servant to come with her into the kitchen, and she said, "Fire, ignite yourself, and heat the oven."

All of a sudden there was a bright light in the oven, and when it was completely hot she crawled inside and stayed there a while. When she came out again she had become even more beautiful than she had been, and when she opened her glistening braids, pearls and jewels fell to the ground. Then she took them and filled the platter with them and ordered the servant to carry them to the prince.

"Tell the prince that he is to accept the pearls and jewels out of love for his sister Lettucia."

The servant returned to the palace with his mouth wide open.

"Well, how did things go today?" the prince asked.

When the servant told the prince and his wife what Lettucia had done, the young bride cried out, "Oh, that's nothing. I can do that as well."

"If you can do it, show us your talent," the prince said.

So she went into the kitchen and called out, "Fire, ignite yourself and heat the oven." But no fire appeared.

"How stubborn the fire is today," she said. "Cook, heat the oven for me."

When the oven was thoroughly heated, she crawled inside, but she suffered miserable burns, and when they pulled her out, she was dead. Then the prince went to Lettucia and accused her of killing his wives by exhibiting talents that the others wanted to imitate.

"I didn't tell them a thing," Lettucia answered. "They're to blame themselves for wanting to imitate something they couldn't do."

"Oh, Lettucia," the prince begged, "do you still refuse to take me for your husband?"

"I won't marry you," she answered.

"Well, at least tell me whose child you are!"

"I'm the daughter of a dog and a cat. If you don't want me, die and scat."

As soon as she gave him the usual answer, the prince returned sadly to his mother and poured out his sorrow. The old queen, however, convinced him to choose another bride and sent for a beautiful princess, who married the prince.

When they came out of the church, the bride saw that the prince had a sad face and asked him what was wrong. He answered once again that he had argued with his sister and that she refused to attend the wedding.

"Don't worry about it," the bride said. "Tomorrow we'll send her a large platter full of sweets, and she'll be reconciled."

Indeed, this is what they did, and when the servant went to Lettucia, she was sitting on her balcony, warming herself in the rays of the sun.

"Wait a moment," she said as she remained sitting there calmly. When the sun no longer shone into the room but only on the iron railing of the balcony, she moved her chair on top of the railing and sat there. The chair did not tip over, and when the sun disappeared behind the roof, she placed the chair on top of the tile roof. Horrified, the servant ran back to the castle and told the prince and his bride what he had just seen.

"Oh, I can do that, too," the princess said.

"Well, let's see it then," her husband said.

But when she set the chair on the railing of the balcony and sat on it, the chair fell over, and she broke her neck. Now the prince went to Lettucia once more, but no matter how much he asked her to take him for her husband, or at least to tell him whose child she was, she continued to give him the same answers. So he went sadly to his mother and said, "Lettucia won't marry me, and I can't summon any more wives, otherwise they'll be calling me the wife murderer.* What should I do?"

"Well, my son," the queen said, "I really can't help you anymore. Now you've got to find out whose child Lettucia is. Perhaps then she'll marry you."

So the prince kept wondering whose daughter Lettucia might be, but try as he might, he could not discover anything. One day, however, as he was walking in a field, lost in his thoughts and despair, he met an old woman who asked, "Tell me, handsome lad, why are you so sad?"

At first he didn't want to tell her, but she kept insisting until he finally poured out his heart to her.

"I can only give you one word of advice," the old woman said. "Go to Lettucia and tell her you are sick and you'd like her to prepare a cool drink for you. When she calls her instruments to her, take the gold mortar and hold to it tightly without her noticing. Then perhaps her mood will change, and she'll reveal everything to you."

The prince liked this advice and made his way to Lettucia.

"Oh, Lettucia," he said, "I'm feeling ill. Could you please make me a cool drink."

"I'd be glad to," she said and began to call out, "Glass, come here. Sugar, come here. Lemons, come here," and everything she called came to her. The prince saw the gold mortar sitting on the table, and he quickly took it without Lettucia noticing and stuck it between his knees.

The sugar was in big chunks, and Lettucia called out, "Mortar, come here!"

However, the mortar could not come because the prince held it tightly between his legs.

She called for the mortar many times in vain until she finally lost her patience and cried out, "I'm the daughter of the sun, and yet this miserable mortar won't obey me!"

The prince jumped up and cried, "If you are indeed the daughter of the sun, you must also become my wife."

When she realized that he had found out whose child she was, she responded with joy, "Yes, I'll be your wife."

A beautiful wedding was celebrated, and Lettucia invited her mother and her grandmothers, and there was great joy in the entire realm. They remained rich and consoled, and we're just sitting and getting old.

---

*Ammazza-mugghièri.

30

PAPERARELLO

Once upon a time there was a king and a queen who had an only son. However, the queen was a wicked woman and could not stand her son. When the boy was twelve years old, the king died, and his son became king. This made the wicked queen angry because she had wanted to rule alone, and thus she sought to bring about the young king's death.

Now, one day her son told her he was going out to hunt, and she said to him, "My son, I want to accompany you on the hunt."

"Oh, Mother," he answered, "that's not right. You can't go hunting with me."

However, she insisted and accompanied him. During the hunt they became separated from their entourage. Suddenly, an ogre* overpowered them and took them to his house. The duplicitous queen was a very beautiful woman, and when she pleaded with the ogre for her life, he was so moved by her beauty that he did not kill her. Still, she had to remain with him and was not allowed to return to her realm. As for the young king, the ogre beat him to death, tied him to a horse, and let the animal run into the forest.

But this horse was a magic horse, and it rushed to a castle inhabited by fairies and knocked on the door. When the fairies heard the knock-

---

*Dravu. In modern Greek, drakos.

ing, the eldest spoke to one of the others and said, "Go and look out the window and see who's there."

"Oh, my sisters," the fairy cried out, "if you only knew! There's a horse standing below, and a dead boy is tied to its back. I've never seen a more handsome boy in my life!"

So the fairies opened the gate, let the horse enter, and untied the young king. Because he was so handsome, they said, "Let's bring him back to life and keep him here as our dear brother."

After they all agreed and used their magic arts to restore him to life, he stayed with them many years, and they were like brothers and sisters to each other.

When the young king had grown up, the eldest fairy said to her sisters, "I want to marry him now, and he'll be my husband and your brother."

So the young king married the fairy, and they lived with great pleasure in their beautiful castle. Eventually, however, the young king became restless and wanted to see the world. Therefore, one day he went to the fairies and said, "Dear wife and dear sisters, I must set out to see the world, and when I've seen enough, I'll return."

The fairies did not want to let him go, but he insisted, and so eventually they had to let him have his way.

"If you want to leave us," said the eldest fairy, "you can at least take this braid of my hair with you and keep it in a safe place. It will be useful to you."

Upon saying this, she cut off one of her beautiful braids and gave it to him. Then the young king mounted his horse and rode away. When it became evening, he found himself in a desolate area. There was not one person or house to be seen far and wide. "What should I do now?" he thought. "If I set up camp in the open, the wild animals will come and eat me."

All at once he remembered the braid, took it out, and said, "I wish to have a castle with servants, and with all that I need for dinner and sleeping quarters, and with a stable and food for my horse."

No sooner did he say all this than a large solid castle stood there, just as he had wished. When he went inside, the servants brought him food and looked after his horse. Then he lay down to sleep and slept quietly the entire night. The next morning he wished the castle to disappear and rode on.

This was the way he traveled through many countries, and whenever he found himself in unknown territory in the evening, he wished for a castle and spent the night in it. Finally he came to a city ruled by a great king. He left his horse outside the city, put on some tattered old clothes, and went to the royal castle. When the queen saw him standing in front of the castle, she sent a servant down to bring him to her so she could ask who he was.

"I'm just a poor man," the young king responded, "and I'm a stranger here. If there is a position free in the castle, I'd like to have it."

"I'm not sure we could use you," the queen said. "We have a secretary, and there's also a gatekeeper. In short, we have all the servants we need. The only person we need is some one to look after the geese. Do you want to be our paperarello?"*

The young king agreed and became the paperarello. He intentionally pretended to be messy and dressed only in dirty rags, slept in the same pen as the geese, and always looked disgusting and filthy.

"Paperarello, go wash yourself!" the queen would always yell.

"This is the way I'm used to being," he would respond.

Now one day the bread in the city happened to run out, and the king did not have any more bread to feed the soldiers. So he called his cook to him and said, "You must provide me with seven ovens full of bread by early tomorrow morning! If you succeed, you'll get my daughter as your wife. But if you don't, I'll rip off your head!"

"Oh, your majesty, that's not possible," the cook moaned. "How do you expect me to heat the oven seven times in one night and bake bread?"

"It's all the same to me!" the king responded. "Just see to it yourself."

Paperarello overheard this exchange and cried out, "Your majesty, I want to bake the bread!"

"All right," the king answered, "but if you don't succeed, I'll rip off your head."

However, instead of working, Paperarello lay down to have some rest. The other servants called out to him, "Paperarello, get to work! You know you can't fool around with the king."

"First I've got to sleep," he said and began snoring.

After an hour the servants cried out to him again, "Paperarello, get up. Do you want to lose your head?"

"Let me sleep a little longer," answered Paperarello, who continued to snore, and so it went the entire night. The servants kept interrupting his sleep and calling to him, but he always answered, "Let me sleep a little longer," and continued to snore.

---

*Literally, goose keeper, or keeper of the geese.

Finally it turned bright daylight, and the servants yelled full of fright, "Paperarello, the king's coming! Now it's too late, and you're going to lose your life."

"Why are you shouting this way?" Paperarello asked as he pulled out his braid and went into the kitchen. "The bread's already lying there—one, two, three, four, five, six loaves—and the seventh is still in the oven. You just have to take it out."

The servants stood there with their mouths wide open, and the king said, "Bravo, Paperarello! Now you can also have my daughter as your wife."

Meanwhile, the king thought to himself, "This wretch must have some magic gift somewhere."

When the princess heard that she was supposed to marry the disgusting Paperarello, she began to weep bitter tears and refused. But there was nothing she could do, and a splendid wedding was celebrated as Paperarello married the beautiful daughter of the king. Yet he could not be persuaded to wash himself or to take off his dirty rags, and when he went into the bridal suite, he said, "I'd prefer to spend the night with my geese in their pen. I can't sleep in a bed like this."

So he went to the pen and slept with the geese and refused to return to the castle. Meanwhile, the king's sons said, "Father, beat the disgusting Paperarello to death."

"No," replied the king. "I'm sure he has a magic gift, and before I do anything, I must find out what his gift is."

Now it happened just at that time that a war broke out, and the king and his sons had to set off for the battle front. All the king's servants went with him and carried beautiful armor and weapons.

"I want to go off to war, too," Paperarello said, and he went into the stable and chose an old, lame horse, tied a little sword to his belt, and followed the servants at a slow pace. After they had ridden for a while, he said, "My horse can't go any farther. You go on ahead to the war. I'll make some toy soldiers out of clay and play war here."

The servants laughed at Paperarello and left him in the middle of the road and continued on their way. No sooner had they left than Paperarello pulled out the braid, wished for beautiful armor, the sharpest sword, and the most courageous horse. Then he rode after the others. The battle had already begun, and the enemy king was close to winning the war. Just then Paperarello charged into the battle and turned the tide for his king, who became victorious. But nobody recognized Paperarello. Just as he was about to leave the battlefield, the king sent a servant to him to ask him to wait because the king wanted to thank him for his help and wished to offer him anything he desired as a token of his gratitude.

"Tell the king," Paperarello responded, "I want nothing but his pinky."

So the king had to cut off his pinky, and Paperarello stuck it into a pocket and rode back to the spot where the others had left him earlier that morning. When they came by, the dirty Paperarello was still sitting there, still making soldiers out of clay.

"Did you win?" he asked the king. "I also won my battle."

Upon saying this, Paperarello took out his little sword and cut off all the heads of the clay soldiers.

The next morning the king set out to war again with all his servants, and Paperarello rode forth on his lame horse. When they reached the same spot, he stopped and made clay soldiers. The others laughed and mocked him and rode on. Meanwhile, he wished for another beautiful set of armor, another sharp sword, and another brave horse, and rode after them. The enemy was just about to win this battle, and the king said to his servants, "Turn around and see if the unknown knight from yesterday is coming again!"

"We see a knight approaching. He looks even more courageous than the one from yesterday," his servants answered.

The knight charged into the battle, and soon the king won again. Once more he sent a servant to the knight to thank him and to offer him whatever he desired out of gratitude. This time the knight demanded the king's ear, and the king had no choice but to slice off his ear. Paperarello stuck it into his pocket and rode off. When the king and his servants set out for home, Paperarello was sitting on the side of the road with his clay soldiers and cut their heads off with his little sword.

The third day went just like the other two. Paperarello stayed behind again, wished for armor, a sword, and a horse, and they were better and more beautiful than the others. Then he rode off into the battle. The servants looked around anxiously for his help because they were in great danger, and when he came, they reported to the king that an unknown knight was coming who was even more handsome and more courageous than the first two. The unknown knight defeated the enemy king again, and after the battle the king sent a servant to thank him and to tell him to choose anything he desired. The king would not refuse him.

"I don't want anything but the king's nose," the knight said.

So the king had to slice off his nose, and Paperarello stuck it into his pocket. When the king rode home, Paperarello was sitting once again at the side of the road playing with his clay soldiers, and he said to the king, "My, how pretty you look without a nose!"

"Leave me in peace," the king responded.

But Paperarello rode after him and kept saying, "My, how pretty you look without a nose. Of course, I'm just a dirty goose keeper. But at least I have my nose, and all my ears and fingers."

Later, when the king sat down to eat his dinner, Paperarello took out the nose, the ear, and the finger and said, "I'm the unknown knight who helped you three times, and I'm also the son of a king and not a dirty goose keeper as you think."

Paperarello went into another room, washed himself, and put on royal garments. When he returned, he was so handsome that the princess rejoiced with all her heart that he was her husband. But the young king said, "I thank you for your daughter, but I already have a dear wife at home, and now I want to return to her. Before I leave, though, I want to wish you back your nose, your ear, and your finger."

All at once the king was healthy and whole again, and the young king took his leave from everyone. He mounted his horse and rode back to the seven fairies. When they saw him coming, they were very pleased, and he lived in great happiness with his wife. Indeed, they remained rich and consoled, while we are still sitting here and getting old.

31

THE LION, HORSE, AND FOX

Once a lion got caught in a narrow pass* and could not get out. Just then a horse came by, and the lion called out to him, "Help me out of this narrow pass."

"I'll gladly do that," the horse said, "but you must promise not to eat me."

The lion promised, and the horse worked with his hoofs until he had freed the lion. When he saw that he was freed, he said, "Now I'm going to eat you."

"What were the conditions?" the horse asked. "Didn't we agree that you wouldn't eat me?"

"That doesn't matter now," the lion cried out. "But if you want, we can go to a judge."

"Good," replied the horse. "Whom should we choose?"

"The fox," said the lion.

The horse agreed, and they went to the fox. Once there, the lion explained the situation.

"Yes," said the fox. "It seems to me that you are right, Mr. Lion, but before I can pronounce my judgment, I must first see exactly where and how you both were standing."

---

*Strittu.

So all three of them returned to the narrow pass, and the horse took his place where he had been standing, and the lion asked the fox to shove him back into the narrow pass.

"Is that how you were standing?" the fox asked.

"This leg was squeezed a bit more," the lion responded.

"Well then, shove yourself a little farther into the pass. You must be exactly where you were at the moment that you asked the horse for help."

The lion squeezed into the pass even more, and the fox asked again, "Is that exactly how you were standing?"

Finally, the lion had squeezed back into the pass so much that he could not get out again.

"So," the fox said, "now you're exactly where you were before, and the horse can decide whether he still wants to help you."

The horse refused and instead threw stones down into the pass until the lion was killed.

Yes, yes, the fox is sly!

32

GIUSEPPINU

Once upon a time there was a king and a queen, and they would have liked to have a little son or little daughter. The queen was very devoted to Saint Joseph and turned to him for help.

"Oh, holy Saint Joseph!" she said. "If you grant me a child, I'll name it Giuseppe or Giuseppina."

Soon thereafter she became pregnant, and when her time came, she gave birth to a son and named him Giuseppinu. The boy grew and became handsomer and stronger with each passing day. When he reached the age of thirteen or fourteen, he had a great yearning to see the world and said to his parents, "Dear Father and dear Mother, let me set out. I must go out into the wide world."

"Oh, my dear son," they answered, "where do you want to go? Stay with us. You have everything you want here."

Because his parents did not want to let him depart, he secretly set out one morning and fled the castle. After he had wandered for a long time, he came to a city where another great king was ruling, and he had a beautiful daughter. Giuseppinu went to the royal palace and began walking back and forth. The princess was standing on the balcony, and when she saw the handsome boy, she took such a liking to him that she went to her father and said, "Dear Father, there is a boy down below, and if you only knew how handsome he is! Please take him into your employ."

The king loved his daughter so much that he could never refuse a request she made, so he had Giuseppinu summoned to him immediately and said, "If you want to enter my service, I shall make you our stable boy."

Giuseppinu agreed, and the king employed him as stable boy. Now he stayed there for a long time, and the princess became more and more fond of him. One day she said to her father, "Dear Father, Giuseppinu is much too good to be a stable boy, please make him a servant so that he can work in the palace itself."

Once again the king granted her wish, and Giuseppinu became a servant. In the meantime there was a little horse among the king's horses, and Giuseppinu liked it so much that he often went to the stable to pet the horse. At the same time the princess became even more fond of Giuseppinu until she fell so passionately in love with him that she went to the king and said, "Dear Father, please give me Giuseppinu as my husband."

Now the king became mad and said, "That's not possible! You deserve a monarch as a husband and not a miserable servant."

But the princess did not let up and kept asking her father with tears in her eyes, and he finally said, "I shall speak to my councillors, and whatever they advise, that's what I shall do."

So he called together all his councillors and said, "My daughter insists on marrying the servant Giuseppinu, and she weeps day and night because I have refused to permit this. Tell me what I should do."

"Your royal majesty," they said, "tell Giuseppinu that he is to marry the princess, but before he can do this, he must take a journey and bring back great sums of money and treasures. We shall provide him with a poor ship for this task, and it will sink, and he will drown. Then the princess will forget him."

The king was pleased with this advice, and he called Giuseppinu to him and said, "Giuseppinu, I want to give you my daughter as your wife, but before you can marry her, you must take a journey and bring back money and treasures. Otherwise, I'll have your head cut off."

So poor Giuseppinu went to the little horse in the stable, petted it, and said, "Oh, my dear little horse, now I must say farewell to you. The king is sending me on a journey. Oh, where shall I go? I'm in a miserable way!"

As he was lamenting his fate, a little old man suddenly appeared in a monk's habit. It was Saint Joseph, but Giuseppinu did not know this.

"Why are you crying?" the little monk asked. After Giuseppinu told him about his troubles, Saint Joseph answered, "Just say to the king that you want to take this trip, but that you want a ship full of salt. I shall travel with you, and you'll see how fortunate you'll be."

So Giuseppinu went to the king and said, "Your majesty, I want to take the journey, but give me a ship full of salt, and then I'll go."

Now the king was very happy and gave him a ship full of salt. However, the ship was so poor and old that water seeped in from all sides. Indeed, the king wanted Giuseppinu to drown. Now Giuseppinu set sail, and all at once Saint Joseph appeared on board. No sooner did the saint arrive on the ship than it became a large, strong vessel that sailed very fast on the sea.

They traveled a long time and finally came to a foreign country where the people did not have any salt with which to spice their food.

"Listen, Giuseppinu," said the saint, "you remain here. I want to go on land."

Saint Joseph filled the sleeves of his monk's habit with salt and went ashore. As soon as he arrived, he entered a tavern where many people were sitting together. He took a place at a table and began eating. Because the food was cooked without salt, he took some from his sleeve spread it over his plate and continued eating. All at once the people began asking, "What did you spread over your meal?"

"There was no salt in it," he replied. "That's why I added a little."

"What is salt?" the people asked.

"You mean you don't know what salt is?" responded the saint, and he grabbed some more salt from his sleeve and spread some on each person's plate. When the people mixed it with their food, their meals tasted much better, and they said, "Good old man, do you have any more of this delicious salt?"

"Oh, yes. An entire ship full."

"Could you give it to us?"

"Yes, but only if you give me an entire ship full of gold in return."

So the people brought him as much gold as he needed to fill a ship, and in turn Saint Joseph gave them the salt.

"Now, we want to sail back home," he said to Giuseppinu, who was very happy that he had managed to get this much gold. So they traveled home, but when they entered the harbor, the saint disappeared.

The princess was sitting on the terrace and looking out over the sea to see if Giuseppinu might soon be coming. When she caught sight of the ship, she ran full of joy to the king and said, "Dear Father, Giuseppinu is coming with a magnificent large ship."

The king became scared when he heard this news and quickly called his councillors together. He told them what had happened and said, "Give me your advice. What should I do now?"

The councillors answered, "Tell Giuseppinu that what he's brought is not enough. If he does not take another journey, he won't be allowed to marry the princess."

When Giuseppinu arrived and brought the gold, the king said, "This is certainly a pretty amount of gold, but it's still not enough, and if you want to marry the princess, you must make a second journey and bring me even more gold. Otherwise, I'll have your head cut off."

So poor Giuseppinu went to the little horse in the stable and began to moan and weep. As he was lamenting his fate, Saint Joseph reappeared and asked him why he was crying. After Giuseppinu told him his troubles, Saint Joseph said, "Wasn't your first journey a success? Go to the king and tell him that you will make the journey, but he must give you a ship full of cats."

Giuseppinu did this, and the king gave him a ship that was even worse than the first one. But after Giuseppinu had set sail, the saint appeared, and no sooner did he arrive than the ship became strong and new so that they could continue merrily on their way.

They sailed for a long time, and finally they came to a foreign country where there were no cats, and the mice could freely dance on the tables.

"Giuseppinu," said Saint Joseph, "I'm going on land for a little while. You remain here until I return."

He took some cats with him and tucked them in the sleeves of his monk's habit and went on shore. As soon as he arrived, he went to a tavern where many people were eating, and the mice were dancing on the tables and even on the plates. All at once the saint pulled the cats out of his sleeves and placed them on the floor. The cats immediately began to hunt the mice and killed a good deal of them. The people watched with astonishment and asked the saint, "Do you have more of these animals?"

"Oh yes. A whole ship full of them."

"Could you leave them here for us?"

"Why not? But you must give me an entire ship full of gold in return."

So the people loaded his ship with gold, and the saint left the cats with them. Now Giuseppinu could sail back home again with a great amount of wealth. But as they entered the harbor, Saint Joseph disappeared.

The princess sat on the terrace and watched to see if Giuseppinu might soon be coming. When she caught sight of the ship, she ran to the king and said, "Giuseppinu's coming, and he's bringing a ship with him that's even larger and more beautiful than the first one!"

"What's that?" the king remarked. "Something strange is going on here!"

He called his councillors together again and told them everything.

"Your majesty," they answered, "you must send Giuseppinu on a third voyage, and the ship must be in such poor condition that it won't even be able to make its way out of the harbor."

When Giuseppinu went to the king and laid all the gold at his feet, the king said, "You've certainly managed to get a lot of gold, but it is still not enough. If you really want to marry the princess, you must take a third voyage. Otherwise, I'll have your head cut off."

Giuseppinu went to the stable and petted the little horse and cried many tears. All at once Saint Joseph reappeared, and when Giuseppinu told him his troubles, the saint said, "What are you thinking? You've already succeeded two times, and you'll succeed again this time. Go to the king and tell him that you will do what he wants, but he must give you a ship full of soldiers' uniforms."

Giuseppinu did this, and the king gave him a ship that was so old and in such poor condition that Giuseppinu would not have been able to sail out of the harbor if the saint had not appeared and turned it into a large and powerful ship. As they were sailing, they encountered an enemy fleet with many soldiers, and the leader of the enemy forces said to Giuseppinu: "Let's battle one another."

The saint said to Giuseppinu, "Accept the challenge, and tell the leader of the enemy forces that whoever loses the battle must give up a ship to the winner."

So they fought under this condition, and Giuseppinu lost the battle. But the saint said to him, "Don't lose your courage. Just say to the leader of the enemy forces that he can have the ship but not the uniforms that are in it. Tell him you'll do battle with him over the uniforms, and if he loses, you will get his soldiers."

So they fought one more time, and Giuseppinu won the battle. The leader of the enemy had to give up his soldiers, and Giuseppinu ordered them to exchange their clothes for the uniforms that he had on his ship. Then he took charge of the army and marched with the soldiers against the city where the king lived. The princess was again sitting on the terrace and waiting for Giuseppinu, and when she caught sight of so many soldiers, she ran to the king and said, "Dear Father, Giuseppinu is coming, and he has an entire army of soldiers with him."

Now the king became frightened and thought, "If I refuse to give him my daughter, he will rob me of my throne." Consequently, he approached Giuseppinu and received him with many honors.

"You have fulfilled all the conditions, and now you may have my daughter for your wife," the king declared.

Then there were three days of festivities. Giuseppinu wed the beautiful daughter of the king, and it was Saint Joseph who married them. After the wedding he blessed them and said, "I am Saint Joseph, and if you ever need me, just call me, and I shall always help you."

Upon saying these words he disappeared and returned to heaven. Then Giuseppinu sent a messenger to his parents to inform them that he was still living and was the husband of a beautiful princess. His parents were extremely happy, and after traveling to his new country they embraced him with great joy. Afterward they all lived happy and content, and we were left without a cent.

33

CRIVÒLIU

Once upon a time there was a brother and a sister who had neither mother nor father, and they lived together all by themselves. Because they loved each other so very much, they committed a sin that they should not have committed. Later, as her time drew near, the sister gave birth to a boy, and the brother had the boy secretly baptized. Then he carved a cross on the baby's shoulder with the words, "Crivòliu, baptized, son of a brother and sister."* After the little boy had been marked this way, the brother put him into a little chest and threw the chest into the sea.

Now it so happened that a fisherman had gone out to sea and saw the little chest floating about in the water.

"A ship must have sunk somewhere," he thought. "I'll fetch the chest. Perhaps there's something useful in it."

He rowed over and took the little chest into his boat. When he opened it and saw the handsome baby inside, he felt pity for the innocent child, took him home to his wife, and said, "Dear wife, our youngest child is old enough so that we can finish weaning him. Now you can suckle this poor innocent child."

So his wife took the little Crivòliu and began to breast-feed him and loved him as if he were her own child. The boy grew and thrived, and each day he became larger and stronger. However, the fisherman's sons

---

*Crivòliu vattiatu, figghiu di frati e soru.

became jealous that their parents loved the little foundling just as much as they cared for them. One time as they were playing with Crivòliu, they had an argument with him and called him a "foundling." Crivòliu became very upset by this and went to his foster parents.

"Dear parents," he said, "tell me whether I am really your son."

"Why shouldn't you be my son?" the fisherman's wife said. "Didn't I suckle you with my breast?"

At the same time the fisherman forbade the other children to call little Crivòliu a foundling again. When Crivòliu became older, the fisherman sent him to school with his sons. Because the father could not hear them, the boys began once more to mock Crivòliu and call him a foundling, and the other children at the school did this as well. Crivòliu went to his foster parents again and asked whether he was really their son. They talked him out of this idea and kept him with them until he was fourteen. When he could no longer stand being called a foundling, he went to the fisherman and his wife and said, "Dear parents, I want you to swear to me that I am your son."

The fisherman had no choice but to tell him how he had found him and what was written on his shoulder.

"Well now, I want to set out and atone for the sins of my parents," Crivòliu said.

The fisherman's wife wept and moaned and did not want to let him go, but Crivòliu would not let anyone stop him and wandered off into the wide world. He traveled for a long time until, one day, he finally came to a desolate region where he found an inn.

"Tell me, good woman," he asked the innkeeper's wife, "is there a hidden cave near here?"

"Yes, my handsome lad," she said. "I know a cave and shall gladly lead you to it."

Crivòliu took two grani's worth of bread and a small jug of water with him and followed the innkeeper's wife to the cave. It was quite far from the inn, and the entrance was covered by thorns and bushes so that he could barely crawl into the cave. Once inside he sent the woman back to the inn, laid the bread and jug on the ground, knelt down, crossed his arms, and began to do atonement for the sin of his parents.

Many, many years passed this way. I don't know how many, but so many that Crivòliu's knees grew roots and he became attached to the ground. Now it so happened that the pope died in Rome, and a new one was to be elected. The cardinals were called together and let a white dove fly into the air. The man on which the dove landed was to become the new pope. The white dove circled several times in the air but did not land on anyone, so they called all the archbishops and bishops and let the white dove fly again, but it did not land on anyone. Then they called together all the priests, monks, and hermits, but the white dove did not choose any of them. The people were in great despair, and the cardinals had to set out and search throughout the land to see if there was still a hermit to be found, and many people accompanied them.

Eventually they came to the inn located in the desolate region and asked the innkeeper's wife whether she perhaps knew a hermit or a penitent, who might be unknown to other people.

"Many years ago," the innkeeper's wife answered, "a sad young man came this way. He asked me to take him to a cave where he could do atonement. I'm sure that he's dead because he only took two grani's worth of bread and a jug of water with him."

But the cardinals said, "We'd like very much to see if he's still alive. Lead us to him."

So the innkeeper's wife led them to the cave. She could barely find the entrance any more because the bushes were so thick and covered with thorns. In fact, the servants had to first clear away the thorns and undergrowth with axes before they could enter. Once they penetrated the cave, they saw Crivòliu kneeling with crossed arms, and his beard had become so long that it touched the ground. In front of him lay the bread, and next to it stood the jug with water. Indeed, throughout all the years he had not had anything to eat or drink. When they now let the white dove fly, it flew for a moment in a circle and then settled on the head of the penitent. All at once the cardinals recognized that he was a saint and asked him to come with them to be pope. But when they wanted to lift him, they realized that his knees had become tightly attached to the ground and first had to cut off the roots. Then they took him to Rome where he became pope.

About this very same time it so happened that the sister said to her brother, "Dear brother, when we were younger we committed a sin which we've never confessed. Only the pope can absolve us. Let's go to Rome before death surprises us and confess our sins ourselves."

So they set out for Rome, and when they arrived, they went into the church where the pope sat in the confession box. After they had confessed to him with a loud voice—one always confesses publicly to the pope—he said, "I am your son, for on my shoulder you will find the mark that you mentioned in your confession. I have atoned for your sin for many years and you have been forgiven for it. Now I absolve you of your sin, and you will live with me and lead a good life."

So they remained with him, and when the time came the Lord called all three into his heavenly realm.

34

Saint Onirià

Once upon a time there were two hunters who went hunting together. While they were in the forest, they were overtaken by darkness and could not find their way out. They wandered about until they saw a small light in the distance. When they approached it, they found a hut in which a bright fire was burning, but there was not a human soul to be seen. They went inside and found a table covered with food and wine, and sat down and ate and drank to their hearts' content. Afterward they moved their chairs closer to the fireplace to warm themselves. As they were sitting there, one of them said, "Do you smell the heavenly aroma in this hut? I wonder where it comes from."

"It seems to be coming from the fire," said the other hunter, and he ripped apart the burning wood. All at once they found a large beautiful heart beneath the wood, and it was the heart that was spreading a wonderful aroma that they had never smelled before in their lives.

"Let's take it with us," said one of the hunters, and he bent down, took the heart out of the fire, and stuck it into his pocket. The two hunters spent a restful night in the hut, and at daylight they found their way out of the forest.

As they continued on their way, they came to an inn, and one of the hunters said, "I'm hungry. Let's stop at this inn and eat something."

They entered, and the innkeeper brought them something to eat. Because it was a warm day, they took off their jackets and laid them on a chair. Now the innkeeper had an only daughter, who was a beautiful maiden and virtuous and pious as well. She served the two hunters, and each time she went by their jackets, her nose caught the scent of the aroma. She became curious, and while the two hunters were busy with their food, she searched the pockets to see what smelled so good. When she caught sight of the marvelous heart, she could not resist her craving for it and took it with her to her room. The hunters did not notice anything, took their jackets, and went away. The innkeeper's daughter laid the beautiful heart on her table and took pleasure in smelling the glorious aroma that it spread.

One day, as she was looking at it again, she was seized by a powerful craving to eat it, and so she ate it. Soon after this she became pregnant. When her father noticed, he became furious and wanted to beat her to death, but her mother implored him to spare her life even though she had committed a sin. After all, she was their only child.

"What's that to me?" the innkeeper yelled. "She has brought disgrace and dishonor to my house, and if she doesn't tell me who did this to her, I'll beat her to death."

"Oh, Father," the maiden wept. "I haven't done anything wrong."

But he wouldn't believe her and beat her and mistreated her every day.

One day, as he was screaming at her and throwing a fit once again, the maiden's godmother came by. She was a pious, God-fearing woman and loved the girl with all her heart.

"Cousin," she said, "why are you so furious?"

The innkeeper told her in great anger what had happened to his daughter, but the woman said, "Cousin, something's strange here. The girl has usually been pious and virtuous. I'm sure she would not have done anything bad. Do me a favor and don't mistreat her. Sooner or later the truth will be revealed."

The innkeeper refused to listen to her, but the godmother had a marvelous dream that very night. A saint appeared to her and said, "I am Saint Onirià and was consumed by fire. Only my heart remained from which I was to be born again. The innkeeper's daughter ate this heart and has conceived me in her body, but she is a virgin just like Maria was. Tell all this to her father so that he won't mistreat her anymore."

The godmother immediately woke her husband and told him her dream, but he felt it was just a dream and didn't mean anything and went back to sleep.

The godmother also laid down again, but just imagine, she had the same dream a second time. "Something's strange here," she thought, and when it turned day, she went to the innkeeper and told him everything. He refused to believe it and screamed and went wild again, until the godmother said, "Cousin, if you continue to mistreat your daughter, you'll be insulting Saint John* because you're refusing the only request that I am making to you."

When the time came for the innkeeper's daughter to have her child, she gave birth to a beautiful baby boy, who grew and flourished and became more handsome with each passing day. However, his grandfather could not stand him and mistreated him the same way he did his mother.

When the child turned five years old, the innkeeper spoke to the godmother's husband, "Cousin, I'm going into the city. Do you want to come with me?"

"Grandfather, I want to go along too," the boy cried out.

"Go away, you son of a good-for-nothing mother!" the innkeeper screamed. "Why must you always get in my way?"

"Let it be, cousin," the other man said. "I'll take the boy along with me."

So the two men set out on their way with the boy and headed toward Catania. Along the way they came to a spot where there was a great deal of dirt and excrement.

"Look, Grandfather," the boy said. "I wish that you would have to burrow through all that dirt."

"Oh, you lousy child!" the innkeeper yelled. "Is this the kind of godless wish you're harboring? I'm going to beat you to death!"

But the cousin intervened and calmed the innkeeper. After they walked a while, they saw a dead man who had been so poor that there was not enough money left to make him a coffin. Instead, two men carried him on a ladder into the church.

"Look, Grandfather," the boy said. "I wish that you would die a death like this man."

The innkeeper became even more furious and wanted to beat him to death with all his might. However, the cousin protected the child until he was able to calm the innkeeper.

After they went some distance more, they encountered a large funeral procession. A rich man had died, and his corpse was being carried in an expensive coffin in a beautiful wagon, and the monks accompanied it with burning candles.

---

*Protector saint of godparents.

"Why don't you wish that I should die like this man?" the innkeeper asked.

"No, Grandfather," answered the boy. "That's not what I wish for you."

And the innkeeper became so furious again that he wanted to beat him to death, and the cousin had to protect the boy once more.

After they arrived in Catania and finished their business, they began their journey back home. When they came to the spot where they had encountered the large funeral procession, the boy said, "Grandfather, place your ear on the ground and listen a little."

"Do you want me to listen to your every whim?" the innkeeper screamed.

Then the cousin said, "Don't get so angry, cousin, and do what the innocent boy wants."

The innkeeper let himself be persuaded, and when he placed his ear to the ground, he heard a great racket. It was if he could hear blows with iron clubs, shouts, and groans.

"You see, Grandfather," the boy said. "Those are the devils that are torturing the souls of the sinners, and the soul that they just received is the soul of the rich man whom we saw at this spot."

The innkeeper stood up and was struck by all this. He looked at his cousin and said softly, "The child must know more than we do."

After they had gone some distance, they came to the place where they had seen the poor man on the ladder.

"Grandfather, place your ear on the ground, and listen a bit."

This time the innkeeper did not contradict the boy, but immediately put his ear to the ground. All at once he heard the holy angels singing "hallelujah," and all the saints were singing along.

"You see, Grandfather. Those are the holy ones and the saints who are receiving the soul of the poor man with their song. He is the poor man we saw on this spot, and that's why I wished you would die like him and not like the rich sinner."

The innkeeper could not say a word. Instead, he himself took the boy by the hand and led him on their way. After a while they came to the spot where there was dirt and excrement.

"Grandfather, I want you to dig here," the boy said, and when the innkeeper did this, he found a large kettle of gold.

"This money belongs to you, Grandfather," the child said. "Of course, you already are a rich man, but you have not used your money in good ways. You are a cold-hearted man and you've exploited people for profit. You had better improve your ways so that we can see each other again. You see, I am Saint Onirià, and my mother is a virgin like Mary. Kiss her hand and honor her because I am now returning to paradise."

"Won't we ever see each other again, my child?" the innkeeper asked.

"We shall see each other again when the dead man speaks with the living," the saint responded. Then he blessed his grandfather and ascended into heaven.

The innkeeper and the godfather returned home and told everything they had seen, while the innkeeper's daughter wept about her lost child.

Now many years passed, and one day two men happened to spend the night at the inn, and during the night one of the men killed his companion and hid the body beneath some straw. The next morning he said to the innkeeper, "My friend went away during the night because he was in a hurry and he left the money for you with me."

So the innkeeper knew nothing about the murder that had taken place in his house. After some time had passed, several travelers arrived and slept in the same room where the dead man had been hidden beneath the straw. Because they smelled a terrible stench, they examined the straw and found the corpse. So they ran quickly to the court, and the police came and arrested the innkeeper. Everyone regarded him as the murderer, and he was sentenced to death and led to the gallows in the village square. When he was standing on the ladder, a marvelously good-looking young man came riding suddenly into the square on a white horse. He was waving a white piece of cloth and shouting, "Stop! Mercy, mercy!"

When he approached, he was surrounded by people and brought to the judge, who asked him why he had interrupted the execution.

"Come with me into the church where the murdered man is lying, and you will understand everything," the young man said.

So they went into the church followed by many people. Then the young man went over to the coffin and said, "Stand up, dead man, and speak with the living and tell us who murdered you."

All of a sudden the dead man stood up and said, "The innkeeper is innocent. My unfaithful companion is the one who killed me."

When the people heard this, they freed the innkeeper and asked his forgiveness, and the handsome young man said to him, "It's time to return home, and I shall accompany you."

When they got home, the innkeeper's wife and daughter were still weeping bitter tears, and the handsome young man said, "Don't cry. Your husband and father is here again. His innocence has been proven."

Then he went over to the innkeeper's daughter and kissed her hand, even though she wanted to keep it from him.

"Bless me, Mother," he said. "I am Saint Onirià, your son, and I've returned to reveal my grandfather's innocence. Now I must leave you again, but if you all live holy lives, we shall see each other again in heaven."

Then he blessed her and was lifted up to heaven. His mother and his grandparents led a holy life and did much good for the poor, and when they died, they also went to heaven. And may the same thing happen to us as well.

35

THE ABBOT WHO
RESCUED THE PRINCESS

Once upon a time there was a king and a queen who had an only daughter, and they loved her more than anything in the world. Now it happened one day when the princess was seven that she went out on the terrace with her nurse and chambermaid because the sun was shining so beautifully. When they were on the terrace, the princess said to her nurse, "Sit down. I want to comb your hair."

"Oh, your majesty," answered the nurse, "that's not something for you to do."

But the princess insisted, as children often do, and the nurse sat down for her sake and let the princess comb her hair. All of a sudden, however, a black cloud swooped down, completely covered the princess, and swept her away.

Just imagine how grief stricken the chambermaid and nurse were! They ran from the terrace and wept as they told the king what had happened. The queen also began to lament, and everyone in the entire palace mourned the loss of the girl. The king ordered his men to search for her everywhere, but it was all in vain. She could not be found, and many years passed without anyone hearing a word about her.

Now, there was a poor widow living in the same city, and she had an only son. They were so poor that they often did not have anything to eat. A good friend had at one time given the boy a seminary outfit, and he wore this when he went to mass and worked in the churches.

This was how he earned some money to feed his mother and himself, meager though it was.

Eight or nine years had passed since the princess had been abducted, and one day a well rose on the bank of the sea, and it was full of water. All the people were highly astounded, and they went to the king and said, "Your majesty, a well suddenly appeared this morning in the bay. It wasn't there before, and it's full of water."

The king ordered a soldier to keep guard over the well the entire day, and he issued a proclamation that whoever would climb down into the well and bring him news about the underworld below would become king after him. Many men tried this. They let themselves down into the well, but as soon as the water covered their heads, they drowned a miserable death.

One day the widow's son thought to himself, "Many have tried and have not succeeded. Now I want to try my luck, and perhaps things will go better for me." He set out on his way without telling his mother, and came to the well where the soldier was standing guard.

"Hey there, good friend, would you do me a favor and let me down into the well?"

"Go home, fellow!" the soldier answered. "Many men have already waged their lives, and nobody has come back alive."

"Perhaps I'll be luckier," the abbot* said. "Let me go down."

So the soldier tied a rope securely around him, gave him a little bell, and let him down. And just imagine what happened! As soon as his feet touched the water, it separated, and he sank straight to the bottom without danger. The water closed after him, and when he was at the bottom of the well, he looked around and saw a door that was completely made of silver. He went over to it, pushed aside the bolt, and opened it. Then he entered a large room, and across from him he saw another door made of gold. When he shoved aside the bolt and opened the door, he saw a third door made of diamonds across from him. He also opened this one and went into a gorgeous garden in which there were all kinds of flowers blooming, and every kind of tree that grows on the earth. As he crossed the garden, he came to some glistening stairs, and when he climbed them, he came to a beautiful salon, where he found a table covered with many good dishes of food. "Oh ho!" he thought, "this is a glorious spot for me," and he ate and drank to his heart's content.

---

*L'abbatino. The storyteller always called the hero of this story "l'abbatino," although when I questioned her, she flatly denied that this man had been a clergyman.

After he had eaten, he became tired and went into another room where he found a beautiful ready-made bed where he laid down and soon fell asleep.

After a while he heard someone calling him by his name: "Peppino!"

"Who's calling me?" he asked.

"I'm the daughter of the king," the voice declared. "I am the princess who was carried away by a cloud many years ago. A wicked sorcerer is keeping me prisoner here. If you can rescue me, your fortune will be made, and so will mine."

"Tell me what I have to do to rescue you," answered the abbot.

"Just stay here and relax," she said. "Eat and drink and keep up your good spirits. When the moment arrives and you can rescue me, I'll tell you."

Consequently, the abbot remained in the underworld, had good things to eat and drink, and there was nothing he lacked. He also had a fast horse, and he could go riding on it in the garden. In the evenings the beautiful princess would come and talk with him. Approximately a month passed this way, and one evening the princess said to him, "Listen, Peppino, early tomorrow morning you must go back to the bottom of the well and have yourself pulled up to the top. In one month and one day, however, right at midnight, you must be on top of the well again and let yourself down. If you arrive even one minute late, it will be bad for you and bad for me. To make sure that you will have everything you want, I'm giving you this ring, and whenever you need money in your pocket, you need only to turn it around on your finger. If you are not at the well at the exact time you are supposed to be, the ring will lose its power. Pay attention, and don't forget to be there on time."

The abbot promised to do everything that she said. He took the ring, and the next morning he went to the bottom of the well, tied the rope around himself, and rang the little bell. As usual there was a soldier above keeping guard over the well. When he heard the bell ringing from below, he said to himself, "Could it be that someone's below there?" and he pulled on the rope and drew the young man up to the top.

The abbot went directly to the house of his poor old mother, who had wept over his death, and knocked on the door and said, "Dear Mother, open up. It's your son, and I'm here again."

"Oh," she answered, "my son is certainly dead. He left me about a month ago and never returned."

But he cried out once more, "You can rest assured that I'm your son, and I've come back to you with a great deal of wealth."

Eventually she let herself be persuaded and opened the door. When she saw her son, she recognized him and embraced him full of joy. Soon after he bought a beautiful palace across from the royal castle and rich garments for him and his mother, who lived with him in the palace.

When the king heard that a distinguished gentleman had moved into the house across from his castle, he sent a servant to ask him to visit his castle that evening. The young man went to the castle and gambled with the king. When he lost, he simply turned the ring, and his pockets were immediately filled with money. He continued to do this for almost a month. When he realized that there were only a few days left before he was to appear at the well, he turned the ring until he had collected enough money so his mother could live another twenty years without worrying about anything. This was the way he took care of her future.

Finally the evening arrived when he was to be at the well at midnight. He took leave from his mother and went to gamble with the king for the last time. In the heat of the game, however, he forgot to look at the clock. Imagine his horror when the clock suddenly struck midnight!

"Your majesty," he said, "forgive me, but I can't stay any longer. I must take care of some important business right away."

But when he turned his ring, his pockets were empty. He realized that the ring had lost its power and said, "Send a servant to my mother tomorrow. She'll pay all my debts, but I must leave right now."

Quickly he ran to the well and said to the soldier who was standing guard there, "Good friend, please do me a favor and let me down into the well."

"Are you crazy?" the soldier replied. "Do you want to lose your life?"

The young man insisted, and the soldier tied the rope around him and let him down. As soon as his feet touched the water, it separated and closed once his body began to sink. When he arrived at the bottom, however, what did he see? The three doors had been torn down and the walls had collapsed. When he entered the garden, all the trees had been ripped out by their roots. The flowers had wilted. The stable in which his horse had stood had also collapsed, and the horse lay dead on the ground. He rushed to the stairs, but they had been destroyed, and at the foot of the stairs lay the beautiful princess. She was dead, and six dead maidens lay on her right side, and six on her left.

The young man began to moan and groan and cursed himself and his fate.

"Have you returned, you villain?!" a voice spoke all of a sudden, and when he turned around, he saw a very old woman, who scolded him and continued to speak: "Is this the way you keep your word? Look! All this is your doing!"

"Oh, my good old woman," he answered. "You're right. I've made a grave mistake. But you must tell me if there is any way I can make up for my mistake. I'll do anything!"

"What good will it be if I tell you?" the old woman said. "You'll never succeed."

But the young man kept asking her until she finally said, "All right, listen to me. Do you see that destroyed stable? You must climb on top of it and take this sword with you. Then you must spring on the back of the horse, which will jump up and become alive again. Grab the reins and pull out your sword because as soon as the horse jumps up, a powerful dragon will attack you. You'll have to fight the beast, but don't fear because you'll be able to defeat it with this magic sword. Once you've killed the dragon, you're to return here, but there will be a terrifying giant on a horse that will ride toward you and say, 'Oh, you little church fly,* how dare you ride in my garden?' Then you must answer: 'I've come to fight you.' 'What? You want to fight me, you church fly!' he'll say, and you must answer: 'I'm so little and you're so big, but I'll defeat you in the name of God.' Then the giant will fight with you for a long time. When he realizes that he can do nothing against you, he'll let a glove fall to the ground and say to you, 'It's so difficult for me to get down off my horse. Why don't you dismount and fetch my glove for me?' Be on your guard not to do what he asks, otherwise it will be the end of you. Just tell him he can pick it up himself. The giant can't fight without the glove, he'll eventually get off his horse to fetch it. While he is bending over, you must approach and take a swing at his neck with your magic sword so that he'll die. Then examine his clothes, and you'll find a bunch of keys and a bunch of feathers. You must rush into the house. There's a locked closet in one of the rooms. Keep trying to find the right key to the closet, and when you've found it, open it. You'll see many bottles there filled with ointments and potions. Take the bottles with the ointments that bring the dead back to life. When you rub the ointment on the princess, she'll awake and regain her life. If you really have the courage, this is what you must do to rescue her."

The young man became somewhat afraid, but then he thought, "I'm in God's hands, and I'm going to try to do what the woman said."

---

*Musca di chiesa.

He took the sword and climbed carefully on top of the destroyed stable. When he reached the top and got his balance, he sprang on the back of the horse. At the very same moment the horse jumped up, and right below him a gigantic dragon surged up and wanted to swallow the young man. However, he had already grabbed the reins of the horse and pulled out the magic sword and began to fight the dragon. Even though the dragon was strong and powerful, it could not withstand the magic sword. After the young man had taken a few swipes at the beast, he finally cut off the dragon's head, and it fell down dead. Then the young man went in the direction that the old woman had told him to go. He had not gone very far before a huge and powerful giant came toward him and cried out with a loud voice, "Oh, you church fly, how dare you go riding in my garden!"

The young man answered, "I've come to fight you."

"What? You want to fight me!" the giant yelled with a scornful laugh. "You tiny church fly!"

"I'm very small and you're very large," said the young man, "but in the name of God, I'm going to defeat you."

"All right then!" said the giant. "Let's fight!"

So they began to do battle with one another for a long time, but neither one could defeat the other. When the giant realized that the young man had a magic sword and that he would not be able to defeat him with force, he resorted to cunning. Just as the old woman had predicted, he let one of his iron gloves fall and said, "I'm so large that it's difficult for me to get off my horse. Why don't you get down and fetch my glove for me?"

"If you let the glove drop, you can also pick it up yourself," answered the young man.

"Oh, do me a favor and get off your horse," the giant pleaded.

But the young man remembered the words of the old woman and responded, "If my glove were to fall to the ground, I would fetch it myself. So get off your horse yourself!"

The giant was obliged to do this and dismounted his horse because he had lost all his power without the glove. However, when he bent down, the young man jumped over to him and cut off his head with one stroke of the sword, and the head flew off far away. He quickly examined the giant's body, and when he found a bunch of keys and a bunch of feathers, he rushed into the house and opened the locked closet. In the closet he found a lot of little bottles with ointments and potions. He only took the bottle that revived the dead and ran to the beautiful dead princess. As soon as he dipped a feather into the ointment and rubbed her temples and nostrils with it, she suddenly opened her eyes and was completely alive and well. Then he rubbed the other twelve maidens with the ointment, and all at once they became alive again. When the young man looked around him, he saw that the trees were standing straight again, the flowers bloomed in the entire garden, and everything that had been destroyed had completely recovered and was as glorious as it had been before.

They remained for a few more days in the beautiful garden, and then the princess took leave from her twelve maidens who remained in the underworld. The young man and the princess went to the well to have themselves pulled up.

"Listen, Peppino," the princess said, "let yourself be pulled up first. If there's a strange soldier up there, and I come up first, he'll betray you and won't pull you up."

At first Peppino did not want to do what she suggested, but she kept asking so that he finally gave in to her will. He tied the rope around himself and gave the signal with the little bell to be pulled up. There was a soldier standing guard, and when he heard the ringing, he thought, "Is it possible that someone's down in the well? I might as well pull the rope."

So he pulled the rope, and the young man succeeded in making his way to the top. Then he untied himself and threw the rope back down.

"Is there still somebody down there?" the soldier asked.

"Yes," the young man answered. "Help me pull."

When the gorgeous princess eventually appeared, the soldier thought to himself, "If she had come up first, I would have never pulled him out!"

The young man took the princess home to his old mother, who was very happy when she saw her dear son again.

"What do we do now?" the young man asked. "Should I take you right to your father?"

"No," she answered. "Do what I say. Go to my father this evening to gamble. After you've been playing for a while, you're to say to him, 'Your majesty, we play here every evening. How would it be for a change if each one of us told a story?' Certainly my father will tell the story of how I was abducted. Then ask him: 'Your majesty, if someone brought back your daughter, what reward would you give him?' Then bring me his answer."

That evening the young man went to the court and gambled with the king. After a while he said, "Your majesty we've already played the entire evening. How would it be for a change if we each told one another a story?"

"Oh," responded the king, "all you others can tell stories, but I can only tell about one sad event from my life."

"What is that, your majesty? Tell us."

Then the king told how his only daughter had disappeared many years ago and since then had not heard anything about her.

"But tell me, your majesty," the young man said after the king had finished his story, "what would you give as a reward if some one brought your daughter back to you?"

"Oh," the king answered, "if some one should return my dear daughter to me, he would receive her as his wife and become king after me."

The young man did not say anything more. The next morning he told everything to the princess, who said, "Good, this evening you are to tell the king that you have a sister and would like to know whether he would permit you to bring her to the court."

When the young man was with the king again that evening, he was having a conversation with him and asked, "Your majesty, I have a sister at home who is really a very beautiful maiden. If you would allow me, I'd like to bring her here one time."

"Do that," the king answered. "I shall be glad to see her."

The young man took the king's answer to the princess, and she said, "This evening I'll accompany you."

When they went to the court that evening and entered the royal hall, she was so beautiful that everyone was astounded and stared at her. The king had her sit across from him, and while they were playing cards, he constantly looked at her. It seemed to him that he knew her.

"Look at this beautiful maiden," he said to his ministers. "Doesn't she look like my lost daughter?"

"Oh, what are you thinking, your majesty?" the ministers answered. "Your daughter has been missing for many years. It couldn't be her."

But the king called for his the queen and said, "Take a look at that maiden. Doesn't she resemble our daughter?"

"Yes," the queen said. "I can see the same traits."

But when the princess saw that her parents were looking at her, she could no longer keep herself composed and cried out, "Dear Father and dear Mother, I am truly your long lost daughter!"

Just imagine the great commotion! The queen fainted out of shock and joy, and people rushed to her side to help her. The king, too, was at a loss and couldn't control himself. Finally he said, "If you are our daughter, then tell us what happened to you."

Then she told the entire story and ended by saying, "This young man is the one who freed me from the power of the evil sorcerer."

When the king and queen heard everything, they became very happy and embraced their daughter and the young man with great joy.

"You have rescued my daughter," the king said, "and now she shall become your wife, and you shall become king after me."

A splendid wedding was held, and there were many festivities. Afterward they lived happy and content, and we were left without one cent.

36

FATA MORGANA

Once upon a time there was a powerful king who had three handsome sons, and among them the youngest was the handsomest and smartest. The king lived in a magnificent castle with a splendid garden. There were many trees with rare fruit and beautiful flowers in the garden, and the flowers had a lovely aroma.

Now one morning the king happened to go into the garden to look at his fruit and discovered that the fruits were missing on one tree. "That's very strange," he thought. "The garden has a tall wall. How could some one get in here?" So he called his sons and told them what had happened, and the eldest said, "Dear Father, don't you worry about this. I'll keep watch this evening and discover who the thief is."

In the evening the prince took his sword and sat down in the garden. Toward midnight he was overcome by a deep sleep. When he awoke, it was bright daylight, and the fruit was missing on another tree. The king and his two younger brothers came up to him, and the eldest said, "What do you want? When it got late, I couldn't stay awake any longer, and someone came again and stole more fruit."

"Well, I'm going to keep watch this evening," the second son announced. "Perhaps things will go better for me."

But they did not go any better for him because he was overcome by a deep sleep toward midnight, and when he awoke, it was broad daylight, and the fruit from another tree had been stolen.

"Dear Father," the second son said to the king, "it's not my fault. I couldn't stay awake. Somehow the thief returned and plundered another one of the trees."

"Well, tonight it's my turn," the youngest son declared. "I'm going to see if I can stay awake."

That evening he took his sword and went into the garden. However, he did not sit down but walked back and forth. All of a sudden at midnight he saw a gigantic arm reach over the wall and pick some fruit. Swiftly he drew out his sword and cut off the arm. The giant uttered a loud cry and ran away. The prince quickly climbed over the wall and followed the traces of blood because the giant had been wounded. Finally he came to a well where the traces of blood stopped.

"Good," thought the prince. "I'll find you again tomorrow." And he returned to the garden and calmly lay down to sleep. The next morning the king came into the garden with his two brothers to see what the youngest had done, and he showed them the giant's arm and said, "Now, my dear brothers, let's set out and pursue the giant."

They took a long rope and a small bell with them and made their way to the well, where the eldest brother said, "Whew! That well's really deep! I'm certainly not going to climb down into it."

The second brother looked down into the well and said the same thing, but the youngest said, "What kind of heroes are you!? Tie the rope around my body. I'm not afraid to try to go down."

They tied him securely, and he took the little bell with him and let himself be lowered into the well. It was very deep, but eventually he came to the bottom and stood in the middle of a beautiful garden. All of a sudden three beautiful maidens appeared in front of him and asked, "What are you doing here, handsome lad? You had better flee while you still have time. If the wicked sorcerer finds you here, he'll eat you because some one hacked off his arm this past night, and he's even more evil than usual."

"Don't you worry, beautiful maidens," the prince replied. "I've come here because I want to murder the sorcerer."

"If you want to murder him, you'd better hurry," the maidens said. "As long as he's still asleep, perhaps you can defeat him."

They led him into a great hall where the giant was lying on the ground sleeping. The prince crept quietly over to him, and with one stroke he sliced off the giant's head so that it flew far into a corner of the room. The beautiful maidens rejoiced and thanked him.

"We are three princesses," they told him, "and the wicked sorcerer kept us here as his prisoners. Because you have rescued us, one of us shall become your wife."

"For now," he answered, "we just want to get out of this underworld and return to the world above. We can talk about this once we reach the top of the well."

So first he tied the eldest sister tightly with the rope, gave the signal with the bell, and his two brothers pulled her up. When the eldest brother caught sight of the beautiful maiden, he cried out, "Oh! What a beautiful face! I want her for my wife!"

But she answered, "First pull up my sisters, and then we can discuss the rest."

When the second sister was pulled up, she was even more beautiful than the first one, and the eldest son cried out again, "Oh, what a beautiful face! I want her for my wife!"

Now the youngest sister was still down below, and when the prince tied the rope around her, he said, "You must wait for me, one year, one month, and one day. If I don't reappear, you may marry."

Then he gave the signal with the little bell, and his brothers pulled up the youngest sister. As she climbed over the rim of the well, she was more beautiful than the sun and the moon, and the eldest brother cried out, "Oh, what a beautiful face! I want her for my wife!" And wicked thoughts entered his mind.

"Oh," the princess said, "throw the rope back down to your brother. He's waiting for it at the bottom of the well."

So they threw the rope down, but the youngest prince was smart, and because he did not trust his brothers, he took a large heavy rock and tied the rope around it. As the other two princes began pulling the rope, they thought they were pulling their brother. When they believed he was half way up the well, they cut the rope, and the rock fell to the bottom and broke into a thousand pieces.

The prince saw how terrible his brothers were and what they had in store for him, and had to remain down below. "Oh," he thought, "how shall I ever get out of here?" He wandered through the entire castle down below and finally came to a stable where he found a beautiful horse. As he began petting it, the horse opened its mouth and said, "You are the one who killed the giant, who was my lord and master, and now you shall be my master. If you want to take my advice, then stay here until I tell you."

So the prince remained in the underworld and found everything he needed in the palace. Meanwhile, his brothers returned to their father with the three maidens. They told him everything that had happened and that the rope had ripped as they were pulling up their youngest brother. The unlucky prince, they said, had fallen back down into the well and was dead. The king began to weep and lament very loudly and could not be consoled.

After some time had passed, the eldest son married the eldest princess, and the second son took the middle princess for his wife. But the youngest princess did not want to get married. Afterward, the two brothers lived in peace and quiet and did not think about their youngest brother, whom they had murdered. However, the king could not forget his youngest son and wept day and night over him, and he eventually lost his sight due to all the crying. All the doctors of the kingdom were summoned to the palace, but none of them could help him. They all said, "There is only one way to save him, and that's the water of the Fata Morgana. Whoever washes his eyes with this water can regain his sight. But who can find this water?"

So the king said to his sons, "Have you heard what the doctors said, my sons? Set out and find the water of the Fata Morgana for me so that I can regain my sight."

The two brothers began their quest and traveled throughout the entire world, but it was in vain. They could not find Fata Morgana anywhere.

But let's leave them for now and see what's happened to the youngest brother in the underworld.

He was still living comfortably in his underground castle, and he had everything he wanted. One day the horse said to him, "Shall I tell you something? Your father has become blind because he wept so much for you, and the doctors told him that nothing can help him except the water of Fata Morgana. Therefore, your brothers set out to find it, but they won't find it because they don't know the way to Fata Morgana. But I know where Fata Morgana is living because she is my sister. So, get on my back and we'll set out to fetch the water."

The prince mounted the horse, and they began their journey. Along the way the horse said, "It will take a great deal to fetch the water because my sister is strong and powerful, and we can only get it from her if we are cunning. So listen to my words and pay close attention to what I say. First you'll come to a large gate that keeps opening and shutting so that nobody can get through. Take an iron rod with you, and stick it between the wings of the gate. That will create space enough to allow us to get through. Then you'll see a gigantic scissors that keeps opening and closing and cuts everything in two that it encounters. Take a roll of paper with you, wet it, and place it between the scissors. That will create an opening large enough for us to get through. Once we've escaped the scissors, two lions will come charging at us and want to swallow us. Therefore, you must take a goat with you, and you must throw half of it to the lion at the left, and the other half to the lion at the right. They'll become so occupied with the goat that they'll let us pass by. Then we'll enter a beautiful garden, and in the garden there's a fountain with water that is my sister's sweat. This is the water you're to fetch. Place a little bottle beneath it so that you can catch the drops. Next to the fountain you'll see a pomegranate tree with beautiful apples. Pick three from the tree because we shall need them."

The prince promised to follow everything exactly as the horse said. He continued riding the horse until he finally came to the large gate, which opened and shut with a great noise so that nobody could get through it. The prince stuck a strong iron rod between the two wings. This quieted the gate, and there was a crack through which the prince could force his way with the horse. Then he came to a gigantic scissors that opened and closed, and it was so huge and sharp that it could easily cut a man in two. However, the prince stuck a roll of wet paper between the blades, and while the scissors tried to cut the paper, he made his way through on the horse. No sooner had he escaped the scissors than two fierce lions came charging at him to swallow him. So he tore the goat into two pieces and threw one half to the right and the other to the left, and the lions pounced on the meat and let him and his horse pass by.

Finally he entered the beautiful garden in which the fountain was standing. He got off the horse, pulled out his little bottle, and put it beneath the fountain to catch some drops of the precious water. Then he picked three pomegranates and put them in a safe place. Now he should have followed the horse's instructions and waited patiently until the little bottle was full, but because the water only came out drop by drop, he became restless and thought, "While the little bottle is being filled, I could take a look at the castle a bit and see what it looks like inside." So he climbed the stairs and entered the castle, where he saw more treasures and precious things than anyone could imagine. The more he moved about the castle, the more splendid things he found. Finally he came to a magnificent room in which Fata Morgana was lying on a bed, and she was so beautiful that her beauty shone through all the seven veils that she was wearing. The prince bent over her and removed the seven veils, and when he saw how beautiful she was, he fell passionately in love with her and leaned over to kiss her. No sooner did he give her the kiss, however, than he was seized by such a terrible fright that he fled the room with the seven veils and ran out of the castle. In the meantime the little bottle had become full. He grabbed it, jumped on the horse, and dashed away.

Now, Fata Morgana had been wakened by the kiss, and when she saw that the veils had been taken off, she sprang out of bed to pursue the prince.

"Oh, lions," she shouted, "why did you let the prince pass through? Come and help me pursue him!"

All at once the lions jumped up and began to follow the prince.

"Turn around," said the horse, "and tell me what you see."

"Oh, my dear little horse," the prince cried, "the beautiful Fata Morgana is following us with two ferocious lions!"

"Don't be scared, and throw a pomegranate behind you."

The prince threw a pomegranate behind him, and all of a sudden a wide river rose flowing with sheer blood. Fata Morgana and the lions were held up by this river, but eventually they made their way over it. The prince had a good lead on them, but Fata Morgana was faster and soon was able to catch up with him.

"Turn around," the horse said, "and tell me what's happening."

"Oh, dear little horse," the prince cried out, "Fata Morgana is right on our heels."

"Don't be scared, and throw the second pomegranate behind you."

Then the prince threw the second pomegranate behind him, and all at once a mountain totally covered with thorns arose. When Fata Morgana and the lions tried to make their way over the mountain, they were miserably stuck by the thorns. However, they persisted and eventually made their way through the thorns with great difficulty and continued to pursue the prince.

"Turn around," the horse said, "and tell me what's happening."

"Oh, my dear little horse," Fata Morgana is right on our heels again."

"Don't be scared, and throw the last pomegranate behind you."

The prince threw the last pomegranate behind him, and all at once a mountain of fire arose. When the lions tried to make their way over, they were burned by the flames. As for Fata Morgana, she gave up the pursuit and returned to her castle.

After the prince rode for a little while longer, the horse said to him, "Look, there come your brothers! They're searching for the water of Fata Morgana. Tell them that you have it, and when they ask you for it, let them have the little bottle."

The prince did what the horse told him to do. He went toward his brothers and said, "Welcome, dear brothers, where are you heading?"

"We've been traveling to search for the water of Fata Morgana for our blind father so that he'll be able to see again."

"Oh, dear brothers," the prince said, "you'll never succeed. I've just managed to obtain a small bottle, but it almost cost me my life, and I know how difficult it is to get there."

When the two brothers heard this, they threatened to murder him if he did not give them the bottle. So he gave them the water, which they took to their old father. When he washed his eyes with the water, he could see again, and he was so pleased that he gave each one of his sons half of his kingdom.

Meanwhile, the horse carried the youngest prince back to the underworld, and he remained there for some time. One day the horse said to him, "Your brothers returned to your father and cured him of his blindness. Now it's time that you return to the world above."

So the prince put on royal garments and wished for a royal retinue. Then he mounted the horse and rode until he came to his father's realm. As he approached the city, he looked so gallant that people quickly spread the news to his brothers that a powerful king was coming with a large retinue. His brothers rode toward him, and when the little horse saw them coming, it said, "Here come your brothers. If they try to take you prisoner, don't resist."

As soon as the two brothers recognized their youngest brother, they said to one another, "Is that our youngest brother coming with such a large retinue? We are in for trouble. He'll certainly tell our father all about what we did to him. We had better take him prisoner right away and tell our father that a foreign king came to declare war against us, and we defeated him."

And, indeed, this is what they did. They pounced on their brother, who let himself be taken prisoner and said, "Just grant me permission to take my little horse into prison with me."

They gave him permission, and the prince was led into the prison with his horse. However, his retinue disappeared for it had only been created out of magic.* When the prince was in the prison with his little horse, the horse said, "Now pay attention to my words, and do what I tell you to do. Take this heavy club and beat me until I fall down dead. Then take a knife and cut my body open. This will bring both us our fortune."

"Oh, my dear little horse, I don't have the heart to do this! You've done so much good for me. How can I repay you this way? No, no, I won't do it!"

---

*Fataciumi.

"But you must do it," the horse said. "It is the only way to free me."

So the prince took a heavy club and beat the horse. With each blow he cried out, "Oh, my dear little horse, forgive me if I'm hurting you! I'm only doing your command."

But the horse said, "Be strong, and just keep beating me. Otherwise I won't die, and then you and I shall suffer a misfortune."

So the prince beat the horse harder and harder until the horse fell down dead. Then the prince took a sharp knife and cut open his body very carefully. All of a sudden, a handsome young man popped out and said, "I'm Fata Morgana's brother and was enchanted in the body of the horse. Because you've freed me, I'm going to help you now."

All at once he wished himself and the prince out of the prison, and suddenly the doors opened, and the two of them went out and walked to the outskirts of the city. When they were outside the city gate, they wished for royal garments and a mighty army. All of a sudden an army appeared behind them much larger than the king's. The army began to attack and shoot and scare the entire city. Meanwhile, the prince sent a messenger to his brothers who said, "Your youngest brother has arrived with a large army to punish you for all that you have done to him."

When his brothers heard this, they became very frightened, and their hearts became as thin as paper.[*]

"We had better go to our youngest brother," they said to each other, "and throw ourselves at his feet and beg forgiveness."

So they went out, fell to their knees, and asked for forgiveness.

"I shall forgive you for all the evil things you have done against me," their brother responded, "but you can no longer be kings. You must hand over my father's realm to me to rule alone. Now lead me to my dear father."

They led him to the old king, and the prince told him everything that had happened. The old king was very glad when he saw his dear son again and embraced him and kissed him.

While they were together and rejoicing, the door sprung open all at once, and a tall, beautiful lady entered dressed in magnificent robes followed by a large entourage. "I am Fata Morgana," she said, "and this young man stole my seven veils and kissed me while I was asleep. Therefore he must become my husband, and I shall make him into a

---

[*]U soi cori si fisiru quantu un filu di capiddu. Literally, their hearts became as thin as hair.

powerful king. As for the youngest princess, who is still single, she will become my brother's wife."

And this is what happened. There were festivities for three days, and the prince married the beautiful Fata Morgana and moved with her to her realm. At the same time he gave his father's kingdom to his brother-in-law, who married the youngest princess. And so they remained happy and content, and we did not receive a cent.

37

THE PIG KING

Once upon a time there was a king and queen who had no children, but very much wanted to have one. One day the queen went for a walk, and a pig ran across her way with her piglets.

"Oh, God, such a dumb beast has so many little ones, and you haven't even given me one despite all my prayers. Oh, if only I could have a child, even if it were a little pig!"

Shortly thereafter it seemed that the queen was going to have a baby, and soon her hour came. However, she gave birth to a tiny piglet. You can imagine the great astonishment and sadness in the castle and the entire land. Nevertheless, the queen declared, "This piglet is my child, and I love him just as if he were a handsome little boy that I had brought into this world."

So she suckled the piglet and loved it with all her heart. In turn, the piglet thrived and grew rapidly day by day. When it had become much larger, it began to roam around the castle and grunt, "I want a wife! I want a wife!"

So the queen said to the king, "What should we do? We certainly can't give our son a princess. There is none that would take him. Let's speak to the washerwoman. She has three beautiful daughters. Perhaps she'll give one of them to our son for his wife."

The king was satisfied with this proposal, and the queen summoned the washerwoman.

"Listen," she said to her, "you must do me a favor. My son would like to marry, and you must give your eldest daughter to him as his wife."

"Oh, your majesty," responded the washerwoman, "should I really give my daughter to a pig?"

"Yes, you should," the queen said. "Look, your daughter will be treated like a queen, and I'll give you whatever you want."

The washerwoman was a poor old lady and let herself be persuaded to carry out the queen's will. So she went to her eldest daughter and said to her, "Just think, my daughter, the king's son wants to marry you, and you'll be treated just like a queen."

To be sure, the daughter did not want to marry a pig. She thought, however, she would have beautiful clothes and all the money she wanted and said "yes." So, a splendid wedding was celebrated, and the festivities lasted for three days. The daughter of the washerwoman was dressed in expensive clothes. While she was sitting in her beautiful dress all spread out, the pig came running up to her. He had been waddling in mud and wanted to rub the dirt off on her precious dress. She brusquely shoved him away and cried out, "Oh, you disgusting beast! Go away! You're dirtying my beautiful dress," and no matter how often he came close to her, she drove him away with unfriendly words.

On the evening of the third day, after the marriage had been performed, she was led into the bridal chamber and laid down on a bed. The pig waited until she had fallen asleep before he entered the room. Then he locked the door, stripped off the pigskin, and turned into a handsome, noble young man. All at once he took his sword and sliced off his wife's head. When morning came, he slipped back into his pigskin, ran around the castle, and grunted, "I want a wife! I want a wife!"

The queen was worried and thought, "What if he has killed the girl?"

When she went into the bridal chamber and found the dead bride in the bed, she was deeply distressed and said, "What should I tell her poor mother?"

Meanwhile, the pig ran around the castle and demanded a wife. So the queen summoned the washerwoman and tearfully told her about the unhappy fate of her daughter.

"Now you must do me a favor and bring your second daughter to me so that she can become my son's wife," she said.

"How can I send my poor child to her death?" the washerwoman yammered loudly.

"You must do it," the queen said. "Just remember that if it works out, your daughter will be the first lady in the entire realm after me."

The washerwoman agreed once more and took her second daughter to the castle. The wedding was celebrated with great splendor for three days and the bride wore a beautiful dress. When she sat there in her gorgeous gown, the pig came running into the room. He had waddled in mud and wanted to climb onto her lap. But she cried out, "Oh, you disgusting beast! Go away! You're dirtying my beautiful dress."

On the evening of the third day she was led into the bridal chamber, and things did not go any better for her than they had gone for her older sister. When she was sound asleep, her husband entered the chamber, stripped off the pigskin, and turned into a handsome young man. Then he cut off her head. The next morning the queen came into the room and found the dead bride in the bed, while her son was running around the castle grunting, "I want a wife! I want a wife!"

What could be done?

The queen had to summon the washerwoman once more to inform her about the sad fate of her daughter and to request that she send her youngest daughter. Then the poor woman began to weep and said, "Am I to lose all my children?"

She did not want to give away her third daughter, but the queen continued to ask and suggested that her youngest daughter was much smarter than the other two. Perhaps she might succeed where the others failed. After a while the washerwoman let herself be persuaded and brought her youngest daughter to the castle. Indeed, she was very intelligent and more beautiful than the sun and the moon. All at once the pig came running toward her, and she bent over and called it "My pretty little beast." Soon a splendid wedding was celebrated for three days, and the bride received the most beautiful clothes. When she was sitting down in a magnificent gown, the pig entered. It had been waddling in mud and wanted to clean itself off on her gown. So she said, "Just climb up on my lap, you dear beast. Even if you make my gown dirty, it doesn't matter. I'll put another one on later."

No matter how often she changed her gown, the pig came and dirtied her garments. She tolerated everything and never lost her patience. On the evening of the third day she was led into the bridal chamber, and while she was sound asleep, her husband entered, stripped off the pigskin, and laid down next to her. Before she woke up, however, he slipped back into the pigskin so that she did not know what a handsome young man she had for a husband.

In the morning the queen entered the room with a heavy heart, and when she found the bride bright and cheery, she thanked God that everything had turned out so well.

For some days things continued like this. One evening, however, the young woman did not fall asleep, and when her husband stripped off the pigskin, she saw him in his true shape and immediately fell in love with him with all her heart.

"Why didn't you let me know how handsome you are?" she asked.

He answered, "Don't tell anyone what I look like. If you do, I must go away, and you must wander for seven years, seven months, and seven days, and you must wear out seven pairs of iron shoes before you can rescue me."

So she promised to keep quiet and not to tell a single person about him. Indeed, she kept her promise for many days. However, one day she could not resist an urge to tell the queen about her son.

"Oh, dear mother," she said, "if only you knew how handsome my husband is when he strips off his pigskin in the evening!"

At that very same moment the prince vanished, and no matter how much the people at the castle searched for him, he could not be found anywhere. So the young woman began to weep and said, "I'm responsible for his misfortune. He told me what would happen. So, I'll now wander seven years, seven months, and seven days until I find him again."

She had seven pairs of iron shoes made for her, and even though the king and queen did not want her to depart, she remained insistent and departed. She wandered for many many days until she came to a small cottage in which a good old woman lived.

"Oh, please," the young woman requested, "let me rest here for one night. Otherwise, I shall die of thirst."

The old woman welcomed her in a friendly way, and when she heard why the princess had left the castle she said, "Oh, you poor girl, you must wander in the underground until you have worn out four pairs of shoes."

So she gave her a small lamp and showed her the entrance to the underworld in which she had to wander, and the poor young woman began to walk. She traveled four years, four months, and four days beneath the earth until she had used up four pairs of shoes.

After this long time had passed, she returned to daylight and wandered on the earth once more. At one point she came to a dense forest and could not find a way out. Eventually she saw a light in the distance, and as she approached it, she saw a cottage and knocked on the door. A very old man opened the door. It was a hermit, who asked her what she wanted.

"Oh, father," she answered. "I'm a poor maiden and have been wandering and looking for my husband," and she told him the entire story.

"Oh, you poor child," the hermit said, "you must still wander farther, and I can't help you. But my older brother lives a day's journey deeper in the woods. Perhaps he can give you some counsel. You may rest here tonight. Tomorrow I'll wake you."

The next morning the hermit woke her, showed her the way, and gave her a hazelnut on her departure.

"Keep it in a safe place. It will be of use to you," he said. Then he blessed her and let her depart.

She wandered the entire day, and when it became evening, she came to the second hermit's hut where she spent the night and told him about her troubles.

"You poor child," he answered. "I can't help you, but my older brother lives a day's journey from here deeper in the woods. Perhaps he can give you good advice."

Upon her departure the hermit gave her a chestnut and said, "Keep it in a safe place. It will be of use to you."

Then she wandered another whole day in the dark woods, and in the evening she came to the third hermit's hut. She spent the night and told him about her sorrows, but he could not help her. Instead, he directed her to his eldest brother who lived deeper in the forest. Upon her departure he gave her a nut and said, "Keep it in a safe place. It will be of use to you."

On the evening of the fourth day she finally came to the eldest hermit who was so ancient that she was almost frightened of him. When she told him why she was wandering about, he said, "You poor child, you must continue wandering until the seven years, seven months, and seven days are up. Then you will arrive in the city where the prince is living. Take this magic wand. That night you are to go in front of the royal castle and hit the ground with the wand. All at once a marvelous castle will rise up, and you can live in it."

Then he blessed her and let her depart.

So she continued to wander until she had used up the seven pairs of shoes, and the seven years, seven months, and seven days had flown by. Finally, one evening, she came to the city where the Pig King lived. To be sure, he had his human shape, for the magic spell had finally been cast off, but he had forgotten his faithful wife, and a beautiful woman held him captive. In a few days they were to be married. When the poor young woman heard this, she felt sick in her heart, but she did what the hermit had told her to do. During the night she went before the royal castle and hit the ground with the magic wand. All at once a magnificent castle arose, and it had large rooms and halls and many servants. Of course, she went inside and began living there.

The next morning, when the Pig King went to the window, he saw the beautiful castle and was very puzzled. He called the queen so that she could see it, too. Meanwhile, the young woman had cracked the hazelnut, which the hermit had given to her, and just imagine, a beautiful gold hen with many gold chicks came out! They were very cute to see. She took the hen along with the chicks and set them on the balcony where the king and queen could see them. When the queen saw the hen and chicks, she felt a great desire to possess them. So she called her loyal chambermaid and said to her, "Go over to the lady in the castle and ask her whether she will sell the hen and the chicks to me. I'll give her whatever she wants for them."

The chambermaid went over to the palace and delivered the message from the queen.

"Tell your mistress," the young woman answered, "the hen and the chicks are not for sale. However, I'd gladly give them to her as a gift if she would allow me to spend one night in her bridegroom's chamber."

When the chambermaid returned with this message, the queen thought, "No, I can't let this happen. It's impossible!"

But the chambermaid said, "Why not, your majesty? We can give the king a sleeping potion tonight. Then he won't notice a thing."

So the queen agreed to the proposal, and the young woman gave the gold hen and the chicks to her and was led into the room of the king. Then she began to weep and lament: "Have you completely forgotten me? Seven years, seven months, and seven days I have wandered in rain and storm, and in the fierce heat of the sun, and I have worn out seven pairs of iron shoes in order to rescue you. And now you are going to be unfaithful to me?"

She wailed and groaned this way the entire night, but because the king had taken the sleeping potion, he could not hear her, and she had to leave the room the next morning without having wakened him.

Beneath the king's room there was a prison, and during that night the prisoners had heard everything that the poor woman had said, and they were astounded by it all. Meanwhile, she went home, cracked open the chestnut, and found a little teacher made of gold with her little pupils who were knitting and sewing. They were very pretty to see, and they were all made of gold. So she took the toys and set them on the balcony. When the queen saw the figures, she had a craving to posses them and sent her chambermaid over to the young woman to see if they were for sale.

"Tell your mistress," the young woman said, "I shall gladly give them to her as a gift if she will let me spend a night in her bridegroom's room."

The queen resisted, but the chambermaid said, "Why not? We'll give the king another sleeping potion so that he won't notice a thing."

When evening arrived, and the king was sitting at the table, the queen mixed a sleeping potion in his wine so that he fell sound asleep. Later, when his real wife came, he could not hear how she wept and wailed the entire night. But the prisoners heard it, and when the king awoke, they requested that he come to them for a few moments. They had something to tell him. So the king went to the prisoners, who said, "Your majesty, for two nights we've been hearing moans and groans from a lady's voice in your room."

"How is it possible that I haven't heard a thing?" responded the king. "Tonight I won't drink any wine."

Meanwhile his poor wife was very sad and had already gone home. When she arrived, she cracked the nut and found a beautiful gold eagle that shone in the sun with great splendor. She took the eagle and placed it on the balcony as she had done with the other figures. No sooner did the queen catch sight of it than she wished to possess it and sent her chambermaid over to buy the eagle at any price, but the young woman continued to give the same answer: "Tell your mistress I'll be delighted to give it to her as a gift if she lets me spend a night in her bridegroom's room."

"All right," thought the queen, "I'll just give the king another sleeping potion."

When it became evening and the king was sitting at the table, he took great care not to drink any of the wine that the queen offered him. Instead, he poured it out beneath the table. He pretended that he had been overwhelmed by sleep and went to bed where he began to snore as though he were sound asleep. All at once the door opened, and his real wife entered, sat down on the bed, and began to lament: "Have you completely forgotten me? Seven years, seven months, and seven days I wandered. In storms and rain, and in the glowing furious heat of the sun, and I wore out seven pairs of iron shoes to save you, and now you want to be unfaithful to me?"

When the king heard all this, he remembered his faithful wife, jumped up, embraced her, and kissed her.

"Yes," he said, "you are my dear wife. Don't worry. We shall flee this place tomorrow."

The next morning, after his wife had left him, he freed all the prisoners as a gesture of thanks for warning him, and secretly equipped a ship in the harbor without the queen noticing it. That night he went on board the ship with his wife and sailed home to his parents. You can imagine how they rejoiced when they saw their son and their dear daughter-in-law again! They celebrated with a beautiful party, and they remained rich and consoled, and we're just sitting here and getting old.

38

THE COURAGEOUS PRINCE AND
HIS MANY ADVENTURES

Once upon a time there was a king and a queen who had three sons whom they loved more than anything in the world. One day the king had to take a journey and said to the eldest son, "Tomorrow I must take a trip. Do you want to come with me?"

"Yes, Father," the son replied, and the next morning they set out and took some good food for their noon meal and were accompanied by a large retinue.

After they had traveled very far from their home, they came to a beautiful high valley, and it was so beautiful that the prince was extremely delighted by it and said, "Dear Father, how wonderful it is here! Let's stay and eat lunch."

"Let's go just a little farther," replied the king. "We'll soon be at another spot that's even more beautiful."

They traveled farther and came to a very barren and strange region, and after they made their way through it, they came to a second high valley that glistened with pure gold. Everything was made of gold, including the ground and mountains.

"Dear Father, how beautiful it is here," the prince said. "Now you must do me a favor and have a small house built for me here because I don't want to return to the city."

"My son, are you crazy?" cried the king, "How can you live here so far away from your mother and me? And who will stay with you?"

"Father, I'm asking this from you as a favor, and you must grant it to me."

In order to satisfy his son, the father called for bricklayers and carpenters from the city and ordered them to build a country house within three days. When it was finished, the king returned home, and the prince remained alone in his new dwelling. He ate and drank and fully enjoyed himself. Finally, when it became late, he laid down in his bed. At midnight, however, he heard a terrible noise—the rattling of chains and thunder. Indeed, he became so scared that he ran out of the house. No sooner did he leave the house than it collapsed with a great bang. Now he became even more frightened and ran back to the city as fast as he could. When he suddenly reappeared at home, his mother became extremely happy, for she had constantly wept about her lost son. As for the king, he asked his son, "Well, are you here again to stay?"

"It was impossible to stay there," the son replied. "If you only knew what a terrifying noise exploded all of a sudden!"

The second son made fun of his elder brother and cried out, "Look at our hero here! He couldn't even stand a little bit of noise. Father, now you must grant me the same favor and have a country house built for me on the same spot."

"My son, what's gotten into your head?" his mother cried. "No, you can't leave me."

And the king added, "What ideas you all have! Stay with us and forget this foolishness."

But the prince was stubborn and continued to ask for this favor until the king finally yielded and had a country house built in the same high valley, more solid than the first one. He accompanied his middle son there, and afterward left him alone. The prince ate and drank and was very happy about his beautiful house. When it became night, he laid down in his bed and fell asleep. At midnight he was wakened by a terrible noise, just as his brother had been, and he was so frightened that he ran out of the house, which collapsed at the same time. Indeed, he returned to the city as fast as he could.

The king and queen received him with great joy, but the youngest brother began to mock his older brothers. "Well, you two are something! How's it possible that neither of you could stay there? Father, now you must do me the favor and build me a house at the same spot."

The queen began to lament and complain very loudly because the youngest son was her favorite. The king, too, was angry and said, "I'd like to know what kind of pleasure you'd get out of such an adventure!

Your brothers were fortunate to have escaped with their lives. Who knows what will happen to you. I refuse to let you go there!"

But the prince answered, "You did favors for my brothers, and now you won't grant me one?" He gave his father very little peace until the king finally gave the order to send the carpenters and brick-layers to the same spot to build another country house. When it was finished, the king accompanied his third son to the country house and then left him alone.

The prince ate and drank, and when it turned dark, he did not lie down to sleep. Instead, he turned on a lamp and placed it on a table. Next he put a chair before it, sat down on the chair, lit his long pipe, and smoked comfortably and calmly. At midnight the same terrible noise was heard again, but he did not let himself be disturbed. Rather he continued to smoke very calmly.

"Bam! Bam!" the noise exploded throughout the entire house. The doors popped open by themselves, and a wild man entered.

"How dare you build your house on my property!" he roared at the prince, who did not say anything. Instead he kept on smoking, and no matter what the wild man said, he did not let himself lose his calm. The wild man moved around the room, looked at everything, and threatened the prince every now and then. When the clock struck one, however, he disappeared, and everything became quiet again. Then the prince laid down in his bed and slept peacefully until morning. When he awoke, he saw that the entire house had become gold—the walls, the floors, the roof—everything was made of pure gold and glistened in the sun.

Meanwhile, the king and queen waited for their son. When he did not come, they said, "Let us all set out and see what's become of him."

So they traveled to the valley with their two elder sons, and when they saw the gold house shining from afar and the prince standing at the window in good shape and looking well, they were very happy and embraced and kissed him. Then he led them through the entire house, and they ate and drank together. After the meal the youngest son said to his brothers, "Let's take a little walk."

They agreed, and all three of them set out. After they had gone for some time, they came to a very deep well in which there was no water.

"That's strange," one of the brothers remarked. "Here's a well without water. Let's climb down and see what's at the bottom."

"Yes," the other two cried out. "Let's draw lots to see who'll be the first to go down."

So they drew lots, and the eldest won. They tied a rope around his body, and he took a little bell with him as they lowered him. Deeper and deeper he went until, all of a sudden, there was so much noise caused by the rattle of chains, thunder, and lightning that he became scared, rang the little bell, and let himself be pulled up as fast as possible.

Now it was the middle brother's turn, but it did not go much better for him. When he heard the racket, he became so frightened that he rang the little bell and had himself pulled up.

"You two are some heroes!" the youngest cried out. "I see already, I've got to go down there."

So he tied the rope around his body, took the little bell, and lowered himself. As he was descending, he heard the terrible noise—the thunder and the rattle of the chains—but he paid no attention. Rather he calmly continued on his way, and when he came to the bottom of the well, he untied himself and looked around and realized that he was in a splendid garden. Right in front of him stood a beautiful maiden who said softly, "You unfortunate man, do you want to lose your life here? Flee as fast as you can!"

"Why should I flee?" the prince asked.

"Don't you know?" she replied. "A wild man is living here, and he's holding me and my two older sisters as prisoners, and when he sees you, he'll certainly eat you."

"Don't you worry," he said. "I'll free you and your sisters. Just let me know me when the wild man falls asleep. Then I'll creep into his room and kill him."

The beautiful maiden was very happy. She showed the prince where he could hide and told him that she was the daughter of king.

When the wild man was asleep, she called the prince, who pulled out his trusty sword, crept into the room, and sliced off the wild man's head. The three sisters thanked him, and then all four of them went to the bottom of the well to let themselves be pulled up. The prince tied the eldest princess first and rang the little bell. When the brothers heard the signal, they pulled on the rope and thought they were pulling up their brother, but when they saw the beautiful maiden who told them how their brother had rescued her and her sisters, they were very glad. Immediately they threw the rope back down and pulled up the second princess.

"Listen," said the youngest sister to the prince, "let yourself be pulled up first, otherwise your brothers may betray you."

"Oh no," he responded, "I'm sure they won't do that. Anyway, how can I leave you alone down here?"

"Oh, do it out of love for me, and let yourself pulled up first!" she kept insisting, but he refused to listen to her and she finally let herself be tied to the rope. Before she did this, she gave him a magic wand and said, "If things turn bad for you, this wand will help you."

He took the wand, and in turn he gave her a ring with a stone.

"Keep this ring in a safe place," he said. "When the ring begins to shine, it will be a signal that I'm near you."

Well, after the brothers had pulled up the third princess, they were overcome by envy toward their youngest brother because he had accomplished so much. They threatened the sisters and said, "If you don't swear to tell our parents that we were the ones who rescued you, we'll kill you. And if they ask about our youngest brother, you must say that you've never seen him."

The three sisters did not want to do this and begged the wicked jealous brothers not to betray their unfortunate brother.

"Don't you see?" they said. "We're three, and you're three. Why do you want to abandon him?"

But the two brothers answered, "If you don't swear to do what we say, we're going to kill you!"

Consequently, the poor maidens had to swear to do as they said, and the two brothers took them to their parents and declared, "Look, dear Father and Mother, we freed these maidens from the power of a wild man."

The king and queen were extremely pleased and said, "Well then, two of them should become your wives. But where is your youngest brother?"

"He separated from us," they said, "and we haven't seen him since."

When the youngest son did not come home, the queen began to lament his fate, and there was great sadness in the entire land. After some time had passed, the two brothers married the two eldest princesses. The youngest maiden did not want to get married, even though the king and queen continually asked her to choose a husband.

Let's leave them now and see what happened to the poor youngest prince.

He waited a long time for the rope to be sent down again. Finally, he had to admit to himself that his brothers had indeed betrayed him.

"The princess was right," he thought. "I should have had them pull me up first.

But he did not lose his courage. Instead he took out his magic wand and said:

"Listen to my command!"

"What do you command?"

"An eagle!"

All at once an eagle swooped down into the well and asked what he desired.

"Take me on your back, and carry me to the world above."

"Good," the eagle answered. "But take some meat with you."

The prince went into the garden where there was a whole herd of oxen. He slaughtered one of them, cut it into a thousand pieces, and put them in a sack. Then he sat down on the eagle's back and the bird began to soar upward. As the eagle flew, however, it constantly demanded meat, and the prince gave it a piece of the ox each time the bird asked. Now the well was very deep, and the meat ran out before they had reached the top. Well, the eagle asked for some more meat with a loud voice, and the prince thought, "If I don't feed it, the eagle will let me fall and I'll plunge to my death."

Because he did not have anything else, he cut off both his legs and gave them to the bird. When the eagle screamed for even more meat, the prince cut off both his arms and gave them to the bird. Only his torso remained. When they reached the top, the eagle put him down and said, "Now you can go home."

"How can I go in this condition?" the poor man answered.

When the eagle saw him so crippled, he asked, "Why did you do this to yourself?"

"You kept demanding meat, and because the ox was finished, there was nothing else to do except to give you my own flesh."

The eagle was very moved by this and brought up the legs and arms again and healed the prince. Meanwhile, the young man put on common clothes, blackened his face, and wandered to the city where the king and queen were living. As he approached the city, the princess's ring began to shine, and she thought, "What's going on here? My ring's beginning to shine so my friend is probably near here."

And even though the king and queen kept pushing her to look for a husband, she kept answering, "I don't have any desire to marry, and there's no one who pleases me among all the suitors."

When the prince entered the city, he went to the royal tailor and said, "I'm a stranger in this city, and I'm a poor wanderer. If you hire me as an apprentice, I'll faithfully serve you."

"I can't give you anything more than food and a room to sleep in," the tailor responded.

"That's good enough for me," said the prince and remained with the tailor and worked for him. However, he refused to wash himself and dress neatly, and he soon looked very dirty.

In the meantime, the king and queen continued to try to convince the princess to marry and presented with new suitors to her every day, but she would not accept any of them. Then one day the king said to her, "Look, my child, we are both old, and life and death are in God's hands. If something should happen to us, you would be left completely alone. Therefore, for the love of us, please choose a husband. Tomorrow I shall proclaim that all the princes, counts, and rich gentlemen are to gather here and participate in a great tournament* for three days. Each one of them will have to ride by on his horse in front of your balcony, and you are to throw your handkerchief to whoever pleases you most."

After a great deal of convincing the princess finally agreed, and the king had it proclaimed everywhere that he was going to hold a large tournament, and all the princes, counts, or barons were to gather at his castle so that the princess could choose one of them for her husband. At the same time the queen said, "Let's have royal garments prepared so that she can marry the very same day she chooses a husband."

The queen summoned her royal tailor and ordered him to make the clothes for the princess. "They must be finished within three days," she said, "otherwise, you'll pay for it with your head."

The tailor promised to do as she commanded, but because he had many other garments to sew, he could not make the clothes for the princess. The first two days passed, and on the evening before the third day he had not even begun to work on the garments. Consequently, his wife burst out lamenting, "Oh, why didn't you tell the queen that you couldn't make the clothes? Now you'll lose your head tomorrow!"

When the prince heard her hue and cry, he asked what the matter was.

"Oh Peppe, dear Peppe," the wife cried out, "can you help us? My husband must have these clothes finished by tomorrow, otherwise he'll lose his life, and he hasn't even begun working on them."

"What concern of it is mine?" Peppe grumbled, "You'll have to find a way out of this yourselves."

But the woman did not stop yammering and complaining, and he finally said, "All right, stop with your noise! Bring the clothes into my room, and I'll see whether I can help you."

They brought the clothes into his room, and he lay down to sleep. But the tailor and his wife were so anxious that they could not sleep, and they ran back and forth to his door. One time the wife peeked through the keyhole and said, "Oh, he's still sleeping, and he hasn't even begun working yet."

So they knocked on his door and cried out, "Peppe, dear Peppe, please start working!"

---

*Giustra.

"Leave me in peace!" Peppe roared, and they had to go back to their bed. After an hour passed they ran to his door again and saw that he still had not begun to make the clothes, "Peppe, you unfortunate child! You'll be the ruin of us!"

"Stop making so much noise!" Peppe growled. "I can't get a wink of sleep!"

They continued to bother him throughout the night, and the next morning when the tailor and his wife were not standing outside his door, the prince took out his magic wand and said, "Listen to my command!"

"What do you command?"

"A gorgeous royal dress, more beautiful than any other in the world!"

All at once a gorgeous dress lay before him, one that no other tailor could have made, and when the tailor and his wife knocked on the door again, he opened it and gave them the beautiful dress. Of course, they were full of joy and embraced him and thanked him. The wife brought him a beautiful cup of coffee, and the tailor said, "Now I'll take this dress to the princess right away, and I want you to carry it and receive the gift from the princess."

"Leave me in peace," said Peppe. "I don't want anything to do with the princess. I don't want any money."

"Please come with me," the tailor said. "Why should anyone else receive the present that you deserve."

Peppe let himself be convinced. So he took the dress and went with the tailor to the royal palace. As they approached the palace, however, the stone in the princess's ring began to shine even more brightly so that she became joyful and thought, "My friend is certainly very near. Oh, if only he would appear!"

As she was thinking this, a servant came and announced that the tailor and his apprentice were outside and had brought the dress that had been ordered.

"Let them come in," she said, and when they entered the stone beamed so bright that even the face of the princess appeared to be transfigured. Meanwhile, her heart said to her, "This dirty apprentice is none other than your friend." She examined the dress, and it pleased her so much that she took a purse filled with gold coins and handed it to Peppe.

But he said to her, "What should I do with your money? I don't want anything!"

"Please take it," said the tailor. "Then I can make you a clean suit."

The tailor kept insisting until Peppe took the money, while the princess kept thinking, "If he were really a poor apprentice, he would not have refused the money. There's no doubt in my mind that this apprentice is my friend."

After the tailor and Peppe left the room, the stone lost a good deal of its shine.

Now the time arrived for the tournament to begin, and on the first day the tailor said to Peppe, "Come with me. We can watch the beautiful show."

"Your beautiful shows don't interest me," Peppe growled. "Go without me."

When all the suitors had mounted their horses, they rode by the royal castle—first the princes, then the counts, and finally the barons and other rich gentlemen. The princess stood on the balcony and held a white handkerchief in her hand, and each one of the men thought: "She'll certainly throw it down to me." But she did not throw it to any of them, and the next day all the suitors had to ride by the castle a second time. Exactly the same thing happened, and she did not throw the handkerchief to any of them. Finally, the third day came.

"Peppe," the tailor said to his apprentice, "today you must go with me. I'm sure you'll like the tournament."

"Leave me in peace," Peppe growled. "What do I care about your tournament!"

However, the tailor would not leave him alone until Peppe was persuaded to go with him. When they came before the castle, most of the suitors had ridden by, and the princess was still holding the white handkerchief in her hand. However, when she saw her ring start to shine all at once, she realized that the prince had to be nearby. When she caught sight of the tailor and his dirty apprentice, she bent over the balcony and let the handkerchief fall on Peppe.

When the king and queen saw which man the princess had chosen as her husband, they became very angry and said, "Why have you scorned so many rich suitors and cast your eyes on a dirty tailor's apprentice? Well, then you can have him! We want you to leave the palace this very day, and we won't be giving you a dowry!"

"As you wish," she said, "but this man will become my husband, and nobody else."

The wedding was held, and Peppe and the princess had to leave the castle right after the ceremony and move to a small cottage that stood straight across from the royal palace. Peppe still did not reveal himself to his wife, but her ring sparkled and glistened so that it was a splendor to see.

Now one day, the two older brothers said to one another, "Let's play a trick today on dumb Peppe. We'll take him on a hunt, and then we'll make a bet to see which one of us can shoot the most birds."

When they went into the forest, they separated, and each one went in a different direction. However, no matter how much the brothers ran around, they did not find one single bird. On the other hand, Peppe shot such a large bunch of birds that he was not able to carry them all. Later, when they came together, and the two brothers saw how lucky the dumb Peppe had been, they said, "Oh, dear Peppe, give us the birds that you've shot, and we'll give you whatever you want."

"If I am to give you my birds," Peppe responded, "you will both have to allow me to make two black marks on your shoulders."

Because the brothers wanted to have the birds so very much, they thought, "Nobody will ever see these marks." They pulled their shirts from their shoulders, and Peppe made two black marks and gave them the birds. Of course, when they returned home, they boasted that they had shot numerous birds.

Some time passed, and the prince let everyone call him "dumb Peppe," and they continually mocked him. Finally he said to himself, "Enough's enough." During that night he took out his magic wand and said, "Listen to my command!"

"What do you command?"

"I want my house transformed into a beautiful palace with all the furnishings that go with it."

When the princess awoke the next day, she was in a magnificent bed, and her simple room had become large and beautiful. As she started wondering how this had come to pass, the door opened, and the prince entered. He had washed himself and put on royal garments and was even more handsome than he had been before. All at once she recognized him, embraced him full of joy, and said, "The ring told me, of course, that you were my dear husband. Why didn't you reveal yourself to me?"

"Because I wanted to test my brothers first," he answered.

When the queen awoke and saw the beautiful palace across the way, she was also most astounded and said, "What is that over there? Yesterday, there was only the little cottage where Peppe was living, and now there's a magnificent palace."

Immediately she sent a servant who told the princess that the queen wanted to invite her to dinner with Peppe. When the princess appeared with the handsome young man, the queen said to her, "Now that you've come with this fine gentleman, may I assume that you've had your fill of your Peppe."

"Dear queen," she answered. "This is Peppe, my dear husband."

Then the prince said, "Dear Mother, don't you recognize me anymore? I'm your youngest son. My brothers betrayed me and left me back in the well. I was able to make it back to this world and returned to the city in disguise. The princess recognized me and chose me as her husband."

When the king and queen heard this, they became very happy and embraced their dear son.

"After my death," the king said, "you are to become king. As punishment for their act, your brothers will be banished from my kingdom."

And that is what happened. The two jealous brothers had to leave the kingdom. Meanwhile, the king celebrated the return of his youngest son with great festivities. And so they remained rich and consoled, and we just sit here and are getting old.

39

THE KING WHO WANTED
A BEAUTIFUL WIFE

Once upon a time there was a king who wanted very much to get married. However, his future wife had to be more beautiful than the sun, and no matter how many ladies he saw, none of them were beautiful enough. So he called his faithful servant to him and ordered him to search everywhere to see if he could find a lovely maiden. The servant set out and traveled through the entire country, but he did not find any young woman that he thought was beautiful enough for the king.

One day, however, he had once again been wandering for some time and had become very thirsty. He came to a small cottage, knocked on the door, and asked for a drink of water. In this house there were two very old women, one who was eighty years old and the other ninety, and they made their living by spinning. Because the servant had asked for some water, the eighty year old stood up, opened the top of the door, and handed him the water. Due to all her spinning, her hands had become very white and fine, and when the servant saw only her white hand, he thought, "This must be a beautiful maiden if her hand is so white and fine." Consequently, he rushed back to the castle, went to the king, and said, "Your majesty, I've found what you've been looking for. Listen to what happened to me." And he told the king his story.

"Good," answered the king. "Go back again, and try to see her."

The servant went to the cottage, knocked on the door, and asked for some water. This time, however, the old woman did not open the top of the door. Instead she handed him a jug through a crack in the top part of the door.

"Do you live here all by yourself?" the servant asked.

"No," she answered. "I live here with my sister. We are poor maidens and make a living through our handwork. I'm fifteen, and my sister is twenty."

The servant went back to the king and reported everything, and the king said, "I want the fifteen year old. Go there and bring her back to me."

When the servant returned to the two old women and told them that the king wanted the younger of the two for his wife, she answered, "Tell the king that I'm ready to do his will, but you must know that since the time I was born, I have never been touched by a ray of the sun, and if a ray of the sun or light hits me, I shall become completely black. So I would like you to ask the king to send me a closed carriage in the evening. Then I shall travel to his castle."

When the king heard this, he sent her royal clothes and a closed carriage. When it became night, the old woman concealed her face with a thick veil and traveled to the castle. The king received her with great joy and asked her to take off the veil. But she answered, "There are too many candles burning here, and their light would turn me black."

As a result, the king married her without having seen her face. When she entered the king's chamber later on and took off the veil, the king saw for the first time what an ugly old woman he had taken for his wife, and in his rage he ripped open the window and threw her out. Fortunately, there was a nail on the wall. Her clothes got caught on it, and she hung there as if she were dangling between heaven and earth. By chance four fairies came by, and when they saw the old woman hanging there, one of them called out, "Look, sisters, that's the old woman who tricked the king. Do you think we should have her dress tear and let her fall to the ground?"

"Oh, no! Let's not do that," responded the youngest and the most beautiful of the fairies. "I'd prefer if we wished her something good. For my part, I wish her youth."

"And I wish her beauty."

"And I wish her wisdom."

"And I wish her a good heart."

This is what the fairies cried out, and while they were talking, the old woman became a gorgeous young maiden more beautiful than anyone had ever seen.

The next morning when the king went to the window and looked out, he saw the beautiful maiden hanging there and became very frightened.

"How unlucky I am!" he said to himself. "What have I done?! Where were my eyes last night?"

He ordered his servants to bring long ladders and to bring her down with great care. Then he asked her forgiveness and said, "Let's celebrate now with a big party and be joyful."

So they enjoyed a splendid party, and the young queen was the most beautiful woman in the entire city.

Now, one day the ninety-year-old sister went to the castle and wanted to visit her sister, the queen.

"Who is this ugly creature?" the king asked.

"An old neighbor who's half crazy," the queen answered quickly.

But the old woman kept looking at her sister who had been rejuvenated and said, "How did you manage to become so young and beautiful? I want to become young and beautiful, too."

She kept asking the same question the entire day, and the queen finally lost her patience and said, "I had my old skin stripped off me, and this new smooth skin appeared beneath it."

So the old woman went to a barber and said to him, "I'll give you whatever you want, but you must strip off my skin so that I'll become young and beautiful again."

"But, my good woman, you'll die if I strip off your skin."

Despite his protests the old woman would not listen to him, and the barber finally did what she wanted. He took his knife and cut her forehead open.

"Oww!" screamed the old woman.

"Whoever wants to look beautiful must suffer pain and trouble,"* the barber answered.

"Well then, slice away, master!" the old woman said.

As the barber continued to skin her with his knife, the old woman suddenly fell down and was dead.

---

*Cu bedda voli pariri,
  Peni e guai hav' a suffriri.

40

FERRAZZANU

Now I want to tell you the story about Ferrazzanu, the king's valet, a wild mischief maker, who was always playing dumb jokes on people. One day the queen said to him, "Ferrazzanu, I've heard that you have quite a pretty wife. Why don't you bring her here? I'd like to meet her."

"Of course, your royal highness," Ferrazzanu answered. "I'd be glad to do this, but my wife is so deaf that she doesn't hear well unless you scream at her very loudly."

"Oh, that doesn't matter," the queen said. "You can count on me to speak loudly enough. Just bring her here."

Then Ferrazzanu went to his wife and said, "Listen, the queen would very much like to meet you. Get dressed and come with me. But you must speak very loudly because the queen is so deaf that she doesn't hear a thing."

When his wife met the queen, she curtsied and screamed with a loud voice: "*Bene diceti*, how is your royal highness?"

The queen was not at all astonished that the woman screamed so loudly. Instead, she thought, "Poor woman. She speaks so loudly because she herself is so deaf." She answered in a voice that was just as loud: "I'm pleased to see you. I assume that you are Ferrazzanu's wife?"

When she heard the queen screaming, Ferrazzanu's wife also thought that the queen was speaking so loudly because she herself was deaf. As a result, the two of them held a conversation made up of such terrible cries that they could be heard throughout the entire castle. Meanwhile, Ferrazzanu stood behind the door and laughed about his prank to his heart's content.

When the king heard the noise and the screaming, he came running and asked the queen what was happening.

"Oh," she answered in her natural voice, "Ferrazzanu's wife has been visiting me today, and the poor woman is so deaf that you must speak very loudly to her."

"Who said I was deaf?" Ferrazzanu's wife stood up and exclaimed. "You're the one who's really deaf, your majesty. My husband told me so."

When the queen realized that Ferrazzanu had gotten the better of her, she became furious. The king summoned his valet and scolded him a great deal for his behavior, but he did not want to punish him because he loved him so much. Nevertheless, the queen insisted so often and so much that the rascal Ferrazzanu had to be punished for playing a joke on her. Therefore, the king decided to pacify her, and he wrote a letter to the captain of the fortress stating that the bearer of the message was to be given one hundred blows with a stick. This letter was to be carried by Ferrazzanu.

When Ferrazzanu took the letter from the king, he looked at it from all sides, smelled it, turned it, and kept doing this until the king asked why.

"Your royal majesty," he answered, "I cannot deliver this letter because it stinks."

"What, you scoundrel! How can you say that something stinks when it comes from my hand?"

"Indeed, your royal majesty," the clever Ferrazzanu replied, "it doesn't stink for you, but there's something rotten in it for me."

The king was delighted by his clever valet and would have liked to have canceled the punishment, but because the queen grew even more angry, he commanded Ferrazzanu to deliver the letter, otherwise he would banish him. So the despondent Ferrazzanu took the letter and set out on his way to the captain of the fortress. Along the way he met a strong peasant boy, and he called him to his side and said, "Listen, my handsome young fellow, would you like to earn a gold coin?"

"Of course. But first you must tell me how," the boy answered.

"Deliver this letter for me," the clever Ferrazzanu said. Then he gave him a coin and the letter, and to make sure things worked, he quietly followed him.

After the captain had read the letter, he quickly had his soldiers tie up the peasant boy and give him a hundred blows with a stick.

Ferrazzanu was delighted and returned to the castle. When the king saw that he was in one piece, he was very astonished and thought to himself, "Did he really deliver my letter?"

Then he heard the clever valet outside, singing loudly. "Not a bad deal for me today. What luck! I paid only one gold coin and escaped one hundred blows!"

When the king and queen heard this, they had to laugh so hard about the clever Ferrazzanu that they could no longer be angry with him.

41

SCIAURANCIOVI*

Now listen to the story about Sciauranciovi, who was just as smart as Ferrazzanu.

One time it so happened that Sciauranciovi ran out of money and had only some thalers left. However, he knew a nobleman, who was his patron and came to visit him every day. When it was about the time for the nobleman's usual visit, Sciauranciovi went into the stable and stuck the few thalers he had beneath the tail of his donkey. Soon thereafter the nobleman came, and when he saw Sciauranciovi in the stable, he went over to him and asked him what he was doing.

"Oh, your excellency," Sciauranciovi replied, "if you only knew what a magnificent talent my donkey possesses! He's a gold donkey, and he gives me nothing but hard thalers."

As he was saying this, he tickled the donkey so that it lifted its tail and let the thalers drop.

When the nobleman saw this, he cried out, "Listen, Sciauranciovi, you've got to sell me this beast. How much do you want for it?"

"Me? Nothing at all." Sciauranciovi answered. "The donkey's not for sale. Otherwise, how could my wife and I support ourselves?"

---

*In other words, he who smells or scents anchovies. Also Sciauranciove.

But the nobleman continued to ask, "I'll give you what you want. Just sell me the donkey."

"All right," Sciauranciovi finally said, "only because it's you, I'll let you have the donkey for four hundred ounces of gold."

"Are you crazy?! Four hundred ounces for this old ass!" the nobleman screamed.

But Sciauranciovi held his position until the nobleman finally agreed and bought the donkey from him for four hundred ounces of gold. Now Sciauranciovi was extremely pleased and ate and drank to his heart's content.

"What will the nobleman say about this when he sees that you've tricked him?" his wife asked.

"Let me worry about it," answered Sciauranciovi.

The next day about the time that the nobleman usually came to visit, Sciauranciovi ordered his wife to break out some stones from the kitchen floor and make a hole. Then she was to pour burning coals into it and cover it with stones. Finally, she had to place the kettle with boiling vegetables on top, and the kettle kept on merrily bubbling.

Soon after she did this, the nobleman came, and he was furious that he had bought a wretched normal donkey for four hundred ounces of gold and immediately began accusing Sciauranciovi: "So this is the way you cheat me after I've done so much for you!"

"Me? Cheat you?" responded Sciauranciovi. "Something like that would never occur to me."

"Yes, it would. You sold me a donkey and said it was a gold donkey, but it's only a plain ordinary donkey who hasn't provided me with one single thaler."

"But why should I be blamed for this?" Sciauranciovi declared. "Yesterday you saw with your own eyes how the donkey gave me hard coins, and if he isn't doing this at your place any more, it's a sign that he has lost his magic power because of the change of houses."

The nobleman was gradually pacified, and when he saw the vegetables cooking in the kettle on the ground, he was astounded and asked how something like that was possible.

"Well," replied Sciauranciovi, "the kettle has a special power. Whenever my wife sticks vegetables, meat, or water inside, the kettle boils everything all by itself, and she can let the kettle stay there and do this as she likes."

The nobleman was once again fooled by the clever Sciauranciovi and cried out, "You've got to sell me the kettle. I'll give you whatever you want."

"No, I'm not going to do this," Sciauranciovi answered. "You've already ruined my donkey, and I have nothing else to support me and my wife."

But the nobleman pleaded with him until Sciauranciovi finally said, "All right, just because it's you, I'll let you have the kettle for three hundred gold ounces."

"What? The old kettle for three hundred ounces?!" the nobleman screamed.

But Sciauranciovi responded, "Mind you this is not your ordinary kettle, and I can't give it to you for anything less."

Consequently, the nobleman gave him the three hundred ounces and took the kettle home with him.

"What do you want to make for dinner tonight?" he asked his wife.

"A vegetable stew,"* she replied.

The nobleman asked for the vegetables, put them into the kettle with some salt and water, and placed the kettle on the ground.

"Now we can take a walk," he said.

"Are you crazy?" his wife exclaimed. "What kind of a meal is this supposed to be?"

"Let me worry about it," said the nobleman, and he took his wife for a walk until it was time for dinner.

"Now let's go home," he said, "and we'll find our vegetables nicely cooked."

But when they returned to their home, the kettle was just as it was when they had left it, and they had nothing to eat for dinner.

The nobleman became very angry, and the next morning he went to Sciauranciovi once again. But Sciauranciovi was very sly and knew in advance that the nobleman would be furious, so before the nobleman arrived, he went to his wife and showed her two small gray rabbits and said, "I'm going to leave a rabbit here. When the patron arrives tell him that I'm not at home, but you know how to get in touch with me. Then say to the rabbit, 'Go quickly and call your master,' and let it loose."

So he gave his wife a rabbit and hid himself near the house. Soon afterward the nobleman arrived and asked for Sciauranciovi.

---

*Minestra.

"My husband is not at home," his wife replied, "but I'll call him right way." She turned to the rabbit and said, "Quick, my little one, go and fetch your master."

Upon saying these words she opened the door and let the rabbit run out. In a little while Sciauranciovi entered the house carrying the other rabbit in his arms, stroking and fondling it. The nobleman was so astonished by this that he soon forgot his anger and cried out, "How is this possible? Sciauranciovi! Did the rabbit really go and fetch you?"

"Certainly, your excellency," Sciauranciovi replied. "I can go wherever I want, and this little rabbit always finds me. That's why my wife sends him out whenever anyone asks for me."

"Sciauranciovi," the nobleman insisted, "you must sell me the rabbit. I'll give you whatever you want."

Sciauranciovi pretended that he did not want to sell the rabbit, but he finally let himself be persuaded and said, "Since it's you, I'll let you have the rabbit for two hundred ounces of gold."

The nobleman gave him two hundred ounces and carried the rabbit to his home, where he said to his wife, "I'm going out now. If anyone comes and asks for me, say to the rabbit, 'Quick, my little one, go and fetch your master,' and let it out the door."

When the nobleman had been away for a while, someone came to see him.

"My husband is not at home," his wife answered, "but I'll have him called." Then she said to the rabbit, "Quick, my little one, go and fetch your master," and she opened the door and let the rabbit outside.

But the rabbit hopped into the field instead and was no more to be seen. His wife waited and waited for her husband, but he did not appear and the visitor became impatient and went away. When the nobleman came home late that night his wife told him what had happened, and he realized that Sciauranciovi had tricked him a third time and swore that he would get revenge. The next morning he called four strong men to his house and gave them a large sack. Then he ordered them to stick Sciauranciovi into the sack and throw him into the sea. He went with them to make sure that Sciauranciovi would really be killed. So the four men forced Sciauranciovi into the sack and carried him away. When they left the city, they heard the bells of a small church ringing for mass, and because the nobleman was pious, he said to the four men, "Let's go and hear the mass. Set the sack down here next to the wall."

They did what he said and went with him into the church. Nearby there was a shepherd with a herd of sheep, and he was whistling a little tune. When the clever Sciauranciovi heard it, he began to shout from inside the sack: "I won't do it! I won't do it!"

The shepherd stopped whistling and looked around him in astonishment to see who had spoken. When he noticed the sack from which Sciauranciovi had cried out, 'I won't do it,' he approached it and asked, "What won't you do? Why are you shouting like this?"

"Oh," Sciauranciovi answered, "they want to drag me and force me to go to the king and make me marry the king's daughter, but I don't want to."

"Oh, if only I were in your place!" the shepherd exclaimed. "I'd marry the princess right away!"

"You know what?" Sciauranciovi responded. "Let me out and take my place. That way both of us will get what we want."

The shepherd agreed with great joy, and he untied the sack and let Sciauranciovi out. Then he crawled into the sack by himself, and Sciauranciovi tied it and was delighted to go off with all the sheep.

When the mass ended, the nobleman and the four men left the church, picked up the sack, carried it to the sea, and threw it into the water.

"So!" thought the nobleman. "I've finally got my revenge on that impudent creature!"

However, as he was on his way back to the city, what did he see but Sciauranciovi, who was cheerfully driving a heard of sheep before him.

"Sciauranciovi? Where did you come from?" the nobleman cried out.

"Oh, your excellency," Sciauranciovi responded. "If you only knew what happened to me! After you had me thrown into the water, I sank softly to the bottom where I found a whole lot of sheep. So I drove as many as I could together and came back to the top."

"Are there still many sheep on the bottom?" the nobleman immediately asked.

"More than you can imagine!" Sciauranciovi replied.

"Take me to the place right now," said the nobleman. "I want to get my share."

So they went to the seashore, and the nobleman crawled into the sack, which Sciauranciovi had to tie and throw into the sea. The nobleman sank to the bottom and drowned. Meanwhile, Sciauranciovi drove his herd of sheep to his home and remained from then on happy and content, but we still don't have a cent.

42

CACCIATURINO

Once upon a time there was a king whose wife died and left him with seven daughters, one more beautiful than the next, but the youngest was the most beautiful and the smartest. His ministers constantly advised the king to remarry and said, "The queen of the neighboring country is a widow and has seven handsome and strong sons. Listen to our advice and try to marry her, and you can give your seven daughters to her seven sons."

The king was very pleased with this advice, and he sent a messenger to the queen to ask her whether he could have the honor of marrying her and wedding his seven daughters to her seven sons. The queen agreed, and all eight marriages were celebrated on one day with great splendor. Thanks to God's blessing, the seven princesses soon became pregnant.

Now one day a war happened to erupt, and the king had to go off to the battlefield with his seven sons-in-law. So the seven princes went to their mother and said, "Dear Mother, we want to place you in charge of our wives. Look after them well when the time comes for them to give birth."

Upon saying this they went off to war. However, the queen was a wicked woman who could not stand her daughters-in-law, and because she saw them constantly weeping and moaning, she became impatient and called her henchmen.*

---

*Sicilian, i tiranni; German, Schergen.

274

"Take these seven women!" she commanded. "They do nothing but cry and lament every today. Drive them deep into the dense part of the forest, poke their eyes out, and leave them to their fate. But make sure that you bring me back seven pairs of eyes."

Consequently, the poor princesses had to leave the castle, and the henchmen led them into the densest part of the forest, where they attacked them and poked their eyes out without caring the least about their crying. Then they left them to their fate and brought their eyes to the queen. Meanwhile, the poor princesses were left in a sorry condition and could not help themselves. They had to remain in the forest and feed themselves from the pitiful herbs and roots they found.

Finally the time came for the eldest princess to have her baby, and she gave birth to a beautiful tiny girl. Because the poor princesses suffered so much from hunger, they killed the innocent child and ate her. A short time later the second princess also gave birth to a girl, and they ate her just as they had the first child. Altogether, six baby girls were born, one after the other, and they were all eaten. Finally the youngest princess gave birth to a beautiful tiny boy, and she said, "Dear sisters, let this child live. It's a boy, and he might be helpful to us later. Let's raise him and take care of him."

So they let this baby live, and his mother named him Cacciaturino. Indeed, he began to grow and became more and more handsome and stronger with each passing day.

But let's leave him in the forest with his mother and aunts, and let's look and see what has happened to the poor princes who spent a long time fighting in the war.

When they came home, their first question was about their wives.

"They're all dead," the wicked queen answered.

Just imagine the despair of the seven princes.

"And my wife died, too? My child as well?" each one of them asked.

"Each and every one of them is dead!" said the mother.

The seven princes became so sad that they all became sick and refused to be consoled. This went on for three or four years.

One day, however, their mother happened to send them into the forest to go hunting because she believed that this might distract them from their bleak thoughts. As they were hunting in the forest, they suddenly saw a gorgeous young boy about three or four years old, and he was so handsome that they called to him and asked, "What's your name, child?"

"Cacciaturino!"

"Who do you live with in this forest?"

"With my mother."

"Would you like to come with us and stay with us at the court? We are actually princes and we would treat you as our own child."

"Wait for me here a little bit," Cacciaturino said. "I must ask my mother first."

So he went to his mother and told her what the seven hunters had said to him.

"Tell the princes," she answered, "you'd like to go with them, but only if they allow you to visit me in the forest once a week."

So Cacciaturino went back to the princes, and they took him with them to the court and regarded him as their son. In particular, the youngest prince loved him with all his heart. But the queen had a sister, who was a wicked ogress. When Cacciaturino became twelve, the queen went to her sister, who said, "Do you realize who the little Cacciaturino is whom your sons regard as their son? It's really the child of your youngest son and the youngest princess. His mother is still living with her sisters in the forest, and you'll see, one day Cacciaturino will learn who he is and will kill you."

"My dear sister," the queen implored, "help me and give me some good advice. How can I get rid of him?"

"I'll tell you what to do. When you go home, pretend to be deathly sick and summon a doctor you have already bribed so that he will say that only the blood of an ogre* can save you. Then you are to send little Cacciaturino to fetch the blood, and the ogre will swallow him up."

The queen was pleased with this advice and went directly to the doctor and bribed him so that he would say what she wanted him to say. When she returned home, she lay down in her bed right away and wept and moaned, "I'm dying! I'm dying!"

"My dear wife," the king cried out very concerned. "What's the matter with you?"

"Quick, have the servants fetch a doctor for me."

The doctor was called right away, and when he saw the queen lying in bed he said, "If the queen does not receive a little flask of the ogre's blood, she will die."

"Oh, how can we possibly get that?" the king cried out. "Nobody can go to the ogre."

"Send Cacciaturino !" the queen responded. "He knows where the ogre lives, but do it fast or I'll die."

---

*Dragu.

So the king summoned poor Cacciaturino and said to him, "Cacciaturino, get yourself ready because you have to go and fetch a flask of blood from the ogre. The queen is sick and she will not get well unless she has this."

"Your majesty," Cacciaturino replied, "I'll carry out your command. Just grant me permission to go into the forest one more time to take my leave from my mother."

"You have my permission," said the king, and Cacciaturino went into the forest to his mother.

"Just think, dear Mother," he said when he was with her, "the king has given me a special task," and he explained to her what happened.

However, the youngest princess was very smart and said to her son, "Have the king give you a sharp knife and a flask, and then set out on your way to the ogre without any fears. When you get there, he will be lying asleep beneath a tree. As soon as you approach him, he'll grab you and swallow you. Don't be afraid. Just grab your knife, cut open his arteries inside his body, and fill the flask with his blood. Once you've cut his arteries, he'll die and his mouth will open. Then you can crawl out. Just obey your mother, my child, and no harm will come your way."

Cacciaturino went to the king and said, " Your majesty, give me a knife and a flask, and I'll go fetch the ogre's blood."

The king gave him a sharp little knife and a flask, and Cacciaturino went to the ogre, who was lying asleep beneath a tree. As Cacciaturino approached him, the ogre awoke and grabbed the small boy right away and swallowed him. Cacciaturino was somewhat scared when he was inside the ogre's body because it was so dark, but he remembered his mother's words, pulled out his knife, and cut the ogre's arteries. Now the ogre could not live much longer, and when he died, his mouth opened like a large gate. Cacciaturino filled the flask with his blood, crawled out, and rushed happily back to the king. Naturally, the king was very glad when Cacciaturino brought him the blood, and the queen pretended that the blood had cured her.

The next morning Cacciaturino went into the forest and told his mother that he had carried out everything as she had instructed, and his mother said, "Very good, my child. Just always follow my advice, and things will go well for you."

But the queen could not find any peace, particularly because Cacciaturino had come back safe and sound. Once again she went to her sister and said, "Dear sister, Cacciaturino has come back and the ogre did not manage to eat him."

"Yes, dear sister," the ogress replied. "I know. So now we must think up something else to bring about his downfall. When you go home, you must pretend as though you've suddenly become blind. Make sure you bribe the doctor again so that he tells the king that if you do not get the water of bona vista,* you will remain blind. The only person who has this water is me, and when you send Cacciaturino to me, I'll make sure that he never returns to you."

The queen went directly to the doctor and bribed him so that he would say what she wanted. Afterward, when she returned home, she began to groan, "Oh, help! Help! I've suddenly become blind!"

The king became frightened and rushed to her right away.

"Dear wife, what's the matter? Don't you recognize me?"

"Oh, if only I could recognize you. I don't see anything anymore!"

The king had the doctor summoned right away, and after he examined the queen for a long time, he said, "If the queen does not get the water of bona vista to wash her eyes, she'll never be able to see again."

"Oh," said the king, "where can we fetch this water?"

"Send Cacciaturino for it," the queen said. "He knows where to find it."

So the king summoned poor Cacciaturino and said to him, "Cacciaturino, you must set out right away and fetch a flask of water of bona vista. The queen has become blind and will not be able to see again unless she gets this water."

"Your majesty," Cacciaturino answered, "I shall carry out your command, but first grant me permission to go into the forest and take my leave from my mother."

"You have my permission," said the king, and Cacciaturino went into the forest and told his mother what the king had commanded him to do.

"Don't lose your courage," she said to him, "and listen to my words. Nobody else but the ogress possesses this water. Go back to the king and request a horse because it is too far to go by foot. When you get to the ogress's palace, you must be careful never to get off your horse. She will greet you in a friendly way and invite you to dine with her, but you must answer, 'If you want me to dine with you, you must provide me with a table that is high enough so that I can eat off it while sitting on my horse.' She will do this and will bring two plates, one with very good food and the other with poisoned food. Before you take a bite from the poisoned plate she offers you, you must drop your fork to the ground

---

*L'acqua di la bona vista. The water of good sight.

and ask the ogress to fetch it for you. She will offer you another fork, but don't take it. Instead, you must oblige her to bend over and pick up your fork. While she is bending, you must quickly exchange the plates so that she eats from the poisoned plate and will die. When she is dead, you must rip apart her dress and take the magic wand that she keeps by her breast. In the closet you'll find fourteen eyes. They are my eyes, and the eyes of my sisters that you are to bring back to us. Finally, fill the flask with the water of bona vista and come back to us before you take the flask to the king."

Cacciaturino rushed to the king and asked him for a horse as his mother had told him to do. Then he stuck his own fork into a pocket, mounted the horse, and rode to the ogress. When he came to her palace, she was standing at the window and called to him in a friendly way, "Hey, handsome lad, why don't you get off your horse and come inside and dine with me at my table?"

"If you want me to dine with you," Cacciaturino answered, "you must have a table set up so that I can eat off it while I am on my horse. This is the way I'm accustomed to eating."

Because the ogress wanted to poison him, she did what he wanted and had a tall table set up so that he could sit on his horse and eat. However, she herself needed a small ladder to get up to him. She brought two plates, which she put before Cacciaturino and said, "Just eat, my handsome fellow."

Cacciaturino responded, "I'm not accustomed to eating with strange forks. Would you mind if I used my own."

When he took his fork out of his pocket, he pretended that it slipped out of his hand and let it fall to the ground.

"Oh, noble lady," he said, "please be so kind and fetch my fork for me. I can't leave my horse."

"Here's another fork," the ogress replied.

"No, no, noble lady," he declared. "I'm accustomed only to eating with my own fork."

So she climbed down to pick up the fork, while Cacciaturino quickly exchanged the two plates. After the ogress climbed back up and took some bites of her food, she suddenly fell down and was dead. Then Cacciaturino ate until he was full, climbed off his horse, and ripped her dress apart. Right near her breast he found the magic wand and took it. Afterward he looked around the palace and found the fourteen eyes in a glass closet, and he took them all. Finally, he filled the flask with the water of bona vista, mounted his horse, and rode back to the forest in good spirits.

"Are you here again, my dear son?" his mother asked full of joy.

"Yes indeed, dear Mother," he responded, "and I've brought back your eyes."

Upon saying this, he rubbed the water of bona vista in her eye sockets, placed her eyes inside, and all at once she could see. This was also the way he restored his aunts' eyesight. Then he took out the magic wand and wished for magnificent clothes for his mother and her sisters and two gold coaches drawn by noble horses. Finally, he wished for a splendid palace that was to face the royal castle.

No sooner had he wished for all these things than they were there. They got into the coaches and drove to the beautiful palace where there were a great deal of servants and maids awaiting them. Indeed, the servants and maids bathed the poor princesses with sweet-smelling water until they were once again well and beautiful. The next morning the king went onto the balcony and he saw the glorious palace across from him. At one of the windows there were several women with a marvelous-looking boy. Because he was curious, he sent a messenger to invite the strange boy and the beautiful ladies to his castle. But when the messenger went to deliver the invitation, Cacciaturino replied, "Tell the king, my ladies do not leave their palace. Therefore, we would like him to honor us by coming to dinner this evening with the queen and her seven sons."

When the king heard this, he said, "Very well then. Let it be." And later he went to the palace with the queen and his seven sons-in-law.

Now just imagine how the table must have been set, and what splendid food they had. It's just enough to know that everything was made by a fairy. Cacciaturino only had to order his magic wand, and everything stood there and was more splendid than anything a king could order. At the table, Cacciaturino had each prince sit next to his wife. After they had finished eating, the king said, "How would it be if each one of us told a story?"

"As you wish, your majesty," Cacciaturino said, "and you deserve to begin."

"No, no, you must begin," the king insisted. "You are the youngest."

"Your will is my command, your majesty," Cacciaturino replied, "but only under one condition. You must give your royal word that no one may leave this room while I tell my story."

"You have my royal word," the king said, and ordered that all the doors be locked shut.

Now Cacciaturino began to speak, and he told the entire story, just as the one I've told you, beginning with the time when the king began to court the queen. With each word he spoke, the queen became more and more pale and would have liked to have left the room, but the king did not allow it because he had given his royal word. After Cacciaturino had told the entire story, he said to the king, "Your majesty, I am Cacciaturino. Here are my mother and father, and you are my grandfather. The wicked queen is the one to blame for the disaster that happened."

"And she will be punished for all this!" the king exclaimed. "Quick—seize her and put her into a kettle with boiling oil and throw her to the dogs."

And this is what happened. The wicked queen was cooked in a kettle with boiling oil and then thrown to the dogs. The old king lived happily and content with his seven daughters and their seven husbands. Cacciaturino succeeded so well because he had listened to his mother's words. Indeed, God does not abandon the just, and whoever does good will be repaid in kind.

43

THE VIRGIN MARY'S CHILD

Once upon a time there was a priest, and his neighbors found him very annoying because he did not let anyone come into his house. He washed and cooked everything himself and lived completely alone.

"This miserly priest!" the people said. "He lives completely alone and doesn't spend any money to hire any of us to help him."

So, they thought of a way to play a joke on him.

Now it so happened that there was a poor young woman who was living in the village at that time, whose husband had recently died. She gave birth to a wonderful, pretty daughter and died soon after the child was born. The neighbors took the poor little child and placed her at the threshold of the priest's house, for they thought: "He certainly won't be able to raise this small child alone. He'll have to hire one or more of us, and then we can earn some money."

When the priest stepped outside the door to his house and saw the innocent child, who was sobbing very loudly, he felt sorry for the baby, lifted her in his arms, and took her to one of his neighbors, who breast fed the baby. The priest gave her a certain sum of money every month for doing this. However, when the child turned four, the priest kept the child in his house, and the neighbors did not receive any more money from him, just as it was before. The little girl slept in the corner of a room where there was a little niche with the statue of the Virgin Mary,*

---

*La bedda madre or the beautiful mother.

who watched over the girl so she would grow and become more beautiful with each passing day. The girl called her "Mother" and spoke to her as if she were speaking to her own mother. The Virgin Mary taught the child how to read, write, and knit. When the priest came home and found the child doing some work, he asked her, "Who taught you how to do that?"

Then the child would answer, "My mother."

And the priest was astounded by this.

When the girl turned fourteen, the priest looked at her one day and realized how beautiful she had become, and he was overcome by lustful desires. So he climbed up on the pulpit and said, "My friends, I need your advice. Many years ago I found a young hen. Do you think I should sell her to you or enjoy the chicken myself?"

"Because you were the one to find the hen, you should enjoy it yourself," the people answered.

So when the priest returned home, he said to the girl, "I'm afraid of the night so I want you to come and sleep with me this evening."

The girl went to the Virgin Mary and told her what the priest said.

"Do you want to leave your poor mother?" the Virgin Mary spoke. "It's better if you stay with me. When he calls you, give him this drink. He'll fall asleep right away, and you can come back to me."

The Virgin Mary gave the child a sleeping potion, and the girl handed it to the priest when he called for her. After the priest was sound asleep, the Virgin Mary stepped out of her niche, took the girl in her arms, and fled with her. When they reached a desolate region, they found a small cottage, and the Virgin Mary stopped there and lived with the young girl who became more beautiful with each day.

Now, one day the king happened to be hunting in the forest and wandered into this desolate region. All of a sudden, he saw a marvelously beautiful maiden in front of him, and he found her so beautiful that he said to her, "You are to become my wife."

So he took the girl on his horse to his castle, while the Virgin Mary followed them. When the wedding was celebrated, the Virgin Mary went to the young queen and said, "I can't remain with you any longer, but when you are in trouble, you just have to call me."

Upon saying this the Virgin Mary disappeared. Now the king and his young wife lived happily together, and after a year had passed, the queen gave birth to two handsome boys. However, let's leave the queen and see what happened to the priest.

When he awoke that morning and could not find the girl anywhere in the house, he was filled with anger and swore that he would get revenge. So he set out and wandered through the entire country, through every village and every city searching for the maiden. Finally he came to the city where the young queen was living. It was just about the time that the great festival of Saint Agatha was being celebrated, and all the people were on the streets or on their balconies. "Good," thought the priest, "I'll go through all the streets and look up at all the windows until I find her."

When the priest walked by the royal castle and raised his eyes, he saw the young queen standing next to the king, and he recognized her right away. Then he had a servant inform the king that he was a clergyman and asked permission to watch the parade from the king's balcony as a favor. The king received him with great respect and took him also to the queen, who did not, however, recognize him. When the parade went by and everyone was watching the people carry a statue of Saint Agatha, and even the children's nurse was on the balcony, the priest slipped unnoticed into the children's bedroom, where they were in a beautiful cradle, and cut their throats with a sharp knife. Then he returned to the balcony and put the bloody knife into the queen's pocket without her realizing it. After the nurse had watched the parade, she rushed back to the babies, who were dead and swimming in blood. She uttered a great cry, and the king and queen rushed into the room. Just think of how grieved they were to find their children in such a condition!

"Who did this?" the king yelled in rage.

"Your majesty," the priest mumbled. "Look at the queen's dress. It has specks of blood all over it. I'm convinced that she has a bloody knife in her pocket."

The king grabbed hold of his wife and searched her pocket with his hand until he found the knife.

"Listen!" he cried. "If I don't murder you, it's only because I love you so much. But I don't want to see you any more. Take your dead children and leave the castle right away."

So the queen took her two dead children in her arms and left the castle in tears. When she was now alone on the road, she was overcome by grief and screamed out loud, "Oh Mother, where are you now? Have you deserted me completely?"

All at once the Virgin Mary appeared next to her and said, "Don't cry, and give me your children."

As she said this, the Virgin Mary closed the fingers on one of her hands and spit on them. Then she rubbed the fingers on the throats of the babies, and they immediately returned to life and smiled at their mother. The Virgin Mary took one of the boys in her arms, and the young queen took the other, and they continued wandering together.

"We must do something to earn a living," the Virgin Mary said. "So let's set up an inn on the road, and this way we'll be able to support ourselves."

So they had an inn built alongside the road, and the queen had to work from morning to dusk. The boys grew stronger and became more handsome than the sun and the moon.

Now let's leave the queen with her children and see what's become of the king.

He grieved so much over the loss of his dear wife and pretty children that he became very sad and could not be consoled. Meanwhile, the priest remained with him and always accompanied him. Many years passed in this way, and one day the king happened to take a trip and took the priest with him. During their journey they came to the inn where the Virgin Mary and the queen were living, and because there was a pretty garden with flowers, the king said, "There is such a pleasant shadow over there. Let's stop and rest here a while."

They entered the garden, and the queen received them, but the king did not recognize her. However, she knew him right away and rushed to tell the Virgin Mary, who said, "Let your children play in the garden with the golden apples that I gave them as a gift."

When the boys entered the garden and began to play with the golden apples, the king watched them. His heart was moved, but he didn't know why. Then he began to play with them without the apples and was delighted by the way they spoke to one another. Meanwhile, the Virgin Mary secretly took the golden apples and hid them in the king's pocket without his noticing it. When the boys wanted to resume playing with the golden apples, they could not find them and began to weep. Then the Virgin Mary said to the king, "Why have you done this to the innocent children? We received you with hospitality, and as thanks you've taken away the golden apples from the boys."

"Why would I have wanted to take the golden apples from the poor children?" the king cried. "See for yourselves. My pockets are empty."

However, when the Virgin Mary searched his pockets, she withdrew the golden apples.

While the king stood there speechless, she said, "Just as these apples were found in your pocket and you declare that you did not place them there, there was once a bloody knife that you found in your wife's pocket, and she knew nothing about it."

Then the king recognized his wife and his dear children and embraced them full of joy. At the same time, the Virgin Mary pointed to the wicked priest and said, "There's the murderer. Tie him up and give him the punishment that he deserves!"

The king ordered his men to seize the priest and put a pitch black garment on him. Then he was burned at the stake and his ashes were strewn in the air. Meanwhile, the Virgin Mary blessed the king, the queen, and their children and vanished. Then they returned to their castle and lived happily and content.

44

The Story About Ohmy

Once upon a time there was a poor old woodcutter who had three beautiful granddaughters. The youngest was called Maruzza,* and she was also the most beautiful and the most clever among them. The grandfather had no way of earning a living, had no money, and did not know how to support his granddaughters.

One day as he was gathering wood in the forest, he became so tired and exhausted that he sat down on a large rock and sighed very loudly, "Oh my!"

All of a sudden a large man appeared and asked him, "Why have you called me?"

"I didn't call you," the woodcutter said, visibly terrified.

"Didn't you cry out 'Ohmy'? That's my name," the huge man said. "You look as though you are a poor lost soul, so I'm going to help you. Bring your oldest granddaughter to me. She will serve my wife. Then I'll reward you with rich gifts. Lead her to this spot, call out my name, and I'll soon appear."

Upon saying these words, he gave the old man some money. Then the old man, full of joy, ran home to his granddaughters.

---

*The diminutive of Maria.

"Just think," he said to the oldest granddaughter, "you have been blessed with good luck. A distinguished gentleman wants to hire you to serve his wife. Now you'll be looked after."

When his granddaughter heard this, she kissed the ground and said, "I thank you, my Lord!"

After a few days had passed, she got herself ready, and her grandfather took her into the woods and called out loudly, "Oh my!"

Ohmy appeared, and when he saw the beautiful maiden, he said, "You've kept your word, and now your daughter will have it good. You may come here once a week and ask about her." Then he gave the grandfather a beautiful gift, took the girl by the hand, and led her to a large stone wall. Once they stood in front of it, the wall opened so that they could enter into splendid rooms that were filled with marvelous treasures and valuable things.

"Where is the mistress of the house?" asked the girl.

"The mistress is you," Ohmy answered. "And if you obey me and do everything I command you to do, you'll also become my wife."

With these words he led her through the entire castle and showed her the beautiful things. Finally, they came to a room in which there were many murdered young women.

"Do you see these women?" Ohmy said. "None of them obeyed me. None of them did their duty. That's why I had to punish them. So let this be a warning to you."

"If they did not obey you," she said, "then they got what they deserved. I'll certainly do my duty."

So the maiden remained with Ohmy and had a good life. After some days had passed, however, Ohmy came to her and said, "I must go away for three days, and I want you to carry out my orders while I am gone. If you don't do this, you'll pay for it badly."

"What do you want me to do?" she asked.

Ohmy gave her a dead leg and said, "You must eat this leg, and when I return, I don't want to see any trace of it."

Upon saying this he left her, but she remained filled with worries.

"How can I eat a dead leg?" she thought. "It's such a dirty, disgusting thing. Well, Ohmy will have to wait an eternity before I eat this!" She threw the leg out the window and believed that Ohmy would not notice it. However, when he returned home, his first question was, "Did you do your duty?"

"Yes, master."

Then Ohmy cried out, "Where are you, leg?"

"I'm here!"

"Come here to me."

Then the leg appeared, and Ohmy said to the maiden, "Because you've lied to me and not done your duty, you shall now receive your punishment!"

Immediately he grabbed hold of her, dragged her into the room where the numerous dead girls were lying, and murdered her.

After some days had passed, the old woodcutter came back to the woods and cried out for Ohmy, and when the large man appeared, the grandfather asked him, "How are things going with my granddaughter?"

"Oh, she's doing very well," Ohmy answered. "My wife treats her as if she were her very own daughter and would like to hire your middle granddaughter as well. Bring her to me here, and I'll give you another beautiful gift."

The old woodcutter ran home once more full of joy and told the second granddaughter that the distinguished gentleman wanted to hire her as well. She was very content, and the grandfather led her into the woods.

"Oh my!" he cried out, and immediately Ohmy appeared and took charge of the granddaughter. He led her through the stone wall into his palace and showed her the marvelous rooms with many treasures.

"Where is my sister?" she asked.

"I'll show you your sister right away," he answered and led her into the room where she saw her dead sister among all the other corpses.

"You see, your sister did not obey my commands. That's why I had to punish her this way. And if you don't obey me, you will suffer the exact same fate."

"Oh, I'll certainly do my duty," she replied, but she was trembling in her heart and thought, "Who knows what terrible command he gave to my poor sister?"

Some days passed, and one morning Ohmy came to her and said, "I must go away for three days. In the meantime I want you to carry out my command. Otherwise, something terrible will happen to you."

With these words, he gave her a foot from a dead person that she was supposed to eat. Then he departed, and the maiden was left with great worries and thought, "How can I eat this disgusting, dirty foot? I'm going to throw it onto the roof and tell that vicious thing Ohmy that I've eaten it." So she did this and believed that Ohmy would not notice it, but when he returned home, his first question was: "Did you carry out my command?"

"Yes, master!"

"Foot! Where are you? Come to me right now!"

Then the foot appeared, and Ohmy exclaimed, "Did you think you could really lie to me? Because you didn't do your duty, I'm going to kill you."

Then he dragged her into the room where the other dead young women were and murdered her as well.

After some days had passed the woodcutter returned to the woods to ask about his granddaughters.

"Oh, they are leading a good life," answered Ohmy. "My wife has taken a great liking to them as if they were her own daughters. Now she would like to have your third granddaughter as well."

The poor woodcutter felt he would explode from joy now that all his granddaughters would be well looked after. So he rushed home to his youngest granddaughter and said, "Maruzza, get yourself ready quickly. The distinguished gentleman wants to hire you as well." Then the grandfather led her into the woods, where Ohmy was very friendly to her and led her through the stone wall.

"Where are my sisters?" Maruzza asked.

"I'll show them to you right away," he responded and opened the door to the room in which all the corpses were lying.

"You see your sisters. They're lying there because they didn't do their duty."

Poor Maruzza's heart trembled, but she only said, "You did the right thing by punishing them if they didn't do their duty. You can order me to do anything you want. I'll do whatever say."

After a several days had passed, Ohmy said to Maruzza, "I've got to go away for three days, and now the time has come when you can show me how obedient you are. You see this arm from a dead person. You must eat it while I'm gone, and I don't want to see the slightest trace of it when I return."

With these words he departed and left poor Maruzza troubled by her worries and thoughts.

"Oh," she thought, "what should I do now? Oh, I'm so unlucky! How can I eat the arm of a dead person! Oh blessed soul of my mother, come and tell me what I should do!"

All of a sudden she heard a voice that called out to her, "Maruzza, don't weep. I shall help you. Heat the oven and make it as hot as possible, and leave the arm inside until it its burned into coals. Then grind the coals into powder and wrap them in a fine cloth around your waist. Ohmy will not notice a thing and won't harm you."

This voice was the blessed soul of her mother. Indeed, Maruzza did everything the voice told her to do. She heated the oven and placed the arm inside until it was burned into coals. Then she ground the coals, wrapped the powder in a fine cloth, and tied it around her waist.

When Ohmy returned home, he asked right away, "Did you carry out my command?"

"Yes, master!"

"Arm, where are you? Come to me now!"

"I can't come," the arm answered.

"Where are you?"

"I'm in Maruzza's body."

When Ohmy heard this, he became very happy and cried, "Well, Maruzza, you will become my wife, for now I know that you're honest and obedient."

From then on Maruzza led a good life with him. Ohmy loved her and gave her everything she wished. One day he also showed her all his closets in which he had many bottles with potions and salves.

"Look," he said. "Here is a salve for dead people. When you rub the salve on them, they return to life. I'm showing it to you because I know that you are loyal to me."

After he had shown her everything, he led her also to a locked door and said, "Look, Maruzza. Everything that's in this castle belongs to you, and you may do whatever you wish with it. However, you may never open this door. If I ever notice that you've opened it, I'll kill you."

No sooner had Ohmy gone on his next trip, however, than Maruzza took her bundle of keys and opened the door. When she entered the room, she saw a marvelously handsome young man lying on the ground as if he were dead, and a dagger was stuck in his heart.

"Oh!" Maruzza thought full of sympathy. "What a poor unfortunate young man! This is why that wicked Ohmy didn't want me to open the door."

So she ran out and fetched some of the salve. Then she returned to the young man, pulled the dagger from his heart, and rubbed the wound with the salve. All of a sudden the young man opened his eyes and was healed.

"Beautiful maiden," he cried. "You've saved me. Let me tell you that I'm a prince, and the evil Ohmy dragged me here and has kept me a prisoner."

"Oh," she responded. "What's the use now that you're cured? Ohmy will soon return, and when he sees that you're healthy and have regained your life, he will kill both of us. So you had better lie down again, and I'll stick the dagger into your heart. Then I'll see what we can do to murder the wicked Ohmy."

And this is what they did. The prince lay down again, and Maruzza stuck the dagger into his heart while shedding many tears, especially because she had fallen passionately in love with him.

When Ohmy returned home, she went with him into the garden and flattered him with many sweet words.

"Tell me, dear master, if you ever had the misfortune of being pursued by someone who wanted to take your life, what would he have to do to kill you?"

"Why are you asking me this?" Ohmy replied. "Do you want perhaps to betray me?"

"Oh, how can you think such a thing like that!? Aren't I your obedient, faithful Maruzza? It was just a thought that went through my head."

"Well, because I know I can trust you, I'll tell you," Ohmy said. "Look, no one can kill me, but if someone were to take a twig from this herb right here and stuff it into my ear, then I would fall asleep and never wake up again."

"Now, now, don't tell me any more. I don't want to know anything about it," Maruzza responded, but secretly she leaned over, broke off a twig of the herb, and put it into her pocket.

"Now, sit down over here," she said to Ohmy, "and I'll clean the lice from your hair."

After she sat down, he laid his head in her lap, and she began picking the lice from his beard until he fell asleep. Then she quickly took the herb and stuffed it into both ears so that he fell into a deeper sleep. Afterward she left him in the garden and rushed back to the house, took the salve, and rubbed it on the prince so that he came back to life once more. Then she ran into the other room where the dead maidens were lying, and she rubbed all of them with the salve. First her sisters, then all the other young women whom the evil Ohmy had murdered one by one. When they were all alive once again, Maruzza gave them rich gifts and sent them back to their homes. She and the prince took the rest of the treasures and traveled to the prince's realm. Just think of the joy of the king and queen as their son came home, for they had wept for many years and had thought that he was dead. Now he had returned and even brought with him a beautiful and clever maiden. So a splendid wedding was celebrated, and the prince married the beautiful Maruzza and lived with her happy and content.

In the meantime, Ohmy lay in the garden and slept and slept for many years. Eventually, however, the herb became old and rotten because of the wind and rain, and one day it fell out and Ohmy awoke from his sleep.

"Where am I?" he thought. Then he jumped up and ran into the house. When he saw nothing but empty walls he became furious and yelled, "That good-for-nothing Maruzza! She betrayed me after I had placed so much trust in her. Just wait—I'll get my revenge on her!"

So he set out and wandered through many countries in search of Maruzza. He wandered far and wide, until one day he finally came to the city in which Maruzza lived. When he went through the streets, he accidentally raised his eyes and saw the beautiful Maruzza standing at a window.

"Ho-ho!" he thought. "You're here, and you're living gloriously in a royal palace!? Just you wait! I'm going to get you yet!"

So he went to a shop and made a statue out of silver that was just as large as he was himself, but hollow on the inside. Then he placed many instruments inside to make music, called for a young man, and said to him, "I'll give you a beautiful gift if you carry this statue on your back through the entire city and charge people money to see it. After you've done this, you're to take it to the king and leave it with him for several days."

The young man promised Ohmy that he would take care of everything, and Ohmy locked himself in the statue. The young man carried the statue through the streets of the entire city and cried out, "Hey, look at the beautiful Saint Nicholas, and listen to the beautiful music he can make!"

When the people heard the young man, many of them called him over and asked, "Let Saint Nicholas stay here for some days so that we can enjoy his music. We'll give you a beautiful gift if you do this."

So the young man took the statue into different houses, and Ohmy played so wonderfully that everyone in the city spoke about the marvelous statue and nothing else, and everyone wanted to see and hear it. Gradually, the news spread to the king and to Maruzza, and she said, "Oh, call the young man with the statue to come to us. I'd like to keep the statue here with us for a few days."

So the king had the young man summoned to the castle and gave him a beautiful present so that he would leave Saint Nicholas with them for a few days. The king had the young man carry the statue into his bedroom, where he enjoyed the beautiful music with Maruzza. In the evening, however, when both of them had lain down to sleep, Maruzza suddenly heard a soft noise and cried out, "Help!"

"What's the matter?" the king asked, and all the people in the palace were terrified and gathered together.

"I heard a noise near the statue," Maruzza said, but when the servants looked through the entire room they found nothing, and the king thought that Maruzza must have dreamed something. When everything was quiet, the same noise could be heard again. Maruzza cried out once more and the servants came running, but they could not find anything, and the king said, "Maruzza, you're dreaming. When you cry out again, I don't want anyone to come."

Meanwhile, in the statue, Ohmy heard this, and it was exactly what he wanted. When the king fell back to sleep, he quietly opened the statue and came out. Maruzza screamed out loud, but no one came because Ohmy quickly placed a bottle with a potion on the bed. As soon as he did this, the king and all the people in the palace fell into a deep sleep. No one woke up. Only Maruzza remained awake and saw Ohmy approach her and grab her by the arm.

"You betrayed me!" he cried. "And you thought you were safe here! Now you're in my power and won't escape your punishment."

Then he went into the kitchen, started a large fire, and placed a huge kettle with oil on the fire. When the oil was boiling just right, he rushed back into the room, grabbed the poor Maruzza, and started to drag her into the kitchen to throw her into the kettle of boiling oil. She wept and screamed, but nobody heard her because the king and everyone in the castle had been put under a spell. As she sought to defend herself, the bottle with the potion fell off the bed and broke on the ground. All of a sudden the king awoke, and the servants came storming into the room. Maruzza cried out, "Help! Help! This vicious monster wants to murder me!"

Then the servants grabbed hold of the evil Ohmy, and the king recognized him and ordered the servants to throw him into the same kettle with boiling oil in which he had wanted to kill Maruzza. And this is what happened. The wicked Ohmy was thrown into the boiling oil and was miserably burned to death, but the king and Maruzza lived for a long time still, rich and consoled, and we have nothing as we get old.

45

THE DAUGHTER OF
PRINCE CIRIMIMMINU

Once upon a time there was a prince named Cirimimminu, whose wife died and left him with a daughter who was very beautiful. Because he did not have a wife, he sent his daughter to a teacher every day, and this woman taught her how to sew and work. Before she went to the teacher, she usually went to the balcony each morning to water the jasmine.

Now the son of the king happened to live across from the house of her father. He also stood on his balcony every morning and watched the beautiful maiden water the jasmine. One day he spoke to her:

"Daughter, daughter of Cirimimminu
Count how many leaves the jasmine may have."*

The prince's daughter, however, was speechless and did not know how to answer him. Later, when she went to the teacher, she told her what the king had said to her.

"Now, put your mind at rest," the teacher said. "When he says the same thing to you tomorrow, you're to answer:

"Son of the king, by the crown of your father,

---

*Figghia, figghia di Cirimimminu,
    Cunta, quanti fogghi c'è ntrô gersuminu.

Count the stars on the dome of heaven.
Son of the king and the queen as well
Count how many feathers the chicken may have.”*

The next morning, as the beautiful maiden was watering her flowers again, she heard the son of the king cry out:

“Daughter, daughter of Cirimimminu
Count how many leaves the jasmine may have.”

Then she answered him with a certain impudence:

“Son of the king, by the crown of your father,
Count the stars on the dome of heaven.
Son of the king and the queen as well
Count how many feathers the chicken may have.”

The son of the king became very upset and thought, “What impudence! Wait, I’ll pay you back for answering me that way.”

He went to the teacher and said, “I’ll give you whatever you want if you do me a favor. I’m going to pass by here today disguised as a fisherman, and I’ll be carrying a basket with the most beautiful fish. Then I’ll cry out: ‘Whoever gives me a kiss will have all these fish for nothing.’ Then send out the daughter of Prince Cirimimminu so that she’ll kiss me.”

Later, when the beautiful maiden was sitting with the teacher and the other girls, a fisherman came by carrying a basket full of the most beautiful fish and called out, “Whoever gives me a kiss will have all these fish for nothing.”

“Do you hear that?” the teacher spoke to the daughter of Prince Cirimimminu. “You are the most pretty maiden here. Go and give the man a kiss.”

But the maiden resisted and said that there were other girls who could just as well go and give him a kiss, but the teacher kept insisting, “You’re the one to go because you are the most beautiful.”

Finally she let herself be persuaded, went outside, and gave the fisherman a kiss. But, when the fisherman received the kiss, he scampered away with all the fish, and she was left standing there somewhat

---

*Figghiu, figghiu di re nourunatu
  Cunta quanti stiddi c’è ntrô stiddatu.
  Figghiu, Figghiu di rè e di riggina
  Cunta, quanti pinni teni na gaddina.

bewildered. The next morning the king's son was standing again on the balcony, and when the beautiful maiden came out to water her flowers, he called over to her:

"Daughter, daughter of Cirimimminu
Count how many leaves the jasmine may have."

"Son of the king, by the crown of your father,
Count the stars on the dome of heaven.
Son of the king and the queen as well
Count how many feathers the chicken may have."

"Oh how beautiful was your kiss,
and just think of all the fish you have missed!"*

"So, you were the fisherman," the beautiful maiden thought. "Just you wait. Now the joke will be on you."

Immediately thereafter the maiden went to her father and said, "Dear Father, please give me the most beautiful horse that can be found in the city."

Once she had the horse, she disguised herself in men's clothes and rode back and forth in front of the king's window. The ministers happened to be standing on the balcony right at that moment, and they called the king's son and told him that a young man was riding a wonderful horse, and they had never seen any horse like it in the entire city. When the king's son saw the horse, he wanted to buy it, and sent a mini-ster down to the street to ask the young man how much he wanted for the horse.

"I won't sell the horse," the young man said. "But whoever gives the horse three kisses on its leg can have it for nothing."

When the king's son heard this, he thought: "Three kisses for such a horse! I might as well give them," and he rushed down to the street.

As he leaned down to give the kisses, the beautiful maiden hit the horse with her spurs so that it jumped up, neighed, and dashed off.

The next morning the king's son was on the balcony again. When the maiden came out to water her flowers he cried out:

"Daughter, daughter of Cirimimminu
Count how many leaves the jasmine may have."

---

*Chi fu bedda dda basciata, e pisci non n'avisti!

"Son of the king, by the crown of your father,
Count the stars on the dome of heaven.
Son of the king and the queen as well
Count how many feathers the chicken may have."

"Oh how beautiful was your kiss!
And just think of all the fish you have missed."

"Oh how sweet was the kiss on the horse's leg,
And just think of how you have missed the horse!"*

The king's son realized immediately that she had been the young man and thought of another way to trick her. So he went to the teacher and promised to give her whatever she wanted if she would get the beautiful daughter of Cirimimminu to sleep at her place and let him hide beneath the bed.

The next day, when it had become evening and the beautiful maiden wanted to go home, the teacher asked her, "Oh, please stay with me tonight. I'm afraid to be alone."

So the maiden stayed with her, and meanwhile, the king's son hid underneath the bed and had long needles and stuck the maiden through the mattresses.

"Oh!" she cried out. "Teacher, there are bugs and fleas in your bed!"

"Calm down, my child," the teacher answered. "You're only imagining things."

But the king's son did not let her get any rest, and she could not sleep that entire night. The next morning she went home to water her flowers, and the king's son was standing at the window and called out:

"Daughter, daughter of Cirimimminu
Count how many leaves the jasmine may have."

"Son of the king, by the crown of your father,
Count the stars on the dome of heaven.
Son of the king and the queen as well
Count how many feathers the chicken may have."

"Oh how beautiful was your kiss,

---

*Chi fu bedda dda basciata, sutt'a a cuda du cavaddu, e cavaddu non n'avisti!

And just think of all the fish you have missed."

"Oh how sweet was the kiss on the horse's leg,
And just think of how you have missed the horse!"

"And how sweet was the entire night:
Oh teacher, bugs and fleas in your bed!"*

"Aha," thought the beautiful maiden. "You were hiding beneath the bed! Just you wait. I'll make you pay for this."

So she summoned one of the king's servants and said to him, "I'll give you whatever you want if you let me spend the night in the room of the king's son."

That evening she put on a large black coat that also covered her face. When the king's son went to bed, she went into his room and spoke to him with a hollow voice:

"Death has won
The poor king's son.
Death is here with his evil eye,
It's time to say good bye!"†

But the king's son cried out:

"Let me live, Death, at least until dawn,
Until I can see Cirimimminu's daughter once more."‡

Death answered:

"If you really want me to wait until the next day
I want every hair from your beard and right away!"§

---

*E chi fu bedda na nuttata: Ai, Signura Maistra, pulici, e cimici c'è ntrô vostru lettu!

† Veni la morti
   Cu l'anchi storti!
   Lu figghiu du rè
   Si l'avi a pigghià!

‡ No, morti, lassami nsinu a matinu
   Quantu vidu la bedda di Cirimimminu.

§ Si t'hâ a lassari nsinu a matinu,
   T'hâ a scippari la barba a filu a filu!

Now the king's son had a handsome large beard, and because he was so frightened by death, he let each and every hair be pulled from his beard. Finally, when the beautiful maiden thought she had made him suffer enough, she went away.

The next morning the maiden began to tease him once more and called out:

"Daughter, daughter of Cirimimminu
Count how many leaves the jasmine may have."

"Son of the king, by the crown of your father,
Count the stars on the dome of heaven.
Son of the king and the queen as well
Count how many feathers the chicken may have."

"Oh how beautiful was your kiss,
And just think of all the fish you have missed."

"Oh how sweet was the kiss on the horse's leg,
and just think of how you have missed the horse!"

"And how sweet was the entire night:
Oh teacher, bugs and fleas in your bed!"

"How beautiful was your beard
each hair plucked out!"*

When the king's son heard that she had been death and had ripped out his handsome beard, he swore he would avenge himself and somehow get control of her. So, he went to Prince Cirimimminu and told him that he wanted to marry his daughter. The prince was, of course, very happy about this and told his daughter. But she replied, "All right, dear Father, but you must make a doll for me out of sugar and honey. It's got to be as large as I am and look like me. Around it's neck there has to be a string so that the head will nod when the string is pulled."

The prince did as she requested, and the wedding was celebrated in full glory. When the king's son wanted to lead the beautiful daughter of Prince Cirimimminu into the bridal suite, she said, "Let me go first. I'll get into bed, and then you follow."

---

*Chi fu bedda la barba scippata a filu a filu!

She placed the doll in the bed and instead hid beneath the bed and held the string that was tied to the head of the doll. When the king's son entered the room, he held a shining sword in his hand, ready to cut off her head.

"Are you the one who forced me to kiss the horse's leg?"

The beautiful maiden pulled on the string so that the doll nodded with her head.

"Are you the one who plucked out my beard?"

The doll nodded once again with its head.

"And after all the things you did, were you the one who so shamefully refused to ever answer me?" he screamed angrily, charged the bed, and sliced off the head of the doll. Then he licked the blade of the sword to get rid of the blood, but when he tasted the honey, he began to regret that he had killed her and started to weep and groan. "Oh, if only I had known how sweet you are, I would never have killed you!"

Then she crawled delightedly out from under the bed and cried out, "You didn't kill me. It was only a doll.

A doll made of sugar and honey and everything nice
we can eat it together as husband and wife!"*

The king's son was extremely pleased, and they ate the doll together and lived happy and content. But we still can't pay the rent.

---

*E la statua di zuccaru e meli,
  Ni la manciamu, maritu e mugghièri!

46

THE GODCHILD OF
SAINT FRANCIS OF PAULA

Once upon a time there was a king and a queen who did not have any children and would very much liked to have had one. The queen had a special affection for Saint Francis of Paula, whom she revered.* So the queen prayed to him and implored him to let her have a child. She would call it Paul or Pauline. Not long thereafter the queen gave birth to a beautiful baby girl, whom she named Pauline.

As Pauline grew, she became more and more beautiful. When she turned seven, her parents sent her to school, and whenever she went with the servant to the school, they always had to pass a small alley, which was very long and ran between two walls. There was no way out, and there were also no houses. One time Pauline said to the servant, "Wait a minute for me. I'll come right back." She went into the alley, where she saw a little monk who waved to her and said, "Dear Pauline, I'm your uncle. Come over here and be nice to me."

The little monk was none other than Saint Francis, who gave Pauline some sweets and said, "Every morning when you go to school, come into this little alley. But you mustn't tell anyone that you meet me here."

Pauline promised, and each morning she would leave her servant and go and kiss Saint Francis's hand. One day the saint said to her,

---

*A riggina era divota di S. Franciscu i Paula.

"Dear Pauline, ask your mother whether it is better to suffer in one's youth or one's old age, and bring me the answer tomorrow."

When Pauline came home from school, she asked her mother right way, "Dear Mother, tell me whether it's better to suffer in one's youth or one's old age."

"Oh child," her mother replied, "what kind of a question is that? Who put such stuff into your head? You won't suffer at all."

But Pauline said it was just a thought that occurred to her and insisted her mother answer her. Finally her mother responded, "Well then, my child, it really doesn't mean anything for you, but if you must know, then it's certainly better to suffer in one's youth so that one has some peace in old age."

The next morning Pauline went into the little alley once again and brought the saint the answer. In turn Saint Francis said, "Very well, my child, come with me," and he took her in his arms, and they disappeared.

Meanwhile, the servant waited at the entrance of the little alley. When she did not return after a while, he went into the alley looking for her, but Pauline was nowhere to be found.

"How is that possible?" he thought. "There is no way out of this alley. There are no houses. She certainly is not able to climb over the high walls."

Then the poor man ran filled with fright to the teacher and asked whether the girl had perhaps come to school in some other way. But Pauline was not there. The teacher accompanied him to the castle and informed the king what had happened. They sent their servants all over the place to look for the maiden, but it was all in vain. The grief of the poor parents was very great, and the queen said, "My poor child will have to contend with her destiny."*

Well, let's leave the parents and see what's happened to Pauline.

Saint Francis took her to a very desolate region and placed her in a tower that had no door and only one window. He lived there with Pauline and raised her and taught her everything that was appropriate for someone of her social class. Pauline grew and became more beautiful with each day. She had marvelous long hair, and whenever Saint Francis would return from his excursions, he would always call out, "Pauline, Pauline, let down your beautiful braids and pull me up."† Then Pauline

---

*Avrà a passare qualche destino.

† Paulina, Paulina
  Cala sti beddi trizzi e pigghia a mia.

would let down her beautiful braids, and Saint Francis would climb up into the tower.

Now it happened that one day, when Pauline was grown, the king went hunting and made his way into the region near the tower. When he came across this strange tower and began staring at it, he noticed a little monk in the distance and heading straight for the tower. The king hid himself behind a bush because he was curious to see how the little monk was going to get into the tower, but Saint Francis was aware that the king was hiding behind the bush and therefore called out, "Pear and quince, let down your beautiful braids and pull me up."*

Pauline recognized the saint's voice and let her braids down. When the king saw the marvelous braids, he became even more curious to find a way to get inside the tower. So, when the saint soon left the tower, he walked over, took a place beneath the window, and called out, "Pear and quince, let down your beautiful braids and pull me up."

Pauline believed that the saint had returned and let down her braids, and the king climbed up. She could barely pull him up because Saint Francis had always made himself very light for her so that she never felt his weight. When the king jumped through the window and saw the beautiful maiden, he stood there completely speechless. However, she was terribly frightened by the man's appearance and fled horrified through all the rooms. The king rushed after her and tried to calm her down with tender words.

"Noble lady," he said, "don't be frightened by me. I don't want to harm you. Come with me to my castle. My mother will receive you in friendly fashion, and you shall become my wife."

Gradually, she calmed down and listened to him. But then she said she couldn't go with him because she had to wait for her uncle. However, the saint did not return because he wanted Pauline to go with the king. So, when Saint Francis still did not appear, the king finally convinced the maiden to follow him, and he took her to his mother and said, "Dear Mother, this maiden is to become my wife."

But because nobody knew who Pauline was, his mother did not want him to marry her. However, she loved her son very much, and consequently received Pauline in friendly fashion and let her stay with the king. After one year passed, Pauline gave birth to their first son. However, during the night Saint Francis came, took the child away, smeared Pauline's mouth with blood, and took away her ability to speak.

---

*Pira e cutugnu,
  Cala sti beddi trizzi cu.
  E supra sugnu.

The next morning, when the old queen came into the room, the baby was gone, and the young mother could not say what had happened to him. The queen erupted and screamed for the king.

"You've brought me a werewolf* from the forest who eats her young! Just look at how her mouth is smeared with blood."

The king did not want to believe this, but when he went over to Pauline, she could not tell him where their child was. The king was very despondent, but he loved her so much that he did not want to banish her from his court. Meanwhile, poor Pauline wept the entire day and constantly prayed to Saint Francis for help.

After a year had passed, she gave birth to her second son, and during the night the saint appeared once more and returned the gift of speech to her.

"Oh, Saint Francis," she begged, "please leave my children with me. Look at how much I have suffered."

"Yes, my child," the saint said, "don't you remember what your mother said, 'It's better to suffer in one's youth and to have peace in one's old age?' So you must suffer in your youth, and you'll enjoy your old age."

Then he took the second child away, smeared her mouth with blood, and again deprived her of her ability to speak. When the child was found missing the next morning, the old queen was completely enraged and wanted to banish Pauline. But the king refused because he still loved her very much.

Another year passed, and Pauline gave birth to a baby girl. When the saint appeared during the night, Pauline pleaded with him, "Oh, Saint Francis, let me at least keep this little girl."

"I must take the child," he responded. "But be consoled. Your sufferings will soon come to an end."

Upon saying this, he took the baby, smeared Pauline's mouth with blood, and again deprived her of her ability to speak. The next morning the old queen was so furious that she locked Pauline in a secluded room, placed some guards before it, and refused to let her son enter.

"This werewolf must die," she said, "and you should marry a woman who is your equal in birth."

The king was very upset, and because he could not go and visit Pauline, he sent his servant to look through the keyhole and tell him what Pauline was doing.

---

*Lupa di voscu. Also, madreselva.

"She was kneeling on the ground," he answered to him, "and she was praying to Saint Francis. She was asking the saint to release her from her suffering."

In the meantime the old queen brought a neighboring princess to the court and said to her son, "You will marry this princess today."

The king was deeply troubled and refused, but his mother insisted. So a beautiful wedding meal was prepared, and after the meal the wedding was to be celebrated. Meanwhile, Saint Francis appeared in poor Pauline's prison and brought her three children with him. Each one was more beautiful than the next. Then he gave her splendid clothes and a royal cape, and he brought three small golden chairs for the children and said to Pauline, "Get dressed in these royal clothes, and sit down with the children. When the time comes, I'll call you."

At the same time the king said to his faithful servant, "Go to the room one more time and see what my poor Pauline is doing."

The servant went to the room and returned with a horrified look.

"Your majesty, you have no idea what I've just seen!"

"What did you see?" the king asked.

"Just think, she's sitting in a royal cape with a crown on her head, and next to her are three children sitting on three golden chairs. They are as beautiful as three angels."

The king wanted to look through the keyhole himself, but the guards prevented him from doing so and he was taken to the wedding meal.

When they were all sitting at the wedding table, Saint Francis called Pauline and her children. He led them out of their prison, and the guards let them pass because they realized that the little monk was a saint. Saint Francis let the children run before him into the wedding hall, and the two eldest ran right up to the king and the old queen, kissed their hands, and said, "Good day, Papa, good day, Grandma. We want to eat. Where are our places?"

When the king saw the children, he was very happy and said, "You are for sure my dear children!" And he embraced them.

Then Pauline entered. She was even more beautiful than before and could speak once again. Beside her was Saint Francis, who said to the king, "I am Saint Francis. It was I who took the children away, but now your sufferings are at an end. Let us be of good cheer and eat together, and afterward I shall marry you to Pauline."

When the new bride heard this, she fainted and had to be carried away. Later, when she recovered, she went back to her father. Meanwhile, Saint Francis presided over the marriage of the king and

Pauline, gave them his blessing, and disappeared. Afterward they lived happy and content, and we still haven't paid the rent.

47

The Story About the Merchant's Son Peppino

Once upon a time there was a merchant who was enormously rich and had even more treasures than the king himself. He lived with his wife in peace and harmony, and the only thing they lacked in their lives was a child. So, one day the merchant's wife called upon Saint Joseph and said, "Dear Saint Joseph, if you grant me a child, I'll build beautiful churches in your name, and every year on your birthday I'll hold a great feast* and shall give you a child made of pure gold, and my own child shall bear your name."

After some time had passed, the merchant's wife became pregnant, and when her hour arrived, she gave birth to a wonderful and handsome baby boy named Giuseppe. Just think how joyful the merchant and his wife were about their only son! In their gratitude they built a magnificent church for Saint Joseph and had a small child made of gold, which they gave as a gift to the church. When Saint Joseph's holiday arrived, they held a great feast to which they invited people from all the different social classes: the rich ate with the rich, the middle class with the middle class, and the poor with the poor, and this feast was repeated each year.

---

*On March 19, which is Saint Joseph's Day, many people are accustomed to holding a feast for the poor, who are celebrated on this occasion. This is called "fare convito a San Giuseppe." The feast usually happens as a result of an oath, but most of the time only as a pious custom.

Little Peppino* grew every day and became the handsomest child in the world. How could it have been any other way? He was created through a miracle, a work of Saint Joseph. Well, when he was about seventeen years old, he went to his father one day and said, "Dear Father, I shall soon be seventeen, and I've seen nothing of the world. Please give me permission to sail on the next ship you send out so that I can take a journey and see the world."

"Oh, my son, what do you want to do out there in the world? You're rich and don't need to bring trouble on yourself. Stay with us. What would we do without you?"

His father continued lamenting, but Peppino would not let himself be persuaded to abandon his project and kept asking his father for permission to leave. Because he was his only son, his father eventually had to grant his request and said he would let him sail on the next ship.

When his mother heard that her only son wanted to depart, however, she began to moan and weep: "Oh, how can I trust the malicious seas with my son!" But all her complaints were in vain. Peppino could not be convinced to stay at home.

When the father was set to send off a ship, he had it well equipped for his son, called the captain, and said to him, "I'm placing my son in your hands. You are responsible for him. If you bring him back in good health, I'll reward you like a prince."

The captain promised that he would look after Peppino with all the powers he had, and then he sailed away with Peppino on board the ship. Meanwhile, it was just their bad luck that a terrible storm arose only a few days after they had departed, and the captain thought that the ship would sink. He let a small boat down into the sea and believed he would be able to save the merchant's son this way, but no sooner had Peppino stepped into the boat than it capsized, and the young man disappeared without a trace. The captain and his men searched from all sides of the ship to try to rescue him, but Peppino did not reappear.

Because he could do nothing more, the captain sailed back home. "Oh," he thought, "how can I appear before his poor father with this news? Who should tell him?"

Meanwhile, the merchant was standing on his balcony and was thinking about his son. All of a sudden he saw a ship with lowered sails moving into the harbor, and he recognized it as the ship on which his son had set sail.

---

*The diminutive form of Giuseppe.

"Oh, no!" he thought. "My son has certainly drowned and is now dead."

When the captain landed and told the parents how their son had drowned, there was great sorrow and mourning in the palace. The merchant had the entire house draped in black and all his servants had to wear mourning garments. Meanwhile, he locked himself in a room with his wife. They did not see a soul and did nothing but grieve over their lost son. Indeed, they even reproached Saint Joseph and said, "Oh holy Saint Joseph, how could you cause us such pain and suffering? Why did you give us a son only to tear him away from us? From now on we shall not be holding a feast on your birthday."

To be sure, when Saint Joseph's Day came, they did not celebrate it.

But let us leave the weeping parents for the time being. Let's see what really happened to their son.

When the boat capsized, a huge wave caught hold of him and threw him onto some rocks. When he managed to recover and look around, he saw that the rocks were opening in front of him. Beautiful maidens came out and spoke to him in a friendly fashion. "Handsome lad, come with us and stay here. You'll have it good here."

He let himself be led by them, and they took him through the rocks into a marvelous garden, where splendid flowers were blooming and the sweetest fruit was growing. The beautiful maidens served him and brought him whatever he wished. And so it went until evening, and when he became sleepy, they led him into a magnificent room with a wonderful bed. They brought him a light, and after he had lain down in the bed, they took the lamp away. When he turned over in the bed, he noticed to his astonishment that a fine, tender female figure was lying next to him. She spoke to him and said, "Just stay here, handsome lad. This will be your good fortune."

When he awoke the next morning, however, the female figure had disappeared, and he did not catch a glimpse of her. For the next year his life continued this way, and he lived as if in paradise. The beautiful maidens served him and fulfilled his every wish. In the evening, after they had taken away the lamp, the beautiful maiden lay next to him and talked with him in such a fine and friendly way that he fell passionately in love with her. He had a great desire to see her in daylight, but every morning when he awoke, he was alone.

One day, when the year had rolled by, the beautiful maiden said to Peppino, "Peppino, would you like to visit your parents?"

"Oh yes!" he answered. "I'd very much like to console them and let them know I'm alive. I'm sure they believe I'm dead."

"Yes, that's what they believe," the maiden answered, "and that's why they are no longer honoring Saint Joseph. His holiday is to be celebrated again very soon. Take this magic stick and hit the rocks with it in the morning. The rocks will open so you can go through. Go to your parents, and be happy and enjoy yourself with them, but remember that you must return here as soon as the feast of Saint Joseph has ended. Otherwise, it will be your misfortune."

The next morning Peppino put on regal garments, hit the rocks with the stick, and they opened. Outside he found a magnificent horse and a large retinue, which resembled that of a king, waiting to accompany him. When he came to his home city, a rumor quickly spread that a great ruler had arrived, and the nobles and richest people of the city approached Peppino and thought he was a king. Each nobleman requested that he dismount and visit his home. However, he sent a messenger, who announced to his father: "A rich king has entered your city and would like to pay you a visit."

The merchant answered, "Oh, my house has been sad and desolate for a year ever since my only son was lost. But I cannot oppose a king's will, so I shall receive him in my house."

Then he had his palace adorned in the most splendid way, and the stairs were covered with the finest rugs. When the king came, the merchant and his wife came down the stairs to greet him, but when Peppino saw his parents, he quickly dismounted, kissed his father's hand, and said, "Bless me, dear Father!"

Then he kissed his mother's hand and said, "Bless me, dear Mother!"

Now just think of how joyful his parents were to see their son whom they had believed to be dead! Just think of how thankful they were to Saint Joseph for his grace and pardon. Peppino told them everything that had happened to him, and as he talked about the beautiful maiden whom he had never seen in the daylight, his mother said, "You can be sure that I'll give you some good advice about how to handle that."

After a few days had passed, it was time to celebrate the holiday of Saint Joseph, and Peppino's parents held a feast that was more splendid and sumptuous than any they had ever held before, and they invited the entire city to attend. When the feast ended, however, Peppino said, "Now I must leave you, for I must return to the rocks. If I don't, it will be my misfortune."

His mother began to weep and did not want to let him depart, but Peppino insisted and said, "Mother, if you keep me from going, it will be my misfortune."

When his mother saw that she would not be able to prevent him from leaving, she gave him a little candle and bottle and said to him: "Listen, my son, if you want to see the beautiful maiden, then follow my advice. After she has fallen asleep, put the candle into the little bottle. It will light up by itself, and then you'll be able to see who the beautiful girl is."

Peppino took the candle and the little bottle, embraced his parents, and rode with his retinue along the seashore until he came to the rocks. No sooner had he approached the rocks than they opened. The beautiful maidens surrounded him and joyfully led him inside. Meanwhile, he could barely wait for the evening to arrive when he hoped to see the beautiful maiden. After he went to bed, the maidens took the lamp away, and just as they did this, the tender figure lay next to him and asked him, "Well now, Peppino, did you enjoy yourself? Were your parents in good health?

"Yes, my noble lady," he answered. "But please don't ask any more questions tonight. I'm tired from the long trip and would like to sleep."

As she fell asleep, however, he quickly took out the candle and put it into the little bottle. All of a sudden the bottle burned brightly. In the light he could see the maiden, who had such wondrous beauty that he could not take his eyes off her and kept staring at her full of delight. When he leaned over her to kiss her, however, a drop of wax fell on her cheek. Just as this happened, the entire beautiful castle disappeared, and he found himself in the dark night, naked and alone on top of a mountain covered by snow.

"Oh!" he sobbed. "What's to come of me? Who will help me?"

No one was there to help him, and so he crawled on his hands and knees with great effort until he reached the foot of the mountain the next morning. He saw a farmyard not very far away and headed straight for it. He knocked on the door and after the farmer opened it, Peppino said to him: "Oh, my good man, could you possibly give me some work to do on your farm so that I can earn something to eat?"

"Who are you?" the farmer asked.

"Oh, I'm just a poor peddler," he answered. "And this past night, as I came across the mountain, I was attacked by robbers, and they plundered me. They even took my clothes."

"Well then, you poor man," the farmer said. "Stay with me, and I'll give you something to eat and some clothes. In return I want you to look after my sheep, but you must not drive them into that forest over there because there is a powerful dragon with seven heads living there. He would eat you as well as my sheep."

So Peppino remained with the farmer, wore poor clothes, was given little to eat, and had to lead the sheep into the meadow every day. Some time later, as the sheep were grazing one day, he suddenly heard a loud voice calling to him: "Oh, Peppe!" He looked around but did not see anyone. Then the voice called out once more and said, "Follow the voice!" So he followed the sound of the voice and came to a cliff where a marvelously beautiful woman was standing. She handed him three brushes and said, "Keep them in a safe place, and if you are in need of something, burn them."

After she said that, she disappeared. Meanwhile, Peppino kept the three brushes beneath his shirt. Several days passed, and he heard a voice again, "Oh, Peppe!" And when he turned around and followed the sound of the voice, he came to the same cliff, where the beautiful woman was standing. This time she gave him three feathers and said, "Keep them in a safe place, and if you are in need of something, burn them."

Once again, after a few days had passed, she called him a third time and gave him three strands of hair with the same words. Now much more time passed, and it so happened that the prince, who owned all the estates and land, sent a message to the farmer that said, "The patron demands that all the accounts be brought to him in three days."

However, the farmer had not put the accounts in order for many years and sat there very despondent. He racked his brains trying to think how he should do the accounts. When Peppino saw this, he said, "Master, do you want me to help you? I can do the accounts."

The farmer was happy with this, and Peppino put all the accounts in order. After three days the farmer could go to the city and take all the accounts to the prince. When the prince had gone through all of them, he said, "Did you do all these accounts yourself?"

The farmer thought, "I'm sure that dumb Peppe made some mistakes," and he answered in a low voice, "Oh, your excellency, please be lenient with me. One of my peasants did the bills."

"That's certainly not a peasant," the prince responded, "but a gentleman. Bring him here. I could use an administrator like him."

"Oh, your excellency, I can't bring him to you because he's wearing such poor and threadbare clothes."

"Don't you worry about that," the prince said, and he gave him some garments and a horse so that Peppino could come to the city in proper fashion. So the farmer was delighted and returned home and said to Peppino, "Oh, Peppe! You are in luck. The prince says that you are too good to be a peasant, and that you should become his administrator."

So Peppino washed himself and put on the fine clothes, and when he stood there so neat and clean, the farmer saw for the first time how handsome he was. So Peppino went to the city and stayed with the prince as his administrator, and the prince loved him like his own son.

Now the prince had just one daughter, who was a very beautiful maiden. When she saw the handsome young man, she fell in love with him, and her only wish was to have him as her husband. She often said to him, "Oh, Peppino! If my father allowed it, I would like very much to marry you."

But he answered, "Oh noble lady, you deserve to marry a prince and not a poor fellow like me."

Indeed, Peppino constantly thought about his beautiful bride, and whenever he finished his work, he went to the seashore and sighed, "Oh, if only a favorable wind could lead me to her!"

This was how Peppino lived the next seven years. Finally, he went to the prince and said, "Your excellency, I have served you faithfully now for a long time, and I've come to ask your permission to allow me to depart. I can no longer stay with you."

The prince was very saddened by this request, and his daughter wept until her eyes were red, but Peppino remained firm in his request: "I can no longer stay with you."

Because the prince realized that he could not prevent Peppino's departure, he gave him many gifts and let him set out. Peppino went straight to the harbor, and when he saw a ship that was about to set sail, he asked the captain, "Where are you going?"

"We're heading to the west."

"Take me with you and I'll give you a hundred gold coins. I've got to travel in the same direction."

So the captain took him on board, and they sailed west. After they had journeyed many days, Peppino finally saw the rocks in which the beautiful castle was enclosed, and he had the ship stop so that he could go on land. Then the ship departed and he was alone on the seashore, but the rocks remained closed. He had to wait a long time before they eventually opened, but nobody came to greet him. He went inside and found everything exactly as he had left it. The beautiful maidens brought him food and drink, but they did not converse with him nor were they as friendly as they had been in the past. When he went to bed in the evening they did not take away the lamp, but the beautiful maiden lay next to him and asked him in a mocking tone, "Well, why don't you tell me how things were on top of the snowy peak? Did you like working for the farmer and looking after his sheep? And why didn't you stay with the prince's beautiful daughter?"

Peppino answered her in a humble tone and asked for her forgiveness, and he kept at it until she finally became friendly again and said,

"Listen to me, Peppino, I'm an enchanted princess, and if you had controlled your curiosity on that one evening, I would have long since been rid of the magic spell. My father was a powerful king, and I am his only daughter. He never wanted me to marry, and when the time came for his death, he cast a spell over me and had me locked in this rocky castle, where I am kept prisoner by his spirit."

"Is there no way to release you from the spell?" Peppino asked.

"Yes, there is a way," she answered. "But I'm afraid you'd never be able to do it."

"Please tell me what it is," he requested. "You'll see. I have what it takes."

"All right. Now listen closely to what I have to say. If you want to rescue me and yourself, early tomorrow morning you must leave the rocks and take this magic stick with you. Then you must go into the forest inhabited by the dragon with the seven heads. At the edge of the forest you are to hit the ground with the stick, and a horse will emerge from the ground along with a magic sword. Mount the horse, tie the sword onto your belt, and ride into the forest where you are to summon your courage and do battle with the dragon. Indeed, you'll defeat him and cut off his seven heads, which you are to take to the farmer who had pity on you and took you into his service. Tell him he's to take the heads to the prince and ask his permission to cut wood in the forest for twelve years. Then you are to return to the forest, where you will use the magic stick to conjure up a rabbit and a dog. The dog will hunt the rabbit and bring it to you. As soon as you cut it open, a white dove will fly out. The dog will also hunt the dove and bring it to you. Cut it open, and you'll find an egg inside that you must keep in a safe place. Finally, at midnight, you will see me lying and sleeping on the ground in the forest. Above me will be my father's ghost. Approach quietly, take good aim, and throw the egg at his forehead. Then he will fall over into a pit and disappear forever. If you can do all of this, I shall be released from his spell."

"But how am I supposed to conjure up the rabbit and dog?" Peppino asked.

"You must take care of that yourself," she replied.

The next morning Peppino left the rocks. He took the magic stick with him and traveled for many days until he came to the forest inhabited by the dragon. He hit the ground with the stick, and all at once a splendid horse emerged from the earth along with a glistening sword. He attached the sword to his belt, swung himself on top of the horse, and rode into the forest. It did not take long before he encountered the dragon, which sought to devour him. But Peppino bravely pulled out his sword and fought the dragon until he had sliced off all seven heads. Then he went to the farmer and said, "You were so good to me when I was poor and miserable. Well, now that I've become rich and powerful, I want to give you these seven heads. I killed the dragon, and these heads are his. Take them to your lord and give him the good news with the condition that he must allow you to chop wood in his forest for twelve years."

"Now I'm a made man!" the farmer cried with joy. "Nobody has entered the forest to chop wood for many years because the terrible dragon was living there. So I'm sure that the prince will gladly grant the condition."

Afterward Peppino took his leave of the farmer and continued to travel in the forest while he contemplated how he was going to conjure up the rabbit and dog, for he had no idea how to do this. Suddenly he remembered the three brushes that the beautiful lady had given him. This beautiful lady was none other than the enchanted princess. So he burned the three brushes, and as soon as he did this, a rabbit sprang from the grass and ran into the woods. Then Peppino burned the three feathers, and as soon as he did this, a dog sprang up, and it hunted the rabbit and brought it back to Peppino, who cut it open. A white bird flew out, and again the dog hunted it down and brought it to Peppino, who cut it open and found an egg exactly where the princess had told him it would be. He put the egg away carefully, and when midnight arrived, he crept quietly into the forest where he saw the princess lying on the ground and sleeping. Above her was her father's ghost. He moved closer, and when he was very near, he softly took out the egg, aimed, and threw it at the ghost and hit him right in the middle of his forehead. No sooner did he strike him than there was a terrifying noise. The old king rolled into a pit and was no longer to be seen. The princess awoke and rushed into his arms full of joy. A magnificent castle stood before them with glorious treasures.

"You've released me from the spell!" the princess cried. "Now all these treasures belong to you. Let's take them with us and go to your parents. Then we'll celebrate our wedding."

So they took all the valuable treasures with them and returned to Peppino's home city. When the merchant and his wife saw their dear son return and that he was bringing his beautiful bride with him, they thanked Saint Joseph with joy in their hearts and held a magnificent wedding. And so they remained rich and consoled, while we keep sitting here and are getting old.

48

SPADÒNIA

Once upon a time there was a king who was pious and godfearing, and he honored the holy souls in purgatory in a special way. Every morning he had a large oven full of fresh bread baked for them to show them some kindness. The Lord also sent him a little donkey with two baskets made out of rafia,* in which the king packed the bread, and the little donkey took everything to the holy souls in purgatory. Soon, however, the king became sick, for his time had come. When he felt that he was about to die, he called his only son, Spadònia, to him and said, "It's time for me to die. Promise me that you will do the same thing I've done for so many years. Every morning you must have bread baked for the poor souls in purgatory and load it onto the little donkey."

Spadònia promised, and the king died. The son continued to have the bread baked every morning, and the Lord sent him the little donkey, which the son sent with the bread to the poor souls in purgatory.

One day, however, Spadònia thought, "I've been loading the bread onto the donkey for some time now and don't actually know whether I'm doing good or bad."†

---

*Zimmili.

† Actually, whether I'm sinning or doing something that's meritable. Se pecu o meritu.

So he called his loyal servant to him and said, "Peppe, you must do me a favor. Tomorrow morning, when the little donkey comes, you must get on it and ride to its destination. I want you to find out whether I'm doing something good or bad by having the bread baked every morning. When the donkey returns the following morning, you can tell me everything that you've seen and heard."

The next morning when the little donkey came to receive the bread, the servant sat down on top of it and rode to wherever it would take him. Along the way he came to a stream with clear water, and it was a joy to see it because the water was so bright and pure. He rode over it and came to a second stream flowing with pure milk. After some time passed he came to another stream that was flowing with pure blood. After he rode a little farther, he saw a beautiful piece of green land with abundant and splendid grass. However, the cows that were grazing on it were lean and pitiful. Immediately thereafter he came to another piece of land with a little dried-out poor grass, but the cows grazing on it were splendid fat animals. Finally he came to a forest filled with many trees, small and big, all mixed together. A handsome young man stood in the middle of them and was chopping down the trees with his ax, first a small one, then a large one. The servant continued riding, and after a while he arrived at a large gate that opened by itself, and the little donkey entered. All at once the servant saw Saint Joseph and Saint Peter and all the dear saints. Among them was the eternal Father,* and the servant said to him, "Oh eternal Father, my master has sent me here and would like to know whether he's doing good or bad by loading the donkey with bread every morning."

"Just continue riding," the eternal Father answered, "and you'll find your answer."

So the servant rode farther on and saw many saints, and among them were the king and queen, the parents of Spadònia, who called out to him and said, "Oh, Peppe! Is that really you? How did you manage to get here?"

"Your son sent me here," Peppe answered, "and would like to know whether he's doing something good or bad every morning by having the bread baked."

"Didn't I order him to do this?" the king asked. "Never mind. Just ride a little farther, and you'll find your answer."

---

* Sicilian, Patri eterni; German, Gott Vater.

So the servant continued riding and finally came to our savior, who was sitting with his beautiful mother* on a throne, and it was the highest and most beautiful in the heavenly realm. Once there, Peppe knelt down and said, "Oh dear Savior, my master has sent me here and would like to know whether he's doing something good or bad when he gives the little donkey the bread each morning."

"He's doing something good," the Savior answered. "Yes, he's doing a good deed for the poor souls in purgatory. I want you also to tell your master that he should marry. However, command him to marry only a maiden with the name Sècula. After he gets married, he is to build an inn, and anyone who arrives should be allowed to stay as long as he wants and eat as much as he wants. Finally I want him to receive my holy blessing, and you are to receive it as well."

"Oh, my lord Jesus Christ," the servant said, "may I ask you a question? On my way here I came to some clear water. Could you tell me what it was?"

"The water was filled with the good deeds of people that were done for the good of the poor souls in purgatory and refreshes them."

"I also saw a stream that was flowing with pure milk," Peppe said. "Oh Lord, tell me what that was."

"It's the milk that the beautiful Mother Mary used to nourish the Christ child."

"Then I also came to a stream with pure blood. What was that?"

"That is the blood which I shed for you sinners."

"Oh Lord, answer me one more question. After I passed the stream of blood, I saw a splendid piece of land, but how come the cows grazing there were lean and pitiful?"

"Those are the profiteers that suck the belongings and blood of the poor people and can never get enough."

"Then I saw another piece of land that was just the opposite of the first. The ground was covered only by poor grass, but the cows were fat and nicely fed. How come?"

"Those are the poor people who have very little and meager food to feed themselves. But they have faith in God, and God blesses them so they can flourish."

"Finally I also saw a handsome young man who was chopping down trees in a forest with a bare ax, some small and some large. What was that about?"

---

*In Sicilian, bedda matri; in German, Mutter Gottes.

"That is Death, who calls the young and the old indiscriminately when their time has come. Do you have any more questions?"

"No," the servant replied, and the Lord blessed him once more, and then he rode home to his master.

When Spadònia saw him coming, he cried out, "Well, what did you see?"

The servant told him everything that he had seen, and what the Lord had commanded. Now Spadònia was not particularly eager to get married, but because the Lord had ordered him to do so, he had a proclamation issued and carried throughout the land calling for a maiden by the name of Sècula to come to the court where he would make her his wife. But not one single maiden appeared.

"Oh," Spadònia thought, "our Lord certainly has his own whims!"* And he set out on his way and rode through the entire world to search for the maiden. As soon as he arrived in a city, he sent a boy throughout the streets to shout: "If there is a maiden here by the name of Sècula, show yourself! The king wants to make you his wife!" But it was all in vain. Spadònia could not find any maidens by the name of Sècula.

After he had traveled the entire world for nothing, he became very sad and said, "Oh, Lord, what a heavy cross you've given me to bear! Now I must return home without accomplishing a thing. However, please regard me with mercy, oh Lord. My intentions have been good."

So he sadly headed toward his home. After he had ridden some distance, he came to a small well, and because he was thirsty, he got off his horse to fetch a drink. At the well there were many poor maidens with pitiful skirts, filling their jugs with water. While Spadònia was standing near them, someone suddenly cried out, "Oh, Sècula!"

Spadònia turned around and saw a little old man standing with an old woman in the distance, and they cried out again, "Oh, Sècula!"

"I'm coming!" one of the maidens responded.

"Is your name Sècula?" Spadònia asked the maiden.

"Yes, noble sir!"

"Oh, Lord, I thank you!" Spadònia cried out, "And you, beautiful Sècula, must follow me because you are to become my wife."

Upon saying these words, he placed her on his horse and rode over to the old people, who were her parents, and said to them, "Your daugh-

---

*So passa certi caprici.

ter is to become my wife, and you must come with me and stay with me
as long as you live."

Imagine the joy of these poor people who had taken care of their
daughter for so long! Spadònia took them all back to his realm and married the beautiful Sècula. After the wedding he had an inn built. A man
had to stand the entire day before the inn and call out to each passerby,
"In this inn you can eat and sleep for nothing as long as you like." And
the inn was always full.

Now when some time had passed, the Savior turned to the Twelve
Apostles one day and said, "Let's set out and go to the inn that Spadònia
built."

This was exactly the time when the inn had run out of food, and
there was not one single piece of bread. The innkeeper sent a message
immediately to Spadònia, and the messenger said: "Twelve travelers
have just arrived, and we've run out of food. Could you send some?"

So Spadònia sent over the very best food right away, and everything else that was necessary. Then Sècula said, "My dear husband, I
feel somewhat strange. I'd like to go over and see these travelers for
myself."

So the two of them went to the inn and found the Lord with the
Twelve Apostles sitting at a table.

"Look, Spadònia, how handsome the old man is!" Sècula said and
pointed to our Lord. "Let's serve him ourselves."

So they served the Savior and the Twelve Apostles, and when they
wanted to go to bed, Sècula brought the Lord another pillow from her
own bed so that he could rest his head more softly. The next morning she wanted to give him some money for his journey, but the Lord
refused and said, "Give the money to some other poor people. It will do
them good. I don't need it."

After the Savior and the Twelve Apostles had departed, Sècula
went to the bed in which the Lord had lain, and she saw the image of
a crucifix printed on the sheet. Then she fell to her knees and called
Spadònia to her.

"Just think who spent the night here!" she exclaimed. "It was our
Lord! Let's run and catch up with him and beg him for his blessing."

But when she and Spadònia left the house, the Lord sent a rain
storm, and everyone became frightened and had to turn back and stay
inside. However, Sècula did not let the rain storm shake her faith.
Rather, she said, "Spadònia, we must catch up with the Lord in spite of
the storm and rain."

So Spadònia set out with her, and they ran through the rain as best
they could until they caught up with the Lord. When they saw him

from a distance, Sècula called out, "Oh Lord, please stop and wait a moment for us."

The Lord stood still, and when Spadònia and Sècula threw themselves down at his feet, he asked, "What do you want from me?"

"Lord," Spadònia answered, "we ask you to forgive us for our sins, and we wish eternal blessings for us and all our relatives."

"May it be as you wish!" the Lord declared.

"When will you be summoning us?" Spadònia asked.

"Get yourselves ready on holy Christmas evening," the Lord answered. "Then I shall come and lead you to my table."

Upon saying this, he blessed them and disappeared from their sight. Spadònia and Sècula returned to their home and gave all their money and property to the poor, and when Christmas Eve arrived, they confessed and took holy communion as did Sècula's old parents. While they sat there peacefully with one another, they departed, and their souls flew to heaven, and may God show us mercy and take us to him when our time comes.

49

KING CARDIDDU

Once upon a time there was a poor shoemaker who had three very beautiful daughters, but the youngest was the most beautiful of all. He was indeed very poor, and although he ran about the entire day and looked for work, he rarely earned much money. When he returned home each evening with empty hands, his wife scolded him with harsh words, and even his daughters reproached him.

One day when he had wandered around for a long time and had not earned a thing, he came to a forest, and because he was very tired, he sat down on a rock and began speaking in despair, "Oh, how terrible I feel!"

No sooner did he say this than a handsome young man stood before him and asked, "Why have you called me?"

"I didn't call you, your lordship," the shoemaker replied.

"Yes, you did!" the young man declared. "When any one sits down on this rock and cries out, 'I feel terrible!' I must always appear."

Then the shoemaker told him how bad things were going for him, and the handsome young man said, "Come with me. I'll give you something."

So he led him through an underground entrance to a magnificent castle, and he gave the shoemaker something to eat—as much as his heart desired. Then he filled his pockets with money and said, "Return to your family, but within a week, I want you to bring me your youngest daughter. I can't marry her yet, but the day will come when I'll be able to make her my wife."

The poor shoemaker set out in good spirits, and along the way he bought some things for his family and returned home. When he knocked, he could already hear his wife and daughters who said, "There he is again empty-handed, and we're almost starving." However, when he showed them his treasures, they became quite friendly, and his daughters embraced him and called him their dear little father.

"Well?" he said. "Now I'm your dear little father!"

Then he told them what had happened to him and told his youngest daughter that he had promised to take her to the young man. She was content with this, and after a week had passed, she set out with her father. When they came to the large rock, the shoemaker sat down on it and cried out, "Oh, how terrible I feel!"

All of a sudden the handsome young man appeared, led them to his underground castle, and gave them a splendid reception. Then the shoemaker embraced his daughter and went home.

Now the maiden led a splendid life. The handsome young man showed her all the rooms of the castle and said to her, "You may do whatever you wish with all these treasures, and when your sisters visit you, you may give them as much as you want." Toward the end he showed her a small locked room and said, "You may never open this room. Make sure that you do not let your sisters persuade you to open it. It would be your misfortune. Pay attention to what I'm telling you because I shall not be with you all the time. I must take frequent trips sometimes for two or three days, and I can't tell you where I am going."

The handsome young man was indeed a king—King Cardiddu—and had been banished by an old witch[*] to live in this underground castle because he had refused to marry her daughter. He was also compelled to go to this old witch whenever he went on a two- or three-day journey. In this room, however, there were some helpful fairies who made clothes destined for the children of the shoemaker's daughter.

Now it happened one day that the king had to take a trip once again for several days, and before he departed he warned the shoemaker's daughter sharply to remember what he had told her. While he was away, her sisters came to visit her. She gave them a splendid reception, showed them the entire castle, and gave them many gifts. When they came to

---

[*]*Mama draja*, in Greek. *Drakana*, a cannibalistic witch, in French, *ogresse*. Usually the common witch is called *mavara* (magara); the beautiful sorceress, who is not always well-intentioned, is called *maga*; and the fairy, *fata*.

the locked door, however, one of her sisters said, "Open the door, and let us see what's inside."

"No," she answered. "I'm not allowed to go into this room. The king has forbidden it."

"Oh, please," the sisters said. "He is miles away. He won't notice a thing."

She remained firm, however, and refused to open the door. Then the sisters said, "Once we leave here, you'll certainly open it."

Upon saying this, they left, and shortly thereafter the king returned home.

"Weren't your sisters here?" the king asked. "And didn't you open the locked door for them?"

"No," she replied. "I followed your orders."

However, she no longer had any peace of mind and constantly thought about fulfilling her curiosity. When her husband fell asleep, she quietly took a candle and leaned over him to make sure that he was sleeping. As she did this, she tipped the candle and a drop of wax fell on to the king's forehead. All of a sudden she found herself on a large rock in the forest, and the king stood next to her and said, "Now do you see why your curiosity is your misfortune. I can no longer keep you with me. You must wander off into the wide world. When you, however, do what I say, you may still become my wife. You are now to go straight ahead until you come to the house of the old witch, where you are to sit down. Then the witch will call you and tell you to come upstairs. Be alert—she will want to eat you. Don't go upstairs until she swears on the name of King Cardiddu that she will not eat you. Then you may go up without worrying and begin to serve her."

After the king said all this, he disappeared, and the poor woman remained alone in the dark forest. So she began to wander and wept bitter tears, and when it became day, she arrived at the house of the old witch. She sat down in front of the door and looked despondently down at the ground. When the witch caught sight of her, she thought, "She'd make a nice roast for me," and she called to her in a friendly way, "Beautiful maiden, why don't you come upstairs to me?"

"Oh, no," she replied. "I won't come because you just want to eat me."

"Something like that would never occur to me," the witch responded. "Now come."

"I'll only come to you if you swear on the name of King Cardiddu that you won't eat me," the woman said.

Then the witch swore on the name of King Cardiddu, and the poor woman went upstairs and began serving the witch as her maid. But the witch was not satisfied that she could not eat her, and constantly tried to lure the woman into a trap. One day she called to her new maid and said, "I've got to go to mass. While I'm gone, I want you to sweep the house and not sweep the house."

Now the poor woman stood there completely puzzled and did not know how she should carry out this command. Out of fear she began to weep bitterly, and all of a sudden King Cardiddu appeared and asked why she was weeping. She told him about her unfortunate situation.

"So," he said, "you can't think of a way out? Why don't you call your sisters? They usually give you such good advice. Perhaps they could help you now?"

When he saw that she continued to weep, he said, "All right, stop your crying. I'll help you. Sweep the house as clean as you can, but then take the basket with all the dirt that you have swept and roll it down the stairs."

She did all this, and when the witch returned home, she saw that her command had been correctly carried out and became angry, but there was nothing she could do against her maid. The next morning, however, she called her again and said, "I'm going to mass. Start the fire and don't start it."

Now the poor woman was puzzled again and began to weep. King Cardiddu appeared once more and said, "So, again you don't know what to do. Why don't you call your sisters? They'll certainly be able to help you."

"Oh," she answered, "if you only are here to mock me, then leave me in peace."

But he felt sorry for her and said, "Now, don't weep. Just arrange the wood as if you were going to light a fire. Place the kettle above it, and put the cinder wood next to it, but don't light the wood."

She did all this, and when the witch came, she saw that the task had been done according to her command. "If I only knew who was helping you!" she said.

The poor maid replied, "Who could possibly help me? There's nobody else here."

On the third morning the witch went to mass again and said, "Make the bed and don't make it."

Now the poor woman began to weep again because she did not know what to do. King Cardiddu appeared, and even though he teased her about her sisters, he helped her because he loved her with all his heart.

"Do you know what you have to do?" he said. "Take off the sheets and covers and fold them, but leave the mattresses as they are."

She did all this, and so her third task was also carried out in the proper way. However, the witch was not at all satisfied and thought of something new. She took all of her white clothes, dipped them in ox blood, and made a heavy bundle out of everything. Then she gave it to the poor woman and said, "You must wash, bleach, mend, iron, and fold all these clothes by this evening. Otherwise, I'm going to eat you!"

So the poor woman took the heavy bundle, which she could barely carry, and wandered around with great difficulty in search of a brook. As she did this, tears flowed down her cheeks. Suddenly, King Cardiddu appeared and asked her why she was weeping.

"Oh," she answered, "poor woman that I am, I am supposed to wash, bleach, mend, iron, and fold all these white clothes by this evening, otherwise the witch will eat me. And she didn't even give me a piece of soap."

"Can't your sisters help you?" the king asked. "Now don't cry. Just climb that mountain over there. The king of the birds is sitting on the top. Take your laundry to him and tell him that King Cardiddu sent you."

So she climbed the mountain with great effort and took her bundle to the king of the birds. Then she said that King Cardiddu had sent her. Well, the king of the birds whistled, and immediately his fairies appeared from everywhere. They took the laundry, and within a matter of seconds, all the clothes were washed, bleached, mended, ironed, and folded. The poor woman lay down and slept until it was evening. Later, when she took the laundry to the witch, the old woman was extremely astonished and angry that the chore had been so properly carried out, and she immediately thought about a new task.

Now she took all the mattresses, showed them to the poor woman, and said, "By this evening I want you to separate all these mattresses, wash and dry the wool, wash the sheets and iron them, and bring them to me nice and fluffy. If you don't, I'll eat you."

Then the poor woman took the mattresses one after the other and carried them with great difficulty into a field, but she realized that she would never be able to fulfill this task. So she sat down and wept, and then the faithful King Cardiddu appeared, and she told him how much she was suffering.

"Go to the mountain again," the king said, "and tell the king of the birds that King Cardiddu has sent you."

However, because she could not carry the heavy mattresses to the top of the mountain, he helped her. When she came to the king of the birds, he whistled for his fairies once again and they did all the work, and she slept soundly until the evening. Then she took the mattresses to the witch, who did not know what to do with her anymore, and therefore decided to send her to her sister, who was an even more terrible witch. She gave her maid a letter and a small box, which she was to take to the witch's sister.

The poor woman set out with great despair and wept. Then King Cardiddu appeared all at once and asked her why she was crying again, and again she revealed all her suffering.

"Now then, don't cry," he said. "Just pay attention to what I tell you. You are supposed to take this small box to the sister, but make sure that you don't open it along the way. First, you will come to a rippling stream in which blood and water are flowing. Just say: 'Well, well, how beautiful this stream is!' Then the stream will calm down, and you'll be able to make your way across it. Then you will see a donkey and a dog. The donkey will have the bones that belong to the dog in its mouth, and the dog will be eating the hay of the donkey. If they don't let you pass, take the bones out of the mouth of the donkey and give them to the dog, and give the donkey the hay. Finally, you'll arrive at the witch's castle. The door will flap back and forth so that you will not be able to enter. Then you are to say, 'Well, how beautiful this door is!' and the door will stop flapping. You will go up the stairs and give the witch the letter and the little box. The witch will tell you to wait until she has read the letter. Be careful not to do this because the letter says that she should eat you. Instead, you are to flee as fast as you can, and the door, the donkey, the dog, and the stream will let you pass."

Now the poor woman continued on her way with more hope, but when she looked at the small box, she became curious to see what was inside it, and she thought, "Nobody will notice if I open it up." No sooner did she touch the top cover, however, than the box began to ring, and it continued to ring and ring. Of course the poor woman was terrified, but the more she tried to stop the box from ringing, the louder the box rang. She began to weep bitter tears, and immediately King Cardiddu appeared.

"Didn't I warn you?" asked King Cardiddu. "Why can't you understand? If I hadn't been nearby just by chance, I wouldn't have been able to help you. This is the last time I am going to help you. After this, be reasonable."

So he stopped the music, returned the box to her, and she set out on her way. Before long she came to a roaring stream in which blood and water were flowing. Then she said, "My, how beautiful this stream is!" As soon as she said this, the water became smooth, and she could cross without danger. Soon she saw a donkey holding a bone in its mouth, and a dog that had hay in its mouth. They were arguing so much that she could not make her way through them, so she took the bone away from the donkey and gave it to the dog, and gave the hay to the donkey. Then they let her pass. When she finally arrived at the witch's castle, she had to go through a door that flapped back and forth so that she was prevented from entering.

"Well, how beautiful this door is!" she said, and the door immediately stopped flapping and let the poor woman through. Now she climbed the stairs and knocked, and when the witch came out, she gave her the letter and the small box.

"Wait a moment," the witch said, "until I've read the letter."

While she went into another room, the poor woman ran down the stairs, and when she came to the door, she repeated what she had said before and was allowed to pass. When she came to the animals, she gave them what was rightly theirs, and they, too, let her pass. Finally, when she came to the stream, she complimented it and fortunately made her way across.

When the witch realized that she had fled, she ran after her and called out to the door from the distance, "Oh, door, don't let her pass!"

But the door answered, "Why shouldn't I let her through? She said that I was beautiful while all you do is curse me."

The door did not want to stop flapping for the witch, so she had to push her way through as best she could. Then she called out to the animals to stop the woman from fleeing, but the animals answered, "Why shouldn't we let her pass? She changed our food so that we finally had some peace and quiet. You never did this, and that's why we're not going to let you pass."

So the witch had to make a great detour in order to get by, and then she cried out to the stream to stop the woman from fleeing. But the stream answered, "Why should I stop her? She told me that I was beautiful, but you constantly curse me, and that's why I'm not going to let you cross."

So the stream began to roar, and when the witch tried to cross, she fell and drowned a pitiful death.

After the poor woman returned to her mistress, she saw that preparations had been made for a glorious wedding. King Cardiddu was to marry the witch's daughter. The poor woman was expected to help in the preparations, and she did this with a heavy heart because she was very much in love with the king. When evening came, the king spoke to the witch, "Let the maid kneel at the end of the bed with two burning candles."

So the poor woman had to kneel at the end of the bed with two burning candles, while the witch's daughter lay in bed. The old witch wanted to use her magic powers at midnight to open the floor on which the maid was kneeling so that she would fall and die, but King Cardiddu knew this, and after a while he said to the witch's daughter, "Listen, I feel sorry for that poor woman, especially in her condition. Why don't you take the candles, and let her sit a while."

So the witch's daughter had to get up and kneel at the end of the bed while the true bride sat in a chair at the head of the bed. Then the king whispered to her, "Come and lie down quietly in the bed."

So she moved nearer and lay down in the bed. When it turned midnight, there was a tremendous noise, and the floor collapsed so that the witch's daughter fell down into the cellar. Then the king and his true bride stood up quietly and fled.

When daylight arrived the witch wanted to see how her daughter was. After she entered the room, she found nobody there and ran terrified into the cellar. When she realized that her own daughter had fallen to her death, she began to cry aloud and swore she would avenge herself. So she pursued the king and his true bride, and after a while she nearly overtook them. However, when the king saw her coming, he said, "You are to become a vegetable garden, and I shall become the gardener."

So his wife became a vegetable garden, and the king was the gardener working in it. Shortly thereafter the witch arrived and asked the gardener, "Tell me, good man, have you seen a man and a woman who came by here?"

"What?" the gardener answered. "You want fresh peas? But they're not ripe yet."

"No," she said. "I asked you whether you saw a man and a woman come by here."

"How can you ask for carrots?" he replied. "It's not their time."

This is the way he answered every question the witch posed until she became impatient and ran away. The king and his bride assumed their human forms again and continued to flee. However, the old witch spied them again and pursued them.

"You are to become a church, and I'll become the sacristan," the king said, and in that very moment she became a church, and he became the sacristan. When the witch came by, she asked him, "Have you perhaps seen a man and a woman who came by here?"

"Mass begins in just another hour," the sacristan answered. "The priest has not arrived yet."

No matter what she asked, he gave similar answers. So the witch became impatient and ran away. The king and his bride assumed their human forms again and continued on their way.

It did not take long, however, for the witch to spot the two of them again.

"You are to become an eel," the king said, "and I'll become the pond in which you swim." And just as he said that, he became the pond, and his wife, the eel.

When the witch came by, she wanted to catch the eel, but no matter how often she grabbed the eel with her fingers, the eel managed to slip through them. Finally, the witch realized that she would never be able to catch either of them in this way. But before she went home, she said, "Just you wait! I'll get my revenge."

When she returned to her house, she sat down at a window, placed her folded hands between her knees, and said, "May the bride of King Cardiddu not be able to give birth until I release my hands from my lap."

In the meantime the king and his bride wandered farther until they came to the royal castle. No sooner had they arrived than it was time for his bride to give birth. However, she could not bear her child because the witch had cast the spell on her. So the king called a faithful servant and sent him to all the churches of the city with the order that the sacristans were to ring the death bells. Then the servant was to stand before the witch's house. When she saw him there, she asked him, "What's the meaning of all the death bells in the churches?"

"King Cardiddu has died," the servant answered.

The witch was so overjoyed that she forgot about her hands and began clapping. At that very moment the king's bride gave birth to a handsome baby boy. Now the servant had to run back to all the churches and commanded the sacristans to ring the bells of glory. When he returned to the witch's house, she asked him, "Why are the bells of glory ringing now?"

"The king's bride has given birth to a splendid baby boy."

Then the witch realized she had been deceived, and in her rage she slammed her head against the wall so hard that she fell down dead. Soon thereafter the king celebrated a beautiful wedding, and there was great joy in his castle. The young queen invited her parents and sisters, and they lived happily and content, and we can't even pay the rent.

50

THE PRINCESS AND KING CHICCHEREDDU

Once upon a time there was a king and a queen who did not have any children, and the queen always sobbed, "Oh, if only I had a child!" Then the king summoned an astrologer and asked him whether the queen would ever bear a child.

"The queen will give birth to a baby girl," the astrologer said, "but the child will go through many trials and tribulations in her fourteenth year."

Soon after the queen gave birth to a little girl who was more beautiful than the sun and blossomed into an attractive maiden. However, when the princess turned fourteen, she suddenly became melancholy, and no one could get her to laugh. Her parents did all they could to distract her, but nothing helped. Finally, the king had a beautiful fountain built on the square in front of the palace. Oil flowed from the fountain, and the king announced that anyone who wanted oil could come and take it from the fountain. His daughter, however, had to sit at a window so that she might be amused by the view. People from far and wide came and soaked up the oil, but the princess continued to remain sad. Finally, when the oil had stopped flowing, an old grandmother came, and she was carrying a little pitcher. When she saw that the oil had stopped flowing, she took a little sponge and dipped it into the oil that remained in the fountain's basin. Then she squeezed the oil into the pitcher and continued doing this until it was full. When the princess saw this, she began to laugh aloud, and arrogant as she was, she picked up a little stone and threw it at the old woman's pitcher, breaking it and spilling all the oil. The old woman became enraged and called out: "May you keep running until you have found King Chicchereddu!"

Then the princess retreated from the balcony and became even sadder than she had been before.

After some time had passed, she went to her parents and said, "Dear parents, let me roam the wide world, for I no longer have any peace of mind at home."

"Oh child," her parents answered, "where do you want to go? You are but a tender maiden. If you need anything, just tell us. You have a good life with us and all your wishes will be fulfilled."

"If you don't let me set out into the world," she responded, "then I shall die from my longing to travel."

So, with great grief, her parents had to relent and gave her whatever she desired—the most beautiful horse from the stable, a bundle of clothes, and some money. Then she embraced her parents, mounted the horse, and rode all alone into the world. She rode straight ahead for many days until she had used up almost all her money. Then she sold her clothes and rode for a few more days. However, she had to sell her horse and wander on foot until she reached another realm that did not belong to her father.

When she had spent all her money and was practically starving, she encountered a rich lady who asked her who she was, for she was surprised to see such a beautiful and tender maiden all alone. The princess answered: "I am a stranger in this country and would like to find some work. Could you help me find a position?"

"The king is looking for an attendant for his sick son," the woman replied. "The prince has been sick for many years, and no doctor has been able to help him. It's a hard job, and I don't know whether you will be able to stand the work."

"I want to try," the princess said, and she went with the lady to the royal castle, where she was presented to the king. In turn, the king took her to his sick son lying sick in a bed. He was a handsome young man, but as thin as a skeleton and so weak that he could scarcely speak. The king told the new attendant what she was to do and showed her a bed in a small corner of the room where she was to sleep day and night to be near his son. No one knew what kind of sickness the prince had, but he continually lost weight even though he ate the entire day with great hunger.

"There's something wrong here," the princess thought, and she decided not to sleep the first night. When it turned evening, she did indeed lay down to sleep, but she did not fall asleep. At midnight the door suddenly sprang open, and a tall beautiful woman entered, approached the prince's bed, and asked him how he felt.

"Oh, I'm not feeling all that well," the prince replied.

"Take this drink," she said. "It will do you good."

However, it was a sleeping potion, and as soon as the prince had taken it, he fell asleep. Then the woman took out a sharp little knife, cut open his arteries, and drank his blood. At one in the morning she disappeared. The princess had witnessed all of this, and the next morning she told the prince and said, "Now I know why you have such a great appetite the entire day and yet don't regain your strength despite all the good food you eat. Just be calm. Tonight I'll take care of her. Just don't drink the potion that she offers you."

When the king and queen came, their son was still not better, but the princess did not tell them what she had observed. In the evening she took the prince's sharp sword, pulled it out if its sheath, and stuck it into her bed. At midnight the beautiful figure appeared once more, sat down on the prince's bed, and offered him a drink again. The prince pretended to drink, but let the potion flow into the bed and closed his eyes as though he were sleeping. As the woman bent over him to open his arteries with her knife, the princess jumped out of her bed with the sword and cut off her head. Then she shoved her body and the head beneath the bed and brought the prince a strong soup right away. Afterward the two of them slept peacefully the entire night.

The next morning when the king and queen came, the prince sat upright in his bed and could also speak again.

"I feel much better, my dear parents," he remarked, "and this maiden is to be my wife."

The king and queen were so happy to see their son so much better that they joyfully gave their approval. But the princess stepped forward and said, "I am most grateful for your kind offer, but I cannot accept it, for I must continue to wander before I may rest."

The prince became very sad and asked her to stay, and the king and queen also tried to persuade her to remain, but the princess was steadfast in her decision and continued to say, "I can't rest. If you really want to do me a service, then give me a good horse, a bundle of clothes, and some money, and let me set out on my journey."

So they gave her a magnificent horse and led her into their treasury so she could take as much money as she wanted. But she took only a little money and a bundle of clothes and mounted the horse. She rode for many days, and when she had spent her money, she had to sell first her clothes and then her horse and continued to wander on foot. By the time she entered another realm she was close to starving. Fortunately she met a noble lady and asked her to help her obtain a position somewhere.

"Our king is looking for an attendant for his sick son," the lady answered. "He has not eaten a thing for many years and is completely mute. However, this is very hard work, and I don't know how well you will hold out."

The princess replied that she wanted to try and was presented to the king, who took her to his son. This young man was very handsome but also much thinner and weaker than the first prince. In a corner of the room there was once again a bed ready for the attendant. The princess immediately thought: "Something's wrong here. I'm going to stay awake again. If I succeeded with the first, then I'll certainly succeed with the second." So she lay down on the bed but did not fall asleep.

At midnight the door sprang open and a beautiful lady entered, sat down on the bed, and pulled out a little gold key from under the pillow. She used the key to open the prince's lips so he could speak and had a conversation with him. Then she locked his lips again, placed the little key beneath the pillow, and disappeared at one in the morning. The princess jumped from her bed, took the little key, and opened the prince's lips just as the lady had done. Afterward she brought him a strong soup, and the two of them slept soundly until morning. When the king and queen entered, their son was very cheerful, could speak again, and told them what had happened. Then he said, "This maiden freed me and is to become my wife."

His parents gladly gave their approval, but the princess thanked them and said, "I must wander much more before I can rest."

The prince was very sad, but she said, "You will marry a noble princess and be happy with her. Please let me set out on my journey."

Then she asked for a horse, a bundle of clothes, and some money, and when she had them all, she rode off. But things did not go much better for her than they had in the past, and she had to sell everything and was on the brink of starvation when she met a noble lady and asked her to help her find some work.

"I know of a position," this woman said, "but I am not sure that you will be able to do the job. The king is looking for an attendant for his insane son, who's been mad for many years, and no doctor has been able to help him."

The princess thought: "It seems to be my fate to help sick princess" and she said she wanted to try. So she was presented to the king, who led her to his son in a deep, dark cellar that only had a small window. They gave her a lamp and locked her inside with the prince, who was a very handsome young man, but he was completely crazy, did not recognize anyone, and kept hitting his head against the wall. The princess crouched somewhat frightened in a corner of the cellar and thought, "No, I don't think I'll be able to hold out here. If it were daytime again, I'd leave right away!"

All of a sudden a gust of wind extinguished her lamp, and she was in complete darkness. She went to the little window to see if it would soon be day, and she saw a little fire burning in a thicket a few steps from the window. "I'm going to go and light my lamp," she said to herself. "At least I won't be in total darkness." So she took her lamp, climbed carefully up to and through the window, and went toward the fire. Once there, she saw an elderly little woman who was spinning and spinning. In front of her was a kettle with boiling water set upon the fire.

The princess approached the old woman and said, "Oh, dear auntie, what are you doing here? How long has it been since we've seen each other?"

The old woman was half blind and really believed it was her niece and greeted her in a friendly way.

"It's such a dark night. What are you doing outside?" the princess asked.

"Don't you know that the prince is insane?" the old woman replied. "Many years ago he laughed at me one time and mocked me, and I swore that I'd avenge myself. Ever since then I've been turning my spinning wheel, and as long as I spin, he can't be cured."

"Well, you must be very tired, poor auntie," the clever maiden said. "Let me spin a little, and you can rest for a while."

The old woman let herself be persuaded, and the princess began to spin while the old little woman lay down and fell asleep right away. Because she was sleeping soundly, the princess grabbed the old witch and threw her into the kettle of boiling water. Then she broke the spinning wheel into a thousand pieces, lit her lamp, and returned calmly to the cellar where she found the prince sleeping peacefully. Then she lay down herself and slept soundly until morning. When the king and queen entered, the prince awoke, looked around with great surprise, and asked, "Why am I in this dark cellar and not in my beautiful rooms?"

Immediately they realized that he had been cured and were most happy. However, the princess told them what had happened the night before, and when the prince heard her story, he desired to have her for his wife. Once again the princess thanked the prince and said, "I must wander about for a long time before I can rest. If you want to do me a favor, then give me a horse, men's clothes, and some money, and let me set out on my journey."

So they gave her a beautiful horse and as much money as she wanted. Then they had some men's clothes made for her. She put them on, mounted her horse, and rode off. It was not long before she came to another kingdom, and when she asked who the king was, she was told that he was King Chicchereddu. So she rode to the castle and began riding back and forth in front of it. The king was on the balcony, and when he saw the handsome young man, he called to him and asked him where he came from. The princess replied, "I'm a stranger in these parts and would like to find some employment."

"Do you want to become my secretary?" the king asked.

So the princess entered the king's service and became his secretary. In time the king took a great liking to his new servant and wanted to have him always at his side. At the same time, it occurred to him that his secretary might be a maiden.

Now the king had a mother who was an evil sorceress and knew very well who the alleged secretary was, but she wanted her son to marry another princess. When the king told her he thought the secretary was a maiden disguised in men's clothing, she talked him out of this. One day, however, he went to her and said, "Mother, I've got to find a way to be certain about this. Just look at his hands. They're not the hands of a man!"

"You're really a blockhead! Why are you insisting that he's a maiden? Take him into the garden. If he's really a maiden, he'll take great pleasure in smelling the flowers and picking them for a bouquet."

The king did what his mother recommended and went into the garden with his secretary.

"Just look at the beautiful flowers," he said. "Would you mind picking some for me and making a bouquet?"

"I really don't know much about flowers," the clever princess answered. "I'd prefer if we'd just walk in the garden."

The king was not satisfied with this response and went to his mother again.

"He didn't pay any attention to the flowers, but I'm not convinced he isn't a maiden."

"You know what," his mother said, "tell him you want him to accompany you to the men's baths. If he accepts, then there should be no more doubt in your mind that he's a man."

So the king called his secretary and said, "Come with me. The day's very hot. Let's take a dip in the baths."

"Very good," the clever princess replied and went with him. When they were very close to the bath house she said, "We've forgotten to take some towels with us. I'll run quickly and get them."

So she ran quickly back to the castle and into her room, where she took a few pieces of paper and wrote:

I came as a maiden.
I'll leave as a maiden.
Ah, King Chicchereddu
You know you've been fooled!*

She placed one of the papers on her desk, attached another one firmly to the gate, mounted her horse, and rode back to her parents.

In the meantime the king waited for his secretary, and after a while he decided to return to the castle, where he saw the note stuck to the gate. When he went into his study, he found the second one lying on top of her desk. The secretary could not be found, and his horse was also missing. Now it was very clear that he had been right, and he became very sick and melancholy, for he loved the princess with all his heart. The old queen became enraged that a young maiden had gotten the best of her son and swore that she would gain vengeance. She took two doves and cast a magic spell. Then she called a peasant and ordered him to take the two doves to the princess and sell them to her. The peasant traveled until he came to the city in which the princess lived and sold the two doves to her. He was a man with good intentions, and when he sold them to her, he said, "Listen to the warning of an honest peasant and do not feed the doves at the same time. You must feed one dove on one day and the other dove the next day."

The princess followed his advice faithfully and found a lot of joy in the pretty doves. One day, however, she had to go to mass and did not have time to feed one of the doves. So she called her chambermaid and said to her, "Feed this dove—it's her turn today. Make sure that you do not give the other one anything to eat."

The chambermaid was, however, negligent, and after the princess left for church, she forgot her mistress's orders and fed both of the doves. At the very same moment that she did this, the princess was transferred back to the castle of King Chicchereddu. Once there the old queen forced her to take off her beautiful clothes and to wear more humble garments and do demeaning work as a kitchen maid. The queen treated her badly and gave her little to eat and beat her a great deal. The

---

*Schetta vinni, schetta mi n'annai, lu Re Chicchereddu u gabbai.

king felt sorry to see the princess in this condition because he still loved her, but he could do nothing against the will of his mother.

Then one day when the princess was being mistreated, he summoned his courage, took her and carried her in his arms into his room. From then on she lived with him, and the old queen could not get her hands on her even though she thought day and night of ways in which she could hurt her. Soon she learned that the princess would be giving birth to a child, and when the time arrived, the old sorceress sat at her window, stuck her folded hands between her knees, and said, "The princess will not be able to give birth to her baby until I take my hands out of this position."

So she sat like this, did not eat or drink, and the poor princess lay in bed with terrible cramps and could not give birth to her child. So the king called a peasant and said to him, "Go to all the churches in the city, give each one a beautiful gift, and order all the sextons to ring the death bells. Then go and stand beneath the window where my mother is sitting. When she asks the meaning of the death bells, you're to answer that King Chicchereddu has died. Then she will lift her hands in grief and begin to pull out her hair, and the magic spell that she's cast on my wife will be broken. Then you're to go and order the sextons in all the churches to ring their bells of gloria, and when my mother asks again what is happening, you're to tell her King Chicchereddu's wife has given birth to a baby."

The peasant went and did as the king commanded. When the old witch heard the death bells, she asked him who had died. The peasant answered, "King Chicchereddu has died."

"Oh, my son, my son!" the queen cried and began tearing her hair out. At the very same moment the princess gave birth to a handsome baby boy. Then the peasant went to the churches and had the sextons ring the bells of glory. When the queen heard them, she asked the peasant, "Why are the bells of glory ringing when my son has died?"

"King Chicchereddu's wife has given birth to a handsome young boy," the peasant replied.

Then the old witch realized that she had been fooled, and in her anger she slammed her head against the wall so many times that she fell down dead. Then King Chicchereddu celebrated a spectacular wedding, and the young queen had her parents come to the castle, where they all lived happily and content, but we were left without a cent.

51

THE CLEVER MAIDEN

Once upon a time there were two brothers. One had seven sons, and the other had seven daughters. Whenever the father with the seven sons met his brother, he would greet him by saying, "Oh brother, you with your seven flower pots, and me with my seven swords! How's it going?"*

These words aggravated the brother enormously, and when he came home, he was always in a bad mood and irritable. His youngest daughter, however, was marvelously beautiful and also very clever. One day, when she saw that her father was constantly in a bad mood, she asked him what was wrong.

"Oh, my child," he responded, "it's because of my brother. He always mocks me for having only seven daughters and no sons. And he does this whenever he sees me. 'Oh brother, you with your seven flower pots, and me with my seven swords! How's it going?'"

"You know what, father," the clever maiden said, "when your brother says something like that next time, you're to respond that your daughters are much smarter than his sons and you want to make a bet: Tell him he's to send out his youngest son, and you'll send out your youngest daughter, and whoever's first to rob the prince's crown will win the bet."

"All right, I'll do that," the father said, and the next time he met his brother, who began teasing him, he said, "You know what, brother, my

---

* O ssu frate, vui cu setti grasti, e ju cu setti spadi.

daughters are much smarter than your sons, and to show you that I'm right—I'd like to make a bet with you. Send out your youngest son, and I'll send out my youngest daughter, and we'll see which of the two can steal the prince's crown first."

The brother agreed, and the maiden and the young man set out. After they had traveled for a while, they came to a little river* with a great deal of flowing water. The maiden took off her shoes, lifted her skirt, and waded cheerfully through the water. But the young man thought, "Why should I get my feet wet? I'll wait until all the water has all flown by and the bed is empty." So he sat down, and in order to help the water flow faster and disappear, he took a nutshell and used it to bail water from the stream onto the bank and into the sand. In the meantime his cousin kept going until she met a farmer boy. "Oh, what a handsome young man!" she said, "Give me your clothes, and I'll give you mine in exchange."

The boy agreed, and the maiden took his clothes and put them on. Then she continued on her way until she came to the city in which the prince lived. As soon as she found the royal palace, she began walking up and down in front of it. The prince stood on the balcony, and when he saw the handsome young man, he called out and asked him what his name was.

"My name's Giovanni, and I'm a stranger here," she answered. "I'm looking for a job and was wondering whether I could enter your service."

"Do you want to be my secretary?" the prince asked.

She agreed, and the prince took her into his service. Soon he became fonder and fonder of her with each passing day. When he looked at her beautiful white hands, he kept thinking: "Those are not the hands of a man. Giovanni is certainly a maiden!" So he went to his mother and told her what he thought, but she answered, "I can't believe this. Why should Giovanni be a maiden!"

"No mother," the prince said. "I'm certain that Giovanni is not a man. Just look at his fine white hands.

> Giovanni walks to the writing stand
> and writes with a fine, exquisite hand.
> He's got a woman's style and way
> and makes me lovesick the entire day.†

---

* Fiumara.

† Giuvanni scrivi
  Cu manu suttili
  Modu di donna
  Ca mi fa muriri.

"Well, my son," the queen said, "if you want to be certain about all of this, take him into the garden. If he picks a pink carnation, then he's a maiden. But if he picks a rose, he's definitely a man."

The prince did exactly what his mother told him to do. He called his faithful servant and said, "Let's take a little walk in the garden."

"Of course, your majesty," the clever maiden answered, and they went into the garden, but she kept herself from looking at the tulips. Instead, she picked a rose and put it in her lapel.

"Just look at the beautiful pink carnations!" the prince exclaimed.

But the maiden answered, "Why should we care about pink carnations? After all, we're not girls!"*

Now the prince went to his mother, who said, "You see, I told you so!"

"No, mother," he answered. "I won't let you talk me out of this, for

> Giovanni walks to the writing stand
> and writes with a fine, exquisite hand.
> He's got a woman's style and way
> and makes me lovesick the entire day.

"You know what," the queen said. "Why don't you propose that you go swimming in the sea together? If he accepts, then you shall know for certain whether he is a man or woman."

Then the prince called his secretary to him and said, "Giovanni, it's so warm today. Let's go swimming in the sea."

"Why not?" the clever maiden answered. "Let's go right now, your majesty."

When they reached the beach, however, the maiden said all of a sudden, "Oh, your majesty, I forgot to bring towels with us. Wait here a moment while I return to the castle and fetch them."

So she ran back into the castle, went to the queen, and said, "The prince wants his gold crown right away and has asked that you give it to me without delay."

The queen gave her the gold crown, and the clever maiden wrote on a piece of paper:

---

* The girl prefers pink carnations because, even though they do not stand out, they have a wonderful aroma, while the boy is more concerned with beauty. Moreover, the carnation is a symbol of happy love. The girl throws a carnation to her lover when she accepts his proposal.

I came as a virgin
I go as a virgin.
The prince's been tricked
with cunning and wit.*

She fastened the sheet of paper on the gate, mounted a horse, and rode away with the crown. When she came to the little stream, her cousin was still sitting there and bailing water with his nutshell. She showed him the gold crown and laughed at him.

"Wasn't my father, right?" she said. "We are indeed smarter than you are!"

Upon saying this, she rode through the stream and returned home in good spirits. In the meantime, the prince was still waiting for his secretary, and when he finally lost his patience and went home, he saw the sheet of paper on the gate from a distance. After he read it, he ran to his mother and was stricken with grief.

"Didn't I tell you," he said, "that Giovanni was a maiden? Now she's gone, and I wanted to have her for my wife."

He ordered his horse to be saddled and set out on his way to search for the beautiful maiden. He rode straight ahead for a long time, and whenever he met some people, he asked them whether they had seen a handsome young man come riding by, but nobody could give him any information. Finally he came to the little river where the son of the other brother was still bailing water with the nutshell.

"Hey, my handsome lad," he called out, "did you by chance see a young man with a gold crown come riding by here?"

"That was my cousin," the fellow answered. "She's certainly home by now."

"Well then, lead me to her," the prince said, and they went to the maiden's home together. In the meantime, she had put on women's clothes and looked even more beautiful. When the prince caught sight of her, he rushed to her and said, "You are to become my wife!"

Then he took her to his castle, and she invited her father and sisters to come. Indeed, they all celebrated a splendid wedding and remained happy and content, but we just sit here and gaze at each other the whole day long.

---

* Schetta vinni
  Schetta mi nni vaju,
  E lu figghiu ddu rè
  Gabbatu l'aju.

344

52

THE ROBBER WITH A WITCH'S HEAD

Once upon a time there was a king who had three beautiful daughters, but the youngest was the most beautiful and the smartest among them. One day the king called her and said, "Come, my child, and clean the lice from my head."

The youngest daughter did this and found a louse. The king put the louse in a large jar with fat and kept it there for many years. Then one day he had the jar split open. The louse had grown into such a monster that everyone was terrified, and the king had it killed. Afterward he ordered the monster to be skinned and had the skin nailed to the door and said, "Whoever can guess the animal from which this skin came can have my oldest daughter as his bride."

Princes and noblemen came from far and wide and sought to court the beautiful princess, but nobody could solve the riddle, and so they all had to die a miserable death.

Now there was also a robber who lived alone in a wild region. He had a witch's head* that he kept in a small basket, and he always obtained good advice from the head whenever he wanted to undertake anything. He had heard how many princes and noblemen had lost their lives because they could not solve the difficult riddle, so he went to the

---

* Testa di mavara.

witch's head and asked, "Tell me, head, which animal's skin did the king have nailed over the door?"

"A louse," the head answered.

Now the robber was in good spirits and set out for the city. Along the way people asked him where he was going.

"I'm going to the city and want to woo the king's oldest daughter," he answered.

"Well, you're heading toward certain death," the people told him.

When he arrived in the city, he had the servants announce to the king that he wished to try to solve the riddle. The king had him enter, showed him the skin, and asked, "Can you tell me which animal's skin this is?"

"A rabbit?" said the robber.

"Wrong!"

"Perhaps, it's from a dog?"

"Wrong!"

"Is the skin perhaps the skin of a louse?"

Since the robber did indeed solve the riddle, the king gave him his oldest daughter as his wife. When the wedding ceremony was over, the robber said to the king, "I want now to return home with my wife."

The princess embraced her father and her sisters and departed with her husband. After they had roamed a long time, they came to a wild, desolate region, and the princess said, "Oh, where are you leading me?! It's so ugly here!"

"Just follow me!" the robber answered.

Finally they arrived at this house, which was so dark and unattractive that the princess said again, "Do you really live here? Oh, how unfriendly it is!"

"Just come inside," the robber answered.

Now the poor princess had to live in this house and work hard. On the second day the robber said, "I've got to go and look after some business. You take care of the house."

Then he turned to the witch's head and spoke softly, "Pay attention to what she says about me."

As soon as the robber was away, the princess could no longer keep everything within herself and began to curse her husband because she had not really wanted to marry him and could not stand him at all.

"This villain!" she said. "I wish he would break his neck! I hope he has bad luck for the rest of his life!" And she went on and on.

But the witch's head heard everything and told the robber when he returned home. Then the robber grabbed the princess, cut off her head, and threw her into a little room in which there were other corpses of young women whom he had murdered in the same way. The next day

he set out for the king's court, and when he arrived, the king asked him, "How is my daughter doing?"

"My wife is in very good health and happy," the robber answered, "but she is somewhat bored and would like to have her middle sister keep her company."

So the king gave him the second daughter, and he took her into that wild region.

"Oh, brother-in-law," the princess said, "how spooky this region is! Where are you taking me?"

"Just follow me!" the robber answered.

When they arrived at the robber's house, the princess asked again, "Oh, brother-in-law, is this your house? This ugly house?"

"Just come inside," the robber said.

"Where is my sister?" she asked.

"You don't have to worry about your sister. Just do the work I tell you to do."

So the princess had to work hard, and her heart became filled more and more with rage and hate against her brother-in-law. One day he said to her, "I must go and look after my business and won't be home until this evening."

Then he went to the witch's head and said, "Pay attention to what she says about me."

Now the princess gave vent to her hatred and began cursing the robber. She called him a villain and wished him nothing but bad luck. However, when the robber returned home, the witch's head told him everything, and the poor princess was not treated any better than her sister.

Now the robber journeyed to the court once more, and the king asked him how things were going with his two daughters.

"Oh, very well," the robber replied. "But they would love to have their youngest sister with them so they could all be together."

So the king also gave him his youngest daughter, who was, however, very smart, and when they went into the wilderness, she said. "Oh no, brother-in-law, how beautiful this region is! Do you really live here?"

And when they came to the house, she said again, "Oh my, how beautiful this house is!"

When they went inside, she took care not to ask about her sisters. Instead she began cheerfully doing her work. Then the robber went to look after his business once more and the witch's head had to pay attention to everything the princess might say. When she completed her work, she kneeled down and prayed loudly for the robber and wished him all the best. In her heart, however, she wished that he would be struck by bad luck. In the evening the robber returned and asked the witch's head right away, "Well, what did she say about me?"

"Oh, we've never had a maiden like her here before!" the head said. "She prayed for you the entire day and had nothing but pious wishes for you!"

The robber was very happy and said to the princess, "Because you have been more intelligent than your sisters, you will have it good here, and I'll also show you where your sisters are."

So, he led her into the little room and showed her the dead sisters.

"You did the right thing, brother-in-law, in killing them if they did not honor and respect you," the clever princess said.

Now things went well for her with the robber, and she was the mistress in the house. But one day when the robber had gone away for several days, she went into his room, looked around, and noticed the witch's head. It was in its basket nailed above the window. Since she was so smart, she called to the head, "What are you doing up there? Why don't you come down to me. It will be better for you."

"No," the head answered. "I feel much better up here and have no desire to come down there."

But the princess flattered the witch's head so much that the head was fooled and finally let itself be brought down.

"My, you have such tangled hair!" the princess said. "Come with me and I'll comb it so that it is fine."

So the witch's head followed her into the kitchen, and the princess took a comb and began combing the head. She had just heated up the oven to make some bread, and while she was combing the head's hair, she carefully wound the long braid around her arm and all at once flung the head into oven. Then she shut the door and calmly let the head burn.

Now the robber's life was tied to the life of the head, and while it burned, the robber felt his health and his life weaken, and he died. In the meantime the princess climbed up to the window where the basket had been hanging and had served as the head's dwelling place. There she found a small jar with an ointment, and when she took it and rubbed it on her sisters, they returned to life. Then she revived all the other young women, who took as much of the robber's treasures as they could carry and returned to their parents. As for the three sisters, they went back to their father and lived with him happily and content until they married three handsome princes.

53

The Clever Farmer's Daughter

Once upon a time there was a young king who went hunting. When it gradually turned dark, he realized that he had become separated from his entourage, and only his messenger was still with him. By nightfall they could no longer find their way home out of the dense forest, so they wandered about for many hours until they finally noticed a light in the distance. When they approached it, they saw that it was a cottage, and the king sent his messenger to wake the people inside. He knocked at the door, and soon a farmer appeared and asked from inside, "Who's knocking so late at night?"

"His majesty, the king, is standing outside," the messenger responded. "He cannot find the way back to his castle. Would you please give him food and a place to stay?"

The farmer quickly opened the door, woke his wife and daughter, and told them to slaughter a chicken and broil it. When the meal was ready, they asked the king to make do with the little they could offer him. The king took the chicken and divided it. He gave the father the head; the mother the breast, and the daughter the wings; he kept the thighs for himself and gave the feet to the messenger. Afterward they all went to bed.

The mother, however, said to her daughter, "Why did the king divide the chicken in such an unusual way?"

"It's quite clear," she answered. "He gave the head to father because he is the head of the family. He gave you the breast because you nurture us as our dear old mother.* He gave me the wings because I'll fly away from here one day. He kept the thighs because he is a rider, and he gave his messenger the feet so that he can run much faster."

The next morning they prepared breakfast for the king and showed him the right path home. When the king arrived at his castle, he took a beautiful roasted chicken, a large cake, a little barrel of wine, and twelve thalers. Then he called his messenger and ordered him to take every-thing to the farmer with the assurance that he would always be in the monarch's good graces.

It was a long way to the farmer's cottage, and the messenger became tired and hungry. Finally, he could no longer resist his appetite, and cut off half the chicken and devoured it. After a while he became thirsty and drank half the wine. When he traveled a bit farther and looked at the cake, he thought, "It's surely good!" and he also ate half the cake. Now he thought: "If I'm going to take half of everything, I might as well be fair and go all the way," and so he took six of the twelve thalers.

Eventually he reached the farmer's cottage and delivered half the chicken, half the cake, half a barrel of wine, and half of the thalers. The farmer and his family were extremely pleased by the honor the king showed them, and they asked the messenger to express their gratitude to him. However, when the daughter saw that everything was half of what it should have been, she told the messenger she would like him to give a special message to the king that he was to repeat word for word.

"First you must say to the king: Why is it, my God, that he who sings in the night sings only halfway? Can you remember this?"†

"Oh, yes!" the messenger answered.

"Then you also have to say to him: It is half moon. But why, my God, half the moon? Can you remember this?"

"Certainly," the messenger answered.

"Then you must also say to him: it was closed on top and closed on the bottom. But why, my God, only half? You won't forget that, will you?"

---

* Pirchí siti vecchiaredda.

† Chiddu chi a notti canta
   O Diu, menzu pirchí?
   La luna a quinta decima,
   O Diu, menza pirchí?
   Stuppatu susu e jusu
   O Diu, menza pirchí?
   Li dudici misi did l'annu
   O Diu, sei pirchí?

"Certainly not," the messenger said.

"Finally, you must say to him: The year has twelve months. Then, why God, just six?"

The messenger promised to say everything exactly as she told him and set out on his way. Just to make sure he would remember everything, he kept repeating it along the way. When he arrived at the castle, the king asked him, "Well, did you deliver everything as I told you?"

"Yes, your majesty," the messenger answered. "But I'm also supposed to deliver a message to you from the farmer's daughter. First, she said: 'Why is it, my God, that he who sings in the night sings only halfway?'"

"What!" cried the king. "You ate half the chicken?"

"Please, your majesty," the messenger said, "first hear my entire message. Then she said: 'It is half moon. But why, my God, half the moon?'"

"What?" yelled the king. "You also ate half the cake?"

"Please, your majesty," the messenger replied. "Let me finish. The third thing she said was: 'It was closed on top and closed on the bottom. But why, my God, only half?'"

"What?" the king yelled again. "You also drunk half the barrel of wine?"

"Please, your majesty," the messenger said. "Let me finish my message. Finally she said: 'It is half moon. But why, my God, half the moon?'"

"Well, you also stole half the thalers, didn't you?" the king cried.

Then the messenger fell to his knees and asked for the king's forgiveness. Indeed, the king was so pleased by the maiden's cleverness that he forgave the messenger. As for the maiden, the king sent a magnificent coach with beautiful clothes, and he took her for his wife.

They remained happy and content
But we can't even pay the rent.

54

THE COUNT AND HIS SISTER

Once upon a time there was a count who had a very beautiful sister, more beautiful than the sun. In fact, the count refused to let her marry because he thought that no man would ever be good enough for her. So when he himself married, he kept his sister in his house, and whenever he gave his wife a beautiful dress as a present, he gave his sister the same one.

Now the king lived across from the count's house, and one evening the count's beautiful sister said to her lamp:

> My golden lamp,
> Silver wick so fine,
> Send me a sign
> to find the king.
> Tell me just what he wants to make.
> Is he asleep? Is he awake?*

---

* Lampa mia d'oru,
  Micciu miu d'argentu,
  Chi fa lu re? Dormi o vigghia?

Since the lamp was a magic lamp, it answered,

Step softly, mistress, step softly,
the king is sleeping soundly.*

So the beautiful young lady rushed across the street and went into the king's chamber. When the sun began to rise, she rushed back to her house, and nobody knew where she had gone. She did the same thing the next evening, and the king fell into great despair because he could not learn who the beautiful lady was who had slept with him two nights in a row. He told this to the count, who advised him to do the following: "When the beautiful lady discards her dress tonight, hide it. This way we'll be able to learn who she is."

The king did what he said, and when the beautiful young lady came into his room again and took off her dress, he took it away and hid it, and when she wanted to flee at sunrise, she could not find her dress and had to leave without it. The king showed the dress to the count, who was shocked and thought, "This was the dress that I recently gave to my wife and my sister. Could it be one of them?"

His wife showed him her dress right away, and then he went to his sister and asked her to show him her dress.

"I'll fetch it right away," she answered. "I've been keeping it in a closet."

However, she went quickly to her brother's wife and said to her, "Dear sister-in-law, please lend me your dress for a moment," and then she brought it back to her brother. Since the dresses were exactly alike, the count was completely fooled. But now the beautiful lady no longer went to the king.

Soon the count's sister noticed that she was going to have a child, so she hid herself from her brother, and when her time came, she gave birth to a lovely boy. She placed him in a basket and covered him with the most beautiful, sweet smelling flowers and sent him to the king. When the king took off the flowers and caught sight of the gorgeous child, he thought for sure it was his son and summoned the count.

"Some unknown woman has sent this child to me," he said. "I'm sure it was the beautiful lady who came to me. I wish I knew how to find her."

---

* Ntrasti, Signura,
  Chi lu re dormi a st'ura.

"Your majesty," the count answered, "why don't you organize a big party and invite all the ladies of the city to attend. Then have your servants build a huge fire and bring out the child. Once he is there, pretend that you want to throw the baby into the fire, and you'll see that the mother of this child will reveal herself."

So the king threw a large party. All the ladies of the city came together, and among them was the count's sister. In the middle of the party, the king had his servants bring out a huge basin with burning fire. Then he pointed to the baby in the basket and said, "Do you all see this lovely child? An unknown woman has recently sent this babe to me. What should I do with the child? I think I want to burn it."

All at once there was a voice that cried out in lament, "Oh, my son, my son!"

The count's sister rushed to the baby. When the count heard her cry, he pulled out his sword and wanted to murder his sister, but the king grabbed him by the arm and declared:

> Stop, oh count, forget the shame. Don't take her life.
> Your sister will soon become the king's own wife.*

Soon thereafter a beautiful wedding was celebrated, and the count's sister became queen. Then they lived happy and content, and we are left without a cent.

---

* Fermati Conti, vergogna non è!
  Soru di Conti e mugghièri di re!

55

CLEVER PEPPE

Once upon a time there was a poor washerwoman who had an only son named Peppe, and everyone regarded him as dumb. Now one time during Carnival, all the people began cooking macaroni and roasting sausages in their homes, and only the poor washerwoman had nothing to eat but dry bread. So Peppe said, "All the people have good things in their homes today. Why should we alone eat dry bread? Give me your chicken. I want to sell it and buy some macaroni and sausage with the money I get."

"Are you crazy?" his mother replied. "Do you want me to sell my last chicken? Then I'll have nothing at all."

But Peppe kept asking her until she finally relented and gave him the chicken. When he went to the market place, he offered his chicken for sale, and a man came and asked him, "How much do you want for the chicken?"

"Three tari."

"Is it nice and fat?" the man asked and took the chicken in his hands as if he wanted to weigh it. Before Peppe realized what was happening, however, the man disappeared along with the chicken. Just think of how poor Peppe began to moan.

"Oh, now my mother will beat me and kill me! What should I do?"

All of a sudden he saw the thief standing in front of a macaroni shop. He quietly sneaked up behind him and heard the man say, "Put aside twenty pounds of macaroni. Here's the money. Tomorrow I'll send a boy with a white donkey, and you can give him the macaroni."

Now this man was the captain of some robbers and had eleven men under his command. After the robber had bought the macaroni, he went to a sausage shop, and Peppe carefully followed him again.

"Put aside twenty pounds of sausage for me," the captain of the robbers said to the butcher. "Here's the money for it. Tomorrow a boy with a white donkey will come, and you can give him the sausages."

Then the robber went into a cheese shop and also bought twenty pounds of cheese that he left aside to be picked up the next day. Peppe kept sneaking after him and noted everything the robber said and did.

When he returned home, his mother asked right away, "How much did you get for the chicken?"

"Oh mother, listen to what happened to me," and he told her his story.

When the woman heard how he had let the chicken be stolen from him, she took a large stick and gave Peppe a good beating.

"Let me go, mother!" he pleaded. "I'll make sure that the robber pays you back. Just get me a white donkey, and tomorrow I'll give your heart reason to rejoice."

"Oh, what do you want with a white donkey?" the washerman cried. "You numbskull! You're not even capable of selling a chicken!"

But Peppe kept asking until she relented and borrowed a white donkey from a neighbor. The next morning Peppe got up very early and drove the white donkey to the macaroni shop.

"Hey there, good friend, my master has sent me to pick up the twenty pounds of macaroni that he bought here yesterday."

The baker saw the white donkey and thought, "That must be the boy that the customer from yesterday promised to send." So he gave Peppe the macaroni without thinking about it much. Peppe loaded it on to the donkey and drove the animal to the butcher shop.

"Give me the twenty pounds of sausage that my master bought here yesterday" he said, and when the butcher saw the white donkey, he thought it was all right to deliver the sausages to Peppe. Peppe also went to the cheese shop and picked up the twenty pounds of cheese there. Afterward he brought everything to his mother and called out, "Mother, let's eat and drink. Now we've been paid back a fourth of what our chicken was worth."

In the meantime the real boy sent by the captain of the robbers arrived at the macaroni shop with a white donkey and wanted to fetch the macaroni.

"You can't have the macaroni a second time," the baker said. "You were already here once."

"That wasn't me," the boy said.

"Well, I can't help you," the baker responded. "A boy came with a white donkey, and I gave him the macaroni."

The butcher and cheese dealer said the same thing, and the boy had to return to the band of robbers with empty hands, while Peppe and his mother filled themselves with the macaroni and the sausages. The next morning Peppe said, "Mother, the man who stole our chicken has paid us back only one fourth of what it was worth. Fetch me some girl's clothes. I'm going to get him to give me the rest of what he owes us."

When his mother brought him some girl's clothes, he disguised himself as a maiden and went out walking until he came to the house where the twelve robbers lived. Once he was there, he sat down on the threshold and began to weep. Soon after a robber came to the window, looked out, and asked, "Why are you crying, beautiful maiden?"

"Oh, my father told me that I should wait for him here, and now it's almost night and my father still hasn't returned. How can I find my way back home?"

"Now, just calm down," the robber said. "You can stay here, and you'll have a good life with us."

So Peppe went inside, and the twelve robbers gave him food and drink. When it became night, the captain of the robbers said, "This maiden belongs to me, and tonight she will sleep in my room."

"Oh, no," said Peppe. "I can't do that. I would be too ashamed."

"Don't be dumb," the robber said, and he led the supposed maiden into his room, where Peppe saw a great deal of gold and silver lying around, and in a corner was a gallows.

"What is that black thing over there?" Peppe asked.

"That's a gallows," said the captain. "We hang all the people who have insulted us on it."

"How do you do it?" Peppe inquired.

"The person puts his head through the noose," the robber replied, "and then we pull the rope until the person dies."

"Oh, I don't understand how that works. Why don't you show me?"

So the robber stuck his head through the noose, and all of a sudden Peppe jumped over to the gallows and pulled on the rope, but he was not strong enough to strangle the robber. Nevertheless, the robber could barely breathe and could not speak at all. Then Peppe grabbed a large club and beat the robber until he was half dead.

"Oh, you villain, don't you recognize me? I'm the boy whose chicken you stole!" Peppe called out in between beatings. When he finally became tired from hitting the robber, he filled his pockets with gold coins, crept quietly out of the house, and ran back to his mother full of joy.

"Here, mother, take this money. Now half the chicken has been repaid."

The next morning the robbers waited hour after hour for their captain to wake up. When everything remained quiet until noon, they finally broke down the door and found him half strangled and half beaten to death. So they took off the noose and put him to bed, and he could only cough in a low voice, "It was the boy whose chicken I stole."

"Let's get a doctor," the robbers said, and one of them went to the window to see whether a doctor was in the vicinity. All at once he saw a doctor on a donkey riding by. So he called to him and invited him to come inside. However, the doctor was none other than Peppe, who had disguised himself to get back at the robbers one more time.

When the robbers called him, he climbed the stairs slowly and deliberately and was then led to the robber's bed.

"This man is very sick," he said. "I can make him healthy with my medicine, but I shall need some supplies to heal him."

So he sent the robbers out of the house, and each one was to fetch something different, and he remained alone with the sick man.

"Do you recognize me again, you villain?" Peppe asked. "I'm the boy whose chicken you stole."

"Oh, mercy! Don't beat me to death! I'll give you a hundred ounces of gold!"

"I can get that money by myself," Peppe answered. "But you have to repay me for the beating that I received from my mother."

Upon saying this he grabbed a club again and beat the robber until he could no longer continue. Then he filled his pockets with gold coins, left the robber laying in bed half dead, and rode happily back home.

"Here, mother, you see this money. Now we have been repaid three fourths of what the hen was worth."

"Oh, my son, be careful that the robbers don't recognize you."

"What can they do to me?" Peppe said, and the next morning he disguised himself as a street cleaner,* loaded the large waste baskets†

---

* Munnizzàru.

† Zimmili. These were large sacks that were woven out of coarse raffia or straw, and one loaded them with dung and dirt or vegetables and fruit.

on the donkey, and set out on his way to the street where the robbers' house was located.

Meanwhile the robbers were having a discussion among themselves: "What should we do with our captain? Instead of getting better, he's getting worse. Perhaps we should take him to a hospital, but we don't have a way of getting him there."

Just then they looked out the window and saw a street cleaner riding by, and it was Peppe.

"Hey, you handsome fellow," they called, "if you do us a favor, we'll give you an ounce of gold."

"What do you want me to do?"

"We've got a sick man here, and we want to put him in one of your large baskets, and then you can take him to the hospital."

"Good," Peppe answered, and he cleaned out a basket so that the robbers could put their sick captain into it. Then they gave him a gold ounce and tied a money belt around the robber that was filled with gold coins. Peppe pretended now to head for the hospital, but when he was out of the sight of the robbers, he drove the donkey into the mountains on a rocky path.

"Where are you taking me?" the robber asked.

"Just come along, you villain! Don't you recognize me anymore? I'm the boy whose chicken you stole."

"Oh, mercy! Let me live. I'll give you all the money I'm carrying with me."

"I can take that by myself," said Peppe, and he untied the money belt and threw the robber into a ditch and left him lying there.

When he returned home, he gave all the money to his mother and cried out, "So, mother, now the chicken has been paid for. Now we are rich people and can live without any worries."

So from then on, Peppe was no longer regarded by the people as dumb, but as sensible and clever.*

---

* Spertiu. This is from the word spertu, esperto. In German, klug.

56

MARIA, THE EVIL STEPMOTHER, AND THE SEVEN ROBBERS

Once upon a time there was a man whose wife died, and he was left with only a small daughter called Maria.

Maria went to a school where she learned sewing and knitting from a woman. Before she went home each evening, this woman told her time and again, "Make sure you give my warm greetings to your father."

Because she seemed to be so kind, Maria's father thought, "she'd make for a good wife," and so he married her. But when they were married, the woman became quite nasty to poor Maria, for that's the way stepmothers have always been. Finally she could not stand Maria at all, and she said to her husband, "The girl eats too much of our bread. We've got to get rid of her."

But the man said, "I'm not going to kill my own child!"

"Take her with you tomorrow into the fields," the woman said. "Leave her there alone. She won't be able to find her way back home."

The next day the man called his daughter and said to her, "Let's go work in the forest, and we'll take some food with us."

He took a large loaf of bread with him, and they set out on their way. However, Maria was shrewd and had filled her pockets with bran. As she walked behind her father, she threw heaps of bran on the path from time to time. After they had walked for several hours, they came to a steep cliff where the man let the loaf of bread fall over and cried out, "Oh, Maria, the bread fell over the cliff!"

"Don't worry, father," Maria said, "I'll climb down and fetch it."

She went down to the bottom of the cliff and found the bread. But when she returned to the top, her father had disappeared, and Maria was alone. She began to weep, for she was very far from their house and in a strange spot. But then she thought about the heaps of bran and summoned her courage again. Slowly she followed the bran and returned home late at night.

"Oh, father!" she said. "Why did you leave me so alone?"

The man comforted her and talked to her until she calmed down, but the stepmother was angry that Maria had found her way back home. After some time had passed, she told her husband once again to take Maria into the fields and leave her alone in the forest. The next morning the man called his daughter again, and they set out on their way. The father carried a loaf of bread with him once more, but Maria forgot to take bran with her. Once they were deeper in the forest and reached another even steeper cliff, the father let the loaf of bread fall again, and Maria had to climb down to fetch it. When she returned to the top, her father was gone, and she was alone. So she began to weep bitter tears and ran around for a long time looking for the way home, but she only managed to go deeper into the dark forest. Gradually as it turned dark, she suddenly saw a light. She went toward it and came upon a cottage in which she found a table set for dinner and seven beds, but there were no people. Indeed, the house belonged to seven robbers, and therefore Maria hid herself behind the oven. Soon the robbers came home. They ate and drank and then laid down to bed. The next morning they went forth and left their youngest brother there so that he could cook* and clean the house. While they were away, the youngest brother also left to buy a few things†. Then Maria came out from behind the oven and began cleaning the entire house. She finished by sweeping the room and setting the kettle on the fire to cook the beans. Then she hid behind the oven again. When the youngest robber returned, he was astonished to see everything so clean, and when his brothers came home, he told them what had happened. They were all very puzzled and could not imagine how all this had come to pass. The next day the second youngest brother remained behind. He pretended that he had to go away, but he returned right away and saw Maria come out of her hiding place to bring things in order. Maria was terrified when she caught sight of the robber.

---

* Fasola c'à pasta.

† Pi fari a spisa.

"Oh," she pleaded, "please don't kill me. For God's sake!"

Then she told him about her evil stepmother, and how her father had abandoned her in the forest, and how she had hidden herself for two days behind the oven.

"You don't need to be afraid of us," the robber said. "Stay with us. Be our sister and cook, sew, and wash for us."

When the other brothers came home, they, too, were satisfied with Maria, and so Maria remained with the seven robbers, kept house for them, and was always quiet and diligent.

One day as she was sitting at the window and sewing, a poor woman came by and asked for alms.

"Oh!" said Maria. "I don't have much, for I myself am a poor, unfortunate maiden. But I shall be glad to give you whatever I have."

"Why are you so unfortunate?" asked the beggar woman.

Then Maria told her how she had left home and had made her way to the robber's house. The poor woman left and later told the evil stepmother that Maria was still alive. When the stepmother heard this she was very angry and gave the beggar woman a ring to take to poor Maria. This ring was a magic ring. After a week passed, the beggar woman went to Maria again to ask for alms, and when Maria gave her something, she said, "Look, my child, I have a beautiful ring. Since you have been so kind to me, I want to give it to you as a gift."

Without suspecting anything, Maria took the ring, but when she put it on her finger, she fell down dead. After the robbers returned home and found Maria on the floor, they were very distressed and shed bitter tears. Then they made a beautiful coffin, and after they had adorned her with the most beautiful jewels and placed a great deal of gold inside, they put Maria into the coffin and placed it on a cart drawn by two oxen. When they approached the king's castle, they saw that the door to the stable was wide open and drove the oxen and the cart inside. All this caused the horses to become unsettled, and they began to kick and make noise. When the king heard the racket, he sent a servant to the stable to-ask the stable master what had happened. The stable master replied that a cart had come into the stable, but no one was driving it and there was a beautiful coffin on the cart.

The king ordered his men to bring the coffin to him and had them open it. When he glanced at the beautiful dead maiden in the coffin, he began to weep bitter tears and could not bear to leave her. Then he ordered four large wax candles to be set up and lit at the four corners of the coffin. Afterward he sent all the people out of the room, locked the door, fell on his knees next to the coffin, and burst into tears. When it came time for dinner, his mother sent servants to fetch him, but he did not even answer. Instead, he kept weeping even more uncontrollably. So the old queen herself went and knocked on the door and asked him to open up. Still, he did not answer. Then she looked through the keyhole. When she saw her son kneeling next to a corpse, she had her servants break open the door. However, when she saw the beautiful maiden, she herself was very touched and leaned over Maria and took her hand. When she noticed the beautiful ring, she thought it would be a shame to have the ring buried with the girl. So she slipped it off. All of a sudden the dead Maria was alive again, and the young king was extremely pleased and said to his mother. "This maiden is to be my bride!"

"Then it will be as you say!" his mother responded and embraced Maria.

So Maria became the wife of the king and a queen as well, and they lived in glory and happiness until the end of their days.

57

BENSURDATU

Once upon a time there was a king and a queen who had three beautiful daughters, and they loved them more than anything in the world. Indeed, they did everything possible to make them happy and content.

One day the three princesses said, "Dear father, we'd very much like to take a trip into the country today and eat lunch there."

"All right, my dear children, let's do it," the king said and gave the orders right away.

A beautiful lunch was prepared, and the king and the queen and their daughters took a trip into the countryside. After they had eaten, the maidens said, "Dear parents, we'd like to take a walk in the garden for a while. When you're ready to return home, just call us."

No sooner did the maidens go into the garden, however, than a large black cloud came down and carried them off. After some time had passed, the king and queen wanted to return home and called their daughters, who were nowhere to be found. They searched throughout the garden, in the house, and in the fields—all in vain. The three maidens had disappeared, and the situation remained that way. Just think of the grief the king and queen suffered! The poor mother lamented the entire day, while the king issued a proclamation that whoever returned his daughters could have one of them for his wife and become his successor as king.

Now there were two young generals at the court, and they discussed the matter: "Let's set out and search for the princesses. Perhaps this will be our fortune."

So they began their quest, and each one of them had a beautiful horse, a bundle of clothes, and some money. They had to travel for a long, long time, and their money ran out and they had to sell their horses. Finally, they had only the clothes they were wearing on their backs. Since they had become hungry, they went to an inn and ordered something to eat and drink. When they were supposed to pay, they said to the innkeeper, "We don't have any money. The only things we have are the clothes on our backs. Take our clothes as payment, and give us some common garments. We'll stay here and serve you."

The innkeeper agreed, after he brought them some old clothes, the two generals stayed and worked for him.

Meanwhile, the king and queen yearned to see their dear children and kept waiting for them to return. But they did not return, nor did the generals.

Now the king had a poor soldier named Bensurdatu, who had loyally served him for many years. Bensurdatu saw that the king was always sad and said to him one day, "Your majesty, I want to set out and look for your daughters."

"Oh, Bensurdatu, I've lost three daughters and two generals. Do you want me to lose you as well?"

But Bensurdatu said, "Let me depart, your majesty. You'll see. I'll bring back your daughters."

After many conversations the king agreed, and Bensurdatu set out on the same path the generals had taken before him. Eventually he arrived at the same inn and demanded something to eat. The two generals came to serve him. Although they were dressed in poor clothes, he recognized them and was so astonished that he asked what had happened to them. They told him everything, and Bensurdatu called the innkeeper to him and said, "Give them back their clothes. I'll pay you what they owe you."

Once the innkeeper brought back the clothes, the generals got dressed and continued with Bensurdatu on their quest to find the King's beautiful daughters. Again they wandered for a long time and finally came to a desolate, wild region where there was no human dwelling to be seen far and wide. Just as it was getting dark, they noticed a light in the distance, and when they approached it, they found a small cottage and knocked on the door.

"Who's there?" a voice asked.

"Oh, please have mercy, and give us shelter for the night," answered Bensurdatu. "We are tired travelers and have lost our way."

A wise old woman lived in the house, and she opened the door and asked them in.

"Where have you come from, and where are you going?" she asked.

"Oh, my good old woman," Bensurdatu answered, "we've taken on a difficult task. We've set out to search for the king's three daughters."

"Oh, how unfortunate you are! You'll never be able to complete your task. The princesses were abducted by a black cloud, and no one knows where they are now."

Bensurdatu pleaded with the old woman and said, "If you know where they are, then tell us. We want to try our luck."

"Even if I tell you," the old woman said, "you still won't be able to rescue them because you'll have to go down into a deep well. When you reach the bottom, you'll find the princesses, but the two eldest are being guarded by two giants, and the youngest is being held captive by a dragon with seven heads."

When the generals heard all this, they became frightened and did not want to go any farther. But Bensurdatu said, "We've come this far, and now we must finish our work. Tell us where this well is. Early tomorrow morning we shall go there."

The old woman told them and gave them cheese, bread, and wine so that they could strengthen themselves, and after they had eaten, they all laid down to bed. The next morning they thanked the old woman and continued on their journey. They traveled until they came to a well, and one of the generals said, "I'm the eldest and want to go down first."

He tied a rope around himself, took a small bell, and began to descend. No sooner had he gone some distance than he heard such thunder and noise that he became frightened and rang the little bell and let himself be pulled up as fast as he could. Now it was the second general's turn, and things did not go any better for him. When he heard the racket, he became so scared that he rang the little bell and let himself be pulled up in a hurry.

"What brave men you are!" Bensurdatu cried. "Now just let me try."

So he tied the rope around himself and cheerfully began his descent into the well. When he heard the thunder, he thought, "Just make all the noise you want. You can't harm me." As he came to the bottom of the well, he found himself in a very large and beautiful room, and the eldest princess was sitting in the middle. In front of her sat a powerful giant, and she had to clean lice from his hair. As she was doing this, he had fallen asleep. When she saw Bensurdatu, she gesticulated with her hand as if to ask him why he had come. He drew his sword and wanted to approach the giant, but she quickly gave him a signal indicating that he should hide himself. The giant was waking up, and he roared, "I smell human flesh!"

"Oh, where do you think the human flesh could have come from?" the princess answered. "No person could possibly come here. Go back to sleep and rest."

As soon as the giant had fallen asleep again, however, Bensurdatu made a sign to her that she should bend back a little. Then he withdrew his sword and chopped off the giant's head with one slice so that it flew off into a corner. The princess was extremely happy. She thanked him and gave him a gold crown as a gift.

"Now show me where your sisters are," Bensurdatu said. "I want to rescue them."

So the princess opened a door and led him into a second room where the second princess was sitting with a giant. She, too, had cleaned the lice from his hair until he had fallen asleep. When Bensurdatu and her sister entered the room, she signaled them that they should hide themselves. Indeed, the giant awakened and roared, "I smell human flesh!"

"Were do you think the human flesh could come from?" she answered. "No person could possibly come here. Go back to sleep and rest."

As he was sleeping, however, Bensurdatu came out of his hiding spot and lopped off the giant's head so that it went flying far away. The princess thanked him and rejoiced. She also gave him a gold crown as a gift.

"Now I want to rescue your youngest sister as well," Bensurdatu said, but the princesses responded, "Oh, you'll never succeed in doing that. She's under the power of a dragon with seven heads."

"Take me to her," answered Bensurdatu. "I intend to fight him."

The princesses opened a door for him, and when he entered, he stood in a huge hall where the youngest princess was chained to a wall. In front of her lay the dragon with seven heads. It looked ghastly and stood up ready to swallow poor Bensurdatu, but he did not lose his courage. Instead, he began fighting with the dragon until he had cut off all seven heads. Then he took the chains off the princess, and she embraced him full of joy and gave him a gold crown as a gift.

"Now let's return to the world above," said Bensurdatu.

He led them to the bottom of the well and tied the rope firmly around the eldest daughter, and when he rang the bell, the generals pulled her up. Then they threw the rope back down, and Bensurdatu tied the rope securely around the second princess.

Now only the youngest sister and Bensurdatu were left, and she said, "Dear Bensurdatu, please let yourself be pulled up first. Otherwise, the generals may betray you."

"No, no," answered Bensurdatu, "I won't leave you alone down here. Don't worry. My companions won't betray me."

"All right, if you won't do otherwise," the princess said. "I'll let myself be pulled up first. But you must promise me one thing. You must come to marry me, and if you don't come, I shall never marry anyone else."

Upon hearing this he tied the rope securely around the princess, and the generals pulled her up. However, when they were supposed to throw the rope back down to Bensurdatu, their hearts became filled with envy for the poor soldier, and they betrayed him and left him there. Moreover, they threatened the princesses and forced them to swear that they would tell their parents that the two generals had rescued them.

"And if they ask you about Bensurdatu, you're to say that you never saw him," they said.

So the princesses had to swear, and the two generals took them back to the court. The king and queen were full of joy when they saw their dear children again, and since the generals told them they had rescued their daughters, the king gladly gave them the two eldest daughters as wives.

Let's leave them now and see what happened to poor Bensurdatu.

He waited a long time, but when the rope was not thrown back down, he realized that his companions had betrayed him and thought, "Oh, I'm in trouble! How can I get out of here?" So he went through all the rooms, and in one of them he saw a beautifully covered table. Since he was hungry, he sat down and ate. But he had to remain in the underground for a long time because he could not find a way to climb out of the well. One day, however, as he was going through the rooms, he saw a purse filled with money hanging on a wall. When he took it down, he realized it was a magic purse because it cried out: "What is your command?"

His first wish was to get out of the well, and as soon as he was out, he wished for a large, beautiful ship with a crew and ready to sail. No sooner did he make this wish than a magnificent ship lay before him, and on top of the masthead there was a flag with the inscription: "The King of Three Crowns." So he boarded the ship and sailed to the city where the king lived, and as he entered the harbor, he ordered the canons of the ship to be fired. When the king heard this and saw the beautiful ship, he thought, "What a powerful ruler he must be! He's got three crowns, and I only have one."

Consequently, he got into his coach, went to greet him in the harbor, and invited him to come to his castle. "He would make a nice husband for my youngest daughter!" he thought. His youngest daughter was still not married, and no matter how many men wooed her, she refused to get married.

When the king returned with Bensurdatu, the princess did not recognize him because he was wearing such splendid royal garments. The king said to him, "Noble lord, let us eat and be merry, and if it is possible, it would be an honor for me if you would take my youngest daughter for your wife."

Bensurdatu agreed, and they sat down at the dinner table and ate and were merry. However, the youngest daughter was sad because she thought of Bensurdatu. Then the king said to her, "This noble ruler wants to elevate you and marry you."

"Oh, dear father," she answered, "I have no inclination to marry."

Then Bensurdatu turned to her and said, "What's this, noble maiden? If I were Bensurdatu, you would certainly marry me, wouldn't you?"

And as she looked at him with astonishment, he continued, "Yes, I am Bensurdatu." And he told his story.

When the king and queen heard this, they became extremely happy, and the king said, "Dear Bensurdatu, you are to have my youngest daughter for your wife, and when I die, you shall inherit my throne." Then he turned to the generals sitting at the table and declared, "As for you traitors, you must leave my realm now and never let yourselves be seen again!"

So the two generals had to leave the realm. For three days there were festive celebrations arranged by the king, and Bensurdatu married his youngest daughter. Indeed, they remained happy and content, and we were left without one cent.

58

The Rooster Who Wanted
to Become Pope

Once upon a time there was a rooster who wanted to go to Rome and have himself elected Pope. So he set out on his way. During his journey he found a letter, which he took with him. At one point he met a hen who asked him, "Mr. Rooster, where are you going?"

"I'm going to Rome and want to become Pope."

"Will you take me with you?" she asked.

"First I must check my letter to see if you can come," the rooster said and looked at the letter. "All right, you can come. When I become Pope, you can become Mrs. Pope."

So Mr. Rooster and Mrs. Hen continued on their way together, until they met a cat.

"Where are you going, Mr. Rooster and Mrs. Hen?" the cat asked.

"We're going to Rome and want to become the Pope and Mrs. Pope."

"Will you take me along?"

"Wait until I've checked my letter to see if you can come," the rooster responded. "All right. Come along. You can be our chambermaid."

After a short while they met a weasel,[*] who asked them, "Where are you going, Mr. Rooster, Mrs. Hen, and Mrs. Cat?"

"We're going to Rome," the Rooster answered. "I want to be the Pope there."

"Will you take me along?"

"Wait until I check my letter," said the Rooster, and after he had looked at it, he continued, "All right. Come along."

So the animals continued traveling on their way to Rome. When it became dark, they came to a little cottage inhabited by a witch, but she had just gone out. So the animals chose a place according to their pleasure. The weasel laid down in the closet, the cat on the warm ashes in the hearth, while the rooster and the hen flew on top of the beams above the door. When the witch came home, she wanted to fetch a candle from the closet, but the weasel hit her in the face with his tail. She wanted to light the candle and went to the fireplace, but she mistook the shining eyes of the cat for glowing coals and tried to light the candle with them. As she stuck the candle into the eyes of the cat, the cat sprang at her face and scratched her terribly. When the rooster heard all the noise, he began to crow very loudly. All at once the witch realized that they were not ghosts but simple animals. So she took a club and chased all four of them out of the house.

The cat and the weasel no longer had any desire to continue the journey, but the Rooster and the Hen continued on their way. When they finally reached Rome, they went into an open church, and the Rooster said to the sacristan, "Let all the bells ring. I'm here to become the Pope."

"All right," said the sacristan. "We can do this. Just come with me."

Then he led Mr. Rooster and Mrs. Hen into the sacristy, where he closed the door and grabbed hold of them. Once he had them in his hands, he twisted their necks and put them into a cooking pot. Then he invited his friends to dinner, and they ate Mr. Rooster and Mrs. Hen with great relish.

---

[*] Luca, padottola.

59

THE BRAVE PRINCE

Once upon a time there was a king and queen who did not have any children, and they would have very much liked to have had either a son or a daughter. So the king summoned an astrologer, who was to tell him the truth about whether his wife would ever give birth to a child. The astrologer answered: "The queen will give birth to a son, but when he grows up, he will cut your throat."

The king was terrified and ordered a high tower without windows to be built in a desolate region. When the queen gave birth to a son, the king had the baby locked in the tower with a nurse. Now the child lived in the tower and grew by leaps and bounds and became stronger and handsomer with each day. He only knew his nurse and thought that she was his mother.

One day he happened to be eating a piece of goat and found a sharp bone in it. He saved the bone, and later, just for fun, he began to scratch open the wall. Indeed, he was enjoying himself so much that he continued doing this until he had made a small hole through which the sun cast its rays into his room. Astounded by this, he dug further with the bone until the hole was so large that he could stick his head outside. When he now saw the beautiful field with thousands of flowers, the blue sky, and the wide sea, he called his nurse and asked her what all of this was. She told him about the large countries and the marvelous cities that existed, and he felt an irresistible urge to set out into the world and to see all these marvelous things.

"Dear mother," he said, "I can't stand to be in this dark tower anymore. Let's go out and see the world."

"Oh, my son," the nurse said. "Why do you want to go off into the world? We have it good here. I think it's best if we stay where we are."

However, since he begged so fervently and asked her to go with him, and since she loved him so much and could refuse him nothing, she finally relented, tied her things together in a bundle, and set out into the wide world with him.

After they had traveled for a long time, they came to a desolate spot and could not find anything to eat. Just as they were on the brink of starvation, they saw a beautiful castle in the distance and headed straight toward it in order to ask for some food. When they approached the castle, however, they could not see a human being anywhere. They climbed the stairs and walked through all the rooms, but no one was there. However, in one of the rooms there was a table covered with delicious food.

"Mother," the prince said, "there's nobody here. Let's sit down and eat."

So they sat down and ate some of the food. Then they got up and walked through the rooms again looking at all the rich things they contained. All of a sudden the nurse saw a band of robbers approaching.

"Oh, my son," she cried, "they're certainly the men who own this castle. If they find us here, they'll definitely beat us to death."

The prince quickly put on a full armor, took the best sword from the wall, chose the best horse from the table, and waited for the arrival of the robbers. When they came closer, he began to fight, and since he was so strong, he soon killed every one of them except for their chief.

"Let me live," he cried out to the prince. "If you do, I'll marry your mother, and you'll be my dear son."

So the prince let the chief of the robbers live. The robber chief married the nurse, but he could not forget that the prince had killed all his companions. Since he was afraid of the young man's enormous strength, however, he thought of a scheme that might bring about the prince's downfall. He called his wife and said, "Your son repulses me, and I want to get him out of my sight. Pretend to be sick and tell him you can only be cured if he brings you some lemons. Then I'll send him into a certain garden, and you can be sure he'll never return."

The nurse wept bitter tears and said, "How could I possibly cause my son's death? Let him live. He's done nothing."

But her husband threatened her: "If you don't do this, I'll chop off your head and your son's head."

So she had to obey him and pretended to be sick.

"Dear mother, what's the matter with you?" the prince said. "Tell me what you desire and I'll surely get it for you."

"Oh, my dear son," she answered, "if only I had a few lemons, I'd certainly get well."

"I'll fetch them for you, dear mother!" the young man declared. "Do you know where I can find them?"

"You must go to a certain garden," she replied and told him it was far away in a desolate region and guarded by wild animals.

So the prince set off on his journey. When he came to this region, the animals attacked him and sought to tear him to shreds, but he drew his sword and killed all of them. Then he calmly picked some lemons and returned home in good spirits. When this stepfather saw him approaching, he was terrified and asked him what had happened.

"Oh," the young man answered, "there was a bunch of wild animals in the garden, but I managed to kill them all."

The robber chief was even more frightened and found it even more difficult to tolerate the prince's presence, so he said once more to his wife, "Your son repulses me, and I want him out of my sight. Pretend to be sick and ask him to fetch you some oranges."

"No, no," the nurse spoke. "I'm not going to do this again. Let the poor young man live."

Her husband threatened her until she finally had to obey him, and she pretended to be sick.

"Dear mother, are you sick again?" the prince asked. "I'm sure you want something. Just tell me what it is, and I'll fetch it for you."

"Oh, my son," she answered, "if I only had some oranges to quell my burning thirst!"

"Is that all," he cried, "I'll fetch them for you in no time."

So the stepfather sent him to another garden, which was full of even more wild animals that tried to plunge on top of him and tear him apart. But he drew his sword and killed them all. Then he picked some of the most beautiful oranges and brought them to his mother.

The robber chief was now frightened beyond belief when he saw the prince, who told him how he had killed all the wild animals. Indeed, the robber's fear and hatred grew, and he kept thinking of a way to get rid of him. So he ordered his wife to pretend to be sick again, and she was to tell the prince that nothing could help her get well except for a little bottle of sweat from the sorceress Parcemina. The nurse wept and did not want to do this at all, but her husband threatened her, and she had to obey. So she pretended to be sick, and when the prince came to her, she sighed, "Oh, how sick I am, how sick I am!"

"Mother," the young man said, "isn't there anything that will help you get well? Just tell me. Then I'll travel through the entire world and look for it."

"Oh, my son," the nurse answered, "there is a way. If I had a little bottle of the sweat of the sorceress Parcemina, I would soon recover."

"Mother," he cried, "I'm going to set out and find the way, and if it can be found somewhere in the world, I'll bring it to you."

So he set out, and since he did not know the way, he wandered aimlessly here and there for many days until he came to a dark forest. As soon as he entered it, he became lost, and by evening he could no longer find his way out. All of a sudden he noticed a light in the distance, and as he approached it, he saw a small hut inhabited by a hermit. He knocked at the door and a haggard old man asked him what he desired.

"Oh, father," he answered, "I've lost my way and would like to spend the night here."

"Oh, my son," the old man replied, "what's brought you to this wild region at this time of night?"

"My mother is sick," he said, "and the only thing that can help her get well is a small bottle of the sorceress Parcemina's sweat. That's why I've set out to fetch it."

"Oh, my son," the old man responded, "give up your foolish undertaking. Many princes have tried to obtain the bottle, but none have come back."

But the prince would not let himself be dissuaded, and when dawn arrived, he wanted to continue his quest. The hermit gave him a chestnut and a little bottle and said to him, "I can't advise and help you, but my older brother lives a day's journey farther in the forest. Keep this chestnut in a safe place. It might be of use to you one day. If you succeed in finding the sweat, I'd also like you to bring me a small bottle filled with it."

Then the old man gave him his blessing and let him go. After the prince had traveled an entire day, he noticed light in the distance, and when he approached it, he saw the hut inhabited by the second hermit. He knocked on the door, and the hermit opened it for him. He was even older than his brother. Then the prince told him why he was wandering about the dark forest, and the hermit tried to dissuade him as much as he could from pursuing his quest, but it was all in vain. The next morning the hermit said, "I can't help you, but my brother, who's even much older than I am, lives a day's journey from here deeper in the forest. Perhaps he'll be able to help you. Take this chestnut and put it in a safe place. It will be of use to you one day. If you succeed in obtaining the sorceress Parcemina's sweat, I'd like you to bring me a little bottle full of it."

Upon saying this, the hermit gave him a chestnut, a little bottle, and his blessing, and he let him go. Late that next evening the prince came once again to a hermit who was much older than his brothers and had a long white beard. When this hermit heard about the young man's quest, he also tried to dissuade the prince from continuing his journey, but it was all in vain. The prince did not want to return home without the sweat of the sorceress Parcemina. The next morning, when the hermit let him depart, he gave him a chestnut and a little bottle and showed him the way to his fourth brother who lived a day's journey farther into the forest.

Once more the prince wandered an entire day deeper into the forest, and when it turned dark, he came to the fourth brother. This man did not even live in a hut, but rather in a basket that hung between the branches of a tall tree. He was so ancient that his white beard hung out of the basket and almost reached the ground. He, asked the prince what he desired, and the young man told him why he was traveling in the dismal forest.

"Camp out beneath the tree," the hermit said. "Early tomorrow morning I'll tell you what you have to do."

The next morning the hermit woke the prince and said to him: "If you absolutely want to seek your fortune, then go with God. Do you see that steep mountain over there? You must climb it. On top there's a garden with a fountain, and behind it a beautiful castle, whose doors are closed. The keys are lying on the edge of the fountain. Fetch them and open the doors quietly, climb the steps, and walk through all the doors, but make sure that you don't touch a single one of the treasures that are lying about. In the last room you'll find a marvelously beautiful woman lying asleep on the bed. This is the sorceress Parcemina, and the sweat flows down her cheeks. Kneel down next to her, collect the sweat with a sponge, and squeeze the sweat into the bottles. As soon as they are full, flee as fast as you can. Be careful and nimble, and may God be with you."

Upon saying this he blessed him, and the prince set out toward the steep mountain. The higher he climbed, the steeper the mountain became, but he thought about his mother and bravely continued climbing. Finally he reached the top and found everything just as the hermit had predicted. He quickly took the keys from the edge of the fountain, opened the door, climbed the stairs, and walked through the rooms. In the last chamber he found the sorceress Parcemina, who lay on a bed and slept, and the sweat flowed in streams down her face. He kneeled down, took a little sponge, collected the sweat with it, and squeezed it into the little bottles. As soon as they were full, he fled as fast as he could. When he closed the door to the castle, the sorceress Parcemina awoke and began to shriek to wake the other sorceresses. Although they all awoke, they could do nothing against the prince because he had jumped down the mountain with great leaps and bounds. As soon as he entered the forest, he went to the eldest hermit and thanked him for his help.

"Listen, my son," the wise man said, "you're about to return home to your parents, and I'm going to give you this donkey and this sack so you can travel faster. When you see your stepfather, he will burst into a great rage because you succeeded in your quest. Then he'll grab hold of you. Let him do this, and just ask him to put you into the sack after he kills you and to load you on top of the donkey."

So the prince mounted the donkey and rode home. Along the way he stopped at the huts of the other hermits and gave them each a small bottle of the sweat. When he eventually came near his house, he saw his stepfather coming toward him from a distance, and the vicious robber was filled with deadly anger. As he approached the prince, he threatened him and began reproaching him for being so late.

"Father," the prince said, "I realize you can't stand me and want to let out your anger on me. Well, do whatever you want with me, but I have one request. When I'm dead, put me into this sack and tie me tightly onto this donkey so that he can carry me out into the wide world."

Then he surrendered without a fight, and his stepfather kicked and trampled him in his rage until he finally cut off his head and hacked his body into small pieces. When he had satisfied his fury, he thought he might as well fulfill the last wish of the poor prince. So he put all the pieces into the sack and tied it onto the donkey. No sooner did the donkey feel the load he was to carry than he raced straight away with it and ran without stopping until he came to the old hermit who had given the donkey to the prince. The hermit took the pieces from the sack, laid them carefully together, and brought the young man back to life. Then he said to him: "Listen, my son, you cannot return to your parents. At any rate, they're really not your parents, for you are the son of a king, and your father is still ruling in a certain realm. So go there and return to your real parents."

The prince set out and wandered until he came to his father's realm. But before he entered the city, he exchanged his armor for some tattered clothes and wrapped his head in some cloth. Then he said to the people, "I've got some nasty scabs," and they started calling him "scabhead."*

When he finally entered the city he saw that all the houses were ceremoniously decorated, and many people were gathering before the royal castle. He asked a man on the street what was happening.

---

* Tignusu.

"Today is a great holiday," he answered. "In one hour the king will drop a white scarf from the top of the tower, and whoever it falls on will get to marry the king's daughter."

This was the first time that the prince learned that he had a sister, but he did not let anyone notice his surprise. "Well," he remarked, "I want to go there and see if the scarf might fall upon me."

The people laughed at him and cried, "No, no! Just look, scabhead wants to marry the beautiful princess!"

But he did not pay any attention to them. Instead he mixed among the people, and just then, as the king threw the scarf from the top of the tower, it floated down and landed on the dirty scabhead. He was brought before the king, and even though the princess was weeping she had to take him as her husband. The wedding was to be celebrated that evening. However, the prince went to the priest and said, "Father, you're supposed to wed me tonight to the princess, but I don't want you to say the customary words that will unite us. I must tell you in all due confidence that she's my sister. Don't marry us because it's not time yet to reveal who I really am."

In the evening the wedding was celebrated, but the prince remained in his tattered dirty clothes and did not want to wash or put on clean clothes. When the young married couple was led into the bedroom, he bellowed: "Do you expect me to sleep on a bed like that!? Throw a mattress on the floor over there."

So they did that, and he slept on a corner of the mattress.

Now it so happened one day that a war erupted, and the enemy forces had gathered outside the gates of the city. A great battle was to take place, and the old king was compelled to go to war. That same day the princess went to Scabhead and said, "My mother and I want to view the battle from the walls of the city. Do you want to come?"

"Leave me in peace," he roared. "I really don't care who wins the battle."

But no sooner did they leave him than the prince opened one of the chestnuts given to him by one of the hermits and found a complete suite of armor, the most beautiful in the world, and a horse more royal than any king had ever possessed. Then the prince washed himself, put on the armor, and stormed into the battle where the king's troops had begun to yield. His presence filled the knights with renewed courage, and the enemy was defeated. When the king called for the unknown knight to honor him and thank him for his help, the stranger had disappeared. The prince sat in his corner again and was wearing his dirty tattered clothes.

The next day the enemy forces came with reinforcements, and the king had to enter the battle again. The princess went to the city walls with her mother, and no sooner did they leave than the prince opened his second chestnut and found armor and a horse even more magnificent than the one of the previous day. Now he charged into the battle again, and his presence decided the outcome of the battle once more in favor of the king. After the battle he vanished without a trace, just as he had done on the first day, but he had been wounded in the leg by a lance. That evening the princess noticed that Scabhead had a bandage around his leg and asked him was wrong.

"Nothing," he answered, "I bumped into something."

But she told her parents the next day and said, "Don't you think that he may be the unknown knight who has been so loyal to us?"

However, the king and queen made fun of her. Meanwhile, the king had to do battle with his enemy for a third day. When the prince was left alone, he quickly opened the third chestnut and found armor and a horse that were the most magnificent of all. When he appeared in the midst of the battle, the fortunes of the king shifted, and he defeated the enemy forces so badly that they did not return. Once again the unknown knight disappeared just as quickly as he had on the first day.

That evening there was a great feast in the court to celebrate the glorious victories, and the princess adorned herself for the special event and said to Scabhead, "Here are some royal clothes for you. Don't you want to get dressed up and attend the event?"

"Leave me in peace," he roared. "What should I do at your feasts and celebrations?"

No sooner did she leave, however, than he put on the royal clothes and entered the large hall that was illuminated by candles, and since he was such a handsome young man, everyone stared at him in astonishment. Then he stepped before the king and said, "I'm the dirty scabhead. I'm also the unknown knight who appeared three times in the battle."

The king embraced him and thanked him, but then the prince said, "I'm also your son, my dear father."

The king became terrified and said, "How could you have committed such a sin and have married your sister?"

"Calm down, dear father," the prince replied. "I never married my sister. The priest can testify to this."

Indeed, when the priest spoke and revealed the truth, there was great joy, and the king and queen were very happy to have their handsome son with them. Then they lived happily and content, and we can't even pay the rent.

60

THE INNKEEPER'S BEAUTIFUL DAUGHTER

Once upon a time there was a woman who ran an inn where travelers spent the night. She had a daughter who was extraordinarily beautiful, but because she was so beautiful, her mother could not stand her. Therefore, she kept her daughter locked up in a room so that no one could ever catch sight of her. Only one maid knew about her, and she was the one who brought her food every day.

Now one day the king happened to come by and wanted to stay over night at the inn. Just as he arrived, the maid was taking some food to the daughter. Because the maid was called to come quickly and prepare the king's room, she forgot to close the door to the daughter's room. When the innkeeper's daughter noticed this, she became curious and wanted to see the king just once. So she stuck her head through the doorway, and when the king came down the hall, she quickly pulled back her head. However, he had seen her and was completely dazzled by her beauty.

"Where is that beautiful girl whom I saw in the hallway?" he asked the maid who was serving him.

"Oh, your majesty," she replied, "that's the daughter of the innkeeper. She's just as good as she is beautiful, but her mother keeps her locked up so that no one has ever caught a glimpse of her."

The king was so delighted by her great beauty that he wanted to make the innkeeper's daughter his wife, but because he could not ask the mother right then and there for her daughter's hand in marriage, he called the maid and said, "I've decided to spend several days here. I

382

want you to speak to the daughter and see if she is willing to become my wife."

So the maid went to the innkeeper's daughter and said, "Just think, my little mistress, the king wants to marry you, and wants to know whether you will flee with him from this house, which only causes you misery."

"Oh," the poor girl answered. "How can I flee? My mother keeps such a close watch over me!"

"You let me worry about that," the good maid responded. Then she went to the king and said, "I know of only one way for you to succeed. Tomorrow you must depart as if you were returning home. Instead, stop at some spot nearby. At the same time, the daughter must pretend to be sick. Then I'll say to the innkeeper that her daughter's sickness is caused by her being locked up all the time, and she should let me take her for a walk outside. I'll bring her to you, but you must take me with you because I won't be able to return to the inn without her."

The king promised to do this, and the next morning he pretended to leave for home, but he only went a short distance and stopped at another inn in disguise so that he would not be recognized as king. Meanwhile, the daughter feigned an illness and said she could not eat anything and became thinner and thinner.

"What's wrong with my daughter? What's causing this sickness?" the innkeeper asked the maid.

"The poor child has no choice and will always get sick," the maid answered, "because she's always cooped up and never has any fresh air. Let me take her to mass tomorrow morning. If she goes for a short walk, I'm sure she'll get well again."

The innkeeper agreed, and the next morning the maid took her to mass. No sooner were they out of the mother's sight than they rushed to the king, who had a coach ready for them. He lifted the beautiful maiden into the coach and drove away. As for the loyal maid, he gave her so much money that she could move to another country with her entire family.

Now the king arrived at his castle and introduced the innkeeper's daughter to his mother.

"This is my dear bride," he said. "And now we want to celebrate a splendid wedding."

The maiden was so beautiful that the old queen took an immediate liking to her. There was a glorious wedding feast, and the king and his young wife lived happily and content together.

After a year had passed a war erupted, and the king had to depart for the battlefield. So he said to the old queen, "Dear mother, I must go off to war. I'm placing my precious wife in your hands. When she gives birth to our child, I want you to let me know about this right away, and I want you to take good care of her."

Upon saying this, he embraced his mother and his wife and set out.

Soon thereafter the young queen have birth to a baby boy, and the old queen took good care of her and sent the king a letter right away to inform him about the birth of his son. However, the messenger, who was to take the letter to the king, stopped to rest at the inn owned by the young queen's mother. He ordered some food, and while he was eating, the innkeeper asked him where he was coming from and where he was going. Then he told her that he was being sent to take the king good news about the birth of his son. When the innkeeper heard this, she decided to get revenge on her daughter because she had fled the inn. When the messenger laid down to sleep a while, she carefully pulled the letter from his pocket and stuck another one inside that said the young queen had been terribly unfaithful to him and deserved the most severe punishment. It was this letter that the messenger took to the king.

When the king read the letter, he became enormously sad because he loved his wife so much, but he wrote his mother that she should continue to take care of his wife and do nothing until he returned. The messenger took this letter and departed. When he passed by the inn, however, he stopped to eat something. The innkeeper asked him whether the king had sent back a reply.

"Yes, indeed," the messenger said. "The letter's in my pocket."

When the messenger took a nap after the meal, the innkeeper carefully drew the letter from his pocket and placed another one inside. This letter said that the old queen was to chop off the hands of the young queen, and afterward tie the child to the stumps of her arms and send her out into the wide world.

When the old queen received this letter, she began to weep bitter tears because she loved her daughter-in-law very much. But the young queen spoke to her with humility.

"I'll do whatever my husband and master commands."

So her hands were chopped off, and the child was tied to her arms so that she could suckle it. Then she embraced the old queen and wandered off far away into a dark forest. After she had roamed for a long time, she came to a little brook, and since she was so tired, she sat down beside it. "Oh," she thought, "if I at least had my hands, I wouldn't be so helpless. I could wash my baby's diapers and give him some clean clothes. If things continue this way, my innocent child will probably die very soon."

While she was speaking to herself and weeping, a venerable old man suddenly stood before her and asked her why she was crying. She explained to him why she was suffering so much grief and told him she was truly innocent and yet was being punished for something that she had not done.

"Don't cry," the old man said, "and come with me. Everything will go better for you."

He led her a little farther into the forest where he hit the ground with a cane. All of a sudden a castle appeared, and it was much more beautiful than the royal castle in which she had been living. There was also a garden that was better than the king's. Indeed, the old man was none other than Saint Joseph, and he had come to help the poor innocent queen.

Now the queen lived with Saint Joseph and her son in the beautiful castle, and since she was so virtuous, Saint Joseph caused her hands to grow back. Meanwhile, the child became tall and strong and more and more handsome with each day that passed. But let's leave the queen and her son for the time being, and see what's been happening with the king.

When the war was over he returned to his castle in great sadness, for his wife's unfaithfulness broke his heart in two.

"What did you do with my wife?" he asked his mother.

"Oh, you terrible man!" the old queen burst into tears and said, "How could you demand that your innocent wife be put through such terrible grief?"

"What" he cried. "Didn't you write to me that she was unfaithful and guilty of a terrible crime?"

"That's not what I wrote!" the queen replied. "I sent you the good news about the birth of your son, and you answered me that I should have her hands chopped off and sent into the wide world with her child."

"I never wrote that!" the king exclaimed.

They fetched the letters, and both insisted that they had not written them.

"Oh, my poor, innocent girl," the old queen moaned. "I'm sure that you are dead by now!"

There was great mourning in the castle, and the king became so melancholy that he was soon overcome by a serious illness. Eventually he recovered, but he continued to remain very sad. Then, one day, the old queen said to him, "My son, the weather is so beautiful. Don't you want to go hunting a little? Perhaps it will take your mind off things."

So the king mounted his horse and set out sadly into the forest without hunting, and because he was so sad, he did not pay attention to where he was going and lost his way in the dense forest. His entourage did not dare speak to him. When it was almost dark, the king wanted to turn around, but nobody knew the right way out of the forest, and so they rode deeper into the woods. Finally they saw a light burning in the distance and headed straight for it. Eventually they came to the beautiful castle in which the young queen was living. When they knocked on the door, Saint Joseph opened it and asked them what they wanted.

"Oh, good old man," the king answered, "could you please give us shelter for the night? We're lost and can't find our way back home."

Saint Joseph asked them to enter, gave them something to eat and drink, and showed them to some good beds. However, the queen and her child did not let themselves be seen.

The next morning, while the king was having breakfast, Saint Joseph went to the queen and said, "The king has spent the night here. Now the moment has come when all your sufferings will end."

So the queen dressed her son in nice clean clothes, and Saint Joseph told him to go to the king, kiss his hands, and say, "Good morning, papa, I'd also like to have breakfast with you."

When the king glanced at the handsome child, he was very moved and did not know why. Then the door opened, and the young queen entered with Saint Joseph and curtsied before him. The king recognized his dear wife right away and hugged her tightly in his arms, and he also embraced his son. Then Saint Joseph approached them and said, "All your sufferings are now at an end. Live happily and content, and if you have a wish, just call, for I am Saint Joseph."

Upon saying this, he blessed them and disappeared. At the same time, the castle vanished as well, and the king and the queen with her son and the entourage stood in the forest. In front of them, however, they saw the way that led out of the forest and to the king's castle. Soon they returned to the old queen, who was most grateful to see her dear daughter-in-law and her little grandson again.

Then they lived happy and content,
And we can't even pay the rent.

71

THE BEAUTIFUL MAIDEN
WITH THE SEVEN VEILS

Once upon a time there was a king and queen who did not have any children, and yet they would have liked to have some very much. So the queen turned to Madonna del Carmine and prayed: "Oh holy Mother of God, if you grant me a child, I swear to you that I shall have a fountain built in the castle courtyard in his fourteenth year, and oil will flow from this fountain for an entire year."

Not long after this the queen became pregnant, and when her time came, she gave birth to a magnificently handsome boy who grew bigger and became even handsomer and stronger with each passing day. When he turned fourteen, his parents remembered their oath and had a fountain constructed in their courtyard. Once it was finished, oil began to flow from it. The prince liked to stand at the window and observe the people who came from far and wide in order to fetch some oil.

Now the year had passed, and the fountain had barely any oil left. An old woman heard about this and thought: "If I had only heard about this fountain sooner. Who knows if there is really any oil left flowing?" So she took a small pitcher and a sponge and set out toward the fountain. It had already stopped flowing, but there was some oil lying in the basin. The old woman took the sponge, soaked up the oil, and squeezed it out into the pitcher. She continued to do this until the pitcher was full. The prince stood on the balcony and observed everything, and in his arrogance he took a stone and threw it at the little pitcher so that it broke and the oil spilled out. The old woman became enraged and cursed him with a spell: "May you never marry until you've found the beautiful maiden with the seven veils."

From that day on the prince was melancholy and could think of nothing but the beautiful maiden with the seven veils. Then one day he went to his parents and said, "Dear father and mother, please give me your holy blessing, for I want to set out into the wide world and seek my fortune."

"Oh, my son," his mother cried, "what fortune do you want to seek? You have everything that you can possibly wish for. Stay with us, my son. You're our only child, and you were given to us only after we made a great oath."

But the prince could not be persuaded to change his mind and said, "Dear mother, if you refuse to give me your blessing, I shall have to depart without it. I can no longer remain here."

His parents heard these words clearly, and thus they granted him permission to depart and gave him their blessing. He took some money, mounted a beautiful horse, and rode away. He journeyed for a long time, straight ahead, for he was not certain where he might find the maiden with the seven veils. Finally, after many days, he came one evening to the edge of a large forest. At the edge of the forest stood a pretty cottage that housed a peasant, his wife, and children.

"I want to spend the night here," thought the prince, "and tomorrow I'll enter the forest." So he knocked on the door and asked for shelter, and the peasant and his wife kindly took him in. The next morning he thanked them, said farewell, and began riding to the forest. Just then the peasant's wife called after him: "Where are you riding, my handsome young man? Don't you dare enter the dark forest, for you don't know what dangers await you. There are terrible giants and wild animals in this forest, and they guard the beautiful maiden with the seven veils. You'll never be able to get through."

But the prince responded, "If this way leads to the maiden with the seven veils, then I am on the right path and must take it."

"I'm warning you," the peasant woman said. "You don't know how many princes and kings have entered this forest, and none of them have ever returned."

The prince would not let himself be persuaded to abandon his mission. This is why the woman finally said, "If you insist on trying your luck, then listen to some good advice. There's a pious hermit who lives deep in the forest about a day's journey from here. Go straight to him this evening and seek his counsel."

The prince thanked the good woman for her advice and rode into the forest, deeper and deeper, until he arrived at the hermit's cottage at dusk. When he knocked, a low voice asked, "Who are you?"

"I'm a poor wanderer who's looking for shelter," the prince answered.

"Keep out in the name of God," the hermit said and crossed himself.

"No, don't keep me out," the young man said. "I have been baptized."

Then the hermit opened the door, let the prince enter, and asked him where he was coming from and where he was going. When he heard, however, that the prince was searching for the beautiful maiden with the seven veils, he said, "Oh my son, let me warn you to return to your home right away. You'll be devastated if you continue your journey."

But the prince refused to listen to the hermit's warning, and the old man finally said, "I can't help you, but I'll give you some good advice. If you see a door that flaps open and shut, then bolt it down. Now go and rest. Tomorrow I'll show you the way to my brother who lives deeper in the forest about a day's journey from here. He can certainly help you. I can give you half of my bread to eat and some water. Each morning an angel comes from heaven to give me a pitcher of water and some pieces of bread that nourish me."

Then they shared the bread and water, and at daybreak the young man set out on his way. As it began to turn dark, he saw some light in the distance. When he approached it, he glimpsed the cottage of the second hermit, who kindly gave him shelter like his brother. He asked the prince what he was doing in such a wild region. After the prince told him everything, the hermit also tried to convince him to turn back, but the young man remained steadfast, and the hermit finally said, "My brother has given you some good advice, and now I'll tell you something more. When you see an ass and a lion, and the lion is holding the ass's hay in his mouth, and the ass has the bones that belong to the lion, then you are to go bravely to them and help them by giving each of them what rightly belongs him: the ass the hay, and the lion the bones. Now get some rest. Tomorrow I'll show you the way to my oldest brother who lives deeper in the forest about a day's journey from here."

The next morning the prince set out on his way, and at dusk he arrived at the third hermit's cottage. He was so old that his beard touched the ground. The hermit kindly gave him shelter and asked him what he desired. After the prince had told him everything, the hermit said, "Good. Now get some rest. Tomorrow I shall tell you what to do."

The next morning the hermit said to the prince, "Listen carefully to each and every word I tell you, for if you forget anything, you'll be lost. There are three things that you must take with you: some bread, a pack of brooms, and a bundle of feather dusters* to fan the fire. If you continue along this path, you'll first meet an ass and a lion. The ass will be holding the lion's bones in its mouth, and the lion the hay of the ass, and they will be arguing. Follow the advice of my second brother, and they will let you pass. Then you'll come across some giants who'll be hitting an anvil with enormous iron clubs. Wait until all of them lift their clubs at one time so that they cannot see you, and then run under the clubs as fast as you can. Next you will see a date tree standing along the way, and it will be bearing tiny meager fruit. Pick some of the dates, but don't throw them away. Instead you are to eat them and to praise the tree. After you have passed the date tree, you'll finally arrive at a large palace. This is where the horrible ogress lives who guards the three beautiful ladies with the seven veils. You must make your way into the palace, but there is a door that flaps open and shut, and it will prevent you from entering. Don't forget the advice of my first brother, and you'll be able to enter. Now some ferocious lions will rush toward you to eat you, but if you throw them some bread, they won't do a thing to you. Go up the palace stairs, and you will see the ogress's servants charging toward you. They'll be carrying large sticks because they don't have any brooms and they clean the floor only with sticks. Show them the brooms that you have and how to clean the floor with the brooms. Then they will no longer stop you. Once you are upstairs, the ogress's cooks will approach you. Give them each a feather duster, and they will let you pass because they don't have any. Finally you'll reach the ogress who will be sitting on a large throne. There will be three small caskets next to her elbows, and in each one of the caskets there is a beautiful maiden with seven veils. Give the ogress this letter, which she will read and then say to you that you must wait while she writes the answer in another room. She'll be going into that room, however, to sharpen her teeth so she can eat you. Therefore, don't wait for her. Instead, quickly grab one of the caskets and flee. It doesn't matter which casket you take, but don't take more than one. All the guards will calmly let you pass, but you must mount your horse and ride as fast as you can so that the ogress does not overtake you. Make sure that you do not open the casket until you have left the forest and are near a fountain because when you open the casket, the beautiful maiden will cry out: "Water!" and if you do not have water right there for her, she will die. If you follow

_____

* Muscalori.

each and every one of my words exactly, perhaps you'll be fortunate and return here."

Upon saying this, the hermit blessed the prince and let him depart. The young man continued riding until he saw the lion and the ass arguing, just as the hermit had said they would be. So he went toward them and gave them what belonged to them. The angry beasts settled down and let him pass. When he rode further, he heard a terrible racket in the distance. It was caused by the giants who hit the anvil with their heavy iron clubs. So he waited until they all raised their clubs at the same time and then drove his horse beneath them so fast that they did not even notice him. After he had the good fortune of escaping the giants, he saw a date tree along the way that was full of fruit. He picked some dates, and even though they were small and puny, he ate them and said, "How sweet these dates are!" As he rode along, he came to the palace in which the ogress was living. The door was flapping back and forth, so he got off his horse and bolted the door with a strong hand, and then hacked through it. No sooner did he enter the palace than the raging lions rushed toward him and wanted to eat him, but he threw them some bread and they let him pass. Just as he began climbing up the stairs, the ogress's servants approached him. They were carrying large sticks and cleaning the stairs. When they caught sight of him, they wanted to beat him to death, but he took one of the brooms and called out, "Look, you should all have this kind of a broom. Then you wouldn't need so much time to clean all the steps." He began to sweep the stairs, and the servants were so happy about this that they took the brooms and divided them among themselves and no longer paid attention to the prince who continued along his way. He did not go very far, however, when the ogress's cooks came toward him. They did not have any feather dusters, and so they always had to fan the fire with their breath. When he gave them his dusters and showed them how to use them, they were very happy and let him pass without any trouble. Finally he came to a great hall where the ogress was sitting on a large throne and looked terrifying. Near her elbows were three little caskets. After the young man bowed, he gave her the letter, which she read.

"Wait here a moment, my handsome lad," the ogress said. "I'm going to write the answer."

But the prince knew that she was really going to sharpen her teeth, so he quickly grabbed one of the caskets and fled. He was fortunate to pass the cooks, the servants, the lions, and the door. Then he mounted his horse and rode away like the wind. Here, too, the date tree, the giants, the lion and the ass let him pass.

When the ogress came out of her room and saw that the prince had disappeared, she quickly counted the caskets and found that one was missing. "I've been betrayed! Betrayed!" she screamed and began running after the prince.

"Why did you let him pass?" she yelled at the cooks.

"We've served you so many years," they replied, "and you never gave us dusters to make our work easier. This young man was kind to us, and that's why we let him through."

Then she ran to her servants and said, "Why didn't you beat him to death with your sticks?"

"We've served you so many years," they answered, "and you never gave us a broom to make our work easier. This young man helped us, so why should we have beaten him to death?"

"Lions, why didn't you eat him?" the ogress screamed at the beasts.

"If you don't be quiet, we'll eat you. When did you ever give us bread like the handsome young man did?"

"Why didn't you stop him?" the ogress spoke to the door.

"I've locked your house for so many years," the door answered. "but it never occurred to you to bolt me down when I flapped back and forth."

"Oh, date tree," the ogress cried, "why didn't you stop him?"

"You've passed by me every day for so many years," the date tree replied, "and you've never taken a date and eaten it. But the handsome young man did this and praised my fruit."

Then the ogress ran to the giants and scolded them for not having killed the prince with their clubs. But they answered, "Why have you forced us to beat the anvil the entire day? When we raise our clubs, we can't see anyone who's passing by."

The ogress continued running and also scolded the lion and the ass for not having eaten the prince. "Be quiet," the lion responded. "Otherwise I'll eat you. You've passed by us for so many years, and you never thought to give either one of us the food that belongs to us, but the young prince did that."

So the ogress had to turn around and go back to her palace because nobody wanted to help her pursue the prince. In the meantime, the prince rushed through the forest with the casket, and as he passed the three hermits and the peasants, he thanked them all for their help. When he came out of the forest, he thought about opening the little casket. So he rode further until he came to a fountain. There he dismounted the horse and opened the casket.

"Water!" a voice cried out, and as soon as the prince poured some water into the casket, a magnificently beautiful maiden arose. She was so beautiful that her beauty shone through the seven veils that she was wearing, and she was wearing nothing but the seven veils. Then the prince said to the beautiful maiden with the seven veils, "Climb this tree and hide yourself in the thick branches. Just stay there while I rush home and get you some clothes to wear."

"Yes," she replied, "but don't let your mother kiss you. Otherwise you'll forget me and will only remember me after one year, one month, and one day.

The prince promised to do what she asked and rode home. When his parents saw him and approached him, he called out, "Dear mother, please don't kiss me, Otherwise, I'll forget all about my dear bride."

Since it was already evening, he thought he would spend the night with his parents and return to the beautiful maiden in the morning. He laid down to sleep, and while he was sleeping, his mother went into his room to look at him once more, and since she had such a great yearning to kiss him, she bent over him and kissed him. Consequently, he forgot his bride and stayed with his parents. Meanwhile, the beautiful maiden waited for him, and when he did not come, she became very sad and thought, "He must have certainly let his mother kiss him, and now he's forgotten me. Well, I'll just sit here in this tree for one year, one month, and one day, and wait for him."

After a year had passed, an ugly black slave happened to pass by the fountain one day in order to fetch some water. When she looked at the water, she saw the reflection of the beautiful maiden with the seven veils and thought it was her own. "Am I really that beautiful?" she cried. "If this is me, why should I have to go to the fountain with this pitcher?"* Well, she broke the pitcher and went home. When she returned to her mistress and was not carrying any water, her mistress scolded her and asked her where she had left the pitcher.

"I've seen my reflection in the water," the slave answered, "and since I am so beautiful, I'll no longer go to the fountain to fetch water."

Her mistress laughed at her and sent her immediately back to the fountain, this time with a copper pitcher. The slave looked into the water once again, and when she saw the beautiful reflection, she raised her eyes in astonishment and saw the beautiful maiden with the seven veils in the tree.

---

* Sugnu tantu bedda, e vaju all' aqua cu a quartaredda?

"Beautiful lady," she called, "what are you doing up there?"

"I'm waiting for my beloved," the beautiful maiden replied. "He is a handsome prince, and he will come to me in one month and one day to make me his wife."

"I'd like to comb your hair a bit," the slave said. So she climbed the tree and began combing the maiden's hair. She had a long needle with a black button, and she suddenly stuck the needle into maiden's head, but the beautiful maiden did not die. Instead, she turned into a white dove and flew away. Now the ugly black slave sat in the tree and waited for the prince, who was still with his parents and no longer thinking about his beautiful abandoned bride.

In the castle where the prince was now living, there was an ancient chambermaid who was so old that she could no longer speak correctly, and every time she spoke, the prince laughed at her. One day, when he laughed at her and was peeling an orange at the same time, he cut his finger, and a drop of blood fell on the white marble floor. The old woman cried out: "May you never marry unless you find a bride who is as white as the marble floor and as red as blood."

At this very same moment, a year, a month, and a day had passed and the prince called out, "Why do I have to look any longer? I already have a beautiful bride like this."

So he took a splendid coach and magnificent clothes and drove to the tree where he had left the beautiful maiden. However, when he arrived and caught sight of the ugly figure in the tree, he was horrified and cried out: "What's happened to you?"

In response, she said:

The sun came
and took my color.
The wind blew,
My voice has left me.*

"If I am to blame for what has happened," the prince responded, "I shall marry you no matter how you look."

Then she put on the beautiful clothes, got into the magnificent coach, and traveled to the royal castle. When the queen saw her, how-

---

* Vinni lu suli, mi cangiau lu culuri, vinni lu ventu, mi cangiau lu parlamentu.

ever, she said to her son, "This is the ugliest girl I've ever seen! Is this the beautiful maiden who caused you to suffer so much?"

"I abandoned her," the prince answered, "and the wind, the rain, and the sunshine have changed her looks. That's why I want to marry her no matter how she looks."

Therefore, a beautiful wedding was celebrated, and the prince married the deceitful slave. But the next morning when the cook was cleaning the antechamber, a white dove flew into the room and sang:

> Cook, cook, working away
> What's the prince doing with the slave?*

Then the bird flew away, but toward noon, as the cook was preparing the food for the royal table, the dove came once more and sang:

> Cook, cook, working in the kitchen,
> What's the king doing with the queen?†

This happened every day, and the prince gradually became angry and wanted to send the clumsy cook away. But the cook confessed the truth and told him how a white dove came twice a day and asked him how things were going with him and the queen.

"Very well," the prince responded, "tomorrow you are to line the window sill with glue, and when the dove comes, you are to call me."

When the dove came the next morning, the prince was already hiding in the kitchen and saw how the dove landed on the window sill and sang:

> Cook, cook, working in the kitchen,
> what's the king doing with the queen?

But when the dove wanted to leave, she was stuck to the glue and could not fly away. Then the prince jumped from his hiding place, took the bird in his arms, and stroked it. As he did this, he noticed the black button of the needle and thought, "You poor bird, who could have tortured you this way?" So he pulled out the needle, and as soon as he did this, the beautiful maiden with the seven veils stood before him. She had

---

* Cocu, cocu ddi la sala, chi fa lu re cu la schiava?

† Cocu, cocu ddi la cucina, chi fa lu re cu la riggina?

become even more beautiful and spoke, "I am the bride you abandoned in the tree. The black slave, whom you took for your wife, was the one who stuck the needle into my head so that I became a white dove. Then she took my place."

Then the prince had the beautiful maiden dressed in magnificent clothes and had her brought to the castle in a splendid coach, as if she had come from a long distance. Meanwhile, he told the slave, "A maiden from another foreign court has arrived. I want you to receive her with all the appropriate honors. She is to dine with us today."

The slave was content to do this, and when the beautiful maiden came, she did not recognize her. After they had eaten, the prince said, "Noble maiden, would you please tell us the story of your life."

Then the beautiful maiden told everyone what had happened to her, and the slave was blind to the truth and did not notice anything.

"Well, what do you think about all this?" the prince asked his wife. "What do you think this deceitful slave deserves?"

"She deserves nothing better than to be cooked in a kettle of boiling oil and then dragged through the city by the tail of a horse," the slave answered.

Then the prince cried out, "You've spoken your own sentence, and this is what will happen to you."

The slave was thrown into a kettle with boiling oil, and afterward tied to a horse's tail and dragged through the entire city. The prince, however, celebrated a splendid wedding and married the beautiful maiden with the seven veils. They remained rich and consoled, and we just keep sitting here and getting old.

62

THE MERCHANT'S CLEVER
YOUNGEST DAUGHTER

Once upon a time there was a merchant who had three daughters. The youngest, Maria, was very beautiful and at the same time smart and clever. One day the father had to take a trip, so he called his daughters and said, "Dear children, I must go away. Watch out for yourselves, for these are uncertain times. Be careful."

Upon saying this, he departed. For a while it was very quiet and peaceful. One day, however, a beggar came to the door and asked for alms. But this beggar was a robber in disguise.

"Don't let the stranger enter," Maria called to her sisters.

But when the beggar began to groan, "I'm so tired, my dear girls. It's been such a long time that I've had anything warm to eat or a decent rest," the two older sisters let him enter. After the beggar had eaten, he said, "Is it already dark? Where shall I find shelter? Oh, dear girls, please let me spend the night here."

"Don't do it," Maria warned, but her sisters did not listen to her. Instead they prepared a bed for him and told him to stay there. Maria could not sleep at all, for she suspected that he was really not a beggar, and she could not rid her mind of this suspicion. Now, when everything in the house was quiet, she got up, crept to the room where the beggar was sleeping, and hid herself nearby. It was not long before the door opened quietly, and the alleged beggar stepped out and cautiously looked around him. He sneaked down the stairs, opened the door, and whistled to his comrades to gather around him. Then they broke into the merchant's store. Maria immediately decided what to do. Like lightning she sprang through a back door into the open and ran to the police, who came running right away. They managed to seize the one robber who had disguised himself as a beggar. The others fled and left behind the merchandise. Then Maria went to her sisters, who were still sleeping. She woke them and said, "Just look at the consequences of your carelessness! Let me tell you what happened."

When their father returned, he heard how courageous and smart his daughter had been and was very happy, but the chief of the robbers could not accept that a young maiden had thwarted his plan, and he swore he would avenge himself. He took the most beautiful clothes from his treasures, mounted a splendid horse, and entered the city where Maria lived. Once there he posed as a grand and rich gentleman and occupied a beautiful house. Then he went to the shop owned by Maria's father, where he bought all kinds of stuff and had a friendly conversation with the merchant. He pretended to be the son of a rich baron and told the merchant all about his wealth and his beautiful castle. The next day he returned, and his visits continued until the merchant had taken a great liking to him. Now the robber asked permission to marry his youngest daughter, and her father went to her, very pleased by the great honor, and said, "Just think, my child, the young baron wants to marry you."

But Maria answered, "Oh, dear father, I feel very well here, and none of us knows this young man. How can we really be sure that he is what he says he is?"

However, her father was blinded by the robber's wealth and by the high rank of the young man, and he tried time and again to convince his daughter to marry him. Finally, Maria said, "Well, do what you want."

So a spectacular wedding celebration was arranged, and on the wedding day the bridegroom brought a letter from his mother in which she wrote to her son that she unfortunately could not attend the wedding, but she hoped that her son would come and visit her with his young wife. Therefore, after the wedding, the couple mounted their horses and rode off to visit the mother.

The road became steeper and steeper and more and more desolate. Maria realized that she was in a wild region that she did not know at all. All of a sudden the chief of the robbers turned to her and spoke in a rough voice: "Get off your horse now! Did you really believe that I was the son of a rich baron? I'm the chief of the robber band, and one of my men was hung because of you, and now I'm going to get my revenge."

Maria got off her horse and began to tremble.

"Now, take off your shoes and stockings," the robber continued, "and climb that mountain over there."

What could Maria do? She had to obey, and climbed the steep mountain with her tender feet. When they reached the top, the robber tore off her clothes, tied her to a tree, and began to whip her with a stick.

"Just wait," he exclaimed. "Now I'm going to call my comrades, and we'll whip you to death."

Upon saying this, he left her. Maria stood there tied to the tree and could not do anything to help herself. The whip lashes were so painful that she could do nothing but moan and groan. However, not far from the tree there was a narrow path, and on this path a peasant and his wife were riding to the market with some sacks of raw cotton. When they heard Maria's groans, they thought she was a ghost. They crossed themselves and wanted to move on as fast as they could, but Maria heard them and called out: "Oh, dear people, I'm a baptized soul like you. Don't leave me!"

So the peasant got off his mule, and when he saw Maria, he quickly took a knife from his pocket, cut the rope with which she had been bound, and set her free. However, what were they to do, for the robbers could appear at any moment! Thinking quickly, the peasant told Maria to get into one of the sacks, which she did, and the peasant stuffed as much cotton into the sack as he possibly could. Then he tied the sack on the mule, sat down on top of it with his wife, and rode away as fast as he could.

Soon the robbers appeared, but they were astonished to see that Maria was no longer there. The chief swore that he would kill her and set out after her. Shortly thereafter he caught up with her, the peasant, and his wife, and ordered them to stop with a grim voice. Because they were scared to death, they obeyed the robber, who took his sword, stuck it into the cotton, and wounded Maria many times. She did not make a sound, and because the sword had to pass back and forth through the cotton, the blood stains were wiped off, and the robber was fooled. He allowed the peasants to continue on their way. But after a short time he decided to pursue them and forced them to halt. When he stuck his sword into the sacks, he was foiled one more time and finally let the people continue on their way.

When they came to the next city, they stopped at a friend's house and said, "Please do us a favor, good mother. Give us your best bed, for we are carrying a poor wounded maiden, and we want to place her in your care."

So they put Maria in the bed, and because they had to move on, they entrusted her to the old woman. Maria remained with her until she had completely recovered, and when people in the city asked who she was, the old woman would always say, "She's my niece."

One day, when Maria was well again, she said to the old woman, "I'm healthy again and don't want to burden you any longer. See if you can find a job for me."

The old woman inquired and learned that the king was seeking a chambermaid. Maria applied for the position, and because she pleased the king so much, he took her into his employ. The more the king saw her, the more she pleased him, and one day he said to her, "You're to become my wife, and no one else!"

Then she had to tell him that she was married, and why she had been given away to the robber chief.

"Oh," the king declared, "if that's all there is to it, we'll catch him, and when he's hung you'll no longer be his wife."

So Maria was looked upon by all the people as the king's wife.

One day as she was sitting at her window, the chief of the robbers rode by.

"Oh no!" he thought, "you're still living, and you're even the king's wife! Just wait. I'll get you yet!" Then he went straight to a goldsmith and said, "Master, you must make me a silver eagle, hollow on the inside, and large enough so that I can stand inside it. I want it finished within three days."

The goldsmith promised to do it and gathered together a group of his apprentices who had to work day and night to finish the eagle. When the work was done, the robber called a porter and said to him, "I want you to walk back and forth with this eagle in front of the king's window until he feels an urge to buy it." Then he locked himself inside the eagle, and the porter carried him on his back and walked in front of the king's window. The king was standing with his wife Maria on the balcony once again, and as soon as he saw the beautiful silver eagle, he cried out, "Look, Maria! How beautiful! Let's buy it."

But Maria had recognized the robber as he had passed by the previous time. Therefore, she was suspicious and said, "Oh, your majesty, you already have so many beautiful things. Why do you want to give away your hard earned money!"

However, the king liked the eagle so much that he bought it and had the porter bring it up into the castle and place it in his room. When the king and Maria were sleeping that night, the robber unlocked the eagle and stepped out. He carefully crept to the king's bed and placed a piece of paper on the pillow. As long as it laid there, neither the king nor the other people in the castle could wake up. Then he moved to Maria, grabbed her, and dragged her into the kitchen.

"You thought I wouldn't find you here!" he said scornfully, and he took the large kettle, filled it with oil, and set it on the fire. "I'm going to boil you in this kettle!"

Now Maria was in a bad situation, but she did not lose courage. Instead she said, "If I have to die, so be it! But let me fetch my rosary beads so that I can pray for the last time."

The robber permitted this, and Maria rushed into her room and called the king. But no matter how much she called, nothing happened. She kicked and pulled him, all in vain. In despair she grabbed hold of his beard and shook him. When his chin moved, it caused the sheet of paper to fall off the pillow. Suddenly the king and all the other people in the castle awoke. Maria led them into the kitchen where the robber was still stirring the fire. To his surprise, they grabbed him and threw him into the boiling oil. Afterward Maria married the king, and it was a spectacular marriage. She had her father and sisters attend the wedding, and they continued to live happy and content, but we were left without a cent.

63

Maruzzedda

Once upon a time there was a poor shoemaker, who had three beautiful daughters. The youngest, however, was the most beautiful, and she was called Maruzzedda.* The older sisters, however, did not like Maruzzedda because she was so unusually beautiful. The shoemaker was poor and frequently had to wander about the countryside for many days in order to earn money.

One day he said to his eldest daughter, "I want you to accompany me when I look for work. Perhaps I shall be a bit luckier. So his eldest daughter went with him, and he earned a tari. Then he said, "Listen, I'm very hungry. Let's eat ten pennies worth of food, and we'll take just ten pennies to the others."

So they bought something to eat and brought the others half of the money. The next day the shoemaker took his middle daughter and earned three carlini. Then he said, "Let's eat fifteen pennies worth of food, and we'll take the others just fifteen pennies."

So they bought something to eat and brought the others just half of the money. On the third day the shoemaker took Maruzzedda with him, and this time he earned two tari. "Listen, Maruzzedda," he said, "let's eat one tari worth of food, and we'll take the others just one tari.

---

* Diminutive of Maria.

"No, father," she replied. "I'd prefer to go home right away, and then we can all eat with one another."

When the father returned home, he told his other two daughters what had happened, and they said, "Just look at our ill-bred sister! Shouldn't she always do what you want?"

They used these words and more to stir their father against the innocent Maruzzedda. The next morning he took her with him again and earned three tari. "Listen, Maruzzedda," he said once more, "Let's eat three carlini worth of food, and we'll take the other three to your sisters."

"No, dear father," she said. "I'd prefer to go home right away. Why shouldn't we all eat together?"

When the father returned home, he told his older daughters about this once again, and they had even harder words for their sister. "Why do you want to keep that shameless person in your house any longer? Chase her out! Get rid of her!"

However, their father did not want to do this. So the sisters proposed: "Take her with you tomorrow, and leave her behind in some desolate spot so that she won't be able to find her way back home."

The father was blinded by their jealousy and let himself be duped by the sisters, and, so the next morning he took Maruzzedda with him. After they had wandered very far and had come to an unfamiliar region, he said to her, "Wait a moment and rest a while. I'll be right back."

So Maruzzedda sat down, and the shoemaker went away. She waited and waited, but her father did not return. The sun began to set, and the father still did not return. Finally, she was very sad and thought, "My father clearly wants to throw me out of the house. Well then, I'll set off into the wide world."

So she wandered away and continued to wander until she was tired and it had become evening. She had no idea where she might find shelter for the night. Suddenly, however, she saw a splendid castle in the distance. She went toward it, entered, and climbed the stairs, but she encountered nobody inside. She went through the rooms, which were lavishly decorated, and in one of them there was a table that had been fully set, but still there were no people. Finally she reached the last room, where she saw a beautiful maiden lying on top of a black frame used for coffins. She was dead.

"Well, since there is nobody here, I'm going to stay until someone comes and chases me away."

She sat down at the table, ate, and drank to her heart's content. Then she laid down in a beautiful bed to sleep. She lived this way for a long time, and no one disturbed her.

One day, however, her father happened to pass by while she was looking out the window. When he saw her, he greeted her, for he was sorry that he had abandoned her, and he asked her how she was doing.

"Oh, things are just fine," Maruzzedda responded. "I've found some work here as a servant, and they treat me well."

"May I come up for a while?" the father asked.

"No, no," she replied. "My master is very strict and has forbidden me to let anyone enter. Farewell, and greet my sisters for me."

The shoemaker went home and told his daughters that he had found Maruzzedda, and once again they deceived him with false words so that he became angry with the innocent Maruzzedda. After some days had passed, the jealous sisters baked a cake with some poison inside, and gave it to their father to take to the poor maiden.

During that very same evening, while Maruzzedda was asleep, the dead maiden appeared to her in a dream and called: "Maruzzedda! Maruzzedda!"

"What do you want?" Maruzzedda asked, half asleep, half awake.

"Tomorrow, your father will bring you a wonderful cake. But beware and do not eat it. Give the cat a piece. The cake has poison inside."

Maruzzedda awoke and saw that she was alone, and thought, "I must have probably dreamed this," and she fell back into a pleasant sleep.

The next day she saw her father coming. She allowed him to climb the stairs, but she would not let him enter.

"If my master should see you, he would discharge me from his service."

"Don't worry, my child," the shoemaker answered. "Your sisters have sent their greetings along with this cake."

"Tell my sisters that the cake is very beautiful," Maruzzedda responded, "and I thank them very much for sending it."

"Don't you want to try a little piece," the father asked.

"No, I can't right now," Maruzzedda answered. "I have work to do. Later, when my work is finished, I'll try a piece."

Then she gave him some money and told him to go. When he was gone, however, she gave the cat a piece of the cake, and the cat died immediately. Then she realized how true the dead maiden's warning had been and threw the cake away.

Meanwhile, the jealous sisters became restless at home because they wanted to know what had happened to Maruzzedda. Therefore, the shoemaker traveled to the castle again the next morning. When he knocked at the door, Maruzzedda came toward him, cheerful and in good health.

"How are things going, my dear child?" he asked.

"Everything is fine, dear father," she answered.

"Why won't you let me see the castle just one time?" he said.

"What are you thinking?" she replied. "That would cost me my job."

Then she gave him some money and sent him away. When the father arrived home and told his other daughters that Maruzzedda was completely healthy, they hated their poor sister even more than before. So they made a beautiful enchanted hat, and whoever put it on would become stiff and paralyzed. The father had to take this hat to Maruzzedda.

During the night, however, the dead maiden appeared to Maruzzedda in a dream once more and called out: "Maruzzedda! Maruzzedda!"

"What do you want?" she asked.

"Tomorrow morning your father will bring you a beautiful hat," the dead maiden said. "Beware, and don't put it on. Otherwise, you'll become stiff and paralyzed."

The next morning the shoemaker did indeed appear and brought his daughter a beautiful hat.

"Tell my sisters that the hat is very beautiful, and I thank them very much," she said to her father.

"Don't you even want to try it on so that I can see how it looks on you?" the father asked.

"No, no, I have to work now," she replied. "Later, when I go to mass, I'll put it on."

Upon saying this, she gave him some money and told him to go. She put the hat into a chest, but did not tear it up as she should have done. Meanwhile, her sisters were convinced that Maruzzedda had been destroyed by the hat, and they were no longer concerned about her.

About this time the dead maiden had been granted permission through God's grace to enter the heavenly paradise. She appeared to Maruzzedda for the last time in a dream and said, "God has permitted me to go to my final resting place, and I am leaving this castle and everything in it to you. Live a happy life, and enjoy all this splendor."

Upon saying this, she disappeared, and the black frame on which she had been lying was now empty.

Many months passed, and one day Maruzzedda decided to clean out all the chests and boxes in the castle. As she was doing this, she came upon the enchanted hat. Since she had received it so long ago, she had forgotten who had sent it to her and thought, "Oh, what a pretty hat! I'm going to try it on." No sooner did she put the hat on her head than she became stiff and paralyzed and could not move anymore. That evening the dead maiden appeared, for the Lord gave her permission to return to earth. She took poor Maruzzedda and placed her on the black frame. Then she flew back to paradise. Maruzzedda lay there as if she were dead, but she did not became pale or cold.

One day, after she had been lying like this for a long time, the king happened to go hunting, and the hunt took him into the vicinity of the castle. At one point he saw a beautiful bird, took aim, and hit it, but the bird fell right into the room where Maruzzedda was lying on the frame. The king wanted to enter the castle, but all the doors were locked, and nobody responded to his knocking. There was nothing else to do but climb through a window, and since the window was not very high, he ordered two of his hunters to climb through it. When they succeeded and saw the wonderful maiden, they forgot all about the bird and the king and kept staring at the dead Maruzzedda. The king became impatient and finally called out: "What are you doing inside there? Hurry up!"

The hunters went over to the window and asked the king to climb up. They told him there was a maiden inside, and that they had never seen anyone so astonishingly beautiful as she. So the king climbed through the window into the room, and as soon as he caught sight of Maruzzedda, he could not take his eyes off of her. When he bent over her, he noticed that she was still warm and cried out, "The maiden is not dead, just unconscious! Let's bring her back to life!"

They tried to wake her. They rubbed her and loosened her clothing, but it was all in vain—Maruzzedda remained stiff. Finally the king took off her hat in order to cool off her forehead, and all at once she opened her eyes and awoke from her slumber. Then the king announced, "You shall be my wife," and he embraced her.

However, the king had a mother, who was an evil sorceress, and consequently he was afraid to take Maruzzedda back to the castle with him. "Stay here," he said to her, "and I'll come to you as often as I can." From then on Maruzzedda lived in the castle and was secretly married to the king, and the king came and visited her whenever he went hunting. After one year she gave birth to their first son and called him Tamo.* After another year, she gave birth to a second son and called him Tamai.† And when she gave birth to a third son the following year, she called him Tamero.‡

---

* T'amo. Translation: I love you.
† T'amai. Translation: I loved you.
‡ T'amerò. Translation: I'll love you.

The old queen had gradually noticed, however, that her son often went hunting and stayed away from the castle for a long time. When she investigated things, she learned about his marriage. So she called a loyal servant and said, "Go to the castle where the king's wife is living and say to her: "My majesty, the queen, will grant you a pardon when you send your oldest son to her today.""

The servant did this, and poor Maruzzedda was fooled and gave the man her eldest son. The next day the old queen had the second son fetched, and soon afterward, the third son. When she had the three children in her castle, she called her cook and said to him, "You must kill these three children and bring me their hearts and livers as proof that you have followed my orders."

The cook had children himself, and his fatherly heart took pity on the poor innocent children and he did not kill them. Instead, he took them to his house and hid them there. As for the queen, he brought her the heart and liver of three billy goats.

Meanwhile the king became sick and laid in his bed. The queen sent another messenger to Maruzzedda and told him to say: "Your husband is sick. You are to go to him and take care of him."

Maruzzedda put on three dresses, one on top of the other, and went to the castle. When she entered the courtyard, there was a huge fire burning, and the old queen was standing beside it and called out, "Throw the girl into the fire!"

"First, let me take off my clothes," Maruzzedda requested, and she took off the first dress, threw it into the fire, and cried with a loud penetrating voice, "Tamo!"

But the queen had placed a group of musicians in front of the king's door, and they had been ordered to play their instruments with all their might so that the king would not be able to hear what was happening in the courtyard. However, he heard his wife's cry, even if it was very weak.

"Stop playing your music," he said, but the musicians continued to play as loudly as they could. Then Maruzzedda threw off the second dress and cried out even louder: "T'amai!"

This time the king heard it much better and called out: "Stop your music!"

But the musicians had received orders not to obey him and continued to play. Then Maruzzedda took off the third dress and yelled from the bottom of her anxious heart as loudly as she could, "Tamero!"

The king heard the cry, jumped out of bed, and ran down into the courtyard. Just as he arrived, the servants were about to throw poor Maruzzedda into the fire. He commanded them to stop and to tie up the queen instead and to throw her into the fire. Then he embraced his wife and said, "Now you will be the queen."

"Oh," she responded, "before anything, take me to my children."

"Where are the children?" the king asked.

"What? They're not here?" the poor mother cried. "Oh my children, my dear children!"

Then she told the king how his mother had sent messengers to fetch the children, but nobody knew anything about this, and there was great sadness in the castle. Then the cook asked to see the king and said, "Your majesty and my queen, console yourselves! The old queen had ordered me to kill your children, but my heart took pity on them, and I let them live."

Then the three children were brought to them, and they embraced them with great joy. The king and queen celebrated with a splendid feast and gave rich gifts to the cook.

And so they lived happy and content,
But we can't even pay the rent.

64

ARMAIINU

Once upon a time there was a king who had three beautiful daughters. One day, while the princesses were enjoying themselves in the garden, three frightening giants broke in and made off with the maidens. Consequently, the king had it proclaimed throughout his realm that whoever brought his daughters back to him could choose one of the princesses for his wife and would become king after him. Many men arrived and set out to find the princesses, but none of them ever returned from their quest.

Now one day, three princes arrived. They were brothers and had themselves announced to the king.

"Your majesty," they said, "we've come to rescue the princesses."

"Oh," answered the king, "many men have set out on this quest, and none have returned. Let's hope that you'll have better luck."

So the three princes began their journey and continued to wander for one year, one month, and one day until they came to a large beautiful castle that lay in the middle of a huge estate. By this time they had lost the courage to travel any farther and said to each other, "Let's stay here until we learn something more concrete about where we might find the princesses. This estate is beautiful, and there's more than enough game to hunt so we can feed ourselves."

So they remained there, went hunting, and led a splendid life in the beautiful castle. Meanwhile the king continued to wait for his daughters and their rescuers, and because no one came, he finally thought, "They've certainly gone missing like the others," and became very sad.

However, he had an old gatekeeper who had once been a soldier, and because he had lost an arm and a leg in a war and could not work, he had become the king's gatekeeper and was called Armaiinu. Well, this man went to the king and said, "Your majesty, I'm going to set out and search for the three princesses and the three princes and bring them back to you."

"Oh Armaiinu!" the king laughed and said. "If so many strong young men have been destroyed trying to find my daughters, how do you expect to succeed?"

But Armaiinu would not let himself be dissuaded from going on this quest, and the king finally granted him permission to leave. So Armaiinu set out on foot and carried a small sword that caused people to laugh when they saw it. However, it was a magic sword, and whoever owned could not be stopped. Armaiinu wandered and wandered, and since he was old and lame, he needed two years, two months, and two days until he came to the castle where the three princes were staying. Finally he reached it, entered, greeted the princes and said, "I've come to look after you and to help you recover the princesses."

The princes laughed, but they also gave him a hearty welcome.

"All right," said Armaiinu, "let's stay here for another few days, and one of us will take a turn and stay in the castle and cook while the others go hunting."

The princes agreed, and on the first day the eldest brother remained in the castle. As he began plucking a wild duck, a powerful giant burst into the castle and asked him with a threatening voice, "Who gave you permission to live in my castle?"

"We've been living here already for two years," the prince answered. "Why has it occurred to you just now to see who's living here?"

"Is that the way you answer me?" the giant shouted and lifted a large club and beat the prince until he lay on the ground half dead. When the others returned, the duck was only half plucked, and the prince was lying on the ground and groaning.

"I felt such a terrible pain in my body," he said, "that I couldn't finish my work."

On the second day the middle brother stayed behind, and things did not go any better for him. While he was plucking a wild duck, the giant appeared and asked him who had allowed him to live in the castle, and because he gave the same answer as his brother, the giant beat him as well and left him lying on the ground half dead. When the others returned, they found the duck only half plucked and the prince on the floor.

"Ohhh!" he groaned. "All of a sudden I had such a terrible headache that I could not continue working."

Consequently, they had to go to bed on empty stomachs again. However, the eldest brother said to the middle one, "Tell me, did the giant perhaps beat you?"

"Yes," answered the other. "But let's not tell the others. If we received a beating, why shouldn't they as well?"

The next morning the youngest brother remained at home, and things did not go any better for him. When the others came home, the duck was only half plucked, and the prince lay on the ground and groaned, "Ohh, I suddenly didn't feel so well. That's why I couldn't make anything."

"Well, that's real nice!" said Armaiinu. "The three of you are strong young men, but we've had to go to bed hungry three nights in a row. One of you felt a terrible pain in his body, the other had a headache, and the third felt sick. I see now that tomorrow your poor Armaiinu will have to remain home and do the work for all three of you."

"Yes," thought the brothers. "Now you'll be home to get the beating that we had to taste."

So on the fourth day Armaiinu remained at home, and just as he was plucking the duck, the giant appeared and said with a threatening voice, "Well, are you still here? Just wait! I'm going to murder you today!"

But Armaiinu pulled out his magic sword and attacked the giant. With one fell swoop, he lopped off the giant's head. Then he roasted the duck, and when the others came back, he was waiting for them by the door in good spirits.

"You're come just at the right time," he called out to them. "Dinner's ready."

The brothers were very astounded and asked him whether anyone had come to the castle.

"Oh yes," Armaiinu responded. "A man came, and since he was so impolite, I cut off his head."

The princes became frightened and thought, "Something strange is going on here!"

The next morning Armaiinu said, "Let's go now and rescue the princesses. Behind the castle there's a large cistern. One of us will have to be let down into it because the poor maidens are being held captive there."

"Good," answered the eldest prince. "I'll try it."

So they took a large basket and tied it to a rope. Then the prince got into it and took a little bell with him. They agreed that whenever he rang the bell, he would be pulled up by the others. However, to land on the floor of the cistern he had to go through a huge wind, a great deal of fire, and lots of water. As soon as the prince encountered the wind, he became so scared that he rang the bell and had himself pulled up.

Now the middle prince wanted to try his luck and was brave enough to make it through the huge wind, but when he felt the water on his feet, he lost his courage and had himself pulled up. Next in turn was the youngest prince, who went courageously through the wind and water, but when he felt the fire, he did not want to go any further and had himself pulled up.

"Now your poor Armaiinu will have to try his luck," the old man said. Then he stepped into the basket and had himself lowered into the cistern. Fortunately he was able to make his way bravely through the wind, water, and fire and landed at the bottom. Once there he climbed out of the basket and wandered a while in a dark room until he saw a door with a light shining beneath it. When he opened it, he saw a beautiful salon in which the eldest princess was sitting before a magnificent mirror. In front of her lay a giant whose head was on her lap. Armaiinu drew out his magic sword and chopped off the giant's head before the monster could awake. Then the princess pointed to a door, and when he opened it and went through, he came to a second salon, in which the second princess was sitting before a mirror. In front of her lay the second giant with his head on her lap. But Armaiinu slashed his head off and went through a door into the third salon where the youngest princess sat like her sisters in front of a mirror holding the giant's head on her lap. Once again Armaiinu chopped off the head of this giant, and thus he liberated all the princesses. Then he led them to the place where the basket was still hanging and rang the little bell. The princes pulled the first princess up to the top and let the basket down again. Armaiinu put the second princess into the basket, and after the basket returned, he set the youngest in it. After the three princes had pulled all the daughters to the top, they talked with one another and said, "Let's leave the old gatekeeper sit there. Then we can share the reward for rescuing the princesses just among ourselves."

They threatened the maidens and said that they would murder them if they did not swear a holy oath to keep quiet and left the place as fast as they could. When they arrived at the king's court, they said, "Your majesty, after a long battle and great difficulty, we succeeded in freeing your daughters and killing the giants."

The king was extremely happy when he heard this news. Afterward he arranged for a magnificent wedding, and each prince married a princess. In the meantime Armaiinu waited in the cistern for a long time and kept ringing the little bell, but the basket did not reappear. Finally he realized that the princes had betrayed him. He went back into the beautiful salons and looked at all the treasures that had been gathered there, but felt only anger because he thought that none of the treasures could help him so long as he was trapped in the cistern. As he stood before the mirror the oldest princess had used, he was so overcome by his rage that he took a large stone and threw it against the mirror, which broke into a thousand pieces. To his surprise, however, a splendid emperor's robe and crown fell out of the mirror.

"What use are this beautiful robe and crown if I can't get out of the cistern?" he cried as he ripped the robe into a thousand pieces. Then he went into the second salon and smashed the other mirror. All at once another emperor's robe and crown fell out of the mirror, and they were even more splendid than the others. Armaiinu wanted to tear apart this robe as well, but when he saw how superbly embroidered it was, he did not want to ruin it. He went to the last salon, where he broke the third mirror. All at once a small flute fell out, and when he put it to his mouth and blew it, a voice cried out: "At your command!"

"I wish to become a handsome young man," Armaiinu responded, and suddenly he was transformed into a gorgeous young man. Then he put on the robe, set the crown on his head, and looked like a powerful emperor. So he whistled again and wished himself out of the cistern, and within seconds he stood in free air. Next he wished for a large retinue and a coach with six horses, and he drove to the king's court.

When the king heard that the emperor of the world* was coming to his realm, he rushed out to meet him and fell at his feet, but Armaiinu lifted him up in a friendly fashion and said he wanted to dine with the king.

So a magnificent dinner was prepared, and after the meal each person was to tell a story.

"I want to tell you the story about a poor gatekeeper," Armaiinu said and began to tell his own story. The three princes, who were sitting at the table with their wives, became very frightened when they heard this story, and Armaiinu cried out, "Yes, your majesty, and I am that poor Armaiinu, and these three princes are the traitors who deserted me, and if you need some proof, just look at how all three are twisting in their seats and have become so pale."

The king ordered the three princes to be led out of the room and to be hung. Afterward he said to Armaiinu, "Choose one of my daughters, and after I die, you will become king."

---

* L'imperaturi di tutto lu munnu.

"No, your majesty," Armaiinu responded, "your daughters deserve to marry three princes. I wish nothing more than to die in your service as your faithful Armaiinu just as I was before."

So he wished himself back into his former shape and became the lame, one-armed Armaiinu he had previously been and remained the king's gatekeeper until he died. As time went by, the three princesses married three princes and remained happy and content, but we did not receive one cent.

65

THE GOLDEN LION

Once upon a time there was a rich merchant who had three sons. One day the eldest said to him, "Father, I want to set out to see the world. Give me a beautiful ship and a lot of money, and let me go."

So the father ordered a beautiful ship to be equipped for his son, and the son sailed off. After he had traveled for some time, he landed at a magnificent city where he saw a proclamation written by the king that said, whoever could find his daughter within a week could have her for his wife. But if he did not succeed, it would cost him his head.

"Well," thought the young man, "this shouldn't be all too difficult."

So he went to the castle and informed the king that he wanted to find the princess within a week.

"Good," the king answered. "You can look in the entire castle. If you don't find her, you will lose your head."

So the young man stayed in the castle and had everything he wanted to eat and drink, and he was allowed to go anywhere he desired to go in the castle. Yet no matter where he searched, in each and every corner, and no matter how many closets he opened, he could not find the princess, and after a week he was beheaded.

When he did not return home, the second son said, "Father, give me a ship, too, and a large sum of money. I want to set out and search for my brother."

So the father ordered a second ship to be equipped, and the son set sail. The winds led him to the same shore where his brother had landed, and when he saw his brother's ship still anchored in the harbor, he thought, "Well, my brother can't be far from here," and he went on land. All at once he saw the same proclamation by the king, who announced that whoever could find his daughter within a week could have her for his wife, but whoever did not succeed would lose his head. "I'm sure my brother tried to find the beautiful princess and lost his life," the young man said to himself. "Now I'll try, and I'm sure I'll succeed."

So he had himself announced to the king and tried to find the princess, but he had no better luck than his brother. No matter where he searched he could not find the beautiful princess, and on the eighth day he was beheaded.

Now only the youngest son remained at home. When he saw that his brothers did not return, he, too, had his father give him a ship and a large sum of money and set out to search for his brothers. The winds drove him to the same shore where he saw his brothers' two ships. When he landed, he entered the city and saw the king's proclamation. "So," he thought, "Whoever can find the king's daughter is to get her for his wife? I'm sure my brothers tried to find her and lost their heads. Now I'm going to try my luck."

While he walked toward the castle with these thoughts in his head, a poor woman came up to him and begged for some money: "My handsome lad, give an old woman some alms."

"Leave me in peace, old woman," he responded.

"Oh, please don't turn me away," the woman said. "You're such a handsome young man. You certainly wouldn't refuse to give an old woman some alms."

"I'm telling you, old woman, leave me in peace."

"Do you have some troubles?" the old woman asked. "Tell them to me, and I'll help you."

He told her that he was searching for the beautiful princess and was trying to think of a way to find her.

"Well, I can help you," the old woman said, "but only if you have a good deal of money."

"Oh, I've got plenty," the young man replied.

"Well then, let a goldsmith make a golden lion for you," the old woman said. "It should have crystal eyes and be able to play a pretty song. After that I'll help you some more."

So he had a golden lion made, and it had crystal eyes and played a merry little song. When the old woman came, she stuck the young man inside the lion and took it to the king. Since the lion pleased the king so much, he asked the old woman whether she would sell it to him.

"The lion doesn't belong to me," she answered, "and my master refuses to sell it at any price."

"Well, at least let it stay here for a short time until I've shown it to my daughter," the king responded.

"Yes, I can do that," the old woman said. "But tomorrow my master must have it back."

When the old woman went away, the king took the golden lion into his room, and at a certain spot, he lifted up part of the floor. Then he climbed down some stairs with the lion in his arms, opened a door, and then another one and another one until he had opened seven, each one with a special key. Meanwhile, the young man who was hiding in the lion saw everything. Finally they came to a beautiful hall in which the princess was sitting with eleven playmates. They all looked exactly like the princess, and they all wore the same clothes.

"How unlucky I am!" thought the young man. "Even if I make it to here, how am I going to tell the princess apart from all the others? They all look alike."

The princess was very pleased by the golden lion and asked, "Dear father, let the cute animal stay here for the night so that we can enjoy it."

After the king had locked her in the hall again, the maidens continued to have fun with the pretty golden lion and then laid down to sleep. But the princess took the golden lion into her room and placed it next to her bed. After a while the young man began to speak: "Oh beautiful princess, just look and see how much I've suffered in order to find you."

Then she started to scream, "The lion! The lion!"

However, her friends thought she was screaming in her sleep and did not move.

"Oh, beautiful princess," the young man spoke again. "Don't be afraid. I'm the son of a rich merchant and wish to become your husband. I've only hidden myself in this golden lion in order to find you."

"What's the use of it all?" she responded. "Even if you get this far, you won't be able to tell me apart from my companions, and you'll still lose your head."

"You can take care of that," he suggested. "I've already done a lot for you. Now you can do something for me."

"All right then," the princess said. "Listen to me. On the last day of the week I'll wrap a white sash around my hips. Then you should be able to recognize me."

The next morning the king came and took the golden lion away and returned it to the old woman who was already at the castle. Then the old woman carried the lion out of the castle and let the young man out. As soon as he was out of the lion, he went to the king and announced that he wanted to find the beautiful princess.

"Good," the king answered, "but if you don't find her, it will cost you your head."

So the young man stayed in the castle, ate and drank, and pretended every now and then to search for the princess. On the eighth day he entered the king's room and gave an order to his servants: "Rip open the floor at this spot."

The king became frightened and said, "Why do you want to rip open the floor? She's certainly not hiding beneath it."

However, the young man did not let himself be misled. Instead, he gave the order a second time for the floor to be ripped open. Then he climbed down the stairs, and when he came to the door, he called out, "Where is the key to this door?"

Then the king had to unlock the door, and also all the other doors, and when they entered the hall, the twelve maidens were standing in a row, and they all looked so much alike that one could not tell them apart. But the princess quickly wrapped a white sash around her hips, and the young man went right toward her and cried out, "This one is the king's daughter, and I very much want her for my dear wife."

Since he had made the right guess, the king could no longer say no, and he organized a splendid wedding. After the wedding the king heaped treasures on him, and the young man took his beautiful wife and sailed home to the old merchant. Before they left, however, they gave a splendid gift to the old woman. In the end they remained man and wife, but we sit here and stare at one another without much life.

66

THE TWELVE ROBBERS

Once upon a time there were two brothers who were both poor and miserable. They had many children and little money. One day, one of the brothers said to his wife, "I want to go into the country to see if I can find some work. Perhaps I'll be able to earn some money."

So he set out on his way and traveled straight ahead until he came to a tall mountain. Then he sat down and began thinking about his sad fate. As he was sitting there, he suddenly saw twelve robbers coming toward him. "Oh, how unlucky I am!" he thought. "If they find me here, they'll murder me." Fortunately, he saw a thick bush nearby where he decided to hide himself until the robbers rode by. However, instead of moving along, the robbers began to climb the steep mountain and were carrying treasures with them. When they reached a large rock, the first robber said, "Open up, door!"*

As soon as he said these words, a door in the rock opened, and all twelve robbers went inside. Then the rock closed itself behind them. After a while they came back out, and the last robber said, "Close, door!"† And the door closed behind them.

---

* Gràpiti, cicca.

† Chiuditi, cicca.

"Oh," thought the poor man, "there are things I can fetch in that cave!" And when the robbers had disappeared, he crawled out from the bush, climbed the mountain, and stood in front of the rock.

"Open up, door!" Immediately the door opened so he could enter. "Close, door!" Immediately the door closed behind him. Then he saw all the treasures of the world that were stored there because the robbers brought everything they stole to this cave. Indeed, the poor man kissed the ground when he saw all the gold and so many treasures. Then he filled his pockets with as many gold coins, as he could carry and said, "Open up, door!" The door to the rock opened, and he went out and said, "Close, door!" so the rock would close again. Then he went home delighted and said to his wife, "God has sent us an abundance of good things so that we can now live comfortably and without worries."

So he set up a small business with the money, and God blessed him so that everything went well for him. But when his brother saw how well things were going for him, he went to him and said, "Dear brother, how did you manage to get all this money? Tell me so that I can also go there and fetch a little.

"Let me tell you what happened to me," said his brother, who began to tell his story. "If you want to go there, you'll still find a huge pile of gold, but you must pay attention to one thing. When the robbers enter, you must count them, and when they come out, you must count them again so that you know whether any one of them has remained inside."

The brother set out and soon came to the tall mountain where the robbers lived. He hid behind a bush, and shortly thereafter the robbers came. He counted them, and there were eleven. When they had returned home some time before, they had found that some of their money was missing, and the captain of the robbers had said, "From now on, one of us will remain at home because the rascal who stole from us will probably come a second time."

Neither of the two brothers could have known this, and when the poor brother who hid himself behind the bush saw the robbers come out again, he counted them once more, and there were eleven again. "Well," he thought, "eleven went inside, and eleven have come back out. So now I can safely go inside."

He took a place in front of the rock and said, "Open up, door!" The door opened up, and he went inside, where he found the gold in great piles. No one could be seen, so he filled his pockets with gold. However, when he wanted to go back outside, the twelfth robber suddenly sprang out at him and killed him.

After the robbers came back home and saw the murdered man, they said, "Well, you scoundrel, now you've received your payment."

Meanwhile, the other brother continued to wait for his poor brother, and when his brother did not come, he thought, "I'm sure the robbers caught him and killed him." So he asked the wife of his brother and their children to come and live with him and looked after them. He remained happy and content, and the old woman sits there without a toothpick or a tooth to pick.

67

THREE GOOD PIECES OF ADVICE

Once upon a time there was a man who had a wife, whom he loved with all his heart. When his wife became pregnant, she said to him one day, " My dear husband, I have such a great craving for a piece of liver. If only I could have some liver!"

"If that's all you want, just a piece of liver," her husband answered, "I'll easily get it for you."

So the man went to a relative who was a butcher and said, "Cousin, be so kind and give me one and a half pounds of liver. My wife has a great craving for some liver."

"I'll be with you right away, cousin. Wait a moment until I've finished serving these other customers."

The man waited and waited. The customers went away, and others came, and his cousin still did not give him a piece of liver.

"Cousin, please wait on me. My wife is sitting at home and cannot sit still because she's got such a great craving for a piece of liver."

"Wait a moment, cousin, until I've finished serving these customers," the butcher answered and continued to serve the other customers one after the other, keeping his own cousin waiting. Finally his cousin lost his patience.

"Is my money not as good as these other people?" he thought, and all at once he grabbed a club and split the butcher's head in two so that he fell dead to the ground. When he saw the butcher lying dead on the ground, he became scared and ran home to his wife.

"Dear wife," he said, "I must get away from here, far away from here. I've met with some bad luck.* My cousin kept serving all the other customers and put me off. But I was thinking of you and felt sorry that you had to wait so long. Finally I lost my patience and hit him with a club and split his head in two. That's why I've got to go off into the wide world and leave you alone."

His wife moaned and wept, but what use was it? In her condition she had to remain alone, and her husband set off into the wide world. As he roamed about, he came to Rome and thought, "Better here than anywhere else. I'll stay here and enter the pope's employ."

So he took a job with the pope and served him faithfully for forty years, and the pope became very fond of him. When the forty years were over, he thought one day, "I've been away from home so long and don't know whether my wife is still living, or whether I have a son or a daughter. I want to return to my hometown. I'm sure that nobody will remember the dead butcher anymore."

So he went to the pope and said, "Your excellency, I have served you faithfully for forty years. Please let me now go back home."

"Good," said the pope, "and since you have served me so faithfully, take this money."

Upon saying these words, he gave him three hundred ounces of gold. The man thanked the pope, put the money in his pocket, and kissed the pope's hand. When he was about to leave the pope called him back and said, "I have a piece of good advice for you. Will you give me a hundred ounces for it?"

"Excellency, take what you would like," the man answered and gave him back a hundred ounces.

"Just remember," the pope said, that this piece of advice has cost one hundred ounces, so pay attention. When something unusual happens to you on your way home, do not say anything about it."

The man promised to do what the pope advised, kissed his hand, and wanted to go, but the pope called him back a second time and said, "If you give me another hundred ounces, I'll give you another piece of good advice."

"Excellency, do whatever you please," the man answered, and put another hundred ounces on the table. Then the pope said, "Just remember that this piece of advice has cost one hundred ounces, so pay

---

* In Sicilian, ci succidìu una disgrazia; in German, mir ist ein Unglück begegnet.

attention to my words. You are to take the exact same path home that you took forty years ago when you first came here."

The man kissed the pope's hand and wanted to leave, but the pope called him a third time and said, "Give me another hundred ounces, and I'll give you a piece of good advice."

"Excellency, take what you want," the man answered and gave the last hundred ounces back to the pope. Then the pope said, "Listen carefully to my words, and don't forget that this advice has cost you one hundred ounces. Let the anger that grips you in the evening rest until the next morning. If you are gripped by anger again in the morning, let it rest until the evening. Remember my words. They will serve you well. And now that you have served me for forty years, you can stay with me for one more day and bake me a whole oven full of bread."

So the man went into the kitchen and kneaded a beautiful white bread, and the pope had the three hundred ounces of gold secretly stuck into the largest loaf and baked with the rest of the bread. When the man came the next day to say farewell, the pope gave him the largest loaf of bread and said, "Take this beautiful white bread with you and eat it only when you are in good spirits."

Then he blessed him and let him depart. The man wandered straight ahead to his hometown. One day, as he was moving along, he became hungry, and since there was an inn along the way, he entered and ordered something to eat. The innkeeper brought him some fish with bread and wine and placed everything in front of him. He also set a dead skull next to him. The man wanted to ask what it meant, but then he remembered what the pope had said: "When you encounter something extraordinary, you should not say anything," and so he kept quiet. After he had eaten the innkeeper said to him, "You're the first person who did not ask me why I set the skull next to him, and this has saved your life. Let me show you what's happened to all those who could not control their curiosity."

Upon saying these words he led him into a drab cellar, where there were many corpses and bones. They were the corpses of those people who had asked the innkeeper why he had placed a skull next to the food. So the man thanked the pope in his heart for the good advice and thought, "To be sure it cost me a hundred gold ounces, but the advice has saved my life."

Now he continued his journey and wandered for many days again. One day he met a lot of workers, who were going into the countryside to pull out the flax, and they said to him, "Do you want to go to Catania? Why are you going that way? Come with us. We're taking a much shorter way."

The man thought about the second piece of advice he received from the pope that he was to take the very same path back that he had taken to reach Rome, and so he answered, "You go your way, and I'll go mine."

He was about a mile away when he heard loud screams. The poor workers were being attacked and murdered by robbers. So he thought: "The pope's advice cost me one hundred ounces of gold, but it saved my life. Blessed is he who gave me this advice!"

Finally, after some days had passed, he arrived late in Catania and went straight to the house where his wife had lived forty years ago. Now, she had given birth to a son at that time, and he had become a priest and lived with his mother. When the man knocked on the door, the son ran down the stairs, opened the door, and asked him what he wanted. When the man saw the priest, he was overcome by great anger and thought, "Who's this cleric living with my wife?"

It would not have taken much for him to murder the priest, but the man thought about the good advice that the pope had given him: "Let the anger that grips you in the evening rest until the next morning." And he answered, "I'm just a poor pilgrim. Could you please give me shelter for the night?"

So his son led him inside, and his wife, whom he had not seen for such a long time, was sitting in the living room.

"Come in, poor man," she said. "Rest a while until I've finished making dinner."

Then she set the table for the evening meal and invited him to eat with them. During the meal the pilgrim said, "Tell us a story, good woman. I'm sure you know many."

"Oh," she answered, "What other story should I tell you but my own sad tale about how I lost my husband shortly after my marriage."

"How did that happen?"

"I was pregnant, and one day I said to my husband that I had a craving for a piece of liver. So he went to the butcher shop to buy it, but because the butcher kept him waiting so long, he picked up a club in anger and split the butcher's head in two. Therefore he had to flee, and I haven't heard from him in forty years. When the time came for me to have my baby, I gave birth to this son, who has become a priest."

When the man heard that the priest was his own son, he thanked the pope in his heart for his good piece of advice. "I might have done something unfortunate in my anger," he thought to himself, and then he spoke to the woman, "It's remarkable! My story is similar to yours, good woman. I had been married only a short time, and my wife was pregnant. One day she said to me, 'Oh, dear husband, I've got a craving for a piece of liver. If only I could have a piece of liver!' So I went to the butcher to buy it, but the butcher served all the customers except for me so that I finally lost my patience and split his head in two. Then I had to flee and leave my poor wife behind. Since then I have heard nothing about her, and now, after forty years, I've returned to see whether she's still living."

As he told his story, his wife kept looking at him, and she could not take her eyes off him. When the story ended, she recognized him and embraced him with many tears and great joy. Then he embraced his son and was glad that he had become such a tall handsome man.

After they had calmed down somewhat and wanted to eat some more, the man took the bread out of his backpack and said, "This bread is all that I've brought for you, and the pope told me that I should eat it when I was in good spirits. When could I ever be happier than I am now that I've found you again? So let's eat this bread."

Upon saying these words, he sliced the bread, and just imagine— three hundred ounces of gold fell out. He was now a rich man and lived many more years with his wife and son in happiness and without any worries.

68

TOBIÀ AND TOBIÒLA

Once upon a time there was a man named Tobià, and his wife was called Sara and his son Tobiòla. Tobià was a pious, God fearing man, and he used all his money and possessions to do good for the poor. All the poor people who died were brought to his house, and then he carried them outside the city on his back and buried them at his own cost. His wife often reproached him for this: "Oh, Tobià, what will happen to us when you give all your money and possessions to the poor? You'll see, there'll come a time when we ourselves will have to go and beg.

"Let it be, dear Sara," he answered. "Whoever does good, will have good done to them."*

Now one day Tobià happened to hear that a poor man had died in the city.

"Bring him here to me," he said. "I'll bury him this evening."

So the people brought the dead man and laid him under the bed. In the evening Tobià took the dead man on his shoulders and carried him outside the city. After he had buried him, he became so tired that he laid down to sleep beneath a tree. Now a swallow happened to have her nest in this tree. While Tobià slept under the tree, some of the refuse from the swallow fell down into his eyes so that he became blind. When

---

* Cu beni fa, beni trova.

he awoke, he could not see anything, and it was only with great effort that he made his way back home. When his wife saw him coming in this condition, she raised her hands to her head and moaned and groaned, "Oh, Tobià, what's happened to you?"

"There's nothing I can do about it," Tobià said. "I laid down to sleep beneath a tree to rest for a while, but there was a swallow that had built her nest there, and some of her refuse fell into my eyes, and I became blind."

"Oh, how unlucky we are! What's going to happen to us now that you can't work, and now that you've given all our money and possessions to the poor?"

"Calm down," Tobià said. "Whoever does good will have good done to him, and God does not abandon the just."

Tobià was now faced with a difficult time because he could no longer work, and soon he ran out of money. So, one day he said to his wife, "Dear wife, we have no more money. Not far from here there's a city where an acquaintance of mine is living, and I loaned him some money some time ago. Let's send our son Tobiòla to him and ask him to repay the loan."

So Tobià called his son Tobiòla and said to him, "My son, you must go to the city where my acquaintance lives and fetch the money that I loaned to him. However, I don't want you to travel there alone. Go to the marketplace and see if you can find a traveling companion."

So Tobiòla went to the marketplace and saw a handsome, slender young man, who asked him, "Tobiòla, are you taking a trip?"

"Yes, to the city over the mountain."

"I've got to go there, too. We can travel together."

Tobiòla was very pleased when he heard this, and he took the young man to his parents and said, "Dear father and mother, I've found a traveling companion. Give me your holy blessing, and let me depart."

So Tobià and his wife blessed their dear son and embraced and kissed him. Soon after Tobiòla set out with the young man, but the city to which they were traveling would take many days to reach.

One day, as they were on their way, they came to a river in which a fish was swimming, and it swam close to the bank.

"Tobiòla," the young man said, "grab the fish and cut out its gallbladder and liver. They'll be useful to you."

Tobiòla did what the young man told him to do. He grabbed the fish, cut out its gallbladder and liver, and put them in a tin can. Soon they reached their destination, where Tobiòla was to fetch the money.

"Where are you going to spend the night?" the young man asked him.

"My father has an acquaintance here, and he's a relative. So I'm going to stay with him," Tobiòla said.

Now this relative had a daughter who was very beautiful, and had already had seven husbands, but they all died during the wedding night. When Tobiòla and the young man went to the relative, Tobiòla said, "Uncle, I'm the son of your cousin Tobià and his wife Sara."

"Oh nephew, what a pleasure!" the man exclaimed. "Come into my house and stay with me, you and your companion."

Tobiòla and the young man entered, and the beautiful uncle's daughter brought them something to eat and drink.

"Do you know what I've thought, Tobiòla?" the young man asked. "I want you to marry the beautiful maiden."

"Oh, my brother,"* Tobiòla answered, "that will be the death of me. This maiden has already had seven husbands, and they were all found dead in bed the morning after the wedding."

"Just calm down, Tobiòla. If you do what I tell you to do, nothing will happen to you."

After the young man said this, he went to the uncle and said, "Good friend, my companion Tobiòla wants to marry your beautiful daughter. Please allow him to have her, and let us return to our home."

The father refused and said, "Don't you know that my daughter is burdened by this terrible fate? She has already had seven husbands, and they all died during the wedding night."

"Who knows," the young man answered, "perhaps Tobiòla won't die. Give him your daughter."

The father finally agreed, and the wedding was celebrated. After the wedding, Tobiòla's companion took him aside and said, "Listen to my words and follow them exactly as I tell you. Tonight, when you are led into the room with your young wife, lock all the doors and windows, and place the gallbladder of the fish on the coal stove so that it burns and you and your wife inhale it. Then you and your wife are to throw yourselves down on your knees, and do atonement for three hours because your wife is plagued by a devil named Romeò. This devil has possessed her because her other seven husbands never atoned for their sins."

Tobiòla remembered everything the young man told him, and when he was led into the room with his wife, he closed all the doors and windows so that the smoke could not get out. Then he took the gallbladder out of the tin can and burned it on the coal stove, and the smoke filled

---

* Fatri meu.

the entire room. Tobiòla and his wife threw themselves down on the ground and did atonement for three hours, and the beautiful maiden wept bitterly. Indeed, her heart was full of anxiety. After three hours they went back to bed and slept peacefully until morning.

When daybreak came, the uncle and his wife got up and were filled with worry.

"Go into the room," the man said to his wife, "and see whether the unfortunate Tobiòla is still alive."

When she entered the room, she saw that the two of them were still sleeping peacefully and soundly. All at once there was great joy in the house, and everyone praised God and thanked him for his mercy. Tobiòla remained a few more days in this city, and after he received his father's money, he said to his uncle, "Dear father-in-law, I must return home to my parents. Give us your blessing and let us depart."

So the uncle loaded the dowry of his daughter on a few mules, blessed his daughter and son-in-law, and let them depart.

At home, Tobiòla's mother Sara still wept because her son had been away for such a long time and she had heard nothing from him. Every evening she had climbed a high mountain to see if he might soon be returning home. When she returned to the top of the mountain on this particular evening and stood there with tears in her eyes looking for Tobiòla, she suddenly saw two men and a woman coming with many packed mules, and when she took a second clearer look, she saw that one of the men was her son Tobiòla.

"God be praised!" she exclaimed full of joy. "My son is coming, and what a beautiful maiden he has with him! That's a certain sign that things went well."

When Tobiòla recognized his mother, he ran toward her and kissed her hand, and the beautiful maiden also kissed her hand, and so they continued on their way home in good spirits.

Now just imagine the joy of the old, blind Tobià when he heard that his son had returned! Meanwhile, the young man said to Tobiòla, "Now take the liver of the fish and rub your father's eyes with it. Then his sight will be restored."

So Tobiòla took the liver of the fish out of the can and rubbed his father's eyes with it, and as soon as he did this, his father could see again. While they were rejoicing about this miracle, the young man transformed himself into a handsome angel and said, "I am the Angel Gabriel and was sent by God to help you because God saw how pious and God fearing you are. Lead a holy life, and you will be happy, and when you die, God will receive you in his paradise."

69

JOSEPH THE JUST

Once upon a time there was a great king who had three sons, and the youngest was called Joseph. The king was more fond of this son than the others, and they became filled with envy. Now the king had large estates in Chiana and had to send this sons there frequently to inspect how the wheat was doing as well as the oxen and the horses. However, he sent only his two elder sons. The youngest he kept with him.

Now one day his elder sons said to him, "Father, we're the ones who always have to go to Chiana while Joseph stays peacefully at home. Why don't you let him accompany us once? Otherwise, if you don't, it's a sign that you love him more than you love us."

"My sons," the king answered, I love you all the same because you are all my children, but your brother is still young, and I fear that the wild animals might eat him."

"And you're not afraid that the same thing might happen to us? Now we clearly see that you love our brother more than you love us!"

What could the king do? In order to satisfy his elder sons, he called little Joseph to him and said, "Your brothers must travel to Chiana again, and you, my son, must accompany them."

So the three brothers set out together for Chiana. However, the hearts of the two elder brothers were filled with envy and anger, and the eldest said to the second one, "I can't stand the sight of our brother anymore. Let's throw him down into the empty well over there, and he'll die of hunger."

So, they tied poor Joseph on a long rope and let him down into the well and waited on top and waited for him to die. While they were waiting there, a powerful king came riding by, much more powerful than their father, and he asked them, "What are you doing at this well?"

"We have to guard the boy down there," they answered. "He's supposed to die."

When the king looked down into the well and saw the marvelously handsome boy, he felt pity for him and said, "Pull him up. I'll buy him from you."

So the princes pulled their brother up, and the king gave them some money and took poor Joseph with him. Meanwhile, the brothers took his shirt away from him, slaughtered a goat, and dipped the shirt into the blood. When they returned home, the king asked them right away, "Where's your brother Joseph?"

"Oh, father!" they cried out. "Wild animals ate him. Look, here is his bloody shirt."

Just imagine the grief of the poor father! He beat his chest, pulled out his hair, and moaned. "Oh, my son, my dear son, the wild animals have eaten you!"

Now let's leave the father and see what happened to his son.

The powerful king took Joseph with him to his land and had him instructed in everything. Joseph continued to grow and became the wisest and most just man in the country, and the king placed him in charge of all his estates and named him Joseph the Just.*

Many years passed, and one day Joseph went to the king and said, "Your majesty, listen to my words, and follow my advice. Seven years will come, and they will be so fruitful that your people will not know what to do with all the wheat and corn. During these seven years you are to order great warehouses to be built and filled with the wheat and corn because seven bad years will come after, and everything will be ruined. If you don't collect and save wheat and corn before this, you and your people will starve to death."

And everything happened just as Joseph had prophesied.

Seven years came in which everything flourished, and so much wheat and corn grew that they barely had room to collected everything. The king ordered large warehouses to be built and filled them with the wheat and corn, as Joseph had recommended. After the seven fruitful years came seven years that were so bad that nothing ripened. No wheat,

---

* Giuseppi Giustu.

no barley, no fruit. Nothing. There was a great rise in the price of food in all the countries, and the king placed his loyal Joseph in charge of the food stocks and let it be known that there was still a great deal of wheat and corn in his country. Many people came from other countries to buy wheat and corn.

At this time the other king, Joseph's father, spoke to his sons, "Dear sons, there is no more wheat and corn in our country. Therefore, I want you to go to the realm where the king has collected and saved wheat and corn and buy some for our country."

The two sons set out for the other realm. When they were led before Joseph the Just, they did not recognize him, but he recognized them.

"What do you want?"

"Your highness, we've come to buy wheat and corn."

So Joseph had their sacks filled with the most beautiful wheat and corn. Then he invited them to dine with him and gave them something to eat and drink. Indeed, he was extremely friendly to them. After they had eaten, the brothers said, "Now we must return to our father in our country."

When they were not looking, Joseph secretly stuck a gold cup in one of the sacks of wheat and let his brothers depart. When they were scarcely a mile away, he pursued them with his servants, and when he had overtaken them, he said, "What have you done? Is this the way you repay my hospitality? I received you as though you were my best friends, and then you stole my gold cup!"

The brothers were extremely shocked and said, "Oh, my lord, we didn't steal anything from you. We are honest people. If you want, you can search our sacks."

"You can be sure I'll do that!" Joseph exclaimed, and he examined the sacks himself and found the gold cup in the very first sack.

You can imagine how shocked the princes were, but Joseph cried out, "You see yourself how you've paid me back! Therefore, one of you shall sit in prison, and the other will return home and fetch your father here so that I can speak to him."

So one of the princes was taken to the prison, and the other returned to his home country. When the king saw him return alone, he asked him immediately, "Where is your brother?"

The son told him everything that had happened, and the king began to weep and moan very loudly.

"Am I to lose all my children? One of them was torn apart by wild animals. The other's sitting in prison. Oh, how unlucky I am!"

Soon he set out and traveled to the country where Joseph was living. When he was led before Joseph, he wanted to fall at his feet, but Joseph lifted him, and his heart was trembling when he saw his old father again. Then the king told him how he had lost his first son, and how he was so unfortunate to see his second son in danger, and he pleaded for his life. However, Joseph could no longer control himself and cried out, "Do you wish to see your youngest son Joseph again?"

"Oh, if only God would permit that!" the old king answered.

"Dear father!" Joseph exclaimed. "I am your youngest son, Joseph! Wild animals did not eat me. My brothers sold me to the king of this land, and I am in his service."

When his brothers heard this, they fell to their knees because they thought that Joseph would take revenge on them, but he lifted them up, embraced them, and forgave them for everything they had done. Then he went to the king of the country and told him how he had found his father again and wanted to return home with him. So he took his leave, and they returned to their home country and lived happy and content, and we were left without a cent.

70

THE TWO BROTHERS

Once upon a time there were two brothers who were both very handsome. However, they were poor and led a wretched existence. Indeed, they barely supported themselves through fishing. Now one day they happened to go out to sea in their boat, and they caught a tiny fish.* So the older brother said, "What a miserable voparedda this is! When I return home, I'll cook it and eat it myself."

"Let me live!" the little fish cried out. "Throw me back into the sea, and I'll bring you good fortune."

"What do you think I am, you dumb fish!" the young man responded. "I caught you, and now I'm going to eat you."

But the younger brother intervened and said, "Oh, why don't you let the little fish live? What use will it be to you if you eat it. It's so small that you'll swallow it in one bite. Do what it wants and throw it back into the water."

"If you let me live," the voparedda said, "you will find two splendid horses on the seashore tomorrow, and they'll be carrying everything you need to become fine knights and to set out into the world."

"All this is so stupid!" the older brother cried. "How do I know that you're telling the truth?"

---

* Voparedda, which is a poor kind of small fish.

"Let the fish live," the younger brother pleaded with him. "Even if it's not telling the truth, we'll most likely catch it again. But if it's really telling the truth, we'd be throwing away our good fortune if we killed it."

So the older brother let himself be persuaded, and he threw the voparedda back into the sea. When they went to the seashore the next morning, two splendid horses, already saddled and bridled, were standing there, and next to them were gorgeous clothes and armor, two swords, and two large purses filled with money.

"Do you see?" the younger brother said. "Weren't we lucky that we didn't kill the little fish? Now we can set out into the wide world and seek our fortune. You go that way, and I'll head off in this direction."

"All right," the older brother responded. "But how are we to fix things so we know whether the other is alive or not?"

"Do you see that date tree over there?" the younger brother said. "If we want news of one another, we'll come here and take a slice of the trunk of the tree with our swords. If milk flows from the tree, it will be a sign that the other is still alive. If blood flows from the tree, then the other is either dead or in danger of dying."

So the two young men put on their armor, fastened their swords, and attached the money purses. Afterward they embraced each other with tenderness, mounted their horses, and rode off into the world, one brother in one direction, the other in another direction.

The older brother rode straight ahead until he came to a foreign realm. When he crossed the boundary, he reached a river, and alongside sat a lovely maiden. She was bound and weeping bitter tears, for there was a wicked dragon with seven heads that lived in this river, and every morning the king sent one of his people to the river for the dragon to eat. If the king did not do this, the dragon would devastate the entire realm. Because the king had already sacrificed nearly all the people, he finally had to send his own daughter to the dragon. When the young man saw the beautiful maiden weeping bitterly, he asked, " Why are you crying, beautiful maiden?"

"Oh," the princess answered. "I've been tied up here so that a wicked dragon with seven heads can come and eat me. You'd better flee, my handsome young man! Otherwise, the dragon will devour you, too."

"I'm not going to flee," the youth responded. "I'm going to rescue you."

"Oh, how's that possible? This monster is terrible! There's nothing you can do against it."

"Let me worry about that, beautiful maiden," the young man declared. "Just tell me from what direction the dragon will be coming."

"All right, if you insist on freeing me, then at least listen to my advice. Stand back a bit when the dragon rises from the water, and I'll say, 'Oh, dragon, today you can eat two humans. Take that young man over there first because I'm tied up and can't get away from you.' Perhaps then you'll be able to defeat the dragon."

The young man took some steps backwards. Soon the water began to roar, and a terrible dragon rose out of the river and wanted to hurl itself at the princess to eat her. But she cried out, "Oh, dragon, today you're getting two humans to eat. Take the young man over there first because I'm tied up and can't get away from you."

So the dragon charged at the young man and tried to swallow him, but he took out his sword and fought until he finally defeated the dragon with the seven heads. After he made sure the dragon was dead, he untied the princess, and she embraced him with great joy and said, "You've rescued me from the dragon, and now you'll become my husband. My father had announced that whoever killed the dragon could have me as his wife."

However, the young man answered, "I can't become your husband now because I must continue my journey. Wait seven years and seven months for me. If I don't return by then, you can marry someone else. Just so you will recognize me again, I'll take the seven tongues of the dragon with me."

So he cut out the seven tongues of the dragon, and the princess gave him an embroidered scarf in which he wrapped the tongues. Then he mounted his horse and rode off.

Soon after he departed, one of her father's slaves arrived. He had been sent by the king to see what had happened to his poor daughter. When the slave arrived, he found the princess alive and well. At her feet lay the slain dragon.

"If you don't swear to your father," he said, "that it was I who killed the dragon, I'll murder you on the spot."

What could the poor maiden do? She promised the slave to do as he demanded, and he took the seven heads and lead the princess to the king. Just imagine how happy the king was when he saw his daughter again, for he believed that she was dead. The entire city rejoiced, and when the slave told everyone that he was the one who had killed the dragon, the king cried out, "Now you may have my daughter as your wife."

However, the princess threw herself at her father's feet and said, "Father, you have given your royal word, and therefore you must keep it, but I beg you to grant me a favor and let me remain single for another seven years and seven months. Then I'll marry the slave."

The king granted her request, and she waited seven years and seven months for her bridegroom, and she wept day and night for him.

Meanwhile, the young man had traveled around he entire world, and when the seven years and seven months were up, he returned to the city where his bride was living. To be exact, he arrived in the city a few days before the wedding between the slave and the princess was to take place. The true bridegroom had himself announced to the king and said, "Your majesty, it is me who deserves your daughter, for I was the one who killed the dragon. Just look at the seven tongues of the dragon and your daughter's embroidered scarf."

"Yes, dear father," the princess spoke, "this young man is telling the truth and is my bridegroom, for the slave made up his story. Still, I think you should pardon him."

"I find it impossible to pardon such a traitor!" the king cried out. "Off with his head! And I mean immediately!"

So the deceitful slave was beheaded, and the king arranged a glorious wedding celebration. The princess married the handsome young man, and they lived happy and content with one another.

Now one evening it so happened that the young man was looking out the window and saw a large bright light on top of a mountain.

"What's that bright light doing over there?" he asked his wife.

"Oh," she answered, "don't look at the light. An evil sorceress lives up there, and no one has been able to defeat her."

He soon began feeling the urge to set out and defeat the wicked witch, and the next morning he mounted his horse. No matter how much the princess cried and complained, he rode off toward the mountain where he had seen the bright light. He had to ride for a long time, and it became dark before he arrived so that he could no longer see his way. Nevertheless, the light was so bright that he rode straight toward it. Finally he came to a beautiful castle, and the bright light was beaming from the windows. He entered and climbed the stairs. All at once he saw an ugly old woman, who was sitting in a room.

"With just one hair from my head I can change you into stone," she-said.

"I don't believe you," the young man cried. "Be quiet, you old woman! Do you think your hair can really harm me?"

In response the witch touched him with one of her hairs, and he was immediately turned into stone and could no longer move.

About this same time his brother happened to think about him and said, "I'm going to return to the date tree to see whether my brother is still alive."

So he went to the date tree and stuck his sword into it, and suddenly he saw blood gush out of the trunk.

"Oh, I feel so terrible! My brother is either dead, or his life is in danger. I must go and search for him throughout the world."

So he mounted his horse and said, "Get going, horse. Run like the wind!"

And he searched the entire world until one day he came to the city where his brother had married. The poor princess was still waiting for her husband and wept bitter tears because he was gone. On this particular day she was standing on her balcony, looking for her husband. All at once she saw his younger brother riding through the city, and since this young man looked just like the older brother and wore the same armor, she thought he was her husband and ran toward him full of joy and cried out, " Oh, you've finally returned! My dear husband! How long I've waited for you!"

When the young man heard this, he immediately thought, "My brother must have been here, and this beautiful maiden is my sister-in-law."

However, he did not say anything. Instead, he let her believe that he was her husband. Meanwhile she led him cheerfully to the old king, and he, too, was very happy to see his son-in-law again, and they ate and drank together. In the evening the young man had to go with the princess to her room. When he got undressed, he took his double-bladed sword and placed it between himself and his brother's wife. She was frightened when she saw the double-bladed sword, but did not dare to ask him why he had done this. So it went for many more days.

One evening, while the young man was looking out of the window, he also saw the bright light on top of the mountain,

"Oh!" the princess cried out. "Are you looking at that light again? Do you want to set out again to defeat the wicked witch?"

All at once he realized that his brother must be in the power of a sorceress, and the next morning he mounted his horse and said, "Get going, horse. Fly like the wind!" And he secretly rode off.

Just like his brother, he had to ride the entire day. Toward evening he encountered a little old man, who was in truth St. Joseph.

"Where are you going, handsome young man?" he asked.

"I want to rescue my brother," the youth told him. "A wicked witch has him in her power."

"Do you know what you must do?" the saint asked. "The witch's power lies only in her hair. Therefore, when you speak to her, jump at her and grab her by the hair, and she will lose her power. Make sure, however, that you don't let go of her. Take her to your brother and force her to revive him. She has a salve that can wake up the dead. As soon as she restores your brother to life, cut off her head because she is an extremely evil witch."

The young man thanked Saint Joseph and continued to ride until he came to the castle. Then he entered and climbed the stairs and saw the same ugly old woman, who called out to him, "With one hair of my head I can turn you into stone."

In response he jumped at her, grabbed her by the hair, and said, "You wicked old woman! Tell me right away where my brother is. Otherwise, I'll cut off your head on the spot."

Because the witch no longer had any power over him, she said, "I'll lead you to your brother, but you must let go of me. I can't walk this way."

"Don't think about it, you ugly witch!" the young man cried out and did not let go of her. So she led him into a room in which there were many petrified people.

"There's your brother," she said.

He looked at all the people and said, "My brother is not here. Beware, old witch! Otherwise, I'll cut off your head!"

So she led him through many other rooms, and in each one she said, "Here's your brother."

But he did not let go of her. Rather, he kept saying, "My brother is not here. Lead me to him or I'll cut off your head."

Finally, in the last room, he saw his brother lying on the ground. Then he said. "This is my brother. Now bring the salve that you use to wake the dead."

She went a closet in which there were many salves and potions, while he kept a tight hold on her hair. Whenever she showed him a false salve, he threatened to kill her. Finally she showed him the right one, and he forced her to rub the salve on his brother. When his brother opened his eyes, he sliced off the witch's head. Meanwhile, his brother rubbed his eyes and said, "Oh, how long have I been sleeping? Where am I?"

"The wicked witch kept you prisoner here," his brother said, "but now she's dead, and you're freed of her power. Now let's go and revive all the other knights whom she cast under her magic spell."

So they rubbed the salve on all the other petrified knights, and they became alive again, were happy, and thanked their rescuers. Then they divided the treasures and precious things that the witch had amassed and returned to their homes. The older brother kept the healing salve and set out with his brother to return to his castle.

As they were riding side by side, the younger brother said, "Oh what a fool you were to ride out and defeat a witch while you left such a pretty wife alone at home! When I arrived, she mistook me for you, and I even shared her bed with her."

When his brother heard this, he exploded violently with jealousy, took out his sword, and cut off his brother's head. Then he entered the city where the princess had been weeping for him day and night. When she saw him coming, she ran toward him full of joy, embraced him, and said, "Oh, how long I've been waiting for you! Now I won't let you set out on another adventure again!"

She led him to the old king, and the entire realm rejoiced because of his safe return. In the evening, as he prepared to go to bed, his wife said to him, "Why did you lay a double-edged sword between us every evening after your previous return?"

All at once he realized how faithful his brother had been, and when he thought how he had killed him, he began to groan very loudly and wanted to ram his head against the wall. Then, suddenly, he remembered the salve that he had brought with him, and he stood up and rushed to the place where he had left his brother. Once there, he rubbed the salve on his neck, set his head on his shoulders, and brought him back to life. The two brothers embraced each other full of joy and returned to the city and held a great banquet. And so they remained rich and consoled, while we just sit and continue to get old.

71

THE SEVEN BROTHERS WITH
MAGIC TALENTS

Once upon a time there was a king who had an only daughter, and he loved her with all his heart. One day he summoned an astrologer, who was to predict the princess's fortune.

"When the princess turns fifteen," the astrologer said, "a giant will come and steal her away."

So the king had the princess carefully guarded so that nobody could make off with her. When the princess became fifteen, however, she was standing at her window, and a giant came by and pulled her to him with his breath. He took her in his arms and fled so fast that no one could catch up with him. The king became very despondent and issued a proclamation throughout the entire realm that whoever brought his daughter back to him could have her for his wife and become king after him.

A poor old woman happened to hear this. She was the mother of seven sons, all endowed with magic talents.* So she called the eldest and said, "If you tell me what your talent is, I'll have a new suit made for you."

"I can take ten men in my arms," he replied, "and can run as fast as the wind."

---

* Actually, they were enchanted, *erano infatati*.

444

Then the mother called the second son and asked him what his talent was.

"When I put my ear to the ground," he answered, "I can hear everything that's happening in the world."

The woman continued to ask all her sons, and each one had a special talent. The third son could break through seven iron doors with one blow of his fist. The fourth could steal something from the arms of people without them noticing a thing. The fifth could build an iron tower with one blow of his fist. The sixth had a rifle, and he could hit anything he aimed at with this weapon. Finally, the youngest could wake the dead when he played his guitar. With these seven sons the mother went before the king and said, "Your royal majesty, my sons want to bring back your daughter."

The king was very happy about this and had a new suit made for each one of them, and so they wandered off together. When they were outside the city in a forest, the second brother put his ear to the ground and said, "I hear the princess weeping. She's sitting in a tower with seven iron gates, and the giant is holding her in his arms."

Then the oldest grabbed all seven of his brothers together and ran with them up to the tower in which the princess was being held.

"Now it's your turn," they said to the third brother, who hit the seven iron gates with such a powerful blow of his fist that they all collapsed. The fourth brother crept into the tower, and while the giant slept, he stole the princess from his arms and brought her out to his brothers. Once again the oldest grabbed all his brothers and the princess together and ran from there as fast as the wind.

When the giant awoke and did not find the princess in his arms anymore, he set out after the brothers, and since he could run faster than the eldest brother, he soon caught up with them. So the brothers called out to the fifth brother: "Now it's your turn."

And when he hit the ground with his fist, a tower appeared in which all eight of them could hide. The tower was so strong that the giant could not destroy it. Therefore he set up camp before the tower and continued to yell: "If you give the princess back to me, I'll let you all go free."

The brothers refused, and finally he said, "Let me just see her pinky. Then I'll let you all leave without harming you."

The brothers thought, "That's something we could do," and they made a small hole in the tower and let the princess stick out her pinky. No sooner did the giant see it, than he pulled her to him with his breath, took her in his arms, and started to run away as fast as he could.

"Quick, shoot him dead," the brothers spoke to the sixth one, who took his rifle, aimed, and shot the giant dead. As they ran to the spot, they saw that he had also shot the princess. All at once the youngest brother took his guitar and began to play. Soon the princess opened her eyes and was revived. Now the oldest took them all in his arms and ran back to the king's castle.

There was great joy in the castle, and the king said, "Which one of you is to have the princess for his bride? Let me hear who performed the greatest feat."

"That was me," the eldest cried, "because I was the one who carried my brothers and the princess together in my arms, and I ran as fast as the wind."

"No, it was me," the second said, "because you would not have known where the princess was without me."

"No, I deserve the princess," interrupted the third brother. "I was the one who knocked down the seven iron doors."

"What use would all that have been if I hadn't stolen the princess from the giant's arms?" asked the fourth brother.

"And if I hadn't built an iron tower," the fifth brother declared, "the giant would have killed us all."

But the sixth brother explained, "No, I deserve the princess because I shot the giant dead."

"And the princess as well," cried the youngest. "And if I had not recalled her from the dead with my guitar, she would still be dead."

"Yes," announced the king. "You're the one who performed the greatest feat, and you shall marry my daughter."

So a splendid wedding was celebrated, and the youngest son married the princess. However, the king was very generous with gifts to the other brothers, and he invited them, along with their mother, to stay in the castle. Indeed, they lived there happy and content, and we don't have one single cent.

72

THE PIOUS YOUNG MAN
WHO WENT TO ROME

Once upon a time there was a poor washerwoman who had an only son, and to be sure, he was very dumb, but he was also good and pious deep down in his heart. The poor woman used to send him into the woods with her mule, and he would search for firewood to sell in the city. This was their miserable existence.

Now one day her son happened to pass by a small church with his mule loaded with firewood. A sermon was being given just at that time, and he tied the mule outside and went into the little church and heard the priest say, "My friends, listen to what the Lord says: Whoever gives to the poor in my name will be repaid a hundredfold." When the young man heard this, he went outside, sold the wood and the mule, and gave the money to the poor.

"Now the Lord must repay me a hundredfold," he thought, and he returned the church and sat down in a corner where nobody noticed him. When all the masses had been held, the sacristan closed the church and did not realize that the young man had remained behind. The young man waited until everything was quiet and climbed up to the altar where there was a large crucifix, and he began speaking to it with the following words. "Hey, listen to me, you!" (Notice how simple-minded he was, for he took the liberty to address Jesus in a very familiar way.) "Listen you," he said, "I carried out your commandment, and I gave everything that I sold to the poor. Now you must repay me a hundredfold. Otherwise, I won't have anything at all to take to my mother."

447

He spoke to the crucifix this way for a long time, and finally the Lord answered him, "I myself am poor and cannot give you any money. But go to Rome—my brother lives there in the greatest church. He is much richer than I am. Perhaps he can give you the money."

"That's true," said the young man. "You must be very poor because you're completely naked."

So he went back to his corner and waited until the sacristan opened the church the next morning so he could leave. Then he set out for Rome without telling his mother anything. He wandered the entire day until it became dark and he came to a monastery.

"Perhaps I can stay here for the night," he thought, knocked on the door, and asked for shelter. He was granted permission to enter, and he and the prior conversed for a while.

"Where are you going, my son?" he asked.

"I must go to Rome and speak with the Lord about a sum of money that he owes me."

At first the prior thought that the peasant boy wanted to make a fool of him, but as soon as he realized how simple-minded he was, he said to him, "You could do me a favor. My monks always have an argument after supper and bash each other's heads until they are bloody. Otherwise, they are very pious and behave themselves. It's as though some evil spirit took possession of them after supper. When you speak with the Lord, ask him where all this comes from, and if you bring me the right answer on your return, I'll give you a gift of one hundred ounces of gold."

The young man promised to do this. Then he rested the entire night in the monastery, and the next morning he set out again on his way to Rome. He wandered the entire day until evening when he came to a small city. All at once he saw a pretty cottage, knocked at the door, and asked for shelter, and the owner granted it to him. This man was a merchant and had three beautiful daughters. When the merchant began talking to the young man, he asked him where he was going.

"I have to go to Rome and speak with the Lord because of a sum of money that he must give me."

The merchant thought he wanted to make a fool out of him, but when he realized how naive the peasant boy was, he said to him: "Do me a favor. I have three beautiful daughters and have not been able to marry off one of them, even though I'm rich. When you speak to the Lord, ask him why this is so, and if you bring me the answer, I'll give you one hundred ounces of gold."

The young man promised to do this, and the next morning he continued his journey. When it turned evening, he came to a farmhouse, knocked on the door, and asked for lodging for the night. The farmer received him in a friendly way, invited him to dinner, and asked him, "Where are you going?"

Once again the young man explained that he was going to Rome to speak to the Lord about a certain sum of money.

"You could do me a great service," the farmer said. "I have a lot of beautiful land, and previously I grew a great deal of fruit on it. But for some years now, the trees have all become barren, and I can no longer grow dates or cherries. When you speak with the Lord, ask him why this is happening. If you bring me the right answer, I'll give you a hundred ounces of gold."

The young man promised to do this, and the next morning he continued his journey. Finally he came to Rome and immediately found the greatest and most beautiful church in which a mass was being held. As soon as he saw the many silk and gold garments of the priests and the gold monstrances covered with precious stones, he thought, "The Lord was right. His brother is much richer. He can certainly give me my money."

So he hid in a corner and waited patiently until the sacristan closed the church door. Then he climbed up to the altar and said, "Listen, you. Your brother sent me to you. He was supposed to give me a large sum of money, but he's too poor, and he told me to tell you that you should give me the money instead of him."

The Lord let him keep making this request for some time, and then he answered him: "Good, my son. Just return home, and along the way you'll receive your money."

"All right," the young man said, "But I still must ask you something. About a half a day's journey from here there's a farmer who owns some land that used to produce a lot fruit. But for some years now the trees have become barren. Why is that happening?"

"Before this," the Lord responded, "the farmer had not built a wall around his property, and when a poor person came by and needed something to eat, he stuck out his hand and took a pear or some other fruit to fill his stomach. But the farmer was greedy and refused to grant the poor people some fruit. That's why he had a wall built around his land, and since then the trees have become barren. If he tears down the wall, the land will once again produce the fruit he wants."

"Tell me something more," the young man continued. "There's a merchant living in a city nearby, and he has three beautiful daughters. Even though he's rich, he's not been able to marry off any of them. Why's that so?"

"The girls are much too interested in their dresses and want to attract men by the clothes they wear. If they were nice and proper and would go to church without makeup, they would soon find husbands."

"Now, I'd like to know one more thing," said the young man. "There's a monastery not too far from here, and the monks are well-behaved and pious the entire day. But when they eat in the evening, they begin to argue and make a racket. Why's that happening?"

"The devil is their cook," the Lord answered. "He's cast a spell over their food so that it causes them strife."

The young man thanked the Lord, and the Lord took something from his side and gave him a stone upon his departure and told him to keep it somewhere safe. The young man hid in the corner again, and when the sacristan came the next morning, the peasant boy went out and began his journey back home.

When he came to the farmer, the man asked him, "Did you speak with the Lord?"

"Yes," he answered, "the trees on your property are barren because you built a wall around your entire land. When the wall is torn down and does not keep the poor from taking fruit from time to time, your land will produce fruit again."

"Wonderful," said the farmer. "I'll try this right away. But you must stay here until the trees bear fruit again, otherwise I won't give you the hundred ounces of gold."

So the young man remained there, and the farmer tore down the wall, and just imagine, in a few days the trees were covered with blossoms! So the farmer gave the young man the hundred ounces of gold, thanked him, and let him go.

Then the young man went to the merchant, who also asked him whether he had spoken with the Lord.

"Yes," he answered. "Your daughters won't get married because they think about make-up and clothes too much. If they were to go to church and be nice and proper, they would soon find husbands for themselves."

"Stay a few days with me so I can see whether your advice is really good," said the merchant. "Then I'll give you the hundred ounces of gold."

So the young man remained there, and the merchant took the make-up and beautiful clothes away from his daughters and sent them to church dressed in a modest and proper way. And just imagine, after a few days, there were so many suitors who wanted to marry the merchant's daughters that the merchant had a large choice to select from! Consequently, he gave the young man the hundred ounces of gold, thanked him for his good advice, and let him depart.

In the evening the young man came to the monastery and was led to the prior, who asked:

"Have you spoken with the Lord?"

"The devil is the cook in your monastery, and he casts a magic spell over the food that causes strife among the monks," the young man answered.

"If that's true," the prior said, "I shall make this sinister spirit disappear right away."

So he took some holy water and dressed himself in holy robes, went into the church, and cast the evil spirit out of the monastery through his sacred acts so that the monks were left in peace from then on. The prior thanked the young man, gave him one hundred ounces of gold, and let him depart.

When he approached the city, the stone, which he had been carrying in a pocket next to his chest, began to illuminate and send such bright wonderful rays that one could see them from miles around. When news reached the priests, they set out ceremoniously and marched toward the wondrous stone. Then the young man told them everything, and because he was found to be worthy of speaking with the Lord, he was also to carry the stone and went among the Baldachin and carried the stone in his hands. When he went into the church and placed the stone on the altar, he fell to the ground and was dead, but his soul flew up to heaven. His mother happened to be in the church and recognized her son, and when she saw him sink to the ground, she rushed to him and took him in her arms. All at once she found the three hundred ounces of gold and took them and led a pious life by doing much good for the poor. And when she died, she was reunited with her son in heaven.

73

⟨⟩⟨⟩⟨⟩

SABEDDA AND HER BROTHER

Once upon a time there was a man whose wife died and left behind two children, a son and a daughter. The daughter was very beautiful, more beautiful than the son, and was taught by a teacher in a school. This teacher had a daughter, who was dark and ugly—uglier than debts. Since the teacher was a shrewd woman, she gave the beautiful girl sweets and said to her, "Tell your father he should marry me, and then I'll give you sweets every day, and you'll lead a good life."

So the child asked her father to marry the friendly teacher, but the father always answered, "Sabedda,* you don't know what you're saying. You'll see. You'll regret this one day."

But Sabedda continued to ask until he lost his patience one day and said, "Good, I'll do what you want, but when things go bad for you, don't come to me and complain."

So the father married the teacher, and at first the stepmother was friendly with Sabedda and her brother. But it did not take long before she became unfriendly, and Sabedda had to do all the hard work: look for wood and carry the water. Moreover, she often received beatings and little to eat. On the other hand, the woman was friendly toward her own daughter and let her do what she wanted. When Sabedda became sad,

---

* Isabella.

452

her father said to her, "You see. Why didn't you listen to me? I told you that you would regret it. Now I can't help you."

One day, after the stepmother had cruelly beaten the poor Sabedda once more, the girl said to her little brother, "Come, let's set out into the wide world and try our luck. I can't hold out any longer the way our stepmother is treating me."

Her brother agreed, and so they stole away and wandered into the-wide world. After they had traveled for a long time, the brother became so thirsty that he was wasting away, and when they came to a brook, he said, "Sabedda, I'm so thirsty. I want to have a drink."

But Sabedda listened to the murmuring water of the little brook, "Whoever drinks my water will be turned into a sheep with gold horns."

However, her brother had already bent over the brook, and no sooner did he take a swig of water than he was transformed into a cute little sheep with pretty gold horns. All at once Sabedda began to weep and continued sadly on her way with the sheep running next to her. On this very same day, the king happened to go on a hunt, and while he was chasing a deer, he encountered the weeping Sabedda, who was so beautiful that he could not take his eyes off her. Then he asked why she was crying, and she answered, "I'm a poor child and have a wicked stepmother at home. She always beats me so much, and that's why I ran away."

"Do you want to come to my castle and become my wife?" the king answered.

"Yes," answered Sabedda, "but my sheep must also come with me."

The king took her up on his horse, and a servant led the little sheep, and so they went to the castle. The king had Sabedda dressed in royal clothes, and a magnificent wedding was celebrated. But Sabedda always looked after her little sheep first, and the animal also had to sleep in her room.

After a year the queen gave birth to a lovely boy who was the great joy of the castle. However, about the same time, the deceitful stepmother heard that Sabedda had not died and had instead become a queen. Therefore, she became completely green with envy and kept thinking of a way to bring about her ruin. So she bought some sweets, put a sleeping potion into a little bottle, adorned herself and her daughter, and went to the castle just when the king had gone out to hunt and Sabedda lay sick in bed.

"Oh, you poor child," the lying stepmother said, "how happy I am to see you so well and alive. Look, I've brought some sweets and this refreshing wine that will do you good. Just try it one time."

Sabedda refused because she feared that her stepmother had something awful up her sleeve, but she did take some of the wine, and no sooner did she swallow some than she fell into a deep sleep. Then her stepmother quickly took off her nightgown and threw her into the cistern, which was in the garden and in which a large fish lived, and this fish swallowed poor Sabedda right away. The stepmother put Sabedda's nightgown on her ugly, one-eyed daughter and put her into the queen's bed. Then the duplicitous stepmother rushed home before the king returned from the hunt.

When the king entered his wife's room and saw the ugly, one-eyed figure lying in the bed, he had a fright and said, "What's happened to you?

"Oh," answered the false queen, "the sheep rammed me with its horns and knocked out one of my eyes."

Well, that terrible animal will no longer live," said the king, who summoned his cook and said to him, "Get your sharpest knives ready because I want you to cut the little sheep's throat tonight."

So the cook grabbed the sheep by the horns, dragged it out of the room, took it into the kitchen, and began to sharpen his knives. Meanwhile, the poor distressed sheep snuck out into the garden where the cistern was, and it began to weep bitter tears and groan:

Sabedda dear, Sabedda mine,
They're sharpening a knife
to cut my throat and take my life.*

When the cook wanted to fetch the sheep to cut its throat, he heard it moaning and groaning and was so horrified by what he heard that he quickly ran to the king and said, "Just think, your majesty, the sheep talks like a reasonable person."

"You're crazy," the king said, but he went with the cook to the cistern where the sheep was still standing and lamenting:

Sabedda dear, Sabedda mine,
They're sharpening a knife
to cut my throat and take my life.

---

* Sabedda, mia Sabedda,
  Pri mia mmolanu li cutedda,
  Pri tagghiari sta carni bedda.

When the king heard this, he sprung forth and cried, "If you can talk, then tell me why you're standing next to the cistern and calling my Sabedda. Otherwise, I'll cut off your head."

So the sheep told him how the stepmother had come and thrown poor Sabedda into the cistern, and that the woman who was lying in the queen's bed was really not the young queen but the stepmother's ugly daughter."

Immediately the king ordered his servants to catch the large fish. Once they had it, they opened it and poured warm oil down the fish's throat until it spit out Sabedda, who was well and alive and had become even more beautiful than she was before. At the same time, the magic that had caused her brother to turn into a sheep vanished, and he became a handsome young man who embraced his sister Sabedda full of joy.

Now the king had his dear wife bathed in precious sweet-smelling water and dressed in her royal garments. He had the ugly daughter cut into pieces, salted in a barrel, and had her head placed at the bottom. Then he sent the barrel to the stepmother and informed her that her daughter was sending her this barrel full of tuna fish. The wicked woman took off the top of the barrel and began to eat the fish. She had a cat that kept springing onto her lap and saying, "Give me something to eat too, and then later I'll also help you weep."

However, she kicked the cat off her and cried, "What? You think I should give you some of this beautiful tuna fish, which my daughter, the queen, has sent to me?"

Now, when she came to the bottom of the barrel and caught sight of the head, she realized that she had eaten her own daughter and began to scream loudly and hit her head against the wall until she sank dead to the ground. But the cat sang: "You didn't want to give me anything to eat, and now I won't help you weep," and it danced around the entire house.

The king and the young queen lived happy and content, and we still don't have a cent.

74

THE CLEVER SHOEMAKER

Once upon a time there was a shoemaker who was very poor and could not find work, and he and his wife almost died from hunger. One day he said to his wife, "My dear, I can't find any work here, so I'm going to set out for the plain of Mascalucia. Perhaps I'll have some luck there."

So he set out and wandered until he came to Mascalucia. No sooner did he begin to yell, "Who wants a shoemaker," than a window opened, and a woman asked him to sew a pair of shoes for her. When he was done, she asked, "How much do I owe you?"

"One tari."

"Here are ten grani, and may the Lord bless you."

The shoemaker began to cry out again, and soon another window opened, and he found some new work.

"How much do we owe you?"

"Three carlini."

"Here are twenty-five grani, and may the Lord bless you."

"Well," thought Master Giuseppe, "things are all right here. I don't think I'll return to my wife just yet. First I'll earn a nice little sum of money, and then I'll ride home on a donkey."

So he remained there many days, found as much work as he needed, and finally earned four gold ounces. Then he went to the marketplace, bought a good donkey for two ounces, and set out on his way back to Catania. As he was going through the forest, he saw four robbers coming at him from a distance. "Oh, now I'm lost," he thought. "They'll certainly take everything from me that I worked so hard to earn." However, he was sly and did not lose his courage. He took the five thalers that were left and stuck them under the donkey's tail. Soon the robbers came upon him and demanded his money.

"Oh, dear friends," he cried, "I'm a poor shoemaker and don't have any money. The only thing I own is this donkey."

But just at that moment the donkey lifted its tail, and the five thalers fell to the ground.

"Well, what is that then?" the robbers asked.

"Yes, my friends," the shoemaker answered, "this donkey is a gold donkey and brings me a good deal of money."

"Sell it to us," the robbers said. "We'll give you as much as you want."

At first the shoemaker refused, and then he pretended to be persuaded by them and sold them the donkey for fifty gold ounces.

"Listen to what I say," he told them. "Each one of you must ride him for one day and one night, one after the other. Otherwise you'll fight with each other over the gold that he produces."

The robbers were delighted and drove their donkey into the forest. Meanwhile Master Giuseppe laughed as he traveled home and rejoiced about the bargain that he had made. He bought a good midday meal, and he and his wife dined with pleasure. Finally, the very next day he bought a pretty vineyard.

Meanwhile the robbers had returned to their hometown with the donkey, and the captain of the robbers said, "I deserve the right to keep the donkey for the first night."

His companions agreed, and so the captain took the donkey to his house, called his wife, and ordered her to spread out a bed sheet in the stable so that the donkey could spend the night on it. She was puzzled by her husband's foolish idea, but he said, "What's it to you? Do what I say, and tomorrow morning we'll find treasures here."

Early the next morning the robber captain rushed to the stable, but instead of treasures he found something else, and realized that Master Giuseppe had tricked them.

"All right," he thought, "Master Giuseppe fooled me, but the others should experience just what I experienced."

When his first companion came to him and asked whether he had gotten a lot of thalers, the captain answered, "Oh brother, if you only knew what wonderful treasures I found! But I don't want to show them to you right now. I'll do it only when we can all show what we've gotten."

So the robber took the donkey with him, but things did not go any better for him than it had for the captain. In short, each one of the four robbers experienced the same thing. When the fourth night flew by and the robbers came together, they decided to attack the shoemaker in his own house and strangle him. They set out on their way and soon came to Master Giuseppe's house. However, he had already seen them coming from a distance and quickly thought of a new trick. He called his wife, took the skin of a sausage, filled it with blood, and tied it around her neck. Then he said to his wife, "When the robbers come, I'm going to tell them that I'll return the money to them, and I'll order you to rush and get the money. But I want you to hesitate a little as if you weren't going to obey me. I'll get mad and stick my knife into this sausage skin, and you'll fall to the ground as if you were dead. When you hear me playing the guitar, I want you to rise up and begin dancing."

It did not take long before the robbers entered the house and began heaping insults and accusing the shoemaker of tricking them.

"You mean, you didn't get any money?" the shoemaker asked in astonishment. "The poor beast probably lost its magic power because it had to change houses. Just calm down. We don't want to argue about something like this. I'll pay you back the fifty gold ounces right away. Agatha, run quickly into the next room and bring these gentlemen the fifty ounces."

"All right," she answered. "But first I must finish chopping the fish. I can't go right away."

"What? Do what I say when I say it!" the shoemaker yelled and pretended to be furious with his wife. "I'll show you!"

Upon saying this, he stabbed her in her neck so that she fell to the ground as if she were dead, and the blood streamed out of the sausage skin.

"Oh, Master Giuseppe, what have you done?" the robbers cried out. "Your poor wife didn't do anything to harm you."

"Oh, let's not waste any words about this," the shoemaker replied, and he took out his guitar and began to play. All at once his wife stood up and began to dance. The robbers stood there with their mouths wide open. Finally they said, "Master Giuseppe, keep the fifty ounces, but tell us how much you want for the guitar. You've got to sell it to us."

"Oh no, gentlemen, I can't do this," the shoemaker said. "Each time I have an argument with my wife, I murder her, and that's the way I cool off my anger. I've become accustomed to this, and if I do this again and don't have the guitar anymore, I won't be able to wake her up and bring her back to life."

But the robbers kept asking him until he finally sold the guitar to them for forty ounces of gold. The robbers were delighted and returned home with the guitar. Then the captain said, "I deserve to try out the guitar the first night."

When he went home, he called his wife and asked, "What's there to eat tonight?"

"Pasta," she said.

"Why didn't you bake any fish?" he screamed and stabbed her in her neck so that she fell down dead. Then he took the guitar and played it, but no matter how much he played, the dead woman did not awake again.

"Oh, that no-good shoemaker! That lousy scoundrel! He's tricked me a second time and I'll strangle him for this!"

But all his shouting could not help him. His wife was dead and remained dead. The next morning one of the other robbers came to fetch the guitar and asked, "Well, brother, how did things go?"

"Oh, wonderful. I killed my wife, and no sooner did I begin to play than she awoke and stood right up."

"Are you serious? Well, then I'm going to try it out this evening."

In short, the four robbers killed their wives, and later, after they came together on the fifth morning and exchanged their stories with each other, they swore they would murder the clever shoemaker. They set out and came to his house, but Master Giuseppe saw them coming from a distance and said to his wife, "Listen, Agatha, when the robbers come and ask where I am, tell them that I went into the vineyard. Then order the dog to call me and chase him out of the house."

Then Master Giuseppe went out a back door into the open and hid himself in a place near the house. Soon thereafter the robbers arrived and asked for him.

"Oh, gentlemen," his wife answered, "he just went into the vineyard. I'll have the dog call him right away." And she turned to the dog: "Go quickly into the vineyard and call your master. Tell him that four men are here to speak with him"

Upon saying this, she opened the door and chased him outside.

"Don't tell us that you're sending the dog to fetch your husband." the robbers said.

"Of course," she replied. "He understands everything, and he'll tell my husband everything that I told him."

After a short time the shoemaker entered and said, "Welcome, gentlemen. The dog told me that you wanted to speak with me."

"Yes, indeed," the robber captain said. "We've come to question you about the guitar. You're to blame for causing us to kill all four of our wives because none of us was able to bring his wife back to life."

"You probably didn't do things the right way," the shoemaker responded.

"Well, we'll forget about all this," the captain said, "but you must sell us your dog."

"Oh no, I can't do this. Just think how much he's worth."

However, the robbers kept asking until Master Giuseppe sold them the dog for forty ounces of gold. The robbers took the dog with them, and the robber captain told his companions that he deserved to have the right to use the animal first. So he took the dog home and said to his daughter, "I'm going to the tavern. When someone comes and wants to speak with me, I want you to set the dog loose and send him to me so that he can call me home."

When someone really came who wanted to speak with him, the daughter set the dog loose and said, "Go to the tavern and call father."

But instead, the dog ran back to the shoemaker.

Later, when the robber came home and did not see the dog anymore, he thought, "He must have returned to his former master." So he set out in the night and went to the shoemaker.

"Master Giuseppe, is the dog here?"

"Oh yes, the poor beast is very attached to me. He'll be like this until he gets accustomed to you."

So the captain took the dog home again and gave him to the second robber the next morning. But he did not tell him the truth about the dog, as the shoemaker had told him. In short, each robber wanted the dog to carry out a task, and each time the dog ran back to the shoemaker and the robbers were compelled to go fetch the dog. When they gathered together on the fifth morning, it became clear that Master Giuseppe had gotten the best of them again, and they decided to strangle him and not to accept anything more from him. So they went to him and began making violent accusations. Finally, they stuck him into a sack and intended to throw him into the sea. Master Giuseppe remained calm and did not resist at all.

As the robbers walked past a church, mass was just about to be held, and the robbers decided to hear the mass first because they were religious people.* So they left the sack outside and went to the church. Nearby a boy was looking after a large herd of pigs and was whistling a

---

* Divozianati.

merry tune. When Master Giuseppe heard this, he began to shout in a loud voice: "I don't want to! I don't want to!"

"What don't you want to do?" the boy asked.

"Oh," replied the shoemaker, "I'm supposed to marry the king's daughter, and I don't want to."

"Oh," the swineherd sighed, "if only I could marry her!"

"Well, there's nothing easier than that," the sly shoemaker responded. "All you have to do is to get into this sack and let me out."

So the swineherd opened the sack and let the shoemaker out. Then he crawled inside himself, and the shoemaker drove the pigs along in great delight. When the robbers came out of the church, they took the sack on their backs and threw it into the sea where it was very deep. On their return home, however, Master Giuseppe came toward them with his herd of pigs, and they stared at him with open mouths.

"Oh, if you only knew how many pigs were in the sea!" he cried. "The deeper you go, the more you find. I got this nice herd and came back up to the shore."

"Are there still more there?"

"Oh, much more than you can bring back," the sly shoemaker said.

"Take us to the spot," they replied.

So the shoemaker led them to the beach and said, "First you all have to tie a rock around your necks. Otherwise, you won't be able to sink deep enough. I already caught all the pigs that were near the top."

Each one of the robbers tied a rock around his neck and jumped into the sea, but they all sank and drowned. On the other hand, Master Giuseppe happily drove his pigs back home and had enough for the rest of his life.

> The sounds of this tale ring from a shell,
> The words of this tale flow from a bowl!
> How beautiful that lady is
> Who told me to tell this tale!*

---

* Faula ntra conca, e faula ntrô bacili,
  Ch'è bedda sta Signura, chi mi l'ha fattu diri!

75

THE TWINS

Once upon a time there was a king who possessed a beautiful and large realm, but he did not have any children. Now a war with another king happened to erupt, and the king had to contend with him and lost the battle. Consequently, all his states were taken from him, and he had to flee from his realm with his wife. They wandered about for a long time until they came to a deserted beach near the sea. They decided to build a little hut there, and the king went fishing while the queen cooked the fish that he brought home, and this was the wretched way they lived with one another.

One day the king happened to catch a gold fish, that spoke to him.

"Listen to me," the fish said, "take me home with you and cut me into eight pieces. Give two to your wife, two to your horse, two to your dog, and bury two in your garden. This will bring you good fortune."

The king did just as the fish said. He took the fish home and cut it into eight pieces. Two he gave to his queen, two to his horse, two to his dog, and two he buried in the garden. Not long thereafter the queen appeared to be pregnant, and when her time came, she gave birth to two handsome boys, who looked so alike that nobody could tell them apart. On the same day, the horse brought two colts into the world, and the dog, two puppies. In the garden two swords grew, and they were made of gold and had magic powers. The two boys grew and flourished, and they became stronger and bigger with each passing day. They were so similar in appearance that their own mother and father could not tell who was who.

When they had become big strong young men, their father told them one day that he had once been a powerful king, but that he had been defeated by a more powerful king and had been robbed of his realm.

"Father," his sons said to him, "we want to set out into the world and regain all your states for you. Give us your blessing and let us depart."

The king and queen were very despondent and did not want to let their dear sons leave, but the brothers answered, "If you do not want to give your blessing, we shall have to leave without it because we are determined to depart."

So their parents gave their blessing, and each one of the brothers took a magic sword from the garden, mounted one of the horses, and took one of the dogs with them. Then they rode off. After they had ridden for some time, one of them said, "Dear brother, here is the spot where we should separate. You go in that direction, and I shall go in the other, and once we have achieved something, we'll meet back here at this spot."

The other brother agreed, and they went their separate ways. One of the brothers rode straight ahead until he came to a city that was decorated for some kind of event.

"Why is your city decorated in such a festive way?" he asked someone on the street, and the man answered, "Our king conquered the neighboring states of a king many years ago. Now he has a lovely daughter, and he has announced to all the knights that he is going to organize a tournament that will to last three days, and whoever is the victor on each one of these days is to marry the princess. As a dowry he is going to give the victor all the neighboring states that he had one time conquered."

"What's the name of your king?" the young man asked.

The man gave him the name of the king, and the youth realized that it was the same king who had conquered his father's states. So he went first to a tavern and refreshed himself with food and drink. Then he mounted his horse, strapped on his magic sword, and rode to the tournament. Many noble knights had gathered there, but the unknown youth defeated all of them because no one could compete with his magic sword. The next day the unknown youth reappeared at the tournament and was victorious again, and on the third day he defeated everyone once more. Then the king spoke to him, "You were victorious on all three days, and now you shall marry my daughter. But tell me, who are you?"

All at once the young man identified himself and said, "I am the son of the king whom you defeated, and whose states you want to give away as your daughter's dowry. I have regained my father's states and am satisfied. So let's enjoy the wedding celebration."

Soon after this they held a splendid wedding, and the prince married the princess, who was more beautiful than the sun. Later he sent a carriage and beautiful clothes to his father, and invited him to return to his realm. In the meantime the prince enjoyed living with his young wife.

One day he decided to go hunting and said to his wife, "I want to go hunting today, and I'll be away for three days.

He took his gold sword, mounted his horse, and was accompanied by his dog. On the same day, however, his brother entered the same city from the other side, and since he looked just like his brother and had the same horse, dog, and sword, everyone thought he was the young king and greeted him in a most reverent way. He was puzzled about this and thought, "Perhaps my brother has already been here."

When he came to the castle, the servants led him up into his brother's quarters, and the princess rushed toward him and said, "My dear husband, you only rode off this morning and told me that you were going to stay away for three days."

"I changed my mind," the prince answered.

So the princess led him to the table for dinner, and in the evening he went with her into the bedroom. When she laid down, however, he took his double-bladed sword and placed it between himself and the princess, who was so frightened by this that she did not dare ask him why he had done it. He continued to do this for two more nights.

When three days had passed, the young husband returned from the hunt, and everyone was astonished when they saw the young king again. He went straight to the castle, and when he saw his brother standing in the castle courtyard, he rushed toward him, embraced him, and cried, "Dear brother, is that you? Now we can really enjoy ourselves."

Everyone was astounded, and he explained to the king and the princess how everything had come about, and the his young wife snuggled up to him and said softly, "I've got to tell you that your bother spent three nights in your bed, but now I know why he always placed a double-edged sword between us."

After a some days had passed and the parents of the two brothers arrived, they traveled once again to their states, where the prince became the king and the beautiful princess, the queen. Later, the other brother married another princess, and so they remained rich and consoled, and we just sit here and continue to get old.*

---

* Iddi ristaru ricchi e cunsulati,
  E nui ristammu ccà sittati.

76

Beautiful Innocenta

Once upon a time there was a king and a queen who did not have a child, and would very much liked to have one. So the king made a promise that if he were blessed with a son, he would have a fountain built when the boy turned twelve, and he would let the fountain flow with oil for twelve hours so that anyone who needed oil could come and fetch some. Shortly thereafter the queen became pregnant, and when her hour came, she gave birth to a splendidly handsome boy. Just think how joyful his parents were!

The child grew and became handsomer with each day that passed. When he turned twelve, the king recalled his promise, had a beautiful fountain built in the castle courtyard, and announced throughout his realm that oil would flow for twenty-four hours. People could come and fetch as much oil as they wanted for nothing. So they came from far and wide and gathered around the fountain to get the oil. The prince stood on the balcony and took pleasure in watching the spectacle. Finally, when the oil had already stopped flowing, an old woman appeared with a small pitcher. When she saw that she would not be able to fill the pitcher, she took a sponge and carefully soaked up the oil that was left in the cracks. The prince stood at his window and watched, and when the pitcher was finally full, he took a stone and, in his arrogance, threw it at the small pitcher so that it broke, and the oil spilled out. Then the old woman called out in anger: "May you never marry until you have found the beautiful Innocenta!"

From that day on the prince thought of no one but the beautiful Innocenta and never enjoyed another peaceful day. When he became somewhat older, he went to his father and said, "Dear father, give me a horse and let me set out to look for the beautiful Innocenta."

"Oh, my son," the father cried in horror. "Are you crazy? Do you know how difficult it is to find the beautiful Innocenta? Do you know that her parents are ogres? Don't think about this anymore, my son, and stay here. You have everything you want, and you're our only son."

But the prince did not stop making his request. He kept asking the king to let him depart until his father finally gave him a horse, blessed him, and let him go.

The prince rode straight ahead for a long time until he eventually came to a wild region where there were no houses to be seen. In the distance he saw a light and went straight toward it. Soon he arrived at a cottage inhabited by a hermit, who was the first guardian of the beautiful Innocenta.

"Who's outside?" he asked in a deep voice.

"I'm a poor young man," the prince answered. "Please let me spend the night here. Tomorrow I'll continue on my way."

"What? Do you intend to kidnap the beautiful Innocenta? I'm going to eat you here and now."

"Don't eat me," the prince responded. "I have no idea who the beautiful Innocenta is. I just want to go hunting for my own pleasure."

So the hermit opened the door, gave him something to eat, and showed him to a bed. The next morning when the prince was about to say farewell, the hermit gave him a staff made of velvet and gold.

"Listen to my advice," he said. "Take this staff. It will be of use to you. My older brother lives a day's journey from here. You should spend the next night with him, and when you take leave from him, let him give you two loaves of bread that will also be of use to you. The day after you will travel to my oldest brother who will give you shelter. When you are sitting at the table with him, tear three hairs from his beard and keep them in a safe pace. They, too, will be of use to you."

The young man thanked the hermit and rode the entire day until he came to the second hermit in the evening. The prince knocked at the door, and the hermit said, "Who's there?"

"I'm a poor young man. Please let me rest here tonight, and tomorrow I'll continue on my way."

"What? Do you intend to kidnap the beautiful Innocenta?" the hermit growled. "I'm going to eat you here and now."

"Don't eat me," the prince responded. "I have no idea who the beautiful Innocenta is. I just want to go hunting for pleasure."

Then the hermit opened the door, gave him something to eat, and a bed for the night. When the prince was about to take his leave the next morning, he asked the hermit, "Please give me two loaves of bread so that I don't die of hunger in this desolate spot."

So the hermit gave him two loaves and bellowed, "Don't get any ideas of kidnapping the beautiful Innocenta or you'll be in for a lot of trouble."

"What concern is it of yours what happens to the beautiful Innocenta?" the prince said and rode off.

Toward evening he came to the third hermit who was ancient and had a long white beard. "Who's outside?" he growled with a deep voice.

The prince asked him for shelter for the night, but the hermit said, "Do you intend to kidnap the beautiful Innocenta? I'm going to eat you here and now!"

But the prince swore that he had no idea who the beautiful Innocenta was, and the hermit eventually let him enter. When they sat down to eat, the prince suddenly grabbed the hermit's beard and tore out three hairs.

"What do you think you're doing?" screamed the hermit. "Now I'm going to eat you."

"Why do you want to eat me?" the prince asked. "A fly became caught in your beard, and as I tried to get rid of the fly, there were three hairs that got caught in my fingers."

The old man settled down and then showed the prince to his bed. The next morning the young man mounted his horse and continued his journey. After he had ridden for some time, he came to some plains and saw a magnificent castle ahead of him. The door stood open, but a gigantic scissors stood in front and moved back and forth opening its blades up and down so that no one could get through. So the prince dismounted, took the staff made of velvet and gold, and stuck it between the scissors. While the scissors cut the staff in two, the prince slipped through the entrance. No sooner had he made his way into the castle than two roaring lions attacked him and wanted to eat him. He threw the two loafs of bread at them, and while they turned their attention to the bread, he rushed up the stairs. In the antechamber there was a vain fly* who began to buzz loudly as soon as anyone broke into the castle so that the witch would hear and rush to the spot. But the prince threw the

---

*Musca vana.

three hairs from the hermit's beard so that the fly became wrapped up in them and no longer thought about buzzing. Finally, the prince entered a large hall in which he found the beautiful Innocenta sitting on a throne, and she was more beautiful than the sun.

"Oh, beautiful Innocenta," he said, "just look at how I've worked and suffered all because of you! Now you must follow me and become my wife."

"How's that possible?" she asked. "My parents have left the castle, but they will return very soon. When they find you here, they will eat you."

"You can take care of that," the prince said. "I've done so much for you. Now you must think of a way to flee this place."

"Good," answered the beautiful Innocenta. "I'll hide you in my room for now, and tonight we shall flee this place."

So she hid the prince in her room, and soon the ogre and his wife came and bellowed, "We smell human flesh! We smell human flesh!"

"Oh, stop it," cried their daughter. "How is it possible for a human to get here? Aren't I completely safe with the buzzing fly, the two lions, and the scissors that keep watch over me?"

Soon after, when the ogre and his wife went to bed, the beautiful Innocenta called the prince, spit on the floor one time, and fled with the young man. After a while the old witch woke up, and since her daughter was not to be seen, she cried out: " Beautiful Innocenta, come and lay down to sleep."

"Soon, I just have to finish sewing this stocking," said the saliva.

"How far are you?"

"I've sewn half a leg."

After an hour the witch called out again, "Beautiful Innocenta, come and lay down to sleep."

"Soon, I just have to finish sewing this stocking."

"How far are you?"

"I'm almost done."

Once again, after a short while, the witch called out, "Beautiful Innocenta, come and lay down to sleep."

"Soon, I must finish sewing the stocking."

"How far are you?"

"I'm sewing the heels."

In the meantime it was nearly day, and the witch cried out one more time. "Beautiful Innocenta, come and lay down to sleep."

Her saliva was already dry, and she no longer answered.

"Beautiful Innocenta, beautiful Innocenta!" the witch cried out, but beautiful Innocenta had long since made her getaway over the mountains.

The witch woke the ogre and cried out, "Our daughter has fled. Come, we've got to follow her."

In order to catch up with the beautiful Innocenta, the ogre and his wife changed themselves into red and white clouds and soon had overtaken the two refugees.

"Look behind you and tell me what you see," the beautiful Innocenta said to the prince.

"I see a red and white cloud," the prince answered.

"Well, I'll become a church, and you'll become the sexton," the beautiful Innocenta said, and she was immediately turned into a church, and the prince into a sexton.

Meanwhile, the ogre and his wife reassumed their natural forms, approached the sexton, and asked him, "Have a man and a woman come riding by here?"

"It's not time yet for mass," he said and pretended as though he did not understand them.

"Have a man and a woman come by here?"

"The priest hasn't arrived yet."

"Have a man and a woman come riding by here?"

"The goblet hasn't been brought yet."

"Have a man and a woman come by here?"

"The host has been forgotten."

"Have a man and a woman come by here?"

"The book for the mass cannot be found."

Well, the ogre and the witch finally lost their patience and returned home grumbling all the way. However, the witch could not settle down and said, "I've got to catch up with them, and if you refuse to come with me, I'm going alone."

So she transformed herself into a white cloud and flew after them.

"Look behind you and tell me what you see," said beautiful Innocenta.

"I see a white cloud,"

"Then I'll become a garden, and you become the gardener."

So she became a garden, and the prince, a gardener. When the witch came, she asked him, "Have a man and a woman come by here?"

"The fennel isn't ripe yet."

"Have a man and a woman come by here?"

"I can't give you any lettuce yet."

"Have a man and a woman come by here?"

"Why are you looking for lettuce at this time of the year?"

"Are you mocking me?" the witch yelled at the gardener and wanted to attack him, but just then the beautiful Innocenta cried out, "You become a rosebush, and I'll become a rose."

Suddenly the prince became a rosebush with a wonderfully beautiful rose budding on it. The witch knew for sure that the rose was her daughter and wanted to pick it, but the rosebush stuck her with its thorns so that she became scratched all over. Still, she kept trying to pick the rose and stuck out her hand so that the beautiful Innocenta cried out again, "You become a fountain, and I'll be the eel in it."

All of a sudden the bush disappeared, and instead there was a fountain standing there, filled with clear water and an eel that was playing in it. The witch wanted to catch the eel, but just as she thought she had the eel in her fingers, it would slip through them.

"Beautiful Innocenta, beautiful Innocenta," she called. "Come with me or else you'll regret everything."

However, no matter how often she cried out to her daughter, the beautiful Innocenta would not listen to her. Finally the witch yelled, "May the prince forget you with the first kiss that his mother gives him!"

Then the witch returned to her castle.

In the meantime, the beautiful Innocenta and the prince continued on their way, and when they approached the city where his parents were living, he said to her, "Beautiful Innocenta, it's not proper at this time to enter my father's castle like this. Stay here until I go and announce your arrival to my father. Tomorrow I'll return with a splendid coach and large entourage, and I'll lead you in triumph to the castle."

"Oh, no," she said. "Don't leave me here. When your mother kisses you, you'll forget me."

"Don't worry," he answered. "I won't kiss my mother, and I'll return tomorrow."

So he led her to one of his father's peasants and left her in a farmhouse. When he arrived at the castle, his parents were full of joy to see their son again. However, he said to his mother, "Dear mother, I'm afraid you can't kiss me, otherwise I'll forget my dear bride. You see, I've found the beautiful Innocenta, and tomorrow I want to drive out with a large entourage and bring her here."

In the evening, however, after he had laid down to sleep, the queen could not resist her desire to kiss her son and thought, "I'll be able to remind him about the beautiful Innocenta." So she went into his room and kissed him, and right away he forgot the beautiful Innocenta. When he awoke, he had no idea who Innocenta was.

"My dear son," his mother said to him, "don't you want to set out and fetch the beautiful Innocenta?"

"Who is the beautiful Innocenta? I don't have any idea who she is, and I don't want to know," the prince replied.

So he stayed with his parents and led a splendid life. After some time had passed, he decided to marry another woman, and their wedding was to be celebrated soon.

The farmer with whom the beautiful Innocenta remained used to go to the city every now and then. When he came home one day, Innocenta asked him what news there was in the city. "The prince has chosen a bride for himself, and the wedding is to be celebrated in the near future."

"Do me a favor," the beautiful Innocenta said. "Buy me seven rolls of sugar and honey, and seven rolls of almond dough."

After the farmer brought her the sugar, honey, and dough, she formed two beautiful doves out of these things and cast a magic spell. Then she gave the doves to the farmer and said, "take these to the royal castle, and have them placed secretly in the prince's room."

The farmer did exactly as she wished, and when the prince went into his room, the doves were sitting there.

"Oh, how pretty these doves are," he said and as he approached them, one of the doves began to sing, "Kirr, kirr, do you remember how I fled with you in the night and spit on the floor so that my saliva would answer for me instead of myself?"

"Yes."

"Kirr, kirr, do you remember how my parents followed us, and I changed myself into a church and you into a sexton? Do you remember how they asked whether a man and woman came by and you answered that the priest had not come, and that the goblet and the host had not arrived yet, and that the book for mass could not be found?"

"Yes."

"Kirr, kirr, do you remember how my mother overtook us, and I changed myself into a garden and you into a gardener? Do you remember how she asked you whether a man and a woman had come by, and you spoke instead of fenchel, lettuce, and cabbage?"

"Yes."

"Kirr, kirr, do you remember how you became a rosebush, and I a rose, and how my mother wanted to pick me, and how you scratched her with your thorns?"

"Yes."

"Kirr, kirr, do you remember how you became a fountain, and I became an eel in it, and how I slipped through my mother's fingers?"

"Yes."

"Kirr, kirr, do you remember how my mother cried out to me, 'beautiful Innocenta, come with me, otherwise you'll regret everything,' and I did not listen to her? Instead I left my mother and father to follow you. Do you remember then how my mother cursed me by saying that the prince will forget me with the first kiss that his mother gives him?"

"Yes."

"Kirr, kirr, do you remember how you left me in the farmhouse, and promised to come back to me?"

When she spoke about the farmhouse, the prince remembered everything that had happened and rushed to the king and said, "Dear father, send my bride back to her home, for I already have a bride, my beautiful Innocenta, the one for whom I have suffered a great deal."

Then he got into a magnificent coach and took splendid clothes with him as well as a large entourage and drove to the farmhouse to fetch the beautiful Innocenta.

"Didn't I tell you that you shouldn't leave me here?" she said.

"My mother kissed me while I was sleeping," he answered. "That's why I forgot you. But now all our suffering has come to an end, and I've come to take you to my castle."

So she put on the beautiful clothes and sat down next to him in the magnificent coach and rode to the royal castle in honor. The king and queen were very happy about their son's beautiful bride and arranged a wonderful wedding. So they finally became man and wife, and now the story is done.

77

$$\sim\!\!\infty\!\!\sim$$

THE WICKED SCHOOLMASTER AND THE
WANDERING PRINCESS

Once upon a time there was a king and a queen who had just one daughter, and they loved her very much. They sent her to a teacher, who looked after other children in his school as well. However, the teacher was a wicked man and often hit the poor children.

Every day he would say to them, "Children be still and quiet until I return." Then he went into his room and only came out again after many hours had passed. As a result, the children became curious, and one day they said, "Let's crawl to the door and look through the keyhole."

But the princess was afraid and did not want to do what the others had decided to do.

"If we all go there, you must come with us as well," they insisted and continued to push her until she decided to go along. So they crept up to the door and looked through the keyhole and saw that the teacher was occupied with a dead person, but they could not see exactly what he was doing because he approached the door very quickly. They all ran back to their places, but the princess lost a shoe on the way and had to return to her place with one missing. When the schoolmaster entered with the shoe, she pulled her foot beneath her skirt so he could not see it.

"Which one of you has lost a shoe?" he asked.

All of the other children showed their feet and cried out: "Not me!"

The poor little princess, however, refused to show her foot, and the teacher said, "Well then, you were the one who was looking through the keyhole. Just you wait. Your punishment will come."

At noon when the other children went home, the servant came to fetch the princess, but the teacher said, "Tell your majesty that the girl would like to eat with me today. She'll come home this evening."

The princess wept, but she had to remain there. When all the children left, the teacher beat the poor child and mistreated her in a terrible way. Finally, he placed a curse on her. "Seven years, seven months, and seven days you shall spend in your bed, and when you are eventually cured, a cloud will come and carry you to the top of Mount Calvary."*

The poor child went home and became sick, so sick that she had to go to bed. She remained sick for many years, and there was not a single doctor who could help her. When the seven years and seven months had passed, however, she became completely healthy and turned into a astonishingly beautiful young woman.

Then, one day, a chambermaid said to her, "It's such a beautiful, sunny day. Come out on to the terrace.† I shall comb your hair."

At first the princess refused, but the chambermaid persuaded her to climb out onto the terrace. When they were on top, the chambermaid took down her beautiful braids and wanted to comb her hair, but she noticed that she had forgotten the ribbons for her hair and said, "I just have to go and fetch the ribbons. I'll return right away."

"Oh, stay with me," the princess said. "It doesn't matter. You can comb my hair without the ribbons."

"No, no," the chambermaid responded. "I want to make you look pretty. I'll be back in a moment."

As she rushed down the stairs, a cloud came by, sank down to the terrace, and swept the princess away to Mount Calvary. When the chambermaid returned to the terrace, she saw that her young mistress had disappeared and she began to yammer. "Oh, if only I hadn't left!" Then she ran to the queen and told her what had happened. The entire castle was in an uproar, and everyone searched for the princess all over, but she was nowhere to be found. Her parents were deeply distressed, and her mother said, "My poor child is certainly cursed."

Let's leave the parents now and see what happened to the princess.

---

* Munti Calvàriu.

† Lastrino.

The cloud carried her to the top of Mount Calvary and set her down there. It was such a terribly steep mountain that no one had ever managed to climb it. Because she did not want to remain there, she placed herself in the hands of our dear Lord and began to climb down the mountain. The thorns and stones ripped her clothes and wounded her tender arms and legs. Finally, however, she reached the foot of the mountain. She wandered until she came to a large magnificent castle, which she entered and went through all the rooms. She did not see a single human soul, but she could not help but notice the most beautiful treasures and a table covered with delicious food. When she reached the last room, she saw a handsome young man lying on the ground. He seemed to be dead, and next to him was a note that read: "If a maiden rubs me for seven years, seven months, and seven days with the grass from Mt. Calvary, I shall return to life, and she shall become my wife."

Then the princess thought: "I'm indeed a poor maiden. I can't find my way back to my parents. I don't have anything to do, so I might as well do a good deed."

So she made the strenuous climb back up Mt. Calvary without worrying about the thorns that ripped her tender arms and legs. Once she was on top, she cut the grass and made many bundles, which she threw down the mountain. Then she climbed down and reached the bottom more dead than alive. After she had somewhat recovered, she began to carry the bundles of grass into the castle and set herself to work rubbing the young man, day and night without sleeping or resting. But once a day she got up to eat something from the delicious food on the table.

This was how seven years and seven months passed. When there were only three days left of the seven, she became so tired that she could barely continue. All at once she heard someone offering a slave for sale on the street and thought, "I could buy this slave and let her rub a little while I rest for a few hours." So she bought the slave who was as black and ugly as one's debts,* and she commanded her to rub the handsome young man while she rested. When she laid down, however, she was so tired that she slept for three days without waking, and when she awoke, the seven years, seven months, and seven days were over. The handsome young man had awakened, regarded the ugly black slave as his savior, and said to her, "You have rescued me. So you shall be my wife." When the princess now appeared, he asked, "Who is this beautiful maiden?"

"She's my kitchen maid," the slave said.

---

*Brutta comu i debiti.

Therefore, the poor princess had to go to the kitchen and do the most demeaning kind of work. Meanwhile, the entire castle became alive with servants and foresters and the entire entourage of a king, for the handsome young man was a prince who had been under a magic spell. Now he celebrated a splendid wedding with the black slave, and the princess had to work in the kitchen.

However, once the king's marshal saw her, he found her so beautiful and good that he developed a great fondness for her. One day, when he had to go on a journey, he called her and said, "I must travel to Rome. Would you like me to bring you anything?"

"Bring me a knife and a stone of patience."

The marshal left, and while he was in Rome, he searched for a long time until he found a stone of patience, which he brought back to her with a knife. Now, of course, he became curious about why the princess wanted these things. So he crept after her and saw that she went into her room and closed the door. When he looked through the keyhole, he saw that she placed the stone of patience and the knife on a table, and she began to complain: "Oh stone of patience, listen to what has happened in my life." Then she told her entire life history beginning with the first day of school. As she told her story, the stone began to swell, and she said, "Oh stone of patience, if you are swelling when you hear about my sufferings, just think how I must feel."

When the marshal heard all this, he rushed to the prince and asked him to come with him and witness this marvelous event. So the prince went with him and looked through the keyhole and heard the princess tell how she had rubbed the handsome young man for so many years and had gone to fetch the grass on top of Mount Calvary. In the meantime the stone became even more swollen, and finally, when the princess told how she had been betrayed by the deceitful slave after all her efforts and work, the stone burst with a powerful bang.

"Oh, stone of patience," she cried, "if you burst upon hearing the story of my life, then I no longer wish to live." As she said this, she grabbed the knife and wanted to kill herself, but the prince knocked down the door, took her by the arm, and said, "You and no other shall become my wife, and the lying slave will pronounce her own sentence."

So he went to the slave and said, "Today my cousin is coming to visit. I want you to give her a good reception."

When the cousin arrived, it was none other than the princess who had meanwhile dressed herself in costly garments so that the slave would not recognize her. After they sat down at the table, the prince asked the slave, "What does a maiden deserve who has betrayed her mistress?"

The slave was distracted and answered, "The best thing to do would be to put her into a barrel of boiling oil and to let her be dragged by a horse through the entire city."

"You've spoken your own sentence," the prince said, "and I want the sentence carried out now."

So she was put into a barrel of boiling oil and dragged through the entire city. Meanwhile, the prince married the beautiful princess, who informed her parents about her wedding. And then they all lived happily and content, but we were left without a cent.

78

THE FOUR PRINCESSES

O nce upon a time there was a king who had four beautiful
daughters. One day he summoned a fortuneteller who was to
tell him the fate of the princesses.

"Before the youngest princess turns fourteen," the fortuneteller
said, "a cloud will come and carry off the four sisters."

As a result, the king had his daughters locked up in the castle, and
they were not allowed to go even into the garden. Since the cloud never
appeared, however, he finally came to the conclusion that the fortuneteller
had made a mistake, and one day, when the princesses had a great yearning to go into the garden, he allowed them to do so. Unfortunately, there
were only a few days left before the youngest princess would complete
her fourteenth year. No sooner did the princesses enter the garden than
a large cloud sank down and whisked away all four of them. Now the
king was very sad, and he issued a proclamation announcing throughout
his kingdom that whoever brought back his daughters would be able to
choose one of them for his wife and could succeed him as king.

Three brothers heard about the proclamation, sons of a neighboring king, and they set out to search for the four princesses. They kept
traveling straight ahead because they did not know where the princesses
were staying. One day they encountered an old woman who asked them,
"My handsome lads, where are you heading?"

"We've set out to find the four princesses who were carried away by
a cloud," the youngest answered.

"Oh, you poor children!" cried the old woman. "You'll have to put up with many dangers and difficulties. After you have traveled for a long time, you'll come to a cistern, and you'll have to climb down into it. But at the bottom is a dragon with seven heads, and this monster guards the princesses. You will have to kill it to rescue them."

The princes thanked the friendly old woman for the information and continued their journey. After they had wandered for many days, they finally came to the cistern in which the dragon was living.

"Let me go down first," the eldest brother said, "and when I ring this bell, pull me up quickly."

So they tied a rope around his body and let him down into the cistern, and he held the little bell in his hand. It was so very dark and eery in the cistern that he soon lost his courage and rang the bell. His brothers pulled him up at once, and the second had the rope tied around his body and wanted to try his luck. But he did not go much further than the eldest. He, too, lost his courage and gave the signal to have himself pulled up. Now it was the youngest's turn. He had the rope tied around him like his brothers and took the little bell with him. However, because he had more courage than the other two, he landed successfully at the bottom of the cistern. Then he entered a large space where the princesses were chained to the wall, and in the middle stood the dragon with seven heads, who looked fierce and horrible. The prince pulled out his sword and began to fight the dragon. Whenever he became exhausted, he looked at the youngest princess who inspired him so that he regained his strength and finally managed to cut off the seven heads of the dragon. The princesses were full of joy, and the prince undid their chains and led them to the place where his brothers were supposed to pull him up. Yet no matter how often he rang the bell, no one responded or pulled the rope up because his brothers had become impatient and had abandoned him.

"What shall we do now?" the prince asked the princesses.

They didn't know how to get out of their dilemma either. Finally the youngest princess said, "Every day an eagle comes and flies down into the cistern. If we ask the bird in a friendly way, perhaps it will carry us above with its wings."

So they waited patiently until the eagle came flying down into the cistern, and they asked the bird whether it would carry them on its wings.

"I'll gladly do this," the eagle replied, "but you must feed me until I'm full.

"That can easily be done," responded the prince. "Right here we have the dragon lying on the ground."

Upon saying this he cut the dragon into tiny pieces and gave them to the eagle to eat. The bird ate until it was full and carried the eldest princess to the top of the cistern. When he returned, he ate another piece of the dragon and carried the second princess up to the spot where there was daylight. Then he took the third and finally the fourth as well.

Only the prince was left, but the eagle had eaten the entire dragon and said, "Unless you give me something to eat, I won't carry you up."

"Where do you expect me to find something in this desolate spot?" the prince replied to the eagle. "Once we get to the top, I'll give you what you want."

But the eagle would not be moved by the prince's plea and said, "Cut some of your flesh from your arms and legs, and give it to me. Then I'll be satisfied."

"I have nothing to lose because I'll be dead if I don't do what the bird asks," the prince thought. "I might as well try this last way to save myself."

So he cut some flesh from his arms and legs and offered it to the eagle. After the bird devoured the flesh, it carried him to the top. When the princesses saw how bloody he was, they were horrified. They immediately dressed his wounds and took care of him until he was healthy again. Then the prince led the princesses to their father and chose the youngest for his wife. Afterward they celebrated a splendid wedding, and when the king died, the prince received the crown and lived happily and content, but we did not receive a cent.

79

ZAFARANA

Once upon a time there was a merchant who had three daughters. They were all very beautiful, but the youngest was the most beautiful of all. When he went on his business trips, he always asked his daughters what he could bring back to them.

One day he had to take another trip, so he went to his daughters and said, "Dear children, I must travel to France. What should I bring back to you?"

The two eldest chose beautiful clothes and jewelry, but the youngest, Zafarana, said, "Dear father, just greet the son of the King of France for me."

When the merchant had ended all his business in France, he asked for permission to see the king's son and gave him his daughter's greetings. Then the prince replied: "I want to marry your daughter Zafarana."

The merchant was very happy about this and took the prince on his ship and returned home. When they arrived at the strait of Messina, however, they heard a threatening voice:

"Do not touch Zafarana! She is mine!"

The father became so frightened by this that he changed his mind and was unwilling to give his youngest daughter to the prince. So the merchant had him marry his oldest daughter.

After some time had passed, the merchant had to travel again and asked his daughters what he should bring back to them. The second daughter asked for some beautiful jewelry, but Zafarana said, "Dear father, just greet the son of the King of Portugal from me."

When her father had finished all his business, he asked permission to see the prince and conveyed Zafarana's greetings. In reply, the prince said, "I want to marry your daughter, Zafarana."

So they boarded the merchant's ship and set sail for Messina. However, when they entered the strait, they heard the same voice, which was even more threatening: "Do not touch Zafarana! She is mine!"

Now the father was very distressed and thought, "There must be some magic spell on my daughter. Who knows what lies ahead for her." So he did not want to give his youngest daughter to the prince. Instead, he gave him the middle daughter.

Now Zafarana lived alone with her father who could not forget the threatening voice. Moreover, he could not think at all of traveling again because he was afraid to leave her alone. However, finally he could not put off his business any longer, so he called together all his servants and said, "I have to take a trip, and I am placing you in charge of my daughter. Do everything that she wishes and keep her out of danger."

The servants promised to do his bidding, and he departed with a heavy heart. But Zafarana had everything that she desired, and the servants did whatever she wanted. One day she felt a desire to drive out somewhere and take a walk. So she went to the coachman and asked him to take a drive into the woods. Once she was there, the coach stopped, and she got out and told the coachman, "I want to walk by myself a while. Wait here, and I'll return soon."

Then she began to climb a hill. When she reached the top, a cloud sank down and took her away. At first the servant waited a while, but when his mistress did not reappear, he followed the way she went up the hill. But no matter how much he called and searched, he could not find a trace of her. Soon it became dark, and there was nothing he could do except to return to Messina.

"Oh," he thought, "what am I going to say after the master returns?"

When the coachman returned home, the chambermaid came running and called out, "Why did you stay out so late? It's already pitch black. What's the matter? Where's our mistress?"

Now the coachman explained that Zafarana had disappeared, and all the servants began to moan and groan. They set out in search of the maiden, but it was all in vain. When the father returned from his journey, his servants met him with such sad faces that he became very anxious and asked right away: "Where is my daughter?"

Then they had to tell him how she had disappeared. The unfortunate father could not console himself at all and kept on saying, "I knew it. There's a magic spell on my daughter!"

In the meantime Zafarana was carried by the cloud through the air and set down in a beautiful castle. A very old man lived there, and she had to serve him. He was, however, an enchanted prince. Zafarana served him faithfully, and the old man was always friendly to her. One day he called her to him: "Zafarana, come into the garden with me, and clean the lice from my hair."

When they were sitting together the old man said, "I have some news to tell you. Your oldest sister has given birth to a beautiful baby boy."

"Oh," Zafarana said, "would you do me a favor and let me make a short visit to my sister?"

"No," the old man answered. "If you go and visit your sister, you certainly won't return."

But Zafarana kept asking and promised for sure that she would return so that the old man finally consented. He gave her the most beautiful clothes and a beautiful coach in which she was to travel to her sister. Before her trip he took her into a room in which there were three chairs—the first was made of gold; the second, silver; the third, lead.

"Look," he said to Zafarana, "you may go, but you are not allowed tell anyone where you live. And as soon as you hear my voice, you must return right away. Then you are to come into this room. If I am sitting on the golden chair, it is good for you. If I am sitting on the silver chair, it will be neither good nor bad for you. If I am sitting on the lead chair, it will be unfortunate for you."

Now Zafarana departed and traveled to her oldest sister, who was very happy to see Zafarana again, especially because she had been absent for such a long time. But no matter how much people asked her questions, she told them nothing about her life. After she had many conversations with her sister, she suddenly heard the voice of the old man calling to her. So she embraced her sister on the spot, rushed out, and traveled back to the castle. As she entered the room with the chairs, the old man was sitting on the gold one. "Thank God," she thought. "That's a good sign."

Some weeks passed by, and the old man called her to him once more and said, "Zafarana, come into the garden and clean the lice from my hair."

When they were sitting in the garden together, the old man said, "I've got some more news for you. Your middle sister has given birth to a beautiful baby girl."

"Oh," Zafarana cried, "dear master, let me go to her so that I can see my little niece."

The old man did not want to consent, but he finally yielded. Her sister was very happy to see her again when she arrived, and they had many delightful conversations. All of a sudden Zafarana heard the old man calling to her. She pretended not to hear his voice and remained seated. After a while the old man called again: "Zafarana!" She became scared, embraced her sister, and returned to the castle. When she entered the room, the old man was seated in the silver chair. "Now," she thought, "even if it doesn't mean anything good, at least it doesn't mean anything bad."

Once again, some weeks passed, and the old man called her into the garden, and when they were sitting together, he said, "Zafarana, I've got some more news for you. I'd prefer not to tell it, for you'll certainly want to leave again, and that will be your misfortune."

"Then you shouldn't have told me," said Zafarana. "You've already told me too much, now you must finish what you began to say."

"Your father has died," the old man said.

Zafarana began to weep and said, "I was unable to see my father once more while he was still alive, and I want at least to see him dead."

The old man did not want to let her go. "You'll see. It will be your misfortune!" he said.

But Zafarana wept such bitter tears and kept asking for such a long time that he finally consented. Then he had a beautiful mourning dress made for her and sent her to her father's house. She went up the stairs and entered the room where her father was lying on a bed, and candles were burning all around him. Zafarana threw herself on top of him, wept bitterly, and kept crying out: "Father, dear father!"

When the old man called, she heard him, but she did not pay attention because of her great suffering. He called a second time, and once again she did not obey. When he called a third time, she had to obey and returned weeping to the castle.

As she entered the room, the old man was sitting on the lead chair, and he gave her such a strict and serious look without saying a word that she became very frightened. They sat down together at a table and had their evening meal, but the old man did not say a word. He kept staring at her with the same look. When she went to bed and midnight arrived, the old man called, "Zafarana, get up. Open the window and see what the weather is like."

She obeyed and saw the sky was overcast, and it had started to rain. When she told this to the old man, he said, "Good. Now go back to sleep."

After a half an hour had passed, he called again: "Zafarana, get up and see what the weather is like."

"Oh," she said, "let me sleep. You've never called me so much before."

It did not help. She had to get up and see what the weather was like. She saw that it was raining more heavily, and it was thundering and lightning. She told the old man, and he said, "Good. Go back to sleep."

After half an hour he called her a third time: "Zafarana, get up and see what the weather is like."

"Why are you continually waking me up?" Zafarana asked. "You usually don't do this."

However, she had to obey, got up, and looked out the window. She saw such a storm and such bad weather that she quickly closed the window out of fright.

"I believe the world's falling apart," she said. "I've never seen such weather like this in my entire life."

"Good," the old man answered. "Get dressed and go. You can't stay here any longer."

Zafarana began to moan and said, "I've served you faithfully for a long time. You couldn't be so cruel now as to throw me out!"

But the old man kept saying, "You can't stay here any longer. I told you so. I told you it would be your misfortune."

He gave her a bundle of clothes and three pig bristles and said, "Keep them in a safe place. They'll be of use to you."

Then Zafarana had to go out in the dark of night into the terrible storm. At first she managed to make some progress, but as the weather became more and more awful, she crouched down behind a barn door and waited for daybreak. When dawn came, she stood up and wandered into the open with a heavy heart. Soon she came upon a cottage, and a peasant was sitting in front of it. She approached him and said, "My good man, would you please do me a great favor?"

"What would you like?" asked the peasant.

"Give me your clothes," Zafarana answered, "and I'll give you my clothes and everything that I have in my bundle."

The peasant did not want to do this, for he saw that Zafarana's clothes were much more beautiful than his simple garment. But Zafarana kept asking until he agreed to exchange clothes in his cottage and give his to Zafarana, who went into the cottage and soon came back out disguised as a peasant.

Now she wandered farther until she came to a large beautiful city where she went straight to the king's castle and walked back and forth in front of it. The king's personal coachman stood there, and when he saw the handsome young man, he said to him: "Where do you come from, my handsome young man?"

Zafarana answered, "I'm a stranger here, and I'm looking for some work because I'm poor and must find a way to earn money."

The coachman said, "We need to hire a stable boy for the king's horses. If you will accept the job, I can manage to get it for you."

Zafarana agreed and entered the service of the king. She combed and groomed the horses and was always diligent and orderly, but the king had a daughter who was stubborn, and everything had to be done according to her will. When she saw the young stableboy, she fell in love with him, went to her father, and said, "Dear father, there's a young man in the stable who was hired as stable boy. He looks too fine for such coarse work. I want him to work as a servant in the castle."

The king did just what his daughter demanded right away. He had Zafarana summoned, made a beautiful uniform for her, and she had to work as a servant in the castle. After some time passed, the princess went to her father again and said, "Dear father, none of my servants please me. I want the young man to become my personal page, and no one else."

Once again the king fulfilled her wish.

Now the princess fell more and more in love with Zafarana while she worked as her personal servant. One day the princess called her page and said to him, "Listen, I like you very much and want to marry you. Today I'll ask my father for his consent, and he'll certainly give it to me, for he never refuses me anything."

"Oh, princess," Zafarana answered very frightened. "Don't do this. You deserve a great, rich king, not a poor young man like me."

But no matter what she said, the princess kept insisting, and because Zafarana always responded with the same answer, the princess finally went to the king fully enraged and said, "The young page demanded something inappropriate from me, and because of this he must die."

Now Zafarana was placed in chains and was to die in three days. Finally, as she was being led to the gallows, she thought about the three pig's bristles that the old man had given to her, and when she came to the square where the gallows stood, she asked, "Please grant me one last request, and give me a pail with glowing coals."

Her request was granted, and when the pail was brought to her, she threw the three pig's bristles into it, and they burned. Just as this happened, a cloud of dust whirled in this distance, and a handsome, rich prince approached with his entire entourage. It was none other than the old man who had been released from the magic spell.

"Stop!" he called from a distance. "Stop!"

After he arrived at the square, he asked, "Why is this young man going to be hung?"

Then the king told him how the page had insulted his daughter and had to die because of it.

"All right," the prince responded, "But if I can prove that he never insulted your daughter, she must die in place of the page."

"I swear it on my royal honor!" the king said.

When they returned to the castle, the prince had Zafarana sent to a room where she had to put on royal clothes that belonged to women. Then they all recognized that she was indeed a young woman, and the princess had to die in her place. But the strange prince took Zafarana back to his realm where he became king and she became princess.

They continued to live happy and content,
But we were left empty-handed.

80

PEASANT TRUTHFUL

Once upon a time there was a king who had a goat, a lamb, a ram, and a sheep. Because he loved all the animals, he wanted to put them in charge of someone totally trustworthy. Now the king had a peasant whom he simply called Peasant Truthful* because this man had never told a lie. So the king summoned him to his court and placed the animals in his care. Every Saturday the peasant had to come to the city and give the king a report about the animals. When the peasant appeared before the king, he always took off his cap and said, "Good morning, your majesty."†

"Good morning, Peasant Truthful. How's the goat?"

"It's white and mischievous."

---

* Massaru verità.

† "Bon giornu, Riali Maestà!"
 "Bon gironu, Massaru Verità;
 Comu è la crapa?"
 "Janca e ladra!"
 "Comu è l'agneddu?"
 "Jancu e beddu!"
 "Comu è lu muntuni?"
 "Beddu a vidiri!"
 "Comu è lu crastu?"
 "Beddu a guardari!"

"How's my lamb?"

"It's white and beautiful."

"How's my ram?"

"Beautiful to look at."

"How's my sheep?"

"Beautiful to watch."

After they had spoken to one another this way, the peasant would go back to his mountain, and the king believed everything he said. However, among the king's ministers, there was one who was very jealous of the favor the king showed to the peasant, and one day he said to the king, "Is the old peasant really incapable of telling a lie? I'm willing to bet that he'll lie to you next Saturday."

"If my peasant tells a lie," the king cried, "I'm willing to lose my head."

So they made a bet, and whoever lost was to lose his head. However, the more the minister thought about it, the more difficult it became for him to find some means to get the peasant to tell a lie by Saturday, that is, within three days. He thought in vain the entire day, and when it became evening and the first day was gone, he went home in a bad mood. When his wife saw him in such a terrible mood, she said, "What's bothering you and making you so miserable?"

"Leave me in peace!" he responded. "Why do I have to tell you!"

But she continued to ask in a friendly way so that he finally told her.

"Oh," she said, "it's nothing more than that? I'll take care of everything for you."

The next morning she got dressed in her most beautiful clothes, put on her best jewelry, and placed a diamond star on her forehead. Then she took a seat in her coach and traveled to the mountain where Peasant Truthful had led the four animals out to pasture. When she appeared before the peasant, he stood still as if he had been turned to stone, for she was incredibly beautiful.

"Oh, dear peasant," she said, "would you please do me a favor?"

"Noble lady," the peasant answered, "I'll do whatever you order."

"Look," she said, "I am pregnant and have an irresistible desire for roasted liver from a sheep, and if you don't give it to me, I'll have to die."

"Noble lady," the peasant said, "demand what you want from me, but I can't grant you this wish. The sheep belongs to the king, and I can't kill it."

"Oh, how unfortunate I am!" she cried. "I'll surely die if you don't satisfy my desire. Oh, dear peasant, please don't refuse me! The king

490

wouldn't have to know a thing. You can tell him that the sheep fell off a cliff."

"No, I can't say that," the peasant resisted, "and I can't give you the liver."

The woman began to moan and groan even more. She pretended that she was about to die, and since she was so extraordinarily beautiful, the peasant's heart was finally moved by her pleas. He slaughtered the sheep, roasted the liver, and brought it to her. Then the woman ate it full of joy, took leave of the peasant, and departed. Now the peasant became despondent because he did not know what to say to the king. In his embarrassment he took a stick, planted it in the ground, and placed his small jacket on top of it. Then he took some steps toward it and began: "Good morning, your majesty!" However, when he came to the last question the king usually asked about the sheep, he always remained stuck and could not find an answer. He tried it with lies: "The sheep has been stolen," or "the sheep fell over a cliff," but the lies stuck in his throat. He placed the stick in another place on the ground and hung his jacket on top of it again, but nothing came to his mind. He could not sleep the entire night. Finally, the next morning he thought of an appropriate answer. "Yes," he thought, "that will work." He took his stick and jacket and set out to visit the king's castle, for it was Saturday. Along the way he stopped from time to time, set up the stick with the jacket as if it were the king, and held a conversation. Each time he did this, he liked his answer more.

When he entered the castle, the king sat in the throne room with his entire court, for the bet was to be decided on that day. Then Peasant Truthful took off his cap and began as usual.

"Good morning, your majesty."*

"Good morning, Peasant Truthful. How is my goat?"

---

* "Bon giornu, Riali Maestà!"
"Bon giornu, Massaru Verità!"
"Comu è la crapa?"
"Janca e ladra!"
"Comu è l'agneddu?"
"Janca e beddu!"
"Comu è lu muntuni?"
"Beddu a vidiri!"
"Comu è lu crastu?"
"Riali Maestà!
Ju ci dicu la verità.
Vinni na donna di autu munti,
Janca e bedda, cu na stidda in frunti
Tantu di sciamma a lu cori mi misi
Chi pri l'amuri soi lu crastu uccisi."

"It's white and mischievous."
"How is my lamb?"
"It's white and beautiful."
"How is my ram?"
"Beautiful to see."
"How is my sheep?"
"My lord and king
I scorn the lie . . .
Up in the mountain far away
a woman appeared like a star ablaze
Her beauty struck me as did her gaze
that pierced my heart and made me a wreck—
as for the sheep I broke its neck."

Everyone at the court applauded the peasant, and the king gave him a rich reward. The minister, however, had to pay for his jealousy with his head.

81

ABOUT JOSEPH,
WHO SET OUT TO SEEK HIS FORTUNE

Once upon a time there was a peasant and his wife, and they had just one son called Joseph. These people were poor and led a wretched existence. One day, Joseph went to his mother and said, "Dear mother, give me some clothes and your blessing, for I want to set out and seek my fortune.

"Oh, my son," his mother began to weep and said, "you want to leave us? I have enough troubles already, but when you also go away, my only child, there'll be nothing left for me to do but die."

"Mother," Joseph insisted, "I want to set out to seek my fortune."

Finally his parents yielded. They packed his clothes into a knapsack, added some bread and onions, and let him depart with heavy hearts.

After Joseph had wandered about for some time, he became hungry. He sat down behind a door to eat some of the bread and the onions. While he was eating, a fine gentleman came riding by on horseback and asked him who he was.

"Oh," responded Joseph, "I'm just a poor boy and have set out to seek my fortune."

"If you come with me and serve me faithfully," the gentleman said, "you'll have a good life."

Joseph was satisfied and decided to go along with the stranger, who took him to a magnificent castle that contained a great deal of treasures.

"This is where I live," the gentleman said to Joseph, and he had him take off his peasant clothes and gave him an elegant suit. "You are

to live here with me and enjoy your life. You may take and use as much
money as you want. But once a year you must do something important
for me."

"I'll do whatever you order," Joseph replied, and he lived with
the strange gentleman in splendor and joy. When the year was almost
over, Joseph had a great longing to see his parents. So he went to his
master and said, "Please let me go for a few days so that I can visit my
parents."

At first his master did not want to let him depart because he thought
Joseph would not return, but when Joseph promised to be back within
a few days, he let him go.

When Joseph arrived in his hometown, people on the street wondered, "Isn't that the son of old Joseph?"*

Others thought differently and remarked, "That's a fine gentleman.
Joseph was only a peasant."

Finally Joseph reached the house of his parents, and when he entered,
only his mother was there. He greeted her, and she bowed before the
fine gentleman. Then he said to her: "Isn't old Joseph at home?"

"Oh yes," his mother said, "I'll go and call him right away," and she
went into the garden and said to her husband. "A strange man has come
to our house, and he's asking for you."

The old peasant went into the room, took off his cap, and said,
"What may I do for you?"

Then Joseph began to laugh and said, "Don't you recognize me? I'm
Joseph, your son."

There was great joy in the house, and Joseph had to tell them everything that had happened to him, and he immediately gave them a great
deal of money so that they could live in comfort.

"Unfortunately, I must leave right away and return to my master,"
he announced.

His mother began to weep and asked, "Oh, my dear son, stay with
me."

But Joseph said, "I promised my master that I would return."

So they let him depart and Joseph returned to his master.

After a few days had passed, the strange man said, "Joseph, today
you must do me that service for which I hired you."

And he led him into a room that had hunter's clothes laid out in it,
and Joseph had to put them on. Then the two of them mounted their

---

* Zio Peppe.

horses. There was also a third horse loaded with many empty sacks that Joseph had to lead by the reins. They rode for many hours until they came to some plains with a mountain that soared into the sky. This mountain was so steep that no human could climb it. They dismounted at the foot of the mountain and refreshed themselves with food and drink. Then Joseph's master ordered him to kill the third horse and take off its skin. Joseph did this, and then they lay the skin in the sun to let it dry.

"Now we can rest for a while," the master said.

Soon, however, he called Joseph again, gave him a sharp little knife, and said, "I'm going to sew you in the skin along with all the empty sacks. Then crows will come and carry you to the top of the mountain. Once you're there, you are to cut yourself out of the skin with this knife, and I'll call up to you and tell you what you're to do next."

Joseph was ready to do anything, and his master sewed him into the skin. Right after the crows came, lifted him, and carried him to the top of the mountain where they set him down. Then Joseph cut himself out of the skin with the knife and looked around. The entire peak was covered with diamonds.

"What should I do now?" he asked his master.

"Fill all the sacks with diamonds and throw them down to me," his master yelled.

When Joseph had filled all the sacks and had thrown them down to his master, he called, "What should I do now?"

"Live well," his master responded, "and find some way to get down from there."

Upon saying this, he loaded the sacks onto Joseph's horse and rode away, laughing as he went.

Joseph stood there and did not see any way he could descend the mountain. He stamped his feet in rage, and all of a sudden he heard a noise like knocking on wood. He leaned over, and yes, he was right. He was standing on a wooden door with a lock. He managed to open the door and thought, "At least the wild birds can't eat me here." When he slipped inside, he saw some stairs which he descended carefully, for it was completely dark. Finally he came to a bright hall. As he was standing there and looking around, a door opened and a giant came out.

"How dare you enter my palace!" the giant said in a deep voice.

At first Joseph was terrified, but he soon summoned his courage and replied cheerfully, "Oh, dear uncle, is it you? How happy I am to see you!"

"Are you really my nephew?" asked the giant who was somewhat dumb.

"Certainly," Joseph said, "and I want to stay with you."

The giant was satisfied, and so Joseph lived with him and had a good life.

But soon he noticed that the giant was overcome by some terrible sickness every day at a certain hour that caused him to suffer a great deal.

"Dear uncle," Joseph asked, "where does this sickness come from? Can I help you get better?"

"Oh, dear nephew," the giant answered, "it's possible to cure me, but how could someone like you succeed in doing it?"

"Just tell me, uncle," Joseph insisted. "Perhaps I can help you."

"All right," the giant said. "Every day four fairies come and bathe in the pond in my garden, and as long as they are in the water, I am overcome by this sickness."

"How can I save you from the fairies?" Joseph asked.

"Before they climb into the water," the giant said, "they take off their blouses and leave them on the stone fence. You must hide yourself there, and while they are in the water, you must grab the blouse of the fairy queen* so she cannot fly away, and without her the others will not return."

So Joseph hid himself behind the stone fence. Soon he heard a rustling in the air, and four fairies appeared. They took off their blouses and climbed into the water. Joseph stuck out his hand and took the blouse of the fairy queen. At that very same moment the fairies jumped out of the water with a cry, took their blouses, and flew away. But the fairy queen could not fly away without her blouse. Then the giant stepped forward and put her into chains. Every morning he brought her a slice of bread and some water and asked her, "If you marry my nephew, I'll set you free."

But the fairy always answered, "No, I refuse."

"Then you'll stay in chains," declared the giant.

After a while he brought her a little lamp, placed it next to her head, and said, "If you don't marry my nephew, you will live only as long as there is oil left in this lamp."

"All right," said the fairy, "I'll marry him!"

So the chains were taken off there was a beautiful wedding, and Joseph was very happy.

---

* Capo-fata.

The next day the giant said to him: "You can no longer stay with me. Take your wife and go home to your parents. Here is your wife's blouse. No matter what, do not give it back to her unless someone shows you a snuffbox that looks like this one." And he gave him a gold snuffbox and a magic wand and told him to leave.

So Joseph took his wife and set out on his way. The journey was long, and soon they were tired.

"I wish I were home already," Joseph said, and because he had the magic wand in his hand, they found themselves at his home right after he had spoken those words. Then he wished for a beautiful house with coaches and horses, and servants and beautiful clothes for him and his wife. Afterward he went to his old parents. They were very glad to see him again, and Joseph said, "Come with me to my palace. I want to introduce you to my wife."

They went with him and stayed there. Now Joseph led a glorious life, held great parties, and was the richest and most distinguished man in the entire country. As for the blouse, he gave it to his mother for safekeeping. He also showed her the gold snuffbox, and she had to swear to him that she would not give up the blouse unless someone showed her the same kind of snuffbox, and he always carried his box with him. Meanwhile, his wife remained discontent and kept thinking of ways to get the gold snuffbox, for she missed the other fairies and wanted to return to them.

Now one evening Joseph threw another great ball. A gentleman stepped up to Joseph's wife and asked her to dance.

"I'll be glad to dance with you," the fairy said, "but when we form lines, you must dance near my husband and try to take away the gold snuffbox that he's carrying with him."

The gentleman promised this, and since Joseph did not suspect anything, he was not on his guard. The gentleman succeeded in taking away the snuffbox without being observed, and he gave it to the fairy right away. She was very happy about this and immediately sent her chambermaid to her mother-in-law. The fairy had told the chambermaid to say, "Here is the gold snuffbox. Give me my mistress's blouse in exchange."

When the old woman saw the snuffbox, she innocently gave the blouse to the chambermaid, who took it to the fairy right away. No sooner did the fairy put on the blouse than she disappeared, and with her the beautiful castle vanished along with the servants, coaches, and horses. Joseph sat on a stone on the roadside in his old peasant clothes. He was very depressed for he had loved his wife very much. When he returned to his parents' house he could not console himself, and one day he said, "Mother, give me your blessing. I want to set out to seek my wife."

His mother wept bitter tears and did not want to let him depart, but Joseph insisted, and so his parents finally had to consent. Now Joseph went straight to the place where the strange gentleman had found him and sat down behind the same door. It was not long before the stranger came riding by and asked him again who he was and what his name was. He did not recognize Joseph because he thought that he had long been dead. Joseph answered that his name was Franco. Then the gentleman hired him, and everything went like the first time. After he had lived one year in splendor, he had to accompany his master to the plains where he was sewn into the horse skin and carried by the crows to the top of the mountain of diamonds. However, instead of filling the sacks full of diamonds, Joseph grabbed large stones and began throwing them at his master. Then the gentleman recognized him and yelled, "Oh, it's you! This time it's you who's cheated me!"

But because Joseph kept throwing even more stones, the gentleman had to clear out and ran from the spot as fast as he could. Meanwhile Joseph opened the wooden door, climbed down the stairs, and went to the giant.

"What, my nephew," the giant asked in astonishment, "you're here again?"

Then Joseph told the giant what had happened to him.

"Didn't I tell you that you should keep the blouse in safekeeping?" the giant said. "What do you want from me?"

"I want to search for my wife," Joseph replied, "and you must help me."

"Are you totally crazy?" the giant exclaimed. "You'll never ever be able to find your wife again. Another giant has captured her, and you'll never be able to kill him."

However, Joseph continued to ask for his help until the giant said, "I can't help you anymore, but I'll show you the right direction and give you some bread so that you won't die of hunger."

So the giant showed him the way, and Joseph set out to search for his wife. After he had wandered for a long time, he became hungry and sat down on a rock and began to eat some bread. As he was eating, some crumbs fell on the ground and a bunch of ants suddenly appeared and began pecking at the crumbs.

"Poor little insects! You're all so hungry," thought Joseph, and he broke a large piece of bread into pieces and spread them on the ground. Then the king of the ants came and said, "As thanks for the way you have so kindly fed my ants, I am giving you this ant leg. Keep it safe, for it will be of use to you."

To be sure, Joseph thought that such an ant leg would not be much use to him, but since he did not want to insult the king of the ants, he took the bone, wrapped it in a piece of paper, and stuck it into his pocket. As he continued on his way, he saw an eagle nailed to a tree with an arrow.

"Oh, this poor bird!" he thought, and he pulled the arrow out.

"Thanks a lot," the eagle cried. "Because you were kind enough to save me, I want to give you something. Pull out a feather from my wing. It will be of use to you."

Joseph pulled out the feather and stuck it with the ant leg. After a short while he saw a lion, who was limping and groaning in a miserable way.

"Poor beast!" Joseph thought, "he probably has a thorn in his foot." And Joseph leaned over and carefully pulled the thorn out.

"Because you have been so kind to help me," the lion said, "I want you to have a hair from my beard as thanks. Yank it out, for it will certainly be of use to you."

Joseph took the hair and put it with the other things. After he wandered for a while, he became tired and almost lost heart, for he still had very far to go. Then he remembered the eagle's feather and thought, "I can at least try it one time." He took the feather in his hand and said, "I'm a man and want to become an eagle."*

No sooner than he said these words, he became an eagle and flew through the air until he landed at the giant's castle. Once there he said, "I'm an eagle and want to become a man." As soon as he said this, he was restored to his natural shape. Now he took the ant's leg out and said, "I'm a man and want to become an ant." Then he became transformed into an ant and crawled through a crack in the wall of the palace. He wandered though many rooms until he came to a large hall where he saw his wife, who was tied with heavy chains along with many other fairies who were all chained. Then he said, "I'm an ant and want to become a man." All of a sudden he stood before his wife in his true shape.

When she saw him, she was very happy but also scared.

"Oh, when the giant finds you here, he'll kill you!" she cried.

"Let that be my concern," Joseph said. "Just tell me how I can free you."

"Oh," his wife said, "even if I tell you, what good will it do? You can't free me."

---

* Cristianu sugnu e acula diventu.

499

"Just tell me," Joseph insisted.

Then his wife responded: "First you must kill the dragon with the seven heads that lives in the mountains behind the castle. If you manage to cut off his seventh head, you must split it in two. A raven will fly out, and you must grab hold of it and kill it. Then you must cut out the egg in its body. If you hit the giant right in the middle of his forehead with this egg, he will die. But this is much too difficult for you. You'll never succeed in doing it."

All of a sudden they heard heavy footsteps, and his wife anxiously cried out, "Oh Joseph, the giant is coming!"

Joseph grabbed his ant leg right away, spoke the magic words, and immediately became an ant. Now the giant entered the hall and growled in a deep voice: "I smell human flesh!"

But the fairy said, "How could a human being come to us. You've locked us up so securely."

Upon hearing this the giant became calm. Meanwhile Joseph crawled through a crack into the open and said, "I'm an ant and want to become a man." Then, as a man, he took the feather in his hand, transformed himself into an eagle, and flew with quick beats of his wings to the foot of the mountain where the dragon was living. There he saw a shepherd, who was sitting on the path and looked distressed. Joseph turned himself into a man again, stepped toward the shepherd, and asked him what was wrong.

"Oh," the shepherd said. "I had such a large herd of sheep, and the dragon has eaten so many that I only have a small herd left. But I don't dare drive them on to the meadow because the dragon will eat them."

"If you hire me to serve you," Joseph said, "I can perhaps help you. Give me four sheep and let me drive them on to the meadow."

At first the shepherd did not want to hire him, but Joseph kept encouraging him until the shepherd finally gave him four sheep. Then Joseph began climbing the mountain, and soon he caught sight of the dragon, lured by the smell of the sheep. Immediately Joseph took the lion's hair in his hand and said, "I'm a man and want to become a lion," and he was transformed into a fierce lion so large and strong that there was none his equal. He attacked the dragon, and after a long battle, he succeeded in biting off two heads, but he became so exhausted he could not fight anymore. Fortunately the dragon was also just as exhausted so that it crawled into its cave. Then Joseph assumed his human shape again, gathered his four sheep, which had eaten as much as they wanted, and returned to the shepherd quite pleased with himself. The shepherd was astonished to see Joseph and his four sheep alive again and asked what had happened to him. But Joseph declared, "What's that to you? I've brought back your sheep just as healthy as they were before. Tomorrow I want eight."

The next morning Joseph drove eight sheep to the meadow. The shepherd was curious and quietly followed him. Then he watched as the dragon appeared. Joseph grabbed the lion's hair, said the magic words, and was transformed immediately into a fierce lion, and fought the dragon. On this day he succeeded in biting off four heads, but he became so exhausted that he could not fight anymore, and the dragon had also lost its strength.

"Yes," the dragon said, "if I had a glass from the water of life, I'd show you the power of the king of the dragons!"

"And I," responded Joseph, "if I had a good soup of wine and bread, I'd show you the power of the king of the lions."

When the shepherd heard this, he rushed to his hut, quickly cooked a soup of bread and wine, and took it to the lion. No sooner did the beast eat the soup than all his former strength returned to him. He began to fight once more and bit the seventh head off the dragon. Now he said, "I'm a lion and want to become a man," and he split the seventh head, whereupon a raven flew out and into the air. But Joseph was on top of everything: I'm a man and want to become an eagle," and as an eagle he flew after the raven and killed it. Then he took on his human shape again, cut the egg from the raven's body, and began traveling home once again with the shepherd and his sheep. The shepherd wanted to keep him in his employ and promised him anything he desired if he would only stay on with him. But Joseph answered: "I can't stay with you. I'm glad that I have freed you from the dragon, and I thank you for your quick help."

Joseph flew as an eagle to the giant's castle and crawled through the crack into the hall as ant. "I'm an ant and want to become a man," he said and told his wife about everything he had accomplished and that he had brought the egg.

"The giant's sleeping in the next room," she said. "Now's the time to kill him."

Joseph sneaked into the room next door, aimed directly at the forehead of the giant, and killed him. Then all the fairies were freed from their chains, and his wife embraced him. Afterward she showed him all the treasures that had been gathered there. They took as much as they could carry and traveled home again to Joseph's parents. Once there, they built a house much more beautiful than the first and lived in splendor and joy until their happy end.

82

THE WASTEFUL GIOVANNINU

Once upon a time there was a rich young man named Giovanninu. He had great treasures and wealth, but he did not want to work and attend to his business. Instead, he lived a life of luxury and pleasure, went to all the parties, and gambled and drank away his money. His faithful servant Peppe kept saying to him, "Oh, master, pay attention! You can't continue living like this. If you always give away your money without earning any, you'll soon run out of it."

However, Giovanninu always answered, "It will be a long time before I run out of money. Just let me take care of things."

So he lived from one day to the next, went to each and every party, and gambled away his money.

"Master, be careful," warned the faithful Peppe. But his master did not heed his warnings until one day, all the treasures were used up, and he did not even have enough for Peppe to buy food for the midday meal. Giovanninu began to sell all the silverware and beautiful furniture in the house, but he took the money and used it to return to his former life style.

He did this until he had sold everything and was completely poor and stripped of everything he had.*

"Oh master, I warned you," the poor Peppe said and wept bitter tears.

---

* Ristau poviru e pacciu.

"You were right," Giovanninu said. "There's nothing left for us to do but to seek our fortune. Why don't you head off in that direction, and I'll go in this one, and we'll see whether we can find our fortunes."

So they separated, and Giovanninu wandered forth and had to beg along the way. After he had traveled for a long time, he came one day to a region that he did not know. In front of him stood a magnificent palace, and since the sun was shining so brightly, he sat down on the threshold to warm himself a bit. While he was sitting there, a lovely little white sheep came out of the palace, sat down next to him, and let him pet it. Indeed, he was very happy to have the cute little animal next to him. All of a sudden the sheep opened its mouth and said, "Do you want to go up into the palace with me, handsome lad? You see, I'm an enchanted princess, and if you do everything I tell you to do, you can rescue me from this magic spell."

"Tell me what I have to do," Giovanninu said, "and I'll set you free."

"Come up into the palace," the sheep said. "You'll find some good food and wine and beautiful clothes. There's also a good bed ready for you. If you can survive everything that happens to you each night without making a sound, you'll be able to save me."

Once again Giovanninu promised he would free her from the spell. The enchanted princess led him into the palace, where he ate and drank to his heart's content and then laid down to bed.

Soon he fell asleep and was completely relaxed. When it turned midnight, however, he was wakened by a great noise. The door sprang open, and in marched a long line of people, each one carrying a burning candle.

"Get up and come with us," they said to Giovanninu.

However, he did not answer them and remained quiet. Then they tore him out of the bed and dragged him into the middle of the room, formed a circle, and danced around him. In the process they kicked and hit him and treated him in an awful way, but he withstood everything and did not utter a sound. When morning arrived, they left him half dead on the ground and disappeared. Then the little white sheep entered, dressed his wounds, and brought him food and drink so that he could recover. This is what happened every night for the next two weeks.

One morning, however, a maiden entered his room instead of the little white sheep, and she was so beautiful, it was as if God had created her.*

---

* The customary expression is: as if his mother had made her, comu la fici so matri.

"I'm the little white sheep," she said, "and you have freed me from the magic spell. I'm not going away. I'm just returning to my parents. I can't take you with me yet, but in eight days I'll come again. I'll come three days in a row, each time at noon, and you must wait for me at the palace gate. Make sure that I don't find you asleep, otherwise you'll regret it!"

Giovanninu promised to keep on his guard, and the beautiful princess drove off. When she returned home, her parents rejoiced to see their daughter once more because they had lost her many years ago. Then she said to them, "Giovanninu rescued me, and I want him to become my husband."

When eight days had passed, she climbed on a gorgeous horse, took a large retinue of people with her, and rode to the palace. Giovanninu had been sitting on the threshold and waiting for her, but in the palace there were still many other enchanted maidens, who had been filled with jealousy against the beautiful princess because she was the first one to be freed from the magic spell. They cast a magic spell on poor Giovanninu, and at the very moment that the princess appeared in the distance, he suddenly felt very tired and fell into a deep sleep. When the princess arrived and found him asleep, she became very despondent, climbed off her horse, and cried out: "Giovanninu! Giovanninu! Wake up."

But he did not hear her because he been enchanted by magic. When she realized that she wouldn't be able to wake him, she took a piece of paper and wrote on it: "Look out for yourself! I only have two days left." She stuck the note into his pocket and rode off. When he finally woke up and saw that the sun was setting, he became very frightened and thought to himself, "I'm going to be sorry for this! I'm sure the princess came and found me asleep." When he then put his hand into his pocket and found the note, he became even sadder and lamented, "Oh, how unlucky I am! How could I fall asleep?"

The next day he sat down again on the threshold at the right time and thought,

"Today I'm definitely going to remain awake." But things did not go any better for him than the first time. At the very moment that the princess appeared in the distance, he was overcome by a deep sleep. Because she found him asleep a second time, she was even more despondent and got off her horse and cried out, "Giovanninu! Giovanninu! Wake up!"

When he did not wake up, she took a piece of paper and wrote on it: "Now I'll be coming only one more time. If you are asleep tomorrow, you'll regret it!"

She stuck this note into his pocket, mounted her horse, and rode off. When Giovanninu woke up and found the note, he groaned very loudly and said, "How's this possible? Something strange is going on here—I fall asleep at noon each day."

On the third day he did not sit down. Instead, he walked up and down in front of the palace, but nothing helped him. As soon as the princess appeared in the distance, he was overcome by the magic sleep. When the princess found him asleep again, she cried out, "Well, because you didn't want to be blessed by fortune, you won't have any! If you want to regain me, you'll have to wander a long time before you find me." Once again she put a note in his pocket, mounted her horse, and rode off. Just imagine Giovanninu's sorrow when he awoke and found the note. "How unlucky I am! How shall I ever find her?" he moaned.

There was nothing left for him to do but grab his walking staff once again and wander into the wide world, and since he had nothing but the clothes on his back, he had to beg. Giovanninu traveled for a long, long time, and his clothes became tattered, but he did not find the beautiful princess. One day, as he was lying along the road worn out and weak and could go no further, an eagle flew by and asked him, "Handsome lad, why are you so sad and lying on the ground?"

"Oh," answered Giovanninu, "I'm so weak that I can't go any farther."

"Get on my back," the eagle said, "I'll carry you a good part of the way."

So Giovanninu climbed on the back of the eagle, who flew off with him into the air and soared like the wind. After they had flown for some time, the eagle suddenly cried out, "Meat!"

"What should I do now?" thought Giovanninu. "If I don't give the eagle any meat, the bird will drop me."

Since he had no meat with him, he cut off his left hand and gave it to the eagle. But after a short time passed, the eagle cried out again, "Meat!" Then Giovanninu cut off his left arm and gave it to the eagle, and since the bird continued to demand more, he had to slice off his left foot and left leg. Finally, the eagle swooped down to the ground and said, "Get off my back and continue on your way."

"How can I continue wandering in this condition?" Giovanninu complained.

When the eagle saw him so crippled, it asked, "Why did you do that?"

"You kept demanding meat, and I had no other meat to give you except my own flesh."

The eagle was moved by this and said, "Don't worry. I'm going to heal you."

Upon saying this he brought forth poor Giovanninu's arm and leg.

"I know that you've been wandering in search of the beautiful princess, so listen to my advice. If you travel for another two days, you'll come to a small cottage and find a wise old woman who will help you."

So Giovanninu set out on his way again and wandered two days. On the evening of the second day he came to a cottage just as the eagle said he would. He knocked on the door and an ancient woman came and asked him what he wanted.

"I'm a poor young man," answered Giovanninu. "Please take pity on me and let me rest here tonight."

"Come in, my son," the old woman said as she opened the door. She invited him in and gave him something to eat and drink. "What has brought you to this desolate region?"

Giovanninu told her everything that had happened and afterward he said, "Please tell me how I can find the beautiful princess again."

"Just sleep for now," replied the old woman. "Early tomorrow morning I'll tell you what you're to do."

So Giovanninu laid down and slept peacefully until morning. When he awoke, the old woman gave him something more to eat and said, "The princess is living in the nearby city, and you are to continue wandering until you get there. Here is a magic wand. When you're finally in the city, ask someone where the king's palace is, and during the night, use the wand to create a palace, much more beautiful than the king's, right across from it. Now you will make up for whatever you've had to tolerate because of the princess."

Upon saying this, the old woman gave him the magic wand, and Giovanninu thanked her very much and wandered off. After he traveled for some time, he finally came to the city where the princess was living. He asked for directions to the royal castle and took note of exactly where it was standing. During the night he crept back to the spot with his magic wand and cried out: "Listen to my command!"

"What's your command?" the wand asked.

So Giovanninu wished for a fully furnished palace. In addition he asked for coaches, servants, and horses. All at once a magnificent castle stood before his eyes, more beautiful than any other castle in the world. Servants appeared and washed and dressed Giovanninu in costly garments. He became such a handsome young man that no one recognized him. When the princess saw the magnificent palace the next day, she was astonished and said, "Is there something wrong with my eyes, or has such a beautiful palace really arisen over night?"

While she was still thinking about this, Giovanninu appeared at the window, but she did not recognize him. Since he was such a handsome young man, however, she fell passionately in love with him and said, "This man is to become my husband and no other."

She tried to make his acquaintance, but he pretended not to notice her. The more indifferent he was toward her, the more passionate her love for him became. So she sewed twelve shirts made from the finest cloth, placed them on a silver platter, covered them with a gorgeous embroidered scarf, called her servant, and sent them to Giovanninu. The servant was to say: "The princess who is living across from you sends her greetings and requests that you make good use of them out of love for her."*

When the servant took this message to Giovanninu, he replied, "Very good. I wanted to buy dust rags for the kitchen today, the scarf you can take to the church, and tell your mistress that I am very grateful for the gifts."

The servant returned to the princess very distressed.

"Oh, your majesty," he said, "this man must be much richer than you are. Just think—he had the shirts taken into the kitchen to be used as dust rags for the kettle."

So the princess became very sad, and had a gold candelabra, which was more beautiful than anyone had ever seen, sent to Giovanninu with the message: "The princess sends her greetings. May you use this candelabra as a light next to your bed out of love for her."

However, when the servant went to Giovanninu and took him the message, the young man responded again, "Good. The candelabra comes just at the right time. I wanted to buy a lamp for the kitchen today. Bring the candelabra into the kitchen, and tell your mistress that I am very grateful."

The servant took this reply to his mistress, which caused he princess to become even sadder. She then sent her faithful servant to Giovanninu once more and told him to say: "The princess has fallen passionately in love with you and wants to ask you whether you will honor her by becoming her husband."

When Giovanninu heard this he answered, "If the princess wants to become my wife, I must see her carried through the city in a coffin

---

* Mi voi struditi pi l'amuri soi.

like a dead woman with priests and music until she is brought beneath my window."

When the princess heard this, she had herself placed into a coffin and carried through the entire city. The priests accompanied her with burning candles, and all the people ran after the procession. When she came beneath the window where Giovanninu was standing, he spit and cried out in a loud voice: "How can you let yourself be put to shame just because of a man? Now I've repaid you for everything that I had to suffer because of you!"

All at once the princess recognized him. She jumped out of the coffin, ran to him, and fell down at his feet.

"Giovanninu, my dear Giovanninu, forgive me! Oh, you've made me suffer very much!"

"And I suffered for you very much," answered Giovanninu. "That's why I wanted you to suffer because of me."

They embraced each other, and there was great joy in the entire land. For three days there were festivities, and then they were married. When the old king died, Giovanninu succeeded him. And so they lived happy and content, but we've been left without one cent.

83

THE BANISHED QUEEN AND
HER TWO ABANDONED CHILDREN

Once upon a time there was a woman who had three daughters. They were all very beautiful, but they were poor and had to earn their living by spinning. When the moon shone brightly in the evening, they would sit by their little window and spin. Across the way was the royal castle, and when the king went up and down the stairs, he always had to walk by the girls.*

One time the oldest daughter said, "If I could have the king as my husband, I would bake four loaves of bread and feed an entire regiment, and there would even be some bread left over."†

Then the second daughter said, "If I could have the king as my husband, I would fill an entire regiment with one glass of wine, and there would even be some wine left over."

Finally, the youngest daughter announced, "If I could have the king as my husband, I would bear him two children, a boy with a gold apple in his hand, and a girl with a gold star on her forehead."

They repeated these words each time the king came by, and one time the king heard it and ordered the three sisters to appear before him up in his castle.

---

* There is another variant where this story takes place during the times when kings listened at the doors of their subjects to discover what they were saying, and the king had listened at the door of these girls.

† In the variant this maiden declares that she would provide garments for an entire army with one piece of cloth, and there would be some cloth left over.

"Who are you?" he asked them. "And what are you doing at your window each evening as I come by?"

They answered, "We're poor girls and have to earn our living by spinning. So we sit at our little window each evening and spin. In order to pass the time away, we chat with one another."

"What did you say last evening as I went by?" he asked the oldest.

"Your majesty," she responded, "I said that if I could have the king as my husband, I would bake four loaves of bread and feed an entire regiment, and there would even be some bread left over."

Then the king asked the second sister, "What did you say?"

"Your majesty," she responded, "I said that if I got the king as my husband, I would fill an entire regiment with one glass of wine, and there would even be some wine left over."

At last he asked the youngest sister, "What did you say?"

She was ashamed and did not want to answer. However, she finally had to tell him: "Your majesty, I said that if I got the king as my husband, I would bear him two children, a boy with a gold apple in his hand and a girl with a gold star on her forehead."

After the king heard all this, he said, "You will be my bride."

He ordered beautiful clothes to be made for her, and she became his wife. The two sisters also moved into the castle and lived there in joy and splendor.

Now, after some months had passed, a war broke out and the king had to go off to the battlefield. He called the two sisters to him and said, "I shall expect you to look after my wife while I am gone. When it's time for her to give birth, take good care of her."

But the two sisters were jealous of the youngest sister and her good fortune. When the young queen was about to give birth, they pretended to take care of her, and when their sister really gave birth to two children, a boy with a gold apple in his hand, and a girl with a gold star on her forehead, they placed them in a crate and threw it into the water. In their place the sisters put two puppies next to the young queen.

When the king returned home from the war and wanted to see his children, the sisters said to him, "The young queen has given birth to two puppies."

The king became angry and ordered his servants to build a shed in the courtyard at the foot of the stairs. The queen was to live in it day and night with bread and water. Next to the shed stood a sentinel who forced anyone who went up or down the stairs to spit into the face of the queen.

In the meantime the crate with the poor children was dragged from the water by an old fisherman. When he opened it and saw the two beautiful children, he brought them to his house, and his wife suckled them. The children remained there and became more beautiful and larger as each year passed. After they became older, however, they had an argument with the sons of the fisherman, who had called them bastards. That was when they learned they were not the children of the old couple, and so they said, "Give us your blessing. We want to go and search for our parents."

They wandered into the world, and after a while they met a friendly old man who asked them, "Where are you traveling, and why are you so alone?"

They told him how they had left their home to seek their parents. Then the old man gave them a magic wand and said, "Whatever kind of treasures you wish, this wand will help you obtain them."

They continued wandering until they came to the city ruled by their father and wished for a magnificent house across from the royal castle. No sooner had they made their wish than a splendid palace stood before them. The next morning the two jealous sisters went to the window and could not stop gazing in astonishment at the beautiful palace that had arisen over night. While they were talking about it, they saw the king's two children, and the aunts immediately recognized them by the gold star and apple. They were terrified and called to a poor woman, to whom they used to give alms every Friday, and said to her: "Go over to that house. Some rich people are living there. They will certainly give you something. When the young maiden gives you something, you're to say to her, 'noble lady, you are beautiful, but your brother is more handsome than you are beautiful. If you get some of the dancing water, that will change.'"

Indeed, the terrible aunts thought, the brother will set out to get the dancing water for her, and he will die when he tries to do it. Then we'll also get rid of her in no time. So the poor woman went into the palace and said to the chambermaid, "Tell your mistress that a poor beggar woman is here and is asking for alms."

The maiden herself came, and the poor woman said, "Noble lady, you are beautiful, but your brother is more handsome than you are beautiful. If you get some of the dancing water, that will change."

When the maiden heard this, she felt such a longing for the dancing water that she became very melancholy, and when her brother came home, she told him what the beggar woman had said and asked him to fetch the dancing water for her.

"But dear sister," her brother responded, "you don't know what dangers are involved here. I'll gladly go to fetch it for you, but you'll see, I won't return."

"Oh, I'm sure you'll return," his sister said, and because he loved her so much, he could not refuse her request and prepared himself for the journey. Then he gave her a ring and said, "As long as this ring remains clear and white, I'll return. But if the ring becomes misty, that will be a sign that I cannot return."

Upon saying this he embraced his sister, mounted his most splendid steed, and set out on his way. He had to travel for many days until he came to a dense forest. When it became evening, he could not find his way out. He wandered about and thought, "By morning the wild animals will have eaten me." Suddenly he saw a light in the distance, and as he approached it he saw a small hut. He knocked on the door, and an old hermit opened it.

"Oh, my son," the old man said, "what are you doing in this wild place so alone?"

"Father," the young man answered him, "I've been searching for the dancing water."

"Oh, my son," the old man said, "renounce your foolish quest. There have been many princes, kings, and dukes who have passed by here in search of the dancing water, and none has ever returned."

The young man, however, did not let himself be scared off, for he loved his sister very much.

"Well, if you insist on going ahead," the hermit said, "then go with God. To be sure I can't help you, but my older brother lives about a day's journey farther into the woods. You should seek him out. Perhaps he can advise you what to do."

The next morning the young man continued his travels until it was late at night. He saw a light in the distance and it was the little hut inhabited by the second hermit. The young man knocked on the door, and the hermit opened and asked him what he wanted. When he heard that the young man had set out in search of the dancing water, he tried to warn him even more seriously than his brother had done. But the young man would not abandon his quest, and so the hermit said, "I can't give you any advice, but my oldest brother lives a day's journey farther in the forest, and perhaps he'll be able to help you."

The next morning the young man rode off again, and toward evening he came to the third hermit, who was ancient.

"My son," the hermit asked, "what are you doing in this miserable place?"

When he heard why the young man had set out on his travels, he became horrified and said, "My son, let me warn you. Don't do this. So many have met their ruin in pursuit of the dancing water. How can you possibly succeed?"

Since the young man would not be deterred, the hermit said, "All right, if you insist, may God bless you. Do you see the mountain over there? You must first climb it. But since it is inhabited by wild animals, you must fill your knapsack with meat and throw it to them so they will let you pass. On top of the mountain there is a magnificent castle. Go inside and through all the rooms. Be careful not to touch any of the glorious treasures that you will see there. In the last room there are numerous cups filled with water. Do not touch any of them until you see the water move. Then grab one of the cups and flee as fast as you can."

The old man now gave him his blessing and let him depart.

Meanwhile, the young man bought some oxen, which he had slaughtered and chopped into pieces. He filled his knapsack with the meat and headed for the mountain. When he began to climb the mountain, wild animals sprung up from all sides, but he threw large pieces of meat to them, and they allowed him to pass. Thanks to his luck, he reached the peak of the mountain, got off his horse, and entered the castle, where he saw so much glistening treasure and wealth that he was practically blinded by it all. But he thought about the hermit's warning and did not touch a thing. Indeed, he did not even turn around but strode through all the rooms until he came to the chamber where he found the cups with the dancing water. He waited for the water to gush, and then he grabbed a cup and fled as fast as he could. Along his way home, he stopped to visit the hermits who were happy to see him again so healthy, and finally he returned to his sister, who was glad that he had returned. After he gave her the cup, he placed it in the window and enjoyed watching the gushing water.

When the two aunts saw that their nephew had returned safe and sound, they were terribly frightened and called the beggar woman again.

"When you go over to the house next Friday, we want you to tell the young lady, 'your brother is handsome, but you are now much more beautiful. If you fetch the talking bird, that will change.'"

The woman went to the maiden and did what the sisters had ordered her to do. When the young man came home, he found his sister so sad again that he asked whether he could do something for her that she would like.

"Oh, dear brother," she answered, "you fetched the dancing water for me. Now you must also go and fetch the talking bird!"

"Dear sister," he said, "I'll gladly do this for you, but this time you won't see me again. That's for sure."

But the sister was convinced that he would return, so the young man mounted his horse again and rode until he came to the first hermit.

"Father," he said, "you helped me find the dancing water. Now please help me fetch the talking bird."

"My son," the hermit replied, "you succeeded the first time, but be careful. You will not succeed the second time."

The young man refused to heed his warning and moved on to the second hermit, and then the third, who said to him: "My son, if you insist on trying your luck no matter what, then go with God. Make sure that you have enough meat to throw to the wild animals. When you are in the castle, go through all the rooms, but make sure that you don't touch anything. When you reach the chamber with a great number of birds, wait until the birds begin to speak. Then grab one of them and flee as fast as you can. But make sure that you don't touch the bird unless it speaks."

The young man went up the mountain loaded with meat and was fortunate to be able to pass through the wild animals. He dismounted in front of the castle and went through the rooms. There were even more beautiful things, than before, but he went by them without touching them. When he entered the chamber with the birds, however, he forgot the hermit's warning and grabbed a bird that was not speaking. All of a sudden he was turned into stone, and his horse as well.

Meanwhile, his sister looked at his ring every day and was happy that it remained so clear and bright. Yet one morning, the ring was totally misty. She began to weep and said, "I'm going to set out to save my brother." So she wandered forth for many days until she reached the first hermit in the forest. She knocked on his door, and the old man opened it. When he saw a woman standing there, he said, "Oh my daughter, what are you doing in this wilderness so alone?"

"Father," she answered, "I've set out in search of my brother."

"Yes, daughter," the wise man spoke. "We warned your brother enough times, but he did not want to listen to us."

Then he directed her to the second hermit, and he sent her to the third.

"Oh, daughter," the third hermit said to her. "How can you save your brother? You're just a weak maiden. Do you know the dangers awaiting you?"

She would not let herself be dissuaded, and the wise man told her how to protect herself against the wild animals and continued: "When you enter the castle, go through all the rooms but make sure that you don't touch anything. There is a magnificent bed in the innermost room. The sorceress will be sleeping on it. Beneath the bed are her diamond slippers. Be careful not to touch them. Instead, approach the bed quietly without looking around, stick your hand beneath the pillow without waking the sorceress, and pull out the gold can which is hidden there. Take the salve that is in the can and rub your brother with it. Once you do this, he will come back to life."

The maiden set out on her way, loaded with meat, and she bravely passed through the wild animals while throwing them the meat. Then she strode through the rooms without touching anything. When she reached the room where the sorceress was sleeping, she approached the bed quietly, stuck her hand cautiously beneath the pillow, and pulled out the gold can. Immediately thereafter she rushed through the rooms without making a sound, rubbed her brother with the salve as well as all the other princes and brave men who had been turned to stone, and they were all brought back to life. After this she went down the stairs and rubbed the horses, and once all the men were gathered, they mounted their horses and fled as fast as they could. The brother made sure, however, to take the talking bird with him. When they had all descended the mountain, the sorceress awoke and screamed: "I've been betrayed! I've been betrayed!" But her power was gone, and she could no longer harm anyone. The sister and brother rode to the three hermits and thanked them for their help. Then they returned to their beautiful house and placed the bird next to the cup in the window.

One day the king noticed the wonderful objects and invited the sister and brother to a meal in his castle. When they were climbing the stairs, they passed their mother and lowered their eyes. Although the sentinel told them that the king had ordered everyone to spit into the face of the woman, they did not do it. After the meal, the king said, "You have a cup with dancing water and a talking bird in your window. Might I be able to see them one time?"

The sister and brother sent a servant to their house to fetch the bird and cup and set them on the table. All of a sudden the bird began to speak: "Dear water, I know a beautiful story. Should I tell it to you?"

"Please do," answered the water.

Then the bird told the entire history of the sister and brother, how they had been thrown into the water, and what had happened to them afterward. When the two aunts heard this, they became pale, for the king recognized his children, and there was great joy in the castle. Now his poor wife, the queen, was bathed and given beautiful clothes. Meanwhile the king ordered the two evil sisters be put in a barrel with boiling oil. The barrel was then tied to the tail of a horse that was driven through the entire city.

84

THE PIOUS CHILD

Once upon a time there was a pious God-fearing peasant, who found a poor little child in a field.

"Oh, you innocent little creature!" he cried. "What kind of a vile mother would abandon you to this fate? I'm going to raise you as my own."

So he picked up the child and began caring for him, and after that day, things began to go very well for him. His fruit trees flourished, the grain harvest and wine were good, and the peasant led a comfortable life. The child grew and became a pious young boy, but he was naive and didn't know anything about our savior and the saints. One time, while he was playing with clay, he formed big and small balls and made them into a rosary. The beads were just right. Nothing was missing, not even a gloria patri. When the peasant saw this, he was astonished and decided to take the boy to the city of Catania.

"Do you want to come with me?" he asked one morning. "I'm riding to Catania."

"Whatever you want, master," he replied and went with the peasant to the city.

When they approached the dome, the peasant said, "Why don't you go into the church for a while until I finish my business."

The boy went into the church and saw all the gold and silk robes, the embroidered covers for the altar, and the numerous flowers and candles, and he was very amazed because he had never seen anything like it. Finally he came to the altar where the crucifix was standing, knelt down on the steps to the altar, and spoke to the crucifix: "Little brother, why have you been nailed to this wood? Did you do something bad?"

The crucifix nodded his head.

"Oh, poor little brother, you should never do that again because now you know how much you must suffer for it."

And the Lord nodded his head once more.

This conversation went on for a long time, and he talked with the crucifix until mass was completed and the sacristan wanted to close the church door. When he caught sight of the little peasant boy, he asked him to get up and leave the church.

"No," the boy answered. "I'm staying here. Otherwise, this poor man will be completely alone. First you nailed him to this wood, and now you've abandoned him to his fate. Isn't it true, little brother, you'd like me to stay with you?"

And the Lord nodded his head. When the sacristan heard and saw this, he became frightened and ran and told the priest everything he had just witnessed.

"He must certainly be a holy soul," the priest remarked. "Let the boy stay there and take him a plate of macaroni and some wine."

When the sacristan took the macaroni and wine to the boy he said, "Set it down. I'll eat soon." Then he turned to the crucifix and said, "Little brother, you must be hungry. Who knows how long it's been since you've had something to eat. Have a little macaroni."

Then the boy climbed onto the altar and gave the Lord some macaroni, and the Lord ate it. Then the boy said, "Little brother, you must also be thirsty. Drink a little of my wine," and he gave the Lord some wine to drink, and the Lord drank. Soon after he had shared all his food and wine with the Lord, the boy fell down dead, and his soul flew to heaven and praised God.

The priest had concealed himself behind the altar, and when he saw the transfigured body of the boy, he spread the news throughout the city that there was a saint in the dome, and he had the boy placed in a gold coffin. The people came and saw the boy's transfigured body and prayed to him. When the peasant came, he recognized the little boy he had raised, and he thanked the Lord for having brought the boy to him. Then he went home, and everything he undertook was so successful that he became a rich man. To be sure, he used the money to do many good things for the poor, and he led a holy life until he died and went to Paradise.

May our lives be just like his.

85

KATERINA'S FATE

Once upon a time there was a merchant who had such an enormous treasure that he was richer than any king in the world. In the grand hall where he granted audiences, there were three marvelous chairs. One was made of silver, the second of gold, the third of diamonds. Aside from his wealth, this merchant had a daughter, his only child, named Katerina, and she was more beautiful than the sun.

One day as Katerina sat in her room, the door suddenly sprang open by itself, and a beautiful tall lady entered. She held a wheel in her hands.

"Katerina," she said, "when would you prefer to enjoy your life, during your youth or during your old age?"

Katerina looked at her in astonishment and could not compose herself. The beautiful lady asked once more: "When would you prefer to enjoy your life, during your youth or during your old age?"

Now Katerina thought, "If I say in my youth, then I'll have to suffer in my old age. Therefore, I'd prefer to enjoy my life during my old age, and I'll place myself in God's hands during my youth." So she answered, "During my old age!"

"Let it be as you wish," the beautiful lady said, spun her wheel one time, and disappeared. This tall, beautiful lady was none other than Katerina's Fate.*

---

* Sorte.

A few days later her father suddenly received news that several of his ships had sunk in a storm. A few more days passed, and he learned that more of his ships had capsized. To make a long story short, within a month he lost his entire fortune and had to sell everything that he had. Yet even this money was soon lost and he finally was completely poor and miserable. Eventually he became sick from all the sorrow and died.

As a result, Katerina was completely alone in the world without a cent to her name, and without anyone who might take care of her. So she thought, "I'll go to another city and look for some employment." Soon she set out and wandered until she came to another city. As she walked through the streets, she saw a lady standing at a window who asked her, "Where are you going so alone, beautiful maiden?"

"Oh, noble lady, I'm a poor maiden and would like to find a position so that I can earn a living. Could you use me?"

The lady hired her as her servant, and Katerina was very loyal to her. After some days had passed, the woman said to Katerina one evening, "I must go out tonight and shall lock the door."

"Good," Katerina said, and when her mistress was gone, she took her work, sat down, and began sewing. Suddenly the door flew open and her Fate entered.

"So!" she cried. "Here you are sitting, Katerina, and you think I should leave you in peace!?"

Upon saying these words Fate ran to all the closets, took out all the clothes and linen that belonged to Katerina's mistress, and ripped them to shreds.

"Woe is me!" Katerina thought. "When my mistress returns and finds everything in this condition, she'll certainly kill me."

In her fear she ran through the door and fled, but her Fate gathered together all the torn and destroyed things, made them whole again, and restored everything to its proper place. When the mistress returned home, she called for Katerina, but the girl was nowhere to be found.

"Did she steal anything from me?" the woman thought, but when she checked, there was nothing missing. She was very surprised, but Katerina did not return. Rather the girl continued to travel until she came to another city. As she went through the streets, another lady was standing at a window, and she asked Katerina, "Where are you going so alone, pretty girl?"

"Oh, noble lady, I'm a poor woman, and I'm looking for some employment to earn my living. Could you use me?"

The woman did indeed employ her, and Katerina served her and thought she would finally have some peace. However it lasted only a few days until, one evening while her mistress was out, her Fate reappeared and addressed her with some harsh words: "So, here you sit! Did you really think you could escape me?"

As she said this, her Fate ripped and destroyed everything in sight so that poor Katerina fled, fearing for her life.

To make a long story short, Katerina led this horrible existence for the next seven years. She ran from one city to the next and tried to find a job in each place. But, after a few days her Fate would appear, tear and destroy the things that belonged to her mistress, and the poor maiden had to flee. When she left the house, however, her Fate would restore things to their previous order.

After seven years her Fate finally seemed to become tired of persecuting the unfortunate Katerina. One day Katerina came to a city and saw a lady standing at a window who asked her: "Where are you going so alone, you beautiful maiden!"

"Oh, noble lady, I'm a poor maiden and am looking for some employment to earn a living. Could you use me?"

"I'd very much like to employ you," the woman answered, but you must do something for me every day, and I don't know whether you have the strength to do it."

"Tell me what it is," Katerina said, "and I'll do it if I can."

"Do you see that big mountain over there?" the lady said. "Well, every morning you must carry a large board with freshly baked bread to the top of it, and you must cry out in a loud voice: 'Oh Fate of my mistress! Oh Fate of my mistress! Oh Fate of my mistress!' three times. Then my Fate will appear and take the bread."

"I'll gladly do this," Katerina said, and the lady hired her.

Now Katerina worked many years for this woman, and every morning she took the tray with the freshly baked bread to the top of the mountain, and after she cried out, "Oh, Fate of my mistress" three times, a beautiful, tall woman appeared and took the bread. However, Katerina often wept when she thought about how she had been so rich and was now working as a poor maid.

One day her mistress said to her, "Katerina, why do you weep so much?"

Then Katerina told her how badly things had gone for her, and her mistress said, "Do you know what, Katerina? Tomorrow, when you take the bread to the top of the mountain, ask my Fate if it could possibly convince your Fate to leave you in peace. Perhaps this will help."

This advice pleased poor Katerina. The next morning, when she took the bread to the Fate of her mistress, she told the beautiful lady about her misery and said, "Oh, Fate of my mistress, please ask my Fate not to persecute me anymore."

"Oh, you poor girl," the Fate replied. "Your Fate is wrapped in seven covers. Therefore, she can't even hear you. When you come tomorrow, I shall lead you to her."

After Katerina returned home, the Fate of her mistress went to the girl's Fate and said, "Dear sister, why don't you stop making poor Katerina suffer so much? Let her enjoy some happy days again."

"Bring her to me tomorrow," Katerina's Fate replied. "I want to give her something that should help her out of her misery."

The next morning, when Katerina took the bread to the top of the mountain, the Fate of her mistress led her to her own Fate, who was wrapped in seven covers. Her Fate gave her a skein of silk and said, "Keep it in a safe place. It will be of use to you."

Then Katerina went home and told her mistress, "My Fate gave me a skein of silk as a gift. What should I do with it? It's not worth much money."

"Well," her mistress said, "I would keep it in a safe place. It might do you some good."

After some time had passed, it so happened that the young king was to marry and wanted to have some royal garments made for himself. When the tailor was to make a beautiful suit, he could not find silk of the same color. The king sent out messengers throughout the realm who spread the word that whoever had a certain kind of silk was to bring it to the court and would be well paid for it.

"Katerina," her mistress said, "your skein of silk is this color. Take it to the king so that he will give you a beautiful gift."

So Katerina put on her best clothes and went to the court, and when she came before the king, she was so beautiful that the king could not take his eyes off her.

"Your majesty," Katerina said, "I've brought you a skein of silk of the color that you could not find."

"Do you know what, your majesty," one of his ministers cried out, "let us give the maiden the weight of the silk in gold."

The king agreed, and a scale was brought. The silk was placed on one side, and on the other, gold. Now just think what happened. No matter how many pieces of gold the king placed on the scale, the silk was always heavier. The king ordered a larger scale to be brought, and all his treasures were placed on one side, but the silk still weighed more.

Finally, the king took his gold crown from his head and placed it on top of all the other treasures, and just look: now the side with the gold came down and weighed just as much as the silk.

"Where did you get this silk?" the king asked.

"Your majesty," Katerina responded, "I received it from my mistress as a gift."

"No, that's not possible," the king said, "and if you don't tell me the truth, I'll have your head chopped off."

Then Katerina told everything that had happened to her since the time she had been a rich girl. Meanwhile there was a wise woman who was living at the court, and she said, "Katerina, you have suffered too long. You will now see happier times, and because it was only after the gold crown brought about a balance on the scale, this is a sign that you will become a queen."

"If she is to become a queen," the king declared, "then I shall be the one who makes her one, for Katerina and no one else shall become my wife."

And this is indeed what happened. The king informed his bride that he did not want to marry her anymore, and he married the beautiful Katerina instead. So, after Katerina had suffered so much in her youth, she enjoyed bliss and happiness in her old age, and she remained happy and content, but we still can't pay the rent.

86

GODFATHER DEATH

Once upon a time there was a man who had just one son. In those times many people did not have their children baptized while they were young. Rather, they waited until they were somewhat older. So, when this child reached the age of seven, he still had not been baptized.

When our dear Lord saw this from heaven, he was annoyed and called Saint John to him and said, "Listen to me, Saint John, I want you to go to this village and tell this man that I want to know why he hasn't had his son baptized yet."

So Saint John went to the earth and knocked on the door of this man's house.

"Who's there?" the man asked.

"It's me, Saint John,"

"What do you want from me?" the man asked.

"Our dear Lord has sent me," the saint said, "and he wants to know why you haven't had your son baptized yet."

"Well, it's because I haven't found a good godfather," the man replied.

"If that's the case," Saint John said, "I'll be glad to be your child's godfather."

"I want to thank you," the man said, "but this cannot be. If you become my child's godfather, then you'll have only one wish, and that would be to take him to Paradise as soon as possible, and I don't want that."

So Saint John had to return to heaven without accomplishing anything.

Next, the dear Lord sent Saint Peter to the earth to warn the man, but things did not turn out any better for him. The man gave Saint Peter the same answers as he gave to Saint John and did not want Saint Peter as the godfather.

Then the dear Lord thought, "What does he have in mind? He certainly wants his son to have immortality. Well, I can only send Death to him now."

So the dear Lord sent Death to the man to ask him why he had not had his son baptized. When Death arrived on earth, he knocked on the man's door.

"Who's there?" asked the man.

"Our dear Lord has sent me," Death answered, "to ask you why your child has not been baptized yet."

"Tell the dear Lord," he replied, "that I haven't found the right godfather."

"Don't you want me to be the godfather?"* Death asked.

"Who are you?"

"I am Death."

"Yes," the man declared. "I'd very much like you to be the godfather of my child, and we can let him be baptized right away."

Soon thereafter the child was baptized. Then after several months had passed, Death reappeared to the man, who gave him a friendly reception and wanted to offer him all kinds of good food. But Death said, "Don't go to so much trouble. I've only come to fetch you."

"What?" the man exclaimed. "I especially chose you so that you would protect me, my wife, and my son."

"That's not possible," Death answered. "The scythe cuts all the grass that it finds on its way. I can't protect you."

Then Death took the man into a dark cellar in which there were a lot of lamps burning on the walls.

"You see the lamps?" he asked. "They are the lamps of life. Each person has this kind of lamp, and when it goes out, he must die."

"Which is my light?" the man asked.

Then Death showed him a little lamp in which there was very little oil left, and when it ran out, the man fell down dead.

Did Death also have the son die? Of course. Death cannot protect anyone. When the son's time came, he too had to die.

---

* This should actually be godmother because death is a female in Sicily.

87

BEAUTIFUL ANNA

Once there were three sisters who were all very beautiful, but the youngest was the most beautiful among them, and she was called Anna. The three girls had neither father nor mother, and they made a living through their handicraft. The first spun and made reels of yarn. The second did the weaving, and the youngest sewed shirts and other clothes.

One day, as they were sitting and working in front of the door to their house, the prince came riding by on his way to the hunt. When he saw the three beautiful girls, he cried out, "What a beauty she is, the maiden who's spinning! What a beauty she is, the maiden who's weaving! But the maiden who's sewing will be the end of me!"*

The two older sisters became jealous when they heard that the prince preferred their sister to them, and the eldest said, "Tomorrow I shall do the sewing, and Anna will spin."

When the prince came by again the next morning, however, he said, "What a beauty she is, the maiden who's sewing! What a beauty she is, the maiden who's weaving! But the maiden who's spinning will be the end of me!"

The sisters became even more jealous, and on the third morning Anna had to weave. But the prince said, "What a beauty she is, the

---

* Ch'è bedda, chidda chi 'ncanna, ch'è bedda chidda chi tessi, chidda chi cusi muriri mi fa.

maiden who's sewing! What a beauty she is, the maiden who's spinning! But the maiden who's weaving will be the end of me!"

As a result of all this the sisters could not stand Anna any longer and began to plan how they might cause her ruin. Eventually they decided to lead her to a wild, desolate region where they would leave her so that she would not be able to find her way home. So the oldest sister said to Anna, "Come with me, Anna. We've got some dirty clothes, and we'll have to wash them in a little brook."

Anna agreed to follow her, and so the two of them wandered off. When they came to a wild desolate spot, the sister said, "Oh Anna, I've forgotten to bring some soap with me. Wait for me here a while, and I'll go fetch it."

So beautiful Anna sat down and waited for her sister. She waited and waited, but nobody came. Then she began to shed bitter tears and thought, "She left me here alone intentionally so that I would die. Well, I won't return to my sisters. Instead, I'm going to set out and seek my fortune in the wide world."*

So she set out and wandered until she finally came to a large beautiful house. She knocked on the door and a woman opened and asked her what she wanted.

"Oh, my good woman," the beautiful Anna asked, "please let me rest here tonight. I'm a poor maiden and am completely alone in the world."

"Oh, you poor child," the woman cried. "How did you manage to wind up here? If my husband finds you, he'll eat you. However, I feel sorry for you and shall hide you. Perhaps I'll be able to soften him up."

So the woman hid the beautiful Anna, and soon her husband came home and muttered, "I smell some human flesh! I smell some human flesh!"

"Oh, what are you talking about?" his wife responded. "You're always smelling human flesh. That's what comes from your having already eaten so many humans. Just think, today a maiden came by here, and she was more beautiful than the sun. I believe that if you had seen her, you would have let her live."

As she now saw that she had softened her husband, she brought beautiful Anna from her hiding place, and she was so beautiful that the ogre immediately became very fond of her and did not want to eat her.

---

* Pri circari a me vintura.

"Stay with us, beautiful maiden," he said, "and you will have a good life."

So beautiful Anna stayed with the ogre and his wife and was just like their own child.

When some time had passed, the ogre died and soon after his wife as well. The beautiful Anna remained alone in the large house, and all its treasures belonged to her. One day when she was standing on the balcony, her eldest sister happened to pass by and recognized Anna and asked her how she was.

"I'm doing fine," Anna answered, but she did not invite her sister to come up.

"If I had known that I was going to meet you here, I would have brought you a present," the sister said.

"Thanks," Anna answered. "I don't need anything, nor do I want presents from anyone."

Her eldest sister continued on her way home and said to the second sister, "Just think, I saw our sister Anna, and she's become even more beautiful than she was. She's wearing elegant clothes and lives in a large house."

The hearts of both the sisters became filled with jealousy, and they began thinking how they might be able to bring about Anna's ruin. So they took some grapes* and poisoned them. The next day the eldest sister made her way to the beautiful Anna's house, who was sitting and working on the terrace. When her sister saw her, she went up and called to her in a friendly way: "Oh, dear little sister, how nice it is to see you again. And how beautiful you've become! Look, I've brought you some beautiful grapes. Do me a favor and eat them."

"I thank you," Anna replied. "You see that my garden is full of grapes. I don't need yours."

The sister kept insisting until Anna took a grape and put it into her mouth. As soon as she did, she fell down, and the grape stuck in her throat. Her sister left her lying on the terrace and went home pleased with what she had done.

Now it just so happened one day that the prince went hunting and passed by this house. He saw a beautiful bird on the terrace and he shot it, and the bird fell onto the floor of the terrace. So the prince climbed the stairs and wandered through all the rooms, but there wasn't a human soul to be found. When he came to the terrace, an astonishingly beau-

---

* Un grappu ri curniola.

tiful maiden was lying there, and when he looked at her more closely, he saw beautiful Anna. Then he began to weep and kissed her and said, "How beautiful this little nose is! How beautiful this little mouth! But I'll die just by looking at her tender little neck."*

As he bent over and touched her throat, the grape sprung out of her mouth, and beautiful Anna opened her eyes and came to life. The prince was overjoyed and said, "You shall become my wife!"

But the prince had an evil mother who was living with him, and he could not bring the beautiful Anna to his castle. Instead, he left her in her house, and every day, when he went hunting, he came and visited her. After a year Anna gave birth to a son, and since he was as handsome as the sun, she named him Sunny. The next year she gave birth to a daughter as beautiful as the moon, and she called her Luna. The children grew fast and became even more beautiful, but their mother was not allowed to go to the royal castle. However, the prince came every day and visited her. Then one day he became sick—so sick that he had to remain in bed for many days and could not visit Anna. He cried out loud: "Oh my son, Sunny! Oh my daughter, Luna! What is my wife Anna doing so alone?"†

His mother overheard all this and called her son's faithful servant and said to him, "If you don't tell me right now what the prince is talking about, I'll have your head chopped off."

The servant confessed that Anna was the wife of the prince and Sunny and Luna were his children.

"Very well," the queen said. "Then go immediately to Donna Anna and tell her: 'Your husband has confessed everything to his mother, and she wishes to see her little grandchildren.' Then take the children, murder them, and bring their hearts and tongues to me as proof that you have carried out my command."

So the servant went sadly to beautiful Anna and told her that the prince had sent him to fetch his children, and she put on their very best clothes and gave them to the servant. He took them away, but even though he was supposed to murder them, he took pity on the innocent children. Indeed, he let them live and took them to his own mother. As for the queen, he brought her the hearts and tongues from two billy goats.

The next morning the queen sent the servant to Anna once more with orders to bring her to the castle. The beautiful Anna had three

---

* Ch'è beddu stu nasuzzu, ch'è bedda sta vucuzza, e stu codduzza muriri mi fa.

† Figghiu miu suli, figghia mia luna, comu fa Donn' Anna sula?

dresses adorned with little bells, one dress with silver bells, the second with gold, and the third with diamonds. She put on all three, one on top of the other, and went this way to the castle. There was an enormous fire burning in the courtyard, and on top of it was a kettle with boiling oil. Next to the fire stood the old queen, who ordered the servants to throw Anna into the boiling oil. When Anna heard this, she threw off all her three dresses, which began to ring with their little bells. The sound was so lovely and loud that the prince heard it in his room. He jumped out of bed and saw that the servants were about to grab hold of beautiful Anna and throw her into the boiling oil.

"Stop!" he yelled as he ran to free beautiful Anna from their hands. Then he ordered the evil queen to be thrown into the oil in place of Anna. As he now embraced her full of joy, Anna asked, "Where are my dear children? You summoned them to the castle yesterday?"

"I didn't order our children to be brought here," the prince replied. "It was certainly my evil mother who did this. Oh my children, my dear children!"

All at once the servant came, threw himself at the prince's feet, and confessed everything to him. Then he told the prince that the children were safe and sound with his mother. When the children were fetched, their parents embraced them full of joy. Afterward there were three days of celebrations, and the prince became king and beautiful Anna queen. They remained happy and content, but we still can't pay the rent.

88

THE DRAGON SLAYER

Once upon a time there was a brother and a sister. They had neither father nor mother and loved each other with all their hears. They were very poor and only had two goats, which the sister drove to the meadow every day. One day one of the goats escaped, and she had to run after it. She ran and ran until it became night, and she found herself in a desolate place and could no longer make her way back home. The goat kept running ahead of her, and when it came to a house, it stopped at the door and laid down on the threshold. The girl found the goat and thought, "It's pitch dark, and I can't find my way home. I might as well stay here until it becomes day."

When it began to dawn, she heard a powerful voice in the house that roared, "I smell human flesh!" and all at once a giant came out the door. He was so terrible to look at that the girl became frightened.

"What are you doing here?"

The girl told the giant how she had to run after the goat and had arrived at the house in the dark of the night.

"Good," said the giant. "Come into my house and serve me."

"Oh, no," answered the girl, "you'll certainly eat me."

"Don't worry," he answered. "if you serve me loyally, I won't harm you."

So the girl remained with the giant, served him well, and had a good life with him. Meanwhile, because her brother had not been able to find his little sister, he became sad and continued to miss her very much.

Now one day while he was moping about and looking after the one goat that had remained, the animal escaped. He ran after it over hill and valley until he came to an unknown place and could not find his way back home. The goat ran ahead of him, and when it came to a house, it stopped at the door and laid down. The boy thought, "It's so dark now that I won't be able to find my way back. I might as well remain here until it becomes day."

Now this was the house of the giant in which his sister was staying. The next morning she opened the door and saw a handsome boy lying there. When she took a closer look, she recognized her brother and embraced him with joy, but also with great fear, for she was scared that the giant might kill him.

"Dear brother," she said. "I must hide you, for the giant, my master, will soon wake up and might eat you."

So she hid him in the cellar. When the giant woke up, he roared, "I smell human flesh!"

"Oh, what are you saying?" she answered. "Nobody's here."

He continued to roar: "I tell you, I smell human flesh!"

Then she summoned her courage and said, "I must tell you that my brother's here. As you spared my life, so must you spare his."

The giant promised to do this as long as the brother worked for him as a servant. So now the sister and brother both lived with the giant, served him, and led a good life.

When they became older, they wanted to depart and be with human beings again, but the giant would not let them go. So one day the brother said to the sister, "I can't hold out any longer in his desolate spot. We can't stay here forever. Besides, we can never be sure that he won't do something to us. Who knows whether the giant won't decide one beautiful day to eat us. So try to find out from him how we can get rid of him. Then I'll kill him, and we can get away from here."

His sister agreed with his proposal, went to the giant, and said to him, "Do you want me to clean the lice from your head?"

The giant said "yes," and when they were together, she began to speak: "Why don't you tell me what one would have to do to get rid of you? Of course, I hope it will never happen."

"Well, my dear child," the giant answered, "there's only one way to kill me. Do you see all those rusty swords hanging in my room? The middle one is a magic sword. Whoever wields it can never be defeated, and if it is cleaned so that it shines, this sword can cut off my head. Whoever kills me will be a lucky man because he will find an ointment in my head. Any wound that is rubbed with this ointment will heal right away."

"Oh, stop now!" the maiden cried. "I don't want to hear these stories any longer. May you live a long life."

However, she secretly went to her brother and told him everything the giant had said. The brother waited a few days and began to clean all the swords in the giant's room so that they became bright and shiny.

"What are you doing there?" the giant asked.

"I'm cleaning your swords. Just look how rusty they are," the young man answered.

When he cleaned the magic sword, it glistened so brightly that he never saw anything like it before in his life. One evening when the giant slept, the young man crept into his room and cut off the giant's head with the magic sword. Then he collected the ointment in the giant's head and kept it in a little box. Afterward he and his sister dug a grave for the giant and put him inside. Finally, they took all the treasures that had been stored in the hut and moved to the nearest city, where they bought a pretty house and continued to enjoy living together.

One day, however, the brother said, "Dear sister, I can't stay with you any longer, for I want to see the world and try my luck."

She wept and did not want to let him depart, but he would not let himself be deterred from setting out into the world. He took some beautiful armor, fastened the magic sword onto his belt, and stuck the little box of ointment in a pocket. Then he mounted a beautiful steed and rode away.

He traveled for a good deal of time and finally came to a large beautiful city that was completely decked in black, and all the people wore black clothes. So he asked an innkeeper what all this meant.

"Oh," he answered, "the city is plagued by a dragon with seven heads. It lives on top of that mountain over there, and each year we have to bring him a virtuous virgin. Otherwise, he would devastate the entire city. This year the king's daughter lost the lottery, and today she must be led to the mountain. The king has proclaimed that any knight who kills the dragon can have his daughter for his wife, but nobody wants to try because the dragon is much too terrifying."

"I want to try my fortune," the young man thought. "After all, I have the magic sword."

So he mounted his horse again, fastened the magic sword, stuck the box with the ointment into a pocket, and rode toward the mountain. When he came near the dragon's cave, the monster crawled out because it had smelled human flesh. Then the young man pulled out his magic sword, fought with the dragon, and cut off some of the heads. But, the dragon wounded him on his leg, and also wounded the horse. The young man retreated a bit, took out the little box, and rubbed his wounds and the horse's wounds with the ointment. All at once the two of them were fresh and well again so that he could wield his sword and finally kill the dragon. Then he cut out the seven tongues from the seven heads, wrapped them in a scarf, and returned to the inn.

In the meantime the princess prepared herself for the difficult march to the mountain, and although she wept bitter tears, she finally had to bid farewell to her parents and begin climbing the mountain. One of her father's slaves accompanied her. When they came to the top of the mountain, they saw the dragon lying in his blood. The princess thanked God from the bottom of her heart that she did not have to die, but the slave thought he would make use of this situation. He placed his sword against her breast and said, "If you don't swear me that you'll tell your father I've killed the dragon, I'll take your life."

Struck by fear, she promised him what he wanted, and he took the seven heads that had been cut off as proof that he had killed he dragon. When the princess returned safe and sound from the mountain and said the slave had killed the dragon, there was great joy in the entire land, and the king said to the slave, "You have rescued my daughter and shall have her for your wife."

So a great celebration was arranged. Everyone in the country was happy, but the princess was sad, for she did not want to marry the slave. When the true conqueror of the dragon heard that the slave was to marry the princess, he quickly had a splendid garment made for himself, took the seven tongues in his pocket, went to the castle, and had himself announced to the king.

"Your majesty," he said. "I've heard that a slave has performed a heroic deed and has killed the dragon. Please tell me how everything happened."

"My slave accompanied my daughter to the top of the mountain," the king responded. "Fortunately he had the strength to defeat the dragon and to cut off its seven heads. As proof he brought the seven heads with him."

"May I see the seven heads just once?" the young man asked.

So the king gave the order to fetch the seven heads of the dragon and to show them to the unknown young man.

"Yes, they are certainly powerful heads," the young man said. "I wonder how large the tongues are?"

Upon saying this, he opened the jaws of each one of the heads, but there were no tongues inside. The king and his ministers were very astonished and said, "How's that possible? Did the monster not have any tongues?"

All at once the youth pulled his scarf out with the seven tongues and placed a tongue in each one of the jaws of the dragon's heads, and what do you know, they fit perfectly.

"Isn't it true, your majesty," he said, "that the conqueror of the dragon must be the one who cut out the tongues before the heads were brought to you? I am the one who fought the dragon and defeated him. The slave is a miserable liar."

The king summoned his daughter and asked her once more whether the slave really had killed the dragon. She fell on her knees and said, "Oh no, dear father, he didn't do it. Instead he threatened to kill me if I told you the truth."

The king became very happy and said, "Look, this handsome young man is your rescuer, and he is the one whom you shall have for your husband."

And that's what happened. The deceitful slave was led to the gallows and hung. The unknown youth married the beautiful princess and had his sister join them. Then they all lived happy and content, and we still can't pay the rent.

89

SAINT JAMES OF GALICIA

Once upon a time there was a king and queen who did not have any children and would have liked to have a son or a daughter. At one time the queen turned to Saint James of Galicia* and said, "Oh Saint James, if you will grant me a son, I swear to you that he will make a pilgrimage to you when he becomes eighteen years old."

Soon thereafter the queen became pregnant through God's grace and through the saint, and when her time arrived, she gave birth to a baby who was so beautiful it was as if God had made him. The boy grew rapidly from one day to the next and became bigger and more handsome. When he was twelve years old, the king died, and the queen remained alone with her son whom she loved like her own eyes. Many years passed, and soon the prince was to turn eighteen, but when the queen thought that she would have to separate from him very soon and send him by himself on the pilgrimage, she became very sad and wept the entire day.

One day the prince asked her, "Mother, why do you sob the entire day?"

"It's nothing, my son," she answered. "I only have some worries."

---

* In Sicilian the name San Japicu is used. It is a very old form for Saint James. Compare *La venutadi lu re Japicu a Cantania* of 1287 in the book *Cronache Ciciliane*, ed. V. di Giovani (Bologna, 1865), p. 165.

"What are you worried about?" he responded. "Are you concerned that your estates in Chiana* are not doing well? Let me go there so I can see everything and report back to you."

The queen agreed, and the prince set out on the road to the estates that belonged to his mother in Chiana. He found that everything was in the best condition and returned to his mother.

"Dear mother," he said, "be happy and forget your worries. Everything is in order on your estates. The animals are flourishing, the fields have been plowed, and the wheat will soon be ripe."

"Good, my son," she replied, but she did not become happy, and the next day she began to sob and weep again. So the prince said to her, "Mother, if you don't tell me why you are so troubled, I'm going to set out and wander throughout the world."

"Oh, my dear son," she answered, "I'm troubled because you must separate from me. Before you were born, I yearned so much to have a child that I promised Saint James of Galicia that if he granted me a son, I would send you on a pilgrimage to him when you turned eighteen. This is why I am troubled. You will have to wander off alone and spend many years away from me. You see, it will take a whole year just to journey to the saint."

"If that's all it is, dear mother," the son said, "don't be so worried. Only the dead don't return. If I stay alive, I'll soon come back to you."

So he consoled his mother, and when he turned eighteen, he took his leave from the queen and said, "Farewell, dear mother, and God willing, we shall see each other again."

The queen wept bitterly and embraced him with many tears. Then she gave him three apples and said, "My son, take these three apples, and pay attention to my words. You are not to take this long journey all by yourself. If another young man joins you and wants to travel with you, take him into a tavern and invite him to eat with you. After the meal you are to cut an apple in two parts, one small and one large. Ask the young man to take one of the pieces. If he takes the larger half, you are to separate from him because he won't be a true friend. If he takes the smaller piece, regard him as your brother and share everything you have with him."

Upon saying these words, she embraced her son again and blessed him, and the prince wandered off. He traveled for quite a long time without meeting anyone, but one day he saw a young man who came

---

* This is Piana, the plain of Catania.

along his way. This fellow stopped and asked him, "Where are you going, handsome lad?"

"I'm taking a pilgrimage to Saint James of Galicia. When my mother was younger and could not have any children, she swore to him that if he would grant her a son, this son would take a pilgrimage to the saint when he turned eighteen. So the saint granted her a son, namely me, and because I'm now eighteen, I'm making the pilgrimage to Lizia."

"I've got to go there too," the other fellow said. "My mother had exactly the same experience as yours. So if we both must make the same journey, we might as well travel together."

So they continued their trip together, but the prince was suspicious of his companion and thought, "I had better make the test with the apple."

At one point they came to a tavern, and the prince said, ""I'm hungry. Let's get something to eat here."

The other agreed, and they went inside and ate together. After they had eaten, the prince took out an apple, cut in two uneven parts, and asked his companion to choose one of them. When he took the larger piece, the prince thought, "You're not a true friend," and in order to separate from him, he pretended to be sick and had to stay in a bed there. Then the other fellow said, "I can't wait for you because I have a long trip ahead of me. So I bid you farewell."

"Farewell," replied the prince, and he was happy to get rid of him.

Later, when the prince continued his journey, he thought, "Oh, if only God would lead a true friend to me so that I would not have to travel alone!"

Soon afterward another young man joined him and asked, "Where are you traveling to, handsome lad?"

So the prince told him how his mother had taken an oath to send him on a pilgrimage to Saint James of Galicia, and that he was making this journey."

"I must also travel there," the young man said. "My mother took the very same oath."

"Then we can journey there together!" the prince exclaimed, and they continued their trip together.

When they rode up to the next tavern, the prince said, "I'm hungry. Lets stop here and get something to eat."

So they entered and ate with one another, and after the meal the prince cut the second apple into two uneven pieces and handed them to his companion, who took the larger piece. "You're not a true friend," thought the prince, and once again, in order to separate from his companion, he pretended to be sick and let the other continue the journey alone. Later, however, he set out again with a sad heart and thought, "Oh God, let me find a true friend who will be like a friend to me on this journey." While he was praying to God, he suddenly saw a young man coming his way. He was such a handsome fellow and looked so friendly that he took a liking to him right away and thought, "If only this were the true friend!"

The young man joined him and asked, "Where are you traveling to, handsome lad?"

So the prince told him about the oath his mother made and why he had to make this holy pilgrimage.

"I must also go there," the young man cried out. "My mother made the very same oath."

"Well then, we can travel together," the prince said, and so they continued their journey together.

The young man was so friendly and polite that the prince wished more and more that this fellow might finally show himself to be the true friend. Just as they were riding by a tavern, the prince said, "I'm hungry. Let's go inside and eat something together."

So they entered and ordered something to eat. After the meal the prince cut the last apple into two uneven parts and asked his companion to take one. Now just think, the companion took the smaller piece, and the prince was happy that he had found a true friend.

"My handsome fellow," the prince said, " we must regard one another as brothers. What's mine is also yours, and what's yours is mine. And this is how we should travel together until we come to the saint. And if one of us should die along the way, the other must carry the dead one to the final destination. Let's swear on this!"

Both of them swore this oath, and they regarded each other as brothers and continued on their way. Since it took an entire year to reach the saint, just imagine how much the two had to wander. One day, as they were tired and exhausted and had come to a large beautiful city, they said, "Let's stay here a few days and rest, and later we can continue on our way."

So they rented a small house and lived in it. Across from them stood the royal castle. One morning, when the king went onto the balcony and saw the two handsome young men across from him, he thought, "Well, these two young men are very handsome! One is even more handsome than the other, and I think I'll give him my daughter for his wife."

As it turned out, the prince was more handsome than his companion.

To accomplish his purpose, the king invited both young men for dinner. When they came to the castle, he received them in a friendly way and called his daughter to his side. She was more beautiful than the sun and the moon. Later, before they went to bed, the king slipped the prince's traveling companion a poison drink so he fell down dead in his room. Indeed, the king thought, "when the friend dies, the other will be glad to stay here and no longer think about his pilgrimage. Rather, he will marry my daughter."

The next morning, when the prince awoke, he asked, "Where is my friend?"

"He died suddenly last night and is to be buried right away," the servants replied.

"If my friend is dead, I can't stay here any longer," he responded. "I've got to leave as soon as possible."

"But why don't you stay here?" the king asked. "I want to give you my daughter for your wife."

"No," the prince said. "I can't stay here. But I would appreciate it if you would do me a favor. Give me a horse and let me depart in peace. After I have completed my pilgrimage, I'll return and marry your daughter."

So the king gave him a horse, and the prince mounted it. He carried his dead friend on the saddle in front of him, and gradually he finished the journey. But, his companion was not dead. Rather, he lay in a deep sleep. When the prince came to Saint James of Galicia, he got off his horse and took his friend in his arms like a child and carried him into the church. Then he laid the dead man on the steps of the altar before the saint and prayed: "Oh Saint James of Galicia, look—I've fulfilled my oath and have come to you with my friend! I'm now leaving him in your hands. If you bring him back to life, we shall praise your mercy. If he does not return to life, he at least fulfilled his oath."

Just imagine—as the prince was still praying, his dead friend rose up and was alive again and well! So the two young men thanked the saint, gave him great presents, and set out on their way back home.

When they came to the city where the king lived, they rented the little house again that stood across from the royal castle. The king was very happy that the handsome prince was there again and had become even more handsome. He organized great festivities and ordered a splendid wedding to be celebrated. Thus the prince married the beautiful princess. After the wedding they remained a few months more with her father, but then the prince said, "My mother is waiting anxiously at home for me. Therefore, I can't stay here any longer. I need to set out with my wife and my friend to return to my mother."

The king agreed, and they prepared for the journey. However, the king still had a deep hatred for the poor, unfortunate young man, whom he had one time tried to poison, but who had returned alive to his castle. Now he wanted to harm him again, and so he sent him on an urgent mission over land on the day of the departure.

"Go quickly," said the king. "Your friend will certainly wait for you before he departs."

So the young man rushed off to carry out the king's mission without saying goodbye. Meanwhile, the king said to the prince, "You must hurry and depart. Otherwise you will not reach your first destination before evening."

"I can't leave without my friend," the prince answered.

But the king said, "Just set out on your way. He'll be back in less than an hour and will catch up to you soon with his fast horse."

The prince let himself be convinced, took his leave from his father-in-law, and departed with his wife. The poor friend needed many hours to carry out the king's mission, and when he finally returned, the king said to him, "Your friend is already far away from here. You'd better see how you can best catch up with him."

So the poor young man had to leave the palace and was not even given a horse. He began to run, and he ran day and night until he caught up with the prince. But due to the great stress, he developed a terrible case of leprosy so that he looked sick and miserable. Nevertheless, the prince received him in a friendly way and cared for him like a brother.

Finally they reached home where the queen had been waiting very anxiously and embraced him full of joy. The prince immediately had a bed set up for his sick friend and called together all the doctors of the city and land, but none of them could help him. Since the prince's friend did not get better, the prince turned to Saint James of Galicia and said, "Oh Saint James, you brought my friend back from the dead. Please help him one more time, and let him be cured from this wicked leprosy."

As he was praying, a servant entered the room and said, "There is a strange doctor outside who wants to cure the poor young man."

Well, this doctor was none other than Saint James of Galicia, who had heard the prince's prayer and had come to help his friend. You must also know that the prince's wife had already given birth to a little girl, who was a beautiful, lovely child.

When the saint stepped toward the sick man's bed, he examined him and said to the prince, "Do you really want to cure your friend? At any price?"

"At any price," the prince responded. "Just tell me how I can help him."

"This evening you are to take your child," the saint said, "and cut open all her veins. Then you are to rub her blood into the wounds of your friend, and this is how he will be cured."

Of course the prince was shocked and scared when he heard that he had to kill his little daughter, but he said, "I promised my friend to treat him like a brother, and if there is no other means, I shall have to sacrifice my child."

When it became evening, they took the little child and cut open her veins and rubbed her blood into the wounds of the sick man. All at once he was healed from the wicked leprosy, but the little child became completely white and weak and looked like she was dead. So they placed her in her cradle, and her poor parents were very despondent because they thought that they had lost their child.

The next morning the saint came and asked after the sick man.

"He's well and healthy," the prince answered.

"And where did you put your little daughter?" asked the saint.

"She's lying in her cradle and is dead," the father spoke in a sad voice.

"But just look and see how she's doing," the saint said, and when they went over to the cradle, the child was sitting in it and was once again lively and healthy. Then the saint said, "I am Saint James of Galicia and have come to help you because I saw how true your friendship was. Continue to love one another, and if things should go badly, call upon me, and I shall come and help you."

Upon saying these words he blessed them and disappeared right before their eyes. Meanwhile, they led pious lives and did much good for the poor and remained happy and content, while we still can't even pay the rent.

90

THE HERMIT

Once upon a time there was a pious hermit who lived on top of a high mountain. He fed himself on grass and roots and spent the entire day doing atonement with his forehead always touching the ground. Now one day a company of rich people from the city made an excursion to the very same mountain for pleasure. They ate and drank, and everyone spent a delightful day there. In the evening one of the men called his servant and said to him, "Collect all the spoons and forks that we brought with us. We want to get ready for our return trip."

So the servant collected all the silverware, but instead of packing everything, he stuck one of the silver serving spoons into his pocket. The hermit saw all this but said nothing, and the entire party rode off toward home. Along the way it occurred the gentleman to count the silverware, and it became apparent that the silver serving spoon was missing.

"What's this?" he asked the servant. "Did you perhaps forget the spoon? Let's return and look for it."

When they returned to the same place where they had been eating, a poor pilgrim had appeared in the meantime and was collecting crumbs and bones and eating them to still his hunger.

"I'm sure you're the one who stole the spoon," said the man who was missing the spoon.

"Oh, my dear gentleman," the pilgrim implored. "I've taken nothing but the bones and the crumbs. You may search me, and you'll see that I have certainly not taken your spoon."

"Nothing there! But it could only have been you. No one else has been here other than you!"

All at once they beat him and abused him. They tied him to the tail of a horse and dragged him with them. The hermit saw all this, and his heart began to grumble about God's justice. "What's this?" he thought. "Is this the way things are to happen on earth? Is that thief of a servant to go unpunished while the innocent pilgrim is mistreated in such an awful way? God is unjust to tolerate such things. Therefore, I'm no longer going to do atonement. Instead, I'll return to the world and enjoy my life."

Said, done. The hermit left the mountain and no longer did atonement. Rather he set out to enjoy his life. As he wandered about, he met a strong handsome young man who asked him, "Where are you traveling to?"

The hermit indicated the city to which he was traveling.

"I'm going there too. Why don't we travel together?"

So they continued wandering together. The trip was long, and they soon became tired. All at once a mule driver came the same way.

"Hey, good friend," the young man called out, "would you permit us to ride your mules for a while? We're very tired and weak."

"I'd be glad to," answered the mule driver, "You can ride the mules as far as our paths are heading in the same direction."

So they each sat on a mule and rode along with the mule driver. The young man had noticed that there was a bunch of gold in the back sack of the mule driver, and he began taking the coins out and throwing them on the road without the mule driver noticing it. The hermit saw all this and felt in his heart, "What? This poor man has shown us some kindness, and now my companion's doing this wicked thing!" However, since the young man was so strong, he was afraid to say anything. After they had traveled a good distance, the mule driver said, "Now, my friends, our ways part, and I really can't take you with me any farther,"

They got off the mules, thanked him, and continued traveling by foot, but the hermit said, "How could you be so unfair to the poor man and throw away his money after he was so good to us?"

"Be quiet!" the young man answered. "Mind your own business and not mine!"

In the evening they came to an inn, and when the innkeeper's wife came to them, they said, "Good woman, could you give us shelter for the night? Unfortunately, we don't have any money to pay you."

"Oh, don't even speak about it," the innkeeper's wife said, and she kindly took them in and gave them something good to eat and drink. Then she showed them to a room in which there was a bed for each one of them. There was also a cradle in this room, and the woman's small child was sleeping in it. The next morning, as they prepared to continue their journey, the young man went over to the cradle and strangled the poor little child.

"Oh, you villain!" exclaimed the hermit. "That good woman showed us many kind favors, and yet you've murdered her child!"

"Be quiet!" the young man responded. "Mind your own business!"

So they continued wandering, and the hermit walked silently next to the young man. All of a sudden the young man changed into a beautiful shining angel and said to the hermit, "Listen to me, you simple human being, you who have dared to grumble about God's justice! I am an angel sent by God to open your eyes. That innocent pilgrim whom you saw being abused murdered his father on that very same spot many years ago, and that's why God sent him this punishment. Know that God forgives quickly, but he hesitates to punish. The money, which I threw on the road, did not belong to the mule driver. He had stolen it from someone else. After he discovers he has lost the money, he will perhaps contemplate his life and regret his sin. The woman's child might have become a robber or murderer if he had lived. The mother is, however, pious, and she had prayed every day to God, 'Oh, Lord, if my child will not lead a holy life, then I would prefer you take him to you as long as he is innocent.' Indeed, God heard her prayer. So now you see that God's justice has greater vision and sees further than human beings. Therefore, return to your hermitage and do atonement for your grumbling and see whether you may be forgiven."

As soon as the angel had spoken these words, he flew up to heaven. Meanwhile, the hermit returned to his mountain and became even more committed to doing atonement than before, and he died as a saint.

91

THE PRINCE'S TWO CHILDREN
FROM MONTELEONE

Once upon a time there was a prince, the prince of Monteleone,*
who lived with his wife in a glorious castle. He was enormously
rich and had everything his heart desired. However, he and his
wife were always sad because they did not have any children.

"Oh," she often thought, "who will inherit our treasures one day?"

Finally, after many long years had passed, the princess was going to
have a child. The prince had a tower without windows built in a desolate
region, and he had it lavishly furnished with costly furniture. The princess was, however, no longer to be seen. When her time came, she gave
birth to a son and a daughter. The prince had the babies quietly baptized, hired a nurse, and had her locked in the tower with the children.
There the children thrived. They grew bigger each day† and became
more and more beautiful. When they were older, their father sent them
a clergyman, who taught them to read and write and everything else
appropriate for a good education.

After some years passed the princess became sick and died. Soon
thereafter the prince became very sick, and because he felt that his end
was near, he summoned the clergyman and said, "I feel that I shall have

---

* Principi did Muntiliuni. (Monteleone in Calabria)

† Crisciànu un jornu pi dui.

to die. I am going to put you in charge of my children. You shall be their guardian and in charge of my entire fortune. But do not let them leave the tower until there is a good opportunity for them to marry."

The clergyman promised the prince he would care for the children as though they were his own, and soon the prince passed away. Then the clergyman locked all the treasures in the castle, moved to be with the children in the tower, released the nurse after she promised not to tell anyone about the children, and lived alone with them in their solitary dwelling. Meanwhile, the children became more beautiful from day to day and were hard-working students. When they read about foreign countries and cities in their books, the boy was astounded and wanted to know how the world was made. The older he became, the more he desired to set out and see the world. Since he had now become a handsome young man, he went one day to the clergyman and said, "Uncle, let me out of the tower, for I want to get to know the world."

At first the clergyman did not want to allow him to depart, but the young prince insisted so much that the clergyman finally had to consent. So he had a magnificent ship built for the young man's journey, hired a crew, and filled the ship with valuable treasures. When the prince took leave of his sister, he gave her a ring with a precious stone and said, "As long as this stone is clear, then I am well and alive and shall return to you. However, if the stone becomes misty, then I'll be dead and won't be able to return." Upon saying this, he embraced her, boarded the ship, and sailed away. Everything seemed beautiful to him, the sky, the sun, the stars, the flowers, the sea. Everything was unfamiliar to him and everything made him happy.

After he had traveled a while he arrived at a beautiful city ruled by a king. When he sailed into the harbor, he ordered the guns of the ship to be fired. The king heard the firing, became curious, and went to the harbor, and once he saw the beautiful ship, he wanted to board it. As soon as he was on the ship, he was very well received by the young prince, and the king took such a great liking to the handsome and noble young man that he took him on land and invited him into his castle, where he gave him great honors and made him one of his steady companions. Indeed, he took him everywhere—to the theater, to the balls—but there were many among his ministers who were jealous over the favor shown to the young man, for there is no lack of jealous people in the world.

One day when the king was holding court, the young prince told the king about his sister, how beautiful she was, and that no man had ever laid eyes on her. Indeed, he boasted about her great virtue. One of the minsters shrugged his shoulders and said that his sister would lose her virtue with the first attempt on it, and he bet that he could succeed in tempting her. One word led to the next, and finally the minster and the young man made the bet. Whoever lost the bet would be hung. Now the minister boarded a ship, and after he had searched for the place called Monteleone for a long time, he finally found it. But when he inquired about the daughter of the dead prince, everyone laughed in his face, for they believed that the prince and princess had died without children. No matter where he asked, he could not obtain any news about her. So he became very scared and began to fear for his life.

As he meandered through the streets in a terrible mood, a poor woman asked for alms. He rejected her harshly, and she asked why he was so ill-tempered. Finally, he told her about the bet he had made and that he could not find the princess of Monteleone.

"If someone could only help me," he cried, "I'd give a rich reward."

The woman was none other than the nurse of the two children. Because the minister had promised such a rich reward, she let herself be bribed and said, "Come tomorrow to this same place, and I shall help you."

The next morning the duplicitous woman made her way to the tower and knocked on the door. By chance the clergyman had gone to the city, and the maiden was all alone in the house. When the nurse saw the maiden, she said, "Dear child, I'm your former nurse, and I've come to visit you."

The maiden let her enter, and the old woman strode through the room and inspected everything in great detail. When she went into the maiden's bedroom, she said to her: "Come my dear child, I want to dress you in some pretty clothes."

The maiden had a birthmark on her shoulder with three gold hairs woven together with a thread. She was also wearing her brother's ring that was sewn to a corset. As the old woman began dressing her, she noticed the exact form of the birthmark and stole the ring without being observed. Then she departed and returned quickly to the minister and told him everything that she had noticed and gave him the ring.

Now the minister returned in a great hurry to his country, appeared before the king, and said, "I've won the bet." He described the inside of the house and said. The princess has a birthmark with three gold hairs on her shoulder, and they are woven together with a thread. Finally, she gave me this ring."

When the young prince heard this, he could not contradict the minister, but he became furious and enraged with his innocent sister.

"All right," he said. "I'm prepared to die, and I only ask for an eight-day delay."

The king, who was very sad about the fate of his favorite, granted the delay, and so the young prince called his faithful servant Franz to him and said, "You've served me faithfully up to now. So I'd like you fulfill my last command. Rush to my unworthy sister, kill her, and bring me a little bottle of her blood so that I can drink it. Then I'll be happy to die."

The servant was very distressed by this mission, but he had to obey and thus traveled to Monteleone. When the young princess saw him and noticed how sad he was, she asked him why.

"Oh," Franz replied. "I must kill you, for you've committed a great sin. On account of you my poor master must die."

"What have I done?" asked the poor maiden.

"What? Didn't you receive the king's minister and even let him have the ring that your brother gave you?"

It was only then that she noticed that the ring was gone, and she immediately suspected the nurse who had helped her get dressed a few days before. So she threw herself at the clergyman's feet and cried, "Dear uncle, let me depart. I must go and save my brother."

"Oh child," the clergyman responded, "you'll never succeed!"

But she kept asking until he finally consented.

"Now, dear uncle," she continued. "You must fetch the most beautiful pearls and jewels that belonged to my mother."

The clergyman went to the castle, filled a chest with the most precious stones and valuable pearls, and the maiden set off with Franz to the king's city.

"Now you must rent me a room in an inn," she said. "Then kill some chickens, take my brother a bottle of their blood, and tell him that you've carried out his command."

Franz did everything that his mistress ordered, and after the young prince drank the blood, Franz returned to the inn. Then he accompanied the princess to the best goldsmith of the city, and she said to him, "Master, I want you to make a sandal out of these pearls and jewels within three days, and I want it to be as precious as you can possibly make it."

The master immediately hired a group of apprentices, who had to work day and night but within three days the precious sandal was finished.

Soon, the eight days had passed, and the poor young prince was to be led to the gallows. Now his sister had a small platform constructed along the way her brother would be led to his death. She sat down on it, and in front of it lay a silver tea tray with the sandal. As the procession that accompanied her brother came by, she waited until the king appeared in his coach and called out, "Your majesty, I beg for justice and your protection!"

"What is your wish?" asked the king.

"One of your ministers stole a sandal from me, which belongs to the one that you see on this tea tray. That man over there is the thief."

She pointed to the minister who was responsible for the execution that her brother was about to suffer.

"What!" the minister exclaimed. "How can I have stolen your sandal? If I see you one more time, then I shall have seen you only two times in my life."*

"Oh you miserable creature!" the princess cried. "If you don't recognize me now, how can you boast that you've already enjoyed my favor? I am the sister of this unfortunate young man sentenced to death because of your slander."

When the king heard all this, he ordered the young prince to be freed right away. But the minister was seized and hung on the gallows intended for the prince. Then the king led the sister and brother to his castle, and since the maiden was so beautiful, he took her for his bride. Soon afterward the sister and brother sent for their treasures, and the clergyman was also invited to live with them.

They lived happy and content,
But we were left without a cent.

---

* Si vi vidu n'autra vota, v'aju vidutu dui voti.

92

THE CLEVER FARMER

Once upon a time there was a king who had gone hunting. All at
once he saw a farmer working in a field.

"How much do you earn in a day?" the king asked him.

"Your majesty," he replied. "I earn four carlini per day."

"What do you do with the four carlini?" the king continued to ask.

"I eat the first. The second I use to earn interest. The third I give
back, and the fourth I throw away."*

The king continued riding, but after some time passed, he decided
that the farmer's answer was strange, and he turned back and asked him,
"Tell me, did you mean to say that you eat the first carlino, earn interest
with the second, give the third away, and throw the fourth away?"

"With the first carlino," he answered, "I nourish myself. With the
second I nourish my children, who must take care of me when I get old.
With the third I nourish my father and give him back what he did for
me, and with the fourth I nourish my wife, and so I regard that as throwing it away because I don't gain anything from it."

---

* Unu m'u manciu; unu lu scuntu; unu lu ristituisciu e unu lu jettu.

"Yes," said the king. "You're right. But promise me that you won't tell anyone what you've just told me, not before you have seen my face one hundred times."

The farmer promised to do this, and the king rode happily toward home. When he was sitting down to dinner with his ministers, he said, "I want you to listen to a riddle. A farmer earns four carlini a day. He eats the first. He earns interest with the second. He gives the third away, and the fourth he throws away. What's the meaning of this?"

No one could solve the riddle. Finally, one of his ministers remembered that the king had spoken with a farmer on the day before, and decided to seek out the farmer and get him to tell him the answer to the riddle. When he came to the farmer, he asked him for the solution to the riddle, but the farmer answered, "I can't you because I promised the king not to tell anyone until I had seen his face one hundred times."

"Oh," responded the minister, "I can certainly show you the king's face," and he pulled a hundred thalers out of his purse and gave them to the farmer. On each and every one of the thalers the king's face could be seen. Once the farmer looked at each one of the thalers he said, "Now I've seen the king's face one hundred times. So I can tell you the answer to the riddle," and he told the minister.

The minister was delighted and went to the king and said, "Your majesty, I have found the solution to the riddle. Here's the answer." And he told it to him.

"Only the farmer himself could have told you this!" the king cried, and he had the farmer summoned and took him to task.

"Didn't you promise me not to tell the answer to the riddle until your saw my face one hundred times?"

"Your majesty," the farmer answered, "your minister showed me your picture one hundred times."

Upon saying this he showed the king the sack with the money that the minister had given him. Then the king was pleased with the clever farmer and gave him a generous gift so that he became a rich man for the rest of his life.

93

THE TWO COMRADES*

Once upon a time there were two good comrades, master shoe-makers, who had been suffering from great hunger. One day one of them turned to the other and said, "My friend, what are we doing here? We're not earning any money. Let's take our baskets and set out to find some work."

This is what they did, and as they were walking, one of them said, "It might be better if we separate, my friend. You go that way, and I'll go this way. After we find some work and earn some money, we'll return to our homes."

So, the two comrades separated. One went that way, and the other went this way. Let's leave one of these good men and follow the other who was clever and could do many things. He was called Master Pippu.

Well, this man made his way out into the world, and when it turned dark, he came to a region in the countryside where there were neither houses nor people. So he went to a hill covered with large rocks where he intended to pass the night and protect himself from the wet and cold. While he was settling down in between some rocks, he heard a voice cry out from a cave below: "Open, cicca!"

All at once, part of a rock opened, and twelve robbers came out from inside, one after the other.

---

* This tale and the one that follows, "The Story of the Three Sisters," are two Sicilian fairy tales written down in the dialect of Messina by D. Salvatore Morganti.

"Close, cicca!" the same voice said, and the rock closed.

Master Pippu didn't care how dangerous the situation was. He would have gone as far as hell to find his fortune. So, when the robbers had gone off some distance, he said to himself, "I'd like to see what's inside this cave. Let's see if the rock will obey my voice. – Open, cicca!"

The rock opened, and after Master Pippu entered, he said, "Close, cicca!" And the rock closed. Once inside he saw all the treasures of God: food, wine, valuables, and money. So he began to fill his basket with gold, hats, shoes, and all sorts of things.

"Open, cicca" and "close, cicca," Master Pippu said once he was outside. "Saint Peter, help me!" he continued talking and then began running toward home.

His wife, concerned and troubled, was waiting for him at the door just as she had been doing for many days. As soon as she saw him appear, she ran to greet him and embraced him.

"My wife," Master Pippu said to her, "we're rich, very rich! Oh, what a rich treasure! Let's be quiet and take everything into the house. Then I'll tell you what happened."

When they were inside, they closed the door, and Master Pippu began to take out all the money and place it on the table. Just imagine the astonishment of his wife who was very happy and danced without music!

"Oh, husband, is all this money ours?" she asked. "How did you manage to get it? Who gave it to you? Was it some one you met?"

Master Pippu told her what had happened, and the two of them began to count the money, because, as the old people say, money should be counted even when it is found by accident.

But now let's turn to the other comrade who had returned from his journey before Master Pippu. In fact, he was starving because he had not found any work. He lived next door to Master Pippu, and when he heard the sound of the gold coins, he said to his wife, "Ciccia – for she was called Ciccia – I think that my friend has returned. But what's this noise of money that I hear in his house?"

"You're right," his wife responded. "I've been hearing this noise for quite a while. It sounds like gold coins. Maybe your friend Pippu has found a treasure, or perhaps he's become a prince or a baron? Just wait here. I'll go to their home and find out everything there is to know."

So she went to her husband's comrade, and upon entering his house, she said, "Congratulations, my friend! I just heard about your return and even more about the great treasure that you found. Things are working out better and better for you. My best wishes."

Surprised by what she said, Master Pippu could not hide anything, and since Ciccia was so insistent, he opened up and revealed to her what had happened.

"Well now, I'm going to send my husband there," Ciccia said, "so that we can become just as rich as you are."

"Let me give you some advice, my friend," Master Pippu responded. "Your husband is not the man for such things. It's a dangerous undertaking, and if he goes there, he won't return because I'm sure he will die at the hands of the robbers."

But Ciccia did not want to hear advice like this, and she persuaded her husband to try his luck as well. Master Antoni, for that was his name, set out immediately on his way. Now let's leave him on his journey and turn to the robbers.

When they returned to the cave and saw that some money was missing, they cried out, "We've been tricked! Tricked! Some one knows our secret, and when we leave again, he'll return and enter the cave."

So they discussed everything and decided to leave some one behind to keep guard when they left the cave.

Soon thereafter Master Antoni arrived and hid behind the rocks. When he saw the robbers leave the cave and depart, he ran down, and as soon as he stood before the entrance, he cried out, "Open, cicca," and the rock opened. But he was terrified, for while he was kneeling down to enter the cave, he was stopped by the robber who was keeping guard. This man was fully armed and grabbed him by his shirt.

"Stop, you thief!" he cried out. "You've made the wrong move."

Master Antoni was scared to death when he felt the hands of the robber. He threw himself at the robber's feet and pleaded with him, but it was in vain. When the others returned, they cut off poor Master Antoni's head and hands, and they placed them at the entrance of the cave as an example to anyone else who might try to enter.

Master Antoni's wife waited that day. She waited the next day, and the day after and the day after that, but her husband did not return to his home. His wife continued to weep about her husband and could not find any peace.

"Didn't I tell you, my friend," Master Pippu said, "that your husband would die at the hands of the robbers? Why didn't you listen to my advice? Now I'll go and see what happened."

So Master Pippu set out for the robbers' cave.

The robbers who had killed Master Antoni thought that he was the only person who knew the secret of the cave. So they decided not to keep a guard in the cave anymore, and Master Pippu, who hid behind the same rocks as he had done before, watched them leave the cave and counted them one by one. There were twelve.

"Now there's nobody inside," he said and ran toward the cave. "Open, cicca," and the rock opened. But how great was Master Pippu's fright and suffering when he saw his comrade's head attached to the top of the cave! Without losing any time, however, he entered and gathered together another large bundle of money. Then he went outside and, quick as a deer, raced home. Once he arrived, he told Ciccia the bad news about her poor husband, and to console her and help her get over her suffering, he gave her part of the money. Already rich, Master Pippu threw away his basket, shoe tree, awl, and carving knife and led a life of luxury, eating well and enjoying good times.

Note: According to another version, Master Pippu's wife asks her neighbor for a scale to weigh some herbs. However, the neighbors hear the sound of the gold coins and smear some tar on the scale so that some of the gold coins stick to it. Because of this, the second comrade decides to seek his fortune in the same way that his friend found his.

94

⁂

THE STORY OF THE THREE SISTERS

Once upon a time there were three very poor sisters who struggled to make a living by spinning. The oldest sister used to carry their yarn into town to sell it to the artisans. One day, after she had bought some food with the money that was earned from the yarn, she headed home and carried the food for their dinner in her scarf. As she was passing through a street, a large dog attacked her with all its fury, grabbed the bundle of food from her hand, and ran off as fast as it could. The unfortunate maiden was completely stunned and burst into tears. Then she ran home and told her sisters what had happened.

"Oh, you fool," the middle sister said. "How could this happen? How could you let a dog rob the food?"

"Well, just you wait!" the older sister replied. "The mere look of that big and hungry beast would have frightened you!"

"To tell you the truth, if I had been in your shoes," the middle sister responded, "this would not have happened to me! Tomorrow I'll do the shopping, and we'll see if this same dog can fool me."

The next day the middle sister left and did the shopping. On her way home she passed through the same street, and the dog was already there. It bared its teeth as it approached her, within the twinkle of an eye, the dog grabbed the food from her hands and ran away with it. Totally mortified, the unfortunate maiden returned home.

"I told you that ugly dog would rob you," the eldest sister scolded her.

The youngest sister, who felt very discontent, let out a big laugh.

"I can hardly believe," she said to her sisters, "that you've been so stupid! What the devil has gotten into you? I'm going to take care of this beast. Tomorrow I'll do the shopping, and I assure you, this time we won't go hungry. Until then, let's get to work."

The next day the youngest sister went to do the shopping, and as she returned through the same street, she held on to her scarf tightly with her hands. When the dog appeared and was about to pounce on her, she didn't budge. So the dog grabbed the scarf with its teeth and tried with all its might to pull it out of the maiden's hands. The dog tugged and tugged, and finally it won and carried off the handkerchief with the food. But the maiden was quick and courageous, and she began to follow the dog as it ran through the door of a large palace. When she was close to the dog, she cried out, "I won't leave you alone unless you give me back the food!"

But the dog climbed the stairs, entered a room, and disappeared ahead of her.

"Either I'll find the dog or the owner," the girl said again, "and I'll make them give me back all our stuff."

She ran through the rooms and searched all of them back and forth. However, she couldn't find the dog or the owner. The palace was deserted and abandoned, but there were all the treasures of God – valuables, money, and jewels, and in the middle of one room there was a table covered with all sorts of dishes including wine, sweets, and liquors. Since she had lost her way and wanted to get over her bad mood, she sat down at the table and began to eat and drink. After she finished her meal, nobody appeared, and she thought about her sisters. So she gathered together some valuables and food and ran straight home.

"It's true," she said to her sisters, "that the dog grabbed the food from me, but I followed it to its house, where I ate and drank. And now I've brought you all sorts of good things."

After she had told them what had happened, she persuaded her sisters to go with her to the palace and live there. They all agreed about this plan, and so they set out for the palace. Later when they settled down, it was as if it were their own home. The oldest sister who never stopped working was always the last one to go to bed. One time, after midnight, she heard a voice of a woman at the top of the stairs, and it was lamenting and crying out, "Can I come up? – Can I come up?"

Frightened by this voice, she threw down her work, ran quick as a whistle to her sisters, and jumped into bed without saying a word. The next day when the youngest sister heard her story, she began to mock her. "You missed out," she said. "Why didn't you let her come up the stairs? Didn't you hear that she was asking for permission? Tonight I'm going to check on what happened."

When evening arrived, the two older sisters went to bed, and she remained by herself and continued working. After a while the clock sounded midnight, and she heard the same voice. "Can I come up? – Can I come up?"

"Come up. Come up," responded the maiden.

When she was at the top of the stairs, the youngest sister saw a beautiful lady before her with her hair down, her bare breast covered with blood, and a dagger stuck into her heart.

"Who are you? What do you want?" the maiden asked without losing courage.

"Who am I?" the lady responded. "I am the shadow of the mistress of this palace. The dog that carried off your food is the same shadow under another form. I am dead, and my tomb lies at the bottom of the stairs. My lover became cruelly jealous of me, and without any reason, he took his knife and killed me. Then he dragged me downstairs by my hair and buried me down below. Now listen to me. I'll make you the heiress of this palace and owner of all the money and treasures that are here. However, you must swear an oath and avenge me."

"How?" the maiden asked.

"If you look in the wardrobe," she replied, "you'll find all my clothes and jewelry. Put them on every day and sit down on the balcony with your back always turned toward the outside. My lover, who passes by every day on the street, will mistake you for me and will think that I've recovered. You are to pretend that you've seen him and are to make some signs by nodding your head, but you're not to turn to face him. Gradually he'll want to come up stairs. You are to pretend to be indignant, and you must scold him and treat him badly. And if ever he looks at your face, he may doubt whether it's me. So you're to remember all the particulars of our life and our love that I'll now tell you. Pretend to make peace with him, and when he is together with you and lifts your veil, you are to stab him in the breast with a dagger. When he is dead, you're to drag him down the stairs and bury him in the same hole that my body is in."

"Rest assured," responded the maiden. "I shall avenge you."

The shadow recounted all the circumstances of her life with her lover and disappeared. The next day the maiden put on beautiful garments and dressed herself as if she were the lady of the house. Then she sat down on the balcony with her back turned to the outside. The lady's lover passed by the balcony and then turned back. When he saw the maiden on the balcony, he thought his lover had recovered and went upstairs.

"Are you really my lover?" he asked, timid and bewildered.

"I am," the disguised lady replied. "You're not mistaken. But how could you dare come here and search for me? How could you forget the barbaric way you murdered me? How could you forget the way you stabbed me in the heart with your dagger?"

She continued to recall all the circumstances of their love, and he was persuaded that she was truly his lover. Even if she did not look like her former self, he believed her appearance might have changed because of the suffering she had endured when she died.

"I remember everything," he responded, "and I fall to your feet and ask your pardon for all the suffering that I've caused you. I've changed, and I'll now be your loyal and tender lover until death. Pardon me, my love."

They made peace and went to sit down at the table to eat, but as he approached her to throw himself into the arms of his lover, the maiden quickly took out a dagger and stabbed him in his heart.

"I'm dying," he said as he fell, "by treacherous hands."

The maiden grabbed him by his hair and dragged him down to the foot of the stairs, and she buried him where he had buried his lover. The three sisters became owners of this rich palace, but they were not happy because the price of blood is always bitter.

NOTES

These notes are based on material that I have gathered from the following works:

Aarne, Antti, and Stith Thompson. *The Types of the Folktale: A Classification and a Bibliography*. 2nd rev. ed. FF Communications No. 3. Helsinki: Suomalainen Tiedeakatemia, 1961.

Gonzenbach, Laura. *Sicilianische Märchen*, 2 vols. Leipzig: W. Engelmann, 1870. The notes were prepared by Reinhold Köhler and are in the second volume.

Gonzenbach, Laura. *Fiabe Siciliane*, ed. Luisa Rubini. Rome: Donzelli, 1999. The notes were written by Luisa Rubini, who has also provided source material in her book, *Fiabe e mercanti in Sicilia*. Florence: Olschki, 1998.

Zipes, Jack. *The Great Fairy Tale Tradition: From Straparola and Basile to the Brothers Grimm*. New York: Norton, 2001.

Luisa Rubini's notes are by far the most revealing about parallels to other folk-tale collections in Italy, and she has also provided exhaustive historical material. I have generally kept the references to various tales and collections in the original language. In the cases in which the tales and collections are well known and accessible in English, I have provided English translations and sources. Whenever the name of a folklorist, collector, or scholar is mentioned in the notes without mention of the work, the work can be found listed in the bibliography which follows these notes.

Each tale title is accompanied by the German title and designated number in Gonzenbach's original compilation. The titles are followed by the tale-type classification in Aarne and Thompson's work as a helpful reference.

1. *Sorfarina—Die Geschichte von Sorfarina, Nr. 36*
Tale Type AaTh 891—The Man Who Deserts His Wife and Sets Her the Task of Bearing Him a Child.

Similar versions can be found in Giovanni Boccaccio's, "Giletta di Nerbona" in *Decameron* (1349–1350); Giovan Francesco Straparola's "Ortodosio Simeoni" in *Le piacevoli Notti* (1550–1553); Giambattista Basile's "La Sapia Liccarda" in *Lo cunto de li cunti* (1634–1636); and Marie-Jeanne Lhéritier's "The Discreet Princess, or The Adventures of Finette" ("L'Adroite Princesse, ou les aventures de Finette") in *Oeuvres meslées* (1696). There was another contemporary Sicilian oral version, "Catarina la Sapienti," published by Giuseppe Pitrè in *Fiabe, novelle e racconti popolari siciliani* (1875), and others listed in Sebastiano Lo Nigro's *Racconti popolari siciliani* (1957).

The prince's desire for revenge is also the desire to control a woman. When he finally does try to kill her, he licks the "blood" from the sword because, according to Sicilian folklore, this gesture will prevent him from being tormented by remorse or from being discovered. Of course, the sugar or honey makes him regret his actions even more, and all his efforts to control Sorfarina are frustrated.

2. *The Green Bird—Vom grünen Vogel, Nr. 27*
Tale Type AaTh 432—Prince as Bird.

Versions of this tale were common in the literature of the Middle Ages and Renaissance. One of the most important was the "Lai Yonec" in *The Lais of Marie de France* of the late twelfth century. (Other important literary tales were Giambattista Basile's "The Green Meadow"—["Verde Prato"] in *Lo cunto de li cunti* (1634–1636) and Mme d'Aulnoy's "The Blue Bird"—["L'oiseau bleu"] in *Les Contes de fées* (1697). Giuseppe Pitrè published a Sicilian variant, "Li pall magichi" in *Fiabe, novelle e racconti popolari siciliani* (1875), and other Italian variants can be found in the twentieth-century collections of Calvino, Lo Nigro, Cirese, and De Simone.

3. *The Snake Who Bore Witness for a Maiden—Von der Schlange, die für ein Mädchen zeugte, Nr. 46*
Tale Type AaTh 672 C—Testimony of the Serpent.

This tale about rape is one of the few recorded in Sicilian and Italian folklore. Luisa Rubini points out that Giuseppe Pitrè collected an Albanesian version, "I biri Regghit e Gghialpri" or "Il figlio del Re e il serpente" in *Fiabe, novelle e racconti popolari siciliani* (1875), but this tale is much different because the young woman eventually consents to the advances of the prince. Reinhold Köhler mentions that he found only one similar tale in Abraham Tendlau's *Das Buch der Sagen und Legenden jüdischer Vorzzeit* (1842). In tale 29, a weasel is called upon by a maiden to witness her rape, and later the weasel kills the child of the faithless man.

4. *The Sister of Muntifiuri—Von der Schwester der Muntifuri, Nr. 33*
Tale Type AaTh 403 A—The Wishes.

This tale is similar to "Giovanni and Katerina," Nr. 25, and "Quaddaruni and His Sister," Nr. 28, in Gonzenbach's collection. This story was popular throughout Europe, and versions can be found in the works of Basile, d'Aulnoy, Schneller, Grimm, Grundtvig, Asbjørnsen, and Glinski. The basic plot in all these versions concerns a young man who serves a king. The king learns that he has a beautiful sister, and he wants to marry her. However, when the sister travels to the king's court, her place is taken by an ugly, mean-spirited maiden. Eventually, however, the sister regains her place as the true bride. In most versions the beautiful maiden receives exceptional gifts because of her kindness and friendliness. For an earlier variant, see "The Two Cakes" ["Le doie pizzele"] in Giambattista Basile's *Lo cunto de li cunti* (1634–1636). Other versions can be found in the collections of Giuseppe Pitrè.

5. *The Story About Ciccu—Die Geschichte von Ciccu, Nr. 30*
Tale Type AaTh 566—Fortunatus.

There are also motifs and elements from the tale types of "Ferdinand the True and

Ferdinand the False" (AaTh 531) and "The Boy Steals the Giant's Treasure" (AaTh 328). Gonzenbach's tale reflects the great European interest in the "fortunate" or lucky young man who acquires magical gifts that enable him to gain wealth and power. Numerous tales about this hero arose during the Middle Ages and were printed in chapbooks. There is even a version in the *Gesta Romanurum* (Deeds of the Romans, fourteenth century). Eventually the oral and literary tales led to the publication of a popular German novel, *Fortunatus* (1489) by an anonymous author, which was translated into other European languages.

The mix of the different types led Reinhold Köhler to divide the plot into four parts:
1. Ciccu and the magic objects.
2. Ciccu and the dates.
3. Ciccu and the ogre.
4. Ciccu and the most beautiful woman in the world.

There are many interesting variants that can be found in the works of Straparola, Basile, Mme d'Aulnoy, Rehfues, the Brothers Grimm, and Pitrè.

6. *Count Piro—Vom Conte Piro, Nr. 65*
Tale Type AaTh 545 B—Puss in Boots.

This tale type is one of the most famous and widespread tales in Europe and North America. Reinhard Köhler points out that in many countries, such as Finland, Russia, and Siberia, it is a fox that plays the major role as animal helper as is the case in most Sicilian tales. The cat can be found in the collections of Straparola, Basile, Schneller, Glinski, Haltrich, Asbjörnsen, Afanaskev, Chudjakov, and Radloff. In the literary tradition, the best known versions are those of Straparola ("Soriana" in *Le piacevoli Notti*, 1550–1553), Basile ("Gagliosa" in *Il cunto de li cunti*, 1634–1636), and Perrault ("The Master Cat, or Puss in Boots" ["Le maître chat ou Le chat botté"] in *Histoires ou Contes du temps passé*, 1697). The Brothers Grimm published a version of "Puss in Boots" in the 1812 first edition of *Kinder- und Hausmärchen*, but they deleted it because it was too similar to Perrault's tale. Luisa Rubini indicates that there are also interesting versions and references in the works of Imbriani, Pitrè, Calvino, Lo Nigro, Cirese and Serafini, and De Simone. She remarks that Pitrè's tale, Nr. 88 in *Fiabe, novelle e racconti popolari siciliani* (1875), was told by a twenty-eight-year-old woman, Angela Smiraglia. In her tale the protagonist, named Don Giuseppi Piru, kills the fox at the end of the tale because he doesn't want his wife to discover how the fox helped him use trickery to attain his wealth.

7. *Beautiful Angiola—Von der schönen Angiola, Nr. 53*
Tale Type AaTh 310—The Maiden in the Tower.

Extremely popular throughout Europe, this tale has an illustrious literary history in the following key works: Giambattista Basile, "Petrosinella" in *Lo cunto de li cunti* (1634–1636); Charlotte-Rose de Caumont de la Force, "Persinette" in *Les Contes des contes* (1698); Friedrich Schulz, "Rapunzel," *Kleine Romane* (1790); Jacob and Wilhelm Grimm, "Rapunzel" in *Kinder- und Hausmärchen* (1857); Ludwig Bechstein, "Rapunzel" in *Deutsches Märchenbuch* (1845); and Vittorio Imbriani, "Prezzemolina" in *La Novellaja fiorentina* (1871). The incarceration of a young woman in a tower (often to protect her chastity during puberty) was a common motif in various European myths and became part of the standard repertoire of medieval tales, lais, and romances throughout Europe and Asia. The motif of a pregnant woman who has a strong craving for an extravagant dish or extraordinary food is also very important. In many peasant societies people believed that it was necessary to fulfill the longings of a pregnant woman, otherwise something terrible, like a miscarriage or bad luck, might occur. Therefore, it was incumbent on the husband and other friends and relatives to use spells or charms or other means to fulfill these cravings. Another important motif in Gonzenbach's tale—the dog-face curse placed on Angiola by the witch for having insulted her—is generally a curse by a fairy who is not properly respected or honored. Quite often a girl's face is changed into a goat face or even a cat face.

There is a very important retelling of this motif embedded in Mme. d'Aulnoy's "The White Cat" in *Les Contes de fées* (1697). At one point a young prince meets an enchanted cat, who was once a princess, and she explains to him why and how she was transformed into a cat. She recounts that when her mother had been pregnant with her, she had taken a journey and had such a craving to eat some fruit from the fairy garden that she promised the fairies her baby. Her father protested, and the queen herself regretted her actions. However, the fairies took the princess and built a tower for her without an entrance. The fairies entered the tower on the back of a dragon. The princess was never told about her parents, and her only companions were a talking parrot and talking dog. One day a prince discovered the tower, and the princess and the prince fell in love. The fairies discovered their love and decided that the princess had to marry someone of their own kind, a monstrous fairy king. So the princess and prince decided to flee with the help of the parrot and the dog, and they got married. However, the fairies found them. The prince was devoured by a dragon, and the princess wanted to take her own life, but the fairies transformed her into a white cat. In conclusion, the white cat explains that only when she finds a prince who resembles her dead lover, will she be able to regain her human form.

There is a Sicilian variant, "La Vecchia di l'ortu" in Pitrè's *Fiabe, novelle e racconti popolari siciliani* (1875), and other Italian versions and references can be found in the works of Nerruci, Lo Nigro, Cirese and Serafini, and Calvino.

8. *Betta Pilusa—Von der Betta Pilusa, Nr. 38*

Tale Type AaTh 510 B—The Dress of Gold, of Silver, and of Stars. In the western world the theme of incest took on significance in literature during the eleventh century. Stories dealing with this topic that may have influenced Straparola, Basile, Perrault, and the Grimms appeared in Ser Giovanni Fiorentino's *Il Pecorone* (1378) as "Dionigia and the King of England" and in the fifteenth-century verse romance of *Belle Hélène de Constantinople*, of which there are also prose manuscripts. It became a very popular story and was published in chapbooks and folk collections up to the nineteenth century.

There is generally one plot outline followed in most of the publications: The Emperor Antoine of Constantinople falls in love with his daughter Hélène and manages to obtain a papal dispensation so that he may be allowed to marry her. However, Hélène flees to England before the wedding and meets King Henry, but does not reveal that she is from a royal family and why she has fled Constantinople. Henry falls in love with her and marries her against his mother's wishes. When the pope is besieged by the Saracens, Henry goes off to war to help him. While he is absent, Hélène gives birth to twins, but the queen mother sends a message to her son that Hélène has brought two monsters into the world. Henry writes back that Hélène is to be kept under guard, but his mother changes his message into an execution order. When the Duke of Gloucester, who is the acting regent, reads the order, he has Hélène's right hand chopped off as proof that he has slain her. In reality he sends her off in a boat with her two sons and hangs the hand around the youngest son's neck. In the meantime, he has the hand of his own niece chopped off as replacement, and she is also burned at the stake. After a shipwreck, Hélène's sons are abducted by a wolf and lion who take them to a hermit who names the boy with the hand around his neck Brac and the other Lion.

Meanwhile, Hélène makes her way to Nantes. When Henry learns about Hélène's fate from the Duke of Gloucester, he has his mother executed. By chance he meets the emperor Antoine, who is looking for his daughter. Together Henry and Antoine search for Hélène for a year. At the same time, Brac and Lion commence their quest for their mother. When they come to Tours, they enter the service of Archbishop Martin de Tours, who names them Brice and Martin. Unknown to all, Hélène has also moved to

Tours. When Henry and Antoine encounter Brice and Martin in Tours, they notice the hand around one of the boy's necks, and Henry is united with his sons. Soon Hélène comes upon them and she is reunited with her sons, father, and husband, and her hand is restored to her through a miracle.

Many of the motifs in this legend stem from Byzantine and Greek tales and medieval legends. There is some connection to the marriage customs in the ruling houses in the pre-Hellenistic period. Other important sources are the legend of the famous eighth-century King Offa, John Gower's *Confesso Amantis*, written in the fourteenth century, and Geoffrey Chaucer's *Canterbury Tales* (1387–1389). The father's incestuous desire has always been depicted as sinful, and the second half of the story, the transformation of the princess into a mutilated person or squalid, animal-like servant, has parallels with the Cinderella tales. However, for the most part the heroine is a princess, and the plot revolves around her fall from and return to royalty. Her purity and integrity are tested, and she proves through a ring or shoe test that she is worthy of her rank. Depending on the attitude of the writer, the incestuous father is punished or forgiven. Sometimes he is just forgotten. Some of the key versions are: Giovan Francesco Straparola, "Tebaldo" in *Le Piacevoli Notti* (1550–1553); Giambattista Basile, "The Bear" ["L'Orsa"] in *Lo cunto de li cunti* (1634); Charles Perrault, "Donkey-Skin" ["Peau d'Ane"] in *Griseldis, nouvelle. Avec le conte de Peau d'Ane, et celui des Souhaits ridicules* (1694); Brothers Grimm, "All Fur" ["Allerleirauh"] in *Kinder- und Hausmärchen* (1857).

The Brothers Grimm based their version on a story that was embedded in Carl Nehrlich's novel, *Schilly* (1798). Other literary versions that are related to the topic are Johann Karl August Musäus's "Die Nymphe des Brunnens" in *Volksmärchen der Deutschen* (1782) and Albert Ludwig Grimm's "Brunnenhold und Brunnenstark" in *Lina's Märchenbuch* (1816). There is an old Scottish oral version "The King Who Wished to Marry His Daughter," published in John Francis Campbell, ed., *Popular Tales of the West Highlands* (1860–1862). Most of the tales dealing with incest are also clearly related to another cycle of tales concerned with "The Maiden without Hands." One of the key literary sources here is Philippe de Rémi's verse romance *La Manekine* (c. 1270), which may have been based on oral tales in Brittany connected to the motif of the persecuted woman.

In her essay, "The Donkey-Skin Folktale Cycle (AT510B)," Christine Goldberg demonstrates that the tales about incest, which she calls the Donkey-Skin cycle, are also connected to the Cinderella cycle. She also pays a great deal of attention to other motifs such as the King Lear motif of "Love Like Salt," the old woman's skin and disguised flayer, the hiding box, and the spying. However, she does not deal with the legend of *Belle Hélène*, which clearly is crucial for understanding the historical background of incest tales. Other versions of this tale type can be found in the works of Waldau, Schleicher, Grundtvig, and Pitrè.

9. *Lignu di Scupa—Die Geschichte von Lignu di scupa, Nr. 84*
Tale Type AaTh 500—The Name of the Helper.

The major literary sources for this tale are: Giambattista Basile, "The Seven Bits of Bacon Rind" ["Le Sette Cotennine"] in *Lo cunto de le cunti* (1634); Marie-Jeanne Lhéritier, "Ricdin-Ricdon" in *La Tour ténébreuse et les jours lumineux* (1705); Jacob and Wilhelm Grimm, "Rumpelstilzchen," "The Three Spinners" ["Die drei Spinnerinnen"], and "The Lazy Spinner" ["Die faule Spinnerin"] in *Kinder- und Hausmärchen. Gesammelt durch die Brüder Grimm* (1857).

The importance of spinning in the economy of Europe from the medieval period to the end of the nineteenth century can be documented in the thousands of folk and fairy tales that were disseminated by word of mouth and through print. The most popular spinning tale is, of course, "Rumpelstilzchen." Like many tales about spinning, it reveals how important spinning could be for women: a good spinner could rise in social status and find a husband who would reward her efforts. This is the case even in Basile's comical version in which the peasant girl hates spinning and cannot spin well. Indeed, there are different perspectives on the value of spinning for women in these tales, and many of them that were probably told by women in spinning rooms reveal how the spinners would actually like *not* to spin anymore, but use their spinning to entangle a man and to weave the threads and narrative strands of their own lives.

The origins of the figure and the name "Ricdin-Ricdon" or "Rumpelstiltskin" have never been conclusively determined. Sometimes the character is a demonic figure; sometimes a magical gnome, dwarf, or spirit. Basile's female protagonist relied on the magical intervention of fairies. Mlle. Lhéritier was undoubtedly familiar with Basile's tale, but she changed it immensely to address important social issues concerning the diligence and value of a young woman who unwittingly makes a bargain with the devil. The Grimms were well aware of her tale, but they also knew many others that had an influence on their various spinning tales. Johannes Praetorious (a pseudonym for Hans Schultze) published a humorous version in his book *Der Abentheurliche Glücks-Topf* (1669); Sophie Albrecht's *Graumännchen oder die Burg Rabenbühl* ("The Little Gray Man or the Castle Rabenbühl," 1799) was strongly influenced by Mlle. Lhéritier's "Ricdin-Ricdon"; August Ey combined some motifs of "Beauty and the Beast" in his version "Die goldene Rose" ("The Golden Rose") in his *Harzmärchenbuch* (1862). Sometimes motifs from tales that deal with persecuted heroines were combined with motifs of demonic figures and the guessing of names to form a tale similar to "Rumpelstiltskin." For instance, Ignaz and Joseph Zingerle published "Cistl im Korbl" in *Tirols Volksdichtungen und Volksbräuche* (*The Folk Poetry and Customs of Tyrol*, 1852), which uses motifs from the Grimms' "All Fur" and tales about a demonic helper. In the English tradition, Rumpelstiltskin generally goes by the name of Tom-Tit-Tot, and there are hundreds of different versions of this tale in Great Britain, as the English folklorist Edward Clodd has shown in his book *Tom Tit Tot: An Essay of Savage Philosophy* (1898). Joseph Jacobs published one of the best texts of "Tom Tit Tot" in *English Fairy Tales* (1890). In Italy there are interesting versions of "Rumpestiltskin" in the anthologies edited by Schneller, "Tarandandò," and by Pitrè, "Li sette tistuzzi." Other variants can be found in the works of Lütolf, Strackerjan, and Müllenhoff.

10. *Don Giovanni di la Fortuna—Don Giovanni di la Fortuna, Nr. 72*
Tale Type Aa Th 361—Bear Skin.

This tale type could also be called the wager with the devil. Generally speaking, although the devil never captures the soul of the protagonist, he is often rewarded in the end with the souls of people who are selfish or greedy. Among the more important literary sources are Hans Jakob Christoph von Grimmelshausen's *Simplicissmus* (1621/22–1676) and Jacob and Wilhelm Grimm's "Barenhäuter" or "Bearskin" in *Kinder- und Hausmärchen* (1857). Italian versions (written in German) can be found in the anthologies by Schneller and Knust, and recounted in dialect in Carolina Berti Coronedi's and Giuseppe Pitrè's collections of tales.

11. *Federico and Epomata—Die Geschichte von Feledico und Epomata, Nr. 55*
Tale Type AaTh 313 C—Forgotten Fiancée.

Significant literary sources are: Francesco Bello, *Il Mambriano* (fifteenth century), fifth novella; Celio Malespini, "Matrimonio di Filenia, figliuola del Re d'Egitto" in *Ducento Novelle del Signor Celio Malespini* (1609), and Giambattista Basile, III, 9 in *Lo cunto de le cunti* (1634). In all these versions a king is dying from leprosy and can only be saved if he can bathe in the blood of a prince. The king's daughter saves the threatened prince and escapes, but she cannot avoid her mother's curse, which causes the prince to forget her. While she waits for a chance to help him regain his memory, she plays the role of a prostitute, but she manages to protect her virginity through magic and regain the prince. Other versions of this tale can be found in the collections of Müllendorff, Asbjørnsen, Arnason, and Schneller. The Brothers Grimm published a watered-down version, "The True Bride" ["Die wahre Braut"] in *Kinder- und Hausmärchen* (1857).

12. *The Fearless Young Man—Von dem, der sich vor Nichts fürchtete, Nr. 57*
Tale Type AaTh 326—The Youth Who Wanted to Learn What Fear Is.
This tale is more a humorous anecdote, a *Schwank*, than a fairy tale, and the hero is more a rascal and rogue like Giufà than the typical hero of fairy tales. Some early literary versions are: Giovan Francesco Straparola's "Flamminio Veraldo si parla da Ostia, e va cerando la morte" in *Le piacevoli Notti* (1550–1553) and "The Youth Who Went Out in Search of Fear" ["Märchen von einem, der auszog das Fürchten zu lernen"] in Jacob and Wilhelm Grimm's *Kinder- und Hausmärchen* (1857). Other versions can be found in the collections of Nerucci, Zingerle, Grundtvig, Schneller, and Pitrè. Many of the tales concern death, and Gonzenbach's tale is interesting because the protagonist never learns to fear.

13. *Caruseddu—Die Geschichte von Caruseddu, Nr. 83*
Tale Type AaTh 327 B—The Dwarf and the Giant, AaTh 328—The Boy Steals the Giant's Treasure, AaTh 1119—The Ogre Kills His Own Children, and AaTh 531—Ferdinand the True and Ferdinand the False.
There are motifs in this narrative that can be found in other tale types such as the boy who steals the giant's treasure, the ogre who kills his own children, and Ferdinand the True and Ferdinand the False. Important literary versions are *The History of Tom Thumb*, a chapbook (1621); Mme d'Aulnoy, "The Orange Tree and the Bee" ["L'oranger e l'abeille"] *Les Contes de fées* (1697); Charles Perrault, "Little Tom Thumb" ["Le Petit Poucet,"] *Histoires ou Contes du temps passé* (1697), and Jacob and Wilhelm Grimm, "Thumbling" ["Däumling"] in *Kinder- und Hausmärchen* (1857).

14. *How Saint Joseph Helped a Young Man Win the Daughter of a King— Von einem, der mit Hülfe des heiligen Joseph die Königstochter gewann, Nr. 74*
Tale Type AaTh 513 B—The Land and Water Ship.
The key motif in this tale, which assumed many different forms in Europe, is not really the unusual ship, but the men with extraordinary talents who are "collected" by the young man with the help of Saint Joseph. Some of the more important versions are: Giovanni Sercambi, "De Bono Facto," in *Novelle* (fifteenth century); Giambattista Basile, "Lo 'gnorante' and "Lo Polece" in *Lo cunto de li cunti* (1634); Marie-Catherine d'Aulnoy, "Belle-Belle ou le Chevalier fortuné" in *Les Contes de fées* (1697); and Jacob and Wilhelm Grimm, "How Six Set Out into the World" ["Sechse kommen durch die ganze Welt"] in *Kinder- und Hausmärchen* (1857). Most of these versions do not have the religious element introduced in Gonzenbach's tale.

15. *The Courageous Maiden—Die Geschichte von dem mutigen Mädchen, Nr. 78*
Tale Type AaTh 512 B*—The Ghost Is Avenged.
There are not many versions of this tale, although Gonzenbach included a second variant in dialect, "The Three Sisters," Nr. 94, at the end of this collection. In addition, Pitrè published a similar anonymous tale, "Lu Sangunazzu" in *Fiabe, novelle e racconti popolari siciliani* (1875).

16. *The Humilated Princess—Die gedemüthigte Königstochter, Nr. 18*
Tale Type AaTh 900—King Thrushbeard.
Among the important literary sources are: Giambattista Basile, "Pride Punished" ["La Superbia Punita"] in *Lo cunto de li cunti* (1634–1636) and Jacob and Wilhelm Grimm, "King Thrushbeard" ["König Drosselbart"] in *Kinder- und Hausmärchen. Gesammelt durch die Brüder Grimm* (1857).

The taming of a proud princess or aristocratic woman, who thinks that she is too good to marry any man, especially one who is beneath her in social rank, became an important didactic motif in the medieval oral and literary tradition. In fact, the shaming of a princess by a gardener, fool, lower-class man, or prince disguised as a beggar or peasant became a well-known motif up through the twentieth century. In the thirteenth-century erotic tale written in middle-high-German verse "Diu halbe bir" or "Die halbe Birne" ("Half a Pear"), there is a mighty king who decides to offer his daughter in marriage to the knight who shows his valor and wins a tournament. When a knight named Arnold wins the tournament, he is invited to a feast where pears are served, one for two people. He cuts a pear in half without peeling it. After he eats his half, he offers the princess the other half, and she is so insulted that she berates him before all the guests. Arnold is enraged and departs, swearing revenge. He returns later as a court fool and is allowed to enter the princesses's salon to entertain her and her ladies. She becomes so sexually aroused by his antics that she yields to his amorous advances. Then Arnold leaves, discards his disguise, and returns to the court as knight. When the princess sees him again, she begins to mock him as the knight with half a pear. He responds with a retort that makes her aware of his amorous conquest of the night before, and consequently compels her to become his wife. A similar version can be found in the fourteenth-century Icelandic legend "Clárus" written by Jón Halldórsson. Shakespeare used this motif in *The Taming of the Shrew* (1605), and Luigi Allemanni's novella, "Bianca, figliuola del conte di Tolosa" ["Bianca, Daughter of the Count of Tolouse"] (1531) had a direct influence on Basile. The popularity of the literary tales had a strong influence on the oral tradition, and the mutual development of different versions led to Hans Christian Andersen's "The Swineherd" (1842) and Ludwig Bechstein's "Vom Zornbraten" ("About the Angry Rost") in *Deutsches Märchenbuch* (1845). Giuseppe Pitrè published a Sicilian version, "La Rigginotta sghinfignusa" in *Fiabe, novelle e racconti popolari siciliani* (1875), and there is an Italian variant in Nerucci's collection of tales in 1880.

Ernst Philippson's *Der Märchentypus von König Drosselbart* is an excellent study of the folklore and literary background of this tale type. For the most part, the tales about so called shrews represented a patriarchal viewpoint of how women, particularly courtly women, were to order their lives according to the dictates and demands of their fathers and husbands. In addition, the women fulfill the wish-dreams of men's imaginations, and the sadism of the tale is often concealed by the humorous manner in which a haughty woman must learn humility.

17. *Rags and Leaves—Die Geschichte von Pezze e fogghi, Nr. 77*
Tale Type AaTh 425*—Enchanted Animal Insulted by Guests.

This version emanates from the beast–bridegroom cycle of tales, which includes hundreds of variants. The first and most important literary version was Apuleius's story of the second century, "Cupid and Psyche" in *The Golden Ass*. Giuseppe Pitrè published a tale similar to Gonzenbach's with the title "Lu surciteddu cu la cuda fitusa" in *Fiabe, novelle e racconti popolari siciliani* (1875) as did Gherardo Nerucci with "Il Magnano o Pelo torto 'n barba" (1880). Gonzenbach's "Rags and Leaves" also contains many of the same elements and motifs found in the King Thrushbeard tale type.

18. *The Brave Shoemaker—Vom tapferen Schuster, Nr. 41*
Tale Type AaTh 1640—The Brave Tailor.

There are hundreds of versions of this popular tale, which probably originated in the sixteenth century in Europe and circulated in the Orient before this period. Often the protagonist is not a shoemaker but a tailor, bookbinder, beggar, or poor man. Whatever the profession may be, he is characterized as small and weak, and generally he kills seven flies with one blow of an instrument. This is particularly the case in Jacob and Wilhelm Grimm's "Das tapfere Schneiderlein" ["The Brave Little Tailor"] in *Kinder- und Hausmärchen* (1857). The most important Sicilian version, other than Gonzenbach's, is Giuseppe Pitrè's "Lu malacunnatta" in *Fiabe, novelle e racconti popolari siciliani* (1875). There are fascinating variants in the works of Schneller, Vonbun, Hahn, Kuhn, Pröhle, Zingerle, Birgliner, Wolf, and Schönwerth.

19. *Prince Scursuni—Die Geschichte vom Principe Scursuni, Nr. 43*
Tale Type AaTh 425 A—The Monster (Animal) as Bridegroom.
This tale is similar to "The Pig King," Nr. 37, in Gonzenbach's collection and forms part of the well known beast–bridegroom cycle that has its literary antecedent in the Roman writer Apuleius's "Cupid and Psyche," *The Golden Ass*, which appeared in the middle of the second century. The most important literary versions of this tale, which was widespread in Europe and the Orient, are: Giovan Francesco Straparola, "Galeotto" in *Le Piacevoli Notti* (1550–1553); Giambattiste Basile, "The Serpent" ["Lo serpe"] in *Lo cunto de li cunti* (1634); Marie-Catherine d'Aulnoy, "The Ram" ["Le Mouton"] in *Les Contes de fées* (1697) and "The Wild Boar" ["Le Prince Marcassin"] in *Suite des Contes Nouveaux ou des Fées à la mode* (1698); Henriette Julie de Murat, "The Pig King" ["Le Roy Porc"] in *Histoires Sublimes et Allégoriques* (1699); Jean-Paul Bignon, "Zeineb" in *Les Aventures d'Abdalla* (1710–1714); Jeanne-Marie Leprince de Beaumont, "Beauty and the Beast" ["La Belle et la Bête"]-in *Magasin des enfans* (1756); Jacob and Wilhelm Grimm, "The Singing, Springing Lark" ["Das singende, springende Löweneckerchen"] and "Hans My Hedgehog" ["Hans Mein Igel,"] in *Kinder- und Hausmärchen* (1857).

"Cupid and Psyche" was not a major literary influence until the middle of the seventeenth century in France when there was a kind of revival with a separate publication of Apuleius's tale in 1648, La Fontaine's long story *Amours de Psyche et de Cupidon* (1669), and Corneille and Molière's tragédie-ballet *Psyché* (1671). The focus in La Fontaine's narrative and the play by Moliére and Corneille is the mistaken curiosity of Psyche. Her desire to know who her lover is almost destroys Cupid, and she must pay for her crime before she is reunited with Cupid. These two versions do not alter the main plot of Apuleius's tale and project an image of women who are either too curious (Psyche) or vengeful (Venus), and their lives must ultimately be ordered by Jove. Nor is Cupid a beast.

All this was changed by Madame d'Aulnoy, who was evidently familiar with different types of beast–bridegroom folk tales and was literally obsessed by the theme of Psyche and Cupid and reworked it or mentioned it in several fairy tales: "Le Mouton" ("The Ram," 1697), "La Grenouille bienfaisante" ("The Beneficent Frog," 1698), and "Serpentin Vert" ("The Green Serpent," 1697), "Gracieuse et Percinet" ("Gracieuse and Percinet," 1697), and "Le Prince Lutin" ("Prince Lutin," 1697). By the time the Grimms wrote their version of "The Singing, Springing Lark," which they had heard from Henrietta Dorothea Wild in 1813, there were hundreds if not thousands of oral and literary versions that incorporated motifs from the oral beast–bridegroom cycle and the literary tradition of "Cupid and Psyche" and "Beauty and the Beast." For instance, even before the publication of the Grimms' tale, Charles Lamb wrote the long poem, *Beauty and the Beast: or a Rough Outside with a Gentle Heart* (1811), and there were important versions by Ludwig Bechstein, Walter Crane, Andrew Lang, Vittorio Imbriani, and Giuseppe Pitrè in the nineteenth century.

In Sicilian folklore the snake was considered extremely dangerous, and if one looked into the eyes of a snake, he or she could be paralyzed. Another aspect of Sicilian folklore in Gonzenbach's tale is the preference for women to cure the prince rather than doctors. The Sicilian peasants placed more trust in female healers than doctors. Motifs from the "Cinderella" cycle of tales are present: the wicked stepmother and the good dead mother, who comes to her daughter's aid.

20. *Maria and Her Brother—Von Maria und ihrem Brüderchen, Nr. 49*
Tale Type AaTh 450—Little Brother and Little Sister.
For the most well known literary sources, see Giambattista Basile, "Ninnillo and Nennella" in *Lo cunto de le cunti* (1634–1636); Charles Perrault, "Little Tom Thumb" ["Le Petit Poucet"] in *Histoires ou contes du temps passé* (1697); Marie-Catherine

d'Aulnoy, "Finette Cendron" in *Les contes de fées* (1697); Jacob and Wilhelm Grimm, "Hänsel und Grethel" in *Kinder- und Hausmärchen* (1857).

The popularity and importance of the tales in the European oral and literary tradition may be attributed to the themes of child abandonment and abuse. Although it is difficult to estimate how widespread child abandonment was, it is clear that lack of birth control, famines, and poor living conditions led to the birth of many children who could not be supported and became unwanted. In the Middle Ages it was common to abandon these children in front of churches, in special places of village squares, or in the forest. Sometimes the abandonment and/or abuse was due to the remarriage of a man or woman who could not tolerate the children from a previous marriage. When the children are abandoned in the fairy tales, they do not always have an encounter with a witch, but they do encounter a dangerous character who threatens their lives, and they must use their wits to find a way to return home. Given the manner in which the tale celebrated the patriarchal home as haven, "Hansel and Gretel" became one of the most favorite of the Grimms' tales in the nineteenth century. Ludwig Bechstein wrote a similar version in his *Deutsches Märchenbuch* (1857), probably based on the Grimms' tale, while Engelbert Humperdinck produced his famous opera *Hänsel und Gretel* in 1893. In the Italian tradition, important folk tales of this type can be found in the collections of Pitrè, Imbriani, and Nerucci.

The most thorough treatment of this tale type is Regina Böhm-Korff's *Deutung und Bedeutung von "Hänsel und Gretel"* (1991). This study traces the historical development of different versions and pays careful attention to the motif of food and famine in the tale as well as the motif of abandonment.

21. *Autumunti and Paccaredda—Von Autimunti und Paccaredda, Nr. 54*
Tale Type AaTh 313 C—Forgotten Fiancée.
This story is similar to "Federico and Epomata." See note 11. The unusual motifs and elements in this version concern the vow made by the queen to the Madonna of Altomonte, and the apparition of the Madonna in the boy's dream when he turns seven.

22. *Giufà—Giufà, Nr. 37*
Giufà, who is a fool, rascal, or idiot and takes the world at face value, has different names in Sicily—Giucà and Iuxà. As bumbling idiot, he is certainly related to other fools in Europe and North America such as Jack, Hans, Pierre, Ivan, Giucca, and Pietro, among others. However, Giufà's most important progenitor is Nasreddin Hodscha or nasr ad-din in Islamic culture. Numerous tales were spread about the mythic Nasreddin Hodscha during the medieval ages and mixed to produce the figure of Guha in the Arabic world and Giufà in Sicily. In fact, storytellers in Sicily continue to invent and tell tales about Giufà to the present day. There have been numerous studies of Guha/Giufà, of which the most recent significant collection and analysis is Francesca Maria Corrao, ed. *Le storie di Giufà* (Palermo: Sellerio, 2001).

There are thirteen tale types for the stories related within the framework presented by Gonzenbach:

1. "Giufà and the Cloth," Tale Type AaTh—1643 The Broken Image, and AaTh 1642—The Good Bargain
This story can be found in *Thousand and One Nights*. Giambattista Basile published an important Neopolitan version, "Vardiello" in *Lo cunto de li cunti* (1634).

2. "Giufà and the Door," Tale Type AaTh—Guarding the Storeroom Door.
Versions of this tale can be found in the collections of the Brothers Grimm and Pitrè. As in many of the tales about fools, Giufà takes words literally and carries out instructions with disastrous consequences.

3. "Giufà and the Hen," Tale Type AaTh—Numbskull Sits on Eggs to Finish the
   Hatching.
One of the first printed versions of this story can be found in Lorenzo Astemio,
Ecatomythium secundum (1505). Other variants that followed are in Girolamo Morlini's *De
matre quae filium custoditum reliquit* (sixteenth century), Giulio Cesare Croce's *Le piacevoli e
ridicolese simplicità die Bertoldino* (1600), and Giambattista Basile's *Lo cunto de li cunti* (1634).

4. "Giufà and the Shepherd," Tale Type AaTh—The Fool as Murderer.
Versions of this story appeared in Girolamo Morlini's *De famulo aromatarii qui dominum
interfecit* (sixteenth century), Giovan Francesco Straparola's *Le piacevoli notti* (1550–
1553), and Giuseppe Pitrè's *Fiabe, novelle e racconti popolari siciliani* (1875).

5. "Giufà and His Sister," Tale Type AaTh 1681 B—The Fool as Custodian of Home
   and Animals.
This story is probably connected to incidents of voluntary and accidental fratricide.
There are other versions in the works of Nerucci and Pitrè.

6. "Giufà and the Owl," Tale Type AaTh 1029—The Woman as Cuckoo in the Tree—
This tale is known throughout Europe and continued to be diffused throughout the
twentieth century.

7. "Giufà and the Pigs," Tale Type AaTh 1004—The Hogs in the Mud, The Sheep in
   the Air.
There are many modern versions of this story.

8. "Giufà and the Creditors," Tale Type AaTh 1654—The Robbers in the Death
   Chamber.
Although there are many European versions of this story, its origins may be Native
American. There is also an interesting variant in Giuseppe Pitrè's *Fiabe, novelle e racconti
popolari siciliani* (1875).

9. "Giufà and the Fairies," Tale Type AaTh 1011*—Fool to Spin Flax Destroys It.
The interference of the fairies, who take pity on the fool, is a motif that can be found in
Giambattista's "Le sette cotennine" ["The Seven Pieces of Bacon Rind"] in *Lo cunto de
li cunti* (1634) and also in Gonzenbach's "Lignu di scupa."

10. "Giufà and the Clothes," Tale Type AaTh 1558—Welcome to the Clothes.
This tale was widespread in the Islamic world during the late medieval period and
began to appear in Europe during the sixteenth century. Different versions can be
found in the works of Sercambi and Pitrè.

11. "Giufà and the Bishop."
This tale has not been classified according to the Aarne-Thompson system.

12. "Giufà and the Friends."
This tale has not been classified according to the Aarne-Thompson system. There is an
interesting variant, "Giufà e lu friscalettu" in Giuseppe Pitrè's *Fiabe e Leggende popolari
siciliane* (1888).

13. "Giufà and the Robbers," Tale Type AaTh 1525 D—Theft by Distracting
    Attention.
There are hundreds, if not thousands, of stories about robbers and thieves that have
been spread since antiquity. This particular "Giufà" tale has a variant in Pitrè's *Fiabe,
novelle e racconti popolari siciliani* (1875).

23. The Magic Cane, the Gold Donkey, and the Little Stick That Hits—
Zaubergerte, Goldesel und Knüppchen schlag zu, Nr. 52
Tale Type AaTh 563—The Table, the Ass, and the Stick.

This story is one of the most popular international tales. Some important literary versions that preceded Gonzenbach's narrative are: Giambattista Basile, "The Ogre" ["Il Racconto dell'Orco"] in *Lo cunto de li cunti* (1634); Jacob and Wilhelm Grimm, "The Magic Table, the Golden Donkey, and the Club in the Sack" ["Tischendeckdich, Goldesel und Knüppel aus dem Sack"] in *Kinder- und Hausmärchen* (1857).

The tales by Basile and the Grimms contain three important fairy-tale motifs: the banishment of the sons or son from the home, their or his apprenticeship, and the demonstration of magic skills and gifts. In this respect, the two tales bear a similarity to those tales in which sons go out into the world to learn a craft, especially in the humorous way in which the protagonists manage to bumble their way through life. It is as if the heavens were protecting them. In some of the oral versions it is the devil who helps the awkward and naive youngest brother. In his adaptations of Basile's tales, Clemens Brentano, the German romantic poet, wrote a hilarious political version of "The Ogre" entitled "Das Märchen vom dem Dilldapp" ("The Fair Tale about Dilldapp," written 1805–1811, revised 1815).

Other important variants can be found in the works of Schneller, Zingerle, Baring-Gould, Waldau, Strackerjan, Frere, and Pitrè.

24. The Singing Bagpipe—Vom singenden Dudelsack, Nr. 51
Tale Type AaTh 550—Search for the Golden Bird, AaTh 551—

The Sons on a Quest for a Wonderful Remedy, and AaTh 780—The Singing Bone. The three different types are mixed in this tale, which is known throughout Europe. Perhaps the most important motif concerns the bone that is made into a bagpipe. In other versions the bone is made into a flute or a horn. The tale is also widely known as a ballad. Pitrè published an important variant, "Lu Re di Napuli," in *Fiabe, novelle e racconti popolari siciliani* (1875). Other versions can be found in the collections of Schneller, Suttermeister, Caballero, Wolf, Haltrich, Töppen, and Müllenhoff.

25. Giovanni and Katerina—Von Giovannino und Caterina, Nr. 32
Tale Type AaTh 510A—Cinderella, and AaTh 480—The Kind and Unkind Girls

There are two similar versions, "The Sister of Muntifiuri," Nr. 4, and "Quaddaruni and His Sister," Nr. 28, in Gonzenbach's collection. Although there are two or more tale types mixed in this story, the primary plot is evidently based on "Cinderella," especially the initial part. The most important literary versions are: Giambattista Basile, "The Cat Cenerentola" ["La Gatta Cenerentola,"] in *Lo cunto de li cunti* (1634); Charles Perrault, "Cinderella, or The Glass Slipper" ["Cendrillon ou la petite pantoufle de verre"] in *Histoires ou contes du temps passé* (1697); Marie-Catherine d'Aulnoy, "Finette Cendron" ["Finette Cendron"] in *Les Contes de fées* (1697); Jacob and Wilhelm Grimm, "Cinderella" ["Aschenputtel"] *Kinder- und Hausmärchen* (1857).

There are thousands of oral and literary versions of "Cinderella," one of the most popular fairy tales in the world. There are indications that the tale may have originated in ancient China or Egypt. In the European literary tradition, which first began with Bonaventure des Périers's *Les Nouvelles Recréations et Joyeux Devis* (*New Recreations and Joyous Games*, 1558), it seems that Basile may have played a role in influencing Perrault and d'Aulnoy, who in turn had some effect on the Grimms' tale. Significant in Basile's tale is the active role that Cenerentola plays in determining her future: she kills her stepmother and stops her father's ship from returning from Sardinia. Some of this activism, in contrast to Perrault's narrative, can be seen in the Grimms' version. Because there were so many different versions by the time the Grimms composed their "Cinderella"—for instance, they may have also been influenced by the Bohemian version "Laskopal und Miliwaka" in *Sagen der Böhmischen Vorzeit aus einigen Gegenden alter*

Schlösser und Dörfer (*Legends of the Bohemian Early Period from Some Regions of Old Castles and Villages*, 1808)—it is difficult to establish one source for their work in particular. Clearly, many different literary and oral tales fostered a huge Cinderella cycle in the East and the West. Aside from Basile's version, Giuseppe Pitrè's "La picuredda" (1875) and Vittorio Imbriani's "La Maestra" (1877) are clearly related to Gonzenbach's tale.

Alan Dundes's *Cinderella: A Folklore Casebook* (1982) provides valuable background information and discussions about the cycle and different interpretations. The early literary work of Basile, Mme. d'Aulnoy, and the Grimms certainly played a role in the creation of nineteenth-century plays and musical adaptations, such as Nicolas Isouard's popular fairy opera, *Cendrillon* (1810) as well as in the equally successful opera, *La Cenerentola* (1817) by Gioacchino Antonio Rossini.

26. *The Shepherd Who Made the Princess Laugh—*
Von dem Schäfer, der die Königstochter zum Lachen brachte, Nr. 31
Tale Type AaTh 566—The Three Magic Objects and the
Wonderful Fruits (Fortunato).

The basic plot of this story concerns a young man who loses three magic objects to a sly princess. He regains them by discovering a magic fruit, generally dates, which causes the people who eat them to have leprosy or to grow horns on their heads. This tale bears a great similarity to Gonzenbach's "The Story About Ciccu" (see note 5). The first printed version of this tale type can be found in the *Gesta Romanorum* (Deeds of the Romans, fourteenth century), and the influence of the popular German novel, *Fortunatus* (1489) by an anonymous author, translated into other European languages, is clear. Some interesting Italian variants can be found in the works of Pitrè, Nerucci, and Imbriani.

27. *Beautiful Cardia—Von der schönen Cardia, Nr. 29*
Tale Type AaTh 552A—Three Animals as Brothers-in-Law.

As in many of the tales in Gonzenbach's collection, this story includes motifs and elements from other tale types such as the daughter promised to animal suitor; enraged old woman prophecies for youth; animals help hero win princess; and suitor test: choosing princess from others identically clad. The significant literary versions that precede Gonzenbach's tale are: Giambattista Basile, "The Three King Beasts" ["I Tre Re Bestie"] in *Lo cunto de li cunti* (1634); Johann Karl August Musäus, "Die Bücher der Chronika der drei Schwestern" ["The Books of the Chronicles of the Three Sisters"] in *Volksmährchen der Deutschen* (1782–1787); Friedmund von Arnim, "The Castle of the Golden Sun" ["Vom Schloß der goldenen Sonne"] in *Hundert neue Mährchen im Gebirge gesammelt* (1844); Brothers Grimm, "The Crystal Ball" ["Die Kristallkugel"] in *Kinder- und Hausmärchen* (1857). Italian variants can be found in the works of Comparetti, Knust, and Pitrè.

28. *Quaddaruni and His Sister—Von Quaddaruni und seiner Schwester, Nr. 34*
Tale Type AaTh 403 A—The Wishes, and AaTh 480—The Kind and the Unkind Girls.
There are two similar versions, "The Sister of Muntifiuri," Nr. 4, and "Giovanni and Katerina," Nr. 25, in Gonzenbach's collection. See notes 4 and 25 for background information.

29. *The Daughter of the Sun—Von der Tochter der Sonne, Nr. 28*
Tale Type AaTh 898—The Daughter of the Sun.
There are very few versions of this story that probably originated in the Middle East. It appears to be the traditional tale of a young woman who is locked in a tower for her own protection because of a prophecy, but the tale quickly departs from the traditional plot. There are two other interesting Italian versions: Giuseppe Pitrè, "La Fata muta" in *Fiabe, novelle e racconti popolari siciliani* (1875) and Domenico Comparetti, "Il Palazzo incantato" in *Novelline popolari italiane* (1875).

30. *Paperarello—Von Paperarello, Nr. 67*
Tale Type AaTh 590—The Prince and the Arm Bands

This tale is similar to Gonzenbach's "The Brave Prince," Nr. 54. It was widespread throughout Asia, North Africa, and Europe. In the thirteenth century the Anglo-Norman verse romance, *Beuve de Hampton*, was based on the same plot, which became a popular story in chapbooks and folk collections in Europe: a young prince, betrayed by his mother, stepmother, or parents, is killed and brought back to life by fairies or a hermit. He travels into the world and disguises himself as a dirty common man, often with scabs. Then he performs valorous deeds and reclaims his position as young prince. Versions of this tale can be found in the works of Straparola, the Brothers Grimm, and Pitrè.

31. *The Lion, Horse, and Fox—Vom Löwen, Pferd und Fuchs, Nr. 69*
Tale Type AaTh 155—The Ungrateful Serpent Returned to Captivity.

Normally the major protagonist of this fable is a snake, and it is one of the oldest fables in the world. Its origins can be traced back to the *Panchatantara* (c. 100 B.C.), which began to be circulated in Europe in the eleventh century and was also known under the name *The Fables of Bidapi*. There are also versions in the *Disciplina Clericalis* by Petrus Alfonsi, the *Roman de Renart*, and the *Gesta Romanorum* (Deeds of the Romans, fourteenth century). In Italy the Jesuits published a variant in *L'utile col dolce* (1671–1678). In the nineteenth century Giuseppe Pitrè included "L'Omu, lu lupu e la Vurpi" in *Fiabe, novelle e racconti popolari siciliani* (1875) and Domenico Comparetti included "Gli ingrati" in *Novelline popolari italiane* (1875).

32. *Giuseppinu—Die Geschichte von Giuseppinu, Nr. 76*
Tale Type AaTh 1651—Whittington's Cat, and—AaTh 1651 A Fortune in Salt.

This story is based on the widely popular story of *Richard Whittington and His Cat*, which originated in the twelfth century and recounted how a cat helped a poor young man become a rich merchant. After its publication in a chapbook as *The Famous and Remarkable History of Sir Richard Whittingon* about 1605, it was also spread in folk books, as a play, ballet, and children's book. In Gonzenbach's version the cat is replaced by Saint Joseph, and there are other variants with a priest as helper. Many more versions can be found in the works of Sacchetti, the Brothers Grimm, Busk, Asbjørnsen, Nicolas de Troyes, Waldau, and Nerucci.

33. *Crivòliu—Vom Crivòliu, Nr. 85*
Tale Type AaTh 933—Gregory on the Stone.

This story is a retelling of the legend about Saint Gregory, which stresses the need to cleanse all sins though sincere penitence. The origins of this legend are French and can be traced back to the twelfth century. There is a version in the *Gesta Romanurum*, and other variants can be found in the works of Pitrè and Imbriani. Alessandro D'Ancona published an important study about the history of this legend in *La Leggenda di Vergogna e la Leggenda di Guida* (1869).

34. *Saint Onirià—Vom Sant'Onirià oder Nerià, Nr. 87*
Tale Type AaTh 788—The Man Who Was Burned up and
Lived Again.

This is an unusual legend because there are no known literary sources. Spread by word of mouth, the legend concerns Saint Anthony, who allegedly burned himself because of a sin. However his heart remains, and a young virgin eats it and becomes pregnant. When she gives birth, her son becomes a regeneration of the saint. The legend was popular throughout Europe. Giuseppe Pitrè published a similar version, "Sant' Antria" in *Fiabe e Leggende popolari siciliane* (1888). In contrast to Gonzenbach's tale, it begins by recounting the sin of the saint.

35. *The Abbot Who Rescued the Princess—Die Geschichte von dem Seminaristen, der die Königstochter erlöste, Nr. 63*
Tale Type AaTh 301—A Quest for a Vanished Princess.

This story is similar to "Fata Morgana," Nr. 36; "The Courageous Prince and His Many Adventures," Nr. 38; "Armaiinu," Nr. 63; "Bensurdatu," Nr. 52; and "The Four Princesses," Nr. 78. The basic plot concerns the betrayal of a young man by his brothers, after he has rescued three princesses from an underground prison. The betrayed young man finds a way back to the world—generally with the help of a bird—exposes his brothers, and marries the youngest princess.

This plot is, however, altered a great deal in the different versions with motifs from other tale types. Giuseppe Pitrè published two interesting variants, "La Jisterna" and "Lu malacunnutta" in *Fiabe, novelle e racconti popolari siciliani* (1875).

36. *Fata Morgana—Die Geschichte von der Fata Morgana, Nr. 64*
Tale Type AaTh 301 A Quest for a Vanished Princess, AaTh 551—The Sons on a Quest for a Wonderful Remedy, AaTh 313—The Girl as Helper, and AaTh 314—The Youth Transformed to a Horse.

This story is a mixture of many tale types, but the frame is derived from the plot of the vanished princess and is similar to "The Abbot Who Rescued the Princess," Nr. 35; "The Courageous Prince and His Many Adventures," Nr. 38; "Armaiinu," Nr. 63; "Bensurdatu," Nr. 52; and "The Four Princesses," Nr. 78. Important here is the introduction of Fay Morgana, the sister of King Arthur, who plays a role in many of the French and English romances of the late medieval period. In the Sicilian folk tradition, she lived in the waters of the Messina strait and was considered a powerful fairy/siren.

37. *The Pig King—Vom Re Porco, Nr. 42*
Tale Type AaTh 425A—The Monster (Animal) as Bridegroom.

This tale is similar to "Prince Scursuni." See note 19 for background information to the Beast as Bridegroom tale type. There are clear parallels to Giovan Francesco Straparola's "Galeotto," *Le Piacevoli Notti* (1550–1553); Marie-Catherine d'Aulnoy's "The Wild Boar" ["Le Prince Marcassin"] in *Suite des Contes Nouveaux ou des Fées à la mode* (1698), and Henriette Julie de Murat's "The Pig King" ["Le Roy Porc"] *Histoires Sublimes et Allégoriques* (1699). There are also two important Italian variants: Giuseppe Pitrè's "Lu Sirpenti" in *Fiabe, novelle e racconti popolari siciliani* (1875) and Vittorio Imbriani, "Il Re Porco," *La Novellaja Milanese* (1877).

38. *The Courageous Prince and His Many Adventures— Von einem muthigen Königssohn, der viele Abenteuer erlebte, Nr. 61*
Tale Type AaTh 301—A Quest for a Vanished Princess.

"The Abbot Who Rescued the Princess," Nr. 35; "Fata Morgana," Nr. 36; "Armaiinu," Nr. 63; "Bensurdatu," Nr. 52; and "The Four Princesses," Nr. 78. For background information, see note 35. Other variants can be found in the works of Zingerle, Schneller, Colshorn, and Schleicher.

39. *The King Who Wanted a Beautiful Wife—Von dem König, der eine schöne Frau haben wollte, Nr. 73*
Tale Type AaTh 877—The Old Woman Who Was Skinned.

There is a direct parallel with Giambattiste Basile's "The Old Woman Who Was Skinned" ["La vecchia scorticata"] in *Lo cunto de li cunti* (1634–1636). Other variants can be found in the collections by Schneller and Pitrè.

40. *Ferrazzanu—Von Ferrazzanu, Nr. 75*
Tale Type AaTh 1698 C—Two Persons Believe Each Other Deaf.

This story is a popular humorous anecdote or *Schwank*, which deals with the theme of deafness. Its literary origins can be traced to a story by Raynaldo da Mantova, and this theme was also treated by Matteo Bandello in "Il Gonella fa una burla a la marchesa di Ferrara e insiememente a la proprie moglie," *La prima parte de le movelle del Bandello* (1554). Gonella was the name of a well known jester or buffoon in Italian folklore. Giuseppe Pitrè also published a variant, "Li centu lignati," in *Fiabe, novelle e racconti popolari siciliani* (1875).

41. *Sciauranciovi—Vom Sciauranciovi, Nr. 71*
Tale Type AaTh 1539—Cleverness and Gullibility.

This story is similar to "The Clever Shoemaker," Nr. 74, and there are two important literary antecedents: *Historia di Campriano* (1518) and Giovan Francesco Straparola, "Pre Scarpacifico" in *Le piacevoli notti* (1550–1553). The feats of Sciauranciovi are derived from the clever peasant Campriano and are often attributed to popular jesters in Italian folklore such as Giufà, Ferrazzanu, and Gonella. Giuseppe Pitrè also published a Sicilian variant, "Lu zu Crapianu," *Fiabe, novelle e racconti popolari siciliani* (1875).

42. *Cacciaturino—Die Geschichte vom Cacciaturino, Nr. 80*
Tale Type AaTh 590—The Prince and the Arm Bands, and AaTh 321—
Eyes Recovered from Witch.

For background information, see note 30, "Paperarello," which has a similar plot. There are, of course, major differences that stem from the inclusion of the motif of the eyes of the seven princesses that are poked out. Joseph Jacobs published "The Son of Seven Queens" in *Indian Fairy Tales* (1892), which is much closer in theme and plot than "Paperarello," and Giuseppe Pitrè included two interesting variants, "Filippeddu" and "Lu Ciclòpu" in *Fiabe, novelle e racconti popolari siciliani* (1875).

43. *The Virgin Mary's Child—Von dem Kinde der Mutter Gottes, Nr. 25*
Tale Type AaTh 706—A Help of the Virgin's Statue.

This story is not a religious legend. Rather, it belongs to a cycle of tales about incest and is related to Nr. 8. "Betta Pilusa," Tale Type AaTh 510 B—The Dress of Gold, of Silver, and of Stars. See note 8 for background material. In the tale type, Help of the Virgin's Statue, the virtuous maiden does not need to disguise herself. Instead she relies on the help of the Virgin Mary. Indeed, she must flee her persecutor (generally her father) assisted by the Virgin Mary and marries a king. Because the father is obsessed, he continues his pursuit and makes it appear that his daughter has murdered her own children. Banished a second time, so to speak, she is eventually aided by the Virgin Mary or some other helper, who restores her innocence and brings about the downfall of the incestuous father. Other variants of this tale type can be found in the works of Straparola, Arnason, Wolf, and Pitrè.

44. *The Story About Oh My—Die Geschichte von Ohimè, Nr. 23*
Tale Type AaTh 311—Rescue by the Sister.

This story is clearly related to the conditions of poverty in Sicily. The grandfather is glad to find positions for his granddaughters because they are so poor, and he does not realize that they are going to be abused by a monster or ogre. In many similar fairy tales, it is the youngest sister who redeems the murdered sisters, and "The Story About Oh My" recalls different versions of "Bluebeard" and "The Robber Bridegroom." Compare the different variants of Charles Perrault, "Bluebeard" ["La Barbe bleue"] in *Histoires ou contes du temps passé* (1697) and Jacob and Wilhelm Grimm, "Fitcher's Bird" ["Fitchers Vogel"] and "The Robber Bridegroom" ["Der Räuberbräutigam"] in *Kinder- und Hausmärchen* (1857). In most of these tales and other variants, the daughters leave their home because they think they will improve their living conditions (sometimes they are kidnapped). Whatever the case may be, they always fall into the hands of an evil sorcerer, robber, monster, or ogre. Then the youngest daughter must find a way to rescue her sisters and herself. Other versions can be found in the works of Hahn, Zingerle, and Pitrè.

45. *The Daughter of Prince Cirimimminu— Von der Tochter des Fürsten Cirimimminu oder Unniciminu, Nr. 35*
Tale Type AaTh 879—The Basil Maiden [The Sugar Puppet, Viola], and AaTh 884B*—Girl Dressed as Man Deceives the King.

This tale is similar to "Sorfarina," Nr. 1. The key motifs (the men's clothes, the sugar puppet) concern the deception of the king, who cannot gain control over the daughter of Prince Cirumimminu, no matter how hard he tries. See note 1 for background material. Other variants can be found in the works of Basile, Bandello, Pitrè, and Imbriani.

46. *The Godchild of Saint Francis of Paula—Von dem Pathenkinde des heiligen Franz von Paula, Nr. 20*
Tale Type AaTh 938—Misfortunes in Youth, AaTh 710—Our Lady's Child, and AaTh 310—The Maiden in the Tower.

This religious story has many different variants in Sicily, Italy, Greece, and Turkey, and it is basically a test of faith. This tale is similar to another in Gonzenbach's collection, "Katerina's Fate," Nr. 85. The oldest literary versions can be found in the *Gesta Romanorum* (Deeds of the Romans, fourteenth century) and Jacob de Voragine's *Legenda aurea* (thirteenth century, translated into English as *The Golden Legend* by William Caxton in 1483). Two interesting Italian variants are Giuseppe Pitrè's "Sfurtuna" in *Fiabe, novelle e racconti popolari siciliani* (1875) and Domenico Comparetti, "Il Macchiaiolo," *Novelline popolari italiane* (1875). Other versions are included in the works of Schönwerth, Asbjørnsen, Haupt and Schmaler, Grimm, Schott, Meier, Waldau, and Dasent.

47. *The Story About the Merchant's Son Peppino—Die Geschichte von dem Kaufmannssohne Peppino, Nr. 16*
Tale Type AaTh 400—The Man on a Quest for His Lost Wife, and AaTh 302—The Ogre's (Devil's) Heart in the Egg.

In this story Peppino is named after Saint Joseph, the saint of the poor and orphans who live under deplorable conditions. Though there is a religious element in this tale, it is certainly not a legend, for it incorporates motifs from other fairy tales. Peppino's adventures resemble those of Psyche in "Cupid and Psyche." However, here it is the male who is too curious and must redeem himself for wanting to know the identity of his lover. Peppino's attempts to redeem himself are also tasks he must perform to show his devotion to Saint Joseph. There are other variants in the works of Campbell, Haltrich, Asbjørnsen, Pitrè, and Wolf.

48. *Spadònia—Die Geschichte von Spadònia, Nr. 88*
Tale Type AaTh 470—Friends in Life and Death, and AaTh 471—The Bridge to the Other World.

This story is more connected to the religious legend than to the fairy tale. It originated in the *exempla* of the fifteenth century and was told as a parable to explain the strange happenings in the other world that have a connection to the real world, especially the differences between rich and poor and their rewards. Variants can be found in the works of Schleicher, Grundtvig, Arnason, Bladé, Maurer, Castrén, and Pitrè.

49. *King Cardiddu—König Stieglitz, Nr. 15*
Tale Type AaTh 425A—The Monster (Animal) as Bridegroom, AaTh 428—The Wolf, and AaTh 313 A—The Girl as Helper.

This story is similar to "Prince Scursuni," Nr. 19, "The Pig King," Nr. 37, and "Zafarana, Nr. 79. For background information, see note 19. The particular plot of "King Cardidu" is, however, unusual, and there are very few tales that have the same structure. Two tales collected by Giuseppe Pitrè come the closest in form: "Lu 'Mperaturi Scursini" and "Marvizia" in *Fiabe, novelle e racconti popolari siciliani* (1875). Other variants can be found in the works of Asbjørnsen and Grundtvig.

50. *The Princess and King Chicchereddu—Von der Königstochter und dem König Chicchereddu, Nr. 12*
Tale Type AaTh 425 D—Vanished Husband Learned of by Keeping Inn (Bath-house), AaTh 884—The Forsaken Fiancée: Service as Menial, and AaTh 884B*—Girl Dressed as Man Deceives the King.
The beginning of the tale is reminiscent of the frame tale in Giambattiste Basile's *Lo cunto de li cunti* (1634–1636), in which Princess Zoza cannot laugh until she sees an old woman whose efforts to carry away oil in a jug are thwarted by a mischievous page. When the old woman's jug breaks and the oil spills all over her, Princess Zoza laughs and is cursed by the old woman. However, the plot of the tale is radically different from Basile's frame tale, and mixes motifs from different tale types. At the end of the narrative, the old queen prevents the princess from giving birth by keeping her hands folded. This motif is based on an old Greek superstition that claimed that a birth could be stopped or prevented by folding one's hands. For instance Hercules' birth was at first prevented in this way. This motif also appears in other tales in the Gonzenbach collection: "Autumunti and Paccaredda," Nr. 21, and "King Cardiddu," Nr. 49. Giuseppe Pitrè published two Sicilian variants, "Lu Cavadduzzu fidili" and "Lu Re d'Amuri" in *Fiabe, novelle e racconti popolari siciliani* (1875).

51. *The Clever Maiden—Von dem klugen Mädchen, Nr. 17*
Tale Type AaTh 884—The Forsaken Fiancée: Service as Menial, AaTh 884 B*—Girl Dressed as a Man Deceives the King, and AaTh 1273*—Numskull Bales out the Stream.
This story is more a humorous anecdote or Schwank than a fairy tale. Moreover, it has an unusual "feminist" tendency, for the brother with seven daughters turns out to be more fortunate than his brother with seven sons, thanks to the cleverness of his youngest daughter. Giambattista Basile published an early version of this tale, "The Plot of Garlic" ["La serva d'agulie"] in *Lo Cunto de li cunti* (1634–1636). It was recorded by Vincenzo della Sala and published in the journal *Giambattista Basile: Archivio de letteratura popolare I* (1883): 2–3. Evidently a popular tale told in the region of Campana, "The Two Merchants" reflects on family rivalries and class differences that existed in the countryside from the sixteenth to the twentieth century. Most interesting is the valorous role played by the youngest daughter of a family blessed with too many daughters.

Vittorio Imbriani also published an important tale, related as "Fanta Ghiro, Persona bella" in *La Novellaja Fiorentina* (1877) that is related to "The Clever Maiden." Imbriani's nineteenth-century Florentine tale is similar in some respects to the lengthy tale "Belle-Belle ou Le Chevalier Fortuné" (1698) by Mme d'Aulnoy in *Contes Nouveaux ou les Fées à la mode*. It concerns the third and youngest daughter of a sick king whose realm is under attack. Her name, Fanta-Ghiro, means valorous young girl, according to Imbriani, and she disguises herself as a young knight to save her father's kingdom. When she meets her enemy, a handsome young king, he suspects that she is a woman and falls in love with her. He tries to set traps for her and prove that Fanta-Ghiro is truly a female, but she cannot be caught. Indeed, she wins the battle of wits and prevents the young king from possessing her father's realm. However, in the end, the young king pursues her, declares his love for her, makes peace with her father, and marries the brave and cunning heroine.

52. *The Robber with a Witch's Head—Vom Räuber, der einen Hexenkopf hatte, Nr. 22*
Tale Type AaTh 621—The Louse Skin, AaTh 311—Rescue by the Sister,

and AaTh 302—The Ogre's [Devil's] Heart in the Egg.
This story has a major important literary source in Giambattista Basile's "Lo polece" in
Lo cunto de li cunti (1634–1636). As is often the case, it is the youngest sister who rescues
her older sister or sisters from a robber or ogre. There are also three variants of this
tale in Giuseppe Pitrè, *Fiabe, novelle e racconti popolari siciliani* (1875).

53. *The Clever Farmer's Daughter—Die kluge Bauerntochter, Nr. 1*
Tale Type AaTh 1533—The Wise Carving of the Fowl,
AaTh 875—The Clever Peasant Girl,
and AaTh 875—A Girl's Riddling Answer Betrays a Theft.

This story is part of the tradition of exempla that can be traced to the medieval period
in Europe. These exemplas were often used in church services as stories to instruct the
people and became a vital part of the oral tradition. Two versions of this tale can be
found in Giovanni Gobi's *Scala Coeli* (c. 1350) and Franco Sachetti's *Il Trecentonovelle*
(fourteenth century). Pitrè published three versions, "Lu cuntu du lu 'nniminu" and
"La panza chi parra" in *Fiabe, novelle e racconti popolari siciliani* (1875) and "Lu Re e
la figghia di lu mercanti" in *Fiabe e Leggende popolari siciliani* (1888), and Domenico
Comparetti, one version, "La Ragazza astuta" in *Novelline popolari italiane* (1875).

54. *The Count and His Sister—Vom Grafen und seiner Schwester, Nr. 56*
Tale Type AaTh 1419 E—Underground Passage to Paramour's House,
and AaTh 926—Judgment of Solomon.

This story can be traced back to the late Middle Ages and is found in the anonymous
Seven Wise Men of the thirteenth century among other works. The traditional plot
concerns adultery, not virginity. Generally speaking, it is not a brother who guards
the chastity of his sister and is deceived. Rather, it is a husband who is deceived by an
adulterous wife, who manages to meet her lover through an underground passage. This
theme is common in many of *The Lais of Marie de France* from the late twelfth century.
Variants of "The Count and His Sister" were widespread in India, Turkey, Greece, and
Italy. Giuseppe Pitrè published a version similar to Gonzenbach's story with the title
"La Soru di lu Conti" in *Fiabe, novelle e racconti popolari siciliani* (1875).

55. *Clever Peppe—Die Geschichte vom klugen Peppe, Nr. 82*
Tale Type AaTh 1538—The Youth Cheated in Selling Oxen.

This story, which is more a funny anecdote (*fabliau/Schwank*) about a buffoon than a
fairy tale, can be found in most countries of Europe, but it is not particularly popular.
In the Italian tradition, Rachel Busk published a version, "Ass or Pig" in *The Folk-Lore
of Rome* (1874), and Giuseppe Pitrè included a variant, "Lu scarparu e li monaci" in
Fiabe, novelle e racconti popolari siciliani (1875).

56. *Maria, the Evil Stepmother, and the Seven Robbers—Maria,*
die böse Stiefmutter und die sieben Räuber, Nr. 2
Tale Type AaTh 327—Hansel and Gretel, and AaTh 709—Snow White

The beginning of this story is similar to the beginning of the Hansel and Gretel tale
type. Here Maria is abandoned by her father, who is compelled to do this by the evil
stepmother. Thereafter, the tale resembles "Snow White." Of course, there are major
differences with the traditional Grimms' tale. Instead of dwarfs, there are robbers who
take care of Maria, and she is sent into a death-like sleep by a magic ring, not an apple.
Finally, though Maria is rescued by a king, the stepmother is never punished. Giuseppe
Pitrè published another Sicilian variant, "La 'Nfanti Margarita" in *Fiabe, novelle e racconti popolari siciliani* (1875). There are other versions in Glinski, Bodenstedt, Arnason,
Maurer, Hahn, Wolf, and Schneller. In Gonzenbach's collection, there are two other
similar tales, "Maruzzedda," Nr. 60, and "Beautiful Anna," Nr. 87.

57. *Bensurdatu—Die Geschichte von Bensurdatu, Nr. 62*
Tale Type AaTh 301—A Quest for a Vanished Princess

This story is a mixture of many tale types, but the frame is derived from the plot of the vanished princess and is similar to "The Abbot Who Rescued the Princess," Nr. 35; "The Courageous Prince and His Many Adventures, Nr. 38; "Fata Morgana," Nr. 36; "Armaiinu," Nr. 63; "The Four Princesses," Nr. 78. See note 35 in *Beautiful Angiola*.

58. *The Rooster Who Wanted to Become Pope—Von dem Hahn,*
der Papst werden wollte, Nr. 66
Tale Type AaTh 20 D*—Cock and Other Animals Journey to Rome
to Become Pope, AaTh 130—The Animals in Night Quarters,
and AaTh 210—Cock, Hen, Duck, Pin, and Needle on a Journey.

This story not only mocks the rooster's vanity, but also makes fun of his illiteracy and those of his companions. The tale is a pastiche of different fables that can be found in the works of the Brothers Grimm, Korn, Vernaleken, Haltrich, Waldau, Grundtvig, and Campbell.

59. *The Brave Prince—Vom tapferen Königssohn, Nr. 26*
Tale Type AaTh 590—The Prince and the Arm Bands,
and AaTh 314—The Youth Transformed to a Horse.

This tale is similar to Gonzenbach's "Paperarello," Nr. 30. For background material see note 30.

60. *The Innkeeper's Beautiful Daughter—Von der schönen Wirthstochter, Nr. 24*
Tale Type AaTh 706—The Maiden without Hands.

The major literary sources for this tale are Ser Giovanni Fiorentino, "Dionigia and the King of England" ["Dionigia e il re d'Inghilterra,"] in *Il Pecorone* (1554); Giambattista Basile, "The Maiden without Hands" ["La Penta Mano-Mozza"], in *Lo cunto de li cunti* (1634–1636); Jacob and Wilhelm Grimm, "The Maiden without Hands" ["Das Mädchen ohne Hände"] in *Kinder-und Hausmärchen* (1857).

The mutilation of women, especially daughters, to preserve their virginity or to keep a religious vow has been a common theme in the East and West and can be traced back to antiquity. The fairy tales that involve a maiden who has her hands cut off or cripples herself in some way because of a father who betrays her or wants to sleep with her are related to the fairy tales about incest. Here the plot generally concerns a father who threatens his daughter sexually or makes a bargain with a mysterious power that seeks to attain control over her. She has her hands cut off and runs away. After meeting a prince in a chance encounter, often in his garden as she is seeking something to eat, she weds him, but her jealous mother-in-law or the demonic power from whom she has escaped, interferes with her life when she gives birth to a son and her husband is far away fighting a war or taking care of some urgent business. She is forced to flee with her son into a forest, where she miraculously recovers her hands in a solitary spot. Her husband returns from his journey and learns how he has been deceived. He pursues his wife and is reunited with her and his son.

There were numerous medieval tales in Europe based on the fifteenth-century legends and chapbooks, *La belle Hélène de Constantinople* and the legends about the powerful King Offa of the eight century and that may have influenced Giovanni Fiorentino's "Dionigia and the King of England" and Basile's "The Maiden without Hands." In France, Philippe de Rémi wrote an important verse romance, *La Manekine* (c. 1270), which may have been influenced by French folk tales with the motif of the persecuted woman in Brittany. The plot of De Rémi's verse romance is highly significant because it combines motifs that can be found in all the literary tales about incestuous and traitorous fathers: After ten years of marriage the king and queen of Hungary have a daughter whom they name Joie. Soon thereafter, however, the queen becomes sick, and before she dies, she makes her husband promise that he will not marry unless he finds a woman who looks just like her. Once she is dead, the nobles of Hungary search for a beautiful woman to match the dead queen. Years pass, but they cannot find one until a nobleman realizes that Joie has flowered into the spitting image of her mother. The nobles of Hungary want the king to marry his daughter, but he at first refuses until he eventually falls in love with Joie and explains to her that he must marry her to follow his dead wife's wish. However, Joie cuts off her left hand and throws it into the river. According to the law of the land, the king was not allowed to marry a woman who was missing a part of her body. Furious, the king commands that she be burned at the stake, but when he departs for a distant castle, his steward takes pity on Joie and puts her in a small boat and sets her out to sea. She arrives in Scotland, where she is taken to the young king's court. Though she is missing a hand and keeps quiet about her past, the king is taken by her beauty and desires to wed her. In contrast, his mother is jealous of her and threatens her. When the king becomes aware of this, he takes Joie under his protection and marries her. His mother retreats to her own castle in the country. When Joie becomes pregnant, the king wants to win some glory in a tournament in France, and he departs. Joie gives birth to a handsome son named John, and his steward sends a messenger to France to inform the king about the happy news. However, the queen mother intercepts the message and changes it to read that the queen had given birth to a monstrous creature. When the king reads this message, he writes back that his steward should preserve their lives. Once again, however, the queen mother intercepts the message and exchanges it for one that instructs the steward to have Joie and her son burned at the stake. But the steward burns two wooden statues instead and sets Joie out to sea with her son in a ship without masthead and sail. Somehow the ship manages to make its way to the Tiber River and lands in Rome where a kindly senator takes care of Joie and her son. When the King of Scotland returns home from France, he learns about his mother's treachery and has her buried in a wall alive. Then he sets off in search of his wife and son, and after seven years of wandering, he is reunited with them in Rome. In the meantime, Joie's father, the King of Hungary, has arrived in Rome to beg pardon from the pope for his sin that has been weighing on his conscience. While he is there, Joie miraculously finds her left hand in a fountain and is happily reunited with her father. Finally, the pope prays that Joie's left hand be reattached, and lo and behold, this is what occurs.

In Italy, *La Manekine* became very popular in the fourteenth and fifteenth centuries. Joie was called Olivia and the King of Hungary was Emperor Giuliano. There were verse and prose editions with the title *La Rapresentazione di Santa Uliva*, and chapbooks in the nineteenth century with the titles *Istoria dela Regina Oliva* and *Istoria piazevole della Regina Oliva*. By the nineteenth century there was a similar story, *Stella e Mattabruna*, which had become just as popular in Italy. This tale concerned the step-daughter of the empress of France, who wants to have Stella killed while the emperor goes off to war. Instead, the hired henchman cuts off her hands, and she is later found in a forest by the Duke of Burgundy, who marries her.

Many nineteenth-century variants can be found in the collections of Pröhle, Schneller, Zingerle, Nerucci, and Pitrè, among others.

61. *The Beautiful Maiden with the Seven Veils—Die Schöne mit den sieben Schleiern, Nr 13*

Tale Type AaTh 408—The Three Oranges, and AaTh 313 C—Forgotten Fiancée. This story may have originated in Italy and was widespread mainly in southern Europe and the Orient. The most significant literary source is Giambattista Basile's "Le-tre cetra" in *Lo cunto de li cunti* (1634–1636). This tale served as the basis for Carlo Gozzi's popular play *L'amore delle tre melarance* (1761). Many nineteenth-century variants can be found in the collections of Hahn, Wolf, Simrock, Schott, Zingerle, and Nerucci.

62. *The Merchant's Clever Youngest Daughter—Die jüngste, kluge Kaufmannstochter, Nr. 10*

Tale Type AaTh 956 B—The Clever Maiden Alone at

Home Kills the Robbers, AaTh 311—Rescue by the Sister,
and AaTh 958 E—Deep Sleep Brought on by a Robber.
This story is not a fairy tale but more of a popular romance about a young woman who outsmarts and defeats a ruthless robber. There are many different European variants in the works of Zingerle, Schleicher, Nerucci, Pitrè, and Imbriani.

63. *Maruzzedda—Von Maruzzedda, Nr. 3*
Tale Type AaTh709—Snow White, and AaTh 410—Sleeping Beauty.
This story is similar to "Maria, the Evil Stepmother, and the Seven Robbers," Nr. 51 and "Beautiful Anna," Nr. 87 in Gonzenbach's collection. Here Maruzedda is persecuted twice—once by her jealous sisters at her home and later by her mother-in-law. Giuseppe Pitrè published a variant, "Suli, Perna e Anna" in *Fiabe, novelle e racconti popolari siciliani* (1875).

64. *Armaiinu—Von Armaiinu, Nr. 59*
Tale Type AaTh 301A—Quest for a Vanished Princess.
This story is similar to "The Abbot Who Rescued the Princess," Nr. 35; "The Courageous Prince and His Many Adventures, Nr. 38; "Fata Morgana," Nr. 36; "Bensurdatu," Nr. 52; "The Four Princesses," Nr. 78. See note 35. What is unique in this tale is Armaiinu's refusal at the end of the tale to keep his youth and to marry a princess. He would prefer to remain the loyal old servant until the end of his days.

65. *The Golden Lion—Vom goldnen Löwen, Nr. 68*
Tale Type 854—The Golden Ram.
This story was widespread in Europe, Turkey, and South America. The earliest European literary version is Ser Giovanni Fiorentino's "Arrighetto, figlio dell'Imperadore," *Il Pecorone* (1554). Other versions can be found in Francesco Sansovino's *Cento novelle scelte* (1556), and Lippo Lorenzi and Paolo Minucci's *Malmantile racqvistato* (1688). In most of the tales, the hero, often a prince, conceals himself in the skin of an animal such as a lamb or lion, or transforms himself as a bird (hawk, eagle) to enter the bedroom of a princess to seduce her or to entice her to come with him.

In contrast to Gonzenbach's more pristine version, Giuseppe Pitrè published an interesting Sicilian variant, "L'Acula chi sona" in *Fiabe, novelle e racconti popolari siciliani* (1875), in which a young man arrives as an eagle, and after the princess recovers from her shock, she spends an entertaining evening with him until the early hours of the next morning.

66. *The Twelve Robbers—Die Geschichte von den zwölf Räubern, Nr. 79*
Tale Type AaTh 676—Open Sesame.
This story can be traced back to the Middle Ages in the Orient. Antoine Galland translated it into French as "Ali Baba and the Forty Thieves" and included it in *The Thousand and One Nights* (1704–1713). From this point on, this tale became one of the most popular in the written and oral tradition in Europe and North America. Giuseppe Pitrè published two Sicilian variants, "Li frati scarsi" and "Mastru Juseppi" in *Fiabe, novelle e racconti popolari siciliani* (1875). Gonzenbach included a second dialect version (see N. 93), which more or less places the blame on the greed of Master Antoni's wife rather than on her husband's envy. It is generally the envy or greed of the brother/friend that brings about his death at the hands of the robbers. Other variants can be found in the works of Simrock, Pröhle, the Brothers Grimm, and Otmar, and in English, this tale was made famous through the various nineteenth-century translations of *The Thousand and One Nights* by Edward Lane and Richard Burton.

67. *Three Good Pieces of Advice—Die Geschichte von den drei guten Rathschlägen, Nr. 81*
Tale Type AaTh 910 B—The Servant's Good Counsels,
and AaTh 910—Wise through Experience.

This tale or exemplum was widespread in the medieval and Renaissance periods
throughout the Orient and Europe. Versions can be found in *The Forty Vezirs* and in
The Thousand and One Nights, as well as in many collections of exemplars. There are
variants in the Latin epic *Ruodlieb* (c. 1000), in *El Conde Lucanor* by Don Juan Manel
(1282–1348), and in the *Gesta Romanurum* (Deeds of the Romans, fourteenth century).
In most of the versions, the last piece of advice is always given to prevent the protagonist from murdering his own son and wife. Aside from the good advice, the protagonist
generally receives a loaf of bread or a cake, which he is not to cut open until he reaches
home, or until he is filled with joy. The bread or a cake always contains some kind of
monetary reward or treasure. The motif of murder at the beginning of Gonzenbach's
tale is not always the same. The protagonist leaves his pregnant wife at home for different reasons as is the case in Giuseppe Pitrè's version, "Li tri Rigordi," in *Fiabe, novelle e
racconti popolari siciliani* (1875).

68. *Tobià and Tobiòla—Die Geschichte von Tobià und Tobiòla, Nr. 89*
Tale Type AaTh 507 B—The Monster in the Bridal Chamber.

This story can be traced to the Old Testament of the Bible and to the apocryphal work,
Tobit (c. 200). Given the great diffusion of *Tobit*, the tale was spread in many different
versions throughout Europe and often used as an exemplar. The emphasis in most of
the tales is on charity and the caring of dead souls.

69. *Joseph the Just—Die Geschichte von Joseph dem Gerechten, Nr. 91*
Story of Joseph—There is no classification in Aarne/Thompson.

This story is in Genesis of the Old Testament and was spread widely through word of
mouth and print throughout the Orient and Europe. There are many elements of the
biblical tale missing in Gonzenbach's text. For instance, there is no dream, and there
are three brothers instead of twelve. For the most part, however, the tale emphasizes
the traditional message of forgiveness.

70. *The Two Brothers—Von den zwei Brüdern, Nr. 40*
Tale Type AaTh 303—The Twins or Blood-Brothers,
and AaTh 300—The Dragon Slayer.

This story is similar to "The Twins," Nr. 75, and "The Dragon Slayer," Nr. 88 in
Gonzenbach's collection. One of the most widespread tales in Europe, it is similar to
the literary versions by Giovan Francesco Straparola, "Cesarino, the Dragon Slayer"
["Cesarino de' Berni"] in *Le Piacevoli Notti* (1550–1553); Giambattista Basile, "The
Merchant" ["Il Mercante"] in *Lo cunto de li cunti* (1634–1636); Jacob and Wilhelm
Grimm, "The Two Brothers" ["Die zwei Brüder"] in *Kinder-und Hausmärchen* (1857).

Although there are many romances and tales about dragon slayers in the medieval
period, Straparola's tale was the first literary fairy tale to develop this motif along
with the theme of brotherly love. There are, of course, many other motifs that occur
in the fairy-tale and romance tradition: the unintentional injury, the animal help-
ers, the rescue of the princess, the cutting out of the dragon's tongues, the woman
who enchants men with her hair, the sword that protects the honor of the brother's
wife, the evil witch, the magic plant or balm that saves one of the brothers, and
the reunion of the brothers. All these motifs are used by Straparola, Basile, and the
Grimms in slightly different ways with the animals providing comic relief. Important
in each of these tales are the notions of faith and honor. Basile's tale, "La cerva fata"
("The Enchanted Doe") is also related to the tales in this group. Other variants can
be found in the collections of Hahn, Campbell, Widter-Wolf, Vernaleken, Simrock,
Strackerjan, and Schneller.

*71. The Seven Brothers with Magic Talents—Von den sieben Brüdern,
die Zaubergaben hatten, Nr. 45*
Tale Type AaTh 653—The Four Skillful Brothers.
This story was popular throughout the Orient and Europe, particularly in Italy. The
important literary versions are: Girolamo Morlini, "Three Brothers Who Become
Wealthy Wandering the World" ["De fratibus qui per orbem pererrando ditati sunt"] in
Novellae, fabulae, comoedia (1520); Giovan Francesco Straparola, "The Three Brothers"
["Tre fratelli poveri andando pel mondo divennero molto ricchi"] in *Le Piacevoli Notti*
(1550–1553); Giambattista Basile, "The Five Brothers" ["I Cinque Figli"] in *Lo cunto de
li cunti* (1634–1636); Jacob and Wilhelm Grimm, and "The Four Skillful Brothers" ["Die
vier kunstreichen Brüder"] in *Kinder-und Hausmärchen* (1857).

Most of the material in these tales can be traced to ancient India, especially the
motif of the extraordinary talents acquired by the sons. In the old Hindu collection
Vetalapanchauinsati [*Twenty-five Tales of a Demon*] there is a story in which a beautiful princess named Somaprabha will only marry a man if he has one of the following
qualities: courage, wisdom, or magic power. Three suitors arrive and convince three
separate family members that they are suitable for the princess. Each receives a promise
that he can marry her. However, when the suitors seek to claim her, there are major
problems because the family members had not consulted with one another. But suddenly the princess disappears, and the royal family asks the suitors to help them. The
first suitor, the man of wisdom, informs them that a demon has abducted the princess
and taken her to a forest. The second, the man of magic power, takes them to the forest
in a magic chariot. The third, the man of courage, kills the demon. But the question
remains: who deserves the princess? The answer is the man of courage because the first
two men were created by God to be his instruments and were intended to help him kill
the demon. The first European literary version of this tale type was written in Latin by
Girolamo Morlini, and Straparola translated it into Italian and adapted it. Given the
comic element of the tale and the common problems regarding the education of the
sons, it was popular in both the oral and literary tradition. Basile took delight in the
tale and gave it a special twist at the end by having the father win the princess. The
social conditions of apprenticeship and the father's concern for the future of his sons
served as the social historical background for the humorous adventures. The individual
"trades" that the sons learn formed the basis for other types of folk tales. For instance,
the son's art of thievery is related to the "art" of other master thieves in the oral and
literary tradition of the seventeenth and eighteenth centuries. Other important versions
are Eberhard Werner Happel's tale about three peasant sons in his novel, *Der ungarische
Kriegs-Roman* [*The Hungarian War Novel*, 1685] and Clemens Brentano's important fairy
tale "Das Märchen von dem Schulmeister Klopfstock und seinen fünf Söhnen," ["The
Fairy Tale about the Schoolmaster Klopfstock and His Five Sons" c. 1811–1815], which
was based on Basile's "The Five Brothers."

*72. The Pious Young Man Who Went to Rome—Von dem frommen Jüngling,
der nach Rom ging, Nr. 47*
Tale Type AaTh 460 A—The Journey to God to Receive Reward.
This story has interesting literary antecedents in Giambattista Basile, "Li sette
Palommielle," *Lo cunto de li cunti* (1634–1636) and in Jacob and Wilhelm Grimm "The
Devil with the Three Golden Hairs" ["Der Teufel mit den drei goldenen Haaren"] in
Kinder- und Hausmärchen (1857). Reinhold Köhler traces the tale even further back in his-
tory to the Indian *Pantchatantra*. There are also variants in the works of Zingerle and Pitrè.

73. Sabedda and Her Brother—Von Sabedda und ihrem Brüderchen, Nr. 49
Tale Type AaTh 450—Little Brother and Little Sister,
and AaTh 327—Hansel and Gretel.

This story has literary sources in Johannes de Alta Silva's "Historia septimi spaientis" in *Dolopathos* (thirteenth century), Giambattista Basile's "Ninnillo e Nennella" in *Lo Cunto de li cunti* (1634–1636), and Jacob and Wilhelm Grimm's "Hansel and Gretel" and "Brüderchen und Schwesterchen" ["Little Brother and Little Sister"]. In versions of this popular tale, the brother, transformed into an animal, generally regains his human form. There are some exceptions, as in Giuseppe Pitrè's Sicilian variant, "La Parrastra," *Fiabe, novelle e racconti popolari siciliani* (1875). Here the brother is transformed into a little golden calf.

74. The Clever Shoemaker—Von dem listigen Schuster, Nr. 70
Tale Type AaTh 1539—Cleverness and Gullibility,
and AaTh 1535—The Rich and the Poor Peasant.
This story is similar to "Sciauranciovi," Nr. 41, in Gonzenbach's collection. See note 41 for background information.

75. The Twins—Von den Zwillingsbrüdern, 39
Tale Type 303—The Twins or Blood Brothers.
This story is similar to "The Two Brothers," Nr. 70, and "The Dragon Slayer," Nr. 88, in Gonzenbach's collection. See note 70 for background information. There are two Sicilian versions in Giuseppe Pitrè's collections, "I due gemelli fatati" in *Fiabe, novelle e racconti popolari siciliani* (1875) and "Li dui frati fidili" in *Fiabe e Leggende popolari siciliani* (1888).

76. Beautiful Innocenta—Von der schönen Nzentola, Nr. 14
Tale Type AaTh 408—The Three Oranges,
and AaTh 313—The Forgotten Fiancée.
This story is similar to "The Beautiful Maiden with the Seven Veils," Nr. 11 See note 11 for background information.

77. The Wicked Schoolmaster and the Wandering Princess—Der böse Schulmeister und die wandernde Königstochter, Nr. 11
Tale Type 894—The Ghoulish Schoolmaster and the Stone of Pity,
and AaTh—The False Bride Takes Heroine's Place.
The initial part of this story recalls the frame tale of Giambattista Basile's *Lo cunto de li cunti* (1634–1636). The Princess Zoza must weep three days and fill a jug with her tears in order to wake the enchanted prince Tadeo, who is under a curse. Zoza succeeds, but on the last day she falls unconscious because she is so exhausted. A slave girl assumes her place and takes credit for saving Tadeo. Eventually Zoza regains her rightful place as is the case in another of Basile's tales, "La schiavotella" ["The Slave Girl"] in *Lo cunto de li cunti* (1634–1636). Jacob and Wilhelm Grimm published a variant, "Das Gänsemädchen" ["The Goose Girl"] in *Kinder- und Hausmärchen* (1857). Another variant can be found in Johann Georg Hahn's *Griechische und albenische Märchen* (1864).

78. The Four Princesses—Von den vier Königstöchtern, Nr. 58
Tale Type AaTh 301—A Quest for a Vanished Princess.
This story is similar to "The Abbot Who Rescued the Princess," Nr. 35; "The Courageous Prince and his Many Adventures, Nr. 38; "Fata Morgana," Nr. 36; "Bensurdatu," Nr. 52; and "Armaiinu," Nr. 63. See note 35 for background information. This particular version has an unusual feature to it: the brothers abandon the youngest before he even sends the four princesses back up the cistern. Then he has to fly on an eagle's back with all four sisters.

79. Zafarana—Zafarana, Nr. 9
Tale Type AaTh 425—Beauty and the Beast, AaTh 884—A Girl Disguised as a Man is Wooed by the Queen, and AaTh 425 K—Search in Men's Clothing.
This story is similar to "Prince Scursuni" Nr. 19, "The Pig King," Nr. 37, and "King Cardiddu," Nr. 49. For background information, see note 19. Giuseppe Pitrè published

another interesting Sicilian version, "Rusina 'mperatrici," in *Fiabe, novelle e racconti popolari siciliani* (1875).

80. *Peasant Truthful—Bauer Wahrhaft, Nr. 8*
Tale Type AaTh 889—The Faithful Servant.

This story can be traced back to the medieval period in the Orient and in Europe. There are versions in *The Forty Vezirs* (associated with *The Thousand and One Nights*) and in the *Gesta Romanurum* (Deeds of the Romans, fourteenth century). The variant in the *Gesta Romanurum* recalls the myth of Mercury and Argus in Ovid's Metamorphosis. Giovan Franceso Straparola published an interesting version, "Travaglino," in *Le piacevoli notte* (1550–1553), and there are two other important Italian variants, Giuseppe Pitrè, "Lu Zu Viritati" in *Fiabe, novelle e racconti popolari siciliani* (1875), and Vittorio Imbriani, "Giuseppe 'a Veretà" in *XII Conti Pomiglianesi* (1876).

81. *About Joseph, Who Set out to Seek His Fortune—Vom Joseph, der auszog sein Glück zu suchen Nr. 6*
Tale Type AaTh—The Golden Mountain, AaTh 400—The Man on a Quest for His Lost Wife, and AaTh 302—The Ogre's [Devil's] Heart in the Egg.

There are hundreds of similar popular tales in the world in which the male protagonist discovers a beautiful young woman who is an enchanted animal or bird (seal, mermaid, swan, dove). Before she goes bathing, she takes off her skin. The hero steals her skin so that she cannot escape him, and she must live with him as his wife until she finds a way to recover the skin and escape. Quite often, unlike in Gonzenbach's tale, she does not return to her captor. This tale was popular in the Mediterranean region, and there are two versions in *The Thousand and One Nights*. Giuseppe Pitrè included a Sicilian variant, "Dammi lu velu!" in *Fiabe, novelle e racconti popolari siciliani* (1875).

82. *The Wasteful Giovanninu—Vom verschwenderischen Giovanninu, Nr. 60*
Tale Type AaTh 401—The Princess Transformed into Deer, and AaTh—The Man on a Quest for His Lost Wife.

This story is unusual because it inverts the traditional tale of the male transformed into a beast. Here the dissolute hero must prove his merit by completing chores that are difficult for him to fulfill due to his negligence. Versions of this tale can be found in the works of Campbell, Zingerle, Schneller, and Pitrè.

83. *The Banished Queen and Her Two Abandoned Children—Die verstoßene Königin und ihre beiden ausgesetzten Kinder, Nr. 5*
Tale Type AaTh 707—The Three Golden Sons.

This story has many important literary sources: Giovan Francesco Straparola, "Ancilotto, King of Provino" ["Ancilotto, re di Provino"] in *Le Piacevoli Notti* (1550–1553); Marie-Catherine d'Aulnoy, "Princesse Belle-Etoile and Prince Cheri" ["La Princesse Belle-Étoile et le Prince Chéry"] in *Suite des Contes Nouveaux ou des Fées à la mode* (1698); Eustache Le Noble, "The Bird of Truth" ["L'Oiseau de vérité"] in *Le Gage touché, histoires galantes* (1700); Antoine Galland, "The Two Sisters Who Envied their Cadette" ["Histoire de deux soeurs jalouses de leur cadette"] in *Les Milles et une nuit* (1704–1717); and Jacob and Wilhelm Grimm, "The Three Little Birds" ["De drei Vügelkens"] in *Kinder-und Hausmärchen* (1857). In addition, Carlo Gozzi wrote a play, *La 'ngannatrice ingannata* (1765), based on the tale.

Though this fairy tale may have originated in the Orient, the source is not clear. Straparola's version was widely known by the French writers at the end of the seventeenth century, and it is certainly the source of Mme d'Aulnoy's and Le Noble's tales. However, it may have even influenced Galland's version. His tale of "The

Two Sisters Who Envied Their Cadette" was told to him in Paris by a Maronite Christian Arab from Aleppo named Youhenna Diab or Hanna Diab. There was no Arabic manuscript for this tale, and Galland created it from memory after listening to Diab and may have introduced elements from the European tales he knew. His tale of "The Two Sisters" in *The Thousand and One Nights* and Mme d'Aulnoy's tale of "Princesse Belle-Étoile" had an influence through the French and German eighteenth-century chapbooks (*Bibliothèque Bleue* and *Blaue Bibliothek*) in Europe and in England. Justus Heinrich Saal published his version entitled "Der wahrredende Vogel" ["The Truth-Speaking Bird"] in his book *Abendstunden in lehrreichen und anmuthungen Erzählungen* (1767), and there was also a Scottish adaptation in *Popular Ballads* (1806). The Grimms' source was a tale told in 1813 by a shepherd in a Westfalian dialect, indicating how widespread the fairy tale had also become in the oral tradition.

There tend to be four crucial components in the plot of this tale 1) the wishes of the sisters 2) the envy of the two older sisters and/or mother-in-law 3) the abandonment of the children and unjust punishment of the mother and 4) the reunion of the family often brought about by a singing bird or some magic gift. A bird that reveals the truth is a common motif in many fairy tales throughout the world, and can be found in the collections of Schneller, Hahn, Pröhle, Zingerele, Vernaleken, Peter, Wolf, Curtze, and Saal. Giuseppe Pitrè published a Sicilian version, "Li figghi di lu cavuliciddaru" in *Fiabe, novelle e racconti popolari siciliani* (1875) and Domenico Comparetti, two Italian variants in *Novelline popolari italiane* (1875).

84. The Pious Child—Vom frommen Kinde, Nr. 86
Tale Type AaTh 767—Food for the Crucifix.

This popular story has its origins as a religious exemplar in the thirteenth century and reveals a certain anticonformist spirit because of the boy's simple solidarity with the suffering of Christ, according to Italo Calvino in his collection of *Fiabe italiane* (1956). Giuseppe Pitrè published another Sicilian version, "Lu Puvireddu," in *Fiabe, novelle e racconti popolari siciliani* (1875).

85. Katerina's Fate—Die Geschichte von Caterina und ihrem Schicksal, Nr. 21
Tale Type AaTh 938—Misfortunes in Youth.

This story is similar to "The Godchild of Saint Francis of Paula," Nr. 46, in Gonzenbach's collection. See note 46 in *Beautiful Angiola* for background information. In this particular tale, the role of fate/fortune is extremely important. The Sicilians believed in the mythic power of fate, which could never be clearly described and could either bless or destroy a person's life, which was controlled by a fate or fortune. Everything depended on fate, and a person could not negotiate directly with his or her fate. For more information about the theme of fate, see Elisa Miranda, "Fortuna," in vol. 5, *Enzyklopädie des Märchens* (1987).

86. Godfather Death—Gevatter Tod, Nr. 19
Tale Type AaTh 332—Godfather Death.

This religious story has its origins in the Middle Ages, and it almost always ends on a tragic note. It was widespread in Europe, and there are variants in the collections of Schönwerth, Widter-Wolf, Saal, and the Brothers Grimm. Giuseppe Pitrè published a Sicilian version, "La Morti e so figghiozzu," in *Fiabe, novelle e racconti popolari siciliani* (1875). In both the Gonzenbach and the Pitrè versions, there is an important episode missing: death gives a gift to the son that enables him to become a rich and famous doctor, as in the tale "Godfather Death" ["Der Gevatter Tod"] in the Grimms' *Kinder- und Hausmärchen* (1857).

87. *Beautiful Anna—Von der schönen Anna, Nr. 4*
Tale Type AaTh 709—Snow White, and AaTh 410—Sleeping Beauty.
This story is similar to "Maria, the Evil Stepmother, and the Seven Robbers," Nr. 51, and "Maruzzedda, Nr. 60," in Gonzenbach's collection. See notes 6 and 13 for background information.

88. *The Dragon Slayer—Von dem, der den Lindwurm mit sieben Köpfen tötete, Nr. 44*
Tale Type AaTh 300—The Dragon Slayer,
and AaTh—The Ogre's [Devil's] Heart in the Egg.
This story is similar to "The Two Brothers," Nr. 70 and "The Twins," Nr. 75, in Gonzenbach's collection. See notes 20 and 25 for background information.

89. *Saint James of Galicia—Die Geschichte von San Japicu alla Lizia, Nr. 90*
Tale Type AaTh 516 C—St. James of Galicia.
This religious legend began as a tale about friendship in a *chanson de geste* about Amico and Amelio (c. 1050). The basic plot concerns two young men who resemble each other perfectly and swear a vow of brotherhood to each other. Later one of the young men sacrifices his sons to cure the friend of leprosy with their pure blood. The sons are brought back to life after the sacrifice is successful. The religious element linked to the pilgrimage to St. James was added in the fourteenth century. A prominent example is Kunz Kistener's *Die Jacobsbrüder* (1899), written and circulated in the fourteenth century. Many oral and literary versions as exemplar and legend were spread in verse and prose since that time, and "Saint James of Galicia" became one of the more popular tales about undying friendship in Europe.

90. *The Hermit—Die Geschichte vom Einsiedler, Nr. 92*
Tale Type AaTh—759 God's Justice Vindicated (The Angel and the Hermit).
This story is one of the most popular and widespread exempla and legends in Europe and can be traced back to the Middle Ages. The "classical" plot concerns a hermit or saint who doubts divine justice. Therefore, God sends an angel who takes the hermit on a journey, and the hermit is not permitted to ask any questions as he watches the angel commit inexplicable if not unjust actions. However, in the end everything turns out to be just, and the hermit realizes that he should never doubt God's wisdom and justice. The more important literary sources can be found in Jacques de Vitry, *Sermones Vulgares* (thirteenth century), *Gesta Romanurum* (Deeds of the Romans, fourteenth century), Giovanni Gobi, *Scala Coeli* (fourteenth Century), *Fiore di virtù* (fourteenth century), and Michele Somma, *Quello che sembra inguisto agli occhi degli uomini, è-giusti agli occhi di Dio* (1822). In addition, Giuseppe Pitrè published a Sicilian version, "S. Petru e lu vacili d'argentu," *Fiabe e Leggende popolari siciliani* (1888).

91. *The Prince's Two Children from Monteleone—Die beiden Fürstenkinder von Monteleone, Nr. 7*
Tale Type AaTh 882—The Wager on the Wife's Chastity.
This story is notable for the motifs of the wager, the chastity and dignity of the sister, and the proof of her innocence. There are important literary sources in *Le Comte de Poitiers* (French verse romance, thirteenth century), Giovanni Boccaccio's "Bernabò da Genova" in *Decameron* (1349–1350), and William Shakespeare's *Cymbeline* (1609). In Italy the tale was made popular through a fourteenth-century song *Madonna Elena*, and there are two important nineteenth-century variants: Giuseppe Pitrè, "La Stivala," *Fiabe, novelle e racconti popolari siciliani* (1875), and Vittorio Imbriani, "La novella del signor Giovanni," *La Novellaja Fiorentina* (1877).

92. *The Clever Farmer—Von klugen Bauer, Nr. 50*
Tale Type AaTh 921—The Four Coins,
and AaTh 922 B—The King's Face on the-Coin.

This story was very popular as exemplum in the Middle Ages in the Orient and Europe and was spread in sermons, stories, novellas, and primers. There is a version that dates back to the fourth century, and aside from the variant in the *Gesta Romanurum* (Deeds of the Romans, fourteenth century), there are many similar tales in collections of sermons and exempla from the fourteenth through the nineteenth century. Giuseppe Pitrè published his Sicilian version, "Lu viddanu e lu Re," in *Fiabe, novelle e racconti popolari siciliani* (1875).

93. *The Two Companions – Lu cuntu di li du' cumpari Nr. 93*
Tale Type AaTh 676 Open Sesam

This story is similar to "The Twelve Robbers," Nr. 65 in Gonzenbach's collection. See note 65 for background information.

94. *The Three Sisters – Lu cuntu di li tri soru Nr. 94*
Tale Type AaTh 512 B* The Ghost Is Avenged and AaTh 326 The Youth Who Wanted to Learn What Fear Is

This story is similar to "The Courageous Maiden," Nr. 15, in Gonzenbach's Collection. See note 15 for background information.

Bibliography

Albrecht, Sophie. *Graumännchen oder die Burg Rabenbühl*. Hamburg: Altona, 1799.

Alfonsi, Petrus. *The Disciplina of Petrus Alfonsi*. Edited by Eberhard Hermes. Berkeley: University of California Press, 1977.

Aprile, Renato. *La fiaba di magia in Sicilia*. Palermo: Sellerio, 1991.

Apuleius, Lucius. *The Golden Ass*. Translated and edited by Jack Lindsay. Bloomington: Indiana University Press, 1962.

Arnason, Jón, *Icelandic Legends*. Edited by Eiríkr Magnússon. Translated by George Powell. London: Bentley, 1864.

———. *Icelandic Folk and Fairy Tales*. Edited by May and Hallberg Hallmundsson. Reykjavik, Iceland: Iceland Review, 1987.

Arnim, Friedmund von. *Hundert neue Mährchen im Gebirge gesammelt*. Charlottenburg: Egbert Bauer, 1844.

———. *Hundert neue Mährchen im Gebirge gesammelt*. Edited by Heinz Röllecke. Cologne: Eugen Diederichs, 1986.

Asbjørnsen, Peter Christen. *Norske huldreeventyr of folkesagn*. Christiania: C. A. Oybwad, 1848.

———. *Round the Yule. Norwegian Folk and Fairy Tales*. Translated by H. L. Braekstad. London: Sampson Low, Marston, Seaarle, and Rivington, 1881.

Asbjørnsen, Peter Christen, and Jorgen Moe. *Norske folke-eventyr*. Christiania: J. Dahl, 1852.

———. *Popular Tales from the Norse*. Introduction by George Dasent. Edinburgh: Edmonstron & Douglas, 1859.

Astemio, Lorenzo. *Fabulae [Esopi] ex Greco in Latinum per Laurentium Vallam*. Venice: Joannes Tacuinus, 1495.

Aulnoy, Marie-Catherine Le Jumel de Barneville, Baronne de. *Les Contes de fées*. 4 vols. Paris: Claude Barbin, 1697.

———. *Contes Nouveaux ou les Fées à la mode*. 2 vols. Paris: Veuve de Théodore Girard, 1698.

———. *Suite des Contes Nouveaux ou des Fées à la mode*. 2 vols. Paris: Veuve de Théodore Girard, 1698.

————. *The Fairy Tales of Madame d'Aulnoy*. Translated by Annie Macdonell. Introduction by Anne Thackeray Ritchie. London: Lawrence and Bullen, 1895.

————. *Contes*. Edited by Philippe Houcade. Introduction by Jacques Barchilon. 2 vols. Paris: Société des Textes Français Modernes, 1997–1998.

Bandello, Mateo. *La prima parte de le novelle del Bandello*. Lucca: Il Bustrago, 1554.

————. *Delle novelle del Bandello*. Venice: Francheschini, 1566.

————. *Twelve Stories*. London: Nimmo, 1895.

Barchilon, Jacques, ed. *Nouveau Cabinet des fées*. 18 vols. Geneva: Slatkine Reprints, 1978. Partial reprint of *Le Cabinet des fées*, edited by Charles-Joseph Mayer.

Baring-Gould, Sabine, ed. *Notes on the Folklore of the Northern Countries of England and the Borders*. By W. Henderson. With an Appendix on Household-Stories by S.-Baring-Gould. London, 1866.

Basile, Giambattista. *Lo cunto de li cunti overo Lo trattenemiento de peccerille*. De Gian Alessio Abbattutis. 5 vols. Naples: Ottavio Beltrano, 1634–36.

————. *The Pentamerone of Giambattista Basile*. Translated and edited by N. M. Penzer. 2 vols. London: John Lane and the Bodley Head, 1932.

————. *Lo cunto de li Cunti*. Edited by Michele Rak. Milan: Garazanti, 1986.

————. *Il racconto dei racconti*. Edited by Alessandra Burani and Ruggero Guarini. Translated by Ruggero Guarini. Milan: Adelphi Edizioni, 1994.

Beauvois, Eugène. *Contes populaires de la Norvège, de la Finlande et de la Bourgogne*. Paris: Dentus, 1862.

Bechstein, Ludwig. *Deutsches Märchenbuch*. Leipzig: Wigand, 1845.

————. *Ludwig Bechsteins Märchenbuch*. Leipzig: Wigand, 1853.

————. *Neues Deutsches Märchenbuch*. Vienna: Hartleben, 1856.

————. *Sämtliche Märchen*. Edited by Walter Scherf. Munich: Winkler, 1968.

Behrnauer, Walter. *Die vierzig Veziere oder weisen Meister. Ein altmorgendländischer Sittenroman zum ersten Male vollständig aus dem Türkischen übertragen*. Annotated by W. Fr. Teubner. Leipzig: 1851.

Bello, Francesco. *Il Mambriano*. Venice: Antonelli, 1840.

Bernard, Catherine. *Inès de Cardoue, nouvelle espagnole*. Paris: Jouvenol, 1696; Geneva: Slatkine Reprints, 1979.

Bierling, Friedrich Immanuel, ed. *Cabinet der Feen*. 9 vols. Nürnberg: Raspe, 1761–66.

Bignon, Abbé Jean-Paul. *Les Aventures d'Abdalla, fils d'Hani, envoyé par le sultan des Indes à la découverte de l'île de Borico*. Paris: P. Witte, 1710–1714.

Birgliner, Anton. *Volkstümliches aus Schwaben*. 2 vols. Freiburg: Herd'sche Verlagsbuchhandlung, 1861–1862.

Bladé, Jean-François. *Contes et Proverbes recueillis en Armagnac*. Paris: Franck, 1867.

Boccaccio, Giovanni. *Decameron*. Edited by Vittore Branca. Turin: Einaudi, 1984.

Bodenstedt, Friedrich Martin von. *Märchen vom Zaren Saltan*. Berlin: Euphorion, 1921.

Böhm-Korff, Regina. *Deutung und Bedeutung von "Hansel und Gretel."* Frankfurt am Main: Peter Lang, 1991.

Busk, Rachel Henriette. *The Folk-Lore of Rome Collected by Word of Mouth from the People*. London: Longmans, Green and Co., 1874.

Caballero, Fernán. *Cuentos y Poesías populares andaluces*. Leipzig: Brockhaus, 1861.

Calvino, Italo, ed. *Fiabe*. Torino: Einaudi, 1970.

————. *Italian Folktales*. Translated by George Martin. New York: Harcourt Brace Jovanovich, 1980.

Cambell of Islay, John Francis, ed. *Popular Tales of the West Highlands*. 4 vols. Orally collected and translated. Edinburgh: Edmonstron and Douglas, 1860–1862.

Castrén, M. Alexander. *M. Alexander Castrén's Ethnologische Vorlesungen der altaischen Völker nebst samojedischen Märchen und Tatarischen Heldensagen*. St. Petersburg: Kaiserliche Akademie der Wissenschaften, 1857.

Cénac Moncant, Justin. *Contes populaires de la Gascogne*. Paris: Dentu, 1861.

Chaucer, Geoffrey. *The Canturbury Tales*. Edited by Nevill Coghill. Harmondsworth,

England: Penguin, 1977.

Chodzko, Alexander. *Contes des paysans et des pâtres slaves*. Paris: Hachette, 1861.

———. *Fairy Tales of the Slavs and Herdsmen*. London: Allen, 1896.

Cirese, Alberto, and Liliana Serafini. *Tradizioni orali non cantate. Primo inventario nazionale per tipi, motivi o argomenti*. Rome: Ministero dei Beni Culturali e Ambientali, 1975.

Clodd, Edward. *Tom Tit Tot: An Essay of Savage Philosophy*. London: Duckworth, 1898.

Colshorn, Carl, and Theodor Colshorn. *Märchen und Sagen aus Hannover*. Hannover: Rümpler, 1854.

Comparetti, Domenico. *Novelline popolari italiene*. Turin: Loescher, 1875.

Coronedi Berti, Carolina. *Favole bolognesi*. Bologna: Forni, 1883.

Corrao, ed. *Le storie di Giufà*. Palermo: Sellerio, 2001.

Crane, Thomas Frederick. *Italian Popular Tales*. Boston: Houghton, Mifflin, 1889.

Croce, Giulio Cesare. *Le piacevoli e ridiculose semplicità di Bertoldino figliuolo dell'astuto ed accorto Bertaldo*. Lucca: Marescandoli, 1600.

———. *Le astuzie di Bertoldo e le semplicità di Bertoldino*. Milan: Garzanti, 1993.

D'Ancona, Alessandro. *Sacre rappresentazioni dei secoli XIV, XV, e XVI*. Vol. 3. Florence: 1872.

———. *La Leggenda di Vergogna*. Bologna: Commissione per i testi di lingua, 1968.

Dasent, George. *Popular Tales from the Norse*. Edinburgh: Edmonstron and Douglas, 1859.

De Simone, Roberto, ed. *Fiabe campane*. 2 vols. Turin: Einaudi, 1994.

Delarue, Paul, and Marie-Louise Tenèze. *Le Conte populaire français. Un catalogue raisonné des versions de France et des pays de langue française et d'Outre-mer*. 4 vols. Paris: Maisonneuve et Larose, 1957–1976.

Delarue, Paul, ed. *French Fairy Tales*. Illustrated by Warren Chappell. New York: Knopf, 1968.

Deulin, Charles. *Les Contes de ma Mère l'Oye avant Perrault*. Paris: Dentu, 1878.

Dundes, Alan, ed. *Cinderella: A Folklore Casebook*. New York: Garland, 1982.

Engelien, August, and Wilhelm Lahn. *Der Volksmund in der Mark Brandenburg*. Berlin: Schultze, 1868.

Ey, Karl August Eduard, ed. *Harzmärchenbuch. Oder Sagen und Märchen aus der Oberharze*. 4th ed. Stade: Steudel, 1862.

Fiorentino, Ser Giovanni. *Il Pecorone*. Milan: Giovanni Antonio, 1554; reprinted and edited by Enzo Esposito, Ravena: Longo, 1974.

France, Marie de. *The Lais of Marie de France*. Edited by Glyn Burgess and Keith Busby. Harmondsworth, England: Penguin, 1986.

Frere, Mary. *Old Deccan Days; or, Hindoo Fairy Legends*. London: Murray, 1868.

Gaal, Georg von. *Ungarische Volksmärchen*. Pesth: Heckenast, 1857.

Galland, Antoine. *Les Milles et une nuit*. 12 vols. Vols. 1–4 Paris: Florentin Delaulne, 1704; Vols. 5–7, Paris: Florentin Delaulne, 1706; Vol. 8, Paris: Florentin Delaulne, 1709; Vols. 9–10, Florentin Delaulne, 1712; Vols. 11–12, Lyon: Briasson, 1717.

Glinski, Antoni Jozef. *Polish Fairy Tales*. Translated by Maude Ashurst Briggs. London: John Lane, 1920. Based on Ginski's collection *Bajarz polski* (Vilna, 1862).

Gobi, Jean. *Scala coeli*. Lübeck: Brandiss, 1476.

Goldberg, Christine. *The Tale of the Three Oranges*. Helsinki: Academia Scientiarum Fennica, 1997.

———. "The Donkey Skin Folktale Cycle (AT 501B)." *Journal of American Folklore* 110 (Winter 1997): 28–46.

Gonzenbach, Laura. *Sicilianische Märchen*. 2 vols. Leipzig: W. Engelmann, 1870.

———. *Fiabe siciliane*. Edited and translated by Luisa Rubini. Rome: Donzelli, 1999.

Gower, John. *Confessio Amantis*. Edited by Terrence Tiller. Baltimore: Penguin, 1963.

Gozzi, Carlo. *Opere ed inedite*. Venice: Zanardi, 1801–1802.

———. *Five Tales for the Theatre*. Edited and translated by Albert Bermel and Ted

Emery. Chicago: University of Chicago Press, 1989.

———. *Fiabe teatrali*. Milan: Garzanti, 1994.

Grimm, Albert Ludwig. *Kindermährchen*. Heidelberg: Morhr und Zimmer,1808.

———. *Lina's Mährchenbuch*. Frankfurt am Main: Wilmans, 1816.

Grimm, Jacob, and Wilhelm Grimm. *Kinder- und Hausmärchen. Gesammelt durch die Brüder Grimm*. Berlin: Realschulbuchhandlung, 1812.

———. *Kinder- und Hausmärchen. Gesammelt durch die Brüder Grimm*.Vol. 2. Berlin: Realschulbuchhandlung, 1815.

———. *German Popular Stories, Translated from the Kinder- und Hausmärchen*. Translated by Edgar Taylor. London: C. Baldwin, 1823.

———. *Kinder- und Hausmärchen. Gesammelt durch die Brüder Grimm*. 7th rev. and exp. edition. 2 vols. Göttingen: Dieterich, 1857.

———. *Household Stories from the Collection of the Brothers Grimm*. Translated by Lucy Crane. London: Macmillan, 1882.

———. *The Complete Fairy Tales of the Brothers Grimm*. Edited and translated by Jack Zipes. New York: Bantam, 1987; 3rd rev. ed. New York: Bantam, 2003.

Grimmelshausen, Hans Jakob Christoph von. *Grimmelshausens Simplicissimus Teutsch*. Edited by Jan Scholte. Tübingen: Niemeyer, 1956.

———. *Der abenteuerliche Simplicissimus*. Edited by Alfred Kelletat. Munich: Winkler, 1956.

Grundtvig, Sven. *Gamle danske minder i folkemunde*. Copenhagen: Akademisk Forlag, 1854.

———. *Danish Fairy Tales*. Translated by Jesse Grant Cramer. Boston: Badger, 1912.

Gueullette, Thomas Simon. *Les Mille et Un Quarts d'heure, contes tartares*. Paris: 1715.

Guglielminetti, Marziano. *Novellieri del Cinquecento*. Milan: Ricciardi, 1972.

Hahn, Johann Georg. *Griechische und albenische Märchen*. Leipzig: Engelmann, 1864.

Haltrich, Josef, ed. *Deutsche Volksmärchen aus dem Sachsenlande in Siebenbürgen*. Hermannstadt: Krafft, 1885.

Haupt, Leopold, and Johann Ernst Schmaler. *Volkslieder der Wenden in der Ober- und Nieder-Lausitz*. Grimma: Gebhardt, 1841.

Historia Di Campriano Contadino. Florence: 1579.

Hunt, Robert. *Popular Romances of the West of England*. London: Hotton, 1865.

Imbriani, Vittorio. *La Novellaja fiorentina*. Livorno: F. Vigo, 1871.

Jacobs, Joseph, ed. *English Fairy Tales*. London: Nutt, 1890.

———. *Indian Fairy Tales*. London: Nutt, 1892.

Jamieson, Robert. *Popular Ballads and Songs from Tradition, Manuscripts and Scarce Editions*. Edinburgh, A. Constable, 1806.

Joisten, Charles. *Contes Populaires du Dauphiné*. Vol. 1 Grenoble: Publications du Musée Dauphinois, 1971.

Kistener, Kunz. *Die Jakobsbrüder*. Breslau: M & H. Marcus, 1899.

Knust, Hermann. *Italienische Märchen* in *Jahrbuch für romanische und englische Literatur* VII (1866): 381–401.

Köhler, Reinhold. *Italienische Volksmärchen* in *Jahrbuch für romanische und englische Literatur* VIII (1867): 241–260.

Korn, Johann Friedrich. *Abendstunden in lehrreichen und anmuthigen Erzählungen*. Breslau: 1776.

Kreutzwald, Friedrich. *Ehstnische Märchen*. Halle: Verlag der Buchhandlung Waisenhauses, 1869.

———. *Old Estonian Fairy Tales*. Translated by A. Jogi. Tallinn: Perioodika, 1985.

Kuhn, Adelbert. *Sagen, Gebräuche und Märchen aus Westfalen*. 2 vols. Leipzig: Brockhaus, 1859.

La Fontaine, Jean de. *Les amours de Psyché et de Cupidon*. Edited by Françoise Charpentier. Paris: Flammarion, 1990.

La Force, Charlotte-Rose Caumont de. *Les contes des contes par Mlle ****. Paris: S. Bernard, 1698.

Lane, Edward, ed. and trans. *The Thousand and One Nights*. London: J. Murray, 1859.

Le Noble, Eustache. *Le Gage touché, histoires galantes*. Amsterdam: Jaques Desbordes, 1700.

Le Prince de Beaumont, Marie. *Magasin des enfans, ou Dialogue d'une sage gouvernante avec ses élèves de la première distinction*. Lyon: Reguilliat, 1756.

Lhéritier de Villandon, Marie-Jeanne. *Oeuvres meslées, contenant l'Innocente tromperie, l'Avare puni, les Enchantements de l'éloquence, les Aventures de Finette, nouvelles, et autres ouvrages, en vers et en prose, de Mlle de L'H***—avec le Triomphe de Mme Des-Houlières tel qu'il a été composé par Mlle ****. Paris: J. Guignard, 1696.

———. *La Tour ténébreuse et les jours lumineux, contes anglois, accompagnés d'historiettes et-tirés d'une ancienne chronique composée par Richard, surnommé Coeur de Lion, roi d'Angleterre, avec le récit des diverse aventures de ce roi*. Paris: Veuve de Claude Barbin, 1705.

Lippi, Lorenzo, and Paolo Minucci. *Malmantile racquistato*. Florence: Taglini, 1688.

Lo Nigro, Sedbastiano. *Racconti popolari siciliani: Classificazione e bibliografia*. Florence: Olschki, 1957.

Lütolf, Alois. *Sagen, Bräuche und Legenden aus den fünf Orten Lucern, Uri, Schwyz, Unterwalden und Zug*. Lucerne: Schiffmann, 1865.

Malespini, Celio. *Ducento novelle del signor Celio Malespini*. Venice: Al segno dell'Italia, 1609.

Maurer, Konrad von. *Isländische Volkssagen der Gegenwart*. Leipzig: J. C. Hinrichs, 1860.

Mayer, Charles-Joseph, ed. *Le cabinet des fées; ou Collection choisie des contes des fées, et autres contes merveilleux*. 41 vols. Amsterdam: s.n., 1785.

Meier, Hermann. *Ostfriesland in Bildern und Skizzen*. Leer: H. Securus, 1868.

Milá y Fontanals, Manuel. *Observaciones sobre la poesía popular*. Barcelona: Ramirez, 1853.

Morlini, Girolamo. *Hieronymi Morlini Parthenopei novellae, fabulae, comoedia*. Lutetiae Parisiorum: Jannet, 1855.

———. *Novelle e favole*. Edited by Giovanni Villani. Rome: Salerno, 1983.

Müllenhoff, Karl. *Sagen, Märchen und Lieder der herzogrhümer Schleswig, Holstein und Lauenburg*. Kiel: Schwerssche Buch, 1845.

Murat, Henriette Julie de Castelnau. *Contes de fées*. Paris: Claude Barbin, 1698.

———. *Les nouveaux contes de fées*. Paris: Claude Barbin, 1698.

Musäus, Johann Karl August. *Volksmährchen der Deutschen*. 5 vols. Gotha: Ettinger, 1782–1787.

Nerucci, Gherardo. *Sessanta novelle popolari montalesi*. Florence: Le Monnier, 1880.

Perrault, Charles. *Griseldis, nouvelle. Avec le conte de Peau d'Ane, et celui des Souhaits ridicules*. Paris: Jean Baptiste Coignard, 1694.

———. *Histoires ou Contes du temps passé*. Paris: Claude Barbin, 1697.

Peter, Anton. *Volksthümliches aus Oesterreichisch-Schlesien*. Troppau: Sebstverlag, 1867.

Philippson, Ernst. *Der Märchen Typus von König Drosselbart*. F. F. Commnications No.-50. Greifswald: Suomalainen Tiedeakatemia, 1923.

Pitrè, Giuseppe. *Fiabe e Leggende Popolari Siciliane*. Palermo: L. Pedone Lauriel, 1870.

———. *Fiabe, novelle e racconti popolari siciliani*. 4 vols. Palermo: L. Pedone Lauriel, 1875.

———. *Fiabe e Leggende popolari siciliane*. Palermo: Pedone Lauriel, 1888.

Praetorius, Johannes. *Der abentheuerliche Glücks-Topf*. 1669.

Pröhle, Heinrich. *Kinder und Volksmärchen*. Leipzig: Avenarius and Mendelssohn, 1853.

———. *Harzsagen*. Leipzig: Mendelssohn, 1886.

Rak, Michele, ed. *Fiabe campane*. Milan: Mondadori, 1984.

Rehfues, Philipp Joseph. *Italienische Miszellen*. 2 vols. Tübingen: J. G. Cotta'sche Buchhandlung, 1805.

Roussel, Claude, ed. *La Belle Hélène de Constantinople: chanson de geste du XIVe siècle*. Geneva: Droz, 1995.

Rubini, Luisa. *Fiabe e mercanti in Sicilia. La raccolta di Laura Gonzenbach e la comunità tedesca a Messina nell'Ottocento*. Florence: Olschki, 1998.

Sachetti, Franco. *Novelle di Franco Sacchetti, cittadino fiorentino*. Florence: Borghi, 1833.

———. *Il trecentonovelle*. Edited by Antonio Lanza. Florence: Sansoni, 1984.

Sarnelli, Pompeo. *Posilecheata di Pompeo Sarnelli*. Edited by Vittorio Imbriani. Naples: Morano, 1885.

Schambach, George and Wilhelm Müller. *Niedersächsiche Sagen und Märchen*. Göttingen: Vandenhoeck & Ruprecht, 1855.

Scheidegger, Jean, ed. *Le Roman de Renart*. Geneva: Droz, 1989.

Schenda, Rudolf. *Folklore e Letteratura Popolare: Italia—Germania—Francia*. Rome: Istituto della Enciclopedia Italiana, 1986.

Schleicher, August. *Litauischer Märchen, Sprichwortem Rätsel und Lieder*. Weimar: Wagner, 1857.

Schneller, Christian. *Märchen und Sagen aus Wälschtirol*. Innsbruck: Wagner, 1867.

Schönwerth, Franz Xaver von. *Aus der Oberpfalz*. Augsburg: Rieger, 1857–1859.

Schott, Arthur, and Albert Schott, eds. *Walachische Märchen*. Stuttgart: J. G. Cotta, 1845.

———. *Rumänische Volkserzählungen aus dem Banat*. Edited by Rolf Brednich and Ion Talos. Bucharest: Kriterion, 1973.

Schulz, Friedrich. *Kleine Romane*. 5 vols. Leipzig: Göschen, 1788–1790.

Sercambi, Giovanni. *Novelle*. 2 vols. Florence: Casa Editrice Le Lettere, 1995.

Simrock, Karl Joseph. *Deutsche Märchen*. Stuttgart, 1864.

Stahl, Karoline. *Fabeln und Erzählungen für Kinder*. Nuremberg, 1818.

Strackerjan, Ludwig. *Aberglaube und Sagen aus dem Herzogthum Oldenburg*. Olenburg: Stalling, 1867.

Straparola, Giovan Francesco. *Le piacevoli notti*. 2 vols. Venice: Comin da Trino, 1550/1553.

———. *Le piacevoli notti*. Edited by Pastore Stocchi. Rome-Bari: Laterza, 1979.

———. *Le piacevoli notti*. Edited by Donato Pirovano. 2 vols. Rome: Salerno, 2000.

———. *The Facetious Nights of Straparola*. Translated by William G. Waters. Illustrated by Jules Garnier and E. R. Hughes. 4 vols. London: Lawrence and Bullen, 1894.

Suttermeister, Otto. *Kinder- und Hausmärchen aus der Schweiz*. Aarau: Sauerländer, 1869.

Tendlau, Abraham. *Das Buch der Sagen und Legenden jüdischer Vorzeit*. Stuttgart: J. Cast, 1842.

Töppen, Max. *Aberglauben aus Masuren*. Danzig: Bertling, 1867.

Troyes, Nicolas de. *Le grand parangon des nouvelles nouvelles* (1510). Edited by Krystyna Kasprzyk. Paris: Didier, 1970.

Uther, Hans-Jörg, ed. *Märchen vor Grimm*. Munich: Eugen Diederichs Verlag, 1990.

Vernaleken, Theodor. *Alpenmärchen*. Munich: Borowsky, 1863.

———. *Kinder- und Hausmärchen dem Volk treunacherzählt*. Vienna: Braumüller, 1900.

Vonbun, Franz Josef. *Volkssagen aus Vorarlberg*. Innsbruck: Witting, 1850.

———. *Alpenmärchen*. Stuttgart: Canstatt, 1910.

Villeneuve, Gabrielle-Suzanne Barbot de. *La jeune Amériquaine et Les Contes marins*. La Haye aux dépens de la Compagnie, 1740.

Vitry, Jacques de. *The exempla or Illustrative Stories from the Sermons Vulgares of Jacques de Vitry*. Edited by Thomas Frederick Crane. London: Nutt, 1890.

Waldau, Alfred. *Bohmisches Märchenbuch*. Prague: Gerzabek, 1860.

Wenzig, Josef. *Westslawischer Märchenschatz*. Leipzig: Lorck, 1857.

Wesseleski, Albert, ed. *Deutsche Märchen vor Grimm*. Brünn: Rudolf M. Rohrer, 1938.

Widter-Wolf, Georg, and Adam Wolf. *Volksmärchen aus Venetien* in *Jahrbuch für romantische und englische Literatur* VII (1866): 1–36; 121–154; 249–290.

Wolf, Johann Wilhelm, ed. *Deutsche Märchen und Sagen*. Leipzig: F. A. Brockhaus, 1845.

———. *Deutsche Hausmärchen*. Göttingen: Dieterich, 1851.

Zingerele, Ignanz Vinzenz, and Joseph Zingerele. *Tirols Volksdichtungen und Volksbräuche*. Innsbruck: Wagner, 1852.